S·O·U·R·C·E·S

NOTABLE SELECTIONS IN

Race and Ethnicity

Third Edition

About the Editors

ADALBERTO AGUIRRE, JR., received his bachelor's degree from the University of California, Santa Cruz, and a master's degree and a doctorate in sociology and linguistics from Stanford University. He is a professor of sociology at the University of California, Riverside. His research interests are in sociolinguistics, the sociology of education, and race and ethnic relations. Professor Aguirre has written extensively for such professional journals as *Social Problems, Social Science Journal, Social Science Quarterly, International Journal of Sociology of Language,* and *La Revue Roumaine de Linguistique.* He is the author or coauthor of *An Experimental Sociolinguistic Investigation of Chicano Bilingualism; Intelligence Testing, Education and Chicanos; Language in the Chicano Speech Community; American Ethnicity: The Dynamics and Consequences of Discrimination;* and *Chicanos in Higher Education: Issues and Dilemmas for the Twenty-First Century.*

DAVID V. BAKER received his bachelor's degree in political science from California State University, Northridge, a master's degree and a doctorate in sociology from the University of California, Riverside, and a juris doctorate from California Southern Law School. He is an associate professor of sociology and the chair of the Behavioral Sciences Department at Riverside Community College in Riverside, California. He has held visiting lectureships at the University of California, Riverside, and at Chapman University. His research and teaching interests are in race and ethnic relations with an emphasis on exploring racism in the American criminal justice system. He has contributed works to several professional journals, including *Ethnic Studies, Social Justice,* the *Justice Professional, Criminal Justice Abstracts,* and the *Social Science Journal.* Professor Baker has also received two National Endowment for the Humanities fellowships and is an associate editor for the *Justice Professional.*

Professors Aguirre and Baker are coauthors of *Race, Racism and the Death Penalty in the United States; Perspectives on Race and Ethnicity in American Criminal Justice; Structured Inequality in American Society: Critical Discussions on the Continuing Significance of Race, Ethnicity, Gender, and Class;* and a forthcoming work, with Jenny Chamberlain, on the multicultural dimensions of domestic violence in U.S. society.

S·O·U·R·C·E·S

NOTABLE SELECTIONS IN

Race and Ethnicity

Third Edition

EDITED BY

ADALBERTO AGUIRRE, JR.
University of California, Riverside

DAVID V. BAKER
Riverside Community College

McGraw-Hill/Dushkin
A Division of The McGraw-Hill Companies

This book is dedicated to the loving memory of a father and a brother, Adalberto Aguirre, Sr., and Forrest S. Baker, Jr.

Manufactured in the United States of America

Third Edition

123456789FGRFGR4321

Library of Congress Cataloging-in-Publication Data

Main entry under title:

Sources: notable selections in race and ethnicity/edited by Adalberto Aguirre, Jr. and David V. Baker.—3rd ed.

Includes bibliographical references and index.

1. United States—Race relations. 2. United States—Ethnic relations. 3. Minorities—United States. 4. Racism—United States. 5. Ethnicity—United States. I. Aguirre, Adalberto, Jr., *comp.* II. Baker, David V., *comp.*

305.800973—dc20

0-07-243089-3 ISSN: 1098-5433

Printed on Recycled Paper

Preface

Many people assume that inequality does not exist in the United States. Others believe that if inequality does exist, then it is rooted in individual shortcomings. This view suggests that it is easier to blame the victims of bias for their unequal status than to acknowledge the existence of social processes in society that promote and maintain inequality. Given this kind of thinking, it is not surprising that discussions of inequality in the United States are usually both technical and passionate. Such discussions become technical when distinctions begin to be made between *equality* and *equal rights*. They become passionate when the topic of *victims* and *victimizers* is introduced into the discussion.

We think that inequality is the foundation upon which equality is promoted in U.S. society. Implicit in this premise is the idea that equality is a relative measure of one's quality of life. That is, to be equal someone has to be unequal. Secondly, equality is a comparative social activity That is, one compares oneself with others to evaluate one's level of equality. Interestingly, status characteristics, such as sex, race, and ethnicity, are crucial determinants in shaping social perceptions for equality and inequality. The collection of selections in this book will provide the reader with a variety of notable examples illustrating the social context in which status characteristics shape perceptions of equality and inequality

The Sociological Context for the Study of Inequality

In this book we also look at the patterns and contexts of structured social inequality for racial and ethnic groups. *Social inequality* is both the means and the ends of social stratification. Social stratification establishes a graded hierarchy of superior and inferior ranks in society. The resources and opportunities available in society are distributed according to a person's placement in the social hierarchy. For example, those at the top of the social hierarchy have access to a larger share of social opportunity and resources than those near the bottom of the social hierarchy. The resources that are valued in a society are usually those things that count in any society—namely, material wealth, social status or social prestige, and political power.

The dynamics of a stratified social system are rooted in a disproportionate distribution of valued resources, which results in two culturally distinct groups of people: a culturally dominant group and a culturally subordinate group. The dominant group maintains its social position by controlling the production of valued resources, which they are able to do because they have better access to a larger share of opportunities and resources. For example, by means of property ownership, the dominant group can decide who will have access to valued resources—jobs, home mortgages, etc. In contrast, members of the subordinate group are unable to improve their rank within the social hierarchy because they lack access to the necessary resources.

Structured Social Inequality

The term *structured social inequality* defines a social arrangement patterned socially and historically, which is rooted in an ideological framework that legitimates and justifies the subordination of particular groups of people. In other words, social inequality is *institutionalized.* For example, one can find a record of consistent patterns of institutionalized discrimination in U.S. society that reflect a racial ideology that has resulted in members of particular racial and ethnic groups being systematically denied full and equal participation in major social institutions—education, employment, politics, etc. The discrimination and segregation experienced by African Americans, Hispanic Americans, Native Americans, and Asian Americans in the U.S. educational system have resulted in a pattern of limited occupational and economic growth for each group. Thus, the dynamics of discrimination and segregation have confined the African American, Hispanic, and Native American populations to a subordinate position in U.S. society. Yet participation in these institutions is essential for social mobility—the transition from one social position to another in the stratified system. In a sense, the subordinate position of racial and ethnic groups in U.S. society amounts to a caste system. The structured social relationship of racial and ethnic groups to U.S. society is characterized by closure and rigidity of rank, and institutionalization and acceptance of rigid ranks. Several selections in this book illustrate the extent to which racial and ethnic stratification in the United States is institutionalized.

Structured Discrimination

Racial and ethnic groups in U.S. society are victims of *structured discrimination.* Where social inequality reflects the procedural nature of unequal access to resources in society, structured discrimination identifies the existence of racial and ethnic prejudice. Together, social inequality and structural discrimination define the sociocultural relationship of racial and ethnic groups to society. For example, the limited access of racial and ethnic groups to valued resources constrains their ability to alter their social position in society. Secondly, since their social position is a subordinate one, racial and ethnic minorities are unable to promote their interests as either a group of individuals or as a class of individuals. As a result, racial and ethnic groups are ignored by social institutions that control access to valued resources because the groups do not possess the required resources for legitimate participation within those social institutions. In the end, racial and ethnic minorities become the victims of racial ideologies that serve as the basis for an unequal distribution of and access to valued resources.

Thus, another purpose of this book is to examine the context of structured discrimination for racial and ethnic groups in U.S. society.

Racial and Ethnic Oppression

The intersection between racial ideology, racial prejudice, and structured racial inequality is *racial oppression*. Racial oppression is the cumulative product of discriminatory acts built into social structures and legitimated or sanctioned by cultural beliefs and legal codes. Racial oppression takes on two dimensions: a structural dimension, in which the structural arrangements of social institutions act to physically control members of a perceived inferior group through discriminatory actions; and a *sociocultural* dimension, by which the cultural (prejudicial) beliefs and the statutory (legal) requirements act to legitimate or sanction these physical controls of subordinate groups. One purpose of this book is to provide observations regarding the existence of racial oppression.

The Persistence of Inequality

Racism and its racist ideologies remain pervasive in contemporary society because they are deeply ingrained in U.S. culture. Social critic Mario Barrera, in *Race and Class in the Southwest: A Theory of Racial Inequality* (University of Notre Dame Press, 1980), states that "racial ideologies become embodied in the thought of future generations who have no conception of the exact context in which they originated, and are thus transformed into broad-based racial prejudice even among people whose interests are not served by it."

Oliver Cromwell Cox, in *Caste, Class, and Race* (Monthly Review Press, 1970), adds to this viewpoint by arguing that racial prejudice has become part of our cultural heritage and that "as such both exploiter and exploited for the most part are born heirs to it."

Still another critic, L. Litwark, in "Professor Seeks Revolution of Values," *The University of California Clip Sheet* (May 1987), contends that racism in American society remains pervasive because "new civil rights laws have failed to diminish the violence of poverty, to reallocate resources, to redistribute wealth and income and to penetrate the corporate boardrooms and federal bureaucracies.

These observations reinforce the idea that racial prejudice and the ideology of racism in contemporary American society are irrational, ingrained racial folklore at work.

Despite the intention of the framers of the Constitution to ensure equal rights to every person, social differences between people developed during the historical maturation of the United States. These social differences matured as forms of social, political, educational, and economic inequality. The persistence of racial and ethnic inequality in a society that is committed to individual rights is, therefore, a direct challenge to the historical romanticism surrounding the arrival of immigrants to the United States seeking freedom and opportunity. Race and ethnicity have played a significant historical role in determining the individual rights of certain racial and ethnic immigrant groups in U.S. society.

To borrow an observation from C. Wright Mills in *The Sociological Imagination* (Oxford University Press, 1959): The study of racial and ethnic inequality in the United States is the sociologist's quest for an introspective understanding of equality in American society Thus, we have selected the contributions in this text in hopes of enlightening our readers to this theme. We have selected critical and important discussions on race and ethnic inequality that uncover the social consequences of structured inequality

Although the study of racial and ethnic groups and relations has long been integral to the social sciences, in the United States this field has witnessed revived and renewed attention in recent years. It is a dynamic, challenging, and changing field that captures the attention and passion of sociologists, educators, political scientists, psychologists, policymakers, and social commentators. However, this field of study is not remote from our everyday experiences. Issues related to race and ethnic relations confront all of us personally and are a topic of concern everywhere in our society.

Sources: Notable Selections in Race and Ethnicity, 3rd ed., is an introductory-level college text anthology that contains 23 selections that have shaped the study of race and ethnicity and our contemporary understanding of it. Included here are the works of a wide range of distinguished observers, past and present, and each selection contains essential ideas or has served as a touchstone for other scholars. These selections offer findings from a variety of disciplines and are well suited to courses that attempt to examine in some depth topics related to race and ethnicity. Each selection is preceded by a headnote that establishes the relevance of the selection.

In our shared teaching experience, we have come to see that a preponderance of American college students presumes that the aims of the civil rights campaigns of the 1960s alleviated the gross social inequities suffered by racial and ethnic minorities in U.S. society. Many students believe that members of racial and ethnic minority groups are no longer systematically denied equal participation in the major social institutions of U.S. society. We think that this misconception has been encouraged, in part, by the continued debate regarding the liabilities of affirmative action programs and whether or not majority White group members are the new victims of "reverse discrimination." Our purpose in this book, then, is to introduce students to some of the notable discourse regarding consistent patterns of institutionalized discrimination and forms of racial ideology in U.S. society. The selections in Part 1 introduce students to some basic sociological ideas underlying race and ethnic relations in the United States, namely, race, ethnicity, prejudice, discrimination, and racism. Discussions in Part 2 concern theoretical orientations to the study of race and ethnic relations in the United States. Part 3 focuses on the institutional consequences of race and ethnic inequality in U.S. society, including the educational institution, the political institution, the economic institution, the legal institution, the institution of the family, and the institution of health and medicine. Part 4 discusses the relationship between race and popular culture and explores the ethnic community. And Part 5 involves responses to race and ethnic oppression in U.S. society.

ON THE INTERNET Each part in this book is preceded by an *On the Internet* page. This page provides a list of Internet site addresses that are relevant to the part as well as a description of each site.

CHANGES TO THIS EDITION This edition of *Sources: Notable Selections in Race and Ethnicity* represents a considerable revision from the second edition. Of the 23 classic readings, 10 are new. Six of the 14 chapters are brand new as well: chapter 4, "Assimilationism"; chapter 5, "Power and Conflict"; chapter 10, "The Family Institution"; chapter 11, "The Institution of Health and Medicine"; chapter 12, "The Media"; and chapter 14, "Responses to Racism." Many of these revisions are directly attributable to feedback from the users of the second edition.

A WORD TO THE INSTRUCTOR *An Instructor's Manual With Test Questions* (multiple-choice and essay) is available through the publisher for the instructor using *Sources* in the classroom.

Sources: Notable Selections in Race and Ethnicity is only one title in the Sources series. If you are interested in seeing the table of contents for any of the other titles, please visit the Sources Web site at `http://www.dushkin.com/sources/`.

ACKNOWLEDGMENTS Thanks go to those who reviewed the second edition of *Sources* and responded with specific suggestions for the third edition:

Peter Adler
University of Denver

Cliff Brown
University of New Hampshire

Georgine Dickens
Morgan Community College

Pamela Braboy Jackson
Western Oregon University

Steven Smith
Rutgers University

Richard Stempien
Mohawk Valley Community College

We welcome your comments and observations about the selections in this volume and encourage you to write to us with suggestions for other selections to include or changes to consider. Please send your remarks to us in care of SOURCES, McGraw-Hill/Dushkin, 530 Old Whitfield Street, Guilford, CT 06437.

Adalberto Aguirre, Jr.
University of California, Riverside

David V. Baker
Riverside Community College

Contents

PART ONE

Basic Concepts

On the Internet . . .

Sites appropriate to Part One

The American Civil Liberties Union (ACLU) Freedom Network is the foremost advocate of individual rights in the United States, litigating, legislating, and educating the public on a broad array of issues affecting individual freedom. This page includes links to racial equality, women's rights, criminal justice, and immigrants' rights.

`http://www.aclu.org`

Established in 1957, the U.S. Department of Justice Civil Rights Division is the primary institution within the federal government responsible for enforcing federal statutes prohibiting discrimination on the basis of race, sex, handicap, religion, and national origin. The site includes links to special issues and the full text of select cases and briefs.

`http://www.usdoj.gov/crt/`

The U.S. Commission on Civil Rights is an independent, bipartisan agency first established by Congress to investigate complaints, research information, and appraise federal laws relating to discrimination.

`http://www.usccr.gov`

The primary purpose of the University of Wisconsin Institute on Race and Ethnicity is to conduct and encourage a variety of activities designed to enhance conceptual, theoretical, and empirical inquiry into the phenomena of race and ethnicity.

`http://www.uwm.edu/Dept/IRE/`

CHAPTER 1 Race and Ethnicity

1.1 MICHAEL OMI AND HOWARD WINANT

Racial Formations

For social scientists, one decisive aspect of race is that it is a sociopolitical construct. The maxim that racial distinctions are socially defined is clearly illustrated throughout the sociopolitical history of the United States: Black Africans were easily identified as slaves by the color of their skin, while Whites were always associated with freedom. Mob violence and vigilantism were directed toward the Chinese "coolies," who could easily be identified by their "slanted" eyelids. The U.S. government's extermination policy of Native Americans was possible because Native Americans were easily identified by their skin color and by their hair color and texture. The U.S. repatriation policy toward Haitian political refugees has been identified by many in Congress as racially biased against Blacks. In other words, the biological attributes of race have served as the basis of racial oppression in American history. These historical examples illustrate that beyond its biological importance, race is a political arrangement.

In the following selection from *Racial Formations in the United States From the 1960s to the 1980s* (Routledge, Kegan & Paul, 1986), Michael Omi, a professor in the Department of Ethnic Studies at the University of California, Berkeley, and Howard Winant, a professor of sociology at Temple University, refer to the sociohistorical development of race as the *racialization* of American society. They argue that because race is arbitrarily constructed, the meaning and use of race follows economic and political changes in U.S. society.

Key Concept: the social significance of race in U.S. society

In 1982–83, Susie Guillory Phipps unsuccessfully sued the Louisiana Bureau of Vital Records to change her racial classification from black to white. The descendant of an eighteenth-century white planter and a black slave, Phipps was designated "black" in her birth certificate in accordance with a 1970 state law which declared anyone with at least one-thirty-second "Negro blood" to be black. The legal battle raised intriguing questions about the concept of race, its meaning in contemporary society, and its use (and abuse) in public policy. Assistant Attorney General Ron Davis defended the law by pointing out that some type of racial classification was necessary to comply with federal record-keeping requirements and to facilitate programs for the prevention of genetic diseases. Phipps's attorney, Brian Begue, argued that the assignment of racial categories on birth certificates was unconstitutional and that the one-thirty-second designation was inaccurate. He called on a retired Tulane University professor who cited research indicating that most whites have one-twentieth "Negro" ancestry. In the end, Phipps lost. The court upheld a state law which quantified racial identity, and in so doing affirmed the legality of assigning individuals to specific racial groupings.[1]

The Phipps case illustrates the continuing dilemma of defining race and establishing its meaning in institutional life. Today, to assert that variations in human physiognomy are racially based is to enter a constant and intense debate. *Scientific* interpretations of race have not been alone in sparking heated controversy; *religious* perspectives have done so as well.[2] Most centrally, of course, race has been a matter of *political* contention. This has been particularly true in the United States, where the concept of race has varied enormously over time without ever leaving the center stage of US history.

WHAT IS RACE?

Race consciousness, and its articulation in theories of race, is largely a modern phenomenon. When European explorers in the New World "discovered" people who looked different than themselves, these "natives" challenged then existing conceptions of the origins of the human species, and raised disturbing questions as to whether *all* could be considered in the same "family of man."[3] Religious debates flared over the attempt to reconcile the Bible with the existence of "racially distinct" people. Arguments took place over creation itself, as theories of polygenesis questioned whether God had made only one species of humanity ("monogenesis"). Europeans wondered if the natives of the New World were indeed human beings with redeemable souls. At stake were not only the prospects for conversion, but the types of treatment to be accorded them. The expropriation of property, the denial of political rights, the introduction of slavery and other forms of coercive labor, as well as outright extermination, all presupposed a worldview which distinguished Europeans—children of God, human beings, etc.—from "others." Such a worldview was needed to explain why some should be "free" and others enslaved, why some had rights to land and property while others did not. Race, and the interpretation of racial differences, was a central factor in that worldview.

In the colonial epoch science was no less a field of controversy than religion in attempts to comprehend the concept of race and its meaning. Spurred on by the classificatory scheme of living organisms devised by Linnaeus in *Systema Naturae,* many scholars in the eighteenth and nineteenth centuries dedicated themselves to the identification and ranking of variations in humankind. Race was thought of as a *biological* concept, yet its precise definition was the subject of debates which, as we have noted, continue to rage today. Despite efforts ranging from Dr. Samuel Morton's studies of cranial capacity[4] to contemporary attempts to base racial classification on shared gene pools,[5] the concept of race has defied biological definition. . . .

Attempts to discern the *scientific meaning* of race continue to the present day. Although most physical anthropologists and biologists have abandoned the quest for a scientific basis to determine racial categories, controversies have recently flared in the area of genetics and educational psychology. For instance, an essay by Arthur Jensen which argued that hereditary factors shape intelligence not only revived the "nature or nurture" controversy, but raised highly volatile questions about racial equality itself.[6] Clearly the attempt to establish a *biological* basis of race has not been swept into the dustbin of history, but is being resurrected in various scientific arenas. All such attempts seek to remove the concept of race from fundamental social, political, or economic determination. They suggest instead that the truth of race lies in the terrain of innate characteristics, of which skin color and other physical attributes provide only the most obvious, and in some respects most superficial, indicators.

RACE AS A SOCIAL CONCEPT

The social sciences have come to reject biologistic notions of race in favor of an approach which regards race as a *social* concept. Beginning in the eighteenth century, this trend has been slow and uneven, but its direction clear. In the nineteenth century Max Weber discounted biological explanations for racial conflict and instead highlighted the social and political factors which engendered such conflict.[7] The work of pioneering cultural anthropologist Franz Boas was crucial in refuting the scientific racism of the early twentieth century by rejecting the connection between race and culture, and the assumption of a continuum of "higher" and "lower" cultural groups. Within the contemporary social science literature, race is assumed to be a variable which is shaped by broader societal forces.

Race is indeed a pre-eminently *sociohistorical* concept. Racial categories and the meaning of race are given concrete expression by the specific social relations and historical context in which they are embedded. Racial meanings have varied tremendously over time and between different societies.

In the United States, the black/white color line has historically been rigidly defined and enforced. White is seen as a "pure" category. Any racial intermixture makes one "nonwhite." In the movie *Raintree County,* Elizabeth Taylor describes the worst of fates to befall whites as "havin' a little Negra blood in ya'—just one little teeny drop and a person's all Negra."[8] This thinking flows from what Marvin Harris has characterized as the principle of *hypo-descent:*

> By what ingenious computation is the genetic tracery of a million years of evolution unraveled and each man [sic] assigned his proper social box? In the United States, the mechanism employed is the rule of hypo-descent. This descent rule requires Americans to believe that anyone who is known to have had a Negro ancestor is a Negro. We admit nothing in between.... "Hypo-descent" means affiliation with the subordinate rather than the superordinate group in order to avoid the ambiguity of intermediate identity.... The rule of hypo-descent is, therefore, an invention, which we in the United States have made in order to keep biological facts from intruding into our collective racist fantasies.[9]

The Susie Guillory Phipps case merely represents the contemporary expression of this racial logic.

By contrast, a striking feature of race relations in the lowland areas of Latin America since the abolition of slavery has been the relative absence of sharply defined racial groupings. No such rigid descent rule characterizes racial identity in many Latin American societies. Brazil, for example, has historically had less rigid conceptions of race, and thus a variety of "intermediate" racial categories exist. Indeed, as Harris notes, "One of the most striking consequences of the Brazilian system of racial identification is that parents and children and even brothers and sisters are frequently accepted as representatives of quite opposite racial types."[10] Such a possibility is incomprehensible within the logic of racial categories in the US.

To suggest another example: the notion of "passing" takes on new meaning if we compare various American cultures' means of assigning racial identity. In the United States, individuals who are actually "black" by the logic of hypo-descent have attempted to skirt the discriminatory barriers imposed by law and custom by attempting to "pass" for white.[11] Ironically, these same individuals would not be able to pass for "black" in many Latin American societies.

Consideration of the term "black" illustrates the diversity of racial meanings which can be found among different societies and historically within a given society. In contemporary British politics the term "black" is used to refer to all nonwhites. Interestingly this designation has not arisen through the racist discourse of groups such as the National Front. Rather, in political and cultural movements, Asian as well as Afro-Caribbean youth are adopting the term as an expression of self-identity.[12] The wide-ranging meanings of "black" illustrate the manner in which racial categories are shaped politically.[13]

The meaning of race is defined and congested throughout society, in both collective action and personal practice. In the process, racial categories themselves are formed, transformed, destroyed and reformed. We use the term *racial formation* to refer to the process by which social, economic and political forces determine the content and importance of racial categories, and by which they are in turn shaped by racial meanings. Crucial to this formulation is the treatment of race as a *central axis* of social relations which cannot be subsumed under or reduced to some broader category or conception.

RACIAL IDEOLOGY AND RACIAL IDENTITY

The seemingly obvious, "natural" and "common sense" qualities which the existing racial order exhibits themselves testify to the effectiveness of the racial formation process in constructing racial meanings and racial identities.

One of the first things we notice about people when we meet them (along with their sex) is their race. We utilize race to provide clues about *who* a person is. This fact is made painfully obvious when we encounter someone whom we cannot conveniently racially categorize—someone who is, for example, racially "mixed" or of an ethnic/racial group with which we are not familiar. Such an encounter becomes a source of discomfort and momentarily a crisis of racial meaning. Without a racial identity, one is in danger of having no identity.

Our compass for navigating race relations depends on preconceived notions of what each specific racial group looks like. Comments such as, "Funny, you don't look black," betray an underlying image of what black should be. We also become disoriented when people do not act "black," "Latino," or indeed "white." The content of such stereotypes reveals a series of unsubstantiated beliefs about who these groups are and what "they" are like.[14]

In US society, then, a kind of "racial etiquette" exists, a set of interpretative codes and racial meanings which operate in the interactions of daily life. Rules shaped by our perception of race in a comprehensively racial society determine the "presentation of self,"[15] distinctions of status, and appropriate modes of conduct. "Etiquette" is not mere universal adherence to the dominant group's rules, but a more dynamic combination of these rules with the values and beliefs of subordinated groupings. This racial "subjection" is quintessentially ideological. Everybody learns some combination, some version, of the rules of racial classification, and of their own racial identity, often without obvious teaching or conscious inculcation. Race becomes "common sense"—a way of comprehending, explaining and acting in the world.

Racial beliefs operate as an "amateur biology," a way of explaining the variations in "human nature."[16] Differences in skin color and other obvious physical characteristics supposedly provide visible clues to differences lurking underneath. Temperament, sexuality, intelligence, athletic ability, aesthetic preferences and so on are presumed to be fixed and discernible from the palpable mark of race. Such diverse questions as our confidence and trust in others (for example, clerks or salespeople, media figures, neighbors), our sexual preferences and romantic images, our tastes in music, films, dance, or sports, and our very ways of talking, walking, eating and dreaming are ineluctably shaped by notions of race. Skin color "differences" are thought to explain perceived differences in intellectual, physical and artistic temperaments, and to justify distinct treatment of racially identified individuals and groups.

The continuing persistence of racial ideology suggests that these racial myths and stereotypes cannot be exposed as such in the popular imagination. They are, we think, too essential, too integral, to the maintenance of the US social order. Of course, particular meanings, stereotypes and myths can change, but the presence of a *system* of racial meanings and stereotypes, of racial ideology, seems to be a permanent feature of US culture.

Film and television, for example, have been notorious in disseminating images of racial minorities which establish for audiences what people from these groups look like, how they behave, and "who they are."[17] The power of the media lies not only in their ability to reflect the dominant racial ideology, but in their capacity to shape that ideology in the first place. D. W. Griffith's epic *Birth of a Nation,* a sympathetic treatment of the rise of the Ku Klux Klan during Reconstruction, helped to generate, consolidate and "nationalize" images of blacks which had been more disparate (more regionally specific, for example) prior to the film's appearance.[18] In US television, the necessity to define characters in the briefest and most condensed manner has led to the perpetuation of racial caricatures, as racial stereotypes serve as shorthand for scriptwriters, directors and actors, in commercials, etc. Television's tendency to address the "lowest common denominator" in order to render programs "familiar" to an enormous and diverse audience leads it regularly to assign and reassign racial characteristics to particular groups, both minority and majority.

These and innumerable other examples show that we tend to view race as something fixed and immutable—something rooted in "nature." Thus we mask the historical construction of racial categories, the shifting meaning of race, and the crucial role of politics and ideology in shaping race relations. Races do not emerge full-blown. They are the results of diverse historical practices and are continually subject to challenge over their definition and meaning.

RACIALIZATION: THE HISTORICAL DEVELOPMENT OF RACE

In the United States, the racial category of "black" evolved with the consolidation of racial slavery. By the end of the seventeenth century, Africans whose specific identity was Ibo, Yoruba, Fulani, etc., were rendered "black" by an ideology of exploitation based on racial logic—the establishment and maintenance of a "color line." This of course did not occur overnight. A period of indentured servitude which was not rooted in racial logic preceded the consolidation of racial slavery. With slavery, however, a racially based understanding of society was set in motion which resulted in the shaping of a specific *racial* identity not only for the slaves but for the European settlers as well. Winthrop Jordan has observed: "From the initially common term *Christian,* at mid-century there was a marked shift toward the terms *English* and *free.* After about 1680, taking the colonies as a whole, a new term of self-identification appeared—*white.*"[19]

We employ the term *racialization* to signify the extension of racial meaning to a previously racially unclassified relationship, social practice or group.

Racialization is an ideological process, an historically specific one. Racial ideology is constructed from pre-existing conceptual (or, if one prefers, "discursive") elements and emerges from the struggles of competing political projects and ideas seeking to articulate similar elements differently. An account of racialization processes that avoids the pitfalls of US ethnic history[20] remains to be written.

Particularly during the nineteenth century, the category of "white" was subject to challenges brought about by the influx of diverse groups who were not of the same Anglo-Saxon stock as the founding immigrants. In the nineteenth century, political and ideological struggles emerged over the classification of Southern Europeans, the Irish and Jews, among other "nonwhite" categories.[21] Nativism was only effectively curbed by the institutionalization of a racial order that drew the color line *around*, rather than *within*, Europe.

By stopping short of racializing immigrants from Europe after the Civil War, and by subsequently allowing their assimilation, the American racial order was reconsolidated in the wake of the tremendous challenge placed before it by the abolition of racial slavery.[22] With the end of Reconstruction in 1877, an effective program for limiting the emergent class struggles of the later nineteenth century was forged: the definition of the working class *in racial terms*—as "white." This was not accomplished by any legislative decree or capitalist maneuvering to divide the working class, but rather by white workers themselves. Many of them were recent immigrants, who organized on racial lines as much as on traditionally defined class lines.[23] The Irish on the West Coast, for example, engaged in vicious anti-Chinese race-baiting and committed many pogrom-type assaults on Chinese in the course of consolidating the trade union movement in California.

Thus the very political organization of the working class was in important ways a racial project. The legacy of racial conflicts and arrangements shaped the definition of interests and in turn led to the consolidation of institutional patterns (e.g., segregated unions, dual labor markets, exclusionary legislation) which perpetuated the color line *within* the working class. Selig Perlman, whose study of the development of the labor movement is fairly sympathetic to this process, notes that:

> The political issue after 1877 was racial, not financial, and the weapon was not merely the ballot, but also "direct action"—violence. The anti-Chinese agitation in California, culminating as it did in the Exclusion Law passed by Congress in 1882, was doubtless the most important single factor in the history of American labor, for without it the entire country might have been overrun by Mongolian [sic] labor and *the labor movement might have become a conflict of races instead of one of classes.*[24]

More recent economic transformations in the US have also altered interpretations of racial identities and meanings. The automation of southern agriculture and the augmented labor demand of the postwar boom transformed blacks from a largely rural, impoverished labor force to a largely urban, working-class group by 1970.[25] When boom became bust and liberal welfare statism moved rightwards, the majority of blacks came to be seen, increasingly, as part of the "underclass," as state "dependents." Thus the particularly deleterious effects on blacks of global and national economic shifts (generally rising unemployment rates, changes in the employment structure away from reliance on labor intensive work, etc.) were explained once again in the late 1970s and 1980s (as they had been in the 1940s and mid-1960s) as the result of defective black cultural norms, of familial disorganization, etc.[26] In this way new racial attributions, new racial myths, are affixed to "blacks."[27] Similar changes in racial identity are presently affecting Asians and Latinos, as such economic forces as increasing Third World impoverishment and indebtedness fuel immigration and high interest rates, Japanese competition spurs resentments, and US jobs seem to fly away to Korea and Singapore.[28] . . .

Once we understand that race overflows the boundaries of skin color, super-exploitation, social stratification, discrimination and prejudice, cultural domination and cultural resistance, state policy (or of any other particular social relationship we list), once we recognize the racial dimension present to some degree in *every* identity, institution and social practice in the United States—once we have done this, it becomes possible to speak of *racial formation.* This recognition is hard-won; there is a continuous temptation to think of race as an *essence,* as something fixed, concrete and objective, as (for example) one of the categories just enumerated. And there is also an opposite temptation: to see it as a mere illusion, which an ideal social order would eliminate.

In our view it is crucial to break with these habits of thought. The effort must be made to understand race as *an unstable and "decentered" complex of social meanings constantly being transformed by political struggle.*

NOTES

1. *San Francisco Chronicle,* 14 September 1982, 19 May 1983. Ironically, the 1970 Louisiana law was enacted to supersede an old Jim Crow statute which relied on the idea of "common report" in determining an infant's race. Following Phipps's unsuccessful attempt to change her classification and have the law declared unconstitutional, a legislative effort arose which culminated in the repeal of the law. See *San Francisco Chronicle,* 23 June 1983.
2. The Mormon church, for example, has been heavily criticized for its doctrine of black inferiority.
3. Thomas F. Gossett notes:

   Race theory . . . had up until fairly modern times no firm hold on European thought. On the other hand, race theory and race prejudice were by no means unknown at the time when the English colonists came to North America. Undoubtedly, the age of exploration led many to speculate on race differences at a period when neither Europeans nor Englishmen were prepared to make allowances for vast cultural diversities. Even though race theories had not then secured wide acceptance or even sophisticate formulation, the first contacts of the Spanish with the Indians in the Americas can now be recognized as the beginning of a struggle between conceptions of the nature of primitive peoples which has not yet been wholly settled. (Thomas F. Gossett, Race: The History of an Idea in America (New York: Schocken Books, 1965), p. 16)

Winthrop Jordan provides a detailed account of early European colonialists' attitudes about color and race in *White Over Black: American Attitudes Toward the Negro, 1550–1812* (New York: Norton, 1977 [1968]), pp. 3–43.

4. Pro-slavery physician Samuel George Morton (1799–1851) compiled a collection of 800 crania from all parts of the world which formed the sample for his studies of race. Assuming that the larger the size of the cranium translated into greater intelligence, Morton established a relationship between race and skull capacity. Gossett reports that:

   In 1849, one of his studies included the following results: The English skulls in his collection proved to be the largest, with an average cranial capacity of 96 cubic inches. The Americans and Germans were rather poor seconds, both with cranial capacities of 90 cubic inches. At the bottom of the list were the Negroes with 83 cubic inches, the Chinese with 82, and the Indians with 79. (Ibid., p. 74)

   On Morton's methods, see Stephen J. Gould, "The Finagle Factor," *Human Nature* (July 1978).

5. Definitions of race founded upon a common pool of genes have not held up when confronted by scientific research which suggests that the differences *within* a given human population are greater than those between populations. See L. L. Cavalli-Sforza, "The Genetics of Human Populations," *Scientific American* (September 1974), pp. 81–9.
6. Arthur Jensen, "How Much Can We Boost IQ and Scholastic Achievement?", *Harvard Educational Review,* vol. 39 (1969), pp. 1–123.
7. Ernst Moritz Manasse, "Max Weber on Race," *Social Research,* vol. 14 (1947), pp. 191–221.
8. Quoted in Edward D.C. Campbell, Jr, *The Celluloid South: Hollywood and the Southern Myth* (Knoxville: University of Tennessee Press, 1981), pp. 168–70.
9. Marvin Harris, *Patterns of Race in the Americas* (New York: Norton, 1964), p. 56.
10. Ibid., p. 57.
11. After James Meredith had been admitted as the first black student at the University of Mississippi, Harry S. Murphy announced that he, and not Meredith, was the first black student to attend "Ole Miss." Murphy described himself as black but was able to pass for white and spent nine months at the institution without attracting any notice (ibid., p. 56).
12. A. Sivanandan, "From Resistance to Rebellion: Asian and Afro-Caribbean Struggles in Britain," *Race and Class,* vol. 23, nos. 2–3 (Autumn–Winter 1981).
13. Consider the contradictions in racial status which abound in the country with the most rigidly defined racial categories—South Africa. There a race classification agency is employed to adjudicate claims for upgrading of official racial identity. This is particularly necessary for the "coloured" category. The apartheid system considers Chinese as "Asians" while the Japanese are accorded the status of "honorary whites." This logic nearly detaches race from any grounding in skin color and other physical attributes and nakedly exposes race as a juridicial category subject to economic, social and political influences. (We are indebted to Steve Talbot for clarification of some of these points.)
14. Gordon W. Allport, *The Nature of Prejudice* (Garden City, New York: Doubleday, 1958), pp. 184–200.
15. We wish to use this phrase loosely, without committing ourselves to a particular position on such social psychological approaches as symbolic interactionism, which are outside the scope of this study. An interesting study on this subject is S. M. Lyman

and W. A. Douglass, "Ethnicity: Strategies of Individual and Collective Impression Management," *Social Research,* vol. 40, no. 2 (1973).

16. Michael Billig, "Patterns of Racism: Interviews with National Front Members," *Race and Class,* vol. 20, no. 2 (Autumn 1978), pp. 161–79.

17. "Miss San Antonio USA Lisa Fernandez and other Hispanics auditioning for a role in a television soap-opera did not fit the Hollywood image of real Mexicans and had to darken their faces before filming." Model Aurora Garza said that their faces were bronzed with powder because they looked too white. " 'I'm a real Mexican [Garza said] and very dark anyway. I'm even darker right now because I have a tan. But they kept wanting me to make my face darker and darker' " (*San Francisco Chronicle,* 21 September 1984). A similar dilemma faces Asian American actors who feel that Asian character lead roles inevitably go to white actors who make themselves up to be Asian. Scores of Charlie Chan films, for example, have been made with white leads (the last one was the 1981 *Charlie Chan and the Curse of the Dragon Queen*). Roland Winters, who played in six Chan features, was asked by playwright Frank Chin to explain the logic of casting a white man in the role of Charlie Chan: " 'The only thing I can think of is, if you want to cast a homosexual in a show, and get a homosexual, it'll be awful. It won't be funny... and maybe there's something there...' " (Frank Chin, "Confessions of the Chinatown Cowboy," *Bulletin of Concerned Asian Scholars,* vol 4. no. 3 [Fall 1972]).

18. Melanie Martindale-Sikes, "Nationalizing 'Nigger' Imagery Through 'Birth of a Nation'," paper prepared for the 73rd Annual Meeting of the American Sociological Association, 4–8 September 1978 in San Francisco.

19. Winthrop D. Jordan, op. cit., p. 95; emphasis added.

20. Historical focus has been placed either on particular racially defined groups or on immigration and the "incorporation" of ethnic groups. In the former case the characteristic ethnicity theory pitfalls and apologetics such as functionalism and cultural pluralism may be avoided, but only by sacrificing much of the focus on race. In the latter case, race is considered a manifestation of ethnicity.

21. The degree of antipathy for these groups should not be minimized. A northern commentator observed in the 1850s: "An Irish Catholic seldom attempts to rise to a higher condition than that in which he is placed, while the Negro often makes the attempt with success." Quoted in Gossett, op. cit., p. 288.

22. This analysis, as will perhaps be obvious, is essentially DuBoisian. Its main source will be found in the monumental (and still largely unappreciated) *Black Reconstruction in the United States, 1860–1880* (New York: Atheneum, 1977 [1935]).

23. Alexander Saxton argues that:

    North Americans of European background have experienced three great racial confrontations: with the Indian, with the African, and with the Oriental. Central to each transaction has been a totally one-sided preponderance of power, exerted for the exploitation of nonwhites by the dominant white society. In each case (but especially in the two that began with systems of enforced labor), white workingmen have played a crucial, yet ambivalent, role. They have been both exploited and exploiters. On the one hand, thrown into competition with nonwhites as enslaved or "cheap" labor they suffered economically; on the other hand, being white, they benefited by that very exploitation which was compelling the nonwhites to work for low wages or for nothing. Ideologically they were drawn in opposite directions. *Racial identification cut at right angles to class consciousness.* (Alexander Saxton, *The Indispensable Enemy: Labor and the Anti-Chinese Movement in California* (Berkeley and Los Angeles: University of California Press, 1971), p. 1, emphasis added.)

24. Selig Perlman, *The History of Trade Unionism in the United States* (New York: Augustus Kelley, 1950), p. 52; emphasis added.
25. Whether southern blacks were "peasants" or rural workers is unimportant in this context. Some time during the 1960s blacks attained a higher degree of urbanization than whites. Before World War II most blacks had been rural dwellers and nearly 80 percent lived in the South.
26. See George Gilder, *Wealth and Poverty* (New York: Basic Books, 1981); Charles Murray, *Losing Ground* (New York: Basic Books, 1984).
27. A brilliant study of the racialization process in Britain, focused on the rise of "mugging" as a popular fear in the 1970s, is Stuart Hall *et al., Policing the Crisis* (London: Macmillan, 1978).
28. The case of Vincent Chin, a Chinese American man beaten to death in 1982 by a laid-off Detroit auto worker and his stepson who mistook him for Japanese and blamed him for the loss of their jobs, has been widely publicized in Asian American communities. On immigration conflicts and pressures, see Michael Omi, "New Wave Dread: Immigration and Intra-Third World Conflict," *Socialist Review,* no. 60 (November–December 1981).

1.2 BETH B. HESS, ELIZABETH W. MARKSON, AND PETER J. STEIN

Racial and Ethnic Minorities: An Overview

Through historical patterns of immigration and colonialism, the United States has become a multiracial and multiethnic society. Equal status in U.S. society, however, is denied to various racial and ethnic groups. As a result, U.S. society stratifies people into dominant and subordinate groups defined by race and ethnicity. Subordinate group status is thus synonymous with minority group status. A *minority group* refers to a category of people who (a) share a distinctive racial or ethnic identity that sets them apart from members of a dominant group, and (b) suffer differential or unequal treatment at the hands of the dominant group because of their racial or ethnic characteristics.

In the following selection from "Racial and Ethnic Minorities: An Overview," from their book *Sociology* (Macmillan, 1985), sociologists Beth B. Hess, Elizabeth W. Markson, and Peter J. Stein provide an overview of racial and ethnic minorities in the United States and the forms of mistreatment suffered by these groups throughout American history.

Key Concept: racial and ethnic minorities

RACIAL MINORITIES

Native Americans

Estimates of the size of the Native American population prior to the invasion of Europeans in North America vary; a conservative estimate is 5 million when Columbus discovered America. It was not long after the arrival of Europeans that Native American tribes were reduced to a racial and ethnic group "inferior" to the "more civilized" white newcomers. Because Europeans viewed their own cultures as superior, the physical characteristics of Native Americans were taken as evidence of biological inferiority. All Native Americans were categorized as "Indians" and their widely varying cultures destroyed. Disease was a major factor in reducing the Native American population; frequently, entire communities became ill, halting everyday life and enabling conquest by white settlers. Remarkably, Native Americans had previously been almost free of infectious diseases such as smallpox and measles, and they lacked any biological defenses against epidemics (Thornton, 1987) brought by Europeans.

Because Native Americans were not considered to be entitled to equal status with whites, treaties with the "Indians" were ignored. During the 1800s, whole tribes were resettled forcibly into reservations distant from centers of population and business. The complex interaction of relocation, war, and forced culture change combined with disease to reduce the Native American population to its low point of roughly 250,000 people in 1900 (Thornton, 1987). By the early 1980s, about 53 million acres, or 2.4 percent, of U.S. land was managed in trust by the Bureau of Indian Affairs. These reservations became notorious for their lack of economic opportunities. Moreover, most tribes own only a small part of their reservations.

Native Americans remain the poorest and the most disadvantaged of all racial or ethnic groups in the United States. Contrary to popular belief, only slightly more than half of all Native Americans live on reservations. Many live in metropolitan areas such as Los Angeles, Chicago, Seattle, and Minneapolis–St. Paul. Others are farmers and migrant laborers in the Southwest and north central regions, and many live in New York State and New England. The earnings of metropolitan Native Americans are higher than those of nonmetropolitan Native Americans. Better jobs and higher levels of education of metropolitan Native Americans account for these differences (Snipp and Sandefur, 1988). . . .

Self-determination and economic self-sufficiency cannot be achieved easily when the most basic needs, such as adequate education, housing, and health care, have not yet been met. Death rates from a range of diseases are greater than among the U.S. population as a whole. Mortality from alcohol-related causes among Native Americans remains about 22 times higher than the national average, and the suicide rate is twice the national average. Housing is substandard, and nearly half the hospitals built by the Indian Health Service were built before 1940 and are both understaffed and in need of repairs.

Far from being on the verge of extinction, however, the Native American population is growing faster than the U.S. population as a whole. According to Government statistics, there are around 1.5 million Native Americans, most heavily concentrated in California, Oklahoma, Arizona, New Mexico, and North Carolina. It is difficult, however, to know the precise size of the current Native American population, as the Federal government uses a variety of criteria to count "Indians." Although the birthrate among Native Americans accounts for a small proportion of the increase in their numbers, it seems likely that many people who identified themselves as belonging to some other race or ethnicity in earlier censuses now identify themselves as Native Americans, reflecting a new militancy.

Demonstrations and lawsuits have called attention to the treaties broken by the U.S. government and the unmet needs of Native Americans. Several lawsuits have resulted in a return of native lands and/or reparation payments in the millions. But despite the rising tide of political activity illustrated by the American Indian Movement (AIM), it has been difficult for Native Americans to create a unified political front. The variety among tribes is great, and there is no typical Native American, no one Indian culture, language, religion, or physical type.

African-Americans in America

AFRICAN-AMERICANS AND STRATIFICATION HIERARCHIES In 1989, 30 million African-Americans accounted for almost 13 percent of the total population of the United States. To what extent have African-Americans moved into and up the stratification system?

Although all legal barriers to voting have been removed, African-Americans are less likely to vote than whites, partly because of difficulties encountered in registering and voting in the South but primarily as a result of lower income and less education, which, in turn, are associated with lower voter turnout in general. Also, feelings of powerlessness and alienation reduce the motivation to vote ("What good would it do?"). Although African-Americans constitute about 12 percent of the country's voting-age population, it will not be until 1998 that they achieve parity in voting in congressional elections (National Urban League, 1989).

The number of African-American state legislators rose from about 168 in 1970 to over 400 today. Other elected officials increased, and an African-American political elite has begun to emerge. But the rate of increase of elected African-American officials has declined and is about only one-third of what it was from 1970 to 1976. At the moment, elected African-American officials represent considerably fewer than the almost 13 percent that would reflect their percentage in the American population. . . .

In the arenas of employment, occupation, income, and wealth, African-Americans remain disadvantaged compared to whites. . . . The average income for white families was 78 percent higher than for African-American families in 1987 dollars. Economic disparity between the two racial groups has increased since 1978 (Urban League, 1989). Indeed, analysis of trend data show that the income gap between African-Americans and white men has not lowered since 1948 (Farley and Allen, 1987). About one African-American in three lives below the poverty line today compared to about one in ten whites (U.S. Bureau of the Census, Series P-20, No. 442). At the current rate of progress of African-Americans, parity with whites will not be achieved in individual poverty rates until the year 2148 for individuals and 2158 for families (National Urban League, 1989). The rate of unemployment for young African-American men is three times that of young white men—a disparity increasing since 1948. Among young central-city African-Americans men, unemployment rates (excluding "discouraged workers") are as high as 50 percent (Farley and Allen, 1987). Although African-American women fare somewhat better, their higher income in comparison to white females is primarily due to lower earnings of women regardless of race or ethnicity. In 1980, more than a century after the abolition of slavery, there were still more African-American women employed as domestics than there were African-American women professionals (Farley and Allen, 1987). . . .

High unemployment, poverty, and economic tension have taken their toll among African-Americans. An African-American male teenager is six times as likely as a white male teenager to be a victim of homicide (National Urban League, 1989). African-Americans suffer from higher rates of almost all cancers and are 33 percent more likely to develop diabetes. Higher rates of heart disease and stroke among African-American women account for nearly half of the black-white difference in their life expectancy: cancer, homicide, and strokes account for 50 percent of the six-year difference between African-American and white men (Farley and Allen, 1987). Nearly 40 percent of all African-American mothers receive no prenatal care in the first trimester of pregnancy. One in eight African-American infants is born at a low birth weight, and the infant mortality rate is twice that of white infants. The infant mortality rate for whites ranks with Britain and West Germany; for African-Americans it ranks with Cuba. African-American children are more likely to drop out of elementary or high school and less likely to attend college.

Much has been written about the increasing numbers of African-American families that have moved into the middle class (Wilson, 1980, 1981), but they still work harder for equal rewards. At the same level of education and occupation, African-American wages are lower than those of whites.

Given the political, income, and occupational data just presented, it is evident that sources of personal and social prestige are systematically denied to African-Americans. In one area of most rapid gains, education, advancement may be more apparent than real. . . .

African-Americans have made occupational gains since 1960, but they have not been as significant as those of whites, particularly white males. In football, for example, although 57 percent of total members of the NFL were African-American by 1987, only 6.5 percent of the administrative posts were held by African-Americans. Even African-Americans in positions that pay well and sound prestigious have complained that they have been placed in high-visibility dead-end jobs.

The evidence supports the caste model of stratification in the United States today, although debates over the relative importance of class and race continue. Some analysts (Wilson, 1978, 1986) claim that race itself is less important than the overwhelming effects of poverty. Others cite continuing racism as a major factor in perpetuating the cycle of poverty. That African-Americans have fared poorly in our economic system seems evident. Although African-Americans have achieved higher levels of education and have greater opportunities for political activity, they remain outside the mainstream stratification system. And their disadvantages have been built into the social structure. For generations, despite their familiarity with American customs and language, African-Americans were systematically denied the right to vote, to be on juries, and even to be promoted in the military long after newer immigrant groups had achieved these goals (Lieberson, 1981).

Comparative studies of African-American and white ethnic immigrants indicate that the greater success of whites in achieving middle-class status has been aided by "a set of bootstraps that must be government issued . . . a system of protection that takes the civil rights of groups to acquire property and to pursue a wide range of economic opportunities" (Smith, 1987, p. 168). African-Americans have not been issued similar bootstraps enabling collective entry into the middle class....

Asians in the United States

Like European-Americans, Asian-Americans come from different cultures and religious backgrounds and speak different languages. Yet, a tendency to classify all Asians together has dominated both immigration policy and popular attitudes....

The Asian-American population increased by 142 percent between 1970 and 1980. Despite the growing importance of Asians, the decennial census is the only source of detailed information currently available. Unlike Latinos, on whom data are collected by the federal government each year, Asians are still too small a category to be captured in sample surveys.... Those people described by the Bureau of the Census as Asian are diverse, representing different languages, religions, cultural traditions, time of immigration, and poverty level.... The only other source of national data on Asians comes from the Immigration and Naturalization Service, which collects annual information on immigrants. Immigration data indicate that the three largest groups of Asian immigrants during the past few years have been Chinese, Filipino, and Korean. These three groups make up more than 20 percent of the total number of legal immigrants coming to the United States.

CHINESE In the mid-nineteenth century, young Chinese males were imported to work on the transcontinental railroad. Unable to bring a wife with them or to send for a woman to marry, those who remained in the United States formed an almost exclusively male community, concentrated in a few occupations (Siu, 1987). Chinese men were victims of extreme prejudice, discrimination, and open violence until the outbreak of World War II, when suddenly they became the "good" Asians compared to the "evil" Japanese. Restrictive immigration laws ended in the 1960s, and... 63.3 percent of Chinese-Americans in 1980 were foreign born.

The majority of Chinese live in seven states, with California having the highest concentration (40 percent), followed by New York, Hawaii, Illinois, Texas, Massachusetts, and New Jersey. As older immigrant groups have left the garment industry, an increasing number of immigrant Chinese entrepreneurs in New York have opened small manufacturing plants that do not require large initial capital investments; they have also recruited workers through kin and friendship networks (Waldinger, 1987).

As barriers to discrimination were lifted, Chinese-Americans entered colleges and universities in growing numbers.... A high proportion of both American- and foreign-born Chinese in the labor force held jobs as managers, professionals, or executives in 1980, and this percentage is growing. Although residential discrimination still exists in some areas, it has been less difficult for Chinese than for African-Americans to assimilate culturally or to amalgamate.

JAPANESE According to one social scientist (Kitano, 1976), Japanese immigrants "came to the wrong country and the wrong state (California) at the wrong time (immediately after the Chinese) with the wrong race and skin color, with the wrong religion, and from the wrong country" (p. 31). After the outbreak of World War II, the Japanese in North America were forcibly moved from their homes and "relocated." Inasmuch as hostility toward Japan was high in the United States during World War II, Japanese-Americans provided visible targets for its expression. Their appearance, language, and culture were interpreted as indications of disloyalty to the United States. More than 100,000 West Coast Japanese-Americans were placed in detention camps, with guard towers and barbed-wire fences. Their property was confiscated, sold, or stolen. Among the long-term effects of relocation were a reduction in the relative power of men over women in the family, a weakening of control over offspring, and reinforcement of a sense of ethnic identity.

Has the pattern of Japanese-Americans assimilation been similar to that of other minority... groups, or are they still excluded from the majority society, as their relocation during World War II dramatically illustrated? In the history of U.S. race relations, few nonwhite minorities have established as secure an economic position as whites. The Japanese-Americans in California are a notable exception and have been upwardly mobile in part because of their economic ethnic hegemony. *Ethnic hegemony* refers to the power exerted by one ethnic group over another. Japanese-Americans achieved economic control over produce agriculture, thereby dominating an important economic area that permitted them to interact from a position of power with the majority culture (Jiobu, 1988).

Greater mobility, in turn, has been associated with a shift from jobs in the ethnic community to employment in the corporate economy, and to greater assimilation. For example, third-generation Japanese-Americans have a higher percentage of non-Japanese friends than do first- or second-generation Japanese-Americans. They are also more likely to have non-Japanese spouses, to live in a non-Japanese neighborhood, and to profess non-Japanese religious beliefs (Montero, 1981). Moreover, the Japanese are the only Asian-American group to have a higher proportion of childless couples than do whites (Robey, 1985). In short, as occupational and financial mobility has occurred, greater cultural, structural, and marital assimilation has taken place.

Can the Japanese-American community remain intact or will it be amalgamated into the majority society? The answer will depend on whether Japanese-Americans develop a broader identity as Asian-Americans. But the most highly educated and most successful Japanese-Americans have become the most cut off from their ethnic background; for example, 40 percent have non-Japanese spouses. The irony of this trend toward amalgamation is that the Japanese may lose their roots in the tradition that gave rise to their upward mobility.

THE INDOCHINESE Indochina is a region in southeast Asia that includes Vietnam, Cambodia, Thailand, and Laos. In 1960, a total of only 59 immigrants were admitted to the United States from Vietnam, Laos, and Cambodia combined; all but 3 of these came from Vietnam. However, in the decade following the end of the Vietnam War, about 842,000 Indochinese immigrants, primarily refugees, arrived in the United States. In 1987 alone, more than 50,000 Indochinese immigrated to the United States (*Statistical Abstract, 1989*). Indochinese now represent more than one Asian-American in five.

Within the Indochinese population, there are marked cultural and linguistic variations. Only about one-sixth came as part of the largely elite first wave of South Vietnamese who brought with them money and skills. In contrast, recent arrivals have been both more numerous and more diverse: Vietnamese "boat people," lowland Laotians, almost all of the Hmong or Laotian hill tribes, and Cambodians. Many of these people came from rural backgrounds, had little education or transferable occupational skills, no knowledge of English, and had spent long periods in refugee camps overseas prior to coming to the United States. Moreover, their arrival coincided with inflation, recession, and growing fears of displacement among the native-born population (Rumbaut, 1986). Despite government policies that attempted to settle these new refugees throughout the United States, about 40 percent of Indochinese immigrants live in California, and 8 percent in Texas. Vietnamese also cluster in Washington, Pennsylvania, New York, Louisiana, and the District of Columbia. Laotians can be found in places as diverse as Minnesota, Rhode Island, and Oregon, with a large concentration of Hmong in agricultural central California.

OTHER ASIANS In 1980, there were about 1.7 million people of other Asian ethnicities in the United States. Filipinos accounted for 45 percent, followed by Asian Indians and Koreans. Koreans showed the most remarkable growth, increasing from 69,999 in 1970 to 357,000 by 1980. The welcome given to the arrival of Asian-Americans, like that of most new immigrants who are not of northern European origin, has been mixed. However, Asians, whether from Korea, India, or elsewhere, may be the achievers of the future. An incredible 52 percent of adult Asian Indians and more than one-third of Filipinos are college graduates. (It is important to note that most Asian Indians admitted to this country already had a good educational background upon arrival.)

ETHNIC MINORITIES

The great variety of nationalities is a defining characteristic of American society. To illustrate general themes in the immigrant experiences and to introduce you to the fastest growing ethnic minorities in the United States, our discussion will focus on two recent entrants: Latinos and Middle-Easterners.

Latinos

Latino is a category made up of many separate cultural and racial subgroups bound together by a common language, Spanish (although even language patterns vary by country of origin). In 1989, about 21 million Spanish-speaking people were officially recorded as residing in the United States, and several million others are believed to have entered without official documents.

Because of their generally younger ages and high birthrates, it is likely that Spanish-speaking Americans will soon outnumber African-Americans as the single largest minority group in the United States.

In 1989, the four major ethnic subdivisions within the Spanish-speaking population were Mexican-Americans; Puerto Ricans; Cubans; and people from Central and South American countries, particularly the Dominican Republic, Colombia, and El Salvador.... The remainder were from other Spanish-speaking nations.... Differences within the Spanish-speaking minority are striking, especially in terms of education and income. Each ethnic group has its own immigration history, cultural patterns, and its own internal diversity.

There is a stratification system within the Latino population, based not only on indicators of socioeconomic status but also on skin color. Race and ethnicity combine to determine the relative status of Spanish-speaking Americans, both within the stratification system of the wider society and within the hierarchy of the Latino subculture. These divisions reduce the likelihood of the development of shared interests necessary to build a unified Latino power base.

MEXICAN-AMERICANS When the United States conquered Mexico in 1848 the Southwest had already been settled by Mexicans. A gradual pattern of economic and social subordination of the Mexicans, as well as Native Americans, developed as white Americans ("Anglos") migrated into the Southwest.

Like many other ethnic groups that have not been accepted by the majority group, Mexican-Americans tend... to live in particular geographic areas, such as southern California, south Texas, and New Mexico.... Although the stereotype of the Mexican farm laborer persists, relatively few Mexican-Americans today work on farms, in contrast to the employment pattern of their parents. This change reflects the increasing industrialization of agriculture rather than gains in job status or income. The occupational mobility of Mexican-Americans has been horizontal rather than vertical. That is, the present generation has moved from farm labor into other unskilled jobs, such as work in canning factories. Relatively few have moved into semiskilled or higher-status occupations. Many undocumented workers from Mexico have been employed in low-wage service and manufacturing jobs to keep labor costs low and to prevent unionization.

On various measures of social mobility, Mexican-Americans rank below the average for the population as a whole. In general they have less education than do non-Latinos or African-Americans. The traditional Mexican family is an extended one, with the kinship group being both the main focus of obligation and the source of emotional and social support. Birthrates are relatively high, especially among first-generation and poorly educated women (Bean and Swicegood, 1985). Within the family, gender roles are well defined. Both mothers and daughters are expected to be protected and submissive and to dedicate themselves to caring for the males of the family. For the Mexican male, *machismo,* or the demonstration of physical and sexual prowess, is basic to self-respect.

These traditional patterns protect Mexican-Americans against the effects of prejudice and discrimination, but they also reinforce isolation from the majority culture. An upwardly mobile Mexican-American must often choose between remaining locked into a semi-isolated ethnic world or becoming alienated from family, friends, and ethnic roots (Arce, 198).

PUERTO RICANS Technically U.S. citizens since the United States took the island after the Spanish-American War in 1898, Puerto Ricans began to arrive on the mainland in large numbers in the 1950s because of the collapse of the sugar industry on their island. One-third of the world's Puerto Ricans now reside in the mainland United States. Of the 2.3 million mainland Puerto Ricans, 80 percent live in six states: New York, New Jersey, Connecticut, Illinois, Pennsylvania, and Massachusetts. Although almost two-fifths of the Puerto Ricans in the continental United States have incomes below the poverty level, their expectations of success are higher than the expectations of those who have remained in Puerto Rico.

Although Puerto Ricans are often grouped with Mexican-Americans, the two populations are very different in history, culture, and racial composition. Puerto Rico's culture is a blend of African and Spanish influences, with a heavy dose of American patterns. In Mexico, both Spanish and Native American elements combine.

The Puerto Rican experience on the mainland has included a continuing struggle for stability and achievement in education, politics, the arts, and community control. Puerto Ricans have been elected to the U.S. Congress, to state legislatures, and to city councils. Growing numbers of Puerto Ricans have moved from the inner city to middle-income, homeowner suburbs, and young Puerto Ricans are entering the fields of law, business, medicine, and teaching.... Others continue to have difficulty on standardized English and math tests, to drop out of school, and to face unemployment. About 43 percent of Puerto Rican families are likely to be headed by a woman with no husband present.

CUBANS Cuban immigration to the United States began in large numbers when Fidel Castro came to power in the mid-1950s. Between 1954 and 1978, more than 325,000 Cubans were admitted as permanent residents in the United States, especially in the Miami, Florida, area. In early 1980, an additional 115,000 refugees entered the country in a sudden, somewhat chaotic exodus from Cuba. Although it is too early to determine how these new Cuban immigrants will fare in the United States, many earlier immigrants have achieved success operating businesses within Cuban communities... and a Cuban-American woman from Florida was elected to Congress.

Of all Spanish-speaking subgroups in the U.S. the Cubans are older and better educated; are more likely to live in metropolitan areas, though not the central city; and have the highest median income. Much of their success, however, can be attributed to the educational and occupational characteristics with which they entered America. Theirs was an upper- and middle-class emigration in contrast to that of the Cuban newcomers of 1980, who were, on the average, younger, less educated, and less skilled. Recent Cuban immigrants have also been received with greater hostility and fear, and they are experiencing barriers to mobility within the established Cuban communities as well as outside.

Beth B. Hess et al.

In recent years, a new group of immigrants from the Middle East has begun to emerge as a visible urban minority. The number of immigrants from Middle Eastern countries has averaged more than 18,000 annually since 1970. Yet, little is known about them.... They have come from a number of different countries such as Egypt, Syria, Lebanon, Iran, and Jordan, and they speak a number of languages. Their religious affiliations include Muslim, Coptic Christian, and Melkite Catholic, and they bring with them diverse cultural norms. Many would not describe themselves as "Arabs." They do not speak Arabic or identify with Arabic history and culture. The one common denominator of these different ethnic groups is their Middle Eastern origin. The socioeconomic position of the various ethnic groups also varies: the Lebanese, the Syrians, and the Iranians are primarily middle class, whereas other groups are mostly working class....

In the Detroit area, which now has the largest concentration of Arabic-speaking people outside the Middle East—more than 200,000 Lebanese, Palestinians, Yemenis, and Iraqi-Chaldeans—there has been conflict between Middle Easterners and other ethnic groups. From the limited information available, however, there seems to be little racial tension, juvenile delinquency, or crime within Near Eastern immigrant communities. Tensions are caused by drinking, dating, and language, as younger people become acculturated to the norms of the dominant society and reject traditional values and behavior. As with most other immigrant groups, length of residence in the United States is an important factor both in acculturation and in socioeconomic status.

CHAPTER 2 Prejudice and Discrimination

2.1 WILLIAM JULIUS WILSON

The Declining Significance of Race

For decades, the idea of the *underclass* has been the subject of considerable debate in the social sciences. In short, the underclass refers to individuals who are outside the occupational structure of U.S. society. Often called the *inner-city (ghetto) poor,* their communities are plagued by extreme poverty, perpetual joblessness, drug addiction, street violence, high rates of out-of-wedlock childbirths, and transgenerational welfare dependency. Some commentators argue that the underclass constitutes a culturally deprived segment of the American population that is caught in a tangle of social pathology.

William Julius Wilson is the Lucy Flower Distinguished Service Professor of Sociology and Public Policy at the University of Chicago's Center for the Study of Urban Inequality, where he is currently directing a $2.8 million study on poverty, joblessness, and family structure in the inner city. His publications include *The Declining Significance of Race: Blacks and Changing American Institutions* (University of Chicago Press, 1978).

In the selection that follows, which is from "The Declining Significance of Race," *Society* (January/February 1978), Wilson traces the social history of the underclass and contends that, since World War II, class position has become more significant than race in defining the underclass. That is, the forces of postwar industrialization have diminished the effects of racial discrimination, and through occupational advancement a significant Black middle class has been created.

Key Concept: the underclass

Race relations in the United States have undergone fundamental changes in recent years, so much so that now the life chances of individual blacks have more to do with their economic class position than with their day-to-day encounters with whites. In earlier years the systematic efforts of whites to suppress blacks were obvious to even the most insensitive observer. Blacks were denied access to valued and scarce resources through various ingenious schemes of racial exploitation, discrimination, and segregation, schemes that were reinforced by elaborate ideologies of racism.

But the situation has changed. However determinative such practices were in the previous efforts of the black population to achieve racial equality, and however significant they were in the creation of poverty-stricken ghettos and a vast underclass of black proletarians—that massive population at the very bottom of the social class ladder plagued by poor education and low-paying, unstable jobs—they do not provide a meaningful explanation of the life chances of black Americans today. The traditional patterns of interaction between blacks and whites, particularly in the labor market, have been fundamentally altered.

NEW AND TRADITIONAL BARRIERS

In the pre-Civil War period, and in the latter half of the nineteenth through the first half of the twentieth century, the continuous and explicit efforts of whites to construct racial barriers profoundly affected the lives of black Americans. Racial oppression was designed, overt, and easily documented. As the nation has entered the latter half of the twentieth century, however, many of the traditional barriers have crumbled under the weight of the political, social, and economic changes of the civil rights era. A new set of obstacles has emerged from basic structural shifts in the economy.

These obstacles are therefore impersonal, but may prove to be even more formidable for certain segments of the black population. Specifically, whereas the previous barriers were usually designed to control and restrict the entire black population, the new barriers create hardships essentially for the black underclass; whereas the old barriers were based explicitly on the racial motivations derived from intergroup contact, the new barriers have racial significance only in their consequences, not in their origins. In short, whereas the old barriers portrayed the pervasive features of racial oppression, the new barriers indicate an important and emerging form of class subordination.

It would be shortsighted to view the traditional forms of racial segregation and discrimination as having essentially disappeared in contemporary America; the presence of blacks is still firmly resisted in various institutions and social arrangements, for example, residential areas and private social clubs. However, in the economic sphere class has become more important than race in determining black access to privilege and power. It is clearly evident in this connection that many talented and educated blacks are now entering positions of prestige and influence at a rate comparable to or, in some situations, exceeding that of whites with equivalent qualifications. It is equally clear that the black underclass is in a hopeless state of economic stagnation, falling further and further behind the rest of society.

THREE STAGES OF AMERICAN RACE RELATIONS

American society has experienced three major stages of black-white contact, and each stage embodies a different form of racial stratification structured by the particular arrangement of both the economy and the polity. Stage one coincides with antebellum slavery and the early postbellum era and may be designated the period of *plantation economy and racial-caste oppression.* Stage two begins in the last quarter of the nineteenth century and ends at roughly the New Deal era, and may be identified as the period of *industrial expansion, class conflict, and racial oppression.* Finally, stage three is associated with the modern, industrial, post-World War II era which really began to crystallize during the 1960s and 1970s, and may be characterized as the period of *progressive transition from race inequalities to class inequalities.* The different periods can be identified as the preindustrial, industrial, and modern industrial stages of American race relations, respectively.

Although this abbreviated designation of the periods of American race relations seems to relate racial change to fundamental economic changes rather directly, it bears repeating that the different stages of race relations are structured by the unique arrangements and interaction of the economy and polity. More specifically, although there was an economic basis of structured racial inequality in the preindustrial and industrial periods of race relations, the polity more or less interacted with the economy either to reinforce patterns of racial stratification or to mediate various forms of racial conflict. Moreover, in the modern industrial period race relations have bene shaped as much by important economic changes as by important political changes. Indeed, it would not be possible to understand fully the subtle and manifest changes in race relations in the modern industrial period without recognizing the dual and often reciprocal influence of structural changes in the economy and political changes in the state. Thus different systems of production and/or different arrangements of the polity have imposed different constraints on the way in which racial groups have interacted in the United States, constraints that have structured the relations between racial groups and that have produced dissimilar contexts not only for the manifestation of racial antagonisms, but also for racial group access to rewards and privileges.

In contrast to the modern industrial period in which fundamental economic and political changes have made the economic class position of blacks the determining factor in their prospects for occupational advancement, the preindustrial and industrial periods of black-white relations have one central feature in common: overt efforts of whites to solidify economic racial domination (ranging from the manipulation of black labor to the neutralization or elimination of black economic competition) through various forms of judicial, political, and social discrimination. Since racial problems during these two periods were principally related to group struggles over economic resources, they readily lend themselves to the economic class theories of racial antagonisms that associate racial antipathy with class conflict.

Although racial oppression, when viewed from the broad perspective of historical change in American society, was a salient and important feature during the preindustrial and industrial periods of race relations in the United States, the problems of subordination for certain segments of the black population and the experience of social advancement for others are more directly associated with economic class in the modern industrial period. Economic and political changes have gradually shaped a black class structure, making it increasingly difficult to speak of a single or uniform black experience. Although a small elite population of free, propertied blacks did in fact exist during the pre-Civil War period, the interaction between race and economic class only assumed real importance in the latter phases of the industrial period of race relations; and the significance of this relationship has grown as the nation has entered the modern industrial period.

Each of the major periods of American race relations has been shaped in different measure both by the systems of production and by the laws and policies of the state. However, the relationships between the economy and the state have varied in each period, and therefore the roles of both institutions in shaping race relations have differed over time.

ANTEBELLUM SOUTH

In the preindustrial period the slave-based plantation economy of the South allowed a relatively small, elite group of planters to develop enormous regional power. The hegemony of the southern ruling elite was based on a system of production that required little horizontal or vertical mobility and therefore could be managed very efficiently with a simple division of labor that virtually excluded free white labor. As long as free white workers were not central to the process of reproducing the labor supply in the southern plantation economy, slavery as a mode of production facilitated the slaveholder's concentration and consolidation of economic power. And the slaveholders successfully transferred their control of the economic system to the political and legal systems in order to protect their class interest in slavery. In effect, the polity in the South regulated and reinforced the system of racial caste oppression, depriving both blacks and nonslaveholding whites of any meaningful influence in the way that slavery was used in the economic life of the South.

In short, the economy provided the basis for the development of the system of slavery, and the policy reinforced and perpetuated that system. Furthermore, the economy enabled the slaveholders to develop a regional center of power, and the polity was used to legitimate that power. Since non-slaveholding whites were virtually powerless both economically and politically, they had very little effect on the developing patterns of race relations. The meaningful forms of black-white contact were between slaves and slaveholders, and southern race relations consequently assumed a paternalistic quality involving the elaboration and specification of duties, norms, rights, and obligations as they pertained to the use of slave labor and the system of indefinite servitude.

In short, the pattern of race relations in the antebellum South was shaped first and foremost by the system of production. The very nature of the social relations of production meant that the exclusive control of the planters would be derived from their position in the production process, which ultimately led to the creation of a juridicial system that reflected and protected their class interests, including their investment in slavery.

WORKERS' EMERGING POWER

However, in the nineteenth century antebellum North the form of racial oppression was anything but paternalistic. Here a more industrial system of production enabled white workers to become more organized and physically concentrated than their southern counterparts. Following the abolition of slavery in the North, they used their superior resources to generate legal and informal practices of segregation that effectively prevented blacks from becoming serious economic competitors.

As the South gradually moved from a plantation to an industrial economy in the last quarter of the nineteenth century, landless whites were finally able to effect changes in the racial stratification system. Their efforts to eliminate black competition helped to produce an elaborate system of Jim Crow segregation. Poor whites were aided not only by their numbers but also by the development of political resources which accompanied their greater involvement in the South's economy.

Once again, however, the system of production was the major basis for this change in race relations, and once again the political system was used to reinforce patterns of race emanating from structural shifts in the economy. If the racial laws in the antebellum South protected the class interests of the planters and reflected their overwhelming power, the Jim Crow segregation laws of the late nineteenth century reflected the rising power of the white laborers; and if the political power of the planters was grounded in the system of producing in a plantation economy, the emerging political power of the workers grew out of the new division of labor that accompanied industrialization.

CLASS AND RACE RELATIONS

Except for the brief period of fluid race relations in the North between 1870 and 1890 and in the South during the Reconstruction era, racial oppression is the single best term to characterize the black experience prior to the twentieth century. In the antebellum South both slaves and free blacks occupied what could be best described as a caste position, in the sense that realistic chances for occupational mobility simply did not exist. In the antebellum North a few free blacks were able to acquire some property and improve their socioeconomic position, and a few were even able to make use of educational opportunities. However, the overwhelming majority of free northern Negroes were trapped in menial positions and were victimized by lower-class white antagonism, including the racial hostilities of European immigrant ethnics (who successfully curbed black economic competition). In the postbellum South the system of Jim Crow segregation wiped out the small gains blacks had achieved during Reconstruction, and blacks were rapidly pushed out of the more skilled jobs they had held since slavery. Accordingly, there was very little black occupational differentiation in the South at the turn of the century.

Just as the shift from a plantation economy to an industrializing economy transformed the class and race relations in the postbellum South, so too did industrialization in the North change the context for race-class interaction and confrontation there. On the one hand, the conflicts associated with the increased black-white contacts in the early twentieth century North resembled the forms of antagonism that soured the relations between the races in the postbellum South. Racial conflicts between blacks and whites in both situations were closely tied to class conflicts among whites. On the other hand, there were some fundamental differences. The collapse of the paternalistic bond between blacks and the southern business elite cleared the path for the almost total subjugation of blacks in the South and resulted in what amounted to a united white racial movement that solidified the system of Jim Crow segregation.

However, a united white movement against blacks never really developed in the North. In the first quarter of the twentieth century, management attempted to undercut white labor by using blacks as strikebreakers and, in some situations, as permanent replacements for white workers who periodically demanded higher wages and more fringe benefits. Indeed, the determination of industrialists to ignore racial norms of exclusion and to hire black workers was one of the main reasons why the industrywide unions reversed their racial policies and actively recruited black workers during the New Deal era. Prior to this period the overwhelming majority of unskilled and semiskilled blacks were nonunionized and were available as lower-paid labor or as strikebreakers. The more management used blacks to undercut white labor, the greater were the racial antagonisms between white and black labor.

Moreover, racial tension in the industrial sector often reinforced and sometimes produced racial tension in the social order. The growth of the black urban population created a housing shortage during the early twentieth century which frequently produced black "invasions" or ghetto "spillovers" into adjacent poor white neighborhoods. The racial tensions emanating from labor strife seemed to heighten the added pressures of racial competition for housing, neighborhoods, and recreational areas. Indeed, it was this combination of racial friction in both the economic sector and the social order that produced the bloody riots in East Saint Louis in 1917 and in Chicago and several other cities in 1919.

In addition to the fact that a united white movement against blacks never really developed in the North during the industrial period, it was also the case that the state's role in shaping race relations was much more autonomous, much less directly related to developments in the economic sector. Thus, in the brief period of fluid race relations in the North from 1870 to 1890, civil rights laws were passed barring discrimination in public places and in public institutions. This legislation did not have any real significance to the white masses at that time because, unlike in the pre-Civil War North and the post-Civil War South, white workers did not perceive blacks as major economic competitors. Blacks constituted only a small percentage of the total population in northern cities; they had not yet been used in any significant numbers as cheap labor in industry or as strikebreakers; and their earlier antebellum competitors in low-status jobs (the Irish and German immigrants) had improved their economic status in the trades and municipal employment.

POLITY AND RACIAL OPPRESSION

For all these reasons liberal whites and black professionals, urged on by the spirit of racial reform that had developed during the Civil War and Reconstruction, could pursue civil rights programs without firm resistance; for all these reasons racial developments on the political front were not directly related to the economic motivations and interests of workers and management. In the early twentieth century the independent effect of the political system was displayed in an entirely different way. The process of industrialization had significantly altered the pattern of racial interaction, giving rise to various manifestations of racial antagonism.

Although discrimination and lack of training prevented blacks from seeking higher-paying jobs, they did compete with lower-class whites for unskilled and semiskilled factory jobs, and they were used by management to undercut the white workers' union movement. Despite the growing importance of race in the dynamics of the labor market, the political system did not intervene either to mediate the racial conflicts or to reinforce the pattern of labor-market racial interaction generated by the system of production. This was the case despite the salience of a racial ideology system that justified and prescribed unequal treatment for Afro-Americans. (Industrialists will more likely challenge societal racial norms in situations where adherence to them results in economic losses.)

If nothing else, the absence of political influence on the labor market probably reflected the power struggles between management and workers. Thus legislation to protect the rights of black workers to compete openly for jobs would have conflicted with the interests of white workers, whereas legislation to deny black participation in any kind of industrial work would have conflicted with the interest of management. To repeat, unlike in the South, a united white movement resulting in the almost total segregation of the work force never really developed in the North.

But the state's lack of influence in the industrial sector of private industries did not mean that it had no significant impact on racial stratification in the early twentieth century North. The urban political machines, controlled in large measure by working-class ethnics who were often in direct competition with blacks in the private industrial sector, systematically gerrymandered black neighborhoods and excluded the urban black masses from meaningful political participation throughout the early twentieth century. Control by the white ethnics of the various urban political machines was so complete that blacks were never really in a position to compete for the more important municipal political rewards, such as patronage jobs or government contracts and services. Thus the lack of racial competition for municipal political rewards did not provide the basis for racial tension and conflict in the urban political system. This political racial oppression had no direct connection with or influence on race relations in the private industrial sector.

In sum, whether one focuses on the way race relations were structured by the system of production or the polity or both, racial oppression (ranging from the exploitation of black labor by the business class to the elimination of black competition for economic, social, and political resources by the white masses) was a characteristic and important phenomenon in both the preindustrial and industrial periods of American race relations. Nonetheless, and despite the prevalence of various forms of racial oppression, the change from a preindustrial to an industrial system of production did enable blacks to increase their political and economic resources. The proliferation of jobs created by industrial expansion helped generate and sustain the continuous mass migration of blacks from the rural South to the cities of the North and West. As the black urban population grew and became more segregated, institutions and organizations in the black community also developed, together with a business and professional class affiliated with these institutions. Still, it was not until after World War II (the modern industrial period) that the black class structure started to take on some of the characteristics of the white class structure.

CLASS AND BLACK LIFE CHANCES

Class has also become more important than race in determining black life chances in the modern industrial period. Moreover, the center of racial conflict has shifted from the industrial sector to the sociopolitical order. Although these changes can be related to the more fundamental changes in the system of production and in the laws and policies of the state, the relations between the economy and the polity in the modern industrial period have differed from those in previous periods. In the preindustrial and industrial periods the basis of structured racial inequality was primarily economic, and in most situations the state was merely an instrument to reinforce patterns of race relations that grew directly out of the social relations of production.

Except for the brief period of fluid race relations in the North from 1870 to 1890, the state was a major instrument of racial oppression. State intervention in the modern industrial period has been designed to promote racial equality, and the relationship between the polity and the economy has been much more reciprocal, so much so that it is difficult to determine which one has been more important in shaping race relations since World War II. It was the expansion of the economy that facilitated black movement from the rural areas to the industrial centers and that created job opportunities leading to greater occupational differentiation in the black community (in the sense that an increasing percentage of blacks moved into white-collar positions); and it was the intervention of the state (responding to the pressures of increased black political resources and to the racial protest movement) that removed many artificial discrimination barriers by municipal, state, and federal civil rights legislation, and that contributed to the more liberal racial policies of the nation's labor unions by protective union legislation. And these combined political and economic changes created a pattern of black occupational upgrading that resulted, for example, in a substantial drop in the percentage of black males in the low-paying service, unskilled laborer, and farm jobs.

However despite the greater occupational differentiation within the black community, there are now signs that the effect of some aspects of structural economic change has been the closer association between black occupational mobility and class affiliation. Access to the means of production is increasingly based on educational criteria (a situation which distinguishes the modern industrial from the earlier industrial system of production) and thus threatens to solidify the position of the black underclass. In other words, a consequence of the rapid growth of the corporate and government sectors has been the gradual creation of a segmented labor market that currently provides vastly different mobility opportunities for different segments of the black population.

On the one hand, poorly trained and educationally limited blacks of the inner city, including that growing number of black teenagers and young adults, see their job prospects increasingly restricted to the low-wage sector, their unemployment rates soaring to record levels (which remain high despite swings in the business cycle), their labor force participation rates declining, their movement out of poverty slowing, and their welfare roles increasing. On the other hand, talented and educated blacks are experiencing unprecedented job opportunities in the growing government and corporate sectors, opportunities that are at least comparable to those of whites with equivalent qualifications. The improved job situation for the more privileged blacks in the corporate and government sectors is related both to the expansion of salaried white-collar positions and to the pressures of state affirmative action programs.

In view of these developments, it would be difficult to argue that the plight of the black underclass is solely a consequence of racial oppression, that is, the explicit and overt efforts of whites to keep blacks subjugated, in the same way that it would be difficult to explain the rapid economic improvement of the more privileged blacks by arguing that the traditional forms of racial segregation and discrimination still characterize the labor market in American industries. The recent mobility patterns of blacks lend strong support to the view that economic class is clearly more important than race in predetermining job placement and occupational mobility. In the economic realm, then, the black experience has moved historically from economic racial oppression experienced by virtually all blacks to economic subordination for the black underclass. And as we begin the last quarter of the twentieth century, a deepening economic schism seems to be developing in the black community, with the black poor falling further and further behind middle- and upper-income blacks.

SHIFT OF RACIAL CONFLICT

If race is declining in significance in the economic sector, explanations of racial antagonism based on labor-market conflicts, such as those advanced by economic class theories of race, also have less significance in the period of modern industrial race relations. Neither the low-wage sector nor the corporate and government sectors provide the basis for the kind of interracial job competition and conflict that plagued the economic order in previous periods. With the absorption of blacks into industrywide labor unions, protective union legislation, and equal employment legislation, it is no longer feasible for management to undercut white labor by using black workers. The traditional racial struggles for power and privilege have shifted away from the economic sector and are now concentrated in the sociopolitical order. Although poor blacks and poor whites are still the main actors in the present manifestations of racial strife, the immediate source of the tension has more to do with racial competition for public schools, municipal political systems, and residential areas than with the competition for jobs.

To say that race is declining in significance, therefore, is not only to argue that the life chances of blacks have less to do with race than with economic class affiliation, but also to maintain that racial conflict and competition in the economic sector—the most important historical factors in the subjugation of blacks—have been substantially reduced. However, it would be argued that the firm white resistance to public school desegregation, residential integration, and black control of central cities all indicate the unyielding importance of race in the United States. The argument could even be entertained that the impressive occupational gains of the black middle class are only temporary, and that as soon as affirmative action pressures are relieved, or as soon as the economy experiences a prolonged recession, industries will return to their old racial practices.

Both of these arguments are compelling if not altogether persuasive. Taking the latter contention first, there is little available evidence to suggest that the economic gains of privileged blacks will be reversed. Despite the fact that the recession of the early 1970s decreased job prospects for all educated workers, the more educated blacks continued to experience a faster rate of job advancement than their white counterparts. And although it is always possible that an economic disaster could produce racial competition for higher-paying jobs and white efforts to exclude talented blacks, it is difficult to entertain this idea as a real possibility in the face of the powerful political and social movement against job discrimination. At this point there is every reason to believe that talented and educated blacks, like talented and educated whites, will continue to enjoy the advantages and privileges of their class status.

My response to the first argument is not to deny the current racial antagonism in the sociopolitical order, but to suggest that such antagonism has far less effect on individual or group access to those opportunities and resources that are centrally important for life survival than antagonism in the economic sector. The factors that most severely affected black life chances in previous years were the racial oppression and antagonism in the economic sector. As race declined in importance in the economic sector, the Negro class structure became more differentiated and black life chances became increasingly a consequence of class affiliation.

Furthermore, it is even difficult to identify the form of racial contact in the sociopolitical order as the source of the current manifestations of conflict between lower-income blacks and whites, because neither the degree of racial competition between the have-nots, nor their structural relations in urban communities, nor their patterns of interaction constitute the ultimate source of present racial antagonism. The ultimate basis for current racial tension is the deleterious effect of basic structural changes in the modern American economy on black and white lower-income groups, changes that include uneven economic growth, increasing technology and automation, industry relocation, and labor market segmentation.

FIGHTING CLASS SUBORDINATION

The situation of marginality and redundancy created by the modern industrial society deleteriously affects all the poor, regardless of race. Underclass whites, Hispano Americans, and Native Americans all are victims, to a greater or lesser degree, of class subordination under advanced capitalism. It is true that blacks are disproportionately represented in the underclass population and that about one-third of the entire black population is in the underclass. But the significance of these facts has more to do with the historical consequences of racial oppression than with the current effects of race.

Although the percentage of blacks below the low-income level dropped steadily throughout the 1960s, one of the legacies of the racial oppression in previous years is the continued disproportionate black representation in the underclass. And since 1970 both poor whites and nonwhites have evidenced very little progress in their elevation from the ranks of the underclass. In the final analysis, therefore, the challenge of economic dislocation in modern industrial society calls for public policy programs to attack inequality on a broad class front, policy programs—in other words—that go beyond the limits of ethnic and racial discrimination by directly confronting the pervasive and destructive features of class subordination.

2.2 JOE R. FEAGIN

The Continuing Significance of Race: Antiblack Discrimination in Public Places

To dispel the commonly held belief that racial and ethnic discrimination have been effectively eliminated from society, social scientists have documented the life experiences of minority groups. To this end, Joe R. Feagin, a sociology professor at the University of Florida and the author of *Racial and Ethnic Relations,* 3rd ed. (Prentice Hall, 1989), has drawn on several in-depth interviews with members of the Black middle class to ascertain the sites and character of discriminatory actions and the range of coping mechanisms Blacks draw upon to deal with discriminatory actions. In the following selection from "The Continuing Significance of Race: Antiblack Discrimination in Public Places," *American Sociological Review* (February 1991), Feagin discusses his findings, which show that "deprivation and discrimination in public accommodations persist."

Key Concept: the continuing significance of race

Title II of the 1964 Civil Rights Act stipulates that "all persons shall be entitled to the full and equal enjoyment of the goods, services, facilities, privileges, advantages, and accommodations of any place of public accommodation... without discrimination or segregation on the ground of race, color, religion, or national origin." The public places emphasized in the act are restaurants, hotels, and motels, although racial discrimination occurs in many other public places. Those black Americans who would make the greatest use of these public accommodations and certain other public places would be middle-class, i.e., those with the requisite resources....

ASPECTS OF DISCRIMINATION

Discrimination can be defined in social-contextual terms as "actions or practices carried out by members of dominant racial or ethnic groups that have a differential and negative impact on members of subordinate racial and ethnic groups" (Feagin and Eckberg 1980, pp. 1–2). This differential treatment ranges from the blatant to the subtle (Feagin and Feagin 1986). Here I focus primarily on blatant discrimination by white Americans targeting middle-class blacks. Historically, discrimination against blacks has been one of the most serious forms of racial/ethnic discrimination in the United States and one of the most difficult to overcome, in part because of the institutionalized character of color coding. I focus on three important aspects of discrimination: (1) the variation in sites of discrimination; (2) the range of discriminatory actions; and (3) the range of responses by blacks to discrimination.

Sites of Discrimination

There is a spatial dimension to discrimination. The probability of experiencing racial hostility varies from the most private to the most public sites. If a black person is in a relatively protected site, such as with friends at home, the probability of experiencing hostility and discrimination is low. The probability increases as one moves from friendship settings to such outside sites as the workplace, where a black person typically has contacts with both acquaintances and strangers, providing an interactive context with greater potential for discrimination.

In most workplaces, middle-class status and its organizational resources provide some protection against certain categories of discrimination. This protection probably weakens as a black person moves from those work and school settings where he or she is well-known into public accommodations such as large stores and city restaurants where contacts are mainly with white strangers. On public streets blacks have the greatest public exposure to strangers and the least protection against overt discriminatory behavior, including violence. A key feature of these more public settings is that they often involve contacts with white strangers who react primarily on the basis of one ascribed characteristic. The study of the micro-life of interaction between strangers in public was pioneered by Goffman (1963: 1971) and his students, but few of their analyses have treated hostile discriminatory interaction in public places. A rare exception is the research by Gardner (1980: see also Gardner 1988), who documented the character and danger of passing remarks by men directed against women in unprotected public places. Gardner writes of women (and blacks) as "open persons," i.e. particularly vulnerable targets for harassment that violates the rules of public courtesy.

The Range of Discriminatory Actions

In his classic study, *The Nature of Prejudice,* Allport (1958, pp. 14–5) noted that prejudice can be expressed in a series of progressively more serious actions, ranging from antilocution to avoidance, exclusion, physical attack, and extermination. Allport's work suggests a continuum of actions from avoidance, to exclusion or rejection, to attack. In his travels in the South in the 1950s a white journalist who changed his skin color to black encountered discrimination in each of these categories (Griffin 1961). In my data, discrimination against middle-class blacks still ranges across this continuum: (1) avoidance actions, such as a white couple crossing the street when a black male approaches; (2) rejection actions, such as poor service in public accommodations; (3) verbal attacks, such as shouting racial epithets in the street; (4) physical threats and harassment by white police officers; and (5) physical threats and attacks by other whites, such as attacks by white supremacists in the street. Changing relations between blacks and whites in recent decades have expanded the repertoire of discrimination to include more subtle forms and to encompass discrimination in arenas from which blacks were formerly excluded such as formerly all-white public accommodations.

Black Responses to Discrimination

Prior to societal desegregation in the 1960s much traditional discrimination, especially in the South, took the form of an asymmetrical "deference ritual" in which blacks were typically expected to respond to discriminating whites with great deference.... Such rituals can be seen in the obsequious words and gestures—the etiquette of race relations—that many blacks, including middle-class blacks, were forced to utilize to survive the rigors of segregation (Doyle 1937). However, not all responses in this period were deferential. From the late 1800s to the 1950s, numerous lynchings and other violence targeted blacks whose behavior was defined as too aggressive (Raper 1933), Blauner's (1989) respondents reported acquaintances reacting aggressively to discrimination prior to the 1960s.

Deference rituals can still be found today between some lower-income blacks and their white employers. In her northeastern study Rollins (1985, p. 157) found black maids regularly deferring to white employers. Today, most discriminatory interaction no longer involves much asymmetrical deference, at least for middle-class blacks. Even where whites expect substantial deference, most middle-class blacks do not oblige. For middle-class blacks contemporary discrimination has evolved beyond the asymmetrical deference rituals and "No Negroes served" type of exclusion to patterns of black-contested discrimination....

Some white observers have suggested that many middle-class blacks are paranoid about white discrimination and rush too quickly to charges of racism (Wieseltier 1989, June 5; for male views of female "paranoia" see Gardner 1988). But the daily reality may be just the opposite, as middle-class black Americans often evaluate a situation carefully before judging it discriminatory and taking additional action. This careful evaluation, based on past experiences (real or vicarious), not only prevents jumping to conclusions, but also reflects the hope that white behavior is not based on race, because an act not based on race is easier to endure. After evaluation one strategy is to leave the site of

TABLE 1

Percentage Distribution of Discriminatory Actions By Type and Site: Middle-Class Blacks in Selected Cities, 1988–1990

	Site of Discriminatory Action	
Type of Discriminatory Action	*Public Accommodations*	*Street*
Avoidance	3	7
Rejection/poor service	79	4
Verbal epithets	12	25
Police threats/harassment	3	46
Other threats/harassment	3	18
Total	100	100
Number of actions	34	28

discrimination rather than to create a disturbance. Another is to ignore the discrimination and continue with the interaction, a "blocking" strategy similar to that Gardner (1980, p. 345) reported for women dealing with street remarks. In many situations resigned acceptance is the only realistic response. More confrontational responses to white actions include verbal reprimands and sarcasm, physical counterattacks, and filing lawsuits. Several strategies may be tried in any given discriminatory situation. In crafting these strategies middle-class blacks, in comparison with less privileged blacks, may draw on middle-class resources to fight discrimination.

THE RESEARCH STUDY

To examine discrimination, I draw primarily on 37 in-depth interviews from a larger study of 135 middle-class black Americans in Boston, Buffalo, Baltimore, Washington, D.C., Detroit, Houston, Dallas, Austin, San Antonio, Marshall, Las Vegas, and Los Angeles. . . .

Although all types of mistreatment are reported, there is a strong relationship between type of discrimination and site, with rejection/poor-service discrimination being most common in public accommodations and verbal or physical threat discrimination by white citizens or police officers most likely in the street. . . .

The most common black responses to racial hostility in the street are withdrawal or a verbal reply. In many avoidance situations (e.g., a white couple crossing a street to avoid walking past a black college student) or

TABLE 2

Percentage Distribution of Primary Responses to Discriminatory Incidents by Type and Site: Middle-Class Blacks in Selected Cities, 1988–1990

	Site of Discriminatory Incident	
Response to Discriminatory Incident	*Public Accommodations*	*Street*
Withdrawal/exit	4	22
Resigned acceptance	23	7
Verbal response	69	59
Physical counterattack	4	7
Response unclear	–	4
Total	100	99
Number of responses	26	27

attack situations (e.g., whites throwing beer cans from a passing car), a verbal response is difficult because of the danger or the fleeting character of the hostility. A black victim often withdraws, endures this treatment with resigned acceptance, or replies with a quick verbal retort. In the case of police harassment, the response is limited by the danger, and resigned acceptance or mild verbal protests are likely responses. Rejection (poor service) in public accommodations provides an opportunity to fight back verbally —the most common responses to public accommodations discrimination are verbal counterattacks or resigned acceptance. Some black victims correct whites quietly, while others respond aggressively and lecture the assailant about the discrimination or threaten court action. A few retaliate physically. Examining materials in these 37 interviews . . . we will see that the depth and complexity of contemporary black middle-class responses to white discrimination accents the changing character of white-black interaction and the necessity of continual negotiation of the terms of that interaction.

RESPONSES TO DISCRIMINATION: PUBLIC ACCOMMODATIONS

Two Fundamental Strategies: Verbal Confrontation and Withdrawal

In the following account, a black news director at a major television station shows the interwoven character of discriminatory action and black response.

The discrimination took the form of poor restaurant service, and the responses included both suggested withdrawal and verbal counterattack.

> He [her boyfriend] was waiting to be seated.... He said, "You go to the bathroom and I'll get the table...." He was standing there when I came back; he continued to stand there. The restaurant was almost empty. There were waiters, waitresses, and no one seated. And when I got back to him, he was ready to leave, and said, "Let's go," I said, "What happened to our table?" He wasn't seated. So I said, "No, we're not leaving, please." And he said, "No, I'm leaving." So we went outside and we talked about it. And what I said to him was, you have to be aware of the possibilities that this is not the first time that this has happened at this restaurant or at other restaurants, but this is the first time it has happened to a black news director here or someone who could make an issue of it, or someone who is prepared to make an issue of it.
>
> So we went back inside after I talked him into it and, to make a long story short, I had the manager come. I made most of the people who were there (while conducting myself professionally the whole time) aware that I was incensed at being treated this way.... I said, "Why do you think we weren't seated?" And the manager said, "Well, I don't really know." And I said, "Guess." He said, "Well I don't know, because you're black?" I said, "Bingo. Now isn't it funny that you didn't guess that I didn't have any money" (and I opened up my purse) and I said, "because I certainly have money. And isn't it odd that you didn't guess that it's because I couldn't pay for it because I've got two American Express cards and a Master Card right here. I think it's just funny that you would have assumed that it's because I'm black."... And then I took out my card and gave it to him and said, "If this happens again, or if I hear of this happening again, I will bring the full wrath of an entire news department down on this restaurant." And he just kind of looked at me. "Not [just] because I am personally offended. I am. But because you have no right to do what you did, and as a people we have lived a long time with having our rights abridged...." There were probably three or four sets of diners in the restaurant and maybe five waiters/waitresses. They watched him standing there waiting to be seated. His reaction to it was that he wanted to leave. I understood why he would have reacted that way, because he felt that he was in no condition to be civil. He was ready to take the place apart and... sometimes it's appropriate to behave that way. We hadn't gone the first step before going on to the next step. He didn't feel that he could comfortably and calmly take the first step, and I did. So I just asked him to please get back in the restaurant with me, and then you don't have to say a word, and let me handle it from there. It took some convincing, but I had to appeal to his sense of, this is not just you, this is not just for you. We are finally in a position as black people where there are some of us who can genuinely get their attention. And if they don't want to do this because it's right for them to do it, then they'd better do it because they're afraid to do otherwise. If it's fear, then fine, instill the fear.

This example provides insight into the character of modern discrimination. The discrimination was not the "No Negroes" exclusion of the recent past, but rejection in the form of poor service by restaurant personnel. The black response indicates the change in black-white interaction since the 1950s and 1960s, for discrimination is handled with vigorous confrontation rather than deference. The aggressive black response and the white backtracking underscore Brittan and Maynard's (1984, p. 7) point that black-white interaction today is being renegotiated. It is possible that the white personnel defined the couple as "poor blacks" because of their jeans, although the jeans were fashionable and white patrons wear jeans. In comments not quoted here the news director rejects such an explanation. She forcefully articulates a theory of rights—a response that signals the critical impact of civil rights laws on the thinking of middle-class blacks. The news director articulates the American dream: she has worked hard, earned the money and credit cards, developed the appropriate middle-class behavior, and thus has under the law a *right* to be served. There is defensiveness in her actions too, for she feels a need to legitimate her status by showing her purse and credit cards. One important factor that enabled her to take such assertive action was her power to bring a TV news team to the restaurant. This power marks a change from a few decades ago when very few black Americans had the social or economic resources to fight back successfully....

The confrontation response is generally so costly in terms of time and energy that acquiescence or withdrawal are common options. An example of the exit response was provided by a utility company executive in an east coast city:

> I can remember one time my husband had picked up our son... from camp; and he'd stopped at a little store in the neighborhood near the camp. It was hot, and he was going to buy him a snowball. And the proprietor of the store—this was a very old, white neighborhood, and it was just a little sundry store. But the proprietor said he had the little window where people could come up and order things. Well, my husband and son had gone into the store. And he told them, "Well, I can't give it to you here, but if you go outside to the window, I'll give it to you." And there were other [white] people in the store who'd been served [inside]. So, they just left and didn't buy anything.

... This site differed from the previous example in that the service was probably not of long-term importance to the black family passing through the area. In the previous site the possibility of returning to the restaurant for business or pleasure, may have contributed to the choice of a confrontational response. The importance of the service is a likely variable affecting black responses to discrimination in public accommodations....

The complex process of evaluation and response is described by a college dean, who commented generally on hotel and restaurant discrimination encountered as he travels across the United States:

> When you're in a restaurant and... you notice that blacks get seated near the kitchen. You notice that if it's a hotel, your room is near the elevator, or your room is always way down in a corner somewhere. You find that you are getting the undesirable rooms. And you come there early in the day and you don't see very many cars on the lot and they'll tell you that this is all we've got. Or you get the room that's got a bad television set. You know that you're being discriminated against. And of course you have to act accordingly. You have to tell them, "Okay, the room is fine, [but] this television set has got to go. Bring me another television set." So in my personal experience, I simply cannot sit and let them get away with it [discrimination] and not let them know that I know that that's what they are doing....
>
> When I face discrimination, first I take a long look at myself and try to determine whether or not I am seeing what I think I'm seeing in 1989, and if it's

> something that I have an option [about]. In other words, if I'm at a store making a purchase, I'll simply walk away from it. If it's at a restaurant where I'm not getting good service, I first of all let the people know that I'm not getting good service, then I [may] walk away from it. But the thing that I have to do is to let people know that I know that I'm being singled out for a separate treatment. And then I might react in any number of ways—depending on where I am and how badly I want whatever it is that I'm there for.

This commentary adds another dimension to our understanding of public discrimination, its cumulative aspect. Blacks confront not just isolated incidents —such as a bad room in a luxury hotel once every few years—but a lifelong series of such incidents. Here again the omnipresence of careful assessments is underscored. The dean's interview highlights a major difficulty in being black —one must be constantly prepared to assess accurately and then decide on the appropriate response. This long-look approach may indicate that some middle-class blacks are so sensitive to white charges of hypersensitivity and paranoia that they err in the opposite direction and fail to see discrimination when it occurs. In addition, as one black graduate student at a leading white university in the Southeast put it: "I think that sometimes timely and appropriate responses to racially motivated acts and comments are lost due to the processing of the input." The "long look" can result in missed opportunities to respond to discrimination.

Using Middle-Class Resources for Protection

One advantage that middle-class blacks have over poorer blacks is the use of the resources of middle-class occupations. A professor at a major white university commented on the varying protection her middle-class status gives her at certain sites:

> If I'm in those areas that are fairly protected, within gatherings of my own group, other African Americans, or if I'm in the university where my status as a professor mediates against the way I might be perceived, mediates against the hostile perception, then it's fairly comfortable.... When I divide my life into encounters with the outside world, and of course that's ninety percent of my life, it's fairly consistently unpleasant at those sites where there's nothing that mediates between my race and what I have to do. For example, if I'm in a grocery store, if I'm in my car, which is a 1970 Chevrolet, a real old ugly car, all those things—being in a grocery store in casual clothes, or being in the car—sort of advertises something that doesn't have anything to do with my status as far as people I run into are concerned.
>
> Because I'm a large black woman, and I don't wear whatever class status I have, or whatever professional status [I have] in my appearance when I'm in the grocery store, I'm part of the mass of large black women shopping. For most whites, and even for some blacks, that translates into negative status. That means that they are free to treat me the way they treat most poor black people, because they can't tell by looking at me that I differ from that.

This professor notes the variation in discrimination in the sites through which she travels, from the most private to the most public. At home with friends she faces no problems, and at the university her professorial status gives her some protection from discrimination. The increase in unpleasant encounters as she moves into public accommodations sites such as grocery stores is attributed to the absence of mediating factors such as clear symbols of middle-class status —displaying the middle-class symbols may provide some protection against discrimination in public places....

RESPONSES TO DISCRIMINATION: THE STREET

Reacting to White Strangers

As we move away from public accommodations settings to the usually less protected street sites, racial hostility can become more fleeting and severer, and thus black responses are often restricted. The most serious form of street discrimination is violence. Often the reasonable black response to street discrimination is withdrawal, resigned acceptance, or a quick verbal retort. The difficulty of responding to violence is seen in this report by a man working for a media surveying firm in a southern industrial city:

> I was parked in front of this guy's house.... This guy puts his hands on the window and says, "Get out of the car, nigger."... So, I got out, and I thought, "Oh, this is what's going to happen here." And I'm talking fast. And they're, "What are you doing here?" And I'm, "This is who I am. I work with these people. This is the man we want to put in the survey." And I pointed to the house. And the guy said, "Well you have an out-of-state license tag, right?" "Yea." And he said, "If something happened to you, your people at home wouldn't know for a long time, would they?" ... I said, "Look, I deal with a company that deals with television. [If] something happens to me, it's going to be a national thing."... So, they grab me by the lapel of my coat, and put me in front of my car. They put the blade on my zipper. And now I'm thinking about this guy that's in the truck [behind me], because now I'm thinking that I'm going to have to run somewhere. Where am I going to run? Go to the police? [laughs] So, after a while they bash up my headlight. And I drove [away].

Stigmatized and physically attacked solely because of his color, this man faced verbal hostility and threats of death with courage. Cautiously drawing on his middle-class resources, he told the attackers his death would bring television crews to the town. This resource utilization is similar to that of the news director in the restaurant incident. Beyond this verbal threat his response had to be one of caution. For most whites threatened on the street, the police are a sought-after source of protection, this is often not the case....

Responses to Discrimination by White Police Officers

Most middle-class blacks do not have such governmental authority as their personal protection. In fact, white police officers are a major problem.

Encounters with the police can be life-threatening and thus limit the range of responses. A television commentator recounted two cases of police harassment when he was working for a survey firm in the mid-1980s. In one of the incidents, which took place in a southern metropolis, he was stopped by several white officers:

> "What are you doing here?" I tell them what I'm doing here.... And so me spread on top of my car. [What had you done?] Because I was in the neighborhood, I left this note on these peoples' house: "Here's who I am. You weren't here, and I will come back in thirty minutes." [Why were they searching you?] They don't know. To me, they're searching, I remember at that particular moment when this all was going down, there was a lot of reports about police crime on civilians.... It took four cops to shake me down, two police cars, so they had me up there spread out. I had a friend of mine with me who was making the call with me, because we were going to have dinner together, and he was black, and they had me up, and they had him outside.... They said, "Well, let's check you out."... And I'm talking to myself, and I'm not thinking about being at attention, with my arms spread on my Ford [a company car], and I'm sitting there talking to myself, "Man, this is crazy, this is crazy."
>
> [How are you feeling inside?] Scared. I mean real scared. [What did you think was going go happen to you?] I was going to go to jail.... Just because they picked me. Why would they stop me? It's like, if they can stop me, why wouldn't I go to jail, and I could sit there for ten days before the judge sees me. I'm thinking all this crazy stuff.... Again, I'm talking to myself. And the guy takes his stick. And he doesn't whack me hard, but he does it with enough authority to let me know they mean business. "I told you stand still; now put your arms back out." And I've got this suit on, and the car's wet. And my friend's hysterical. He's outside the car. And they're checking him out. And he's like, "Man, just be cool, man." And he had tears in his eyes. And I'm like, oh, man, this is a nightmare. This is not supposed to happen to me. This is not my style! And so finally, this other cop comes up and says, "What have we got here Charlie?" "Oh, we've got a guy here. He's running through the neighborhood, and he doesn't want to do what we tell him. We might have to run him in." [You're "running through" the neighborhood?] Yeah, exactly, in a suit in the rain?! After they got through doing their thing and harassing me, I just said, "Man this has been a hell of a week."
>
> And I had tears in my eyes, but it wasn't tears of upset. It was tears of anger; it was tears of wanting to lash back.... What I thought to myself was, man, blacks have it real hard down here. I don't care if they're a broadcaster; I don't care if they're a businessman or a banker.... They don't have it any easier than the persons on skid row who get harassed by the police on a Friday or Saturday night.

It seems likely that most black men—including middle-class black men—see white police officers as a major source of danger and death. (See "Mood of Ghetto America" 1980, June 2, pp. 32–34; Louis Harris and Associates 1989; Roddy 1990, August 26). Scattered evidence suggests that by the time they are in their twenties, most black males, regardless of socioeconomic status, have been stopped by the police because "blackness" is considered a sign of possible criminality by police officers (Moss 1990; Roddy 1990, August 26). This treatment probably marks a dramatic contrast with the experiences of young white middle-class males. In the incident above the respondent and a friend experienced severe police maltreatment—detention for a lengthy period, threat of arrest, and the reality of physical violence. The coping response of the respondent was resigned acceptance somewhat similar to the deference rituals highlighted by Goffman. The middle-class suits and obvious corporate credentials (for example, survey questionnaires and company car) did not protect the two black men. The final comment suggests a disappointment that middle-class status brought no reprieve from police stigmatization and harassment. . . .

CONCLUSION

I have examined the sites of discrimination, the types of discriminatory acts, and the responses of the victims and have found the color stigma still to be very important in the public lives of affluent black Americans. The sites of racial discrimination range from relatively protected home sites, to less protected workplace and educational sites, to less protected workplace and educational sites, to the even less protected public places. The 1964 Civil Rights Act guarantees that black Americans are "entitled to the full and equal enjoyment of the goods, services, facilities, privileges, advantages, and accommodations" in public accommodations. Yet the interviews indicate that deprivation of full enjoyment of public facilities is not a relic of the past: deprivation and discrimination in public accommodations persist. Middle-class black Americans remain vulnerable targets in public places. Prejudice-generated aggression in public places is, of course, not limited to black men and women—gay men and white women are also targets of street harassment (Benokraitis and Feagin 1986). Nonetheless, black women and men face an unusually broad range of discrimination on the street and in public accommodations.

The interviews highlight two significant aspects of the additive discrimination faced by black Americans in public places and elsewhere: (1) the cumulative character of an *individual's* experiences with discrimination; and (2) the *group's* accumulated historical experiences as perceived by the individual. A retired psychology professor who has worked in the Midwest and Southwest commented on the pyramiding of incidents:

> I don't think white people, generally, understand the full meaning of racist discriminatory behaviors directed toward Americans of African descent. They seem to see each act of discrimination or any act of violence as an "isolated" event. As a result, most white Americans cannot understand the strong reaction manifested by blacks when such events occur. They feel that blacks tend to "over-react." They forget that in most cases, we live lives of quiet desperation generated by a litany of *daily* large and small events that whether or not by design, remind us of our "place" in American society.

Particular instances of discrimination may seem minor to outside white observers when considered in isolation. But when blatant acts of avoidance, verbal harassment, and physical attack combine with subtle and covert slights, and these accumulate over months, years, and lifetimes, the impact on a black person is far more than the sum of the individual instances.

The historical context of contemporary discrimination was described by the retired psychologist, who argued that average white Americans

> ... ignore the personal context of the stimulus. That is, they deny the historical impact that a negative act may have on an individual. "Nigger" to a white may simply be an epithet that should be ignored. To most blacks, the term brings into sharp and current focus all kinds of acts of racism—murder, rape, torture, denial of constitutional rights, insults, limited opportunity structure, economic problems, unequal justice under the law and a myriad of... other racist and discriminatory acts that occur daily in the lives of *most* Americans of African descent—including professional blacks.

Particular acts, even antilocution that might seem minor to white observers, are freighted not only with one's past experience of discrimination but also with centuries of racial discrimination directed at the entire group, vicarious oppression that still includes racially translated violence and denial of access to the American dream. Anti-black discrimination is a matter of racial-power inequality institutionalized in a variety of economic and social institutions over a long period of time. The microlevel events of public accommodations and public streets are not just rare and isolated encounters by individuals; they are recurring events reflecting an invasion of the microworld by the macroworld of historical racial subordination.

REFERENCES

Allport, Gordon. 1958. The *Nature of Prejudice.* Abridged. New York: Doubleday Anchor Books.

Benokraitis, Nijole and Joe R. Feagin. 1986. *Modern Sexism: Blatant, Subtle and Covert Discrimination.* Englewood Cliffs: Prentice-Hall.

Blauner, Bob. 1989. *Black Lives, White Lives.* Berkeley: University of California Press.

Brittan, Arthur and Mary Maynard. 1984. *Sexism, Racism and Oppression.* Oxford: Basil Blackwell.

Doyle, Betram W. 1937. *The Etiquette of Race Relations in the South.* Port Washington, NY: Kennikat Press.

Feagin, Joe R. and Douglas Eckberg. 1980. "Prejudice and Discrimination." *Annual Review of Sociology* 6:1–20.

Feagin, Joe R. and Clairece Booher Feagin. 1986. *Discrimination American Style* (rev. ed). Melbourne, FL: Krieger Publishing Co.

Gardner, Carol Brooks. 1980. "Passing By: Street Remarks, Address Rights, and the Urban Female." *Sociological Inquiry* 50:328–56.

———. 1988. "Access Information: Public Lies and Private Peril." *Social Problems* 35:384–97.

Goffman, Erving. 1956. "The Nature of Deference and Demeanor." *American Anthropologist* 58:473–502.

Griffin, John Howard. 1961. *Black Like Me.* Boston: Houghton Mifflin.

"The Mood of Ghetto America." 1980. June 2. *Newsweek,* pp. 32–4.

Moss, E. Yvonne. 1990. "African Americans and the Administration of Justice." Pp. 79–86 in *Assessment of the Status of African-Americans,* edited by Wornie L. Reed. Boston: University of Massachusetts, William Monroe Trotter Institute.

Raper, Arthur F. 1933. *The Tragedy of Lynching.* Chapel Hill: University of North Carolina Press.

Roddy, Dennis B. 1990. August 26. "Perceptions Still Segregate Police, Black Community." *The Pittsburgh Press,* p. B1.

Rollins, Judith 1985. *Between Women.* Philadelphia: Temple University Press.

Wieseltier, Leon. 1989, June 5. "Scar Tissue." *New Republic,* pp. 19–20.

CHAPTER 3 Racism

3.1 LOUIS L. KNOWLES AND KENNETH PREWITT

Institutional and Ideological Roots of Racism

The mid-1960s witnessed an explosion of racial violence throughout the United States. Between 1964 and 1968 riots broke out in New York, Philadelphia, Rochester, Los Angeles, Chicago, Cleveland, Lansing, Omaha, Cincinnati, Buffalo, Detroit, and Newark. The federal government responded to the disorder by establishing social science commissions to investigate the social troubles—such as unemployment, inadequate education, and domestic violence—inundating the Black community. President Lyndon B. Johnson established the Commission on Civil Disorders, chaired by Otto Kerner, governor of Illinois, to investigate what had happened, why the riots had occurred, and what could be done to prevent further outbreaks.

In this selection from "Institutional and Ideological Roots of Racism," in Louis L. Knowles and Kenneth Prewitt, eds., *Institutional Racism in America* (Prentice Hall, 1969), Louis L. Knowles and Kenneth Prewitt critically evaluate the findings of the Kerner Commission. They argue that the commission did not go far enough in its investigation to discover the root causes of racial violence in the United States. To these authors, the commission simply attributed the civil unrest to "black pathology"—a *blaming the victim* thesis. Knowles and Prewitt instead attribute racial disorder to America's "historical roots of institutional racism," which have prevented Blacks from attaining equality in society.

Key Concept: the historical roots of institutional racism

THE REPORT OF THE NATIONAL ADVISORY COMMISSION ON CIVIL DISORDERS: A COMMENT

The contemporary document perhaps most indicative of the ideology of official America is the influential "Kerner Commission Report." This is an important work. It is being widely read, and we cite from it frequently in the pages to follow. However, since our analysis operates from a premise fundamentally different from the Report, a few comments at this point will help introduce the substantive chapters to follow.

The Report asks: "Why Did It Happen?" A painful truth is then recorded: "White racism is essentially responsible for the explosive mixture which has been accumulating in our cities since the end of World War II." Unfortunately, the Report too quickly leaves this truth and emphasizes the familiar list of "conditions" of "Negro unrest." Paraded before the reader are observations about the frustrated hopes of Negroes, the "belief" among Negroes that there is police brutality, the high unemployment in the ghetto, the weak family structure and social disorganization in the Negro community, and so on.

It is the immediate conditions giving rise to civil disorders which the Report stresses, not the *causes behind the conditions.* Perhaps what is needed is a National Advisory Commission on White Racism. If a group of men sets out to investigate "civil disorders," their categories of analysis are fixed and, from our perspective, parochial. In spite of their admission that "white institutions created [the ghetto], white institutions maintain it, and white society condones it," the categories with which the commission operated screened out the responsibility of white institutions and pushed the commission back to the familiar account of "black pathology."

In the important section "What Can Be Done," this fault is even more clearly seen. Certainly it is true that much accumulated frustration would be relieved if the sweeping recommendations concerning administration of justice, police and community relations, housing, unemployment and underemployment, welfare thinking, and so forth were implemented. The Report merits the closest attention for its statement that issues of race and poverty must receive the highest national priority, and for its further argument that what is needed is a massive commitment by all segments of society. What disappoints the reader is that the section "What Can Be Done" only accentuates the shortsightedness of the section "Why Did It Happen." The recommendations are directed at ghetto conditions and *not* at the white structures and practices which are responsible for those conditions. Thus, while it is true that improved communication between the ghetto and city hall might defuse the pressures building up in the black community, the issue is not "better communication" but "full representation." Black people should not have to communicate with city hall; they should be represented at city hall.

The shallowness of the Report as social analysis is again reflected in its discussion of black protest movements. The Report does not uncover a critical social dynamic: militancy is first of all a response to white resistance and control, not its cause. The naiveté of the Report, and its ultimate paternalism, is nowhere better shown than in its attempt to draw parallels between the black power movement and the philosophy of Booker T. Washington. Accommodation stood at the center of Washington's thought; accommodation is explicitly and forcefully rejected by the ideology symbolized in the "black power" slogan. As Carmichael and Hamilton wrote, "Black people in the United States must raise hard questions which challenge the very nature of the society itself: its long-standing values, beliefs, and institutions."

What we miss in the Kerner Commission Report is the capacity to ask "hard questions." The Commission members are to be saluted for their instinct that "white racism" is the culprit. They are to be faulted for their inability or unwillingness to pursue this theme. We do not have access to the professional resources available to the Kerner Commission, and therefore our study lacks the statistical detail of the national report. But we have tried to push the analysis of the race question into areas where the Report dared not tread: into the heart of institutional, which is to say white, America.

A new realization is dawning in white America. Under the insistent prodding of articulate blacks plus a few unusual whites, the so-called "Negro Problem" is being redefined. Just possibly the racial sickness in our society is not, as we have so long assumed, rooted in the black and presumably "pathological" subculture but in the white and presumably "healthy" dominant culture. If indeed it turns out that "*the* problem" is finally and deeply a white problem, the solution will have to be found in a restructured white society.

Institutional racism is a term which describes practices in the United States nearly as old as the nation itself. The term, however, appears to be of recent coinage, possibly first used by Stokely Carmichael and Charles V. Hamilton in their widely read book, *Black Power*.[1] It is our goal to work with this term until we feel we have come to some full understanding of it, and to present an analysis of specific practices appropriately defined as "institutionally racist." Our strategy is to be self-consciously pragmatic. That is, we ask not what the motive of the individuals might be; rather we look at the consequences of the institutions they have created.

TOWARD A DEFINITION

The murder by KKK members and law enforcement officials of three civil rights workers in Mississippi was an act of individual racism. That the sovereign state of Mississippi refused to indict the killers was institutional racism. The individual act by racist bigots went unpunished in Mississippi because of policies, precedents, and practices that are an integral part of that state's legal institutions. A store clerk who suspects that black children in his store are there to steal candy but white children are there to purchase candy, and who treats the children differently, the blacks as probable delinquents and the whites as probable customers, also illustrates individual racism. Unlike the Mississippi murderers, the store clerk is not a bigot and may not even consider himself prejudiced, but his behavior is shaped by racial stereotypes which have been part of his unconscious since childhood. A university admissions policy which provides for entrance only to students who score high on tests designed primarily for white suburban high schools necessarily excludes black ghetto-educated students. Unlike the legal policies of Mississippi, the university admission criteria are not intended to be racist, but the university is pursuing a course which perpetuates institutional racism. The difference, then, between individual and institutional racism is not a difference in intent or of visibility. Both the individual act of racism and the racist institutional policy may occur without the presence of conscious bigotry, and both may be masked intentionally or innocently.

In an attempt to understand "institutional racism" it is best to consider first what institutions are and what they do in a society. Institutions are fairly stable social arrangements and practices through which collective actions are taken. Medical institutions, for instance, marshal talents and resources of society so that health care can be provided. Medical institutions include hospitals, research labs, and clinics, as well as organizations of medical people such as doctors and nurses. The health of all of us is affected by general medical policies and by established practices and ethics. Business and labor, for example, determine what is to be produced, how it is to be produced, and by whom and on whose behalf products will be created. Public and private schools determine what is considered knowledge, how it is to be transmitted to new generations, and who will do the teaching. Legal and political institutions determine what laws regulate our lives, how and by whom they are enforced, and who will be prosecuted for which violations.

Institutions have great power to reward and penalize. They reward by providing career opportunities for some people and foreclosing them for others. They reward as well by the way social goods and services are distributed —by deciding who receives training and skills, medical care, formal education, political influence, moral support and self-respect, productive employment, fair treatment by the law, decent housing, self-confidence, and the promise of a secure future for self and children. No society will distribute social benefits in a perfectly equitable way. But no society need use race as a criterion to determine who will be rewarded and who punished. Any nation that permits race to affect the distribution of benefits from social policies is racist.

It is our thesis that institutional racism is deeply embedded in American society. Slavery was only the earliest and most blatant practice. Political, economic, educational, and religious policies cooperated with slaveholders to "keep the nigger in his place." Emancipation changed little. Jim Crow laws as well as residential and employment discrimination guaranteed that black citizens remained under the control of white citizens. Second-class citizenship quickly became a social fact as well as a legal status. Overt institutional racism was widely practiced throughout American society at least until World War II.

With desegregation in the armed forces and the passage of various civil rights bills, institutional racism no longer has the status of law. It is perpetuated nonetheless, sometimes by frightened and bigoted individuals, sometimes by good citizens merely carrying on "business as usual," and sometimes by well-intentioned but naive reformers. An attack on institutional racism is clearly the next task for Americans, white and black, who hope to obtain for their children a society less tense and more just than the one of the mid-1960's. It is no easy task. Individual, overt racist acts, such as the shotgun slaying of civil rights workers, are visible. Techniques of crime detection can be used to apprehend guilty parties, and, in theory, due process of law will punish them. To detect institutional racism, especially when it is unintentional or when it is disguised, is a very different task. And even when institutional racism is detected, it is seldom clear who is at fault. How can we say who is responsible for residential segregation, for poor education in ghetto schools, for extraordinarily high unemployment among black men, for racial stereotypes in history textbooks, for the concentration of political power in white society?

Our analysis begins with attention to ideological patterns in American society which historically and presently sustain practices appropriately labeled "institutionally racist." We then turn attention to the procedures of dominant American institutions: educational, economic, political, legal, and medical. It is as a result of practices within these institutions that black citizens in America are consistently penalized for reasons of color.

Quite obviously the social arrangements which fix unequal opportunities for black and white citizens can be traced back through American history—farther back, as a matter of fact, than even the beginning of slavery. Our purpose is not to rewrite American history, although that needs to be done. Rather our purpose in this initial chapter is to point out the historical roots of institutional racism by examining the ideology used to justify it. In understanding how deeply racist practices are embedded in the American experience and values, we can come to a fuller understanding of how contemporary social institutions have adapted to their heritage.

HISTORY AND IDEOLOGY

Some form of white supremacy, both as ideology and institutional arrangement, existed from the first day English immigrants, seeking freedom from religious intolerance, arrived on the North American continent. From the beginning, the early colonizers apparently considered themselves culturally superior to the natives they encountered. This sense of superiority over the Indians, which was fostered by the religious ideology they carried to the new land, found its expression in the self-proclaimed mission to civilize and Christianize—a mission which was to find its ultimate expression in ideas of a "manifest destiny" and a "white man's burden."

The early colonists were a deeply religious people. The church was the dominant social institution of their time, and the religious doctrines brought from England strongly influenced their contacts with the native Indians. The goals of the colonists were stated clearly:

> *Principal and Maine Ends* [of the Virginia colony] . . . ware first to preach and baptize into *Christian Religion* and by propogation of the *Gospell,* to recover out of the arms of the *Divell,* a number of poore and miserable soules, wrapt up unto death, in almost invincible ignorance . . . and to add our myte to the Treasury of Heaven.[2]

Ignorance about the white man's God was sufficient proof in itself of the inferiority of the Indian and, consequently, of the superiority of the white civilization.

The mission impulse was doomed to failure. A shortage of missionaries and an unexpected resistance on the part of the Indian (who was less sure that the white man's ways were inherently superior) led to the dismantling of the few programs aimed at Christianization. It became clear that conquering was, on balance, less expensive and more efficient than "civilizing."

Thus began an extended process of genocide, giving rise to such aphorisms as "The only good Indian is a dead Indian." It was at this time that the ideology of white supremacy on the North American continent took hold. Since Indians were capable of reaching only the stage of "savage," they should not be allowed to impede the forward (westward, to be exact) progress of white civilization. The Church quickly acquiesced in this redefinition of the situation. The disappearance of the nonwhite race in the path of expansionist policies was widely interpreted as God's will. As one student of America's history has written, "It apparently never seriously occurred to [spokesmen for Christianity] that where they saw the mysterious law of God in the disappearance of the nonwhite races before the advancing Anglo-Saxon, a disappearance which apparently occurred without anyone's willing it or doing anything to bring it about, the actual process was a brutal one of oppression, dispossession, and even extermination."[3]

In short, what began as a movement to "civilize and Christianize" the indigenous native population was converted into a racist force, accompanied, as always, by a justificatory ideology. In retrospect, the result is hardly surprising. The English colonists operated from a premise which has continued to have a strong impact on American thought: the Anglo-Saxon race is culturally and religiously superior; neither the validity nor the integrity of alien cultures can be recognized. (The Indian culture, though native to the land, was considered the alien one.) When it became clear that Indians could not be "saved," the settlers concluded that the race itself was inferior. This belief was strengthened by such racist theories as the Teutonic Theory of Origins, which pointed out the superiority of the Anglo-Saxons. The institution of slavery and its accompanying justification would seem to have been products of the same mentality.

It has, of course, been the white man's relationship with the black man which has led to the most powerful expressions of institutional racism in the society. This is a history which hardly needs retelling, although it might be instructive to consider how closely related was the justification of Indian extermination to that of black slavery. It was the heathenism or savagery, so-called, of the African, just as of the Indian, which became the early rationale for enslavement. A particularly ingenious version of the rationale is best known under the popular label "Social Darwinism."

The Social Darwinian theory of evolution greatly influenced social thought, hence social institutions, in nineteenth-century America. Social Darwinists extended the concept of biological evolution in the development of man to a concept of evolution in development of societies and civilizations. The nature of a society or nation or race was presumed to be the product of natural evolutionary forces. The evolutionary process was characterized by struggle and conflict in which the "stronger, more advanced, and more civilized" would naturally triumph over the "inferior, weaker, backward, and uncivilized" peoples.

> The idea of natural selection was translated to a struggle between individual members of a society; between members of classes of society, between different nations, and between different races. This conflict, far from being an evil thing, was nature's indispensable method of producing superior men, superior nations, and superior races.[4]

Such phrases as "the struggle for existence" and "the survival of the fittest" became *lingua franca*, and white Americans had a full-blown ideology to explain their treatment of the "inferior race."

The contemporary expression of Social Darwinian thinking is less blatant but essentially the same as the arguments used in the nineteenth century. The poverty and degradation of the nonwhite races in the United States are thought to be the result of an innate lack of ability rather than anything white society has done. Thus a long line of argument reaches its most recent expression in the now famous "Moynihan Report": the focal point of the race problem is to be found in the pathology of black society.

Social Darwinism was buttressed with two other ideas widely accepted in nineteenth-century America: manifest destiny and white man's burden. Briefly stated, manifest destiny was simply the idea that white Americans were destined, either by natural forces or by Divine Right, to control at least the North American continent and, in many versions of the theory, a much greater share of the earth's surface. Many churchmen supported the idea that such expansion was the will of God. The impact of this belief with respect to the Indians has already been noted. Let it suffice to say that manifest destiny helped provide the moral and theological justification for genocide. The belief that American expansion was a natural process was rooted in Social Darwinism. Expansionism was simply the natural growth process of a superior nation. This deterministic argument enjoyed wide popularity. Even those who were not comfortable with the overt racism of the expansionist argument were able to cooperate in policies of "liberation" in Cuba and the Philippines by emphasizing the evils of Spanish control. Many, however, felt no need to camouflage their racism. Albert J. Beveridge, Senator from Indiana, stated his position clearly:

> The American Republic is a part of the movement of a race—the most masterful race of history—and race movements are not to be stayed by the hand of man. They are mighty answers to Divine commands. Their leaders are not only statesmen of peoples—they are prophets of God. The inherent tendencies of a race are its highest law. They precede and survive all statutes, all constitutions.... The sovereign tendencies of our race are organization and government.[5]

In any case, if racism was not invoked as a justification for imperialist expansion in the first place, it subsequently became a justification for continued American control of the newly "acquired" territories. This was particularly true in the Philippines. "The control of one country by another and the denial of rights or citizenship to the Filipinos were difficult ideas to reconcile with the Declaration of Independence and with American institutions. In order to make these opposing ideas of government compatible at all, the proponents of the acquisition of the Philippines were forced to rely heavily on race theories."[6]

An argument commonly expressed was that the Filipinos were simply incapable of self-government. " 'The Declaration of Independence,' stated Beveridge, 'applies only to peoples capable of self-government. Otherwise, how dared we administer the affairs of the Indians? How dare we continue to govern them today?' "[7] The decision, therefore, as to who was capable of self-government and who was not so capable was left to the United States Government. The criteria were usually explicitly racist, as it was simply assumed that whites, at least Anglo-Saxons, had the "gift" of being able to govern themselves while the inferior nonwhite peoples were not so endowed.

The ideology of imperialist expansion had an easily foreseeable impact on the domestic race situation. As Ronald Segal points out in *The Race War,*

> Both North and South saw and accepted the implications. What was sauce for the Philippines, for Hawaii and Cuba, was sauce for the Southern Negro. If the stronger and cleverer race is free to impose its will upon "new-caught sullen peoples" on the other side of the globe, why not in South Carolina and Mississippi? asked the *Atlantic Monthly.* "No Republican leader," proclaimed Senator Tillman of South Carolina, "... will now dare to wave the bloody shirt and preach a crusade against the South's treatment of the Negro. The North has a bloody shirt of its own. Many thousands of them have been made into shrouds for murdered Filipinos, done to death because they were fighting for liberty." Throughout the United States doctrines of racial superiority received the assent of influential politicians and noted academics. The very rationalizations that had eased the conscience of the slave trade now provided the sanction for imperial expansion.[8]

Another component of the ideology which has nurtured racist policies is that of "the white man's burden." This phrase comes from the title of a poem by Rudyard Kipling, which appeared in the United States in 1899. Whatever Kipling himself may have wished to convey, Americans soon popularized and adopted the concept as an encouragement for accepting the responsibility of looking after the affairs of the darker races. This notion of the "white man's burden" was that the white race, particularly Anglo-Saxons of Britain and America, should accept the (Christian) responsibility for helping the poor colored masses to find a better way of life.

It should be clear that this notion is no less racist than others previously mentioned. Behind the attitude lies the assumption of white supremacy. In exhorting Americans to follow British policy in this regard, the philosopher Josiah Royce stated the assumption clearly.

> ... The Englishman, in his official and governmental dealings with backward peoples, has a great way of being superior without very often publicly saying that he is superior. You well know that in dealing, as an individual, with other individuals, trouble is seldom made by the fact that you are actually superior to another man in any respect. The trouble comes when you tell the other man, too stridently, that you are his superior. Be my superior, quietly, simply showing your superiority

in your deeds, and very likely I shall love you for the very fact of your superiority. For we all love our leaders. But tell me I am your inferior, and then perhaps I may grow boyish, and may throw stones. Well, it is so with the races. Grant then that yours is the superior race. Then you can say little about the subject in your public dealings with the backward race. Superiority is best shown by good deeds and by few boasts.[9]

Both manifest destiny and the idea of a white man's burden, in disguised forms, continue to shape white America's values and policies. Manifest destiny has done much to stimulate the modern day myth that colored peoples are generally incapable of self-government. There are whites who continue to believe that black Afro-Americans are not ready to govern themselves. At best, blacks must first be "properly trained." Of course, this belief influences our relations with nonwhites in other areas of the world as well.

The authors have found the concept of manifest destiny helpful in analyzing white response to "black power." Black power is based on the belief that black people in America are capable of governing and controlling their own communities. White rejection of black power reflects, in part, the widely accepted white myth that blacks are incapable of self-government and must be controlled and governed by whites. Many whites apparently still share with Albert Beveridge the belief that "organization and government" are among the "sovereign tendencies of our race."

The belief in a "white man's burden" also has its modern-day counterpart, particularly in the attitudes and practices of so-called "white liberals" busily trying to solve "the Negro problem." The liberal often bears a strong sense of responsibility for helping the Negro find a better life. He generally characterizes the Negro as "disadvantaged," "unfortunate," or "culturally deprived." The liberal generally feels superior to the black man, although he is less likely to publicly state his sense of superiority. He may not even recognize his own racist sentiments. In any case, much like Josiah Royce, he senses that "superiority is best shown by good deeds and by few boasts." Liberal paternalism is reflected not only in individual attitudes but in the procedures and policies of institutions such as the welfare system and most "war on poverty" efforts.

It is obvious that recent reports and action plans carry on a traditional, if diversionary, view that has long been acceptable to most white Americans: that it is not white institutions but a few bigots plus the deprived status of Negroes that cause racial tension. Such a view is mythical.... We are not content with "explanations" of white-black relations that are apolitical, that would reduce the causes of racial tension to the level of psychological and personal factors. Three hundred years of American history cannot be encapsulated so easily. To ignore the network of institutional controls through which social benefits are allocated may be reassuring, but it is also bad social history. America is and has long been a racist nation, because it has and has long had a racist policy. This policy is not to be understood by listening to the proclamations of intent by leading citizens and government officials; nor is it to be understood by reading off a list of compensatory programs in business, education, and welfare. The policy can be understood only when we are willing to take a hard look at the continuing and irrefutable racist consequences of the major institutions in American life. The policy will be changed when we are willing to start the difficult task of remaking our institutions.

NOTES

1. Stokely Carmichael and Charles Hamilton, *Black Power: The Politics of Liberation in America* (New York: Vintage Books, 1967).
2. Quoted in Thomas F. Gossett, *Race: The History of an Idea in America* (Dallas: SMU Press, 1963), p. 18.
3. *Ibid.*, p. 196.
4. *Ibid.*, p. 145.
5. *Ibid.*, p. 318.
6. *Ibid.*, p. 328.
7. *Ibid.*, p. 329.
8. Ronald Segal, *The Race War* (Baltimore: Penguin Books, 1967), p. 219.
9. Gossett, p. 334.

3.2 EDNA BONACICH

Inequality in America: The Failure of the American System for People of Color

U.S. society is highly stratified: People in the upper echelon of the system control an inordinate amount of the nation's wealth. And the privilege of the upper class contrasts sharply with the poverty of the millions of poor people who struggle for survival on a daily basis.

In this selection from "Inequality in America: The Failure of the American System for People of Color," *Sociological Spectrum* (vol. 9, no. 1, 1989), Edna Bonacich, a professor of sociology and ethnic studies at the University of California, Riverside, argues that people of color are disproportionately relegated to the lower levels of the class structure to the extent that *social* inequality in the United States has become *racial* inequality. During her discussion, Bonacich poses and attempts to answer an interesting question: How unequal is the distribution of rewards in the United States?

Key Concept: class and racial inequality

INEQUALITY IN AMERICA

The United States is an immensely unequal society in terms of the distribution of material wealth, and consequently, in the distribution of all the benefits and privileges that accrue to wealth—including political power and influence. This inequality is vast irrespective of race. However, people of color tend to cluster at the bottom so that inequality in this society also becomes racial inequality. I believe that racial inequality is inextricably tied to overall inequality, and to an ideology that endorses vast inequality as justified and desirable. The special problems of racial inequality require direct attention in the process of attacking inequality in general, but I do not believe that the problem of racial inequality can be eliminated within a context of the tremendous disparities that our society currently tolerates. And even if some kind of racial parity, at the level of averages, could be achieved, the amount of suffering at the bottom would remain undiminished, hence unconscionable.

How unequal is the distribution of rewards in the United States? Typically this question is addressed in terms of occupation and income distribution rather than the distribution and control of property. By the income criterion, the United States is one of the more unequal of the Western industrial societies, and it is far more unequal than the countries of the Eastern European socialist bloc. The Soviet Union, for instance, has striven to decrease the discrepancy in earnings between the highest paid professionals and managers and the lowest paid workers, and as a consequence, has a much flatter income distribution than the United States (Szymanski 1979, pp. 63–9).

To take an extreme example from within the United States, in 1987 the minimum wage was $3.35 an hour, and 6.7 million American workers were paid at that level. That comes to $6,968 a year. In contrast, the highest paid executive, Lee Iacocca, received more than $20 million in 1986, or $9,615 per hour. In other words, the highest paid executive received more in an hour than a vast number of workers received in a year (Sheinkman 1987).

The excessive differences in income are given strong ideological justification—they serve, supposedly, as a source of incentive. Who will work hard if there is no pot of gold at the end, a pot that can be bigger than anyone else's? The striving for achievement leads to excellence, and we all are the beneficiaries of the continual improvements and advances that result.

Or are we? I believe a strong case can be made for the opposite. First of all, the presumed benefits of inequality do not trickle down far enough. The great advances of medical science, for example, are of little use to those people who cannot afford even the most basic health care. Second, instead of providing incentive, our steep inequalities may engender hopelessness and despair for those who have no chance of winning the big prize. When you have no realistic chance of winning the competition, and when there are no prizes for those who take anything less than fourth place, why should you run all out? Third, one can question how much inequality is necessary to raise incentives. Surely fairly modest inducements can serve as motivators. Does the person who makes $100,000 a year in any sense work that much harder than the person who makes the annual $7,000 wage? Altogether, it would seem that the justifications for inequality are more rationalizations to preserve privilege than they are a well-reasoned basis of social organization. The obvious wholesale waste of human capability (let alone life in and for itself) that piles up at the bottom of our system of inequality is testimony to the failure.

Even more fundamental than income inequality is inequality in the ownership of property. Here not only are the extremes much more severe, but the justification of incentives for achievement grow exceedingly thin. First, large amounts of property are simply inherited and the owner never did a stitch of work in his or her life to merit any of it. Second, and more important, wealth in property expands at the expense of workers. Its growth depends not on the achievements of the owner so much as on his or her ability to exploit other human beings. The owner of rental property, for example, gets richer simply because other people who have to work for a living cannot afford to buy their own housing and must sink a substantial proportion of their hard-earned wages into providing shelter. The ownership of property provides interest, rent or profit simply from the fact of ownership. The owner need only put out the capital itself to have the profits keep rolling in for the rest of his or her life.

The concentration of property in the United States is rarely studied—I assume because its exposure is politically embarrassing and even dangerous to those in power (who overlap substantially with, or are closely allied to those who own property). Only two such studies have been undertaken in the last 25 years, one in 1963 and one in 1983. The 1983 study was commissioned by the Democratic staff of the Congressional Joint Economic Committee (U.S. Congress 1986). It seems it may have been a political hot potato since shortly after its appearance, a brief 19-line article appeared in the *Los Angeles Times* stating that the committee withdrew some of its conclusions because of "an error in the figures" (*Los Angeles Times* 1986).

The 1983 study found that the top 0.5 percent of families in the United States owned over 35 percent of the net wealth of this nation. If equity in personal residences is excluded from consideration, the same 0.5 percent of households owned more than 45 percent of the privately held wealth. In other words, if this country consisted of 200 people, one individual would own almost half of the property held among all 200. The other 199 would have to divide up the remainder.

The remainder was not equally divided either. The top 10 percent of the country's households owned 72 percent of its wealth, leaving only 28 percent for the remaining 90 percent of families. If home equity is excluded, the bottom 90 percent only owned 17 percent of the wealth.

The super-rich top half of one percent consisted of 420,000 families. These families owned most of the business enterprises in the nation. They owned 58 percent of unincorporated businesses and 46.5 percent of all personally owned corporate stock. They also owned 77 percent of the value of trusts and 62 percent of state and local bonds. They owned an average of $8.9 million apiece, ranging from $2.5 million up to hundreds of times that amount.

Forbes publishes an annual list of the 400 richest Americans (*Los Angeles Times* 1986). In 1986, 25 individuals owned over a billion dollars in assets. The richest owned $4.5 billion. That is a 10-digit figure. The four-hundredth person on the list owned $180 million. So the concentration of wealth at the very top is even more extreme than the Congressional study reveals. In 1986, for the first time, a Black man made the *Forbes* list—he owned $185 million in assets. The super-rich property owners of this country are generally an all-white club.

By 1987, the number of billionaires in the country (as counted by *Forbes*) had grown from 26 in 1986 to 49 (*Forbes* 1987). The average worth of the top 400 had grown to $220 million apiece, a jump of 41 percent in one year. The top individual now owned $8.5 billion. Together, these 400 individuals commanded a net worth of $220 billion, comparable to the entire U.S. military budget in 1986, and more than the U.S. budget deficit, or total U.S. investment abroad.

RACIAL INEQUALITY

The gross inequalities that characterize American society are multiplied when race and ethnicity are entered into the equation. Racial minorities, especially Blacks, Latinos and Native Americans, tend to be seriously overrepresented at the bottom of the scale in terms of any measure of material well-being.

In the distribution of occupations Whites are substantially overrepresented in the professional and managerial stratum. They are almost twice as likely as Blacks (1.71 times) and Latinos (1.97 times) to hold these kinds of jobs. On the other hand, Blacks and Latinos are much more concentrated in the lower paid service sector, and the unskilled and semiskilled of operators, fabricators and laborers. Whereas only 27 percent of White employees fall into these combined categories, 47 percent of Blacks and 43 percent of Latinos are so categorized. Finally, even though the numbers are relatively small, Blacks are more than three times and Latinos more than twice as likely as Whites to work as private household servants. This most demeaning of occupations remains mainly a minority preserve (U.S. Department of Labor 1987).

Occupational disadvantage translates into wage and salary disadvantage. The median weekly earning of White families in 1986 was $566, compared to $412 for Latino families and $391 for Black families. In other words, Black and Latino families made about 70 percent of what White families made. Female-headed households of all groups made substantially less money. Both Black and Latino female-headed families made less than half of what the average White family (including married couples) made (U.S. Department of Labor 1987).

Weekly earnings only reflect the take-home pay of employed people. In addition, people of color bear the brunt of unemployment in this society. In 1986, 14.8 percent of Black males, 14.2 percent of Black females, 10.5 percent of Latino males, and 10.8 percent of Latino females were unemployed officially. This compares to 6 percent of White males and 6.1 percent of White females (U.S. Department of Labor 1987).

The absence of good jobs or any jobs at all, and the absence of decent pay for those jobs that are held translates into poverty. Although the poverty line is a somewhat arbitrary figure, it nevertheless provides some commonly accepted standard for decent living in our society.

As of 1984, over one-third of Black households lived in poverty. If we include those people who live very close to the poverty line, the near poor, then 41 percent, or two out of five Blacks, are poor or near poor. For Latinos the figures are only slightly less grim, with over 28 percent living in poverty and 36 percent, or well over one-third, living in or near poverty. This compares to an official poverty rate of 11 percent for Whites.

Female-headed households, as is commonly known, are more likely to live in or near poverty. Over half of Black and Latino female-headed families are forced to live under the poverty line, and over 60 percent of each group live in or near poverty. The figures for White female-headed families are also high with over one-third living in or near poverty. But the levels for people of color are almost twice as bad (U.S. Bureau of the Census 1986).

The degree of racial inequality in property ownership is stark—more stark than the income and employment figures.... The average White family has a net worth of about $39,000, more than ten times the average net worth of about $3,000 for Black families. Latino families are only slightly better off, with an average net worth of about $5,000. The differences are even more marked among female-headed households. The average Black and Latino female-headed households have a net worth of only $671 and $478 respectively, less than 2 percent of the net worth of the average White household.

... The richest man in this country owned $8.5 billion in wealth in 1987 and there are a handful of others close behind him. Meanwhile, the average —not the poorest but the average—Black and Latino female-headed household only commands a few hundred dollars. How can one even begin to talk about equality of opportunity under such circumstances? What power and control must inevitably accompany the vast holdings of the billionaires, and what scrambling for sheer survival must accompany the dearth of resources at the bottom end?...

CAPITALISM AND RACISM

I want to consider the ways in which the American political-economic system is bound to racism. It is my contention that the racism of this society is linked to capitalism and that, so long as we retain a capitalist system, we will not be able to eliminate racial oppression. This is not to say that racism will automatically disappear if we change the system. If we were to transform to a socialist society, the elimination of racism would have to be given direct attention as a high priority. I am not suggesting that its elimination would be easily achieved within socialism, but it is impossible under capitalism.[1]

Stripped of all its fancy rationalizations and complexities, the capitalist system depends upon the exploitation of the poor by the rich. Property owners need an impoverished class of people so that others will be forced to work for them. We can see this... on a world-wide scale, where, for example, poor Latin American countries sent to American investors and lenders (between 1982 and 1987) $145 billion more than they took in. And they still owe a principal of $410 billion in foreign debt, and all the billions of dollars of interest payments that will accrue to that (*Los Angeles Times* 1987).

Capitalism depends on inequality. The truth is, the idea of equality cannot even be whispered around here. It is too subversive, too completely undermining of the "American way." Liberals, conservatives, Democrats and Republicans are all committed to the idea of inequality and so, no matter how much they yell at each other in Congressional hearings, behind the scenes they shake hands and agree that things are basically fine and as they should be.

Perhaps not everyone agrees with my formulation, but I do not think anyone can disagree that there is a commitment to economic inequality in this system and that no attempt is made to hide it. It is part of the official ideology. However the same cannot be said for racial inequality today. At least at the official level it is stated that race should not be the basis of any social or economic distinction. Thus it should, in theory, be possible to eliminate racial inequality within the system, even if we do not touch overall inequality.

Even though an open commitment to racial inequality has been made illegitimate in recent years as a consequence of the Civil Rights and related social movements, I believe that it remains embedded in this system. Before getting into the present dynamics of the system, however, let me point out how deeply racism is embedded in the historical evolution of capitalism. First of all, one can make the case that, without racism, without the racial domination implicit in the early European "voyages of discovery," Europe would never have accumulated the initial wealth for its own capitalist "take off." In other words, capitalism itself is predicated on racism (Williams 1966).

But setting aside this somewhat controversial point, European capitalist development quickly acquired an expansionist mode and took over the world, spreading a suffocating blanket of White domination over almost all the other peoples of the globe. The motive was primarily economic, primarily the pursuit of markets, raw materials, cheap labor and investment opportunities. The business sector of Europe, linked to the state, wanted to increase its profits. They sought to enhance their wealth (see Cheng and Bonacich 1984).

The belief in the inferiority of peoples of color, the belief that Europeans were bringing a gift of civilization, salvation, and economic development, helped justify the conquest. They were not, they could think to themselves, hurting anyone. They were really benefactors, bringing light to the savages.

The world order that they created was tiered. On the one hand, they exploited the labor of their own peoples, creating from Europe's farmers and craftsmen an ownerless White working class. On the other hand, of the conquered nationalities they created a super-exploited work-force, producing the raw materials for the rising European industries, and doing the dirtiest and lowest paid support jobs in the world economy. Because they had been conquered and colonized, the peoples of color could be subjected to especially coercive labor systems, such as slavery, indentured servitude, forced migrant labor and the like.

Both groups of workers were exploited in the sense that surplus was taken from their labor by capitalist owners. But White "free labor" was in a relatively advantaged position, being employed in the technically more advanced and higher paid sectors. To a certain extent, White labor benefited from the super-exploitation of colonized workers. The capital that was drained from the colonies could be invested in industrial development in Europe or the centers of European settlement (such as the United States, Canada, Australia, New Zealand and South Africa). The White cotton mill workers in Manchester and New England depended on the super-exploitation of cotton workers in India and the slave South, producing the cheap raw material on which their industrial employment was built.

Although the basic structure of the world economy centered on European capital and the exploitation of colonized workers in their own homelands, the expansion of European capitalism led to movement of peoples all over the globe to suit the economic needs of the capitalist class. Internal colonies, the products of various forms of forced and semiforced migrations, replicated the world system within particular territories. . . .

Still, we can ask: Is it not possible that within the United States, a redistribution could occur that would eliminate the racial character of inequality? Could we not, with the banning of racial discrimination and even positive policies like affirmative action, restructure our society such that color is no longer correlated with wealth and poverty? This is what is meant by racial equality within capitalism. The total amount of human misery would remain unaltered, but its complexion would change.

Assimilationism

It seems to me that, even if people of color are fully distributed along the capitalist hierarchy, resembling the distribution of White people, that does not necessarily spell the end of racism. The very idea of such absorption is assimilationist. It claims that people of color must abandon their own cultures and communities and become utilitarian individualists like the White men. They must compete on the white man's terms for the White man's values.

The notion that the American system can be "color blind," a common conservative position, is, of course, predicated on the idea that one is color blind within a system of rules, and those rules are the White man's. Even though he claims they are without cultural content, this is nonsense. They are his rules, deriving from his cultural heritage, and he can claim that they are universal and culturally neutral only because he has the power to make such a claim stick. There is an implicit arrogance that the White man's way is the most advanced, and that everyone else ought to learn how to get along in it as quickly as possible. All other cultures and value systems are impugned as backward, primitive or dictatorial. Only Western capitalism is seen as the pinnacle of human social organization, the height of perfection (see Bonacich 1987 and Bonacich in press for an elaboration of these points).

The absurdity of such a position need scarcely be mentioned. The White man's civilization has not only caused great suffering to oppressed nationalities around the globe, but also to many of its own peoples. It has not only murdered and pillaged other human beings but has also engaged in wanton destruction of our precious planet, so that we can now seriously question how long human life will be sustainable at all.

Let me give an example of the way in which the White man's seemingly universal rules have been imposed. In 1887 the U.S. government passed the Allotment Act, authored by Senator Henry Dawes. This law terminated communal land ownership among American Indians by allotting private parcels of land to individuals. Dawes articulated the philosophy behind this policy:

> The head chief [of the Cherokee] told us that there was not a family in that whole nation that had not a home of its own. There was not a pauper in that nation, and the nation did not owe a dollar.... Yet the defect in the system was apparent. They have got as far as they can go, because they own their land in common.... There is no enterprise to make your home any better than that of your neighbor's. There is no selfishness, which is at the bottom of civilization. Until this people consent to give up their lands and divide them among their citizens so that each can own the land he cultivates, they will not make much progress (Wexler 1982).

Needless to say, the plans to coerce American Indians into participation in the White man's system of private property did not work out according to official plan. Instead, White people came in and bought up Indian land and left the Indians destitute. People who had not been paupers were now pauperized. It is a remarkably familiar story. The workings of an apparently neutral marketplace have a way of leaving swaths of destruction in their wake.

The Role of the Middle Class

The growth of a Black, Latino and Native American middle class in the last few decades also does not negate the proposition that racial inequality persists in America. In order to understand this, we need to consider the role that the middle class, or professional-managerial stratum, plays in capitalist society, irrespective of race. In my view, middle class people (including myself) are essentially the sergeants of the system. We professionals and managers are paid by the wealthy and powerful, by the corporations and the state, to keep things in order. Our role is one of maintaining the system of inequality. Our role is essentially that of controlling the poor. We are a semi-elite. We are given higher salaries, social status, better jobs, and better life chances as payment for our service to the system. If we were not useful to the power elite, they would not reward us. Our rewards prove that we serve their interests. Look at who pays us. That will give you a sense of whom we are serving (see Ehrenreich and Ehrenreich 1979).

We middle class people would like to believe that our positions of privilege benefit the less advantaged. We would like to believe that our upward mobility helps others, that the benefits we receive somehow "trickle down." But this is sheer self-delusion. It is capitalist ideology, which claims that the people at the top of the social system are really the great benefactors of the people at the bottom. The poor should be grateful to the beneficent rich elites for all their generosity. The poor depend on the wealthy; without the rich elites, where would the poor be? But of course, this picture stands reality on its head. Dependency really works the other way. It is the rich that depend on the poor for their well-being. And benefit, wealth and privilege flow up, not down.

The same basic truths apply to the Black and Latino middle class with some added features. People of color are, too often, treated as tokens. Their presence in higher level positions is used to "prove" that the American system is open to anyone with talent and ambition. But the truth is, people of color are allowed to hold more privileged positions if and only if they conform to the "party line." They are not allowed real authority. They have to play the White man's game by the White man's rules or they lose their good jobs. They have to give up who they are, and disown their community and its pressing needs for change, in order to "make it" in this system....

The rising Black and Latino middle class is, more often than not, used to control the poor and racially oppressed communities, to crush oppression and prevent needed social change. The same is the case, as I have said, with the White middle class. However, there was an implicit promise that the election of

Black and Latino political officials, and the growth of a professional and business stratum, would trickle down to the benefit of their communities. This has worked as well as trickle down theory in general. Regardless of the intentions of the Black and Latino middle class, the institutional structures and practices of capitalism have prohibited the implementation of any of the needed reforms. Black mayors, for example, coming in with plans of social progress, find themselves trapped in the logic of the private profit system and cannot implement their programs (see Lembeke in press).

This state of affairs is manifest on my campus. There has been a little progress in terms of affirmative action among the staff. However, if you look more closely, you discover that almost all of the Black and Chicano staff work under White administrators. Furthermore, those people with professional positions are highly concentrated in minority-oriented programs, like Student Affirmative Action, Immediate Outreach, Black and Chicano Student Programs and the like. Even here they are under the direction of White supervisors who ultimately determine the nature and limits of these programs.

What happens, more often than not, is that professional staff who are people of color become shock-absorbers in the system. They take responsibility for programs without having the authority to shape them. If recruitment or retention of students from racially oppressed communities does not produce results, it is the Black, Chicano and Native American professional staff who are held accountable, even though they could not shape a program that had any chance of succeeding. The staff people of color must accept the individualistic, meritocratic ethic of the institution and cannot push for programs that would enhance community development or community participation in the shaping of the university. They simply have to implement the bankrupt idea of plucking out the "best and brightest" and urging them to forsake their families and communities in the quest to "make it" in America.

Still, even if the ruling class can make use of people of color in middle class positions, I believe there are real limits to their willingness to allow enough redistribution to occur so that the averages across groups would become the same. The powerful and wealthy White capitalist class may be able to tolerate and even endorse "open competition" in the working and middle classes. However, they show no signs whatsoever of being willing to relinquish their own stranglehold on the world economy. They can play the game of supporting a recarving up of the tiny part of the pie left over after they have taken their share. Indeed, it is probably good business to encourage various groups to scramble for the crumbs. They will be so busy attacking each other that they will not think to join together to challenge the entire edifice.

The White establishment manipulates racial ideology. Even when it uses the language of colorblindness and equal opportunity, the words need to be stripped of their underlying manipulation. Right now it pays that establishment to act as though they are appalled by the use of race as a criterion for social allocation. But not too long ago, certainly within my memory, they were happy to use it openly. Have they suffered a real change of heart? Is a system that was openly built on racial oppression and that still uses it on a world scale, suddenly free from this cancer?

The truth is, a system driven by private profit, by the search for individual gain, can never solve its social problems. The conservatives promise that market forces will wipe out the negative effects of a history of racial discrimination. But this is a mirage. Wealth accrues to the already wealthy. Power and wealth enhance privilege.... The market system will not iron out this oppression. On the contrary, its operation sustains it. Only political opposition, only a demand for social justice, will turn this situation around.

NOTES

1. There is a major debate around the question of race versus class. See, for example, Alphonso Pinkney (1984) and Michael Omi and Harold Winant. The question is raised: Which is more important, race or class? Some argue that race cannot be "reduced" to class and that it has independent vitality. A similar argument is made by some feminists regarding gender. I do not contend that race can be reduced to class, but I do not think that race and class are independent systems that somehow intersect with one another. This imagery is too static.

REFERENCES

Bonacich, Edna. 1989. "Racism in the Deep Structure of U.S. Higher Education: When Affirmative Action Is Not Enough." In *Affirmative Action and Positive Policies in the Education of Ethnic Minorities,* edited by Sally Tomlinson and Abraham Yogev. Greenwich, CT: JAI Press.

——. 1987. "The Limited Social Philosophy of Affirmative Action." *Insurgent Sociologist* 14:99–116.

Cheng, Lucie and Edna Bonacich. 1984. *Labor Immigration Under Capitalism: Asian Workers in the United States Before World War II.* Berkeley: University of California Press.

Ehrenreich, Barbara and John. 1979. "The Professional-Managerial Class." Pp. 5–45 in *Between Labor and Capital,* edited by Pat Walker. Boston: South End Press.

Forbes. 1987. "The 400 Richest People in America." 140 (October):106–110.

Lembeke, Jerry. Forthcoming. *Race, Class, and Urban Change.* Greenwich, CT: JAI Press.

Los Angeles Times. "Hemisphere in Crisis." December 29, 1987.

——. " 'Super Rich' Control Misstated by Study." August 22, 1986.

——. "Walton Still Tops Forbes List of 400 Richest Americans." October 14, 1986.

Omi, Michael and Harold Winant. 1986. *Racial Formation in the United States: From the 1960s to the 1980s.* New York: Routledge and Kegan Paul.

Pinkney, Alphonso. 1984. *The Myth of Black Progress.* Cambridge: Cambridge University Press.

Sacks, Karen Brodkin and Dorothy Remy. 1984. *My Troubles are Going to Have Trouble With Me: Everyday Trials and Triumphs of Women Workers.* New Brunswick, New Jersey: Rutgers University Press.

Sheinkman, Jack. 1987. "Stop Exploiting Lowest-Paid Workers." *Los Angeles Times*, September 9.

Szymanski, Albert. 1979. *Is the Red Flag Flying? The Political Economy of the Soviet Union.* London: Zed Press.

U.S. Bureau of Census. 1986. Current Population Reports, Series P-60, No. 152. *Characteristics of the Population Below the Poverty Level: 1984.* Washington, D.C.: U.S. Government Printing Office.

U.S. Congress Joint Economic Committee. 1986. *The Concentration of Wealth in the United States: Trends in the Distribution of Wealth Among American Families.* Washington, D.C.: U.S. Government Printing Office.

U.S. Department of Labor, Bureau of Labor Statistics. 1987. *Employment and Earnings* 34:212. Washington, D.C.: U.S. Government Printing Office.

Wexler, Rex. 1982. *Blood of the Land: The Government and Corporate War Against the American Indian Movement.* New York: Vintage.

Williams, Eric. 1966. *Capitalism and Slavery.* New York: Capricorn.

PART TWO

Theoretical Orientations to the Study of Race and Ethnicity in the United States

On the Internet . . .

Sites appropriate to Part Two

Founded in 1946, the American Immigration Lawyers Association (AILA) is a national bar association of over 5,200 attorneys who practice and teach immigration law. At this site, you can access general background about immigration, descriptions of the services that immigration lawyers provide, and updates on the latest changes to immigration-related laws and regulations.

`http://www.aila.org`

This is an experimental Black cultural studies site created to increase access to resources about ethnicity, race, and gender among populations of the African diaspora. The site lists bibliographical information on cultural workers in such areas as Black literary criticism, Black popular culture, critical race theory, and film theory.

`http://www.tiac.net/users/thaslett/`

This site on the U.S. Immigration and Naturalization Service offers the latest information on immigration law, employment verification, and naturalization. It also provides access to annual statistical reports and downloadable application forms.

`http://www.ins.usdoj.gov/graphics/index.html`

CHAPTER 4

Assimilationism

4.1 MILTON M. GORDON

Assimilation in America: Theory and Reality

Assimilation refers to a process of accommodation by which members of minority groups are absorbed or integrated into a society's dominant or core culture. In this process, racially or ethnically diverse groups of people adapt and become indistinguishable from the dominant group.

In the following selection from "Assimilation in America: Theory and Reality," *Daedalus* (Spring 1961), Milton M. Gordon explores the dynamics of intergroup relations in American society from three conceptual models —Anglo-conformity, the melting pot thesis, and cultural pluralism. In this now classic work, Gordon treats these conceptual models as ideologies of ethnic assimilation and suggests that they bear far-reaching consequences for ethnic diversity in American society.

Key Concept: assimilation theory

Three ideologies or conceptual models have competed for attention on the American scene as explanations of the way in which a nation, in the beginning largely white, Anglo-Saxon, and Protestant, has absorbed over 41 million immigrants and their descendants from variegated sources and welded them into the contemporary American people. These ideologies are Anglo-conformity, the melting pot, and cultural pluralism....

The story of America's immigration can be quickly told for our present purposes. The white American population at the time of the Revolution was largely English and Protestant in origin, but had already absorbed substantial groups of Germans and Scotch-Irish and smaller contingents of Frenchmen, Dutchmen, Swedes, Swiss, South Irish, Poles, and a handful of migrants from other European nations. Catholics were represented in modest numbers, particularly in the middle colonies, and a small number of Jews were residents of the incipient nation. With the exception of the Quakers and a few missionaries, the colonists had generally treated the Indians and their cultures with contempt and hostility, driving them from the coastal plains and making the western frontier a bloody battleground where eternal vigilance was the price of survival.

Although the Negro at that time made up nearly one-fifth of the total population, his predominantly slave status, together with racial and cultural prejudice, barred him from serious consideration as an assimilable element of the society. And while many groups of European origin started out as determined ethnic enclaves, eventually, most historians believe, considerable ethnic intermixture within the white population took place. "People of different blood" [sic]—write two American historians about the colonial period, "English, Irish, German, Huguenot, Dutch Swedish-mingled and intermarried with little thought of any difference."[1] In such a society, its people predominantly English, its white immigrants of other ethnic origins either English-speaking or derived largely from countries of northern and western Europe whose cultural divergences from the English were not great, and its dominant white population excluding by fiat the claims and considerations of welfare of the non-Caucasian minorities, the problem of assimilation understandably did not loom unduly large or complex....

ANGLO-CONFORMITY

"Anglo-conformity"[2] is a broad term used to cover a variety of viewpoints about assimilation and immigration; they all assume the desirability of maintaining English institutions (as modified by the American Revolution), the English language, and English-oriented cultural patterns as dominant and standard in American life. However, bound up with this assumption are related attitudes. These may range from discredited notions about race and "Nordic"and "Aryan" racial superiority, together with the nativist political programs and exclusionist immigration policies which such notions entail, through an intermediate position of favoring immigration from northern and western Europe on amorphous, unreflective grounds ("They are more like us"), to a lack of opposition to any source of immigration, as long as these immigrants and their descendants duly adopt the standard Anglo-Saxon cultural patterns. There is by no means any necessary equation between Anglo-conformity and racist attitudes.

It is quite likely that "Anglo-conformity" in its more moderate aspects, however explicit its formulation, has been the most prevalent ideology of assimilation goals in America throughout the nation's history. As far back as colonial times, Benjamin Franklin recorded concern about the clannishness of the Germans in Pennsylvania, their slowness in learning English, and the establishment of their own native-language press.[3] ...

The attitudes of Americans toward foreign immigration in the first three-quarters of the nineteenth century may correctly be described as ambiguous. On the one hand, immigrants were much desired, so as to swell the population and importance of states and territories, to man the farms of expanding prairie settlement, to work the mines, build the railroads and canals, and take their place in expanding industry. This was a period in which no federal legislation of any consequence prevented the entry of aliens, and such state legislation as existed attempted to bar on an individual basis only those who were likely to become a burden on the community, such as convicts and paupers. On the other hand, the arrival in an overwhelmingly Protestant society of large numbers of poverty-stricken Irish Catholics, who settled in groups in the slums of Eastern cities, roused dormant fears of "Popery" and Rome. Another source of anxiety was the substantial influx of Germans, who made their way to the cities and farms of the mid-West and whose different language, separate communal life, and freer ideas on temperance and sabbath observance brought them into conflict with the Anglo-Saxon bearers of the Puritan and Evangelical traditions. Fear of foreign "radicals" and suspicion of the economic demands of the occasionally aroused workingmen added fuel to the nativist fires. In their extreme form these fears resulted in the Native-American movement of the 1830s and 1840s and the "American" or "Know-Nothing" party of the 1850s, with their anti-Catholic campaigns and their demands for restrictive laws on naturalization procedures and for keeping the foreign-born out of political office. While these movements scored local political successes and their turbulences so rent the national social fabric that the patches are not yet entirely invisible, they failed to influence national legislative policy on immigration and immigrants; and their fulminations inevitably provoked the expected reactions from thoughtful observers.

The flood of newcomers to the westward expanding nation grew larger, reaching over one and two-thirds million between 1841 and 1850 and over two and one-half million in the decade before the Civil War. Throughout the entire period, quite apart from the excesses of the Know-Nothings, the predominant (though not exclusive) conception of what the ideal immigrant adjustment should be was probably summed up in a letter written in 1818 by John Quincy Adams, then Secretary of State, in answer to the inquiries of the Baron von Fürstenwaerther. If not the earliest, it is certainly the most elegant version of the sentiment, "If they don't like it here, they can go back where they came from." Adams declared:[4]

> They [immigrants to America] come to life of independence, but to a life of labor —and, if they cannot accommodate themselves to the character, moral, political and physical, of this country with all its compensating balances of good and evil, the Atlantic is always open to them to return to the land of their nativity and their

fathers. To one thing they must make up their minds, or they will be disappointed in every expectation of happiness as Americans. They must cast off the European skin, never to resume it. They must look forward to their posterity rather than backward to their ancestors; they must be sure that whatever their own feelings may be, those of their children will cling to the prejudices of this country....

Anglo-conformity received its fullest expression in the so-called Americanization which gripped the nation during World War I. While "Americanization" in its various stages had more than one emphasis, it was essentially a consciously articulated movement to strip the immigrant of his native culture and attachments and make him over into an American along Anglo-Saxon lines—all this to be accomplished with great rapidity. To use an image of a later day, it was an attempt at "pressure-cooking assimilation." It had prewar antecedents, but it was during the height of the world conflict that federal agencies, state governments, municipalities, and a host of private organizations joined in the effort to persuade the immigrant to learn English, take out naturalization papers, buy war bonds, forget his former origins and culture, and give himself over to patriotic hysteria.

After the war and the "Red scare" which followed, the excesses of the Americanization movement subsided. In its place, however, came the restriction of immigration through federal law. Foiled at first by presidential vetoes, and later by the failure of the 1917 literacy test to halt the immigrant tide, the proponents of restriction finally put through in the early 1920s a series of acts culminating in the well-known national-origins formula for immigrant quotas which went into effect in 1929. Whatever the merits of a quantitative limit on the number of immigrants to be admitted to the United States, the provisions of the formula, which discriminated sharply against the countries of southern and eastern Europe, in effect institutionalized the assumptions of the rightful dominance of Anglo-Saxon patterns in the land. Reaffirmed with only slight modifications in the McCarran-Walter Act of 1952, these laws, then, stand as a legal monument to the creed of Anglo-conformity and a telling reminder that this ideological system still has numerous and powerful adherents on the American scene.

THE MELTING POT

While Anglo-conformity in various guises has probably been the most prevalent ideology of assimilation in the American historical experience, a competing viewpoint with more generous and idealistic overtones has had its adherents and exponents from the eighteenth century onward. Conditions in the virgin continent, it was clear, were modifying the institutions which the English colonists brought with them from the mother country. Arrivals from non-English homelands such as Germany, Sweden, and France were similarly exposed to this fresh environment. Was it not possible, then, to think of the evolving American society not as a slightly modified England but rather as a totally new blend, culturally and biologically, in which the stocks and folkways of Europe, figuratively speaking, were indiscriminately mixed in the political pot of the emerging nation and fused by the fires of American influence and interaction into a distinctly new type?

Such, at any rate, was the conception of the new society which motivated that eighteenth-century French-born writer and agriculturalist, J. Hector St. John de Crèvecoeur, who, after many years of American residence, published his reflections and observations in *Letters from an American Farmer.*[5] Who, he asks, is the American?

> He is either an European, or the descendant of an European, hence that strange mixture of blood, which you will find in no other country. I could point out to you a family whose grandfather was an Englishman, whose wife was Dutch, whose son married a French woman, and whose present four sons have now four wives of different nations. He is an American, who leaving behind him all his ancient prejudices and manners, receives new ones from the new mode of life he has embraced, the new government he obeys, and the new rank he holds. He becomes an American by being received in the broad lap of our great Alma Mater. Here individuals of all nations are melted into a new race of men, whose labours and posterity will one day cause great changes in the world.

Some observers have interpreted the open-door policy on immigration of the first three-quarters of the nineteenth century as reflecting an underlying faith in the effectiveness of the American melting pot, in the belief "that all could be absorbed and that all could contribute to an emerging national character."[6] No doubt many who observed with dismay the nativist agitation of the times felt as did Ralph Waldo Emerson that such conformity-demanding and immigrant-hating forces represented a perversion of the best American ideals. In 1845, Emerson wrote in his Journal:[7]

> I hate the narrowness of the Native American Party. It is the dog in the manger. It is precisely opposite to all the dictates of love and magnanimity; and therefore, of course, opposite to true wisdom.... Man is the most composite of all creatures.... Well, as in the old burning of the Temple at Corinth, by the melting and inter-mixture of silver and gold and other metals a new compound more precious than any, called Corinthian brass, was formed: so in this continent,—asylum of all nations,—the energy of Irish, Germans, Swedes, Poles, and Cossacks, and all the European tribes,—of the Africans, and the Polynesians,—will construct a new race, a new religion, a new state, a new literature, which will be as vigorous as the new Europe which came out of the smelting-pot of the Dark Ages, or that which earlier emerged from the Pelasgic and Etruscan barbarism. *La Nature aime les croisements....*

It remained for an English-Jewish writer with strong social convictions, moved by his observation of the role of the United States as a haven for the poor and oppressed of Europe, to give utterance to the broader view of the American melting pot in a way which attracted public attention. In 1908, Israel Zangwill's drama, *The Melting Pot,* was produced in this country and became a popular success. It is a play dominated by the dream of its protagonist, a young Russian-Jewish immigrant to America, a composer, whose goal is the completion of a vast "American" symphony which will express his deeply felt conception of his adopted country as a divinely appointed crucible in which all the ethnic division of mankind will divest themselves of their ancient animosities and differences and become fused into one group, signifying the brotherhood of man. In the process he falls in love with a beautiful and cultured Gentile girl. The play ends with the performance of the symphony and, after numerous vicissitudes and traditional family opposition from both sides, with the approaching marriage of David Quixano and his beloved. During the course of these developments, David, in the rhetoric of the time, delivers himself of such sentiments as these:[8]

> America is God's crucible, the great Melting Pot where all the races of Europe are melting and reforming! Here you stand, good folk, think I, when I see them at Ellis Island, here you stand in your fifty groups, with your fifty languages and histories, and your fifty blood hatreds and rivalries. But you won't be long like that, brother, for these are the fires of God you've come to—these are the fires of God. A fig for your feuds and vendettas! Germans and Frenchman, Irishmen and Englishmen, Jews and Russians—into the Crucible with you all! God is making the American.

Here we have a conception of a melting pot which admits of no exceptions or qualifications with regard to the ethnic stocks which will fuse in the great crucible. Englishmen, Germans, Frenchmen, Slavs, Greeks, Syrians, Jews, Gentiles, even the black and yellow races, were specifically mentioned in Zangwill's rhapsodic enumeration. And this pot patently was to boil in the great cities of America.

Thus around the turn of the century the melting-pot idea became embedded in the ideals of the age as one response to the immigrant receiving experience of the nation. Soon to be challenged by a new philosophy of group adjustment (to be discussed below) and always competing with the more pervasive adherence to Anglo-conformity, the melting-pot image, however, continued to draw a portion of the attention consciously directed toward this aspect of the American scene in the first half of the twentieth century. In the mid-1940s a sociologist who had carried out an investigation of intermarriage trends in New Haven, Connecticut, described a revised conception of the melting process in that city and suggested a basic modification of the theory of that process. In New Haven, Ruby Jo Reeves Kennedy[9] reported from a study of intermarriages from 1870 to 1940 that there was a distinct tendency for the British-Americans, Germans, and Scandinavians to marry among themselves—that is, within a Protestant "pool"; for the Irish, Italians, and Poles to marry among themselves —a Catholic "pool"; and for the Jews to marry other Jews. In other words, intermarriage was taking place across lines of nationality background, but there was a strong tendency for it to stay confined within one or the other of the three major religious groups, Protestants, Catholics, and Jews. Thus, declared Mrs. Kennedy, the picture in New Haven resembled a "triple melting pot" based on religious division, rather than a "single melting pot." Her study indicated, she stated, that "while strict endogamy is loosening, religious endogamy is persisting and the future cleavages will be along religious lines rather than along nationality lines as in the past. If this is the case, then the traditional 'single-melting-pot' idea must be abandoned, and a new conception, which we term the 'triple-melting-pot' theory of American assimilation, will take its place as the true expression of what is happening to the various nationality groups in the United States."[10] The triple melting-pot thesis was later taken up by the theologian Will Herberg, and formed an important sociological frame of reference for his analysis of religious trends in American society, *Protestant-Catholic-Jew*.[11] But the triple melting-pot hypothesis patently takes us into the realm of a society pluralistically conceived. We turn now to the rise of an ideology which attempts to justify such a conception.

CULTURAL PLURALISM

Probably all the non-English immigrants who came to American shores in any significant numbers from colonial times onward—settling either in the forbidding wilderness, the lonely prairie, or in some accessible urban slum—created ethnic enclaves and looked forward to the preservation of at least some of their native cultural patterns. Such a development, natural as breathing, was supported by the later accretion of friends, relatives, and countrymen seeking out oases of familiarity in a strange land, by the desire of the settlers to rebuild (necessarily in miniature) a society in which they could communicate in the familiar tongue and maintain familiar institutions, and, finally, by the necessity to band together for mutual aid and mutual protection against the uncertainties of a strange and frequently hostile environment. This was as true of the "old" immigrants as of the "new." In fact, some of the liberal intellectuals who fled to America from an inhospitable political climate in Germany in the 1830s, 1840s, and 1850s looked forward to the creation of an all-German state within the union, or, even more hopefully, to the eventual formation of a separate German nation, as soon as the expected dissolution of the union under the impact of the slavery controversy should have taken place.[12] Oscar Handlin, writing of the sons of Erin in mid-nineteenth-century Boston, recent refugees from famine and economic degradation in their homeland, points out: "Unable to participate in the normal associational affairs of the community, the Irish felt obliged to erect a society within a society, to act together in their own way. In every contact therefore the group, acting apart from other sections of the community, became intensely aware of its peculiar and exclusive identity."[13] Thus cultural pluralism was a fact in American society before it became a theory—a theory with explicit relevance for the nation as a whole, and articulated and discussed in the English-speaking circles of American intellectual life.

Eventually, the cultural enclaves of the Germans (and the later arriving Scandinavians) were to decline in scope and significance as succeeding generations of their native-born attended public schools, left the farms and villages to strike out as individuals for the Americanizing city, and generally became subject to the influences of a standardizing industrial civilization. The German-American community, too, was struck a powerful blow by the accumulated passions generated by World War I—a blow from which it never fully recovered. The Irish were to be the dominant and pervasive element in the gradual emergence of a pan-Catholic group in America, but these developments would reveal themselves only in the twentieth century. In the meantime, in the last two decades of the nineteenth, the influx of immigrants from southern and eastern Europe had begun. These groups were all the more sociologically visible because the closing of the frontier, the occupational demands of an expanding industrial economy, and their own poverty made it inevitable that they would remain in the urban areas of the nation. In the swirling fires of controversy and the steadier flame of experience created by these new events, the ideology of cultural pluralism as a philosophy for the nation was forged.

The first manifestations of an ideological counterattack against draconic Americanization came not from the beleaguered newcomers (who were, after all, more concerned with survival than with theories of adjustment), but from those idealistic members of the middle class who, in the decade or so before the turn of the century, had followed the example of their English predecessors and "settled" in the slums to "learn to sup sorrow with the poor."[14] Immediately, these workers in the "settlement houses" were forced to come to grips with the realities of immigrant life and adjustment. Not all reacted in the same way, but on the whole the settlements developed an approach to the immigrant which was sympathetic to his native cultural heritage and to his newly created ethnic institutions.[15] For one thing, their workers, necessarily in intimate contact with the lives of these often pathetic and bewildered newcomers and their daily problems, could see how unfortunate were the effects of those forces which impelled rapid Americanization in their impact on the immigrants' children, who not infrequently became alienated from their parents and the restraining influence of family authority. Were not their parents ignorant and uneducated "Hunkies," "Sheenies," or "Dagoes," as that limited portion of the American environment in which they moved defined the matter? Ethnic "self-hatred" with its debilitating psychological consequences, family disorganization, and juvenile delinquency, were not unusual results of this state of affairs. Furthermore, the immigrants themselves were adversely affected by the incessant attacks on their cultures, their language, their institutions, their very conception of themselves. How were they to maintain their self-respect when all that they knew, felt, and dreamed, beyond their sheer capacity for manual labor—in other words, all that they *were*—was despised or scoffed at in America? And—unkindest cut of all—their own children had begun to adopt the contemptuous attitude of the "Americans." Jane Addams relates in a moving chapter of her *Twenty Years at Hull House* how, after coming to have some conception of the extent and depth of these problems, she created at the settlement a "Labor Museum," in which the immigrant women of the various nationalities crowded together in the slums of Chicago could illustrate their native methods of spinning and weaving, and in which the relation of these earlier techniques to contemporary factory methods could be graphically shown. For the first time these peasant women were made to feel by some part of their American environment that they possessed valuable and interesting skills—that they too had something to offer—and for the first time, the daughters of these women who, after a long day's work at their dank "needletrade" sweat-shops, came to Hull House to observe, began to appreciate the fact that their mothers, too, had a "culture," that this culture possessed its own merit, and that it was related to their own contemporary lives. How aptly Jane Addams concludes her chapter with the hope that "our American citizenship might be built without disturbing these foundations which were laid of old time."[16]

This appreciative view of the immigrant's cultural heritage and of its distinctive usefulness both to himself and his adopted country received additional sustenance from another source: those intellectual currents of the day which, however overborne by their currently more powerful opposites, emphasized liberalism, internationalism, and tolerance. From time to time an occasional educator or publicist protested the demands of the "Americanizers," arguing that the immigrant too, had an ancient and honorable culture, and that this culture had much to offer an America whose character and destiny were still in the process of formation, an America which must serve as an example of the harmonious cooperation of various heritages to a world inflamed by nationalism and war. In 1916 John Dewey, Norman Hapgood, and the young literary critic Randolph Bourne published articles or addresses elaborating various aspects of this theme.

The classic statement of the cultural pluralist position, however, had been made over a year before. Early in 1915 there appeared in the pages of The Nation two articles under the title "Democracy versus the Melting-Pot." Their author was Horace Kallen, a Harvard-educated philosopher with a concern for the application of philosophy to societal affairs, and, as an American Jew, himself derivative of an ethnic background which was subject to the contemporary pressures for dissolution implicit in the "Americanization," or Anglo-conformity, and the melting-pot theories. In these articles Kallen vigorously rejected the usefulness of these theories as models of what was actually transpiring in American life or as ideals for the future. Rather he was impressed by the way in which the various ethnic groups in America were coincident with particular areas and regions, and with the tendency for each group to preserve its own language, religion, communal institutions, and ancestral culture. All the while, he pointed out, the immigrant has been learning to speak English as the language of general communication, and has participated in the over-all economic and political life of the nation. These developments in which "the United States are in the process of becoming a federal state not merely as a union of geographical and administrative unities, but also as a cooperation of cultural diversities, as a federation or commonwealth of national cultures,"[17] the author argued, far from constituting a violation of historic American political principles, as the "Americanizers" claimed, actually represented the inevitable consequences of democratic ideals, since individuals are implicated in groups, and since democracy for the individual must by extension also mean democracy for his group.

The processes just described, however, as Kallen develops his argument, are far from having been thoroughly realized. They are menaced by "Americanization" programs, assumptions of Anglo-Saxon superiority, and misguided attempts to promote "racial" amalgamation. Thus America stands at a kind of cultural crossroads. It can attempt to impose by force an artificial, Anglo-Saxon oriented uniformity on its peoples, or it can consciously allow and encourage its ethnic groups to develop democratically, each emphasizing its particular cultural heritage. If the latter course is followed, as Kallen puts it at the close of his essay, then,[18]

> The outlines of a possible great and truly democratic commonwealth become discernible. Its form would be that of the federal republic: its substance a democracy of nationalities, cooperating voluntarily and autonomously through common institutions in the enterprise of self-realization through the perfection of men according to their kind. The common language of the commonwealth, the language of its great tradition, would be English, but each nationality would have for its emotional and involuntary life its own peculiar dialect or speech, its own individual and inevitable esthetic and intellectual forms. The political and economic life of the commonwealth is a single unit and serves as the foundation and background for the realization of the distinctive individuality of each *nation* that composes it and of the pooling of these in a harmony above them all. Thus "American civilization" may come to mean the perfection of the cooperative harmonies of "European civilization"—the waste, the squalor and the distress of Europe being eliminated —a multiplicity in a unity, an orchestration of mankind.

Within the next decade Kallen published more essays dealing with the theme of American multiple-group life, later collected in a volume.[19] In the introductory note to this book he used for the first time the term "cultural pluralism" to refer to his position. These essays reflect both his increasingly sharp rejection of the onslaughts on the immigrant and his culture which the coming of World War I and its attendant fears, the "Red scare," the projection of themes of racial superiority, the continued exploitation of the newcomers, and the rise of the Ku Klux Klan all served to increase in intensity, and also his emphasis on cultural pluralism as the democratic antidote to these ills. He has since published other essays elaborating or annotating the theme of cultural pluralism. Thus, for at least forty-five years, most of them spent teaching at the New School for Social Research, Kallen has been acknowledged as the originator and leading philosophical exponent of the idea of cultural pluralism.

In the late 1930s and early 1940s the late Louis Adamic, the Yugoslav immigrant who had become an American writer, took up the theme of America's multicultural heritage and the role of these groups in forging the country's national character. Borrowing Walt Whitman's phrase, he described America as "a nation of nations," and while his ultimate goal was closer to the melting-pot idea than to cultural pluralism, he saw the immediate task as that of making America conscious of what it owed to all its ethnic groups, not just to the Anglo-Saxons. The children and grandchildren of immigrants of non-English origins, he was convinced, must be taught to be proud of the cultural heritage of their ancestral ethnic group and of its role in building the American nation; otherwise, they would not lose their sense of ethnic inferiority and the feeling of rootlessness he claimed to find in them.

Thus in the twentieth century, particularly since World War II, "cultural pluralism" has become a concept which has worked its way into the vocabulary and imagery of specialists in intergroup relations and leaders of ethnic communal groups. In view of this new pluralistic emphasis, some writers now prefer to speak of the "integration" of immigrants rather than of their "assimilation."[20] However, with a few exceptions,[21] no close analytical attention has been given either by social scientists or practitioners of intergroup relations to the meaning of cultural pluralism, its nature and relevance for a modern industrialized society, and its implications for problems of prejudice and discrimination.

NOTES

1. Allen Nevins and Henry Steele Commager, *America: The Story of a Free People* (Boston, Little, Brown, 1942), p. 58.
2. The phrase is the Coles'. See Stewart G. Cole and Mildred Wiese Cole, *Minorities and the American Promise* (New York, Harper & Brothers, 1954), ch. 6.
3. Maurice R. Davie, *World Immigration* (New York, Macmillan, 1936), p. 36, and (cited therein) "Letter of Benjamin Franklin to Peter Collinson, 9th May, 1753, on the condition and character of the Germans in Pennsylvania," in *The World of Benjamin Franklin, with Notes and Life of the Author,* by Jared Sparks (Boston. 1828), vol. 7, pp. 71–73.
4. *Niles Weekly Register,* vol. 18, 29 April 1820, pp. 157–158; see also Marcus L. Hansen, *The Atlantic Migration, 1607–1860,* pp. 96–97.
5. J. Hector St. John de Crèvecoeur, *Letters from an American Farmer* (New York, Albert and Charles Boni, 1925; reprinted from the 1st edn., London, 1782), pp. 54–55.
6. Oscar Handlin, ed., *Immigration as a Factor in American History* (Englewood, Prentice-Hall, 1959), p. 146.
7. Quoted by Stuart P. Sherman in his Introduction to *Essays and Poems of Emerson* (New York, Harcourt Brace, 1921), p. xxxiv.
8. Israel Zangwill, *The Melting Pot* (New York, Macmillan, 1909), p. 37.
9. Ruby Jo Reeves Kennedy, "Single or Triple Melting-Pot? Intermarriage Trends in New Haven, 1870–1940," *American Journal of Sociology,* 1944, 49:331–339. See also her "Single or Triple Melting-Pot? Intermarriage in New Haven, 1870–1950," *ibid.,* 1952, 58:56–59.
10. Kennedy, "Single or Triple Melting-Pot? ... 1870–1940," p. 332 (author's italics omitted).
11. Will Herberg, *Protestant-Catholic-Jew* (Garden City, Doubleday, 1955).
12. Nathan Glazer, "Ethnic Groups in America: From National Culture to Ideology," in Morroe Berger, Theodore Abel, and Charles H. Page, eds., *Freedom and Control in Modern Society* (New York, D. Van Nostrand, 1954), p. 161; Marcus Lee Hansen, *The Immigrant in American History* (Cambridge, Harvard University Press, 1940), pp. 129–140; John A. Hawgood, *The Tragedy of German-America* (New York, Putnam's, 1940), *passim.*
13. Oscar Handlin, *Boston's Immigrants* (Cambridge, Harvard University Press, 1959, rev. edn.), p. 176.
14. From a letter (1883) by Sanuel A. Barnett; quoted in Arthur C. Holden, *The Settlement Idea* (New York, Macmillan, 1922), p. 12.
15. Jane Addams, *Twenty Years at Hull House* (New York, Macmillan, 1914), pp. 231–258; Arthur C. Holden, *op. cit.,* pp. 109–131, 182–189; John Higham, *Strangers in the Land* (New Brunswick, Rutgers University Press, 1955), p. 236.
16. Jane Addams, *op. cit.,* p. 258.

17. Horace M. Kallen, "Democracy *versus* the Melting-Pot," *The Nation,* 18 and 25 February 1915; reprinted in his *Culture and Democracy in the United States,* New York, Boni and Liveright, 1924; the quotation is on p. 116.
18. Kallen, *Culture and Democracy . . . ,* p. 124.
19. *Op. cit.*
20. See W. D. Borrie *et al., The Cultural Integration of Immigrants* (a survey based on the papers and proceedings of the UNESCO Conference in Havana, April 1956), Paris, UNESCO, 1959; and William S. Bernard, "The Integration of Immigrants in the United States" (mimeographed), one of the papers for this conference.
21. See particularly Milton M. Gordon, "Social Structure and Goals in Group Relations"; and Nathan Glazer, "Ethnic Groups in America: From National Culture to Ideology," both articles in Berger, Abel, and Page, *op. cit.;* S. N. Eisenstadt, *The Absorption of Immigrants* (London, Routledge and Kegan Paul, 1954) and W. D. Borrie *et al., op. cit.*

4.2 RUTH W. GRANT AND MARION ORR

Language, Race and Politics: From "Black" to "African-American"

All-encompassing racial and ethnic labels such as *Asian American, Native American,* and *Hispanic* or *Latino American* are the result of populations' minority status in American society. While these labels provide convenient categorizations for social scientists, they systematically overlook or deny cultural variations within groups. For example, the label *Asian American* groups together dissimilar national elements—including Chinese, Japanese, Korean, Vietnamese, Thai, Khmer, and Asian Indian. Similarly, the terms *American Indian* and *Native American* obscure the multitude of tribal distinctions among these groups. These labels are also sensitive to change. For example, the traditional term assigned Asian Americans by Anglos is *Oriental.* Also, from the colonial era to the 1960s, Anglos identified people of African descent as *Negroes.* In response to the growing militancy of the civil rights era, however, people of African descent systematically rejected the White-imposed category of *Negro* and adopted *Black* instead. Most recently, Blacks have embraced the more inclusionary label *African American.*

In the following selection from "Language, Race and Politics: From 'Black' to 'African-American,'" *Politics and Society* (June 1996), Ruth W. Grant and Marion Orr explain the social and political implications of the label *African American* from a sociolinguistic approach. These authors contend that *African American* amounts to an ethnic term that will depreciate the historical struggle of persons of African descent for racial equality.

Grant is an associate professor of political science at Duke University who teaches political theory with particular interest in early modern philosophy and political ethics. The author of *John Locke's Liberalism* (University of Chicago Press, 1987), Grant earned her Ph.D. from the University of Chicago. Orr is an assistant professor of political science at Duke University who teaches urban politics and urban public policy and African American politics. She earned her Ph.D. from the University of Maryland.

Key Concept: racial and ethnic labels

My dear Roland:

Do not at the outset of your career make the all too common error of mistaking names for things. Names are only the conventional signs for identifying things. Things are the reality that counts. If a thing is despised, either because of ignorance or because it is despicable, you will not alter matters by changing its name. If men despise Negroes, they will not despise them less if Negroes are called "colored" or "Afro-Americans."... Get this then, Roland, and get it straight even if it pierces your soul: a Negro by any other name would be just as black and just as white; just as ashamed of himself and just as shamed by others, as today. It is not the name—it's the Thing that counts. Come on, Kid, let's go get the Thing!

—W. E. B. DuBois[1]

One result of the civil rights struggle of the 1960s was the replacement of the term "Negro" by "black." Now, in the 1990s, there is some question whether "black" will itself be supplanted by "African-American" as the preferred term for America's largest racial minority. Is this change in terminology a politically significant event or a distinction without a difference? What's in a name?

Scholars in recent years have become increasingly sensitive to the ways in which language shapes political discourse and hence political options. Changes in terminology matter, it is argued, because terminology shapes conceptualization: some terms make certain conceptual associations seem obvious and others seem problematic; terms can constrain the way we perceive political alternatives; and so on. We have an intuitive sense that this is so. For example, "black separatism" makes conceptual sense in a way that "African-American separatism" does not. Or consider that the term "black" has an obvious opposite whereas the term "African-American" does not. The terms imply a different relation between members of the group and non-members. Terminological changes thus may influence the way we think about our political situation.

In what follows, we analyze the potential impact of the shift from "black" to "African-American." At the same time, we use this case to question, with DuBois, the extent to which language does indeed construct reality. The meaning of a term may be "given" to a certain extent by the circumstances of its use. We argue that, if "African-American" becomes the dominant term, it is likely to take on many of the same characteristics as earlier terms and that, consequently, it too will be challenged eventually, absent real political change in the condition of the races in America. However, this does not mean that the change from "black" to "African-American" is politically meaningless. We argue that it may matter a great deal, though not in the ways that people generally believe. Many proponents of this change believe that the new term will enhance the self-esteem of minority group members and the respect with which they are treated by the majority. The historical record as well as the psychological research do not confirm these expectations.

Politically, the importance of the shift from "black" to "African-American" lies in the fact that it implies a shift from race to ethnicity or culture as the defining characteristic of the group and consequently it evokes the notion of similarities between this group and other ethnic groups. Yet research in the social sciences has repeatedly demonstrated the uniqueness of the black experience in America. The analogy between blacks and immigrant groups is a weak analogy. We thus raise the possibility that the "African-American" label may mask the role of racism in our history and weaken, rather than strengthen, the political claims of this distinctive minority.[2]

LANGUAGE AND POLITICS

The tacit assumption behind the debate over the term "African-American" is that changes in language matter.[3] How and why language matters has been a central concern of scholarly investigation in recent years, particularly in philosophy, sociology, political theory, and linguistics. There has been a great deal of theoretical elaboration of the issue, and a variety of positions have emerged.[4] For our purposes, it suffices to articulate those few basic propositions which might provide essential theoretical support for the expectation that the change from "black" to "African-American" would be a significant change.

The importance of language is rooted in the broader notion that reality itself is socially constructed, rather than objectively or immutably given. Our very conception of ourselves, of our experience, and of the world is constituted by the society in which we live. This is what accounts for the relativity of reality: "what is 'real' to a Tibetan monk may not be 'real' to an American businessman."[5] Many identify language as the primary mechanism by which the social construction of reality takes place. The world is *as* it is only in and through language. "Learning to speak does not mean learning to use a preexistent tool for designating a world already somehow familiar to us; it means acquiring a familiarity and acquaintance with the world itself and how it confronts us."[6] A child learning a language does not merely learn which sounds express which ideas or stand for which objects. He learns a manner of thinking about the world around him. This observation is not new. Jean-Jacques Rousseau made a similar point over 200 years ago when he wrote that language is not

> only the study of words—that is to say, of figures or the sounds which express them... in changing the signs, languages also modify the ideas which these signs represent. Minds are formed by languages; the thoughts take on the color of the idioms.[7]

Our understanding and experience are decisively shaped by the language within which they take place.

Moreover, our self-understanding is similarly constructed. It is for this reason that one might expect a name change to enhance self-esteem. In learning a language, the child learns about his own place in the world. "Language constitutes both the most important content and the most important instrument of socialization.[8] Language provides us with the conceptual classifications that differentiate things from each other, including those classifications that differentiate us from other people. For example, even our classification of ourselves and others as either feminine or masculine can be seen as the product of social and linguistic practices rather than as a reflection of an underlying biological reality. We identify ourselves with those who are called by the same name as we are, and each name carries expected characteristics that are important in the formation of identity. Clearly, naming, viewed in this way, is not a politically neutral process.

Indeed, language can be viewed as essentially political; language necessarily reflects, reinforces and reproduces the power relations within every society.[9] In advocating the adoption of the term "black," Stokely Carmichael and Charles Hamilton used Lewis Carroll to make precisely this point:

> "When I use a word," Humpty Dumpty said in a rather scornful tone, "it means just what I choose it to mean—neither more nor less."
>
> "The question is," said Alice, "whether you *can* make words mean so many different things."
>
> "The question is," said Humpty Dumpty. "which is to be master—that's all."[10]

If words have no fixed meanings, they become merely instruments of power. The process of definition, if not directly controlled by the powerful, at the very least could be said to serve the interests of the powerful. By implication, to attempt to be self defining is itself an important assertion of power. Where language is understood as the crucial medium for the construction of social reality and personal identity, both the control of the language and the terms we adopt take on enormous political significance.

Yet it is possible to make too much of this. Alice may also have a point (one rather like Dubois's) when she wonders "whether you *can* make words mean so many different things." Rousseau too indicates that the potential of language is not limitless. Language is intertwined with reason, mind, character, and so on so as to be both cause and effect. Immediately following the statement quoted above, Rousseau writes, "Only reason is common; in each language, the mind has its particular form. This is a difference that might very well be a part of the cause or of the effect of national characters."[11] Language is not simply an architectonic social force, but one that is itself limited by predetermined structures and realities. The advocates of terminological change may overestimate our ability to transform political reality through the collective manipulation of language.

The ambiguities in the relation of language and politics indicate the complexity of our initial question: "Does the change from 'black' to 'African-American' matter for politics, and if so, how?' In what follows, we suggest that this is a change that both does and does not matter. "African-American," like every term, exists in a linguistic web of relations with associated terms and conceptions. Its web differs from the one that encompasses the term "black." Consequently, the use of "African-American" can be expected to lead us to interpret the world differently than the use of "black." We will think about race relations differently as a result of the change, perhaps in a variety of subtle ways which we may only dimly perceive. But at the same time, the fact that the term "black" so recently replaced "Negro" and that this earlier change was justified in exactly the same terms as the more recent change to "African-American" leads us to question the limits of the linguistic construction of reality and the capacity of language to effect political change. As we will see, the history of racial nomenclature in the United States reinforces that doubt.

A HISTORY OF RACIAL NOMENCLATURE IN AMERICA

The question as to what to call the descendants of African slaves is not new. In fact, the term used to designate America's largest racial minority has never been settled for long at any time since 1619, when the first African indentured servants landed at Jamestown. During most periods of our history, several terms have coexisted in common speech among different groups, and the precise history of the terminological transformations is far from clear. Nonetheless, what is striking about a brief survey of the history of racial nomenclature is that "African," "colored," "Negro" and "black" have each been adopted at one time by blacks themselves for political reasons, only to be rejected at a later time, also for political reasons.

During the colonial era, the most frequently used term by blacks, for free and slave blacks alike, was "African." When blacks organized their first churches they were called the African Episcopal Church or the First African Baptist Church. The first organized self-help organization was designated the Free African Society.[12] Indeed, the preamble of the Free African Society, which was founded in 1887, began: "We, the free Africans and their descendants of the City of Philadelphia or elsewhere . . . "[13] The African experience was still very immediate for most blacks. "The term *African* more often than not reflected a pride in blackness and racial inclusiveness."[14] The name had an "ideological function" and served as a "rallying point."[15]

"African" was widely used from the last quarter of the eighteenth century until the formation of the American Colonization Society in 1816.[16] Organized by wealthy whites, the Colonization Society led a movement to send free Africans "back" to Africa. Colonization was opposed by many blacks. In the North, black opposition reached fever pitch. It was in the reaction of blacks to the colonization movement of the 1820s and 1830s that the era of "colored" began and that of "African" declined.[17] With the establishment of the Colonization Society, growing numbers of blacks avoided use of the term *African,* opting for a safer appellation, *colored,* because to continue to refer to oneself as African might encourage colonizationists to believe one wanted to be shipped "back" to Africa. A heated debate over what they should call themselves took place when they heard that colonizationists were promoting the view that America was not the African's home.[18]

The first switch in nomenclature, then, was initiated by blacks in response to the suggestion by whites that there was no place for Africans on American soil. Blacks responded loudly to this suggestion. Both the free and enslaved African populations were developing a new realization of their role in the development of America.[19] They had helped build this country. "The Africans reasoned that the European-dominated movements to resettle them in Africa would effectively disinherit them of their share of the American pie whose ingredients included not only their own blood, sweat, and tears, but that of many thousands gone."[20] Blacks' belief in the important role they played in the building of the American nation is reflected in a heightened mobilization in the nineteenth century, not to return to Africa, but toward emancipation as Americans.

The black community reacted to the colonization movement by abandoning the "African" designation and adopting instead the words "colored" and/or "free persons of color." Many prominent blacks in the North went so far as to advocate the removal of the word "African" from titles and from the marbles of churches and other institutions.[21] While it is true that terms were used interchangeably, Stuckey reports that "in any case, the term *colored* was by the late 1830's probably used more widely than any other in black leadership circles; it was used by integrationists and nationalists alike."[22] For example, David Walker's (1829) radical appeal calling for open rebellion against enslavement was addressed to the "Coloured Citizens of the World, but in Particular and very Expressly to Those of the United States of America."[23] Frederick Douglass, the leading public figure and abolitionist, used "colored" (as well as "Negro") in his speeches and writings. Even in the early twentieth century, "colored" was still an accepted racial designation. The oldest civil rights organization, founded in 1909, was (and still is) called the National Association for the Advancement of Colored People (NAACP).

"Colored" gradually began to lose its preferred status to "Negro" around the turn of the century, though the two terms coexisted in common usage for quite some time. Booker T. Washington favored the word "Negro" and urged its adoption by the U.S. Census Bureau.[24] Many viewed "Negro" as more accurate than "colored," as grammatically superior, and as the stronger term of the two.[25] Once again, one can see the development of linguistic change in the designation of the first "Negro" national organizations (the American Negro Academy, 1897; the National Negro Business League, 1901). By 1919, the *Negro Year Book* could report, "There is an increasing use of the word 'Negro' and a decreasing use of the words 'colored' and 'Afro-American'; to designate us as a people. The result is that the word 'Negro' is, more and more, acquiring a dignity that it did not have in the past."[26] Moreover, during this same period there was an aggressive campaign, led by the NAACP, for the capitalization of the word "Negro" on the grounds that the capital letter dignified the term by treating it as other group names were treated (e.g., Italian, Irish, etc.).[27] "Negro" continued to gain predominance, particularly during the period of the two world wars, "Although some Negroes continued to use 'colored,' and although some Negro leaders and intellectuals—DuBois among them—balanced 'Negro' with 'black,' 'Negro' became the label of choice, dominating discourse by and about Negroes for over forty years."[28]

By the 1950s "Negro" was accepted as the preferred term by both blacks and whites. But as the civil rights movement began making progress, the term "Negro" itself eventually fell under attack.[29] In its stead, "black" was promoted as a term that would not only designate a certain group of people, but would express at the same time racial pride, militancy, power, and rejection of the status quo.[30]

Perhaps the most famous proponent of the switch from Negro to black was Stokely Carmichael. In 1966 he helped to coin the phrase "black power," In *Black Power,* Carmichael and his coauthor, Charles Hamilton, urged the adoption of the term "black" as a means for black people to "redefine themselves."[31] Carmichael and Hamilton maintained that the designation "Negro" was the "invention" of whites, of the oppressors of black people, though the history we have just surveyed indicates the weakness of this claim.

For Carmichael and Hamilton, the term "Negro," because it was the "white" term, allowed whites to define black Americans, and their definition of "Negroes" carried definite negative connotations—"Negroes" were lazy, apathetic, dumb, shiftless, and so on. By using the term, blacks themselves were led to believe and to internalize the negative images that whites tended to associate with Negroes.

> There is a growing resentment of the word "Negro," for example, because this term is the invention of our oppressor; it is *his* image of us that he describes. Many blacks are now calling themselves African Americans, Afro-Americans or black people because that is *our* image of ourselves. When we begin to define our own image, the stereotypes—that is, lies—that our oppressor has developed will begin in the white community and end there. The black community will have a positive image of itself that *it* created.[32]

For a period of time, "black" continued to carry strong political messages. Slogans such as "black is beautiful" and "black pride" promoted solidarity within the black community.[33] Moreover, "black" was used to describe those who were "progressive," while "Negro" was used for those who were identified with the status quo.[34]

From the early 1970s to the late 1980s, "black" became the dominant designation. Smith presents public opinion data showing that "black" was preferred by a large majority (65 percent) of blacks by 1974.[35] Because of its association with radicals and extremists, whites were slower in adopting the new term.[36] By the mid-1970s, however, "black" had become the accepted term nationally in the press, in official documents, and for the vast majority of Americans in their common speech. But as the term gained acceptance, it also lost its political edge. "Black" was no longer coupled with its original associated term, "power," and it lost nearly all of its radical connotations.

In December 1988, a movement was launched to replace "black" with "African-American." At a meeting of black leaders in Chicago, Ramona H. Edelin, president of the National Urban Coalition, proposed the switch. Once again, the adoption of the new term was defended as a progressive step in the ongoing struggle for black dignity and liberation in contrast to the old term which was characterized as a symbol of oppression.[37] But in this case, the "old" term was one that had been introduced by radical black leaders only 25 years before as a symbol of black pride.

The evolution of racial labels from the early slavery period through the 1980s reveals a clear pattern. The established name is replaced for political reasons and in response to an initiative from within the black community. Each shift functions in part as an attempt to establish a positive black identity in a hostile environment.[38] Of course, the particular political mechanisms behind each name change vary considerably with the historical circumstances. For example, as we have seen, the change from "African" to "colored" was a response to a political movement among whites, whereas the change from "Negro" to "black" was part of an effort from within the Civil Rights movement involving a variety of factors, among them an attempt to change its political direction to address de facto segregation in the North, black self-determination, and so on. Nonetheless, in every case a new name is introduced by blacks themselves as an expression of some real dissatisfaction with their political situation. And as each new name gains acceptance and eventually comes to reflect the status quo, it too becomes subject to challenge by political forces within the black community. "African," "colored," "Negro," and "black" were each the preferred and progressive term at one time, and each lost that position in turn.

It is not the term itself, but its usage, acceptance and status, as well as the condition of that to which it refers, that determine its political significance and meaning. In our eagerness to investigate the impact of language on politics, we sometimes fall to notice the impact of politics on language. History leads us to expect that, should "African-American" become the established term, it too will succumb to a political challenge unless real conditions change. But in the meantime, what difference might the new term make for racial politics in America?

RACE AND ETHNICITY

Our earlier discussion of language and politics suggested that a terminological change might be expected to make a political difference in two quite different, though related, ways. Language can shape, consciously or unconsciously, our cognitive construction of political reality; how we understand our situation, how we perceive the available alternatives, and so on. Language can also function to shape feelings and attitudes, particularly in the process of the formation of identity. We are primarily concerned here with the first possibility, but it is the second that has dominated the discussion of the potential impact of "African-American" to date.

For example, when the new term was introduced at the December 1988 meeting in Chicago, Jesse Jackson, the groups' spokesperson, framed the rationale for the new term with the following statement.

> Just as we were called "colored," but were not that, and then "Negro," but were not that, to be called "black" is just as baseless. Just as you have Chinese Americans who have a sense of roots in China ... or Europeans, as it were, every ethnic group in this country has a reference to some historical cultural base... There are Armenian Americans and Jewish Americans and Arab Americans and Italian Americans. And with a degree of accepted and reasonable pride, they connect their heritage to their mother country and where they are now.... To be called African American has cultural integrity.[39]

The central claim can be succinctly stated: because "African-American" refers individuals to their common cultural heritage, it can provide a basis for justifiable pride in membership in the group.

The expectation was that use of the new term would improve both individual self-esteem and attitudes among the public generally.[40] Interestingly, a similar claim was made on behalf of the term "black" when it was originally introduced, and psychological research was conducted in order to test the twin claims concerning the impact of the new term on blacks and on whites.[41] These studies do show some increases in self-esteem among blacks. However, among blacks who were strong advocates of the Black Power movement, several of these studies found "dramatic differences" in the level of self-esteem.[42] This raises the question of whether we can attribute the increase in black self-esteem to the switch from "Negro" to "black" or whether it is best described as an effect of the movement's emphasis on group pride. Significantly, this early research also suggests that a change in racial nomenclature should not be expected to have a significant impact on the general view of whites toward blacks. Whites' stereotypes of black Americans tend to remain relatively unchanged no matter what racial designation is in vogue.[43] Of course, in the case of the shift to "African-American," it is too early to assess lasting impact. It is certainly possible that the fact that the new name, unlike the old, refers to a cultural heritage will give it a more positive impact, as its proponents claim.

But it is precisely this emphasis on cultural heritage that raises significant questions about the political impact of the new term when we turn to consider its potential effect on our cognitive construction of political reality. In this area too it is difficult to predict: the term "African-American" resonates in a number of different ways in the language, at once suggesting affinities with "Afrocentrism" and with "Irish-American" or "Mexican-American." It is this latter possibility that concerns us here. The new term may subtly alter the way in which we understand the situation of the races in America by leading us to think of this group as part of the general category, "ethnic groups," or "hyphenated Americans." As Jackson's speech emphasizes, the major difference in the switch from "black" to "African-American" is that ethnicity or culture replaces race as the defining characteristic of the group. Jackson explicitly makes the connection between African culture and the cultures of other groups. But more importantly, an analogy between the *experience* of blacks in this country and the experience of immigrant groups is implicit in the term "African-American." How accurate is such an analogy? If such an analogy is false, might not the adoption of the new label tend to distort the general understanding of the black experience?

Some scholars have approached this issue by questioning the accuracy of the claim that there is an African culture that is analogous to the cultures of other groups, and, if there is, whether it has any relation to contemporary black American culture.[44] Controversies have arisen over such issues as whether the reference to a singular "African" culture obscures the diversity of cultures within Africa.[45] The concept of "Africa" itself has been described as an invention of European colonialism.[46] These controversies recall earlier exchanges among historians and other social scientists concerning the extent to which traditional and indigenous African cultural institutions have survived in the contemporary black American community. The writings of E. Franklin Frazier and Melville Herskovits provide the classic debate surrounding the "Negro" past.[47]

It is not our purpose to join in this debate. Instead, we question the accuracy of the analogy, not between African culture in America and immigrant cultures, but between the black experience in America and the experience of ethnic groups historically and politically.[48] Whether or not there is a common African culture that can serve to unite American blacks, there is clearly a common historical and political experience in America, and it is a unique experience,[49] one that differs from the experience of white ethnics even where one might expect to find the greatest similarity, that is, even among the black populations that migrated to the large Northern cities.[50]

Contrary to what several theorists argued in the early 1970s,[51] there seems to be a general agreement among scholars today that blacks and white ethnics had very different experiences historically in the North and that those differences go a long way toward explaining why white ethnics have become much more assimilated into American political and social life than have blacks.[52]

One of the preeminent works that seeks to explain why blacks have fared much worse than white immigrants over the last century is Stanley Lieberson's *A Piece of the Pie*.[53] Lieberson argues that the black experience differed from that of white immigrants in four significant ways. First, because blacks far outnumbered the members of any single, white ethnic group, blacks were unable to establish the job niches which were so crucial to the success of white immigrant groups. Secondly, because the standard of living of black migrants had been lower than that of Eastern European white immigrants, blacks had lower expectations and aspirations than did their white counterparts. Thirdly, though white immigration stopped after the immigration laws of the 1920s were passed, the numbers of blacks migrating to the North continued. Because these black migrants were unemployed and had low levels of skills and education, they served to undermine the ability of Northern blacks as a whole to gain social and political power. And fourthly, this continued influx of blacks to the North only exacerbated anti-black racism among whites as a whole.[54] For these reasons, blacks had a much tougher time establishing themselves in Northern cities than did white immigrants. Their difficulties stemmed from structural and economic conditions rather than from pre-migration (or pre-immigration) cultural characteristics,[55] the explanation that had been offered by Rosen and Glazer.[56]

Studies since Lieberson's work seem to support its basic thesis concerning the differences between blacks and white ethnics. Susan Olzak maintains that the structure of employment opportunities for white ethnics and blacks differed considerably as early as the 1870s.[57] Her research demonstrates that, in most big cities, the structure of opportunity for blacks deteriorated sharply just as occupational mobility for white immigrants improved. This was the case despite the fact that white ethnic groups had lower literacy rates than blacks in the same cities.[58] Thus Olzak questions human capital explanations of racial differences in occupational mobility. She maintains that "when African-Americans and white ethnics came to compete for the same jobs, skills mattered less than racial boundaries."[59] Similarly, Hirschman and Kraly argue that educational differences do not explain all of the discrepancies in black/white income levels in 1940 or in 1950.[60]

In terms of their political fortunes, blacks throughout the twentieth century have fared worse than white ethnics. As Roger Daniels argues, unlike white ethnics, blacks have faced a myriad of legal barriers in exercising their basic right to vote.[61] Dianne Pinderhughes makes similar claims in her study comparing the differences between blacks and white ethnics in Chicago politics. She argues that, contrary to pluralist models which assume few discriminatory structures against blacks, there have been many structures impeding black political success. In virtually all economic and political organizations, blacks have been discriminated against far more than any other ethnic minority.[62]

In a variety of ways, then, economically, legally, sociologically, and politically, blacks have been in a decidedly different and far less advantageous position than members of immigrant ethnic groups. To the extent that the term "African-American" suggests or implies an analogy between the black and the immigrant experience, it is bound to be misleading. The determining features of the black experience are unique and have had a great deal to do with race and racism as well as with historical contingencies. This is the reality that might be obscured, but cannot be altered, by the term "African-American."

CONCLUSIONS

It is not our goal to determine whether "black" or "African-American" is the more appropriate term. Instead, we are concerned both with understanding the significance of changes in racial nomenclature in general and with the possible political implications of the switch from "black" to "African-American" in particular.

With respect to the first concern, our findings would certainly challenge any unqualified claim that language shapes political reality. The historical survey of changes in racial nomenclature indicates instead that political realities often significantly limit linguistic meaning even as they spur linguistic change. The history suggests an ironic twofold conclusion; both that we are likely to see continued periodic terminological changes and that there is little reason to be optimistic about their results. With the recent emphasis on the power of language, perhaps we have paid insufficient attention to the ways in which language is politically constrained and directed. Analyses of language and politics need to be sensitive to both aspects of the relation between the two.

Our second observation turns to the particular implications of the switch from "black" to "African-American." What is distinctive about this most recent change is that it is a change that emphasizes ethnicity over race. In their quest to be accepted more fully and to be recognized as "other Americans" have been (i.e., Irish-Americans, Italian-Americans), black leaders have embraced a "hyphenated American" label. As Jesse Jackson put it, "to be called African-American has cultural integrity." We suggest that the new term is problematic precisely to the extent that it entails the reconceptualization of blacks as an ethnic group. The foundation of such a reconceptualization is a flawed analogy.

As our discussion above illustrated, opportunities for blacks and white ethnics were shaped differently by historical and sociological factors. Racial prejudice has exceeded ethnic intolerance. And moreover, the conduct of racial politics differs significantly from ordinary bargaining among competing interests.

> Because race is a highly evocative American social characeristic that provokes deep political and economic divisions, it is too broad and controversial a matter to be the subject of meaningful trading, or bargaining. It does not, in short, fit a pluralist analytical framework. When political institutions handle racial issues, conventional rules go awry, individuals react irrationally, and constitutional rules are violated.[63]

The danger in the switch from black to "African-American" is that, by emphasizing ethnicity over race, the new term runs the risk of distorting the unique history of American blacks, tacitly encouraging beliefs based on a false analogy, and confusing our understanding of contemporary racial politics.[64] The black experience in this country simply does not compare to the experience of any other group.

We appreciate that there is a real dilemma behind the choice of "African-American" as the new identifying term. Its strength lies in the fact that it is an attempt to refer to something positive, to a cultural inheritance generated from within the group and valued by its members. It is a step away from group identification based entirely on shared victimization, which is a healthy development. Yet, as we have tried to show, that very strength is, at the same time, the source of the problem. The problem lies in the tendency of the new term to distort our understanding of the black experience. A good part of what it means to be a black American is to be part of a group that has both suffered in unique ways and responded with unique strengths to that experience.

Finally, we raise the question DuBois asked Roland nearly seventy years ago: will a change in nomenclature change the "thing"; that is, the subordinate social, economic and political position of black Americans? Of course, it should be acknowledged that there has been substantial progress since then. We have seen over the last thirty years an intense and largely successful movement to end all government-sanctioned racial discrimination. Most socially significant, overt, racially discriminatory practices by private individuals and groups have also been eliminated, and there is now a substantial black middle class. Yet in spite of these developments, the gap between black and white well-being persists. It persists in every area of the country and for every category of educational attainment. Most analyses of socioeconomic data demonstrate conclusively that the gap between the well-being of blacks and whites remains a reality.[65] This is so even though the American economic system experienced unprecedented economic growth and expansion during the last quarter century. The frustrating search by blacks for a group designation reflects their continued subordination within the American political and economic system. Though its character has changed considerably, the "thing" is still very much with us.

Americans might do well to emulate Frederick Douglass who, in the midst of a similar "names controversy," "preferred to focus his energy and mind on changing the conditions that gave rise to the frustrating search for a group name rather than debate the names issue at great length."[66] DuBois was right: "It is not the name—it's the Thing that counts."

NOTES

1. W. E. B. DuBois, "The Name 'Negro'," *Crisis,* March 1928.
2. Ben Martin takes a contrasting view, though the contrast is not as sharp as it seems at first glance. He describes the introduction of "African-American" precisely as an attempt to strengthen black political claims by highlighting shared racial victimization as the basis of group identity. Those promoting the term certainly hope to strengthen black claims, though they do stress culture, national origin, and so on, along with racial victimization as the basis of group identity. We are concerned here with the long-range implications of the change for white attitudes, as well as black, should the campaign to establish "African-American" as the dominant term prove to be successful. See Ben L. Martin, "From Negro to Black to African American: The Power of Names and naming," *Political Science Quarterly* 106 (1991): 83–107.
3. Geneva Smitherman is one participant in the debate over racial terminology who grounds her arguments explicitly in linguistic theory. See, for example, Geneva Smitherman, "Black Language as Power," in *Language and Power,* edited by Chris Kramarae, Muriel Schulz, and William O'Barr (Beverly Hills, CA: Sage, 1984), 101–15; "A New Way of Talkin': Language, Social Change and Political Theory," *Race Relations Abstracts* (1989):5–23; and "What Is Africa to Me?" Language, Ideology, and African American," *American Speech* 66 (Summer): 115–32.
4. For some of the more important examples of the theoretical literature, see Michel Foucault, *The Archaeology of Knowledge,* translated by A. M. Sheridan (New York: Pantheon, 1972); *Language, Counter-Memory, Practice: Selected Essays and Interviews,* translated by Donald F. Bouchard and Sherry Simon, edited by Donald F. Bouchard (Ithaca: Cornell University Press, 1992); Hans-Georg Gadamer, *Philosophical Hermeneutics,* translated and edited by David E. Linge (Berkeley: University of California Press, 1975); *Truth and Method,* translated and edited by Garrett Barden and John Cumming (New York: Seabury, 1976); Jürgen Habermas, *The Theory of Communicative Action,* translated by Thomas McCarthy (Boston: Beacon, 1984); Maurice Merleau-Ponty, *Consciousness and Language Acquisition,* translated by Hugh J. Silverman (Evanston: Northwestern University Press, 1973); *Phenomenology, Language, and Sociology: Selected Essays of Maurice Merleau-Ponty,* edited by John O'Neill (London: Heinemann Educational, 1974).
5. Peter L. Berger and Thomas Luckmann, *The Social Construction of Reality: A Treatise in the Sociology of Knowledge* (Garden City, NY: Doubleday, 1967), 3.
6. Hans-George Gadamer, *Philosophical Hermeneutics,* translated and edited by David E. Linge (Berkeley: University of California Press, 1976), 63.
7. Jean-Jacques Rousseau, *Emile or on Education,* introduction and translation by Allan Bloom (New York: Basic Books, 1979), 109.
8. Berger and Luckmann, *The Social Construction of Reality,* 133.
9. As William E. Connolly observed, "The language of politics is not a neutral medium that conveys ideas independently formed; it is an institutionalized structure of meanings that channels political thought and action in certain directions... For to adopt without revision the concepts prevailing in a polity is to accept terms of discourse

loaded in favor of established practices," *The Terms of Political Discourse,* 3rd ed. (Princeton: Princeton University Press, 1993), 2–3. For analysis of the political uses of language, see also Murray Edelman, *Political Language: Words That Succeed and Policies That Fail* (New York: Academic Press, 1977); and his *The Symbolic Uses of Politics* (Urbana: University of Illinois Press, 1964).

10. Stokely Carmichael and Charles V. Hamilton, *Black Power: The Politics of Liberation in America* (New York: Vintage, 1967), 36.
11. Rousseau, *Emile or on Education,* 109.
12. John Hope Franklin and Alfred A. Moss, Jr., *From Slavery to Freedom: A History of Negro Americans* (New York: Knopf, 1988); Smitherman, "What Is Africa to Me?"
13. Quoted in Lerone Bennett, Jr., "What's In a Name?" *Ebony,* November 1967, 50.
14. Sterling Stuckey, *Slave Culture: Nationalist Theory and the Foundations of Black America* (New York: Oxford University Press, 1987), 199.
15. Smitherman, "What Is Africa to Me?" 118.
16. Franklin and Moss, *From Slavery to Freedom,* 155–57; Stuckey, *Slave Culture;* Bennett, "What's in a Name?"
17. Bennett, "What's in a Name?"; Smitherman, "What Is Africa to Me?" John S. Butler, "Multiple Identities," *Society* 27 (May/June 1990): 8–13; Stuckey, *Slave Culture.*
18. Stuckey, *Slave Culture,* 202.
19. Franklin and Moss, *From Slavery to Freedom.*
20. Smitherman, "What Is Africa to Me?" 119–120.
21. Stuckey, *Slave Culture,* 204.
22. Idem., 208.
23. Quoted in Smitherman, "What is Africa to Me?" 120.
24. Kelly Miller, "Negroes or Colored People?" *Opportunity: Journal of Negro Life* 15 (May 1937): 144.
25. Idem; Tom Smith, "Changing Racial Labels: From 'Colored' to 'Negro' to 'Black' to 'African American'," *Public Opinion Quarterly* 58 (Winter 1992): 496–514.
26. Quoted in Bennett, "What's in a Name?" 51.
27. Irving Lewis Allen, "Sly Slurs: Mispronunciation and Decapitalization of Group Names," *Names* 36 (September-December 1988): 217–23; Stuckey, *Slave Culture.*
28. Smitherman, "What Is Africa to Me?" 121.
29. Smith, "Changing Racial Labels"; Smitherman, "What Is Africa to Me?"
30. "Black" received some competition in this period from "Afro-American" and "African-American."
31. Carmichael and Hamilton, *Black Power,* 37.
32. Idem.
33. Indeed, blacks often imposed sanctions on each other in the form of public ridicule and stereotyping to maintain their sense of community. For examples of literature of this type, see E. Franklin Frazier's *Black Bourgeoisie: The Rise of a New Middle Class* (New York: Free Press, 1957) and Nathan Hare's *Black Anglo Saxons* (New York: Marzani and Munsell, 1965). Both works are biting satires of black middle-class people and their imitations of white behavior. Each justifies hostility toward these blacks because they deny their black culture and cultural heritage.
34. Martin, "From Negro to Black to African American," 93; Smith, "Changing Racial Labels," 499.
35. Smith, "Changing Racial Labels," 502.

36. Ibid., 509.
37. Ibid., 508.
38. Relabeling strengthens group loyalty "by renewing a sense of differences from and grievances toward outsiders," Martin, "From Negro to Black to African American," 91.
39. Quoted in Smith, "Changing Racial Labels," 503–7.
40. Halford H. Fairchild, "Black, Negro, or Afro-American? The differences Are Crucial," *Journal of Black Studies* 16 (September 1985): 54. Martin, in "From Negro to Black to African American," undercuts the importance of this whole issue by arguing that "many studies have shown that blacks have self-esteem equal to or greater than whites," 101.
41. John E. Williams, Richard D. Tucker, and Frances Y. Dunham, "Changes in the Connotations of Color Names among Negroes and Caucasians," *Journal of Personality and Social Psychology* 19 (August 1971): 222–28; Douglas Longshore, "Color Connotations and Racial Attitudes," *Journal of Black Studies* 10 (1979): 183–97; Fairchild, "Black, Negro, or Afro-American?"
42. Williams et al., "Changes in the Connotations of Color Names," 228; Longshore, "Color Connotations and Racial Attitudes," 194–95.
43. Williams et al., "Changes in the Connotations of Color Names," 228; Longshore, "Color Connotations and Racial Attitudes."
44. Martin, "From Negro to Black to African American," 88–90.
45. See Anthony Appiah, "The Uncompleted Argument: DuBois and the Illusion of Race," *Critical Inquiry* 12 (Autumn 1985): 21–37; Molefi Kete Asante, *Kemet, Afrocentricity and Knowledge* (Trenton, NJ: Africa World Press, 1990).
46. V. Y. Mudimbe, *The Invention of Africa: Gnosis, Philosophy and the Order of Knowledge* (Bloomington: Indiana University Press, 1988).
47. Frazier, *Black Bourgeoisie*; Melville Herskovits, *The Myth of the Negro Past* (New York: Harper and Brothers, 1941).
48. We would like to thank Christopher Greenwald for his valuable assistance in helping to prepare this section of the article.
49. See Charles P. Henry, *Culture and African American Politics* (Bloomington: Indiana University Press, 1990); Matthew Holden Jr., *The Politics of the Black "Nation"* (New York: Chandler, 1973), 16–26; Robert C. Smith and Richard Seltzer, *Race, Class, and Culture* (Albany: State University of New York press, 1992); and Hanes Walton, Jr., *Invisible Politics: Black Political Behavior* (Albany: State University of New York Press, 1985), 21–42.
50. Even here, there is little reason to expect perfect similarity since there had been a long history of slavery and racial discrimination against blacks, who were, after all, not newcomers to America, though many were newcomers to the Northern cities.
51. Nathan Glazer, *Affirmative Discrimination* (New York: Basic Books, 1975); Andrew Greeley, *Why Can't They Be Like Us": America's White Ethnic Groups* (New York: E. P. Dutton, 1971); S. Makielski, Jr., *Beleaguered Minorities* (New York: W. H. Freeman, 1973); Daniel P. Moynihan and Nathan Glazer, *Ethnicity: Theory and Experience* (Cambridge: Harvard University Press, 1975).
52. There is a general consensus that blacks have not fared as well as white ethnics even when immigrants have faced significant political difficulties. See Eugene J. Cornacchia and Dale C. Nelson, "Historical Differences in the Political Experiences of American Blacks and White Ethnics: Revisiting an Unresolved Controversy," *Ethnic*

and Racial Studies 15 (1992): 118–21; and Leonard Dinnerstein, Roger Nichols, and David Reimers, *Natives and Strangers: Blacks, Indians, and Immigrants in America,* 2nd ed. (New York: Oxford University Press, 1990), esp. 328–32.

53. Stanley Lieberson, *A Piece of the Pie: Blacks and White Immigrants Since 1880* (Berkeley: University of California Press, 1980).

54. Lieberson also notes that the continued influx of blacks after 1930 helps explain why anti-black racism was so much greater than anti-Asian racism. In addition, Lieberson notes the fact that slavery created negative stereotypes of blacks which have continued to persist throughout the twentieth century.

55. Ibid., 381.

56. B. Rosen, "Race, Ethnicity, and the Achievement Syndrome," *American Sociological Review* 24 (1959): 47–60; Glazer, *Affirmative Discrimination.*

57. Susan D. Olzak, *The Dynamics of Ethnic Competition and Conflict* (Stanford, CA: Stanford University Press, 1992).

58. Ibid., 143.

59. Idem.

60. See Charles Hirschman and Ellen Kraly, "Immigrants, Minorities, and Earnings in the United States in 1950," *Ethnic and Racial Studies* 11 (1988): 332–65. Joel Pearlmann, *Ethnic Differences: Schooling and Social Structure among the Irish, Jews, and Blacks in an American City, 1880–1935* (New York: Cambridge University Press, 1988), takes a similar position in his study of Providence, R.I., arguing that social stratification theories need to account for *racial* differences in order to explain discrepancies between blacks and white immigrants. Further support for Lieberson's general thesis can be found in John Bodnar, Roger Simon, and Michael Weber's *Lives of Their Own: Blacks, Italians, and Poles in Pittsburgh, 1900–1960* (Urbana: University of Illinois Press, 1982). They emphasize the important point that white ethnics were able to establish job niches, or what they call "kinship-occupational systems" primarily because they arrived before the great numbers of black migrants moved to the North after 1930. After 1930, however, the large, Northern, industrialized economy had already been established, thus leaving few occupational opportunities for blacks.

61. Roger Daniels, *The Politics of Prejudice* (New York: Anthenum, 1977), esp. chap. 4.

62. Diane Pinderhughes, *Race and Ethnicity in Chicago Politics* (Urbana: University of Illinois Press, 1987); see also Steven Erie, *Rainbow's End* (Berkeley: University of California Press, 1988).

63. Pinderhughes, *Race and Ethnicity in Chicago Politics,* 261.

64. For one example, see Allen, "Sly Slurs": "The new label [African-American] would please many social scientists, for it would denote ethnicity over color and connote equality in pluralism," 222. If Pinderhughes is correct, there is no "equality in pluralism" where racial groups are concerned.

65. Andrew Hacker, *Two Nations: Black and White, Separate, Hostile and Unequal* (New York: Ballentaine, 1992); Gerald David Jaynes and Robin M. Williams, Jr., eds., *A Common Destiny: Black and American Society* (Washington, DC: National Academy Press, 1989).

66. Stuckey, *Slave Culture,* 223.

CHAPTER 5 Power and Conflict

5.1 LEOBARDO F. ESTRADA ET AL.

Chicanos in the United States: A History of Exploitation and Resistance

Chicanos as an ethnic group emerged from the conquest of Mexico by the United States in the mid-1800s. Chicanos today constitute about 90 percent of the Hispanic population living in the American Southwest. Chicanos have a common ethnic heritage rooted in collectively experienced oppression, exploitation, and social conflict. The capitalist economic system of the United States has been identified as a major factor in the oppression of Chicanos.

In the following selection from "Chicanos in the United States: A History of Exploitation and Resistance," *Daedalus* (Spring 1981), Leobardo F. Estrada and his colleagues state that Chicanos are a colonized people in the United States. According to Estrada et al., the sociohistorical factors that have shaped the presence of Chicanos in the United States continue to relegate the population to the lower echelons of U.S. society. The institutionalization of Anglo dominance in the Southwest occurred during the second half of the nineteenth century, and it included the establishment of a racial division of labor. Overwhelmingly concentrated in the working class, Chicanos became integrated into the economy on a restricted basis, with most located in unskilled manual labor positions and in a reserve army of labor. The pervasive practice of White capitalists of hiring Mexican labor at low wages has further restricted the socioeconomic mobility of Chicanos already living in the United States. The authors conclude that the historical treatment of Chicanos in the U.S. economic society has put them in a position of severe disadvantage today.

Key Concept: the exploitation of Chicanos

This essay seeks to provide material that will contribute to an understanding of Chicanos[1] in the United States today. The task calls for a historical perspective on the Mexican people within the context of the U.S. political economy.

It is essential to examine first the early and continued influence of Mexicans in the development of what is today the southwestern United States. Unlike those who believe that social, political, and economic influences in the region were largely the result of Anglo penetration, we argue that practices and institutions indigenous to Mexicans were largely taken over by colonizing Anglos.[2] The military conquest of the Southwest by the United States was a watershed that brought about the large-scale dispossession of the real holdings of Mexicans and their displacement and relegation to the lower reaches of the class structure. Anglo control of social institutions and of major economic sectors made possible the subsequent exploitation of Mexican labor to satisfy the needs of various developing economic interests....

THE MILITARY CONQUEST

Mexicans were incorporated into the United States largely through military conquest. The period that brought the northern reaches of Mexico under the U.S. flag begins approximately in 1836 with the Battle of San Jacinto, and ends in 1853 with the Gadsden Purchase. The military conquest was preceded by a period of Anglo immigration.

In 1810 Mexico began its struggle to gain independence from Spain, an objective finally achieved in 1821. Mexico, recognizing the advantage of increasing the size of the population loyal to its cause, granted permission to foreigners in 1819 to settle in its northern area, what is now Texas. Two years later Stephen Austin founded San Felipe de Austin: by 1830, one year after Mexico had abolished slavery, it is estimated that Texas had about twenty thousand Anglo settlers, primarily Southerners, with approximately two thousand "freed" slaves who had been forced to sign lifelong contracts with former owners. This trickle of immigrants soon became an invading horde.

Immigrants into the territories of Mexico were required to meet certain conditions: pledge their allegiance to the Mexican government and adopt Catholicism. The settlers' initial acceptance of these conditions, however, soon turned to circumvention. The distance of the settlements from Mexico's capital city, together with the internal strife common in the period, made enforcement of these settlement agreements difficult, almost impossible. The foreigners' attitudes toward their hosts only aggravated the situation. Eugene C. Barker, a historian, wrote that by 1835 "the Texans saw themselves in danger of becoming the alien subjects of a people to whom they deliberately believed themselves morally, intellectually, and politically superior. Such racial feelings underlay Texan-American relations from the establishment of the very first Anglo-American colony in 1821."

A constellation of factors—attitudes of racial superiority, anger over Mexico's abolition of slavery, defiance of initially agreed-upon conditions for settlement, and an increasing number of immigrants who pressed for independence from Mexico—strained an already difficult political situation. Direct and indirect diplomatic efforts at negotiation failed. The result was the Texas Revolt of 1835–36, which created for Anglo-Texans and dissident Mexicans the so-called independent Texas Republic, which was to exist until 1845. This republic, while never recognized by the Mexican government, provided the pretext for further U.S. territorial expansion and set the stage for the war between Mexico and the United States (1846–48).

Despite significant and conflicting regional interests in the war, imperialist interests allied with proponents for the expansion of slavery carried the day. When the United States granted statehood to Texas in 1845, almost a decade after recognizing it as a republic, war was inevitable; it was officially declared on May 13, 1846. It has been argued that U.S. politicians and business interests actively sought this war, believing Mexico to be weak, a nation torn by divisive internal disputes that had not been resolved since independence.

When hostilities ended in 1848, Mexico lost over half its national territory. The United States, by adding over a million square miles, increased its territory by a third. Arizona, California, Colorado, New Mexico, Texas, Nevada, and Utah, as well as portions of Kansas, Oklahoma, and Wyoming, were carved out of the territory acquired....

A final portion of Mexican land was acquired by the United States through purchase. James Gadsden was sent to Mexico City in 1853 to negotiate a territorial dispute arising from the use of faulty maps in assigning borders under the Treaty of Guadalupe Hidalgo. Mexico's dire need for funds to rebuild its war-ravaged economy influenced its agreement to sell more land. Gadsden purchased over 45,000 square miles in what is now Arizona and New Mexico, land the United States wanted for a rail line to California. The Gadsden Purchase territories were in time seen to contain some of the world's richest copper mines.

The importance for the United States of this imperialist war and the later Gadsden Purchase cannot be overstated. Vast tracts of land, rich in natural resources, together with their Mexican and Indian inhabitants, provided conditions very favorable to U.S. development and expansion. The United States had done very well in its "little war" with Mexico.

DISPOSSESSION AND DISPLACEMENT

To make matters worse, the social and economic displacement of Mexicans and their reduction to the status of a colonized group proceeded rapidly, in clear violation of the civil and property rights guaranteed both by treaty and protocol. In Texas, a wholesale transfer of land from Mexican to Anglo ownership took place. That process has started at the time of the Texas Revolt and gained momentum after the U.S.-Mexico War. Mexican landowners, often robbed by force, intimidation, or fraud, could defend their holdings through litigation, but this generally led to heavy indebtedness, with many forced to sell their holdings to meet necessary legal expenses. With depressing regularity, Anglos generally ended up with Mexican holdings, acquired at prices far below their real value.

The military conquest, the presence of U.S. troops, racial violence, governmental and judicial chicanery—all served to establish Anglos in positions of power in economic structures originally developed by Mexicans. Anglos adopted wholesale techniques developed by Mexicans in mining, ranching, and agriculture. Because this major transfer of economic power from Mexicans to Anglos varied by region, it is important to say something about each.

Texas, responding to a significant expansion in the earlier Mexican-based cattle and sheep industries, was quick to cater to increased world demands. Acreage given over to cotton also expanded, helped greatly by improvements in transport facilities. These industries helped create and develop the mercantile towns that soon became conspicuous features on the Texas landscape. Mexicans, instead of reaping the economic rewards of ownership, found themselves only contributing their labor. Mexicans were increasingly relegated to the lower ranks of society. By the end of the century, ethnicity, merged with social class, made Mexicans a mobile, colonized labor force.

The social structure of *New Mexico* in the beginning was quite different from that of Texas. The state, sparsely populated, was more densely settled in the north, in and about Santa Fé, than in the south; communal villages with lands granted to each community were common in the north. Communal water and grazing rights were assigned by community councils; only homestead and farming land were privately owned. Southern New Mexico, by contrast, boasted *haciendas* that had been established by grantees. This system consisted of *patrónes,* with settlers recruited to perform the necessary chores. It was a social structure organized on a debt-peonage system.

Anglo penetration into New Mexico after the war was more limited and did not occur on a large scale until the mid-1870s. Indian and Mexican defense of the territory served to keep out many settlers. Only an established U.S. military presence in the area made it at all accessible to Anglo cattlemen and farmers. Encountering a diversified class structure among the resident Mexicans, the Anglos generally chose to associate with the U.S. armed forces, creating a quasi-military society in the process. By the early 1880s, however, the railroads had helped to stimulate a new economic expansion. There was a further swelling of the Anglo population, and as pressure for land increased, the process of Mexican dispossession also dramatically accelerated. . . .

Arizona offers the example of the development of a colonial labor force in yet another mode. Arizona, not a separate entity at the time of conquest, was originally part of New Mexico, administered from Santa Fé. The small Mexican population was concentrated in the south, largely in Tucson and Tubac. One of the reasons for the sparseness of the settlements was the failure of the Spanish missionaries to impose Christianity on the nomadic Indian inhabitants; another was the aridity of the soil, which made agricultural pursuits difficult. The presence of the U.S. Army in the 1880s began to have its effects on the region. The Army fought the Indians, allowing the mining of copper and silver to resume; it was soon to become a large-scale economic enterprise. As with other industries, Anglo ownership was the norm; Mexicans contributed their labor, employing the familiar techniques they had developed long before. Railroads accelerated the migration of Anglos and the establishment of new towns. The growth of all these major industries called for a cheap wage labor pool. Mexicans who migrated north, mostly to work in these industries, discovered that the wages they received for tasks identical to their Anglo counterparts were considerably lower. Restricted to menial and dangerous work, and forced to live in segregated areas in the mining and railroad communities that had created their jobs, they felt the indignity of their situation.

California differed from the other regions: New England clipper ships had established very early ties with California; Franciscans, founding missions in the area in the 1830s, forced Christianized Indians into agriculture and manufacturing, to work alongside mulatto and *mestizo* Mexicans. This labor force helped to make California—economically, politically, and socially distant—independent of Mexico City. Excellent climate and abundant natural resources contributed to make this the most prosperous province in Mexico. Strong ties bound the missions to the *ranchos.* Missions, given large parcels of land to carry out their Christianizing enterprise, were neighbors of private individuals who owned vast tracts of land. Eventually, however, the privately owned *ranchos* established their supremacy throughout the province. . . .

A few Anglos had come to Alta California before the U.S.-Mexico War; some were recipients of land grants, and many of them apparently assimilated into Mexican society. After the Texas revolt, however, Anglo foreigners coming to California were more reluctant to mingle or assimilate, and openly showed their antagonism towards Mexicans. The U.S. government was at the same time stepping up its efforts to secure California. In 1842, in fact, the U.S. flag was prematurely raised in Monterey, when Commodore Thomas Jones imagined that the war with Mexico had already begun.

The transfer of land titles from Mexicans to Anglos in California differed significantly from the transfer of title in other areas conquered by the U.S. forces. To begin with, the vast majority of Mexicans did not own land in California. The original *Californios* began to lose title to their lands to better-financed Anglo newcomers very early; there was no possibility of competing with wealth established through banking, shipping, railroads, and other such enterprises. The holdings of these new elites ran into the hundreds of thousands of acres early in the nineteenth century.

Congress established the Land Commission in 1851 to judge the validity of grant claims made by *Californios* whose titles came down through the Spanish and Mexican periods. The commission served mainly to hasten the process of dispossession. Litigation costs often involved a contingent lawyer's fee of one quarter of the land in question. Some Mexican landowners borrowed money at high interest rates to carry on their legal fights, and frequently found themselves in the end selling their lands to meet their debts. Anglo squatters only added to the burden; they formed associations to apply political pressure favorable to their own interests, and were generally successful in retaining land forcefully taken from Mexicans. Violence and murder in California, as in other parts of the conquered territories, was the order of the day....

By the turn of the century, Mexicans had been largely dispossessed of their property. Relegated to a lower-class status, they were overwhelmingly dispossessed landless laborers, politically and economically impotent. Lynchings and murder of both Mexicans and Indians were so common that they often went unreported. Long-term residents of the region were reduced to being aliens in their native lands. The common theme that united all Mexicans was their conflict with Anglo society. The dominant society, profoundly racist, found it entirely reasonable to relegate Mexicans to a colonial status within the United States....

THE U.S. SOUTHWEST AND BEYOND, 1900–1930

... The conditions that greeted new immigrants from Mexico were essentially like those Mexicans already in the United States knew only too well. There was powerful racial hostility; Mexicans were thought to be inferior beings and inherently unassimilable and foreign. Their economic niche was insecure; their work was often seasonal in nature. In agricultural and related pursuits they were forced into a dual-wage system where they received low wages, frequently below those received by Anglos for the same type and amount of work. Many found themselves barred from supervisory positions. The situation in mining and related industries was not much different.

The railroad companies offered only slightly better conditions. By 1908 the Southern Pacific and the Atchison, Topeka, and Santa Fe were each recruiting more than a thousand Mexicans every month. The vast majority worked as section crews, laying track and ensuring its maintenance. The major difference between this industry and others in which Mexicans found work was that it seemed somewhat more stable and less seasonal; wages, however, were uniformly low.

The Southwest was growing; its urban centers—in most instances, expanded versions of earlier Mexican towns—were often inhabited by Mexicans overwhelmingly concentrated in the lower range of the urban occupational structure. The wage differentials common to the rural sector were not as obvious in the urban areas. Access to particular occupations and industries, however, was limited and channeled. There was no mobility out of the unskilled and semiskilled positions in which Mexicans found themselves. They formed a reserve labor pool that could be called up as the situation dictated. When the economy expanded and jobs were created, these might be filled by Mexicans in specific sectors. Contractions of the economy relegated Mexicans quickly to the ranks of the unemployed; it was then they were reminded that they could be technically subject to another "sovereign," Mexico.

Mexicans served the industrial economy in other ways, also. As a reserve labor pool, employers used them as a sort of "strike insurance," much as female and child labor were used to undercut unionizing efforts in other parts of the country. Such policies tended to generate ethnic antagonism between working-class Mexicans and working-class Anglos. Trade union practices, which excluded Mexicans and contributed to their exploitation, also helped to maintain them as a reserve labor pool, forcing them in the end to organize their own unions and associations....

The Mexican government regularly lodged formal complaints with the State Department, protesting the abusive treatment its citizens received from industrial, mining, and agricultural enterprises. Those protests went largely unheeded; the U.S. government generally chose not even to verify the assertions, let alone make efforts to correct abuses....

MIGRATION 1900–1930

... The passage of the 1924 Immigration Act made Mexicans conspicuous by their continued free access to the United States. Debate on the issue continued to agitate Congress.... The powerful economic arguments for the continued importation of Mexican laborers had been articulated two years earlier before a congressional committee by John Nance Garner, who was to become Franklin Roosevelt's vice president: "In order to allow land owners now to make a profit of their farms, they want to get the cheapest labor they can find, and if they can get the Mexican labor it enables them to make a profit."

At the same time, control of the "immigrant" population came to include measures that could be applied to the domestic Mexican population. The Americanization activities of the early twentieth century spread throughout the country and were used to bleach all vestiges in the national flock. These activities included intensive English instruction—with retribution for those who chose to speak other tongues—and success defined as a capacity to speak as did the English-speaking middle class; and intensive "civic" classes to socialist the "foreign" population. The norm for success became the Anglo middle class, and standardized IQ and achievement tests measured this success. The widespread institution of high schools that traced the population into occupational or college preparatory curricula, with immigrants and racial minorities tracked into the former—when they entered high schools at all—became common. English oral proficiency became a requirement for immigration, as did English literacy for voting.... Segregated Mexican schools were maintained. In the early 1930s, through federal court litigation, segregation based on race was challenged, and segregation based on grouping for language instruction was initiated and legitimized....

THE GREAT DEPRESSION AND REPATRIATION

The decade of the Great Depression was another watershed for Mexicans. Social forces during this period significantly shaped the lives of Mexicans and are in many ways still responsible for their status half a century later. The decade began with a massive economic collapse that started late in the 1920s and continued until World War II. There was a major decline in economic activities, with wage rates in both industry and agriculture suffering, and rampant unemployment. With this came a major acceleration of government intervention in social welfare, with bureaucracies developing and expanding to meet the urgent needs of a dislocated populace. There was also a large-scale westward migration out of the Dust Bowl. In the Southwest, this was a time of accelerated rates of concentration into larger and larger units in both agriculture and mining, where increased mechanization led to a further displacement of labor. The industrial sector in the Southwest lagged behind the rest of the nation and could contribute little to absorb either the locally displaced labor or the dust-bowl migrants. These major economic dislocations fell on Mexicans with even greater force than on other groups. Already relegated to a marginal status, Mexicans were particularly vulnerable. The situation worked to eliminate for all practical purposes further northward migration from Mexico.

The Great Depression had another sobering effect: it engendered a collective social atmosphere of insecurity and fear that set the tone in allocating blame for the major social and economic traumas. Mexicans were singled out as scapegoats and made to bear the guilt for some of the ills of the period. It was not long before great numbers of unemployed Mexicans, like other citizens in the country, found themselves on the rolls of the welfare agencies.

One response to the strain placed on limited economic resources throughout the country was the demand for large-scale repatriations. To reduce the public relief rolls and agitation to organize labor, the Mexican became both the scapegoat and the safety valve in the Southwest. It is estimated that in the early years of the Depression (1929–34) more than 400,000 Mexicans were forced to leave the country under "voluntary repatriation." Those who applied for relief were referred to "Mexican Bureaus," whose sole purpose was to reduce the welfare rolls by deporting the applicants. Indigence, not citizenship, was the criterion used in identifying Mexicans for repatriation....

Repatriations took place both in the Southwest and Midwest, where Mexicans, recruited to the area by employers with promises of work, had lived since the early twenties. Approximately half of the "returnees" actually were born in the United States. Shipment to Mexico was a clear violation of both their civil and human rights. The Immigration and Naturalization Service, in concert with the Anglo press, identified the Mexican labor migrant as the source of (Anglo) citizen unemployment, for the increase of public welfare costs (and taxes), and as having entered the country "illegally" and in large numbers. The scapegoating tactics of an earlier nativist generation, with its xenophobic memories and myths, were used against the Mexicans. There was a good deal of sentiment also against Mexico's expropriation and nationalization of its oil industry, which U.S. oil companies had once controlled. Repatriation caused widespread dissolution of family and community, and contributed to an even more acute distrust among Mexicans of all government—local, state, or federal....

WORLD WAR II TO 1960

... After a regulated labor pool was firmly reestablished for agribusiness, in 1954 the Immigration and Naturalization Service vigorously launched "Operation Wetback." Undocumented workers, unstable and intractable as a labor source, were now to be removed. An astonishing 3.8 million Mexican aliens (and citizens) were apprehended and expelled in the next five years. Of the total number deported during that time, fewer than 2 percent left as a result of formal proceedings. The vast majority were removed simply by the *threat* of deportation. "Looking Mexican" was often sufficient reason for official scrutiny. The search focused initially on California and then Texas; it soon extended as far as Spokane, Chicago, St. Louis, and Kansas City....

World War II posed a major dilemma for the United States. In its official pronouncements and acts, the country strongly condemned the racism explicit in Nazism. Yet at the same time, the United States had a segregated military force. This was also a time when President Roosevelt issued Executive Order No. 9066, which authorized the internment of Japanese who were U.S. citizens and whose sole "crime" was living and working on the West Coast.

This contradiction also manifested itself in ugly confrontations between Mexicans and Anglos. The press, for its part, helped to raise feelings against Mexicans. The violent confrontations between servicemen and local police against Mexican residents began late in 1942 and continued until mid-1943....

The Mexican community, in responding to the situation of World War II, acted as it had done in previous times of hostility and exploitation—with organizational efforts and litigation, and occasionally with armed resistance. Unity Leagues, created in the early 1940s, had as their principal purpose the election of Mexicans to city councils in Southern California communities; they also conducted voter registration drives, attempted fund-raising, and worked to get voters to the polls. The basic theme uniting these leagues was the fight against racial discrimination, particularly in the schools. The League of United Latin American Citizens (LULAC), founded in South Texas in 1928, expanded into a national organization in the post-World War II period, and was soon heavily involved in anti-discrimination activity, again particularly in the educational arena.

A landmark court decision in 1945 (*Méndez v. Westminster School District*) barred *de jure* segregation of Chicano students. A similar legal action in Texas in 1948 was also successfully pressed. The results of both court actions, as well as others during the 1950s, helped set the stage for the Supreme Court's *Brown v. Board of Education* decision in 1954, and clearly established the illegality of the deliberate segregation of Chicano and Mexican school children on the basis of race, and of bilingual education as a partial remedy for segregation. The success of these efforts served to encourage civil rights suits in other areas, notably against job discrimination in New Mexico....

GROWTH AND NATIONAL VISIBILITY

... The century-old relationship between the United States and Mexico continues to affect both nations. Immigrants, natural resources, and profits continue to flow north. Legal immigration from Mexico to the United States at present allows between forty and fifty thousand visas each year for permanent residence. Those looking for "commuter status," which allows them to work in the United States while living in Mexico, have to endure, barring political connections, a three-year waiting period.

Mexican workers caught in Mexico's economic sluggishness are aware that wages in the United States for identical work are sometimes seven times higher than at home, and many are thus led to risk illegal entry. Such illegal entry is only increased by the active recruitment by "coyotes," who transport Mexicans across the border for a fee. Undocumented workers are a significant part of the U.S. labor force, particularly for work that most American citizens regard as demeaning, low paying, dirty, and unstable. Undocumented workers have always come to the United States in circumstances of multiple jeopardy, as minorities unprotected from employer exploitation and abuse. Such conditions continue unabated today....

CURRENT STATUS

Chicanos lag behind the rest of the U.S. population by every measure of socioeconomic well-being—level of education, occupational attainment, employment status, family income, and the like. Some say that Chicanos are no different from other immigrants who arrived in the United States impoverished, and who managed by hard work to gain advantages for their children, taking the first important step toward assimilation. The substantial achievements of the American-born first generation over that of the immigrant generation are thought to be conclusive. Such an optimistic view overlooks major changes in the society and the historical relationship of over a century and a half of racial discrimination and economic exploitation. Although economic expansion and dramatic social change characterized the postwar years, economic contraction and dislocation, possibly exaggerated by the new conservative retrenchment, are the hallmarks of more recent times.... Although second-generation and later Chicanos made large gains relative to those of the first generation, such gains did not allow for their thorough absorption into the economic and social structure of U.S. society. The data of the late 1970s suggest how different generations of Chicanos have fared. The median education for second-generation Chicanos was 11.1 years, only two years more than for U.S.-born first-generation, but decidedly more than for the immigrant generation (5.8 years).

All generations of Chicano males are underrepresented in white-collar jobs; Mexican-born males are least likely to be found in such positions. Farm labor is the one area where there is a significant difference between the U.S.-born and immigrant Chicano populations. Over 15 percent of Mexican-born men are employed as farm laborers, twice the number for sons of Mexican immigrants, five times the number of third-generation Chicanos. Labor force participation figures, however, also show that second-generation Chicanos had the highest unemployment rate, while the immigrant generation had the lowest. The data on incomes indicate first-generation Chicano families as having the highest median income, with the second-generation following, and the Mexican-born as having the lowest incomes. The range, however, was not great—about $1,500.

That Mexicans who have resided for the longest time in the United States —second generation—have the highest unemployment rates and only very modest representation in white-collar, professional, and managerial categories suggests the limited structure of opportunity for Chicanos. They are entering the industrial sector at a time when its socioeconomic structure is increasingly tertiary, demanding highly trained personnel in high-technology industries such as aerospace, communications, and the like. Although Chicanos may be making "progress" relative to their immigrant parents, they are actually falling farther behind when looked at in the context of the opportunity structure in an increasingly post-industrial social order and compared to the dominant population. Also, there is evidence that Chicano technical and occupational skills will increasingly limit them to the secondary labor market, with its unfavorable wage rates, limited fringe benefits, and general instability. These conditions do not promise either full equity or full participation for Chicanos in the decades immediately ahead. Still, that the Anglo population growth is at or near a steady state, with its income-generating population increasingly aging, suggests that the younger and expanding Chicano work force will be shouldering a growing and disproportionate burden in the future. Social Security, Medicare, Medicaid, and the myriad of other social programs funded from taxes on the work force will be more and more borne by youthful employed Chicanos.

Historically, Chicanos' economic rewards have been disproportionate to their contribution to U.S. industrial development. Now that the society is increasingly post-industrial, Chicanos find themselves still carrying the burden. The federal government, which played a prominent role throughout the history of Mexicans in the United States, has been repressive, supporting industries and employers, and generally frustrating Chicanos' efforts to advance.

NOTES

1. The terms "Chicano" and "Mexican" are used interchangeably in this essay, because the U.S. Southwest and northern Mexico were initially a cultural and geographic unit, the border being only an invisible line between the two nations.
2. The term "Anglo" will be used to refer to U.S. residents of European origin. It is used, for convenience, as a generic term for all European immigrants to the United States.

5.2 LESLIE INNISS AND JOE R. FEAGIN

The Black "Underclass" Ideology in Race Relations Analysis

In the mid-1990s about 38 million people lived in poverty in the United States—about 15 percent of the total U.S. population. The rate of impoverishment has remained persistent over the last several decades, with non-White minorities and children disproportionately represented among the poor. Blacks and Latinos are more than three times as likely to be poor than Whites, and more than half of all Black and Latino children live in poverty. The poor live mostly in female-headed households where the head of the household has a very low level of educational attainment and skill development and is often functionally illiterate. When the poor can find work, it is usually in a dead-end job that pays at or below the minimum wage and has little intrinsic value. Poor people are heavily concentrated in segregated inner-city neighborhoods and in the rural South.

Social scientists are concerned with the persistence of poverty and the development of a permanent underclass. Researchers have developed ideological themes to explain the persistence of poverty, including *blaming the victim,* the *culture of poverty,* and the *Black underclass.* Inherent within these explanatory frameworks is the notion that poor people are themselves accountable for poverty. The following critique of the *underclass* label is from "The Black 'Underclass' Ideology in Race Relations Analysis," *Social Justice* (Winter 1989). In it, Leslie Inniss and Joe R. Feagin contend that these explanations promote the idea of value deficiency and blameworthiness of poor people and essentially ignore discrimination as an exclusionary mechanism precluding poor peoples' accessibility to the opportunity structure of U.S. society.

Inniss is in the Department of Sociology at the University of Texas at Austin. Feagin is a graduate research professor in sociology at the University of Florida. His publications include *The New Urban Paradigm: Critical Perspectives on the City* (Rowman & Littlefield, 1998) and *Racial and Ethnic Relations* (Prentice Hall, 1996), coauthored with Clairece Booher Feagin.

Key Concept: the "underclass"

INTRODUCTION

Consider this city situation. A central city with 25% unemployment. One-third of the residents have moved out. There are many young men with no jobs collecting welfare checks and on the streets or playing pool with friends most of the day. There are many young women watching television all day. There are numerous unemployed adult children living with an unemployed parent. Many of these city residents have a problem with alcohol and drugs. Older men who once did heavy labor have been laid off; most have been out of work for years. Many young unmarried women, especially teenagers, in the public housing complexes are pregnant or have already had illegitimate children Most of the young do not expect to work in the near future. They seem resigned, angry, or fatalistic about their lives. They feel no one in government cares about them. These people certainly fit the definitions of the underclass used in recent literature in the United States.

Where is this "underclass"? What city are we describing? What are the likely racial characteristics of these urbanites? Many would guess the city is Chicago, New York, or Atlanta, but this city is actually Liverpool, England, once a prosperous city and the second great city of the British Empire. Interestingly, the people described are the *white* and British residents of a troubled city. Not one is Black. Many have educations and skills but no jobs in this northern England city, which has been neglected by the Conservative government ensconced in London in the affluent south of England ("Frontline," 1986).

Reflection on these Liverpool data suggest some of the serious problems with the current discussions of the "Black underclass" by scholars and journalists in the United States. Few U.S. scholars would seriously discuss these white, formerly middle-income families and individuals in Liverpool as some type of "underclass," as a new or distinctive class characterized by problematical values, a "subculture of poverty and deviance," teen pregnancies, crime-oriented males, and better-off families moving out.

To explain the tribulations of the white, formerly middle-income residents of Liverpool there is no need to use the interpretive language of individualized pathology and value aberration that is the focus of the Black underclass discussion in the United States. There is no need to consider these people as a self-reproducing subculture of pathological behavior that contrasts with the "healthy" behavior of their better-off counterparts elsewhere. Nor is there good reason to view the poor young women of Liverpool, with their illegitimate children and single-parent status, as major contributors to the larger underclass problem. The principal reason for the personal and family troubles in Liverpool is the flight of capital to more profitable locations outside the north of Britain; disinvestment is the cause of most unemployment and underemployment. Investors decide where the jobs go. Unemployment is reproduced from one generation to the next not by values, but rather through the working of capital investment markets.

The concept of the "underclass," as it has developed in the last decade in the United States, is not only ahistorical and noncomparative, but also highly ideological and political. It represents a casting about for a way of defining the problems of the poor, and particularly the Black poor, without substantial reference to the actions of U.S. investors and capital flight. A number of social scientists have testified before state legislatures and Congress on the problems of the underclass. The "underclass" problem thereby became politically defined and bureaucratized. An adequate interpretation of the underlying causes of the unemployment and poverty-related problems of Liverpool lies in the decisions of investors to invest or disinvest. And there is no reason not to interpret similar "underclass" phenomena in U.S. cities in the same fashion. There is no need for a new conceptual framework called the "Black underclass" theory which explains the Black situation as culturally distinctive. American scholars have largely failed to put the situation of Black Americans in proper international and comparative perspective.

In this article we will examine the origins of the underclass theory, assess why this wrongheaded viewpoint has taken such hold on the (mostly white) American mind, and provide a more accurate view of what is wrong in Black and white America.

THE CONCEPT OF THE UNDERCLASS

Early Conceptions of the Black Lower Class

The concept variously labelled the "rabble," the "dangerous class," the "lumpenproletariat," and the "underclass" has a long history in Western intellectual thought. Many European analysts have feared the cities because of the growth of sizeable, or organized, working populations. And this perspective migrated to North America. In the 1830s one of the founders of sociology, the French government official Alexis de Tocqueville, visited U.S. cities and wrote perhaps the first white assessment of the Black lower class; he noted that

> the lower ranks which inhabit these cities constitute a rabble even more formidable than the populace of European towns. They consist of freed blacks, in the first place, who are condemned by the laws and by public opinion to a hereditary state of misery and degradation.... [T]hey are ready to turn all the passions which agitate the community to their own advantage; thus, within the last few months, serious riots have broken out in Philadelphia and New York (de Tocqueville, 1945:299).

These words are from *Democracy in America,* an influential sociological analysis of the United States, and they reflect the fears of many educated whites about the "rabble" of Blacks and immigrants in the cities. This rabble is seen by white observers as disturbed, emotional, and dangerous. Note, too, that free Blacks in the cities are highlighted as a central part of the urban rabble. Thus, the idea of the Black underclass is not new with the debates of the 1960s or 1980s; the idea is at least a century and a half old. It is also interesting to note that while de Tocqueville saw free Blacks as dangerous and threatening, he also recognized the role of laws and public opinion in perpetuating the oppressive conditions of freed Blacks, a recognition of discrimination missing in much of the current discussion of the underclass.

Recent Discussions of the Black Underclass: The 1960s

According to *The Oxford English Dictionary,* the word "underclass" was first used in English in 1918 (Burchfield, 1986:1069). Its initial use was as a description of a process—for example, a "society moves forward as a consequence of an under-class overcoming the resistance of a class on top of them." It was not until 1963, in Gunnar Myrdal's *Challenge to Affluence,* that the term was used to describe in some detail a population—"an 'underclass' of unemployed and gradually unemployable persons and families at the bottom of society." The link between Blacks and the underclass was apparently first made in 1964. A January 1964 issue of the *Observer* noted that "the Negro's protest today is but the first rumbling of the underclass." Again in 1966 a connection between Blacks and the underclass was made in the August 19 *New Statesman:* "The national economic growth has been bought at the expense of industrial workers and the poor (largely Negro) underclass" (Burchfield, 1986: 1069).

Moreover, by the 1960s U.S. scholars were writing on the subject of the Black underclass, although the more common terms then were "the poor," "the lower class," and "the culture of poverty." The view of poor communities accenting pathological traits was particularly influenced by the culture-of-poverty generalizations of anthropologist Oscar Lewis. His culture-of-poverty perspective emphasizes the defective subculture of those residing in slum areas, at first in Latin America, and by the 1960s in the United States. Developing the "culture of poverty" concept for the U.S. poor in the book *La Vida,* Lewis (1965) argues that this culture is "a way of life which is passed down from generation to generation along family lines." The poor adapt in distinctive ways to their oppressive conditions, and these adaptations are transmitted through the socialization process.

During the 1960s the acceptance of this view by both scholars and policymakers was given greater legitimacy by its being featured in federal government publications. Published by the government, Catherine Chilman's scholarly publication entitled *Growing Up Poor* in effect gave governmental sanction to the culture-of-poverty portrait, with emphasis on personal disorganization, superstitious thinking, impulsive behavior, inadequate childrearing practices, and a lack of ability to defer gratification (Chilman, 1966). A second government publication, entitled *The Negro Family* (1965), focused on the alleged lack of social integration and pathology in *Black* communities. Here social scientist (later U.S. Senator) Daniel Patrick Moynihan argued that:

> at the heart of the deterioration of the fabric of Negro society is the deterioration of the Negro family. It is the fundamental source of the weakness of the Negro community at the present time (Moynihan, 1965:5).

The typical lower-class Black family was broken or disintegrated. Moynihan proceeded to argue that, in contrast, the typical white family "had maintained a high degree of stability." Black family disorganization was, in turn, tied to disintegration in other aspects of Black lower-class life. Moynihan accentuated the "tangle" of pathology and crumbling social relations—which in his view characterized Black communities—and argued further that "there is considerable evidence that the Negro community is, in fact, dividing between a stable middle class group that is steadily growing stronger and more successful and an increasingly disorganized and disadvantaged lower class group" (*Ibid.*, 1965: 5–6).

The policy impact of this lower-class-pathology emphasis in the social science literature can also be seen in the major government reports on Black/white conflict in the 1960s, including the *Report of the National Advisory Commission on Civil Disorders.* Writing about Black America under a heading of "Unemployment, Family Structure, and Social Disorganization," the authors of this report used a variety of disorganization codewords:

> The culture of poverty that results from unemployment and family breakup generates a system of ruthless, exploitative relationships within the ghetto. Prostitution, dope addiction, and crime create an environmental "jungle" characterized by personal insecurity and tension (National Advisory Commission on Civil Disorders, 1968: 7).

Critics of the Culture of Poverty View

There was much debate over the lower-class-pathology perspective during the 1960s and 1970s. Anyone returning to the discussion of the period will have a strong feeling of *déjà vu.* For example, in *Lower-Class Families* Hyman Rodman argues that the lower-class view is a stereotyped view emphasizing negative aspects. Rodman contends that there are numerous responses made by lower-class persons in adapting to deprivation other than the lower-class-pathology adaptation. One response, the "lower-class value stretch," can be seen in the fact that many poor people share dominant middle-class values and aspirations and reflect these in actions, while at the same time reflecting lower-class values; their repertoire of values is usually greater than for middle-class individuals. Thus when conditions change, such as an availability of employment, most of the poor can rapidly adapt.

In the late 1960s and early 1970s, the junior author of this article also developed a critique. One point made then was that, although types of criminal behavior and drug use exist to a disproportionate degree in many Black communities, the extent of this behavior is exaggerated in many assessments of day-to-day life. It is too easy to move from characteristics of a minority of the Black residents of a given urban community, however unconventional or criminal, to ungrounded generalizations about Black areas overall. In addition, there is much unheralded white-collar crime and drug use in white suburban communities, but scholars have not developed a deviant subculture perspective for these communities. Moreover, the quick typification of Black areas in pathological organization terminology, with its overtones of character flaws and individual blame, tends to play down the intimate relationship between these areas and the larger racial system surrounding them (Feagin, 1974: 123–146).

The Underclass Debate

In the 1970s and 1980s, the debates between the neoconservatives and liberals over the character and constitution of the underclass have mirrored the debates of the 1960s. Numerous analysts have underscored the significant growth in the problems confronting central city Blacks since the 1970s. The emphasis on Black problems has coincided with a major economic crisis (for example, disinvestment in many cities) and, thus, a legitimacy crisis for U.S. capitalism. This crisis of legitimacy has involved ordinary Americans questioning the actions and legitimacy of U.S. elites. Commentators and social scientists such as Charles Murray, Glenn Loury, Ken Auletta, Nicholas Lemann, Nathan Glazer, and Daniel P. Moynihan have played an important role in refurbishing the legitimacy of the existing system of inequality by moving the public discussion away from such issues as decent-paying jobs, capital flight, racism, and militarism and back onto the old 1960s' issues of crime, welfare, illegitimacy, ghetto pathologies, and the underclass. For example, in his 1975 book entitled *Affirmative Discrimination,* Nathan Glazer described a "tangle of pathology in the ghetto" which cannot be explained by "anything as simple as lack of jobs or discrimination in available jobs." Although Glazer does not use the term underclass, he does conjure up its image with comments that suggest that many Black youth prefer illicit activities because they do not want to work at regular jobs. From his perspective, neither rapid economic growth nor affirmative action will benefit unskilled and culturally impoverished Black males reluctant to do low-wage work (Glazer, 1975:71–72).

A Cover Story in *Time*

One of the first national discussions of the underclass appeared in the cover story of *Time* magazine in August 1977, not long after the burning and looting of a store by unemployed Blacks during the New York City electrical blackout in July 1977. The *Time* portrait anticipates that which appears later in both scholarly and journalistic sources: "The underclass has been... left behind.... Its members are victims and victimizers in the culture of the street hustle, the quick fix, the rip-off, and, not least, violent crime" (*Time,* 1977: 14). Although the article tends to focus on the culture, welfare involvement, illegitimacy, street values, and feelings of hopelessness among the members of the underclass, it does also discuss the impact of long-term unemployment on the Black underclass' self-esteem and identification. However, the increasing conservatism of the late 1970s can be seen in the emphasis on individual and private sector initiatives. Asserting that there is no political consensus for governmental job creation or War-on-Poverty programs—which the journalists argue would increase inflation—the article retreats to the mostly conservative strategies of education, tougher law enforcement, a lower minimum wage, work requirements for welfare recipients, and giving private business control of job training programs. The conservative tone of much subsequent discussion of the underclass was foreshadowed in this mass media article.

In the late 1970s prominent intellectual magazines began to carry articles defining the situation of the Black poor in terms of the "underclass." For example, Ken Auletta produced an influential series of articles for the *New Yorker*, which he later developed into a book called *The Underclass.* For Auletta the underclass only includes the nine million people who are permanently poor. Auletta discusses the Black, white, and Hispanic underclasses, but the emphasis is on impoverished Blacks. The central issue is class culture. The underclass is grouped by Auletta into four distinct categories: the passive poor, hostile street criminals, hustlers, and the drunks, homeless, and released mental patients who roam city streets (Auletta, 1982: 198–3O4). (He leaves out the underemployed and unemployed Poor.) For Auletta, racism plays no significant part in the formation of the underclass. Auletta uses "Black underclass" to describe those with a lifestyle characterized by poverty and antisocial behavior: "The underclass suffers from behavioral as well as income deficiencies" *(Ibid.,* 1982: 28). These behavioral deficiencies include immorality, broken families, and a poorly developed work ethic. Auletta's accent on the old "culture of poverty" characteristics is linked to his argument that the plight of the Black underclass has little to do with racial discrimination but instead is the product of cultural deprivation. While he makes occasional concessions to environmental factors, the general tone of this analysis indicates that he prefers the culture-of-poverty perspective.

Similarly, in a 1980 *New York Times Magazine* article, Carl Gershman argued that it is the worsening condition of the underclass, not racial discrimination, which requires the greatest policy attention (Gershman, 1980: 24–30). Critical to his argument is the old idea that the conditions of poorer Black Americans are due to the "tangle of pathology" in which they find themselves. He, too, argues that poor Black Americans are locked into a lower-class sub-culture, a culture of poverty, with its allegedly deviant value system of immorality, broken families, juvenile delinquency, and lack of emphasis on the work ethic.

Moreover, in a widely read 1986 article in the *Atlantic Monthly,* Nicholas Lemann wrote that:

> every aspect of the underclass culture in the ghettos is directly traceable to roots in the South—and not the South of slavery but... in the nascent underclass of the sharecropper South.... In the ghettos, it appears that the distinctive culture is now the greatest barrier to progress by the black underclass rather than either unemployment or welfare (Lemann, 1986: 35).

The culture of the underclass is seen as the greatest barrier to Black advancement. The poor Black communities lack positive values. In the 1970s, the ghettos went from being diversified to being "exclusively Black lower-class" and this resulted in complete social breakdown. "Until then the strong leaders and institutions of the ghetto had promoted an ethic of assimilation," but with the movement away of institutions and leaders there was a "free fall" into "social disorganization." Echoes of the 1960s arguments can again be heard in these views; the criminalized underclass flourished because there was no middle class to reign it in.

Moreover, a 1988 article in the *Chronicle of Higher Education* reviewed the research on the underclass and concluded:

> Although the underclass constitutes a minuscule portion of the total U.S. population and a very small proportion of all those living in poverty, the lives of the ghetto poor are marked by a dense fabric of what experts call "social pathologies"—teenage pregnancies, out-of-wedlock births, single-parent families, poor educational achievement, chronic unemployment, welfare dependency, drug abuse, and crime—that, taken separately or together, seem impervious to change (Coughlin, 1988: A5).

The language of pathology was given legitimacy in this important journal of higher education.

The Mass Media Picks Up the Underclass

Not only the intellectual magazines but also the mass media proclaimed the culturally oriented underclass theory in the mid-1980s. Using social science scholarship, the journalistic accounts had their own special twist. For example, a 1987 *Fortune* magazine author commented as follows:

> Who are the underclass? They are poor, but numbering around five million, they are a relatively small minority of the 33 million Americans with incomes below the official poverty line. Disproportionately Black and Hispanic, they are still a minority within these minorities. What primarily defines them is not so much their poverty or race as their behavior—their chronic lawlessness, drug use, out-of-wedlock births, welfare dependency, and school failure. "Underclass" describes a state of mind and a way of life. It is at least as much a cultural as an economic condition (Magnet, 1987:130).

An *Esquire* article excerpted in a 1988 *Reader's Digest* put it this way:

> The heart of the matter is what has come to be called the underclass—those nine million impoverished black Americans (of a total of 29 million blacks), so many of whom are trapped in welfare dependency, drugs, alcohol, crime, illiteracy, and disease, living in isolation in some of the richest cities of the earth (Hamill, 1988:105).

A Leading Scholar: William J. Wilson

In the late 1970s and 1980s, the University of Chicago sociologist William J. Wilson, a leading Black scholar, became an effectual exponent of the Black underclass perspective. Wilson's 1980 work, *The Declining Significance of Race,* had a major influence on the misconceptions surrounding the "Black underclass." Wilson contended that affirmative action programs had actually widened the gap between the Black middle class and the rest of Black America and had produced a Black underclass that has fallen behind the larger society in every aspect. Wilson's book opened the door for assumptions that racial discrimination had little significance for those who were moving up into the Black middle class and, by extension, that class (status) discrimination was more important than racial discrimination. The Black middle class had become a central part of the underclass argument. Racial discrimination, in employment at least, was not considered to be significant for middle-class Black Americans.

More recently, Wilson has argued that the underclass is composed of individuals who lack training and skills and who either experience long-term unemployment or are not a part of the labor force; individuals who engage in street criminal activity and other aberrant behavior; and families who experience long-term spells of poverty or welfare dependency. He developed these ideas most extensively in a widely discussed 1987 book, *The Truly Disadvantaged.* There Wilson targets the underclass and demonstrates numerous fallacies in the recent neoconservative analysis of the Black poor. Wilson shows, for example, that there is no consistent evidence that welfare programs decrease work effort or increase dependency and that the growing percentage of out-of-wedlock Black births is not the result of immorality or welfare, but instead results from the declining birth rate among married women as well as young women's difficulty in finding marriageable Black men—young men who are not chronically unemployed. In reply to the neoconservative emphasis on the subculture of poverty, Wilson develops the concepts of *social isolation* and *concentration effects.* A central Black underclass dilemma is the departure of stable middle-class families from traditional ghetto areas into better residential neighborhoods farther away. The poor thus face social isolation unlike that of the past. Not only are there fewer role models, but there are also fewer supportive institutions, including family stores, churches, and other voluntary associations. This deterioration brings a decline in sense of community, neighborhood identification, and norms against criminal behavior. Coupled with isolation are the concentration effects of having single-parent families, criminals, and the unemployed crowded into one area. Wilson rejects the neoconservative notion that the causes of current Black problems lie in self-perpetuating cultural traits.

Other Black Scholars

By the 1980s the term "underclass" was being used by white and Black social scientists. A number of Black scholars have made use of, and thereby helped to legitimate, the terminology of the Black underclass. However, although they accept the language of pathology, they have tended to accent the structural causes of the underclass dilemma. For example, in a 1984 book Pinkney has argued that

> Perhaps two of the major defining characteristics of the black underclass are their poverty and the social decay in which they are forced to survive.... Often they are forced to engage in criminal activities, a rational response to the circumstances in which they find themselves. And it must be noted that since these people are treated as animals, they frequently respond in kind (Pinkney, 1984:117).

He goes on to place emphasis on the structural conditions faced by Black Americans. Moreover, in a 1987 analysis of the Black family, Billingsly notes in passing the growth of the underclass:

> The black underclass continues to grow, due in part to extensive poverty, unemployment, and family instability.... Composed of those families and individuals at the bottom of the economic and social scales—perhaps a third of all black families—this sector of the population experiences an enormous portion of suffering (Billingsly, 1987:101).

Douglas G. Glasgow published *The Black Underclass* in 1981; his book has been unnecessarily neglected. Although Glasgow uses the underclass terminology by defining the underclass as a "permanently entrapped population of poor persons, unused and unwanted," his analytical focus is on structural factors. He addresses institutional racism as it operates in the educational system and the job market. Programs like affirmative action have failed to improve life for the inner-city poor because these programs have been "aimed at correcting superficial inequities without addressing the ingrained societal factors that maintain such inequities." Moreover, in a recent article Glasgow notes that the concept of the Black underclass has become widespread and generally has negative connotations. The portrait is one of ne'er-do-well welfare recipients an irresponsible fathers of illegitimate children on the dole. Glasgow takes issue with three of the major assumptions in underclass theory: the implication that there is a value deficiency in the Black community which created the underclass; the notion that the underclass problem is mainly a female/feminization problem rather than a racial one; and the notion that it was antipoverty programs that created the underclass. Nonetheless, he does accept the concept of the underclass as useful and suggests that the underclass concept adds another dimension to the traditional class structure of upper, middle, working, and lower class (Glasgow, 1987:129–145).

A Report by Local Government

Just as in the 1960s, governmental reports in the 1980s have picked up on the underclass theory in analyzing urban problems. A report of the New York City Commission on the Year 2000, established by Mayor Ed Koch, reviews the health of that city and finds it to be "ascendant," with a strong economy and the "exuberance of a re-energized city." While this Koch report does recommend some job creation and development control actions, one section provides an underclass interpretation of poverty in the city. Contrasting conditions of earlier immigrants with the contemporary poor, it portrays the latter as not having the churches and other institutions that aided the mobility of earlier immigrants:

> A city that was accustomed to viewing poverty as a phase in assimilation to the larger society now sees a seemingly rigid cycle of poverty and a permanent underclass divorced from the rest of society.

The report takes a limited "the city can only do so much" attitude to the solution of the poverty problem; the first two solutions proposed are for the "city to do what it can to discourage teenagers from becoming pregnant" and to provide troubled families at an early point with a caseworker. Some attention is given to the need to find job training programs for the welfare mothers, and a brief paragraph outlines how the city needs to develop programs to employ in its own division young unemployed males. As in many previous governmental reports, education is accented as the long-term solution to poverty in the city. There is no attention to the role of racial discrimination in Black poverty, nor is there any analysis of urban capital investment and disinvestment. From the beginning the orientation is "to make more sections of the city attractive to business" (Commission on the Year 2000, 1988: 33).

A CRITIQUE OF THE UNDERCLASS THEORY

A Politicized Theory

The concept of the underclass, as it has developed in the last decade, is highly political and represents a defining of the problems of the Black or in ways that do not involve an indictment of the existing structure of U.S. society. Neoconservatives use a reconstituted culture-of-poverty explanation, while liberals like Wilson mix some of the culture-of-poverty language with an emphasis on the social isolation and concentration of the Black poor. All theories, including the underclass theory, reflect the bias and societal situations of the theorists. Much of the underclass theorizing of the neoconservative theorists—and the white policymakers propagating it—is replete with white fears, assumptions, and biases. Liberal analysts, moreover, have generally fallen into the trap of accepting the language of the underclass theory even though they may place emphasis on demographic or structural factors.

The Problem of Definition

A major indicator of the problems in underclass theory is the ambiguity in various definitions. Auletta, for example, excludes the underemployed and includes street criminals, welfare mothers, hustlers, and the homeless. Wilson includes those who are among the long-term unemployed or who lack skills. For some, the underclass includes both rich criminals and the very poor. Most, but not all, see the underclass as made up primarily of minorities.

Behavior seems to be a common theme. Gephart and Pearson (1988: 3) claim that "most current definitions center around the concepts of concentrated and persistent poverty and/or a profile of 'underclass behaviors' that are judged dysfunctional by their observers." Neoconservatives and liberals alike use the language of illegitimacy, disorganization, and pathology. Many use income to count the underclass, but use behavior as the focus of the discussion. This means that the working poor and the elderly are sometimes included in the total count of those in the underclass, but are not part of the behavioral discussion. Even putting numbers on the size of the underclass has been problematical. Some estimates of the underclass include only a small share of the poor, while others expand the notion to include a much larger population. In a 1988 policy journal article, Ricketts and Sawhill have tried to make the definition of the underclass more concrete and specific, and thus to make it more useful for policymakers. They noted that "estimates of the underclass vary widely—from 3% to 38% of the poor. Persistence-based measures generally lead to higher estimates than location-based measures" (Ricketts and Sawhill, 1988: 318). They develop a definition using census data for geographical areas of cities:

> an underclass area [is] a census tract with a high proportion of (1) high school dropouts . . . ; (2) prime-age males not regularly attached to the labor force . . . ; (3) welfare recipients . . . ; and (4) female heads (Ricketts and Sawhill, 1988: 321).

They found that 2.5 million Americans live in these census tracts, although they admit that many nonpoor also live in there. Their final estimate is that there are about 1.3 million non-elderly adults living in underclass areas.

There is also a problem with the use of "class" in the term "underclass." The underclass distinction is not really a class distinction, because it does not focus on the hierarchy of classes or the relationship of classes, as does the tradition of class analysis since Karl Marx and Max Weber. While some argue that the underclass is outside the production (work) system, this is not actually the case, as we will see below. Moreover, if there is a Black underclass, presumably there is an "overclass." Yet the mainstream discussion does not discuss this "overclass."

Capitalism and Capital Flight

The underclass theory has arisen during an era when American capitalism is undergoing great change. There has been much capital flight out of central cities into suburban areas, cities in the Sunbelt, and foreign countries. Capital and corporate flight is at the heart of Black joblessness and poverty. Workers, Black or white, do not have the same ability to flee the community as do large corporations (Feagin and Parker, 1990: 37–50). Indeed, the threat of corporate flight has become a type of coercion, in that it forces workers to agree to wage reductions and other concessions—or in some cases to accept low-wage jobs. In addition, social scientists have functioned to legitimate a view of the U.S. capitalist system which suggests that Black workers should accept low-wage jobs.

Perhaps the strongest feature of Wilson's book, *The Truly Disadvantaged,* is the emphasis on joblessness as an important causal factor in the isolation of the Black underclass. Wilson argues that the scarcity of young Black males with regular jobs substantially accounts for the growing numbers of female-headed households and the increase in out-of-wedlock births. If young men and women cannot afford to get married, rent an apartment, and live together in a stable economic situation, young women set up their own households, raise their children, and often depend on welfare benefits. Wilson concludes his analysis with a call for a traditional job training and full employment policy, coupled with macroeconomic policy to generate a tight labor market and growth.

Among leading industrial nations the U.S. government has provided the weakest job training and creation programs. One important reason for this is that the U.S. state is substantially under the control of corporate capital, whose leadership seeks the freedom to invest or disinvest wherever profit margin and market control dictate and, thus, to weaken labor, cut taxes, and reduce employment programs. Wilson and other liberal analysts generally do not deal critically with the structure and operation of the contemporary capitalist system. The movement of jobs from northern cities to the Sunbelt cities and overseas, which Wilson does note, is not just part of a routine fluctuation in U.S. capitalism, but rather signals that investors are moving much capital, on a long-term basis, to areas with cheap labor and weak state regulation. Without a radical new policy restructuring the undemocratic investment policy of U.S. capitalism, it is not possible to deal fundamentally with job problems of central city dwellers. In *Black in a White America,* Sidney Wilhelm has pointed to the major problem facing large nonwhite groups concentrated in racially stratified low-wage jobs—the abandonment of whole populations as capitalism restructures to meet the chronic need for renewed profits. The U.S. economy no longer needs the majority of Black workers for full-time jobs (Willhelm, 1983).

Neoconservative and liberal analysts suggest that either the private sector or the government can provide enough jobs to solve the Black underclass problem. Yet, to quote from Adolph Reed (1988:170),

> what if there is no upward mobility queue—or at least not one either fat enough to accommodate the large populations of marginalized blacks and Hispanics or sturdy enough to withstand the dynamics of racial and class subordination?

Contemporary Discrimination: The Matter of Race

For most underclass analysts the concept of the Black underclass accents class culture or social isolation and downplays racial discrimination. A major weakness in Wilson's book is the rejection of current race discrimination as a significant reason for Black problems. Underclass analysts fail to consider the ways in which current discrimination perpetuates the effects of past discrimination. This results in, among other misconceptions, an ahistorical analysis, a too positive evaluation of the situation of middle-income Black Americans, and insufficient attention to the effect of discrimination on the Black underclass.

The discrimination of the past is much more substantial and thorough going for Black Americans. There is a view among some neoconservative scholars that "blacks today are like white immigrants yesterday," and that there is no need for governmental intervention on behalf of Blacks. In an article in the *New York Times Magazine* in 1966, social scientist Irving Kristol argued that "The Negro Today is Like the Immigrant of Yesterday" (Kristol, 1966: 50–51, 124–142). In his view the Black experience is not greatly different from that of white immigrant groups, and Black Americans can and will move up, just as the white immigrants of yesterday did. Similarly, Glazer argues that there are some important differences between the experiences of Blacks and those of white immigrants, but that there are more similarities than differences. He emphasizes that the difference is one of degree: "the gap between the experience of the worst off of the [white] ethnic groups and the Negroes is one of degree rather than kind. Indeed, in some respects the Negro is better off than some other groups" (Glazer, 1971: 45–59). Glazer further avers that, for the most part, the employment conditions faced by Black migrants to northern cities were no worse than those encountered by white immigrant groups.

Yet historical research by Hershberg, Yancey, and their associates has demonstrated that economic conditions at the time of entry into cities and the level of anti-Black racism at that time made the experiences of Blacks far more oppressive and difficult than those of white immigrant groups in northern cities. In the case of white immigrant groups, and of their children and grandchildren, group mobility was possible because:

1. Most arrived at a point in time when jobs were available,when capitalism was expanding and opportunities were more abundant;
2. Most faced far less severe employment and housing discrimination than Blacks did; and
3. Most found housing, however inadequate, reasonably near the workplaces (Hershberg, 1981: 462–464).

From an historical perspective there is no new underclass of the Black poor. For more than half a century there have been many Blacks in and outside cities without jobs; from the beginning of urban residence many Blacks have been locked into the segregated housing in cities.

Moreover, much "past" discrimination that reduced Black resources and mobility is not something of the distant past, but rather is recent. *Blatant* discrimination against Blacks occurred in massive doses until 25 years ago, particularly in the South. All Blacks (and whites) over the age of 30 years were born when the U.S. still had massive color bars both North and South. Most Blacks over 40 years of age were educated in *legally* segregated schools of lower quality than those of whites, and many felt the weight of massive *blatant* racial discrimination in, at least, the early part of their employment careers. And the majority of those Black Americans under the age of 30 have parents who have suffered from blatant racial discrimination. Moreover, most white Americans have benefited, if only indirectly, from past racial discrimination in several institutional areas.

A second misconception can be seen in the conceptualization of the Black middle class. By focussing on the middle class, scholars and other writers can argue that the problem of "race" is solved, that the only problem is that of the underclass, which is not racially determined. For example, it is often assumed that Black women hold favored positions in the labor market because affirmative action programs and equal opportunity programs have been most beneficial to middle-class Black women. This in turn leads to the assumption that Black professional women have experiences, interests, and concerns which are very substantially at variance with Black women who belong to the underclass (i.e., welfare mothers). However, whatever their class position, there are certain fundamental commonalties of experiences and perceptions shared by Black women as a racial-gender group.

Research on upper-middle-income Blacks in corporate America shows them to be suffering from widespread discrimination. Jones' research on Black managers has found that the predominantly white corporate environment, with its intense pressures for conformity, creates regular problems. Jones describes one Black manager working his way up the executive ranks. One day he met with other Black managers who wanted his advice on coping with discrimination:

> Charlie concluded that this should be shared with senior management and agreed to arrange a meeting with the appropriate officers. Two days before the scheduled meeting, while chatting with the President at a cocktail affair, Charlie was sobered by the President's disturbed look as he said, "Charlie I am disappointed that you met with those black managers. I thought we could trust you" (Jones, 1986:89).

Jones has also reported racial climate data from his nationwide survey of a large number of Black managers with graduate-level business degrees. Nearly all (98%) felt that Black managers had not achieved equal opportunity with white managers, and more than 90% felt there was much anti-Black hostility in corporations. The leaders in white (male) oriented organizations are willing, often grudgingly, to bring Blacks and women into important positions but in token numbers and under the existing rules (Jones, 1985).

In addition, members of the Black middle class do not have the same long-term financial security of comparable whites. Thus, a 1984 Census Bureau study of wealth found that the median Black household had a net worth of about $3,400, less than one-tenth of the median white household's net worth. This means that a crisis could easily wipe out most Black middle-class families (U.S. Bureau of the Census, 1987: 440–41).

Moreover, in the 1980s many Black workers at all status levels have faced layoffs and sharp reductions in income, including auto and steel workers. A Federal Service Task Force study found that in the early 1980s minority workers were laid off at 50% higher rate than whites. As Robert Ethridge of the American Association for Affirmative Action put it in 1988: "There are a lot [of Blacks] in peripheral areas like affirmative action and community relations, but as companies downsize, restructure, and merge, they want to cut off those fluff areas" (Ellis, 1988:68). The eight years of attacks on affirmative action under the Reagan administration took their toll. There is today less commitment to affirmative action in the business community.

The Reality of Discrimination

White Americans tend not to see the actual racial discrimination that exists in U.S. society, while Black Americans are acutely aware of it. In reply to an early

1980s Gallup poll question ("Looking back over the last ten years, do you think the quality of life of Blacks in the U.S. has gotten better, stayed the same, or gotten worse?"), over half of the nonwhites in the sample (mostly Blacks) said "gotten worse" or "stayed the same" (Gallup Opinion Index, 1980:10). Yet only a fifth of the *white* respondents answered in a negative way. Three-quarters of the whites said "gotten better." The survey also asked this question: "In your opinion, how well do you think Blacks are treated in this community: the same as whites are, not very well, or badly?" Sixty-eight percent of the whites in this nationwide sample said Blacks were treated the same as whites; only 20% felt they were not well treated or were badly treated.

In the spring of 1988, a *Business Week* article reported on a national survey showing that about half of the Blacks interviewed felt that they had to work harder than whites; just 7% of whites agreed. Over half the Blacks interviewed felt that most Blacks are paid less than whites "doing the same job." The comparable percentage for whites was 18%; 70% of the whites interviewed felt there was pay equality. Eighty percent of the Black respondents, and just 32% of the whites, felt that if an equally well qualified Black and white were competing for the same job, that the Black applicant would be less likely to be hired. Furthermore, 62% of Black respondents said that the chances for Blacks to be promoted to supervisory jobs were not as good as those for whites; even 41% of whites agreed (Ellis, 1988: 65).

Residential Dispersion and Desegregation

Current theories of the Black underclass emphasize the importance of Black middle-class flight from previously all-Black areas and into all-white areas. Underclass theorists argue that middle-class Blacks can and do abandon the ghetto to "move on up" to integrated suburban neighborhoods. The implication is that there is widespread housing integration, at least at the middle-class level. However, theories that focus on middle-class abandonment cannot explain the overwhelming statistical evidence of continuing residential segregation at all class levels (Newman, 1978; Peterson, 1981; Johnston, 1984). To take one example, in the city of New Orleans most Blacks at all income levels remain in traditionally Black areas; the four census tracts with the largest concentrations of Blacks are three public housing projects and one large Black suburban subdivision adjacent to poor Black areas (Inniss, 1988).

Black suburbanization has been low. Only one-tenth of Black Americans live in the suburbs today. Housing segregation data suggest that many stable-income, middle-income Black families have not moved far from ghetto areas, but rather live in nearby suburbs on the ghetto fringe. Thus, one study conducted in the 1980s of New Jersey found that most of the increase in Black suburban population in that state occurred in or near existing Black neighborhoods (Lake, 1981). A 1988 study by Denton and Massey also questioned the middle-class abandonment thesis. Using data from the 1980 census, Denton and Massey found that within the 20 metropolitan areas with the largest Black populations, Blacks continue to be highly segregated residentially, at all socioeconomic levels. Even for the best-educated Blacks, those with one year or more of postgraduate work, the index of segregation was very high. They conclude that if the Black middle class is abandoning the Black poor, "they are not moving to integrated Anglo-Black neighborhoods" (Denton and Massey, 1988: 814).

Moreover, in a recent national survey the majority of the whites interviewed said that the percentage Black in their neighborhood had stayed the same or gone down in the past five years; only 29% said the percentage Black had increased—even a little. Among the Black respondents only 10% reported that the percent Black in their neighborhood had gone down in the last five years. Thirty-five percent reported that the percentage had gone up (Ellis, 1988:65). The surveys suggest no great changes in the mid-1980s.

CONCLUSION

The solution to the problem of Blacks in America is neither obscure nor novel. The vestiges and badges of slavery are still very much in evidence in the terrible statistics that the underclass theorists repeat. But these statistics are not the result, at base, of some underclass subculture or isolation from the Black middle class. They reflect past and present discrimination. One problem is that most commentators have gotten so used to Black poverty that their language of pathology and ghettos seems relatively accurate and harmless. Yet like other forms of discrimination and segregation Black "ghettos" go back to, and are a residue of, slavery; we should not speak of them cavalierly as though they were just areas of cities somehow comparable to other areas such as "suburbs." Ghettos are terrible places reflecting the *result* of white racism, no less.

To get rid of these badges and vestiges of slavery, we not only need some broad restructuring of modern capitalism to meet the needs of ordinary workers, Black and white, but in our view we also require race-specific solutions such as expanded—and aggressive—affirmative action. In theory at least, the concept of affirmative action is radical; affirmative action recognizes that past wrongs are structured-in and must be specially addressed with race-specific structural programs. Some previous affirmative action plans have been successful in opening up institutions for Black Americans.

The opponents of equal opportunity and affirmative action have scored a brilliant coup by getting the mass media to discuss affirmative action in terms of the simplistic phrase "reverse discrimination." Yet the term is grossly inaccurate. Traditional discrimination has meant, and still means, the widespread practice of blatant and subtle discrimination by whites against Blacks in most organizations in all major institutional areas of society—in housing, employment, education, health services, the legal system, and so on. For three centuries now, tens of millions of whites have participated directly in discrimination against millions of Blacks, including routinized discrimination in the large-scale bureaucracies that now dominate this society. The reverse of traditional discrimination by whites against Blacks would mean reversing the power and resource inequalities for a long time: for several hundred years, massive institutionalized discrimination would be directed by dominant Blacks against most whites. That societal condition would be "reverse discrimination." It has never existed.

Moreover, Kenneth Smallwood (1985) has argued that white America has historically benefited from huge federal "affirmative action" plans for whites only, programs which laid the foundation for much of white prosperity in the United States. To take one major example, from the 1860s to the early 1900s, the Homestead Act provided free land in the West for whites, but because most Blacks were still in the semislavery peonage of Southern agriculture, most could not participate in this government affirmative action program giving land to U.S. citizens. That billion-dollar land giveaway became the basis of economic prosperity for many white Americans and their descendants. Recent affirmative action plans for Black Americans pale in comparison with that single program. Moreover, most New Deal programs in the 1930s primarily subsidized white Americans and white-controlled corporations. Thus, Federal Housing Administration (FHA) actions helped millions of white American families secure housing while that agency also encouraged the segregation of Black Americans in ghetto communities. Massive New Deal agricultural programs and the Reconstruction Finance Corporation kept many white American bankers, farmers, and corporate executives in business, again providing the basis for much postwar prosperity in white America.

Yet similar, massive multibillion dollar aid programs have never been made available to most Black Americans. Preferential treatment for white Americans has always been legitimate, and was for more than three centuries an essential part of government development in U.S. society. If so, one might add, why not provide three centuries of equivalent, legitimate, large-scale affirmative action to build up the wealth of the Black American victims of white discrimination?

PART THREE

Race and Ethnicity in American Institutions

On the Internet . . .

Sites appropriate to Part Three

This Education World site, sponsored by the American Fidelity Educational Services, offers over 50,000 pages that can be referenced. Search under the topics "race" and "ethnicity" for education resources related to these categories.

http://www.education-world.com

Studies by the National Center for Education Statistics (NCES) cover the entire educational spectrum, providing the facts and figures needed to help policymakers understand the condition of education in the United States today, to give researchers a foundation of data to build upon, and to help teachers and administrators to identify the best practices for their schools. This site provides information about reports and data products that NCES has released and the results of a variety of educational surveys.

http://nces.ed.gov

The U.S. Census Bureau site is a major source of social, demographic, and economic information. This information includes income/employment data and income distribution and poverty data. Search the terms "race, ethnic" to find the results of the 1996 Race and Ethnic Targeted Test (RAETT) and U.S. population projections by race, as well as other race-related information.

http://www.census.gov

CHAPTER 6 The Educational Institution

6.1 NOEL JACOB KENT

The New Campus Racism: What's Going On?

The politics of racial hate, fear, and anger is increasing significantly on U.S. college and university campuses. Hate literature, graffiti in public places, name-calling, denigrating epithets, and violence continue to disrupt the lives of racial minorities attempting to get a college education. The National Institute Against Prejudice and Violence contends that hundreds of incidents of racial violence and assaults have taken place on college campuses within the last several years. Recently, Asian American students at the University of California, Irvine, were threatened via e-mail with being "hunted down and killed."

The following selection is from the republication of "The New Campus Racism: What's Going On?" in the special Fall 2000 retrospective issue of *Thought and Action* (it was originally published in Fall 1996). In it, Noel Jacob Kent contends that the racial and ethnic intolerance on U.S. campuses reflects a growing racial polarization in the greater society that, in turn, is the product of a "profound moral crisis." Kent proposes that to end the escalating campus racism, colleges and universities must adopt "transformative" strategies that include meaningful curriculum reform comprising more realistic explications of racism in U.S. society, faculty awareness of their own personal microcultures, and the adoption of conflict mediation programs. In a postscript to the republication of his article, Kent contends that since the article was originally published, colleges and universities still have not taken the initiative in challenging racism and the widening racial divide on many campuses, that *de facto* apartheid still reigns on many campuses, and that imaginative policies designed to correct for racism on U.S. college and university campuses are needed now more than ever.

Kent is a professor of ethnic studies at the University of Hawaii at Manoa. His research interests focus on ethnic and race relations and U.S. history and political economy. His most recent endeavor of study is on how colleges and universities handle the issues of ethnic and racial diversity and conflict.

Key Concept: campus racism in the United States

"Racism and bigotry are back on the campus with a vengeance."
—Professor William Damon, Clark University

Colleges and universities could once pretend to offer a refuge from the swirling antagonisms of a highly racialized society. But no longer.

The incidence of verbal and physical harassments and abuses directed against Latino, Asian and Jewish-Americans, foreign students, and, above all, African-Americans has been surging on our campuses since at least the late 1980s.

Why so much bigotry and intolerance at institutions long seen as dedicated to reason and the search for truth?

Part of the answer is that life on campus closely mirrors the dominant patterns and attitudes of the larger society. In both, racial structures and meanings are in flux and hotly contested, and racism, driven by a profound "moral crisis," has proven an entrenched and virulent social force.

Another part of the answer: Our economy in the late 20th Century is going through its most profound restructuring since the dawn of the Industrial Age. The consequences of that restructuring—diminished opportunity, stagnating wages, a decline in the quality of life for many families—directly conflict with the mythic American dream. The result: depression, confusion, and wide-ranging anger throughout the society, a reaction that the campus is not immune from.

Here we will attempt to demonstrate how these interrelated phenomena fuel the rise of intolerance on our campuses. We also hope to suggest how campuses might respond to the current crisis with transformative solutions, rather than the current response, which has usually been reactive, after-the-fact, and too little–too late.

The great triumph of the civil rights movement of the 1960s was to end legal segregation in the United States. A consequence of that movement was that white attitudes toward African-American inclusion shifted demonstrably.

The idea of Black participation in formerly white-monopolized spheres of national life became widely accepted throughout the society. A wholly new set of opportunities and possibilities seemed to open up.

The transformation, however, remained both uneven and incomplete—an odd "mixture of striking movement and surface change."[1] The belief in equal opportunity did not lead to widespread acceptance of equal opportunity in practice. Rather than the steady decline of discrimination and maturing of the "colorblind society" envisioned by integrationists, "racial meanings" remained bitterly contested. The battle for full participation continued as "trench warfare" in bureaucracies and courts.[2]

Given the nation's history and the psychological and material advantages that skin pigmentation confers upon whites, the emergence of a "New Racism" is hardly surprising. Anti-Black prejudice continues as a cultural norm central to the white American worldview and identity.[3] Indeed, as a "fluid, variable and open ended process," racism simply plays too many essential roles to be easily abandoned.[4]

If the United States in 1996 no longer perfectly fits the "two societies, one Black, one white—separate and unequal," described by the National Advisory Commission on Civil Disorders in 1969, it is not so very different either. Older theories of biological inferiority and white supremacy have given way to a new view that combines negative Black stereotypes with the glorification of individualism and meritocracy.

The accepted "wisdom" of the "new racism" is that "a racially balanced society" now provides equal opportunity for all to pursue the American Good Life.[5] Individuals can rise above their environment. There is opportunity for all. Failure results from personal inadequacies, splintered families, and a culture of failure.

Minority poverty, labor market ghettoization, segregated neighborhoods, and disproportionate rates of incarceration are attributed to the moral failure of the people involved.[6] Groups "lagging behind are in essence faulted for their own circumstances."[7]

Crudely overt displays of racism represent a second level of the "New Racism." Its proponents are the fairly large number of whites who remain unable "to perceive Black members as legitimate full members of the polity."[8]

These undisguised acts of bigotry take the form of everyday harassment, violence, and intimidation, ranging from street epithets and the primitive stereotypes bandied about during radio talk shows to the vicious assaults orchestrated by vanguard neo-Nazis, Klan, and other white supremacists.[9] What marks the latter groups, notes Robert Cahill, who monitored white supremacist movements in the Northwest, are their "proudly explicit" racial beliefs, "radical alienation from racial amalgamation," and violence.[10]

The "New Racism" also has its political front. The New Right, the champion of white protectionism and identity, has been a key player in an unlikely coalition of Southern whites, Northern blue collars, religious fundamentalists, and the affluent that practically monopolized the White House from 1968 through 1992. The GOP has been especially effective in turning *crime, busing, welfare,* and *quotas* into highly charged codewords.

All these approaches feed into each other. In Professor Mari Matsuda's succinct phrase: "Gutter racism, parlor racism, corporate racism and government racism work in coordination, reinforcing existing conditions of domination."[11]

The timing is certainly opportune: For the first time since the civil rights era, a majority of whites believe equal rights have been "pushed too far in this country." Much of the Republican Party's 1994 electoral success stemmed from playing to white voter anger at federal social programs and "enforced diversity." The leading 1996 Republican presidential candidates uniformly bashed affirmative action programs, and one, Pat Buchanan, made their abolition a central plank of his platform.[12]

In retrospect, the right-wing success in shifting the national debate from the historic foundations of minority poverty and disadvantage toward the twin myths of total individual responsibility and "color-blindness" has been nothing short of phenomenal.

That our colleges and universities are not immune to the racial polarization of society at large should come as no surprise. Well before entering college, young people have gotten the message—subtle and not-so-subtle—from family, peers, and the media about the appropriate racial hierarchy.[13]

Many white college students, those from highly segregated suburbs and smaller cities, carry the larger society's stereotypes of Blacks as violent criminals/willing welfare dependents. Given their narrow cultural framework, it is difficult for these students to accept non-white presence and cultural expressions on campus. For them, African-American students may appear to be intruders. At least some whites associate difference in skin color with disadvantage and, often, deviance.[14]

But there are also many white students who genuinely support the idea of a color-blind society. For them, the intense skepticism of Blacks to this idea is troubling if not bewildering. They have come face to face with a basic obstacle to real communication: the radically differing views Black and white students have about the meaning of racism. That even the most well intentioned whites and Blacks have entirely different reference points becomes startlingly evident not only over campus issues, but in national and international events like the Gulf War, the O.J. Simpson trial verdict, the Million Man March.

Professor Robert Blauner of the University of California at Berkeley argues that there "are two languages of race in America" and that young whites and Blacks are talking past each other when they discuss "racism." What whites see as peripheral and mainly an historic artifact, Blacks view as absolutely "central" to U.S. history and contemporary society. "Whites," he says, "locate racism in color consciousness and its absence in color-blindness," whereas Blacks expand the meaning to include power, position, and equality in the structuring of American society.[15]

Blauner points out that when Black students act in conventionally American *ethnic* ways—by forming Black Student Unions, for instance—whites interpret this as racial exclusion. White students don't understand why "students of color insistently underscore their sense of difference, their affirmation of racial and ethnic membership." In contrast, minorities of color "sense a kind of racism in the whites' assumption that minorities must assimilate to mainstream values and styles."[16]

This is an increasing point of conflict as campus Blacks mirror the "defensive ethnicity" many whites have adopted. Integration has always taken a psychic toll. Now across the spectrum of African-American society—and especially on campuses—cynicism about the entire undertaking is increasing. Black separatism, once a tactic in the integration struggle, has emerged as an end in itself.

African-American students have always had difficulty in "recognizing" themselves and their heritage on white majority campuses.[17] "I know that whites are never going to respect me on face value," says an Atlanta student.[18] "It feels like I don't exist here," commented one Black student in the midst of a 1995 dispute at the College of the Holy Cross over the barring of whites from a Black campus organization.[19]

Since most campuses don't provide a supportive infrastructure, and have a generally unfavorable racial climate, African-Americans increasingly form their own campus enclaves. "It's a Black thing. You wouldn't understand" read the t-shirts worn by college students, who increasingly choose to segregate themselves from whites in dormitories.[20]

To comprehend the larger forces driving campus racism, we should look at recent structural changes in the United States and the flourishing of old and new fears.

The escalating racial polarization of American society is intertwined with what Professor Charles Maier calls a national "moral crisis." Americans are no longer able to make sense of, much less respond to, the massive changes now confronting them.

Moreover, many certainties and rituals that once provided meaning and stability are now threatened. A public—adrift and dislocated—no longer knows what social progress means. That same public has grown disenchanted with traditional political processes incapable of providing protection.[21]

Americans recite a litany of fears, ranging from loss of jobs and medical coverage to rising taxes. The sense of every-citizen-as-victim is mirrored on prime-time television sitcoms and is the food and drink of immensely popular, immensely spiteful talkshow hosts.

Public discussion is saturated with mean-spirited rhetoric catering to knee-jerk instinct and irrationality. Working people rant at being victimized, yet direct their rage at those even more powerless. The inevitable search for different "others" to blame helps to repress both conflicts within the white majority itself and the need to address society's most deep rooted problems.

At the heart of this contemporary crisis is the collision between the American Dream's myth of individual upward mobility and the reality of the radical restructuring of the U.S. political economy.

The American Dream tells us that if you work hard, you succeed. The nation's vast resources, technical ingenuity, and fluid social system will reward the conscientious, thrifty individual—and, if not her or him, then surely, that person's children. "Americans," remarks Paul Wachtel, "have viewed the future as rightfully providing them with more.[22]

Today, however, pessimism reigns. Forty-three percent of those surveyed shortly before the 1994 election expected life to be worse by the end of the century.[23] A 1995 survey found 55 percent convinced the nation was in long-term decline.[24]

Such pessimism flows from a quarter-century of stagnant and declining family and individual incomes and wages. Personal savings have fallen dramatically, along with discretionary incomes. The buying power of most families remains approximately at late 1970s levels.

The more than 10 million new jobs generated during the Clinton era, significant increases in the rate of women working, and multiple job holding have not reversed income stagnation and decline. A large majority of the population has lost ground absolutely or relatively. People in the lowest income groups have lost the most.[25]

Big Business has jettisoned the post-war social contract and consciously conducted anti-union campaigns with a vengeance and outsourced millions of high-paying jobs to cheaper labor areas. "Downsizing" has become this decade's *leitmotif* [dominant, recurring theme]. Internal corporate labor markets now feature a core of stable, relatively privileged employees surrounded by low-paid, casual, contingent workers lacking rights or benefits.[26] Solid primary sector jobs, with middle class incomes, career ladders, and job security, are driven out by what Chris Tilly calls "firms that have adopted a low-wage, low skill, high turnover employment policy."[27]

College educated workers—middle managers, engineers, professionals, and other white collar workers—have been displaced at a previously unimaginable rate, as corporations flatten hierarchies and hire fewer permanent, well-paid staff.

Youth are at the epicenter of this social earthquake. Today's young adult man is less likely than his father was at the same age to own his own home or have a secure career and opportunities for future mobility.[28] American society now mocks young people's needs for a long-term, secure place in society. The decline of homeownership opportunities has led to a sharp increase in the "unexpected homecomings" of married and unmarried 20- to 30-year olds.

Young adults share the prevailing pessimism about the future. Meanwhile, they continue to desperately cling to the disintegrating American Dream. Throughout the '90s, about three-quarters of college freshmen surveyed agreed they are in school "to be able to get a better job" and "to be able to make more money." Large majorities believe that "the chief benefit of college is that it increases one's earning power."[29]

The latter belief does contain some truth. Higher education credentials have become more crucial than ever before for those aspiring to middle class lives.[30] Yet the hopes of collegians for professional jobs and pay are simply out of line with new labor market realities. Higher education no longer offers a guaranteed payoff.

The collapsed job market for college graduates of the 1970s reappeared in the early 1990s. Job prospects for the 1993 graduating class were "dismal," as fewer recruiters arrived on campuses offering fewer jobs.[31] The mid-'90s "prosperity" has improved things only marginally. More college graduates are working at jobs not requiring college level training.[32]

Even students at the most prestigious institutions are digesting the unpalatable truth that they will wind up poorer than their parents. "There's a general sense of helplessness that students have that they're not going to be able to find a job that will pay them enough to live on," notes one college counselor.[33]

This perception drives the often frantic pressures to link college and professional career. Job hunting becomes a preoccupation almost from the freshman year. The college years become more a financial investment in the future and less a *rite de passage*.

Contemporary young people, perhaps more than any other American generation before them, are trapped between the prevailing "psychology of entitlement" and an economic environment that demands austerity and sacrifice.

We have already seen how the "question of color" arrives on the campus laden with extensive ideological baggage. Now the struggle toward the always elusive goal of racial justice takes on the added dimension of scarcity: The possibility of a livable future has become scarce—for whites as well as Blacks.

Given their increasing financial worries and their deteriorating job prospects, white college students readily perceive of themselves as victims. From a zero sum game perspective, affirmative action programs seem to further stack a deck already loaded against them. The feelings of self-doubt, inadequacy, and difficulties in identity formation now epidemic among youth have been identified with the propensity to scapegoat minorities.[34]

In a culture where very often expressions of rage and frustration are directed at race, terms like "reverse racism" and "terminally Caucasian" take on real power. A white student leader organizing against the white student union at the University of Florida has summarized the mood: "There is a growing realization by white males that they no longer have their privileged advantages, who feel they may not do as well as their fathers, and they are looking for scapegoats."[35]

At UC Berkeley, one embittered student complains that "being white means that you're less likely to get financial aid. It means that there are all sorts of tutoring groups and special programs that you can't get into, because you're not a minority."[36]

Underscoring these intense feelings is the fiscal crisis of higher education in the United States, which *is* victimizing white students (among others). Cutbacks in federal, state, and local funding over the last decade have meant that, at a time of growing enrollments, institutions have left faculty and support positions unfilled, pared back classes, eliminated departments, and shortened library hours.[37]

Meanwhile, as tuition and fee increases soar well beyond inflation rates, financial aid awards have diminished. Financial pressures compel many white students to spend more time working and less in school. Ironically, even as students are being whipsawed between the demands of school, work, and family life, counseling services are being cut back, too.[38] Some would-be full-timers are now part-timers with a long trajectory to graduation. A "ratcheting down" process forces many students to attend a lower prestige school than they might have attended only recently.

White students, reacting out of helplessness and free-floating anger, scapegoat minority students. This demonization leads to the overtly racist acts that occur on our campuses.

Colleges and universities have, of course, never been "ivory towers." The racial divisions and economic dislocation that plague society as a whole play themselves out on our campuses. And never more than today.

How to break this vicious cycle of escalating campus racism and polarization? Senator Bill Bradley maintains that racism will thrive as long as "white Americans resist relinquishing the sense of entitlement skin color has given them throughout our history."[39] Seldom, however, does the college experience cause students to question whether such entitlements exist. Neither do they find their own, nor their society's, racial biases seriously challenged by the curriculum they study or the associations they make.

Few institutions mandate study of cultural identities and values. Only infrequently do white undergraduates investigate the framework in which African-Americans (among others) are marginalized by both university and larger society. For the vast majority of white students, then, college does not change their sense of race and race relations in the United States.[40]

College and university administrators trying to address the race issue have tended to be reactive. They draw up guidelines for conduct, promulgate hate speech codes, and mete out punishments for campus offenders. This has raised a storm of protest and a slew of court actions.

Given the campus racial climate, firm rules to define acceptable behavior are certainly needed. Every student has a basic right to a safe and secure campus learning and living environment free from harassment. No college or university should tolerate violations of those rights. But such policies should be part of a transformative strategy that takes as its point of departure white and minority student attitudes, fears, and self-conceptions. This strategy should help students learn "the different languages of race" cited by Blauner. Make these languages mutually intelligible and students will begin to "get it." Mutual empathy is an indispensable step toward mutual respect and cooperation.

Curriculum reform—as when Stanford broadens the canon to include non-western literature and Wisconsin-Madison requires undergraduates to take courses with an ethnic studies component—is probably the most widely used transformative vehicle. Conflict mediation programs, such as the one at UCLA which emphasizes resolving diversity related conflicts, are also critical. But developing empathy across subcultures demands more. Majority white colleges and universities must take some risky initiatives along uncharted ground.

Black sensibilities and experiences must be given wide-spread voice. White students, too, must have a safe and dignified way to express and work out their greivances and fears and find answers to their own questions of identity. We must not underestimate the mutual hunger for honest talk across racial bunkers. Interracial campus activities and dialogues should be encouraged, so students can appreciate each other as (different) equals and members of a community sharing similar goals. White students should have the opportunity to experience the daily realities of being "otherness" by living in a majority African-American dorm, volunteering in a minority neighborhood, or studying abroad.

Faculty are critical agents in the process. As Gay Reed suggests, learning about other cultures and "celebrating diversity" is only a minor part of understanding "the cultural and historical roots of diversity which have made it so problematic in American society." Reed sagely argues that faculty "need to become aware of their own personal microcultures and understand how this microculture affects and is affected by the larger macroculture."[41]

Programs must move beyond the campus to creatively challenge racism in the community. White children and teenagers at the K–12 level need to be educated about the harsh historical realities of who were not allowed to be "We the People of the United States." Researchers at the University of Massachusetts-Amherst are conducting racial and ethnic diversity and tolerance programs in those Boston elementary schools from which the university has drawn some of its more aggressively racist students. Public and private colleges might, as an institutional mission, adopt local schools for race relations education.

Higher education has a vital role to play in reversing the tide of bigotry and hate in the country, but, right now, the best contribution we can make is to begin getting our own academic houses in order.

AUTHOR'S POSTSCRIPT

This article was originally written to help stimulate thinking about the critical need for colleges and universities to take the intiative in challenging racism and the widening racial divide on many campuses. Progress, four years later, is slow: Few institutions have launched programs of "transformative education."

Of course, the obstacles, including limited resources and fear of student and alumni backlash, are as formidable as ever. Sheer denial also remains a potent force—I remember one *Thought and Action* reader, a faculty member at a small Pennsylvania college, calling to say that the article had really excited him and that his college had profound racial conflicts, but the culture of denial was such that new initiatives were probably not possible.

The last four years also show that neither the nation's "Goldilocks" economy, with its hot job prospects for certain categories of graduates, nor the popularity on campuses of Latino and hip hop music, has done much to lessen student racial stereotypes or fears and anxieties. On most campuses, *de facto* apartheid still reigns. Imaginative policies and programs in the "transformative mode" are needed now more than ever.

NOTES

1. Schuman, 1985.
2. Omi and Winant, 1986.
3. Pettigrew, 1975.
4. Sivanadan, 1983.
5. Belz, 1991.
6. Lewis, 1978.
7. Sears, 1988.
8. Reed and Bond, 1991.
9. Walker, 1991.
10. Cahill, 1990.
11. Matsuda, 1989.
12. Walker 1992; "In Louisiana," 1996.
13. Leo, 1993.
14. Jones, 1988.
15. Blauner, 1996.
16. Blauner, 1996.
17. Keeton and Jans, 1992.
18. Whittaker, 1990; *Chronicle of Higher Education,* 1992.
19. Gose, 1995.
20. Gose, 1995.
21. Maier, 1994.
22. Wachtel, 1983.
23. Seelye, 1994.
24. *Money,* May 1995.
25. Schor, 1992; Newman, 1993; Kuttner, 1995.
26. Sweeney and Nussbaum, 1989; Howard, 1995.
27. Tilly, 1989.
28. Matters, 1990; *Business Week,* 1991.
29. "Attitudes and Characteristics of College Freshmen," 1992b, 1994.
30. "K Mart Economy," 1990.
31. *Wall Street Journal,* 1993.
32. Mishel and Bernstein, 1995.
33. Cage, 1992.
34. Yinger, 1983.
35. Wilson, 1990.
36. Institute for the Study of Social Change, 1990.
37. Adams and Palmer, 1993.
38. Cage, 1992.
39. Kramer, 1992.
40. Ramirez, 1988.
41. Reed, 1996.

REFERENCES

Adams, Cynthia and Palmer, David. "Economic Problems and the Future," *Academe*, January 1993.

Belz, Norman. *Equality Transformed A Quarter Century of Affirmative Action*. New Brunswick, Transaction Publishers, 1991.

Blauner, Robert. "Self-Segregation Should Be Accepted," in *Race Relations*. Greenhaven Press, 1996: 216–223.

Business Week, 25 March 1991.

Cahill, Robert. "Plain and Fancy Racism in North America." Lecture at the University of Hawaii Manoa, 1990 2–3.

Chronicle of Higher Education, 2 October 1991: A31.

"Attitudes and Characteristics of Freshmen," *Chronicle of Higher Education* (Fall 1991), 26 August 1992: 17.

Cage, Mary Crystal. "Students Face Pressures as Never Before but Counseling Help Has Withered," *Chronicle of Higher Education*, 19 November 1992.

"Educational Attitudes and Characteristics of College Freshmen," *Chronicle of Higher Education* (Fall 1993), 1 September 1994.

Delaney, Lloyd. "White Racism" in Bowser, Byron and Hunt, Raymond. *Impacts of Racism on White Americans*. Beverly Hills, Sage Publications, 1981: 161.

Gose, Ben. "A Place of Their Own," *Chronicle of Higher Education*, 8 December 1995:A 34.

Howard, Ann. *The Changing Nature of Work*. San Francisco: Josey Bass, 1995.

"In Louisiana, Church Pews are Trenches in GOP War," *New York Times*, 20 January 1996.

Institute for the Study of Social Change. *The Diversity Project. Interim Report to the Chancellor University of California Berkeley*, Berkeley, 1990.

Jones, James. "Racism in Black and White," in Katz. *Eliminating Racism:* 117.

Keeton, Morris and Jans, Reno. "An Uncertain Trumpet Welcoming Diverse Students." *Liberal Education*. 78 (4), September-October, 1992.

"K Mart Economy." *New York Times*, 27 November 1990: Al.

Kilborn, Peter T. "In New Work World Employers Call All the Shots." *New York Times*, 3 July 1995.

Kramer, Michael. "Straight Talk about Race." *Time*, 1 June: 36.

Kuttner, Robert. "Getting to Grips with the Jellyfish Economy," *Guardian Weekly*, 13 June 1995.

Leo, John. 1993. "The Luxury of Black Students." *US. News and World Report*, 25 March 1992.

Lewis, Michael. *The Culture of Inequality*. New York: Meridian, 1978.

Maier, Charles. "Democracy and its Discontents. A Moral Crisis," *Foreign Affairs*, July-August 1994: 48–64.

Matsuda, Mari. "Public Response to Racist Speech Considering the Victim's Story." *Michigan Law Review*, August 1989: 2320–2380.

Mattera, Philip. *Prosperity Lost*. Reading Mass: Addison-Wesley, 1990.

New York Times, 19 November 1995.

Mishel, Lawrence and Bernstein, Jared. *The State of Working America*, 1994–5, Washington: Economic Policy Institute, 1995: 14–16.

Money, 12 May 1995.

Newman, Katherine. *Declining Fortunes. The Withering of the American Dream.* New York. Norton, 1993.

Omi, Michael and Winant, Howard. *Racial Formation in the United States from the 1960s to the 1980s.* New York. Routledge: 68, 1986.

Onishi, Norimitsu. "Affirmative Action Choosing Sides." *New York Times,* 31 March 1995.

Pettigrew, Thomas. 1975. "Racism and Mental Health of White Americans: A Social Psychological View," in *Racism and Mental Health.* (Charles W. Willie ed.). University of Pittsburgh. (1975).

Reed, Adolph Jr. and Bond, Julian. "Equality Why We Can't Wait." *The Nation,* December 1991: 735.

Reed, Gay Garland, 1996. "Cultural Identities and Frames of Mind. Steps Toward Preparing Multicultural Teachers." (unpublished ms.)

Schor, Juliet. *The Overworked American The Unexpected Decline of Leisure.* New York. Basic Books, 1991.

Schuman, Howard, Teech, Charlotte, and Bobo, Lawrence. *Racial Attitudes in America Trends and Interpretations.* Cambridge, 1985.

Sears, David O. "Symbolic Ethnicity," in *Eliminating Racism* (eds.) Phyllis A. Katz and Dalmas A. Taylor, 1988: 53–78.

Seelye, Katherine Q. "Voters disgusted with politics as election nears." *New York Times,* 3 November 1994.

Sivanadan, S. "Challenging Racism: Strategies for the 80s." *Race and Class* 25 (2), 1983: 1.

Sweeney, John J. and Nussbaum, Karen. *Solutions for the New Workforce,* Washington, D.C. SEIU, 1989: 55–75.

Tilly, Chris. *Short Hours, Short Shrift.* Washington: Economic Policy Institute, 1989.

Wachtel, Paul. *The Poverty of Affluence: A Psychological Portrait of the American Way of Life.* New York: Free Press, 1983.

Walker, Martin. "Patriotism in the Roar," *Guardian Weekly,* 7 April 1991: 23.

Wall Street Journal. "Labor Letter." May 18,1993:1.

Whittaker, Charles. "The New Generation of the Nineties," *Ebony,* August 1990.

Wilson, Robin. "White Student Unions Spark Outrage and Worry." *Chronicle of Higher Education,* 18 April 1990: A36.

Yinger, John Milton. "Ethnicity and Social Change." *The Journal of Ethnic and Racial Studies* 6(1983): 399.

6.2 ADALBERTO AGUIRRE, JR.

Academic Storytelling: A Critical Race Theory Story of Affirmative Action

In the United States the term *affirmative action* angers many White people and frustrates many others. For those who get angry, affirmative action is perceived as an attempt by racial and ethnic minorities to shortcut the pathway to social opportunity. For those who get frustrated, affirmative action is regarded as a *minority plan* to deprive White society of social opportunity. Affirmative action is thus perceived by many White people as benefiting minorities only and as resulting from the victimization of White society. But can White society receive benefits from affirmative action?

In the following selection from "Academic Storytelling: A Critical Race Theory Story of Affirmative Action," *Sociological Perspectives* (Summer 2000), sociologist Adalberto Aguirre, Jr., of the University of California, Riverside, examines affirmative action programs for recruiting minority faculty in academia. Writing in a critical race theory framework, the author constructs a narrative to illustrate the implementation of affirmative action programs for minority faculty. Aguirre argues that the manner in which affirmative action programs are implemented can result in unintended benefits for the (White) majority. As a result, affirmative action programs become exclusionary institutional processes for minority faculty. By telling affirmative action stories about academia, Aguirre also argues, one can observe the institutional climate for racial and ethnic minority faculty.

Key Concept: affirmative action in higher education, critical race theory, and academic storytelling

Abstract: The minority (nonwhite) can tell stories about institutional practices in academia that result in unintended benefits for the majority (white). One institutional practice in academia is affirmative action. This article presents a story about a minority applicant for a sociology position and his referral to an affirmative action program for recruiting minority faculty. One reason for telling the story is to illustrate how an affirmative action program can be implemented in a manner that marginalizes minority persons in the faculty recruitment process and results in benefits for majority persons. Another reason for telling the story is to sound an alarm for majority and minority faculty who support affirmative action programs that the programs can fall short of their goals if their implementation is simply treated as a bureaucratic activity in academia.

This is a story about how affirmative action is practiced in academia. The story can be considered a *counterstory,* because it challenges the (white) majority's story, or stock story, about affirmative action in academia. The stock story justifies the world as it is by "perpetuating the distribution of rights, privileges, and opportunity established under a regime of uncontested white supremacy" (Crenshaw et al. 1995:xxix). Not surprisingly, the stock story disguises affirmative action as a vehicle for legitimating the majority's social reality (Delgado 1993). Delgado (1989) provides an example of how the majority tells the stock story in academia. This example focuses on a black lawyer who interviews for a teaching position at a major law school. Despite the law school's stated commitment to affirmative action and the recruitment of a minority law professor, the black lawyer is rejected. Had he been hired he would have become the first minority law professor at the school. In reaching the decision to reject him, the faculty felt that his interest in civil rights law was not compatible with their interests. They decided to wait another few years until the "crop of black and minority law students graduates and gets some experience" (Delgado 1989:2420) but felt that the black lawyer could be considered for a visiting teaching position while they continued their search.

Delgado argues that his example shows how the majority tells the stock story about affirmative action in academia. First, the stock story "emphasizes the school's benevolent motivation ('look how hard we're trying') and good faith" (Delgado 1989:2421). The law school faculty did appear to give the black lawyer a "serious" look, perhaps even more serious than they would a similarly qualified white lawyer.[1] Second, the stock story lessens the possibility that the black lawyer's "presence on the faculty might have altered the institutions' character, helped introduce a different prism and different criteria for selecting future candidates" (Delgado 1989:2421). The law school faculty would rather continue to promote the belief that there are very few black lawyers available than assume responsibility for hiring one and altering the complexion of the faculty.[2] Third, the stock story is neutral; "it avoids issues of blame or responsibility" (Delgado 1989:2422). You cannot blame the law school for not trying to hire a minority person. In the end, the stock story justifies the majority's view—"there are very few black lawyers out there so let's not rush into something, let's wait a while longer." The *wait* is an excuse for not doing anything.[3]

WHY TELL THE STORY?

My story is nested in my experiences during the past twenty-two years as a Chicano professor of sociology in institutional settings dominated by the majority. During my tenure as a faculty member in academia, I have served on numerous committees, especially *the* affirmative action committee, and participated in activities that have focused on faculty recruitment. As a result, I have had the opportunity to listen to majority faculty stories of minority faculty *recruitment* and their stories of *attracting* majority faculty. I suspect that the stories are told by the majority to justify their competing outcomes. The story in this article is gleaned from my participation in those committees and activities. It is representative of what Richardson (1997:32) calls a *collective story:* "The collective story displays an individual's story by narrating the experiences of the social category to which the individual belongs, rather than by telling the particular individual's story or simply retelling the cultural story." My story is about real experience, an experience that is as real as my social reality. It is an experience that is representative of the practices, rules, and customs that minority persons like myself encounter inside and outside of academia (Austin 1995; Essed 1992; Feagin 1991). I tell my story to bring to light an alternative interpretation of institutional practices in academia that support the majority's stock story.[4]

I assume the role of *sociologist as narrator* in my story. Implicit in this role is the premise that sociological work consists of stories. Stories are social events that instruct us about social processes, social structures, and social situations (Maines and Bridger 1992). Stories also "comprise a series of remembered events in the field in which the author was usually a participant" (Van Maanen 1988:102). As a result, sociologists as narrators are "storytellers in producing accounts of social life" (Ewick and Silbey 1995:203). My story is, thus, a social event because it gives meaning to an experience nested in a complex arrangement of social relations that is known as *academia.*

In the role of sociologist as narrator I have also decided what kind of story to tell (Maines 1993). I have decided to tell a story of how an organizational process, affirmative action, is implemented in academia to reflect the unequal power relations between the majority and the minority. I use the terms *minority* (nonwhite) and *majority* (white) to reinforce the perception that the difference in social relations experienced by white and nonwhite faculty in academia is rooted in structure.[6] That is, the difference in social relations is not simply the outcome of racial or ethnic differences, it is an outcome of social position in the organizational structure of academia (Aguirre, Martinez, and Hernandez 1993). In particular, my story becomes a *critical tale* because it attempts to make "it clear who... owns and operates the tools of reality production" in academia

(Van Maanen 1988:128). As a result, I have taken a side in my story. It is very difficult not to take a side. Unfortunately, it is often "whose side" the storyteller takes that determines if the story is legitimate (Baron 1998; Morris, Woodward, and Peters 1998). Taking the minority's side has often resulted in the storyteller being accused of bias. According to Becker (1967:243), "We accuse ourselves of bias only when we take the side of the subordinate.... [W]e join responsible officials and the man in the street in an unthinking acceptance of the hierarchy of credibility. We assume with them that the man at the top knows best. We do not realize that there are sides to be taken and that we are taking one of them." As a story about the minority, my story can be heard and given the credibility associated with the majority's stories.[7]

CRITICAL RACE THEORY AND TELLING STORIES

The story in this article is grounded in critical race theory (CRT) (for a comprehensive review, see Crenshaw et al. 1995; Delgado 1995; Delgado and Stefancic 1993, 1994, 1997; Ladson-Billings and Tate 1995; Matsuda et al. 1993; Russell 1999; Valdes 1997). CRT became noticeable in the mid-1970s when scholars of color realized that the civil rights movement of the 1960s had stalled and that there was a need for alternative and critical explanations for the continuing presence of racism in American society. According to Crenshaw et al. (1995:xiii), "Critical Race Theory embraces a movement of left scholars, most of them scholars of color, situated in law schools, whose work challenges the ways in which race and racial power are constructed and represented in American legal culture and, more generally, in American society as a whole." While rooted in legal scholarship, CRT also examines topics of sociological interest such as the social construction of race (Haney-Lopez 1994; Scales-Trent 1990), the discriminating effects of immigration law on social identity (Fan 1997; Olivas 1995), and the intersectionality of gender and race (Caldwell 1991; Hernandez-Truyol 1997).

The most distinguishing feature of CRT writings is the use of stories or first-person accounts. According to Bell (1995a:899), critical race theory writings are "characterized by frequent use of the first person, storytelling, narrative, allegory, interdisciplinary treatment of law, and the unapologetic use of creativity." Critical race theorists use storytelling as a methodological tool for giving *voice* to marginalized persons and their communities. They tell stories that challenge the majority's stories in which it constructs for itself "a form of shared reality in which its own superior position is seen as natural" (Delgado 1989:2412). As a result, critical race theorists focus on giving *voice* to marginalized persons and communities because they are suppressed in the majority's stories.

According to Litowitz (1997:520), the majority of CRT stories are "drawn from the experiences of minority law professors, detailing not only negative experiences such as name calling and ostracism, but also positive aspects of their heritage, such as racial solidarity, the importance of tradition and honor, and the struggle against oppression." CRT stories are written by minority persons to humanize their experiences in their own eyes and in the eyes of the majority (Delgado 1989). They can "stir our imaginations, and let us begin to see life through the eyes of the outsider," and they can bring to "light the abuses and petty and major tyrannies that minority communities suffer... that might otherwise remain invisible" (Delgado 1990:109). They can cleanse the minority's soul and allow the majority to examine its practices that marginalize the minority (Brown 1995; Delgado 1995). CRT stories thus offer both the minority and the majority the opportunity to "enrich their own reality" and acquire the "ability to see the world through other's eyes" (Delgado 1989:2439).

CRT stories are not simple anecdotal accounts. They organize the minority's "experiences into temporally meaningful episodes" (Richardson 1990:118). For the sociologist, CRT stories are significant social events because they transform the minority into a self-narrating organism that exhibits spatial and temporal features; it has a past, present, and future. Further, CRT stories instruct sociologists about the minority's social reality, especially such issues as oppression and victimization, that is often ignored in traditional sociological research. Last, CRT stories introduce competing interpretations into sociological practice. In short, they are instructive. For example, they can instruct sociologists on how federal Indian laws have been implemented by the majority to subordinate Indians (Williams 1989, 1990); on how federal immigration laws deprive Latinos in the United States of fundamental social and political rights (Murray 1998; Olivas 1990); and on how the political state, when offered the opportunity, deprives black persons of their personal freedom (see "The Space Traders" narrative in Bell 1992:158–94; see also Delgado and Stefancic 1991). In sociology, CRT stories are a communicative form for the minority that frees it from silence by giving it voice.

A caveat about storytelling in sociology: In a discipline that often defines its relationship to persons, objects, and events as empirical statements about social phenomena, storytelling may be suspect. Storytelling, or narrative, however, has been present in sociological research—from case histories and personal interviews to content analysis (Maines 1993). Storytelling can even be found in unexpected corners of sociological research, such as empirical studies that examine narrative events as underlying structures for social and historical contexts of social action (see Gotham and Staples 1996; Griffin 1993; Kiser 1996; Somers 1992). Storytelling is also used as a primary means of gathering and interpreting data in ethnographic work (Van Maanen 1988), as a research strategy in social science research (Ewick and Silbey 1995), and as an interpretive tool for defining sociological concepts, such as *identity* and *community* (Maines and Bridger 1992; Somers 1994, 1995). Richardson (1990), however, suggests that storytelling, or narrative, has been suppressed in sociological research by a *scientific frame* that dominates sociological thinking. Supporters of the scientific frame argue that storytelling is illegitimate scholarship because it "violates reason's mandates in two ways: first, it substitutes passion for reason and emotion for logic; and second, in its celebration of partiality and 'voice,' it substitutes perspective for truth" (Hayman 1998:10).

A CONTENTIOUS TOPIC

The story in this article focuses on affirmative action. Very few topics are as pregnant with controversy.[8] The majority's storytelling about affirmative action focuses on issues of *preferential treatment* and *reverse discrimination*—on "who benefits and who doesn't." According to Wellman (1997:322), the stories majority males tell about affirmative action "articulate the experience and sentiment of white men in both senses of the word: they link and express their aggrieved sentiments. That is why so many men tell the same story about the job they lost to an 'unqualified' woman or person of color. That is how 'all things being equal' came to mean 'reverse discrimination.'" Members of the majority usually ask questions regarding the appropriateness of using a remedy that seeks to alter the unequal distribution of social opportunity in a society that is heavily weighted in their favor.[9] In the eyes of the majority, access to social opportunity is earned on merit; those with "more" access to opportunity have earned it and those with "less" have not. The attempt to alter the distribution of social opportunity through affirmative action results in the majority's observation that the minority seeks to gain opportunity at their expense (Brest and Oshige 1995; Saphir 1996; Wilkins and Gulati 1996). The majority's story reaches the conclusion that society "would have a meritocracy were it not for affirmative action" (Wasserstrom 1977:619).

In its stories about affirmative action, or about related strategies that seek to redress the inequalities experienced by the minority, the majority portrays itself as *innocent victim.* The majority asks in its stores, Are we not innocent victims of affirmative action? Because of the power of the majority's stories, "most of the successful constitutional discrimination cases in the last decade or so have been won by white male plaintiffs" (Kairys 1992:42). To illustrate the power of the majority's story over the minority's story, Hayman and Levit (1996) review three decisions that favored the majority from the 1994–95 term of the United States Supreme Court: Missouri v. Jenkins, 115 S. Ct. 2038 (1995); Adarand Constructors, Inc. v. Peña, 115 S. Ct. 2097 (1995); and Miller v. Johnson, 115 S. Ct. 2475 (1995).

In *Jenkins,* the majority argued that a desegregation initiative to reduce racial inequality between white and black students in the Kansas City, Missouri, School District would result in making black students "feel" superior to white students. The majority argued that desegregation efforts, coupled with affirmative action initiatives, would victimize white students. According to Justice Thomas, "Making blacks feel superior to whites sent to lesser schools—would violate the Fourteenth Amendment, whether or not the white students felt stigmatized, just as do school systems in which the positions of the races are reversed" (quoted in Hayman and Levit 1996:387). In short, the stigmatization of white students outweighed reducing inequality for black students. After all, racial stigmatization is "new" for white students but not for black students. So why should one expect white students to become victims of racial stigmatization?

In *Peña,* the majority argued that a federal affirmative action law designed to increase the participation of minorities in federal contracting created a system of paternalism in which minorities expected to be given preferential treatment. The majority argued that the law was premised on an invalid assumption that minority contractors are disadvantaged in a manner that white contractors are not. The majority's story argued that using "minority status" to overcome disadvantages in federal contracting resulted in a system of "intentional discrimination" against the majority. That is, the majority depicted itself as victim. Interestingly, after "centuries of discrimination against 'individuals' because of their 'race,' it seemed almost absurd to insist that 'individuals' were not entitled to redress because of their 'race' " (Hayman and Levit 1996:392). The Supreme Court thus supported the majority's argument that while minority status (race) could be the target of discriminatory actions that result in disadvantage, it could not be used to seek redress for its disadvantages if such redress victimized the majority. (Ironically, it was estimated that Adarand received more than 90 percent of state roadway construction money in Colorado, while Peña's bid would have amounted to less than 5 percent of that money.)

In *Johnson,* the federal government required the state of Georgia to create three congressional districts, each with a majority of black persons, before approving its congressional redistricting plan. White voters in one of the majority black districts, the 11th district, sued "perhaps because they did not like being in the minority" (Hayman and Levit 1996:393). The majority's story in this case argued that using "race" to create political communities violated the democratic ideal of racial neutrality in governmental decision making. It stressed that "race" could not be a factor in redistricting because political decisions are made in race-neutral contexts. White persons thus became "victims" when "race" was used to redress political inequalities that diluted minority access to a voting process designed to be race-neutral. Perhaps what is buried in the subtext of the majority's story is the majority's awareness that creating voting districts with a majority of black voters would expose the dependence of its privileged position on a political process that deprived black voters of their rights.

The majority's story in the three decisions is also interesting for what it does not tell. In *Jenkins,* the majority's story does not tell about the historical and social outcomes for black students of racial inequality in schools. It does not tell how disparities in educational funding and quality of school facilities result in black students' unequal access to the opportunity structure in U.S. society. In *Peña,* the majority's story fails to tell about uneven playing fields encountered by minority contractors, uneven playing fields that have historically favored the majority. It does not tell how racism and discrimination in trade associations harms minority contractors but benefits the majority. In *Johnson,* the majority's story does not tell how redistricting has been used historically by the majority to disenfranchise the minority in the political process. It does not tell that its use of redistricting to silence minority voters is a signal that the political process is not race-neutral.

The minority is thus portrayed as the oppressor and the majority as the oppressed in the majority's stories. The majority's storytelling about affirmative action does not tell that for more than two hundred years the majority has "benefited from their own program of affirmative action, through unjustified preferences in jobs and education resulting from old-boy networks and official laws that lessened the competition" (Delgado 1991:1225). I believe that a central purpose of the majority's storytelling about affirmative action is to manufacture the perception that its benefits and privileges are under attack from the minority. According to Quindlen (1992:A21), "The worried young white men I've met on college campuses... have internalized the newest myth of American race relations, and it has made them bitter. It is called affirmative action, a.k.a. the systematic oppression of white men." The majority's stories about affirmative action argue that it is under attack because affirmative action uses "racial discrimination as an ever-ready excuse for demanding preferences while disdaining performance" (Bell 1997a:1454). The majority portrays affirmative action as a vehicle that benefits the minority at the majority's expense. Thus the majority portrays itself as *innocent victim* of reverse discrimination in its stories of affirmative action.

AN AFFIRMATIVE ACTION STORY

Setting: A professor and a student are talking in the professor's office. The professor and the student are both white. Stephen Narrows is a tenured full professor and chair of the sociology department. The student, Beverly Owens, is a fourth-year prelaw honors student and editor of the campus student newspaper. The student is interviewing Professor Narrows about minority faculty recruitment in his department.

Beverly Owens (BO): Professor Narrows, your department just completed a search for a senior faculty position in the areas of race/ethnic relations and social inequality. How many minorities were in the applicant pool?

Stephen Narrows (SN): I believe there were three minorities in the applicant pool. A Latino, an African-American male, and an Asian-American female.[10]

BO: How large was the applicant pool?

SN: There were sixty-seven applicants in the pool.

BO: How many of the minority applicants made it to the short list?

SN: From the initial applicant pool of sixty-seven, a short list of five applicants was derived. The Latino applicant made it to the short list.

BO: Who were the other applicants on the short list?

SN: Three white males and a white female.

BO: Did the Latino applicant meet the requirements for the position?

SN: Yes. He was a senior faculty member at an Ivy League school, and he had an impressive publication and research record and excellent teaching evaluations. The recruitment committee was quite pleased when it received his application. The department has been trying to recruit a qualified minority faculty member for quite a while. He appeared to be an excellent choice for this department. Given the lack of minority faculty, the department was really overjoyed with his application.

BO: I understand he would have been the first minority faculty member in your department.

SN: Yes, and it was quite a disappointment when we lost him.

BO: How exactly did you lose him? Did he remove his application from consideration? Did he go to another institution?

SN: It's a rather complicated story. The university has a DOT, Diversity Opportunity Targets, program for recruiting minority faculty.

BO: I'm not familiar with the DOT program. What does it do?

SN: The DOT program is an affirmative action initiative developed by the university to increase the representation of minority faculty on campus. The campus administration has set aside a certain number of faculty positions solely for the DOT program. Departments identify potential candidates for the program from the applicants that respond to a job announcement. The DOT candidate's name is forwarded to the campus administration for their review. The campus administration reviews the candidate's qualifications, along with the department's needs, and makes a decision whether to provide the department with a faculty position for the minority candidate or decline to consider the candidate for a DOT appointment.

BO: So, how did you lose the Latino applicant? I believe his name is Dr. Adrian Dia.

SN: The department felt that Dr. Dia was an excellent candidate for the DOT program and forwarded his name to the campus administration. After about six weeks the department was notified by the campus administration that all of the DOT appointments had been made. By then it was too late for the department to consider Dr. Dia for the faculty position in sociology.

BO: Why was it too late?

SN: By the time we were notified by the campus administration about its decision regarding Dr. Dia, the department had already made an offer to one of the other applicants, Dr. Tom Smith.

BO: Did the department consider suspending the recruitment process until the campus administration made a decision regarding Dr. Dia?

SN: Not really. You see we didn't want to lose any of the other applicants.

BO: Why didn't the department keep Dr. Dia's application active while the campus administration reviewed his file?

SN: Because the department felt that it would be unfair to the other applicants. You see, Dr. Dia would have had two chances for a faculty position, the DOT program and ours, whereas the other applicants would have had only one chance. The department felt that the other applicants could accuse it of reverse discrimination.

BO: But wasn't it worth the risk to recruit Dr. Dia for a faculty appointment? After all, you did admit that minority faculty are hard to find, and that you've been trying to recruit one for a while now.

SN: I suppose it would have been worth the risk. However, the department was concerned with the issue of reverse discrimination.

BO: But couldn't Dr. Dia argue that he was the victim of discrimination by being removed from the applicant pool, especially since his name was on the short list?

SN: I suppose he could. However, in the department's view he was being considered for a faculty position in the DOT program. Remember the campus administration declined the DOT appointment for Dr. Dia. As a department we do not control the administration's decision-making process regarding the DOT program.

BO: So the department believes that it lost Dr. Dia because of the campus administration's decision?

SN: Yes.

BO: Is the department still interested in recruiting minority faculty?

SN: Most certainly. We will continue to use the recruitment process, especially the DOT program, to increase the representation of minorities on the faculty.

[The conversation comes to an end.]

WHAT DOES THE STORY TELL US?

What does the story tell us about affirmative action? First, affirmative action initiatives, such as the DOT program, can be implemented in a manner that results in unintended benefits for the majority.[11] By referring minority applicants to the DOT program, the university administration and the department increase the risk that minority applicants will be suppressed in the hiring process. According to Mickelson and Oliver (1991:161), this is not surprising if one considers that "greater numbers of minority faculty per se are not their [affirmative action programs'] direct goal." Accordingly, Delgado (1991:1224) observes that affirmative action protects the majority by limiting the number of minority persons that are "hired or promoted. Not too many, for that would be terrifying, nor too few, for that would be destabilizing." Similarly, Steele and Green (1976) have observed that an outcome of pursuing affirmative action goals in academia is a decreased effort to *actually* recruit minority faculty. In this sense, affirmative action *cools* minorities in the recruitment process while the majority pursues its own interests.

For example, Professor Narrows suggests that his department's options are limited when it comes to recruiting minority faculty. In his eyes, and the department's, there is really only one viable option, to refer the minority applicant to the DOT program. As an outcome of the referral, however, the minority applicant is removed from consideration for the position advertised by the sociology department. By referring Dr. Dia to the DOT program the sociology department shifts responsibility for recruiting minority faculty from itself onto the campus administration, a much larger bureaucratic structure that serves as a burying ground for institutional accountability: If you must blame someone, blame the administration. Moreover, the department increases the chances that he will be lost in a bureaucratic context designed to deal with campuswide needs and not necessarily departmental needs. The department may have believed that it was increasing its chances of recruiting Dr. Dia through the DOT program. However, the university administration may not have shared its interest in recruiting Dr. Dia. In particular, the sociology department may not have done an adequate job of communicating its interest in recruiting Dr. Dia to the campus administration.

The ability to shift responsibility for recruiting minority faculty between organizational units shields institutions of higher education from its critics, especially minority critics. How can one be critical of an institution for not recruiting minority faculty if the institution defends itself by showcasing its affirmative action plan for recruiting minority faculty? All too often affirmative action plans for recruiting minority faculty are touted for their "promise" in promoting institutional diversity. However, they are not evaluated for their ability to increase the number of minority faculty: "Affirmative action has made a marked difference in the initial stage of the search process, but unfortunately not in the results" (Mickelson and Oliver 1991:153). The institution's ability to shift its responsibility for recruiting minority faculty thus makes it difficult for critics to "blame" someone for not implementing an affirmative action plan that increases the number of minority faculty. In Dr. Dia's case, the sociology department made an adequate effort to recruit him. The university's DOT program also communicated an institutional commitment to recruiting minority faculty. So who does one blame for not recruiting Dr. Dia? Who does one blame for not implementing a DOT program that benefits minority applicants?

By referring Dr. Dia to the DOT program, the sociology department decreased his chances for a faculty appointment by excluding him from competing with the other four applicants on the short list. One must not ignore the fact that the other four applicants were white and that excluding Dr. Dia allowed four white persons to compete among themselves for the faculty position. The DOT program appears to have benefited the white applicants more than it did Dr. Dia, because his referral to the program reduced the competitive context for the white applicants. While the DOT program may not be intended to increase opportunity for members of the majority, its implementation may reflect academia's interest in protecting majority interests. That is, the DOT program is implemented by the administration to protect the majority from minority competition, thereby protecting an institutional culture and environment that promotes majority interests.[12]

Professor Narrows makes the observation that Dr. Dia's consideration for both the DOT program and a sociology position would be unfair to the other applicants on the short list. He implies that Dr. Dia is being considered for two faculty positions. The issue of "fairness" is often used by the majority to avoid drawing attention to the real issue involved—exclusion (Roithmayr 1997; Sturm and Guinier 1996). Professor Narrows raises the question of *reverse discrimination* in his observation.[13] Is reverse discrimination really an issue if one considers that the only applicants remaining for the sociology position are white? Can the issue of reverse discrimination serve as a device for the majority to avoid questions about an all-white applicant pool? Dr. Dia responded to a job announcement for a sociology position. He did not respond to an announcement requesting minority faculty to submit their credentials for review by the DOT program. While the DOT program is allocated faculty slots (FTE) by the administration for recruiting minority faculty, the DOT program is not an academic unit or department. The DOT program can operate only as a recruitment vehicle, and it is only effective if an FTE is available and an academic unit identifies a qualified minority person it wants to recruit. As a result, contrary to Professor Narrows's observation, Dr. Dia can be considered for one faculty position only, the one in sociology, because he cannot be appointed to the DOT program. Who then is the victim of reverse discrimination?

One also needs to consider that the sociology department did not ask Dr. Dia if he would like his application to be forwarded to the DOT program. Perhaps a reasonable approach would have been to inform Dr. Dia about the DOT program and to offer him the option. The sociology department, however, referred his application to the DOT program because it felt that he was an excellent candidate for the DOT program. Also, before referring his application, the sociology department could have asked the administration if there were any FTEs available in the DOT program. In a sense, Dr. Dia's minority status rendered him *powerless* in the recruitment process; the majority faculty in sociology made a decision for him based on the "paternalistic attitudes of the decision-makers" (Reyes and Halcon 1991:176–77). The majority reasoned that it "knew best" for Dr. Dia by referring him to the DOT program. However, assuming "what's best" for Dr. Dia resulted in an unintended benefit for the white applicants. The lack of consultation between the sociology department and Dr. Dia is, I believe, a reflection of an implicit institutional belief that favors the majority: the powerless position of minority persons constrains them in questioning institutional decisions made for them by the majority. After all, the sociology department appears to have done "its best" to recruit Dr. Dia.

For the sake of discussion, let us assume that the sociology department asked Dr. Dia if he wanted his application to be forwarded to the DOT program. If Dr. Dia refuses, does this mean that he will not be considered for the sociology position? If Dr. Dia agrees, does this mean that the DOT program is his only opportunity for being considered for a sociology position? Regardless of whether he agrees or refuses, Dr. Dia is involved in a "nonchoice" situation. That is, either response decreases his chances for a sociology position. For example, by refusing to have his application forwarded to the DOT program, Dr. Dia's application may no longer look "attractive" to the sociology department. In particular, Dr. Dia's application looks less attractive if one considers that the sociology department views his application as a vehicle for obtaining an "extra" faculty position for the department. That is, the sociology department perceives itself as having access to two faculty positions, the FTE available from the DOT program and the one it advertised. Dr. Dia's application is thus a benefit rather than a liability for the sociology department.

In contrast, by agreeing to have his application forwarded to the DOT program, Dr. Dia is removed from consideration for the position advertised by the sociology department because his opportunity for a sociology position depends on the availability of an FTE in the DOT program. Thus, Dr. Dia does not have a *choice* he controls. Where then is the "preferential" issue that could lead to charges of reverse discrimination? What "choice" does Dr. Dia control that gives him "preference" over the white applicants on the short list? Dr. Dia's condition of powerlessness has robbed him of choice and the ability to control his own fate. How then can he control the fate of others, especially the fate of those who can charge him with "reverse discrimination"?

Finally, the recruitment event described in the story suggests that affirmative action can be a device for the application of exclusionary practices in academia. Majority faculty often lament that minority faculty are so hard to find. Olivas (1988) refers to their lament as a "high-demand/low-supply" myth promoted by majority faculty to camouflage their lack of responsibility for recruiting minority faculty. However, one does not hear, Now that we've found a minority faculty person, let's hire them. In contrast, majority faculty, especially males, are often found without anyone looking for them—Professor Tom Smith has expressed interest in joining the department, let's ask the dean for an FTE for him. The recruitment of majority academics by other majority academics for, in most cases, faculty positions that are created for them is attributed to networking in academia, never referred to as affirmative action. Or, borrowing from Scheff (1995), similar to membership in a gang, majority faculty recruit each other for positions they create for themselves in order to maintain their territorial control in academia. In many ways, majority persons have always had a DOT program in academia that serves their interests (Bell 1995b; Delgado 1991; Lamb 1993; Wilson 1995).

An emphasis on recruiting minority faculty requires that academia alter its practices for including minority faculty in its environment. It requires that academia use affirmative action initiatives, such as the DOT program, to enhance the inclusion of minority faculty rather than their exclusion from faculty recruitment practices (Montero-Sieburth 1996; Verdugo 1995). Despite the implementation of affirmative action programs to recruit minority faculty, especially during the past two decades, minority faculty are rarely found in academia (Aguirre 1995a; Cortese 1992; Johnson 1997; Rai and Critzer 2000). For example, between 1980 and 1993 the representation of white persons in the U.S. professorate increased from 87 to 88 percent. In contrast, the representation of black persons and Latino persons in the professorate remained unchanged at 5 percent and 2 percent, respectively, between 1980 and 1993 (National Center for Education Statistics 1986, 1997). Accordingly, a survey of the thirty-four top-ranked sociology departments in the United States documents the relative absence of minority faculty: "Fewer than 15% of the departments have more than one full-time, tenure track African American faculty member and more than one full-time, tenure track Latino faculty member" (Bonilla-Silva and Herring 1999:7). It would appear that the inclusion of minority faculty in the professorate remains an elusive goal.

CONCLUDING REMARKS

Is the story just another story? I suspect that most majority academics, and perhaps even some minority academics, will regard my story as just another story, an imaginative one but certainly not real. That may happen in the outside world, but not in academia, the majority academic might say. I believe that majority academics prefer to ignore the story, because not to do so requires that they examine themselves and their control of academia. It especially requires majority faculty to consider their role in promoting unequal power relations for the minority in academia. The story in this article argues that affirmative action can be implemented in a manner that results in unintended benefits for the majority. Affirmative action programs, such as the DOT program, are usually not the problem; rather, it is their implementation that often turns a technical issue into a moral argument. Their implementation becomes even more problematic if one considers that the institutional environment in academia is designed to enhance the majority's presence, not the minority's pursuit of opportunity.

The affirmative action program described in the story is representative of affirmative action initiatives in academia that are designed to increase the representation of minorities in the professorate (Johnson et al. 1998; Justus 1987; Moore 1996; Moore 1997; Morgan 1996; Myers and Wilkins 1995; Solorzano 1993; Young 1984). These initiatives have been around since the late 1960s, and they have been funded in a variety of ways, from private foundations to challenge grants from corporate sponsors. However, the emergence of broad-based conservative political interests during the 1980s in U.S. society, especially the structuring of conservative political interest in the Supreme Court, seriously constrained the use of affirmative action initiatives (Gamson and Modigliani 1987; Pratt 1999; Sidanius, Pratto, and Bobo 1996). Affirmative action initiatives in academia may have become more susceptible to attack because they appear to have increased the *representativeness* of minority students and minority faculty in academia (Aguirre 1995b; Bowen and Bok 1998; Gose 1998). However, the initiatives have fallen short of reducing the obstacles faced by minorities in academia. For example, minority faculty encounter obstacles rooted in prejudice and discrimination in their pursuit of professional goals, such as tenure and promotion (Aguirre 1981, forthcoming; Kulis, Chong, and Shaw 1999). Also, minority faculty are often expected to alter their professional goals in an institutional environment defined by the professional goals of majority faculty (Aguirre, Martinez, and Hernandez 1993; Bonilla-Silva and Herring 1999). While affirmative action has opened the door to academia for minorities, it has not extended very far beyond the doorway to help them navigate their way in an institutional environmental that is often not receptive to their presence (Johnson 1997).

The story presented here argues that affirmative action can be implemented so as not to benefit the minority. It must be understood that while affirmative action programs, such as the DOT, target minorities, they do so not to discriminate against the majority but to combat the discrimination experienced by the minority. Proposition 209, for example, was voted into law in California because it depicted affirmative action as a threat to the majority's access to opportunity in the state (Bell 1997b). The debate over Proposition 209 questioned the need for affirmative action in academia; its passage increased the chances that minorities would be turned away by academia (Karabel 1997; Tierney 1996). Ironically, one of the outcomes of the passage of Proposition 209 was a decrease in the numbers of minority students applying for admission and the recruitment of minority faculty in institutions of higher education in California (Schneider 1998). Is the decrease in numbers of minority students and minority faculty a signal that affirmative action programs were improving access for minorities? Or are the decreasing numbers a response from an institutional environment that has become less receptive to the minority's presence? I prefer to believe that affirmative action was working to increase the *representativeness* of minorities in academia.

It is because I prefer to believe that affirmative action is necessary for academia to become an inclusive and multicultural institution that I tell the story in this article.[14] But while we may dream about how affirmative action can shape academia into an inclusive and multicultural institution, we should not be deluded about how affirmative action is implemented. A social fact about academia is that it is controlled by the majority; its numerical representation alone convinces the casual observer that it is the dominant group. Another social fact about academia is that most of its activity is designed to promote the majority's interests; even affirmative action was created by the majority (Law 1999). Not surprisingly, the majority practices affirmative action by itself and on itself in academia. In a few cases, the minority derives some benefit from these practices.

My story urges majority and minority faculty members who support affirmative action to examine the implementation of affirmative action programs. One must not lose sight of the fact that affirmative action in academia is implemented in an institutional environment that often has difficulty responding to minority concerns. Affirmative action must be used by majority faculty as a device for pursuing the inclusion of minorities in academia. Perhaps one way in which majority faculty can examine the implementation of affirmative action is by asking themselves if they receive any unintended benefits from the manner in which academia practices affirmative action.

Finally, some stories are difficult to tell, especially if they address uncomfortable topics. The story here is one of those. The storyteller may be accused of addressing a topic, affirmative action, regarded by the majority as benefiting only the minority. Majority persons may ask, Why is he biting the hand that feeds him? As the storyteller, I am aware of the benefits and obstacles that affirmative action places in the path of an academic career. However, after so many years in academia, listening to conversations between majority faculty in mailrooms or in faculty meetings in which I am often invisible to them, I have come to realize that they have their own faculty recruitment system that only benefits their presence in academia. I regard their system as *affirmative action.* It would appear then that both majority and minority faculty benefit from affirmative action in academia. The question is, Who benefits more from affirmative action in academia? That is another story in need of telling.

NOTES

1. The majority in academia often argue that increases in the number of minority law teachers are an outcome of hiring policies (e.g., affirmative action) that favor unqualified minority candidates (Carrington 1992; Collier 1995). In one case, a white male law professor sued the law school because a minority law professor was hired at a higher salary, thus raising the argument that the minority law professor did not *deserve* what he was being paid (Markoff 1990).
2. One of the challenges faced by minority law professors is that white law professors consider their teaching methods and curriculum suggestions as inappropriate

to academic work. As a result, minority law professors are marginalized by white law professors in institutional discussions of curriculum development and teaching approaches (Harris 1992; Jordan 1990–91; Kupenda 1997; Robinson 1997).

3. For a discussion of how stock stories are used to explain the absence of minorities in the legal profession, see Johnson 1997; Otero and Zuniga 1992; Wilkins and Gulati 1996. Also, consider that the lack of minority law professors decreases the chances that minority lawyers will be available to pursue careers in private law firms (Pearce, Hickey, and Burke 1998).

4. Stories or narrative accounts of how the majority regulates the minority's life in academia can be found in the following: Altbach and Lomotey 1991; Bell 1994; Padilla and Chavez 1995; Padilla and Montiel 1998; Turner and Myers 2000; Valverde and Castenell 1998.

5. Patterson and Monroe (1998:315) note that a story also refers to "the ways in which we construct disparate facts in our own worlds and weave them together cognitively in order to make sense of our reality."

6. Social structure is the outcome of social action, where social action is behavior that is bounded by beliefs and perceptions that justify the ranking of persons in society. The difference in social relations between the *majority* and the *minority* is thus fabricated as a mind-set in society that legitimates social structure as *always having been that way* —the *minority* is subordinate and the *majority* is dominant. For a discussion of how race is presented as biological in order to create it as a socially significant dimension in the explanation of social inequality, see Delgado 1998; Haney-Lopez 1998; Hayman 1998; Powell 1997; Ross 1998.

7. Minority stories often go unheard by white academics because they do not consider them reasonable scholarship; that is, they do not reflect the "pattern of scholarship that majority scholars have undertaken" (Culp 1992:1022).

8. A recent NBC News and Wall Street Journal poll found that a majority (53%) of adults in the U.S. population still favor the elimination of affirmative action programs. The opinion survey was conducted by Roper (June 16–19, 1999).

9. The majority's storytelling hides the fact that the distribution of social opportunity is in its favor because it has excluded the minority from the manufacture of American cultural and social ideology (Vargas 1998). The majority's storytelling was implemented in the Constitution, for example, by excluding persons who were not white, male, and landowners (Finkelman 1999).

10. The observation may be made that this is an unusually small number of minority applicants for a position in the areas of race/ethnic relations and social inequality. First, such an observation implies that most minority academics are to be found in those areas. Thus one would expect them to *appear* when a position in those areas is advertised. Second, such an observation implies that the universe of minority academics is large, with the embedded implication that the number of minority doctorates has been increasing over time. The number of minority doctorates, however, has been decreasing, especially in the African-American population (Aguirre forthcoming; Ehrenberg 1992). In addition, minority Ph.D. recipients are found disproportionately in the field of education, not in the social sciences.

11. Bell (1980, 1981) has developed interest convergence theory to argue that the majority tolerates social justice (i.e., affirmative action) for the minority when it is in the majority's interest to do so. According to interest convergence theory, the majority supports affirmative action because it promotes its own interests by minimizing the minority's interests. For example, the majority uses affirmative action as a means for

constraining the minority's ability to compete with it over valued resources, such as faculty positions.

12. For a discussion of how majority academics use words such as *merit* to shield themselves from competition with minority academics, see Alvarez 1973; Cuadraz 1997; Duster 1976; Niemann 1999.
13. Implicit in raising the issue of reverse discrimination is the argument that the majority suffers because the minority is given preferential treatment in academia. However, the research literature shows that the majority, especially males, have not been disadvantaged by affirmative action in academia (Merritt and Reskin 1997; Misra, Kennelly, and Karides 1999).
14. Affirmative action is a vehicle for making academia *diverse* (i.e., beliefs, perceptions, etc.) for both students and faculty. According to a survey of student attitudes toward diversity in two law schools, at Harvard University and the University of Michigan, students feel that *diversity* plays an important part in shaping positive learning experiences (Orfield and Whitla 1999).

REFERENCES

Aguirre, Adalberto, Jr. 1981. "Chicano Faculty in Postsecondary Educational Institutions: Some Thoughts on Faculty Development." *California Journal of Teacher Education* 8: 11–19.

———. 1995a. "A Chicano Farmworker in Academe." Pp. 17–27 in *The Leaning Ivory Tower: Latino Professors in American Universities,* edited by R. Padilla and R. Chavez. Albany: State University of New York Press.

———. 1995b. "The Status of Minority Faculty in Academe." *Equity & Excellence in Education* 28:63–68.

———. Forthcoming. *Women and Minority Faculty in the Academic Workplace.* Washington, DC: ERIC Clearinghouse on Higher Education.

Aguirre, Adalberto, Jr., Ruben Martinez, and Anthony Hernandez, 1993. "Majority and Minority Faculty Perceptions in Academe." *Research in Higher Education* 34:371–85.

Altbach, Philip, and Kofi Lomotey, eds. 1991. *The Racial Crisis in American Higher Education.* Albany: State University of New York Press.

Alvarez, Rodolfo, 1973. "Comment." *American Sociologist* 8:124–26.

Austin, Arthur. 1995. "Evaluating Storytelling as a Type of Nontraditional Scholarship." *Nebraska Law Review* 74:479–528.

Baron, Jane. 1998. "Storytelling and Legal Legitimacy." *College Literature* 25:63–77.

Becker, Howard. 1967. "Whose Side Are We On?" *Social Problems* 14:240–47.

Bell, Derrick. 1980. "Brown v. Board of Education and the Interest-Convergence Dilemma." *Harvard Law Review* 93:518–33.

———. 1981. *Race, Racism, and American Law.* Boston: Little, Brown.

———. 1992. *Faces at the Bottom of the Well: The Permanence of Racism.* New York: BasicBooks.

———. 1994. *Confronting Authority: Reflections of an Ardent Protester.* Boston: Beacon Press.

———. 1995a. "Property Rights in Whiteness—Their Legal Legacy, Their Economic Costs," Pp. 75–83 in *Critical Race Theory: The Cutting Edge,* edited by R. Delgado. Philadelphia: Temple University Press.

———. 1995b. "Who's Afraid of Critical Race Theory?" *University of Illinois Law Review* (1955):893–910.

———. 1996. *Gospel Choirs: Psalms of Survival for an Alien Land Called Home.* New York: BasicBooks.

———. 1997a. "California's Proposition 209:A Temporary Diversion on the Road to Racial Disaster." *Loyola of Los Angeles Law Review* 30:1447–64.

———. 1997b. "Protecting Diversity Programs from Political and Judicial Attack." *Chronicle of Higher Education,* April 4, pp. B4–B5.

Bonilla-Silva, Eduardo, and Cedric Herring. 1999. "We'd Love to Have Them, But . . . The Underrepresentation of Sociologists of Color and Its Implications." *ASA Footnotes* (March):6–7.

Bowen, William, and Derek Bok. 1998. *The Shape of the River: Long-Term Consequences of Considering Race in College and University Admissions.* Princeton: Princeton University Press.

Brest, Paul, and Miranda Oshige. 1995. "Affirmative Action for Whom?" *Stanford Law Review* 47:855–900.

Brown, Eleanor. 1995. "The Tower of Babel: Bridging the Divide between Critical Race Theory and 'Mainstream' Civil Rights Scholarship." *Yale Law Journal* 105:513–47.

Caldwell, Paulette. 1991. "A Hair Piece: Perspectives on the Intersection of Race and Gender." *Duke Law Journal* (1991):365–96.

Carrington, Paul. 1992. "Diversity!" *Utah Law Review* 1992:1105–1203.

Collier, Charles. 1995. "The New Logic of Affirmative Action." *Duke Law Journal* 45: 559–78.

Cortese, Anthony. 1992. "Affirmative Action: Are White Women Gaining at the Expense of Black Men?" *Equity & Excellence in Education* 25:77–99.

Crenshaw, Kimberle, Neil Gotanda, Gary Peller, and Kendall Thomas, eds. 1995. *Critical Race Theory: The Key Writings that Formed the Movement.* New York: New Press.

Cuadraz, Gloria. 1997. "The Chicana/o Generation and the Horatio Alger Myth." *Thought & Action* 13:103–20.

Culp, Jerome. 1992. "You Can Take Them to Water But You Can't Make Them Drink: Black Legal Scholarship and White Legal Scholars." *University of Illinois Law Review* (1992):1021–41.

Delgado, Richard. 1988. *Minority Law Professors' Lives: The Bell-Delgado Survey.* Madison: University of Wisconsin–Madison, Law School. Institute of Legal Studies.

———. 1989. "Storytelling for Oppositionists and Others: A Plea for Narrative." *Michigan Law Review* 87:2411–41.

———. 1990. "When a Story Is Just a Story: Does Voice Really Matter?" *Virginia Law Review* 76:95–111.

———. 1991. "Affirmative Action as a Majoritarian Device: Or, Do You Really Want to Be a Role Model?" *Michigan Law Review* 89:1222–31.

———. 1993. "On Telling Stories in School: A Reply to Farber and Sherry." *Vanderbilt Law Review* 46:665–76.

———, ed. 1995. *Critical Race Theory: The Cutting Edge.* Philadelphia: Temple University Press.

———. 1998. "Rodrigo's Book of Manners: How to Conduct a Conversation on Race-Standing, Imperial Scholarship, and Beyond." *Georgetown Law Journal* 86:1051–73.

Delgado, Richard, and Jean Stefancic. 1991. "Derrick Bell's Chronicle of the Space Traders: Would the U.S. Sacrifice People of Color if the Price Was Right?" *University of Colorado Law Review* 62:321–29.

———. 1993. "Critical Race Theory: An Annotated Bibliography." *Virginia Law Review* 79:461–516.

———. 1994. "Critical Race Theory: An Annotated Bibliography 1993, a Year of Transition." *University of Colorado Law Review* 66:159–93.

———, eds. 1997. *Critical White Studies: Looking Behind the Mirror.* Philadelphia: Temple University Press.

Duster, Troy. 1976. "The Structure of Privilege and Its Universe of Discourse." *American Sociologist* 11:73–78.

Ehrenberg, Ronald. 1992. "The Flow of New Doctorates." *Journal of Economic Literature* 30:830–75.

Essed, Philomena. 1992. "Alternative Knowledge Sources in Explanations of Racist Events." Pp. 199–224 in *Explaining One's Self to Others: Reason-giving in a Social Context,* edited by M. Cody and S. Read. Hillsdale, NJ: Lawrence Erlbaum.

Ewick, Patricia, and Susan Silbey. 1995. "Subversive Stories and Hegemonic Tales: Toward a Sociology of Narrative." *Law & Society Review* 29:197–226.

Fan, Stephen. 1997. "Immigration Law and the Promise of Critical Race Theory: Opening the Academy to the Voices of Aliens and Immigrants." *Columbia Law Review* 97:1202–40.

Feagin, Joe. 1991. "The Continuing Significance of Race: Anti-Black Discrimination in Public Places." *American Sociological Review* 56:101–16.

Finkelman, Paul. 1999. "Affirmative Action for the Master Class: The Creation of the Pro-slavery Constitution." *Akron Law Review* 32:423–70.

Gamson, William, and Andre Modigliani. 1987. "The Changing Culture of Affirmative Action." *Research in Political Sociology* 3: 137–77.

Gose, Ben. 1998. "A Sweeping New Defense of Affirmative Action." *Chronicle of Higher Education,* September 18, pp. A46–A48.

Gotham, Kevin, and William Staples. 1996. "Narrative Analysis and the New Historical Sociology." *Sociological Quarterly* 37:481–501.

Griffin, Larry. 1993. "Narrative Event-Structure Analysis, and Causal Interpretation in Historical Sociology." *American Journal of Sociology* 98:1094–1133.

Haney-Lopez, Ian. 1994. "The Social Construction of Race: Some Observations on Illusion, Fabrication, and Choice." *Harvard Civil Rights–Civil Liberties Law Review* 29:1–62.

———. 1998. "Race, Ethnicity, Erasure: The Salience of Race in LatCrit Theory." *La Raza Law Journal* 10:57–125.

Harris, Cheryl. 1992. "Law Professors of Color and the Academy: Of Poets and Kings." *Chicago-Kent Law Review* 68:331–52.

Hayman, Robert. 1998. "Race and Reason: The Assault on Critical Race Theory and the Truth about Inequality." *National Black Law Journal* 16:1–26.

Hayman, Robert, and Nancy Levit. 1996. "The Tales of White Folk: Doctrine, Narrative, and the Reconstruction of Racial Reality." *California Law Review* 84:377–440.

Hernandez-Truyol, Berta. 1997. "Borders (EN)Gendered: Normativities, Latinas, and a LatCrit Paradigm." *New York University Law Review* 72:882–927.

Johnson, Alex. 1997. "The Underrepresentation of Minorities in the Legal Profession: A Critical Theorist's Perspective." *Michigan Law Review* 95:1005–62.

Johnson, Jerry, Ravishankar Jaycdevappa, Lynne Taylor, Anthony Askew, Beverly Williams, and Bennett Johnson. 1998. "Extending the Pipeline for Minority Physicians: A Comprehensive Program for Minority Faculty Development." *Academic Medicine* 73:237–44.

Johnson, Willie. 1997. "Minority Faculty: Are We Welcome on Campus?" *Thought & Action* 13:113–24.

Jordan, Emma. 1990–91. "Images of Black Women in the Legal Academy: An Introduction." *Berkeley Women's Law Journal* 6:1–21.

Justus, Joyce. 1987. *The University of California in the Twenty-first Century: Successful Approaches to Faculty Diversity.* Oakland: University of California Office of the President.

Kairys, David. 1992. "Prejudicial Restraint: Race and the Supreme Court." *TIKKUN* 7: 37–43.

Karabel, Jerome. 1997. "Reclaiming the High Ground: Can Affirmative Action Survive?" *TIKKUN* 12 :29–31.

Kiser, Edgar. 1996. "The Revival of Narrative in Historical Sociology: What Rational Choice Theory Can Contribute." *Politics & Society* 24:249–71.

Kulis, Stephen, Y. Chong, and Heather Shaw. 1999. "Discriminatory Organizational Contexts and Black Scientists in Postsecondary Faculties." *Research in Higher Education* 40:115–48.

Kupenda, Angela. 1997. "Making Traditional Courses More Inclusive: Confessions of an African American Female Professor Who Attempted to Crash all the Barriers at Once." *University of San Francisco Law Review* 31:975–92.

Ladson-Billings, Gloria, and Williams Tate. 1995. "Toward a Critical Race Theory of Education." *Teachers College Record* 97:47–68.

Lamb, John. 1993. "The Real Affirmative Action Babies: Legacy Preferences at Harvard and Yale." *Columbia Journal of Law and Social Problems* 26:491–521.

Law, Sylvia. 1999. "White Privilege and Affirmative Action." *Akron Law Review* 32: 603–27.

Litowitz, Douglas. 1997. "Some Critical Thoughts on Critical Race Theory." *Notre Dame Law Review* 72:503–29.

Maines, David. 1993. "Narrative's Movement and Sociology's Phenomena: Toward a Narrative Sociology." *Sociological Quarterly* 34:17–38.

Maines, David, and Jeffrey, Bridger. 1992. "Narratives, Community and Land Use Decisions." *Social Science Journal* 29:363–80.

Markoff, Lisa. 1990. "Arizona Professor Sues, Saying White Males Face Discrimination." *National Law Journal* (April 30):4.

Matsuda, Mari. 1988. "Affirmative Action and Legal Knowledge: Planting Seeds in Plowed-Up Ground." *Harvard Women's Law Journal* 11:1–17.

Matsuda, Mari, Charles Lawrence, Richard Delgado, and Kimberle Crenshaw, eds. 1993. *Words That Wound: Critical Race Theory, Assaultive Speech, and the First Amendment.* San Francisco: Westview Press.

Merritt, Deborah, and Barbara Reskin. 1997. "Sex, Race, and Credentials: The Truth about Affirmative Action in Law Faculty." *Columbia Law Review* 97:199–300.

Mickelson, Roslyn, and Melvin Oliver. 1991. "Making the Short List: Black Candidates and the Faculty Recruitment Process." Pp. 149–66 in *The Racial Crisis in American Higher Education,* edited by P. Altbach and K. Lomotey. Albany: State University of New York Press.

Misra, Joya, Ivy Kennelly, and Marina Karides. 1999. "Employment Chances in the Academic Job Market in Sociology: Do Race and Gender Matter?" *Sociological Perspectives* 42:215–47.

Montero-Sieburth, Martha. 1996. "Beyond Affirmative Action: An Inquiry into the Experience of Latinas in Academia." *New England Journal of Public Policy* 11:65–97.

Moore, Ann. 1996. "Career Mentoring as a Career Development Strategy for African American Women in the Academy." *Thresholds in Education* 22:33–36.

Moore, Robert. 1997. "Promoting the Recruitment and Retention of Minority Dental Faculty: Federal, State, and Personal Programs." *Journal of Dental Education* 61:277–82.

Morgan, Joan. 1996. "Reaching Out to Young Black Men: A Dedicated and Determined Group of Scholars Offer the Lure of the Academy." *Black Issues in Higher Education* 13:16–19.

Morris, Karen, Diana Woodward, and Eleanor Peters. 1998. "Whose Side Are You On? Dilemmas in Conducting Feminist Ethnographic Research with Young Women." *International Journal of Social Research Methodology* 1: 217–30.

Murray, Yxta. 1998. "The Latino-American Crisis of Citizenship." *U.C. Davis Law Review* 31:503–89.

Myers, Samuel, and Roy Wilkins. 1995. *MHEC Minority Faculty Development Project: Final Report.* Minneapolis, MN: Midwestern Higher Education Commission.

National Center for Education Statistics. 1986. *Digest of Education Statistics 1985–1986.* Washington, DC: National Center for Education Statistics.

——. 1997. *Digest of Education Statistics 1997.* Washington, DC: National Center for Education Statistics.

Niemann, Yolanda. 1999. "The Making of a Token: A Case Study of Stereotype Threat, Stigma, Racism, and Tokenism in Academe." *Frontiers* 20:111–25.

Olivas, Michael. 1988. "Latino Faculty at the Border." *Change* 20:6–9.

——. 1990. "The Chronicles, My Grandfather's Stories, and Immigration Law: The Slave Traders Chronicle as Racial History." *Saint Louis University Law Journal* 34:425–41.

——. 1995. *Storytelling Out of School: Undocumented College Residency, Race, and Reaction.* Working Paper No. 2. Oakland: University of California Office of the President, Latino Eligibility Study.

Orfield, Gary, and Dean Whitla. 1999. *Diversity and Legal Education: Student Experiences in Leading Law Schools.* Cambridge, MA: Harvard University, Civil Rights Project.

Otero, Lisa, and Juan Zuniga. 1992. "Latino Identity and Affirmative Action: Is There a Case for Hispanics?" Unpublished manuscript, Harvard Law School. On file with author.

Padilla, Raymond, and Rudolfo Chavez, eds. 1995. *The Learning Ivory Tower: Latino Professors in American Universities.* Albany: State University of New York Press.

Padilla, Raymond, and Miguel Montiel. 1998. *Debatable Diversity: Critical Dialogues on Change in American Universities.* New York: Rowan and Littlefield.

Patterson, Molly, and Kristen Monroe. 1998. "Narrative in Political Science." 1:315–31.

Pearce, James, JoAnn Hickey, and Debra Burke. 1998. "African Americans in Large Law Firms: The Possible Cost of Exclusion." *Howard Law Journal* 42:59–70.

Powell, John. 1997. "The 'Racing' of American Society: Race Functioning as a Verb before Signifying as a Noun." *Law and Inequality* 15:99–125.

Pratt, Carla. 1999. "In the Wake of Hopwood: An Update on Affirmative Action in the Education Arena." *Howard Law Journal* 42:451–67.

Quindlen, Anna. 1992. "The Great White Myth." *New York Times,* January 15, p. A21.

Rai, Kul, and John Critzer. 2000. *Affirmative Action and the University: Race, Ethnicity and Gender in Higher Education Employment.* Lincoln: University of Nebraska Press.

Reyes, Maria de la Luz, and John Halcon. 1991. "Practices of the Academy: Barriers to Access to Chicano Academics." Pp. 167–86 in *The Racial Crisis in American Higher*

Education, edited by P. Altbach and K. Lomotey. Albany: State University of New York Press.

Richardson, Laurel. 1990. "Narrative and Sociology." *Journal of Contemporary Ethnography* 19:116–35.

______. 1997. *Fields of Play: Constructing an Academic Life.* New Brunswick, NJ: Rutgers University Press.

Robinson, Reginald. 1997. "Teaching From the Margins: Race as a Pedagogical Sub-Text." *Western New England Law Review* 19:151–81.

Ross, Thomas. 1990. "Innocence and Affirmative Action." *Vanderbilt Law Review* 43:297–316.

______. 1998. "Being White." *Buffalo Law Review* 46:257–79.

Roithmayr, Daria. 1997. "Deconstructing the Distinction between Bias and Merit." *California Law Review* 85:1449–1507.

Russell, Katheryn. 1999. "Critical Race Theory and Social Justice." Pp. 178–88 in *Social Justice/Criminal Justice: The Maturation of Critical Theory in Law, Crime and Deviance,* edited by B. Arrigo. New York: West/Wadsworth.

Saphir, Erich. 1996. "Equality of Opportunity or Reverse Discrimination: Affirmative Action Reconsidered." *Current World Leaders* 39:27–47.

Scales-Trent, Judy. 1990. "Commonalities: On Being Black and White, Different, and the Same." *Yale Journal of Law and Feminism* 2:305–27.

Scheff, Thomas. 1995. "Academic Gangs." *Crime, Law & Social Change* 23:157–62.

Schneider, Alison. 1998. "What Has Happened to Faculty Diversity in California?" *Chronicle of Higher Education,* November 20, pp. A10–A12.

Sidanius, Jim, Felicia Pratto, and Lawrence Bobo. 1996. "Racism, Conservatism, Affirmative Action, and Intellectual Sophistication: A Matter of Principled Conservatism or Group Dominance?" *Journal of Personality and Social Psychology* 70:476–90.

Solorzano, Daniel. 1993. *The Road to the Doctorate for California's Chicanas and Chicanos: A Study of Ford Foundation Minority Fellows.* Berkeley: California Policy Seminar.

Somers, Margaret. 1992. "Narrativity, Narrative Identity, and Social Action: Rethinking English Working-Class Formation." *Social Science History* 16:591–630.

______. 1994. "The Narrative Constitution of Identity: A Relational and Network Approach." *Theory and Society* 23:605–49.

______. 1995. "Narrating and Naturalizing Civil Society and Citizenship Theory: The Place of Political Culture and the Public Sphere." *Sociological Theory* 13:229–74.

Steele, Claude, and Stephen Green. 1976. "Affirmative Action and Academic Hiring: A Case Study of a Value Conflict." *Journal of Higher Education* 47:413–35.

Sturm, Susan, and Lani Guinier. 1996. "The Future of Affirmative Action: Reclaiming the Innovative Ideal." *California Law Review* 84:953–1036.

Tierney, William. 1996. "Affirmative Action in California: Looking Back, Looking Forward in Public Academe." *Journal of Negro Education* 65:122–32.

Turner, Carline, and Samuel Myers. 2000. *Faculty of Color in Academe: Bittersweet Success.* Boston: Allyn and Bacon.

Valdes, Francisco. 1997. "Under Construction: LatCrit Consciousness, Community and Theory." *California Law Review* 85:1089–1142.

Valverde, Leonard, and Louis Castenell, eds. 1998. *The Multicultural Campus: Strategies for Transforming Higher Education.* Walnut Creek, CA: AltaMira Press.

Van Maanen, John. 1988. *Tales of the Field: On Writing Ethnography.* Chicago: University of Chicago Press.

Vargas, Sylvia. 1998. "Deconstructing Homo[geneous] Americanus: The White Ethnic Immigrant Narrative and Its Exclusionary Effect." *Tulane Law Review* 72:1493–1596.

Vasquez, Jesse. 1992. "Embattled Scholars in the Academy: A Shared Odyssey." *Callaloo* 15:1039–51.

Verdugo, Richard. 1995. "Racial Stratification and the Use of Hispanic Faculty as Role Models." *Journal of Higher Education* 66:669–85.

Wasserstrom, Richard. 1977. "Racism, Sexism, and Preferential Treatment: An Approach to the Topics." *UCLA Law Review* 24:581–622.

Wellman, David. 1997. "Minstrel Shows, Affirmative Action Talk, and Angry White Men: Marking Racial Otherness in the 1990s." Pp. 311–31 in *Displacing Whiteness: Essays in Social and Cultural Criticism,* edited by R. Frankenberg. Durham: Duke University Press.

Wilkins, David, and G. Mitu Gulati. 1996. "Why Are There So Few Black Lawyers in Corporate Law Firms? An Institutional Analysis." *California Law Review* 84:496–625.

Williams, Robert. 1989. "Documents of Barbarism: The Contemporary Legacy of European Racism and Colonialism in the Narrative Traditions of Federal Indian Law." *Arizona Law Review* 31:237–78.

______. 1990. *The American Indian in Western Legal Thought: The Discourses of Conquest.* New York: Oxford University Press.

Wilson, John. 1995. "The Myth of Reverse Discrimination in Higher Education." *Journal of Blacks in Higher Education* 10:88–93.

Young, Joyce. 1984. "Black Women Faculty in Academia: Strategies for Career Leadership Development." *Educational and Psychological Research* 4: 133–45.

CHAPTER 7 The Political Institution

7.1 MARGALYNNE ARMSTRONG

Protecting Privilege: Race, Residence and Rodney King

The U.S. federal government legitimated residential discrimination against "inharmonious racial groups" in the 1930s when the Federal Housing Administration (FHA) provided instructions to insurance underwriters on how to prevent minorities from integrating into White neighborhoods. The FHA argued that a change in racial occupancy in White neighborhoods "contributes to instability and a decline in values." It wasn't until the early 1960s that the federal government moved to curb institutionalized racial discrimination in the housing industry. With President John F. Kennedy's issuance of Executive Order 11063 in 1962, the U.S. government conceded that "discriminatory policies and practices result in segregated patterns of housing and necessarily produce other forms of discrimination and segregation which deprive many Americans of equal opportunity." Kennedy directed all executive departments and agencies "to take all action necessary and appropriate to prevent discrimination . . . in the disposition of property, and in the lending practices of institutions with monies insured or guaranteed by the Federal government." Congress challenged housing discrimination a few years later by passing the Federal Fair Housing Law in the Civil Rights Act of 1968.

Nevertheless, housing discrimination against non-White minorities and women remains pervasive in the United States because local, state, and federal governments have not effectively enforced fair housing laws. Despite the development of fair housing laws, the freedom of many non-White Americans to choose where they want to live remains mythical. A nationwide study by the Urban Institute recently found that despite federal housing laws making it illegal to withhold housing from people because of race, national origin, or family status, Blacks and Latinos still encounter discrimination when they try to purchase or rent a home. As a result, roughly three out of four Blacks in American cities currently live in segregated neighborhoods.

In the following selection from "Protecting Privilege: Race, Residence and Rodney King," *Law and Inequality* (June 1994), Margalynne Armstrong contends that the polarization of privileged Whites and unprivileged non-Whites in American society is clearly reflected in residential segregation. She states that residential segregation continues because America's legal system insulates economic discrimination from the civil rights law under the guise of race neutrality. As a result, middle-class Whites have succeeded in isolating themselves from poor minority Americans. Also, housing discrimination affects educational and employment opportunities, access to health care facilities and social services, and even the likelihood of criminal victimization. Since where one lives affects all aspects of peoples' lives, argues Armstrong, housing segregation is a useful indicator of the relative inequality of racial and ethnic groups in the United States.

Key Concept: residential segregation and the protection of White privilege

The 1992 acquittal of the Los Angeles police officers who beat Rodney King, and the resulting devastation of an already ravaged community, is a parable that contains many different lessons about race in America.[1] Although the verdict's most graphic illustrations are about the manner in which our criminal justice system abuses African Americans,[2] the events also reflect a fundamental injustice of another sort—how and where Americans reside.[3] The America represented by Rodney King and South Central Los Angeles lives in segregated cities[4] while the America of the police defendants and Ventura County jurors resides in segregated suburbs.[5]

Metropolitan residential patterns reflect widely held convictions that "good neighborhoods" exclude poor blacks and Hispanics.[6] The segregation of poor minorities, particularly African Americans, in urban ghettos exacerbates their poverty[7] and creates a false sense that urban problems are not the concern of suburban residents. But the suburbs are not insulated from urban crises, "[t]he real city is the total metropolitan area—city and suburb."[8] The urban inner city and outlying suburbs will inevitably clash because American society cannot back away from its proclamations that the segregation which sustains these contrasting worlds will no longer be tolerated.

According to our nation's Constitution and the Fair Housing Act, both governmental and privately imposed discrimination are prohibited.[9] The Fair Housing Act, enacted in 1968, provides that it is unlawful "[T]o discriminate against any person in the terms, conditions or privileges of sale or rental of a dwelling... because of race, color, religion, sex, familial status or national origin."[10] But despite this broad mandate, the law has been interpreted to reach only a narrow spectrum of racial exclusion. The law provides no redress for much of the widespread segregation of poor minority Americans committed under the auspices of privilege, both racial and economic.[11]

This article argues that, rather than prohibit economic discrimination, our legal system insulates it from the reach of civil rights law. Our system allows easy circumvention of fair housing law when discrimination takes the form of financial requirements or if exclusion is attributed to protection of property interests. Such economic discrimination has been accorded a race-neutrality belied by the prevalence of hyper-segregated black urban ghettos.[12] The article will also examine how courts protect commonplace assertions of racial privilege by designating the tendencies of middle-class whites to flee school and residential integration as de facto (and therefore irremediable) segregation. This protection of established racial and economic privilege is so embedded in our society that formal equality is rendered meaningless to poor minority Americans.[13]

To truly eradicate housing segregation, our society must examine and challenge the way our legal system reinforces two underlying assumptions: that white people have the privilege of escaping people of color, and that anyone who can afford to is entitled to abandon the urban poor. By casting economic discrimination as colorblind and as an unassailable right, American law ignores the symbiotic relationship between employment discrimination, urban poverty and contemporary residential segregation.[14]

The Los Angeles uprising echoes a lesson proffered to our nation in the past. Twenty-five years ago, a commission appointed to study the uprisings of the summer of 1967[15] concluded:

> Segregation and poverty have created in the racial ghetto a destructive environment totally unknown to most white Americans. What white Americans have never fully understood—but what the Negro can never forget—is that white society is deeply implicated in the ghetto. White institutions created it, white institutions maintain it, and white society condones it.[16]

The acquittal and the riots of 1992 illustrate the consequences of society's continuing insistence on maintaining spaces where the poor or the black or the brown are sequestered from privileged lives.

I. THE ILLUSION OF SEPARABLE SOCIETIES

The polarization of the privileged and the unprivileged[17] in our society is reflected in the divergent demographics of South Central Los Angeles and Simi Valley in Ventura County. The population of South Central L.A. is 52.8 percent African American and 41.9 percent Hispanic.[18] The South Central region of Los Angeles was once predominantly inhabited by African American working class families employed in manufacturing plants located along a local railroad corridor. Today "those jobs have largely dried up, leaving the area with a negligible source of local employment."[19] The unemployment rate in L.A.'s African American communities is as high as 50 percent.[20] Those who are able to leave these neighborhoods do; the number of black people who live in the city of Los Angeles decreased between 1980 and 1990.[21]

Simi Valley, in contrast, is a "garden spot with safe streets, good schools [and] a nice industrial base."[22] It has a population of approximately 100,000, many of whom left Los Angeles and its substantial population of people of color.[23] Only 1.5 percent of the suburb's residents are African American.[24] Suburban housing tends to be in the form of individually owned houses,[25] whereas "two thirds of the families in South Central Los Angeles rent their small stucco bungalows, and they live there because they cannot afford to live anywhere else."[26] Despite state legislation requiring local governments to establish policies to ensure that the housing needs of all income groups are met,[27] California's suburban communities avoid setting up affordable housing programs using techniques such as under-assessing low income housing needs and enacting ordinances that restrict the supply of housing.[28] But even though the residents of central Los Angeles cannot readily move to the suburbs, the suburbs come to them every day.

Despite rejecting Los Angeles as a place to live, a number of Simi Valley residents maintain weekday association with the city as commuters. Some of these commuters are L.A. police officers: the town has been described as a white, middle-class "bedroom community" for police.[29] Suburbanites tend to see the police as a "thin blue line"[30] or "bulwark against urban chaos and crime."[31] Apparently, during working hours the police are driven by the attitude of revulsion felt by the privileged towards ghetto inhabitants;[32] at night they join the privileged in the suburbs. The police serve as contact points, forced to confine people who have deliberately been left behind in the chaos and who know they have little chance of escaping it.

The acquittal of the officers in the first Rodney King beating trial reflects this view of the police as a breakwater.

> Living just up the freeway and over the hills from Los Angeles, the jurors ended up viewing the four police officers as their own protection against the spread of inner-city crime.... The jurors feared "that if they punished these cops they would be less safe in their little community up there...."[33]

Simi Valley and other suburban residents long ago surrendered Los Angeles to the perceived enemy and attempted to sever any responsibility to the city.[34] But it was impossible to completely sever connections to Los Angeles because no suburb, particularly a "bedroom community" for urban employees, can cut its economic, cultural and infrastructural[35] ties to its urban center. A larger network of interdependency binds the residents of a metropolitan area, and of our nation as a whole.[36] Suburban Americans "cannot escape responsibility for choosing the future of our metropolitan areas and the human relations that develop within them."[37] The connection retained by urban police officers peculiarly reinforces the sense of white entitlement to an area that is off limits to most people of color. To residents who come face to face with urban crime and poverty on the job, Simi Valley must seem a well deserved home and resting place. Here, the besieged police can exercise the "earned" privilege of taking refuge from their work day battles with the unprivileged.

All over the United States, our cities are ringed by Ventura Counties, exclusive enclaves where middle-class people retreat in order to shut out urban problems. Americans have fled the cities in astonishing numbers. The 1992 presidential election was the first in which over 50 percent of the votes were cast by people who lived in the suburbs.[38] Although there has been an increase in black suburbanization, compared to whites, relatively few blacks reside in suburbs, and many of these suburbs are predominantly African American.[39]

Many suburban residents continue to derive their income from the cities they have abandoned, but more and more frequently their employers also forsake the cities.[40] With this exodus, middle class and business interest in the welfare of the city dries up. Consequently, resources are redirected to serving the locus of their perceived interest—the suburbs. The result is a regressive redistribution of the costs of having a society that includes poor people, by which city residents who are least able to pay bear the lion's share of the expenses of poverty.[41]

II. LIVING WHERE YOU WANT

1. Extralegal "Rights"

There are places in America in which you are not supposed to be if your skin is black or brown.[42] Should an African American or Hispanic American (particularly a young male) walk through the streets of certain suburbs, towns, or urban neighborhoods he might notice that the inhabitants view his presence with suspicion, resentment or worse. A person of color can be in danger in such areas, for such areas are inexorably linked with violent attacks on people of color who happen to pass through. Infamous examples are Bensonhurst in Brooklyn, where 16 year old Yusef Hawkins was murdered when he came to the area to look at a used car,[43] and the Howard Beach section of Queens, where Michael Griffin was chased to his death by a gang of local residents.[44] Although some perpetrators of racially motivated violence attribute their actions to security concerns, others openly admit that they believe their neighborhoods should be reserved for whites.[45]

Nonwhite visitors are greeted with palpable hostility in white enclaves because the residents collectively establish and enforce an extralegal "right" to practice racial discrimination. Although statutes explicitly prohibit racial discrimination in most housing transactions, the extralegal right receives more respect and private enforcement than the actual housing discrimination laws. Neighborhood residents protect and implement this "right" to discriminate. Transgressions against this right are redressed rapidly through violence, while violations of the legal right against discrimination require bureaucracy, lawyers, or courts for enforcement.[46] The false "right" arises from notions of entitlement and the primacy accorded property ownership in American legal and constitutional tradition.[47] Some white Americans believe that property ownership carries with it entitlement to racial exclusivity—by earning enough money they acquire the privilege of residing "where they want."[48] Other residents of white segregated neighborhoods explicitly believe that living where you want is a right or privilege incident to being born with white skin.[49]

The continued existence of predominantly white or predominantly minority neighborhoods and suburbs that appear to defy fair housing law has been attributed by some analysts to the cumulative expression of individual choices. This cynical use of "consumer preference" attempts to disclaim government or societal responsibility for segregation. At the same time it falsely implies that freedom of choice works in a neutral manner.[50] Free choice, however, is not available to all Americans. Generally, only white residents of segregated areas are able to actually exclude members of other races from residing in their communities.[51] Although there is a growing movement of people of color who choose to live in predominantly black or brown neighborhoods,[52] minority residents have traditionally been denied participation in shaping the configuration of their residential environments where there is any white interest in the area.[53] Although some African Americans affirmatively choose black neighborhoods, many blacks who live in segregated middle-class neighborhoods would prefer more integration[54] or may have originally moved to an integrated neighborhood that resegregated because of white flight.[55]

The urban minority poor find themselves doubly abandoned due to the exercise of two forms of privilege. Because the privilege of living where one wishes is disbursed on the basis of income as well as race, middle-class Americans of color also attempt to relinquish the urban ghettos to the poor.[56] Some move to middle-class black neighborhoods, but many seek housing in predominantly white integrated communities in which the populations are healthier,[57] and the neighborhoods offer superior services, better schools, and more resources.[58] Urban and suburban areas which are substandard, burdened by crime, environmental degradation,[59] and wretched schools are more likely to house predominantly minority populations.[60] Amenities that middle-class people take for granted, such as banks, supermarkets and stores that provide basic goods and services, are scarce in low income minority neighborhoods.[61] Simply put, it is difficult to enjoy the benefits of a middle-class lifestyle in a poor minority neighborhood.

Indeed, if they wish to remain members of the middle class, black residents are almost forced to leave urban inner city neighborhoods because the areas provide limited opportunity to earn a living legally.[62] The staggering unemployment figures for inner city neighborhoods[63] reflect a vicious cycle whereby the neighborhoods provide little work and the low income populations are too poor to move closer to areas where work can be found.[64] The scarcity of employment opportunity is coupled with rampant employment discrimination against African Americans.[65] In the end, our inner cities are inhabited by people who have no means of leaving. If the choice of abandoning our inner cities was truly available to all Americans, our ghettos would surely become ghost towns.[66]

2. Economic Privilege and Residential Access

Race plays a potent role in access to housing in America,[67] but financial status is probably the primary factor in residential exclusion. The inability to pay the price of housing excludes prospective home-seekers across racial lines. But the fact that financial determinants can operate against the white people as well as against black people does not mean that economic discrimination is race neutral.[68]

Many Americans see nothing wrong with using economic status to distribute access to housing opportunities. Economic discrimination, however, enables our nation to preserve and continue widespread racial exclusivity in the composition of our communities. Although acknowledgement of the racial implications of economic privilege may be psychologically difficult, people who are concerned about integration and equal opportunity must consider the ramifications of economic privilege. When protecting privilege is elevated above the goal of racial equality, the consequence is residential segregation. This segregation will not be limited to economically elite communities because upper-middle-class behavior sets a standard by which success is measured. Therefore, high income whites cannot live in segregated areas and expect lower income whites to abstain from using their racial privilege in similar ways.

Our society uses economic privilege as a means of controlling access to good neighborhoods. Because America is a democracy which promises equality of opportunity, it would be unfair to arbitrarily deny people the prospect of residing in a decent environment. Thus, in order to justify the exclusion of the poor from safe areas with access to public services and good schools, income is used as a measure of worthiness. Economic privilege seems less inequitable if we pretend that it is distributed on the basis of merit.[69]

The 1980s saw a resurgence in blaming poor people for their want of advantage.[70] Being unprivileged was no longer ascribed to misfortune or racism, it became a matter of just desserts. Under this line of reasoning, people who live in substandard areas or who are destitute are unprivileged because of their own decisions. The poor "choose" to drop out of school, to become teenage mothers, to apply for welfare; the unemployed are "determined" not to work.[71] This attitude towards the unprivileged is rooted in the American mythology that any person, through her own will and effort, can work her way out of poverty.[72] Such dogma neutralizes the unfairness of privilege by casting it not as something granted, but as something obtainable by all.

If privilege can be achieved, then lack of privilege is attributable to individual choice, i.e., the only thing preventing the poor from gaining privilege is their own lack of ambition or diligence. Because most people obtain their financial success through employment and do not see themselves as being unfairly advantaged, economic privilege is viewed as "earned." Since we work hard to obtain financial status rather than simply being lucky enough to inherit it as some form of birthright, economic privilege does not appear arbitrary or gratuitous. In fact, many Americans take it for granted that wealth should provide distance from poverty and the poor; they even see it as a reward and incentive for hard work. Such attitudes are blind to the fact that many of the poor work hard, yet are not rewarded with privilege.[73] A disproportionate number of minority Americans are among the working poor or involuntarily unemployed who lack privilege.[74] Our opinions about poor people sentence those who are unable to work, due to no fault of their own, to a world with few options and limited futures. A large number of the poor are children who are unable to "earn" the privilege of living in middle-class neighborhoods.[75] Children in poor and minority areas are often accorded mediocre or substandard educations which further impair their ability to compete for the type of work that could reward them with access to middle-class privilege.[76] In the end, economic privilege distributes benefits and privilege capriciously because, despite hard work, willingness to work, or inability to work, poor minorities are excluded from the opportunity to earn the financial status that provides an escape to areas available to the more privileged. For many people poverty results from structural deficiencies more than from their individual failings.[77] Economic privilege is not uniformly disseminated on the basis of merit and is, at best, an unjust and inadequate rationale for the segregation of the poor. It also serves as a mask to conceal unlawful exclusion for purposes of preserving racial privilege.

Even when we recognize that in denying the poor access to middle- and upper-class neighborhoods economic privilege perpetuates racial segregation, our courts fail to acknowledge the legal wrong. The courts give economic status such primacy that considerations of wealth actually insulate otherwise prohibited housing discrimination from legal scrutiny. These general notions of wealth and earned privilege are replicated and prevail, even in the administration of our fair housing laws.

III. PROTECTING PRIVILEGE

1. The Poor and the Jurisprudence of Housing Discrimination

The idea that race and money entitle people to the privilege of residential choice and the actual prerogative to exclude those who are not similarly privileged is a powerful influence in our society. Concepts of privilege are so firmly held as to effectively constitute a "right" in the minds of many American property owners.[78] Most frequently, courts protect the "right" to engage in racial discrimination as an unspoken corollary of the right to discriminate on the basis of income.[79] Courts also reinforce popular notions of an extra-legal "right" to discriminate on the basis of race by recognizing residential segregation as a legal impediment to judicial intervention in school desegregation cases.[80]

The jurisprudence of housing discrimination generally rejects protecting the poor as a group[81] and there is no fundamental right to housing under federal constitutional analysis.[82] A series of United States Supreme Court cases, decided primarily in the 1970s, refused to recognize poverty as a suspect classification or find that legislation that discriminates against the poor is subject to strict judicial scrutiny.[83]

State and local legislation directed at excluding the poor is a barrier to the effective enforcement of federal civil rights law. Economic rationales, such as keeping property taxes low,[84] provide a very convenient wrapper for concealing impermissible discrimination. Professor John Calmore described the predictable outcome of judicial deference to wealth-determined distinctions in the following manner:

> Although in absolute numbers there are more white poor than black poor, blacks carry a disproportionate burden of poverty, and thus many times their claims for substantive distributive justice are essentially race claims. Often, what begins as a claim concerning the effects of racial discrimination gets transformed in constitutional analysis into a complaint not of racial but economic injustice and then denied in the reformulated terms.[85]

When our courts refuse to recognize economic class as a suspect category they protect legally prohibited racial discrimination, allowing those who discriminate to frustrate civil rights goals and block some of the limited steps American society has taken to eradicate poverty.

Opposition to the placement of subsidized housing in middle-class neighborhoods illustrates the clash of economic privilege and racial justice. Although a handful of federal programs have recognized the need for low income housing and provided funding, local resistance often thwarts their implementation.[86] Opponents of low income housing attempt to block it by protesting that the development will interfere with their property values. Courts consistently find preservation of this economic privilege more compelling than protecting the poor from exclusion. Such cases ignore the tendency of the American public to equate poverty with minority races. When legislators are able to label a concern as economic, examination of the law's racial impact is diverted and discriminatory legislation is permitted to escape exacting scrutiny. This dynamic is illustrated by *James v. Valtierra,*[87] in which the U.S. Supreme Court denied an equal protection challenge to a provision of the California State Constitution. This provision, enacted through the voter referendum process, required voter approval of low rent housing projects. Although the provision singles out housing for the poor for electoral approval, and subjects no other type of development to this requirement, the Court found the provision to embody democratic ideals, writing:

> This procedure ensures that all the people of a community will have a voice in a decision which may lead to large expenditures of local governmental funds for increased public services and to lower tax revenues. It gives them a voice in decisions that will affect the future development of their own community. This procedure for democratic decisionmaking does not violate the constitutional command that no State shall deny to any person "the equal protection of the laws."[88]

James v. Valtierra epitomizes the exclusionary force of economic privilege. A popularly perceived entitlement to exclude the poor is transformed into a constitutional right. Although property owners feel that their ownership entitles them to many "rights" to limit inimical uses of neighboring property, subsidized housing is the only residential land use decision accorded the status of necessitating individual input from the local inhabitants. The *James* decision characterizes the right to exclude as the embodiment of democratic principles. The poor are forever excluded from the community without ever having a chance to participate in the democratic process that banishes them. The Court refused to examine the racial implications of California's constitutional provision, stating that it was "seemingly neutral on its face."[89]

Court decisions in cases brought under the Fair Housing Act have not protected the poor as a class from discrimination any more effectively than have equal protection decisions. In *Boyd v. Lefrak Org.* prospective renters challenged as racially discriminatory the income requirements imposed by a management company that was already subject to a consent decree from a previous pattern and practice suit under the Fair Housing Act.[90] The landlord required that applicants have a weekly *net* income (deducting all taxes, fixed obligations and debts) that was at least 90 percent of the monthly rental (the 90 Percent Rule), or to have a guarantor whose weekly net income was 110 percent of the monthly rental.[91] Expert testimony at trial indicated that the income requirements excluded 92.5 percent of local black and Puerto Rican households, and that white household eligibility would be four times as great as that of black households and ten times as great of as that of Puerto Rican households.[92] The district court found that the defendant's income criteria violated the Fair Housing Act due to a "disproportionately high racially discriminatory impact" and that they did not establish a business necessity or other non-racial grounds for the rule.[93] In reversing the judgment of the district court the circuit court wrote:

> While blacks and Puerto Ricans do not have the same access to Lefrak apartments as do whites, the reason for this inequality is not racial discrimination but rather the disparity in economic level among these groups.... A businessman's differential treatment of different economic groups is not necessarily racial discrimination and is not made so because minorities are statistically overrepresented in poorer economic groups. The fact that differentiation in eligibility rates for defendants' apartments is correlated with race proves merely that minorities tend to be poorer than is the general population.[94]

The court noted that although a disparate impact analysis might be appropriate in a challenge to state action, it could ignore the racially exclusionary results of the defendant's policy because the policy applied uniform economic criteria to whites and minorities.[95] The majority in *Boyd* framed the issue as the ability of a landlord to use economic factors to judge prospective tenants.[96] An alternative characterization of the issues presented could focus on the exclusionary effects of the landlord's economic criteria to determine if they were designed to evade prohibitions against racial discrimination. The opinion instead accords the income requirements the presumption of neutrality, while failing to examine their contextual ramifications. The court ignored the fact that the 90 Percent Rule was devised by a management company while subject to a consent decree for previous violations of the Fair Housing Act.[97] These prior violations might have provided evidence that the requirements were intended to result in prohibited racial exclusion.

In *Boyd,* the right to engage in economic discrimination was more palpable in the eyes of the majority than the racial discrimination it advanced. The plaintiffs had a "right" to not be discriminated against on the basis of race, but were not protected against economic discrimination. Again, a court refused to even examine whether racial discrimination occurred because the defendant could present a theory of economic discrimination.

A state statute that the California courts have held to prohibit arbitrary discrimination in housing, California's Unruh Civil Rights Act,[98] has been limited judicially to exclude discrimination based on poverty. In *Harris v. Capital Growth Investors XIV*[99] the California Supreme Court refused to remedy economic exclusion that caused prohibited discriminatory impact, even when the insubstantial nature of the economic rationale indicated other non-economic motives. Income requirements that went beyond those necessary to protect the economic interests of a landlord were upheld even though these requirements disproportionately excluded female-headed households from the pool of applicants to whom the defendants would rent units.[100] Policies that limit the housing available to female-headed households also exclude a disproportionately high percentage of minorities.[101]

The court refused to examine the defendant's policy because it was applicable to all applicants regardless of race, color, sex, religion, etc.[102] The justices found it unimportant that applying the policy to all people would result in excluding members of statutorily protected groups significantly more than it would exclude households headed by white males. Because the defendant cited economic status as the basis of the exclusion the court could shift its focus to the financial ramifications of the policy. When the balance focused on economic interests, protecting privilege was accorded more importance than the total exclusion of low income people, even those who in fact could pay market rate for the housing. Economic interest again served as a trump card, overriding all other considerations. The *Harris* court explicitly granted considerations of wealth primacy over actual discriminatory impact, even when the biased act was not necessary to protect financial interests.

Thus, the concept of economic privilege is used to justify and sustain the de facto residential segregation of the poor, and, thereby, of many people of color. It has resulted in concentrating low income minorities in center city neighborhoods throughout the United States. Because our society believes that anyone who can afford to live in an affluent suburb is entitled to leave the city and its problems, and since the route to privilege can be achieved by some minorities, it is argued that the existence of urban ghettos is attributable to economic factors rather than to racial discrimination.[103] It is clear, however, that a person of color is much more likely to be excluded from the prospect of earning enough money to "buy" the privilege of escaping to the suburbs, and that income simply reinforces race as a means of keeping blacks in the inner city. Furthermore an African American and a white American with identical educational and financial backgrounds do not have an identical range of housing choices or employment opportunities.[104]

Two problems accompany the great magnitude of judicial deference to economic privilege. One problem is that the deference allows prohibited residential racial discrimination to occur as long as a housing provider can attribute exclusion to economic factors. The second problem with the primacy of economic privilege is that it is distributed unjustly. Economic privilege is not allocated to all who might merit it[105] and is still disproportionately unavailable in African Americans.[106]

2. Protecting Racial Privilege

The second prong of privilege is white racial privilege. White privilege involves advantages and options that are available merely because one is white. A white person need not be a bigot to benefit from racial privilege; simply having white skin will provide access to neighborhoods and jobs which are closed to people of color. Living in such neighborhoods is not, for every resident, an assertion of racial hostility, but many of these areas are sought out by whites because the environment is inhospitable to minorities.

Racial privilege is manifest in the divergent presumptions and perceptions accorded to individuals on the basis of their race.[107] The influence of race as a barrier to better neighborhoods is discounted because the law no longer countenances explicit racial barriers in housing opportunities, therefore the obstacles to escaping ghetto neighborhoods are seen as economic and self-imposed.

Racial privilege tends to be advanced by whites who can work in concert as a community to reinforce exclusion. This is the form of privilege asserted by numerous ethnic groups of European origin who assert that they have the right to maintain segregated enclaves in order to preserve their ethnic or religious identity. Although individuals who are caught discriminating against other identified individuals are subject to state sanction, minorities are kept out of white neighborhoods by a series of factors more complex than individual denials of housing.[108] Punishable acts of discrimination are the exception, so minorities are excluded with legal impunity.

The facts and holding of *City of Memphis v. Greene*[109] present an example of this dynamic. In *Greene,* white residents of Hein Park, a Memphis community bordered to the north by a predominantly black area, requested the city to close a street (West Drive) that served as an artery between the two neighborhoods, ostensibly to reduce traffic and increase safety in Hein Park.[110] The closure would be effectuated by the city's selling a twenty-five foot strip that ran across West Drive to the northernmost property owners in the white area.[111] Residents of the African American community to the north of Hein Park challenged the sale under the U.S. Constitution and 42 U.S.C. §§ 1982 and 1983.[112]

The United States Supreme Court upheld the closing despite Sixth Circuit findings that evidence presented to the district court showed the closing would benefit a white neighborhood, would adversely affect blacks[113] and that the "barrier was to be erected precisely at the point of separation of these neighborhoods and would undoubtedly have the effect of limiting contact between them."[114] Instead the Supreme Court found:

> the critical facts established by the record are these: The city's decision to close West Drive was motivated by its interest in protecting the safety and tranquillity of a residential neighborhood.... The city has conferred a benefit on white property owners but there is no reason to believe that it would refuse to confer a comparable benefit on black property owners. The closing has not affected the value of

property owned by black citizens, but it has caused some slight inconvenience to black motorists.[115]

The Supreme Court majority in *Greene* held that the closing was for traffic safety purposes, ignoring the fact that the closing of West Drive was the only time that the city of Memphis had ever closed a street for traffic control purposes.[116] Although the city and the Supreme Court majority coated the actions of the Hein Park residents with a veneer of neutrality, the motives behind the decision to close West Drive remain apparent. As the dissent in *Greene* noted, "Respondents are being sent a clear, though sophisticated message that because of their race they are to stay out of the all-white enclave of Hein Park and should instead take the long way around in reaching their destinations to the south."[117] *Greene* provided judicial support and legal enforcement for an extralegal white "right" to exclude minorities, even though such a "right" could not be explicitly acknowledged by a court.

Recent cases examining school desegregation and housing discrimination demonstrate that our highest courts are blind to racial segregation that can be attributed to economic privilege. In *Board of Educ. of Okla. City Pub. Sch. v. Dowell,* the Board argued that segregation in its schools was due to private decisionmaking and economics that created residential segregation.[118] The U.S. Supreme Court picked up this theme, embracing without question a right to use financial privilege to resegregate. Again, in *Freeman v. Pitts,*[119] the U.S. Supreme Court lent its imprimatur to racial segregation based on individual privilege and choice. The Court recognized as inevitable, and thus sanctioned, residential segregation based on the preferences of whites:

> The effect of changing residential patterns on the racial composition of schools though not always fortunate is somewhat predictable. Studies show a high correlation between residential segregation and school segregation.... The District Court in this case heard evidence tending to show that racially stable neighborhoods are not likely to emerge because whites prefer a racial mix of 80% white and 20% black, while blacks prefer a 50%-50% mix. Where resegregation is a product not of state action but of private choices, it does not have constitutional implications.... Residential housing choices and their attendant effects on the racial composition of schools, present an ever-changing pattern, one difficult to address through judicial remedies.[120]

Thus, Justice Kennedy decreed that when racial isolation is of societal proportions but results from the free market and individual choice, the Court should not intervene. Neither *Dowell* nor *Freeman* addresses the issue of which individuals get a chance to actively participate in the market and exercise choice. The law can absolve itself from further inquiry if a judge affixes the de facto label, even in cases where the court explicitly recognizes that segregation is occurring. Our courts' refusal to recognize the impact of segregation based on individual choice implicates the legal system as a force that sustains segregation. Even in the absence of de jure segregation, America still finds residential and educational segregation intractable. Racial separation will remain imbedded in our system because it relies on the unassailable concept of economic privilege to obscure deliberate segregation.

IV. CONCLUSION

As suburban America feels increasingly insecure about preserving its status and property, attempts to isolate the middle class from the unprivileged have increased accordingly. Tax revolts, suburban office parks, concrete traffic barriers and walled private neighborhoods and towns are all evidence of a desire to limit contact with the less privileged.[121] The tenet that one of the perquisites of money is to be able to isolate oneself from the unprivileged sustains a societal separation that is illusory and incendiary. Although the urge to reject the urban ghetto is real, the privileged can only pretend to sequester themselves from contact and connection with the unprivileged. The disintegration of the urban center city contributes to the deterioration of the ethical and physical quality of life in society as a whole.[122] Attempts to maintain the illusion that poverty is not a problem for those better off simply magnify the glaring differences between life for the rich and poor and ensure that the inevitable contact of the polarized segments of our society will be explosive.

It is time for our law to recognize that economic discrimination creates a subrosa system of extralegal discriminatory "rights" that directly conflict with our express legal norms prohibiting discrimination. The fact that discrimination on the basis of race in housing transactions is no longer legal does not, by itself, create equal access to communities like Simi Valley. As long as there is no real chance for a family in inner city Los Angeles to choose to move to Ventura County, we cannot honestly say that our society provides equal opportunity at any level. No one believes that the education at a public school in South Central Los Angeles is equal to the education offered at a public school in Simi Valley.[123] Were there truly equal opportunity, many of the families of South Central Los Angeles would move to areas where they could send their kids to the schools that really provide a better chance for the better life.[124] These families do not remain in blighted neighborhoods from a lack of desire for better futures for their children. They simply have little opportunity to choose where they live.

It is also time for the law to stop shielding racial discrimination by labeling it "economic choice." Left to our own devices we Americans make the wrong choices—choices based on obtaining or maintaining privilege, with little thought to the corresponding exclusion of the least fortunate of the American community. A look at the demographics of housing in the United States reveals that many in our nation still choose residential segregation and, by doing so, deny choice to those who would opt for integration. The comparison between life in the neighborhoods of South Central Los Angeles and life for Ventura County residents illustrates that the choice to discriminate imposes burdens on the rest of society.

It is clear that America has never firmly resolved to eradicate residential racial segregation.[125] Thirty years ago Judge Loren Miller wrote "Resistance [to fair housing laws] will persist as long as there is hope that 'white' communities can be maintained at all price levels; it will diminish when the householder who fears Negro occupancy is convinced that he can run but cannot hide from Negro neighbors."[126] But until society genuinely works towards eliminating separate communities for black and white Americans our society will live in constant conflict. The conflict will arise both from our failure to uphold our laws that promise fairness in access and from the resentment of those excluded. The isolation of minority Americans is a barrier to our country's social and economic progress. Unless we move forward in eliminating segregation by recognizing how it is advanced by our protection of economic privilege, we are destined to remain standing still.

We cannot sequester the poor out of existence and we cannot maintain impermeable barriers between the different segments of society without defying basic principles of liberty and equal protection. If our society pretends that its component communities are separate and hostile spheres, the unavoidable interaction will be between angry and fearful factions, as demonstrated in the police beating of Rodney King, the acquittal of the officers, and the upheaval that followed.

As long as the poor do not have any realistic chance of escaping poverty or of leaving the ghetto, they are pinioned to the bottom of society by concepts of privilege that have arbitrarily excluded them from a better life. Although those of us with options that allow us to live where we choose may be more fortunate than meritorious, we erect insurmountable barriers between ourselves and the poor in order to maintain our privileged positions. However, even though the promise of equal access is far from being kept, it has been made and renewed.[127] The lesson our society must learn from the uprising that followed the Simi Valley acquittals is that those to whom the pledge of equality was made have not forgotten America's promises and refuse to allow themselves to be forgotten.

NOTES

1. On March 3, 1991, Rodney King was beaten by police officers during his arrest following a high speed chase. The beating was videotaped by George Holliday, a neighborhood resident, and was broadcast on local and national television. A California grand jury indicted four officers for the beating on assault charges. The state trial originated in Los Angeles County, but venue was moved to Ventura County due to the extensive publicity surrounding the case. On April 29, 1992, a jury in suburban Simi Valley, California acquitted the police officers of all charges except one count of excessive force against officer Laurence Powell. A mistrial was found on that count. Geoffrey P. Alpert et al., *Law Enforcement: Implications of the Rodney King Beating*, 28 CRIM. L. BULL., 469, 471 (1992).

   The four officers were later tried in federal courts for violating King's civil rights. On April 17, 1993, the federal court jury found Sgt. Stacey Koon and Officer Powell guilty.

   An article in the popular press presented some reasons for the opposing verdicts. The state court proceedings were held in

   > a mostly suburban, middle-class area northwest of Los Angeles. The jury there consisted of 10 whites, one Asian and one Latino (sic). By contrast, the federal district encompasses a larger and more socially diverse area that includes the count[y] of Los Angeles.... The federal jury consisted of nine whites, two blacks and one Latino. Experts said that far more important than race were the different experiences and world views of suburban and urban jurors.

Seth Rosenfeld & Marsha Ginsburg, *King Beating Trial Legal Issues*, S. F. EXAMINER, Apr. 18, 1993, at A10. *See also* Mark Hansen, *Different Jury, Different Verdict?*, 78 A.B.A. J. 54 (1992). A discussion of suburban perceptions about race, crime and police brutality appears *infra* at text accompanying note 33.

2. African Americans, particularly African American males, face racial discrimination from each component of the criminal justice system, from law enforcement to prosecution to incarceration. *See Developments In the Law—Race And The Criminal Process*, 101 HARV. L. REV. 1472 (1988) (examining the institutional problem of racial discrimination throughout the U.S. criminal justice system). *See also* Paul Hoffman, *The Feds, Lies and Videotape: The Need for an Effective Federal Role in Controlling Police Abuse in Urban America*, 66 S. CAL. L. REV. 1455, 1459 (1993) ("The predominant, though not exclusive feature of police abuse in Los Angeles is the singling out of young African-American and Latino males for special attention, harassment, detention, physical abuse, brutality, and sometimes death."); Charles J. Ogletree, *Does Race Matter in Criminal Prosecutions?*, 15 CHAMPION 7, 7 (1991) ("Racial disparity and racial prejudice continue to corrupt the criminal justice system, the level of despair there far outdistancing the level of hope."); Cassia Spohn et al., *The Effect of Race on Sentencing: A Re-examination of an Unsettled Question*, 16 L. & SOC. REV. 71 (1981–82) (finding that black males are sentenced to prison at a twenty percent higher rate than white males, while white males are more likely to receive probation, although once the decision to incarcerate is made, no disparity in sentencing was found).

   Even as victims of crime, African Americans fail to receive justice from the criminal law systems. Because murderers of whites are four times more likely to be sentenced to death than murderers of blacks, African American communities are denied equal treatment with respect to those who kill their members. Randall L. Kennedy, McCleskey v. Kemp: *Race, Capital Punishment and the Supreme Court*, 101 HARV. L. REV. 1388, 1391 (1988).

3. A recurring metaphor for the racial configuration of the United States is that of "two nations." The term was used in 1968 to summarize the findings of a federal commission established by President Johnson to investigate the causes of urban "racial disorders" that occurred in cities across the nation during the summer of 1967. The Commission wrote: "This is our basic conclusion: Our Nation is moving towards two societies, one black, one white—separate and unequal." REPORT OF THE NATIONAL ADVISORY COMMISSION ON CIVIL DISORDERS (KERNER COMMISSION REPORT) 1 (1968) [hereinafter (KERNER COMMISSION REPORT).

   Andrew Hacker revives the metaphor "Two Nations" in his 1992 book about the role of race in the United States. ANDREW HACKER, TWO NATIONS: BLACK AND WHITE, SEPARATE, HOSTILE, UNEQUAL (1992). I continue this metaphor in the discussion of different Americas that follows.

4. "The most salient feature of postwar segregation is the concentration of blacks in central cities and whites in suburbs." DOUGLAS S. MASSEY & NANCY A. DENTON, AMERICAN APARTHEID: SEGREGATION AND THE MAKING OF THE UNDERCLASS 67 (1993). "By 1970, racial segregation in U.S. urban areas was characterized [as] a largely black central city surrounded by predominantly white suburbs. . . ." *Id.* at 61. Metropolitan areas throughout the United States experience high levels of black-white residential segregation. Measures of residential segregation for metropolitan areas with the largest black population in 1980 indicated an average index of 77 (where 0 would indicate a random distribution and 100 equals total separation). The index for metropolitan Los Angeles was 79. NATIONAL RESEARCH COUNCIL, A COMMON DESTINY: BLACKS AND AMERICAN SOCIETY 78–79 (Gerald D. Jaynes & Robin M. Williams eds., 1989).

5. According to the 1990 Census, Ventura County had a total population of 669,016. BUREAU OF CENSUS, U.S. DEPT. OF COMMERCE, 1990 CENSUS OF POPULATION, GENERAL POPULATION CHARACTERISTICS, CAL. tbl. 5 at 32 (1992). White residents numbered 529,166 (79.2%), while 15,629 (2.3%) were black. *Id.* The population of the city of Simi Valley was 100,217 in 1990, including 88,345 (88.2%) whites and 1,527 (1.5%) blacks. *Id.*, tbl. 6 at 104. Simi Valley is an area "disproportionately the home of L.A.P.D. officers and retirees." Kimberle Crenshaw & Gary Peller, *Reel Time/Real Justice*, 70 DENV. U. L. REV. 283,286 (1993). Several of the jurors were either in law enforcement themselves or had relatives or close friends in such a job. Nina Bernstein, *Bitter Division in Jury Room; How 12 Ordinary Citizens Met For 7 Days To Produce Verdict That Shook L.A.*, NEWSDAY, May 14, 1992, at 5, *available in* LEXIS, NEWS Library, NEWSDY File. A poll indicated that 24 percent of Ventura County residents have similar connections. *Id.* Three of the four defendants lived in suburban or rural areas of Los Angeles County. Sgt. Stacey Koon lived in Castaic, a hilly town 40 miles north of Los Angeles, an area more rural than suburban. Timothy Wind lived in Santa Clarita which is located near Castaic. Theodore Briseno lived in Sepulveda, a suburb due east of the city of Los Angeles. Leslie Berger & John Johnson, *Officers from Diverse Backgrounds*, L.A. TIMES, Mar. 16, 1991, at A24; *see also A Look at Four Officers Acquitted*, USA TODAY, Apr. 30, 1992, at 2A. I could find no information about the residence of Laurence Powell.
6. Although a number of factors contributed to the postwar suburban expansion "in many metro areas, racially motivated 'White Flight' was undeniably a major factor in suburban growth. 'Good' neighborhoods with 'good' schools often were seen as neighborhoods and schools without any Blacks and, to a lesser degree, without any Hispanics. After the civil rights revolution in the 1960s, neighborhoods and schools without poor Blacks and Hispanics met the 'good' test.

   Racial prejudice played a role in the evolution of overwhelmingly White suburbs surrounding increasingly Black cities." DAVID RUSK, CITIES WITHOUT SUBURBS 29 (1993).
7. MASSEY & DENTON, *supra* note 4, at 130–42.
8. RUSK, *supra* note 6, at 5.
9. U.S. CONST. amend. XIV, § 1, guarantees equal protection of the law from state governments. Despite constitutional guarantees, legislation and government action "undoubtedly played an important part" in the segregation of American cities that occurred with the black migration to northern states after the end of World War I. Richard H. Sander, Comment, *Individual Rights and Demographic Realities: The Problem of Fair Housing*, 82 NW. U. L. REV. 874, 877 (1988).

   The Fair Housing Act, 42 U.S.C. §§ 3601-14 (1988 & Supp. 1992), prohibits racial discrimination in most private housing transactions. Owner conducted sales and rentals in dwellings that contain four or fewer units are exempt from the Act. 42 U.S.C. §§ 3603(b)(1) & (2).
10. 42 U.S.C. § 3604(b). Addressing the enactment of fair housing legislation Prof. Derrick Bell writes:

    it took three years of "protracted and chaotic" legislative effort by Congress before Title VIII was enacted. It became law exactly one week after Dr. Martin Luther King, Jr., was killed by a white assassin. As a further incentive to its enactment, the bill was attached to extremely broad legislation enabling the federal government to prosecute persons involved in riots and civil disorders ... when the self-interest factors that really motivated white support were taken care of (e.g., a symbolic recognition that housing discrimination was wrong, combined with new tough penalties for those convicted of urban disorders planned and activated by some national, black conspiracy), commitment to the cause of fair housing almost disappeared.

> DERRICK BELL, RACE, RACISM, AND AMERICAN LAW 720–21 (2d ed. 1992) [hereinafter RACE, RACISM]; *see also* DERRICK BELL, *The Benefits to Whites of Civil Rights Litigation, in* AND WE ARE NOT SAVED 51, 51–74 (1987).

Despite ample evidence that these proscriptions were enacted to advance majority interests as much as they were directed at benefiting the victims of racial discrimination, the equality of access promised by American law and policy continues to contrast sharply with reality and with popular attitudes. Mary L. Dudziak, *Desegregation as a Cold War Imperative,* 41 STAN. L. REV. 61 (1988).

11. Fair Housing Act coverage does not recognize economic discrimination and does not address the injury that discrimination causes racial groups. *See* Margalynne Armstrong, *Desegregation and Private Litigation: Using Equitable Remedies to Achieve the Purposes of The Fair Housing Act,* 64 TEMP. L. REV. 909 (1991).

12. Since the civil rights laws of the 1960s were enacted

> [h]ousing segregation has changed importantly in ways that make it appear much less severe to whites and a small sector of middle-class blacks, but the overall consequences of the ghetto system for working-class and poor blacks, and for the economic viability of central cities, have become more severe.

Gary Orfield, *Separate Societies: Have the Kerner Warnings Come True?, in* QUIET RIOTS: RACE AND POVERTY IN THE UNITED STATES 100, 106 (Fred R. Harris & Roger W. Wilkins eds., 1988) [hereinafter QUIET RIOTS].

13.

> [T]he attainment of formal equality is not the end of the story. Racial hierarchy cannot be cured by the move to facial race-neutrality in the laws that structure the economic, political, and social lives of Black people. White race consciousness . . . plays an important, perhaps crucial, role in the new regime that has legitimated the deteriorating day-to-day material conditions of the majority of Blacks.

Kimberle Williams Crenshaw, *Race, Reform and Retrenchment: Transformation and Legitimation in Antidiscrimination Law,* 101 HARV L. REV. 1331, 1378–79 (1988).

14. The cycle is illustrated in the following summary of sociologist William Julius Wilson's report on research findings from the Urban Poverty and Family Life Survey:

> Impoverishment . . . [began], in the loss of the blue-collar positions black men could once count on. Men could feed their families with these jobs; they had a sense of control and self-worth. At one time in Chicago, the proportion of blacks in manufacturing had exceeded the portion of whites.
>
> But when those jobs disappeared, joblessness wasn't the only result. The unemployed increasingly found themselves concentrated in problem-plagued low-income neighborhoods. With no one working, no one had ties to the labor market and no one could recommend anyone for available jobs. The despair, isolation and anger . . . soon began feeding on themselves.

Gretchen Reynolds, *The Rising Significance of Race,* CHI. MAG., Dec. 1992, at 81, 83. *See also* William Julius Wilson, *The Plight of the Inner-City Black Male,* 136 PROC. AM. PHIL. SOC'Y 320 (1992).

15. The summers of 1965 and 1966 had seen major uprisings in black ghettos in Los Angeles, Chicago, San Francisco and Cleveland. In 1967 riots triggered by racism, economic deprivation, police brutality and other factors occurred in cities throughout the United States, the most infamous and deadly occurring in Newark, N.J. and Detroit. *See* Fred R. Harris, *The 1967 Riots and the Kerner Commission, in* QUIET RIOTS, *supra* note 12, at 5, 5–15.

16. KERNER COMMISSION REPORT, *supra* note 3, at 1.

17. I use the term unprivileged rather than the euphemism "underprivileged." The latter ironically understates the situation faced by urban minorities, for certainly to possess no privilege is to be accorded less than enough privilege and to thus be more than "underprivileged."

18. Tim Schreiner, *Simi Valley, South Central L.A.—Sharp Contrasts,* S. F. CHRON., May 1, 1992, at A14.

19. DAVID DANTE TROUT, WEST COAST REGIONAL OFFICE, CONSUMERS UNION OF U.S., INC., THE THIN RED LINE: HOW THE POOR STILL PAY MORE 19 (1993).

20. *American Survey: Pull Together?*, ECONOMIST, May 9, 1992, at 25.

21. *Id.* Middle-class African Americans can relocate to middle-class black and integrated communities (if available). Until the 1960s America's inner city neighborhoods featured a "vertical integration of different segments of the urban black population. Lower-class, working-class, and middle-class black families all lived more or less in the same communities. . . ." WILLIAM JULIUS WILSON, THE TRULY DISADVANTAGED 7 (1987).

22. Schreiner, *supra* note 18, at A14.

23. Most of Simi Valley's residents are "from L.A., escaping the big city and its problems." *Id.*

24. *See supra* note 5 for statistics on the racial makeup of Simi Valley and Ventura County.

25. "[T]he officials of affluent jurisdictions have managed to exclude the poor entirely from their communities through the manipulation of zoning and land use controls that bar the construction of housing affordable by low-income families." William L. Taylor, *Brown, Equal Protection, and the Isolation of the Poor,* 95 YALE L. J. 1700, 1729 (1986).

26. Schreiner, *supra* note 18. In South Central Los Angeles 67.7 percent of the housing units are renter-occupied. TROUT, *supra* note 19, at 47. Even when able to afford to purchase homes, African Americans are subject to bias in home mortgage lending.

    In 1992, African-Americans in California were 1.75 times more likely to be rejected for mortgage loans than white applicants by Citibank and 1.5 times as likely to be rejected by Bank of America. . . . Across the country, from California to New York, minorities are disproportionately denied mortgage loans. Disparities in mortgage loan rejections and in application rates raise serious questions about minority borrowers' access to credit.

    MICHAEL A. TERHORST, WEST COAST REGIONAL OFFICE, CONSUMERS UNION OF U.S., INC., THE AMERICAN DREAM: OPENING THE DOOR TO CREDIT AND ENDING MORTGAGE DISCRIMINATION 2–3 (1993).

27. The California Housing Element Law requires local governments to "assist in the development of adequate housing to meet the needs of low- and moderate-income households." CAL. GOV'T CODE § 65583(c)(2) (1994).

28. WILLIAM FULTON, GUIDE TO CALIFORNIA PLANNING 74 (1991). More than 40 percent of the adopted housing elements in California do not comply with the law. *Id.* at 75.
29. Schreiner, *supra* note 18; Don DeBenedictis, *Cop's Second Trial in L.A.*, A.B.A. J., July 1992, at 16.
30. This metaphor has been used repeatedly with respect to the police defendants in the Rodney King beating case. Terry White, the prosecutor in the state trial, said that the jurors saw the police as a "thin blue line separating the law abiding citizens from the *jungle.*" Henry Weinstein, *After the Riots: The Search for Answers*, L.A. TIMES, May 8, 1992, at 3A (emphasis added). The defense attorneys in the federal civil rights trial referred to the police as "a thin blue line that protects the law-abiding citizenry in our communities from the criminal element." *King Case Nears Climax; City On Guard*, CHI. TRIB., Apr. 10, 1993, at 3. The urban jury in the federal case was not persuaded by the metaphor.
31. Jay Mathews, *Playing Politics with Crime*, NEWSWEEK, May 11, 1992, at 40.
32.

> One indication . . . that day-to-day law enforcement might be contravening society's commitment to racial equality is the startlingly disproportionate representation of blacks and other minorities among persons whom police arrest. . . . [T]he argument that police behavior is undistorted by racial discrimination flatly contradicts most studies, which reveal what many police officers freely admit: that police use race as an independently significant, if not determinative, factor in deciding whom to follow, detain, search, or arrest.

Developments in the Law—Race and the Criminal Process, supra note 2, at 1495–96.

33. DeBenedictis, *supra* note 29 (quoting Prof. Bernard Segal). These attitudes raise the question: When suburban cops work in urban jobs, which community is better served by the police, the community that employs them or the communities where the police live? The police perform one aspect of their jobs vigorously, arresting African Americans in numbers that are roughly 100 percent higher than their crime rate. Evan Stark, *The Myth of Black Violence*, USA TODAY MAG., Jan. 1992, at 32, 33. "The National Crime Survey indicates that blacks commit 26.3% of violent crimes, which is roughly twice their percentage in the population. However, they comprise over half of those arrested for violent crimes, four times their percentage in the population." *Id.* Despite this arrest rate, inner city residents receive notoriously poor police protection and service.
34. The metaphor of warfare continues Loren Miller's observations about metropolitan residential patterns, recorded almost three decades ago.

> One of the most persistent bits of urban folklore is that a particular section of a city belongs to the ethnic group that inhabits it at the moment. That set of folk beliefs has a language of its own, bristling with military terminology: Negroes are said to "invade" or "infiltrate" a "white community" when one of their number moves in. Whites are stereotyped as beleaguered and standing heroic guard to repulse black invaders busting blocks and trampling on property values.

Loren Miller, *Government's Responsibility for Residential Segregation*, *in* RACE & PROPERTY, 58, 58 (John H. Denton ed., 1964).

35. Infrastructural connections are particularly important in the Los Angeles metropolitan area. Water, waste-disposal and air quality control problems have required solutions that enable numerous cities and unincorporated areas to work together. *See*

generally WINSTON W. CROUCH & BEATRICE DINERMAN, SOUTHERN CALIFORNIA METROPOLIS: A STUDY IN DEVELOPMENT OF GOVERNMENT FOR A METROPOLITAN AREA (1963).

36. This idea of connection is expressed by Prof. Cornel West:

> [W]e need to begin with a frank acknowledgment of the basic humanness and Americanness of each of us. And we must acknowledge that as a people—*E Pluribus Unum*—we are on a slippery slope toward economic strife, social turmoil and cultural chaos. If we go down we go down together. The Los Angeles upheaval forced us to see not only that we are not connected in ways we would like to be but also, in a more profound sense that this failure to connect binds us even more tightly together. The paradox of race in America is that our common destiny is more pronounced and imperiled precisely when our divisions are deeper.

CORNEL WEST, RACE MATTERS 4 (1993).

37. KERNER COMMISSION REPORT, *supra* note 3, at 226.

38. *America's Cities: Doomed to Burn?*, ECONOMIST, May 9, 1992, at 21. Only 12 percent of the population in the United States now lives in cities with over 500,000 inhabitants. *Id.*

39. "Whereas an average of 71% of northern whites lived in suburbs by 1980, the figure for blacks was only 23%." MASSEY & DENTON, *supra* note 4, at 67. Furthermore, black suburbanization does not necessarily result in integration. Black isolation in most northern areas is remarkably high even though blacks do not exceed 10 percent of the suburban population. *Id.* at 73. This is true of cities including Chicago, Cleveland, Detroit, Gary, and Los Angeles. *Id.*

40. Paul K. Stockman, *Anti-Snob Zoning in Massachusetts: Assessing One Attempt at Opening the Suburbs to Affordable Housing,* 78 VA. L. REV. 535 (1992).

41. *Id.* at 542.

42. The double entendre and the attendant metaphysical implications are intended. *See* RALPH ELLISON, INVISIBLE MAN (1947) ("Since you never recognize even when in closest contact with me... no doubt you'll hardly believe that I exist...").

43. *See* Ralph Blumenthal, *Black Youth Is Killed by Whites; Brooklyn Attack is Called Racial,* N.Y. TIMES, Aug. 26, 1989, at A1.

44. *See* Robert D. McFadden, *3 Youths are Held on Murder Counts in Queens Attack,* N.Y. TIMES, Dec. 23, 1986, at A1. Other predominantly white areas associated with racial bias and violence include Carnarsie in Brooklyn, South Boston and Charlestown in Boston, Canaryville, and Marquette Park, Bridgeport and other Chicago neighborhoods. *See Man Slashed in Carnarsie Bias Attack,* NEWSDAY, Aug. 2, 1991, at 4, *available in* LEXIS, NEWS Library, NEWSDY File; Herbert H. Denton, *In Reborn Boston, Race Hatred Still Festers,* WASH. POST, Dec. 7, 1980, at A1; Howard Witt, *Attack on 2 Blacks Barely Draws Notice,* CHI. TRIB., July 12, 1985, § 2, at 1. For a story of racial bias in ostensibly liberal Northern California see Bill Mandel, *Black Man's Ad is the Talk of the Town,* S.F. EXAMINER Jan. 24, 1993, at B1 (chronicling police harassment of Black resident of Sonoma, California, a town with a 97 percent white population). Of course, Simi Valley, California is now associated with racial exclusion.

45. "We got a neighborhood to protect," and "This is our neighborhood.... You let in one colored, you gotta let in a thousand," were among the justifications proffered for an incident where a racially mixed group of 12 year old students from Brooklyn was attacked by older white teenagers during a school arranged picnic in a Staten Island Park. Howard Blum, *"Bias Incident" at Staten Island's Miller Field: A Tale of Two*

Neighborhoods, in RACE, CLASS, & GENDER IN THE UNITED STATES 67, 68 (Paula S. Rothenberg ed., 2d ed. 1992).

46. *See* Stirgus v. Benoit, 720 F. Supp. 119, 121 (N.D. Ill. 1989) and Pina v. Abington, 1 Eq. Opp. Hous. Cas. (P-H) ¶15,257, 15,495 (E.D. Pa. May 27, 1978), for examples of Fair Housing Act litigation where the facts involved violence against black residents.

47.

> The problem of designing a republican government that could provide security for property was a central one for the Federalists, whose views prevailed at the Constitutional convention of 1787.... Originally invoked as the defining instance of the larger problem of securing justice and liberty in a republic, property indeed came to define the terms of that problem for at least one hundred fifty years.

Jennifer Nedelsky, *Law, Boundaries and the Bounded Self, in* LAW AND THE ORDER OF CULTURE 162, 164 (Robert Post ed., 1991).

48. The widely held but false notion that property ownership gives the titleholder the right to "do anything I want with it" is discussed in the wider context of political discourse in America in MARY ANN GLENDON, RIGHTS TALK 8 (1991).

49. This attitude is illustrated by Bruce Fister, a resident of a white neighborhood on Chicago's south side. In a newspaper article that discussed the Republican party's election strategy of playing on the racial fears of whites to gain votes, Fister said, "I'm against civil rights, open housing, all that stuff.... I've come from too many neighborhoods that turned black and now have the highest crime rate in the city. I'm tired of being pushed away from all my neighborhoods." John Jacobs, *Rust Belt to Decide Campaign Battle,* S.F. EXAMINER, Sept. 27, 1992, at A1, A12. *See also* Cheryl T. Harris, *Whiteness As Property,* 106 HARV. L. REV. 1707 (1993).

50. "Decades of government-sponsored housing discrimination have significantly shaped patterns of residential segregation. Contrary to the notion that racial segregation occurs because of 'natural' migration patterns, ample evidence demonstrates the connection between government actions and private behavior." Robert L. Hayman Jr. & Nancy Levit, *The Constitutional Ghetto,* 1993 WIS. L. REV. 627, 679.

51. The phenomenon of gentrification illustrates this point. A number of African American residents of urban neighborhoods throughout the country have been displaced by whites. Gentrification occurs in areas that are geographically and financially attractive because of comparatively low property costs. White buyers can afford homes in the area but black renters are pushed out. *See* Clarence Johnson, *Gays, Blacks Try to Cool Tensions,* S.F. CHRON., Aug. 28, 1993, at A1 (describing displacement of black homeowners and businesses in a San Francisco neighborhood by urban development and affluent gays); DeNeen L. Brown, *Preserving Low-Income Housing on the Hill,* WASH. POST, June 9, 1988, at J1 (community coalition formed to modify the force of twenty years of gentrification on Capitol Hill); Patrick Reardon, *City's Face is Still Changing, but More Slowly,* CHI. TRIB., Sept. 13, 1987, at 1, 22 (noting gentrification in two Chicago neighborhoods, Lincoln Park and the Near North Side); Philip Lentz, *The Rising Cost of Diversity,* CHI. TRIB., July 20, 1986, at 6 (gentrification in Montclair, N.J.). Some gentrification has resulted from government action to systematically break up black neighborhoods through urban renewal programs. Kaye Thompson, *HUD Accuses Annapolis of Housing-Policy Bias,* WASH. POST, July 28, 1984, at B3.

52. John O. Calmore, *Spatial Equality and the Kerner Commission Report: A Back-To-The-Future Essay,* 71 N.C. L. REV. 1487, 1506 (1993) [hereinafter *Spatial Equality).* Middle-class African Americans are increasingly rejecting predominantly white neighborhoods which are often inhospitable, and deliberately choosing affluent or

middle-class black neighborhoods. *Id.* As more African Americans move to the suburbs (in 1990, 32 percent of blacks in U.S. metropolitan areas lived in suburbs, a 6 percent increase from 1980) the number of predominately black suburbs is also increasing. David J. Dent, *The New Black Suburbs,* N.Y. TIMES MAG., June 14, 1992, at 18, 20. Notably, affluent black suburbs are developing because the individuals want to live in a black community rather than by resegregation due to white flight. *Id.* at 22.

53. Examples include the placement of freeways and urban development projects.

> A state's decision to locate a freeway is often fraught with controversy and politics.... At times, the affected constituency can influence the decision to locate these projects. More often than not, however, the affected population has little to say and even less with which to say it.... The predicaments of discrete and insular minorities tend to be similar. Unable to block project locations themselves, the affected communities attempt to block an adverse governmental decision with other means and through alternative forums.

Anthony N. R. Zamora, *The Century Freeway Consent Decree,* 62 S. CAL. L. REV. 1805, 1820. (1989). The article relates the story of how a coalition of the NAACP, environmental groups and local residents successfully battled the proposed alignment of the Century Freeway through the low income minority neighborhoods of Compton, Lynwood, Watts and Willowbrook. *Id.*

54. A 1989 survey determined that 40 percent of the Black respondents considered living in racially mixed neighborhoods very important, almost double the percent of whites (21 percent) who expressed this view. Richard Morin & Dan Balz, *Shifting Racial Climate: Blacks and Whites Have Greater Contact But Sharply Different Views, Poll Finds,* WASH. POST, Oct. 25, 1989, at A1, A16 (reporting the results of a nationwide *Washington Post*-ABC News Poll of 1249 whites and 371 blacks).

55. *See* Sander, *supra* note 9. "The Black population outside of the central cities of urban areas increased by 2.8 million between 1970 and 1980.... The developing patterns of racial and residential distribution duplicate the traditional patterns of racial segregation of the central city." Robert W. Collin & Robin A. Morris, *Racial Inequality in American Cities: An Interdisciplinary Critique,* 11 NAT'L BLACK L. J. 177, 180 (1989).

56. The notion of living in the "best" place that one can afford is so commonplace that many Americans would consider doing otherwise abnormal. Living in the nicest neighborhood possible is central to the middle-class American dream and is a goal creating incentive to work. This banal mindset can be found in an example of advice to mothers who feel guilty about working outside of the home: "Consider how your job benefits your family. Start with the most obvious—you have a higher standard of living, so you live in a nicer neighborhood and your children are safe and go to decent schools." Dianne Hales, *Letting Go of Guilt,* WORKING MOTHER, Sept. 1992, at 47, 48.

The privilege of living in the "best" neighborhood one can afford is seen as an entitlement to middle-class people of color as well. Although access to some white communities is cut off to them, the exodus of the middle class from urban ghettos has been cited as a factor that has contributed to the disintegration of African American urban communities in the 1970s and 80s. *See* WILSON, *supra* note 21, at 7. Note, however, that Wilson's view is challenged by Professors Douglas Massey and Nancy Denton, who argue that concentrated poverty would have occurred in the ghettos during the 1970s with or without middle-class out-migration. MASSEY & DENTON, *supra* note 4, at 117–18. *see also* Collin & Morris, *supra* note 55, at 180 ("Despite this

Black exodus from the central city, black populations have continued to increase in percentage in American central cities.").

The attempt to create middle-class African American enclaves does not always meet with success.

> Although upwardly mobile blacks, like whites, have sought to carve out neighborhood enclaves that contain only members of their own class, they have been relatively unsuccessful.... Even though the black middle class may not live in ghetto neighborhoods, they often share neighborhoods with the black working poor and near-poor.

Spatial Equality, supra note 52, at 1503.

57. The Department of Health and Human Services reported that death rates are 19 percent higher in large metropolitan counties than in suburban counties. *Growing Disparity in Ethnic Death Rates,* S.F. CHRON., Sept. 16, 1993, at A2. "In the 1980s, death rates had declined by 10 percent in the suburbs but by only half as much in the inner cities." *Id.*

58. *See* RUSK, *supra* note 6, at 29.

59. *See* Luke W. Cole, *Empowerment as the Key to Environmental Protection: The Need for Environmental Poverty Law,* 19 ECOLOGY L. Q. 619 (1992); David Holmstrom, *Pollution In U.S. Cities Hits Minorities Hardest,* CHRISTIAN SCI. MONITOR, Jan. 7, 1993, at 8.

60. *See generally* JONATHAN KOZOL, SAVAGE INEQUALITIES: CHILDREN IN AMERICA'S SCHOOLS (1991).

61. *See generally* TROUT, *supra* note 19.

62.

> The recent shift of manufacturing, office employment and residential development from inner cities to suburban cities has caused large economic and social disparities. The main disparity is that the inner cities have absorbed and retained the lower income minority population while suburban cities have taken in the White population. This departure of industry and jobs has left inner city urban areas without employment opportunities for low income residents, a minority labor force with less marketable skills and a community without an adequate tax base to provide municipal services.

Collin & Morris, *supra* note 55, at 180 (footnote omitted).

63. *See supra* text accompanying note 20.

64. *See* Michael Quintanilla, *Jobs: The Search for Work has Become a Full-time Job.,* L.A. TIMES, Nov. 18, 1992, at J4 (describing the plight of the unemployed poor in Los Angeles who live far from where the jobs are, have no transportation or child-care, and cannot afford to move to areas offering employment).

65. Wilson, *supra* note 14, at 324. "Whether through skills tests, credentials, personal references, folk theories or their intuition, [employers] used some means of screening out the inner-city applicant.... [B]lack job applicants, unlike their white counterparts, must indicate to employers that the stereotypes do not apply to them." Joleen Kirschenman & Kathryn M. Neckerman, *"We'd Love to Hire Them, But . . .": The Meaning of Race for Employers, in* THE URBAN UNDERCLASS 203, 231 (Christopher Jencks & Paul E. Peterson eds., 1991).

66. David Rusk characterizes this phenomenon as "the point of no return" where city populations drop precipitously (up to 44 and 45 percent in Detroit and Cleveland), city-suburb economic disparities drop to a level where city incomes are only about

70 percent of suburban income, and the percentage of minority population in the city climbs due to a continuing exodus of whites. RUSK, *supra* note 6, at 75–77.

67. Black segregation remains high across "all levels of socioeconomic status, whether measured in terms of education, income or occupation." HOUSE JUDICIARY COMM., FAIR HOUSING AMENDMENTS ACT OF 1988, H. R. Doc. No. 711, 100th Cong., 2d Sess. 1, 14 (1988), *reprinted in* 1988 U.S.C.A.A.N. 2173, 2177.

68. *See* discussion of *Boyd v. LeFrak Org., infra* text accompanying notes 90–97.

69. For a discussion of the psychological and philosophical ramifications of this attitude see Michele M. Moody-Adams, *Race, Class, and the Social Construction of Self-Respect,* 24 PHIL. F. 251 (1992–93).

70. *See* WILSON, *supra* note 21, at 13–19.

71. A popular perception, evidenced by callers to radio phone-in shows and in recent books such as Charles Murray's *Losing Ground,* Mickey Kaus' *The End of Equality* and Christopher Jencks' *Rethinking Social Policy; Race, Poverty, and the Underclass,* is that poverty is a lifestyle choice or the result of individual attitudes. The central question in addressing the issue of poverty has become "What's wrong with those people on welfare?", an approach that presumes a lack of merit on the part of the unprivileged. *See* Ruth Coniff, *The Culture of Cruelty,* PROGRESSIVE, Sept. 1992, at 16.

72.

> The ubiquity of work and opportunity, of course, were myths, even in the early Republic. The transformation in economic relations, the growth of cities, immigrations, the seasonability of labor, fluctuations in consumer demand, periodic depressions, low wages, restricted opportunities for women, industrial accidents, high mortality, and the absence of any social insurance: together these chiseled chronic poverty and dependence into American social life.

MICHAEL B. KATZ, THE UNDESERVING POOR 14 (1989).

The opportunity myth is particularly spurious when poverty intersects with race.

> The unspoken and totally facetious maxim is that with self-improvement the opportunity is available for all blacks to be successful. But success for individual blacks demands exceptional skills exercised diligently in settings where their efforts will further or, at least, not threaten white interests. Obviously, no more than a small percentage of blacks is likely to be graced by so felicitous a set of circumstances.

RACE, RACISM, *supra* note 10, at 49.

73. In 1990 6.6 million workers in the U.S. could be categorized as "working poor"—people who devoted more than half of the year to working or looking for work and who lived in families with incomes below the official poverty level. Jennifer M. Gardner & Diane E. Herz, *Working and poor in 1990,* 115 MONTHLY LAB. REV. 20, 20 (1992). Furthermore, even though a person does not have remunerative employment, she may work very hard. The process of maintaining eligibility for benefits and the efforts that go into providing for family needs can be intense and exhausting. *See* Teresa L. Amott, *Black Women and AFDC: Making Entitlement Out of Necessity, In* WOMEN, THE STATE AND WELFARE 280 (Linda Gordon ed., 1990). This difficulty is exacerbated for homeless families.

74. Bureau of Labor statistics data show that Black and Hispanic workers in the labor force for more than half the year are much more likely to be poor than whites. Gardner & Herz, *supra* note 73, at 21. African Americans' poverty rate in 1990 was 2½ times that for whites with similar labor force activity. *Id.*

75. In 1991 about 14.3 million American children (21.8%) lived in poverty. CHILDREN'S DEFENSE FUND, THE STATE OF AMERICA'S CHILDREN 1992 25 (1992). *See also* Gregory Mantsios, *Rewards and Opportunities: The Politics and Economics of Class in the U.S., in* RACE, CLASS, & GENDER IN THE UNITED STATES, *supra* note 45, at 96, 98 (giving statistics on the demography of poverty in the United States).

76. *See generally* KOZOL, *supra* note 60 (describing the state of public schools in several U.S. cities).

77. *See generally* KATZ, *supra* note 72.

78. *See generally* GLENDON, *supra* note 48 (discussing the development of the ideology of "rights" in American society).

79. *See infra* note 83 and accompanying text.

80. *See, e.g.,* Board of Educ. of Okla. City Pub. Sch. v. Dowell, 498 U.S. 237 (1991).

81. A notable exception is Southern Burlington County NAACP v. Township of Mount Laurel (Mount Laurel I), 336 A.2d 713 (N.J.), *appeal dismissed and cert. denied,* 423 U.S. 808 (1975). The Supreme Court of New Jersey held that municipalities may not enact zoning requirements that foreclose housing opportunities for low and middle income people but must affirmatively provide housing for a fair share of lower income area residents. *Id.* The decision has not been particularly effective in increasing low income housing. *See* Southern Burlington County NAACP v. Township of Mount Laurel (Mount Laurel II), 456 A.2d 390 (N.J. 1983).

82. Lindsay v. Normet, 405 U.S. 56 (1972).

83. *See* RUSSELL W. GALLOWAY, JUSTICE FOR ALL? THE RICH AND POOR IN SUPREME COURT HISTORY (1790–1990) 155–58 (1991). Two important decisions of this era, James v. Valtierra, 402 U.S. 137 (1971), and San Antonio Indep. Sch. Dist. v. Rodriguez, 411 U.S. 1 (1973), applied rational basis analysis in cases that alleged discrimination against the poor in public housing and public education funding. Another area in which poverty has not been recognized as a suspect class is abortion rights. *See, e.g.,* Harris v. McRae, 448 U.S. 297 (1980); Beal v. Doe, 432 U.S. 438 (1977); Maher v. Roe, 432 U.S. 464 (1977); Poelker v. Doe, 432 U.S. 519 (1977).

84. *See, e.g.,* the discussion of the facts in Southern Burlington County NAACP v. Township of Mount Laurel, 336 A.2d 713 (N.J. 1975) (town's zoning ordinances exhibited economic discrimination to keep down local taxes on property without regard for non-fiscal considerations affecting people).

85. John O. Calmore, *Exploring the Significance of Race and Class in Representing the Black Poor,* 61 OR. L. REV. 201, 235 (1982).

86. For illustrations of various low income housing programs and local opposition see James v. Valtierra, 402 U.S. 137 (1971) (discussed *infra* notes 87–89 and accompanying text) and U.S. v. Yonkers Bd. of Educ., 635 F. Supp. 1577 (S.D.N.Y. 1986), *cert. denied,* 486 U.S. 1055 (1988).

87. 402 U.S. 137 (1971). Article XXXIV of the California Constitution provides in Section 1:

> No low rent housing project shall hereafter be developed, constructed, or acquired in any manner by any state public body until, a majority of the qualified electors of the city, town or county, as the case may be, in which it is proposed to develop, construct or acquire the same, voting upon such issue, approve such project by voting in favor therefore at an election to be held for that purpose, or at any general or special election.

The provision defines, in telling terms, who it is the local citizenry must vote to admit:

For the purposes of this article only "persons of low income" shall mean persons or families who lack the amount of income which is necessary (as determined by the state public body developing, constructing, or acquiring the housing project) to enable them, without financial assistance to live in decent, safe and sanitary dwellings without overcrowding.

CAL. CONST. art. XXXIV, § 1.

California voters reaffirmed Article XXXIV in the 1993 election. *Final Election Returns,* L.A. TIMES, Nov. 4, 1993, at B6. The electorate rejected Proposition 168, which sought to rescind the voter approval requirement for the construction of low income housing that relies on public money for at least half its funding. *Id.; see* Greg Lucas, *November Ballot's Forgotten Measures,* S. F. CHRON., Oct. 25, 1993, at A17.

88. *James,* 402 U.S. at 143.

89. *Id.* at 141.

90. Boyd v. Lefrak Org., 509 F.2d 1110 (2d Cir.), *cert. denied,* 423 U.S. 896 (1975).

91. *Id.* at 1111.

92. *Id.* at 1117.

93. *Id.* at 1118.

94. *Id.* at 1113.

95. *Id.*

96. *Id.*

97. *Id.* at 1112.

98. CAL. CIV. CODE §§ 51–52 (1994). The Unruh Act has been held to prohibit all "arbitrary discrimination by a business enterprise." *In re* Cox, 474 P.2d 992, 995 (Cal. 1970) (including forms of discrimination that are not specifically mentioned in the Act). *See, e.g.,* Marina Point, Ltd. v. Wolfson, 640 P.2d 115 (Cal.), *cert. denied,* 459 U.S. 858 (1982) (Unruh Act prohibits discrimination against families with children); O'Connor v. Village Green Owners Ass'n, 662 P.2d 427 (Cal. 1983) (Unruh Act prohibits age restrictions, other than in senior citizens complexes).

99. 805 P.2d 873 (Cal. 1991). In *Harris,* low income public aid recipients who could afford to pay the rent charged by the defendants were nonetheless denied apartments because their gross income was not equal to or greater than three times the amount of rent. *Id.* at 874. Although the plaintiff could demonstrate that she was paying a greater rate of rent for the premises that she occupied at the time of applying for defendant's apartment and had not defaulted, the landlord did not have to consider her individual characteristics. *Id.* at 874–75.

100. *Id.* at 889–90. The court held that the landlord's policy could be found to minimize the transaction costs of tenant default, which the court related to maintaining the solvency of the landlord's business. *Id.* at 885–86. The landlord's economic considerations were considered enough to justify excluding the plaintiff despite a demonstrated ability to pay the amount of rent sought by the defendant. *Id.* at 889. Ironically, the woman's status as a poor person forced her to remain in a rental unit that cost a higher percentage of her limited resources than the defendant's apartment.

101. Although the plaintiffs in *Harris* alleged that the defendant's polices had a disparate impact on the protected class of women, African Americans would also be disparately affected by the defendant's policies. In 1991, 46 percent of black families had a female householder and no husband, compared with 13 percent of white families. Carrie

Teegardin, *Census Says More Blacks Face Poverty: 1-Parent Families Key to Slippage,* ATLANTA J. & CONST., Sept. 25, 1992, at A1.

102. *See Harris,* 805 P.2d at 889.

103. *See* WILSON, *supra* note 21, at 121–22.

104. For an examination of discrimination against African Americans in hiring see MARGERY AUSTIN TURNER ET AL., OPPORTUNITIES DENIED, OPPORTUNITIES DIMINISHED: RACIAL DISCRIMINATION IN HIRING (Urban Institute Report 91-9, 1991).

105. *See* Mantsios, *supra* note 75, at 105 ("[S]ome are rich precisely because others are poor . . . one's privilege is predicated on the other's disenfranchisement.").

106.

> By almost all aggregate statistical measures—incomes and living standards; health and life expectancy; educational, occupational and residential opportunities . . . the well-being of both blacks and whites has advanced greatly over the past five decades. [However, by] almost all the same indicators, blacks remain substantially behind whites. . . . Since the early 1970s, the economic status of blacks relative to whites has, on average, stagnated or deteriorated.

NATIONAL RESEARCH COUNCIL, A COMMON DESTINY, *supra* note 4, at 6.

107. Peggy McIntosh eloquently explores the concept of white privilege in *White Privilege and Male Privilege: A Personal Account of Coming to See Correspondences Through Work in Women's Studies* (Wellesley College Center for Research on Women Working Paper No. 189, 1988). Ms. McIntosh describes white privileges as "an invisible package of unearned assets which I can count on cashing in each day, but about which I was 'meant' to remain oblivious." *Id.* at 1. She lists forty-six conditions which she can count on as a member of the white race that may or may not exist for people of color. *Id.* at 5–9. Her list is not exhaustive. *See also* Peggy McIntosh, *White Privilege: Unpacking the Invisible Knapsack,* PEACE & FREEDOM, July/August 1989, at 10.

Perhaps the most telling aspect of white privilege is that whites need not be conscious of their own race or of racial discrimination to survive in America.

> To people of color, who are the victims of racism/white supremacy, race is a filter through which they see the world. Whites do not look at the world through this filter of racial awareness, even though they also comprise a race. This privilege to ignore their race gives whites a societal advantage distinct from any advantage received from the existence of discriminatory racism.

Trina Grillo & Stephanie Wildman, *Obscuring the Importance of Race: The Implications of Making Comparisons Between Racism and Sexism (Or Other -Isms),* 1991 DUKE L. J. 397, 398.

108. Fair housing law is structured and administered under a paradigm of individual rights. The search for individual victims and perpetrators enables the collective expression of privilege to escape legal scrutiny and allows community-based racial exclusion to become more real and enforced more effectively than the actual laws that prohibit discrimination. *See* Armstrong, *supra* note 11, at 916–22.

109. 451 U.S. 100 (1981).

110. *Id.* at 104. Originally the residents requested the closure of four streets that led into the subdivision. *Id.* at 103.

111. *Id.* at 112–113.

112. *Id.* at 129.

113. There was evidence that the closing would cause an economic depreciation in the property values in the predominantly black area. *Id.* at 110.

114. *Id.* at 109.

115. *Id.* at 118.

116. *Id.* at 143 (Marshall J., dissenting).

117. *Id.* at 147.

118. Board of Educ. of Okla. City Pub. Sch. v. Dowell, 498 U.S. 237, 243 (1991).

119. 112 S. Ct. 1430 (1992).

120. *Id.* at 1448 (citations omitted).

121. *See* discussion *supra* of *City of Memphis v. Greene* accompanying notes 109–117. *See also* Tim Schreiner, *Suburban Communities 'Forting Up'*, S. F. CHRON., Sept. 21, 1992, at A1, A12; John Woolfolk, *Charges of Elitism Fly in Traffic Battles,* S. F. CHRON., Aug. 2, 1993, at A15.

122. It becomes more difficult and expensive to keep out the unwanted, and the incursions on individual rights necessary to restrict the movement of "undesirables" threaten everyone's individual rights.

123. *See* Schreiner, *supra* note 18 (comparing the community of Simi Valley with its good schools, to the devastation of South Central Los Angeles). *See generally* KOZOL, *supra* note 60 (describing the disparities between inner city and suburban public schools).

124. Discussing the options available to the low income plaintiffs in *Rodriquez v. San Antonio Sch. Dist.*, one commentator wrote:

> [T]he Rodriquez majority might have replied, "citizens who value public education highly are free to vote with their feet—to relocate to communities where public schools are well financed and taxes are low. The response, of course, is that while this option may be available to some, it is foreclosed to poor people who are barred by zoning, land use controls, or other measures from securing residences in communities that provide the services they desire.

Taylor, *supra* note 25, at 1730.

125. When our government determines that an issue is truly important it rarely leaves social responsibility to individual choice. The state has created powerful bureaucracies to support its military and income taxation politics. If citizens do not go along with the government's choices for us about the draft or income tax, we face the possibility of incarceration. Thus, when our country is honestly committed to its stated policies, the government is able to achieve a fair amount of success in reaching its goals. For example, the U.S. share of Operation Desert Storm was 7.4 billion dollars. *Nunn Says Congress Will Pass Moratorium on Nuclear Testing,* STAR TRIB. (MINNEAPOLIS), July 29, 1992, at 6A. Funds for Desert Storm were allocated quickly with a minimum amount of dissension because the resource of petroleum is prized much more highly than the human beings in our inner cities. *Cf.* Terry Spencer, *Schwarzkopf Says War Was About Oil,* L. A. TIMES, Feb. 14, 1992, at B2. The insincerity of our institutional commitment to desegregation is apparent when the Justice Department chooses to enforce the Fair Housing Act by challenging consent decrees in cases that use racial criteria to maintain integrated housing, yet fails to pursue the patterns and practices that lead to the preservation of thousands of Simi Valleys all over America. *See, e.g.,* U.S. v. Starrett Assocs., 840 F.2d 1096 (2d Cir. 1988). *See also* Armstrong, *supra* note 11, at 918 n.51.

126. Miller, *supra* note 34, at 71–72.

127. Recent renewals of the promise of equality include the Fair Housing Amendments Act of 1988, Pub. L. No. 100–430, 102 Stat. 1619, and the Civil Rights Act of 1991, Pub. L. No. 102–166, 105 Stat. 1071 (codified as amended in scattered sections of 42 U.S.C.).

CHAPTER 8 The Economic Institution

8.1 GEORGE WILSON AND IAN SAKURA-LEMESSY

Earnings Over the Early Work Career Among Males in the Middle Class

The economy is an institutionalized system for the production, distribution, and consumption of goods and services in a society. Labor is the principal mechanism by which people are involved in the economy. Current data show that approximately 134 million people participate in the American civilian labor force. But not all racial and ethnic groups participate fully and equally in the nation's economy. U.S. Department of Labor statistics show that Black workers are 2.2 times more likely to be unemployed than White workers and that Latino workers are 1.7 times more likely to be unemployed than White workers. Earning differentials by race and ethnicity also characterize the American labor market. Recent government figures on income show that the median weekly earnings for White workers is $573, while the weekly earnings for Black workers is $445; it is $385 for Latino workers.

The following selection is from "Earnings Over the Early Work Career Among Males in the Middle Class: Has Race Declined in Its Significance?" *Sociological Perspectives* (Spring 2000). In it, assistant professor of sociology George Wilson of the University of Miami and Ian Sakura-Lemessy, a graduate student at the university, suggest that the earnings gap between male White workers and male minority workers results from the continuing effect of institutionalized discriminatory employment practices in middle-class occupations. Moreover, the widening earnings gap between White and minority workers directly challenges the notion that the significance of race is declining in accounting for opportunities of middle-class Blacks. Accordingly, say Wilson and Sakura-Lemessy, the racial earnings differential between middle-class White and minority workers results from "the well-documented retreat from enforcement of civil rights."

Key Concept: the declining significance of race and institutionalized racial discrimination in the labor market

Abstract: Within the context of William Wilson's "declining significance of race" thesis, this study uses data from the Panel Study of Income Dynamics to examine differences in the income gap among two cohorts of males through the early stages of their work careers in middle-class jobs during the periods 1975–82 and 1985–92. Findings indicate that the racial gap is structured in a manner that is contrary to predictions from the Wilson thesis. In particular, the gap increases over the seven-year period for both cohorts. Further, the gap is particularly pronounced among the more recent cohort. Specifically, it is larger at the outset of the seven-year period and increases more between 1985 and 1992 than between 1975 and 1982. Specific cohort and period effects that explain the racial differences in income are discussed, and directions for future research are identified.

Now more than twenty years old, William Wilson's "declining significance of race" thesis remains the dominant perspective that attempts to explain the complex interplay between race and social class in accounting for the life-chance opportunities of an increasingly differentiated African American population in the post-1965 civil rights era. The influence of the Wilson thesis is manifest in the steady stream of research that has assessed its merits. In this regard, one development in the last decade or so is noteworthy: a growing number of studies have assessed the dynamic of racial inequality among the relatively privileged African American population. In particular, examinations of African Americans who are employed in the middle-class job structure have focused on a range of socioeconomic outcomes, including earnings (Cancio, Evans, and Maume 1996; Thomas 1993; Thomas, Herring, and Horton 1994) and its returns to job authority (Wilson 1997), rates and magnitude of occupational mobility (Farley 1996; Hout 1984), occupational status (Farley 1984), and occupational segregation (Collins 1989, 1993).

However, studies that have assessed the declining significance of race thesis among the middle class have been beset by a methodological limitation: they have relied almost exclusively on cross-sectional data. Significantly, using research designs—such as trend analyses—that are based on cross-sectional data has precluded examining crucial issues relevant to the Wilson thesis such as how inequality unfolds over the work career. In fact, in recent years the analysis of workplace-based rewards over the career span has emerged as a promising area of stratification research. In this vein, sociologists have documented that the study of individual lives through time is particularly suited to capture the crucial role of cohort effects, historical context, and the social influence of age-graded transitions in structuring the distribution of rewards (Rosenfeld 1992; Settersten and Mayer 1997). To date, workplace-based studies focusing largely on gender inequality have validated the importance of temporal analyses: they demonstrate that the male/female gap in outcomes such as earnings and rates of promotion are structured in a curvilinear fashion across the career span (Marini 1997; Moen, Dempster-McClain, and Williams 1992; Smith and Moen 1988).

This study examines racial inequality over a portion of the work career in the middle-class job structure within the context of the declining significance of race thesis. In particular, it uses data from a nationally representative sample to assess racial differences in earnings among two cohorts of male workers through the early years of their work lives in middle-class jobs. It is concerned with two issues: (1) the extent to which the racial gap in earnings is cumulative over the early career years and (2) the extent to which the racial gap in earnings is structured by period effects independent of the work-career cycle. However, before proceeding, it is necessary to elucidate the Wilson thesis and its predictions concerning trends in racial inequality over the career span.

WILSON'S THESIS ABOUT THE AFRICAN AMERICAN MIDDLE CLASS

In *The Declining Significance of Race* (1978), Wilson argued that American society has gone through a series of stages of race relations between African Americans and whites, with each stage representing different forms of racial stratification structured by particular arrangements of both the economy and the polity. As Wilson says,

> My central argument is that different systems of production and/or different arrangements of the polity have imposed different constraints on the way in which racial groups have interacted in the United States, constraints that have structured the relations between racial groups and that have produced dissimilar contexts not only for the manifestations of racial antagonism but also racial group access to rewards and privileges. (1978:3)

The source of controversy surrounding the declining significance of race thesis concerns the rendition of race/class dynamics in the "modern industrial period"—the most recent of the stages. In this regard, Wilson makes arguments about the influence of race and social class both relative to earlier historical stages and in the most recent one. The focus of this study—and indeed, the overwhelming majority of existing studies—has been on the structuring of inequality in the modern industrial period. According to Wilson (1978:3), during this period, which began with the civil rights era in the early 1960s, there has been a "progressive transition from racial inequities to class inequities." In particular, one set of dynamics—macroeconomic changes such as labor market segmentation, the suburbanization of industry, and the decline in the production of goods relative to services—has structured the economy in such a way that African American poverty has become institutionalized, and has produced impoverishment for the urban underclass.

At the same time, a second set of dynamics—the cumulative effects of the dramatic growth of the state sector, active pressure from the state to improve civil rights, economic interventionism, and the implementation of affirmative action policies—has created unprecedented economic opportunities for the relatively advantaged segment of the African American population. According to Wilson, the increased significance of social class permits these African Americans, who have "made it," to muster the resources necessary to sustain their privileged position and encounter an opportunity structure that, with the passage of time, becomes more comparable to whites with similar credentials.

Accordingly, with respect to racial inequality during the modern industrial period, two hypotheses derive from the Wilson thesis:

H1: Work-Career Dynamics: racial inequality should progressively diminish over the work career.

H2: Period Effects: racial inequality should be less pronounced among cohorts of workers who entered the labor force later in the post-1965 period than among cohorts who entered earlier in the period.

PREVIOUS RESEARCH

Research that has assessed the Wilson thesis among the relatively advantaged segment of the African American population has focused primarily on males and suggests the following: (1) the post-1980 period signals a reversal of earlier trends and racial inequality has been steadily on the rise; and (2) inequality increases over the early work career. In particular, several studies support the Wilson thesis in the pre-1980 period: for example, Hout's (1984) examination of race and social class in structuring patterns of intra- and intergenerational occupational mobility among males with data from the "Occupational Change in a Generation" surveys finds that within the first decade of the civil rights era socioeconomic criteria played an increasingly important role in determining the access of African Americans to occupations as well as the possibility of transmitting their relative occupational advantage on to their children. Further, Farley's (1984) analyses of data from the U.S. Census reveal that through the 1960s and 1970s the racial gap in both occupational status and personal income narrowed between African American and white executives, managers, and professionals.

However, studies also provide evidence that trends toward equality have reversed through the decade of the 1980s. For example, Cancio, Evans, and

Maume (1996) utilize data from the Panel Study of Income Dynamics (PSID) to examine differences in the racial gap in earnings between cohorts of young African Americans and white male workers in 1985 and 1976; the authors found that in all census-based occupational categories the proportion of the racial gap in earnings due to discrimination was larger among the more recent cohort. Further, Farley (1996) uses 1980 and 1990 census data to analyze racial differences among males in the probability of attaining upper-middle-class occupation categories; he finds that at every level of educational attainment the odds of African Americans reaching upper-tier jobs lagged farther behind whites in 1990 than a decade earlier. Finally, evidence of deeply entrenched racial inequality emerges from studies that have employed ethnographic techniques to examine the placement of African American managers and supervisors in white-dominated firms in the 1980s (Collins 1989, 1993). Most significantly, these studies document that African Americans are removed from mainstream intrafirm career ladders and suffer from inferior short- and long-term reward trajectories relative to whites pursuant to being channeled into "race-conscious" job functions that are geared to delivering services to African American consumers/clients.

Neither of the two analyses of racial stratification over the work career necessarily compares African Americans and whites at a similar career stage. Thomas, Herring, and Horton (1994) use census data to assess the racial gap in earnings between younger and middle-age male "white" and "blue-collar" workers from 1940 to 1990. Their analyses of successive cross-sectional samples reveal that in the majority of ten-year periods the gap among both categories of workers was smaller among the young than among those of middle age. In addition, Wilson (1997) uses data from the PSID and traces the earnings returns to job authority at two points—1985 and 1976—among his sample of male workers employed in four middle-class occupational categories: he finds that the racial gap favoring whites over African American counterparts for each of the three hierarchical levels of job authority were greater in 1985 than in 1976.

DATA AND METHODS

Data from the Panel Study of Income Dynamics are used to analyze racial differences in earnings among two cohorts of African American and white males through the early work years in middle-class jobs (for a description of the PSID data set, see Hill 1992).[1] The first cohort consists of all non-self-employed white and African American male heads of household in either their first or second year of full-time employment in 1975 who remained employed full-time during the next seven years through 1982; these individuals were interviewed in both 1976 and 1983 about their labor force experiences one year earlier, in 1975 and 1982. The second cohort is comprised of all white and African American male heads of household in either their first or second year of full-time employment in 1985 who remained employed full-time during the next seven years through 1992; these individuals were interviewed in both 1986 and 1993 about their experiences one year before. In addition, to ensure that all sample members were of middle-class status, the sample was restricted to individuals who in both 1975–82 and 1985–92 were employed in one of three 1970 census-based occupational categories. Managers-Administrators, Professional-Technical, and Craftsmen and Kindred Workers.[2] The application of these criteria resulted in a sample of 342 white and 181 African American males in the earlier cohort and 339 white and 207 African American males in the more recent cohort.

Dependent Variable: Earnings

Earnings is measured as the amount of inflation-adjusted earnings (in constant 1992 dollars) made by respondents in the labor market for the years 1975, 1982, 1985, and 1992.[3] Further, as earnings was a criterion for inclusion in the original sample, sample weights provided with data in all sample years were used to adjust for nonrepresentativeness on this variable.

Independent Variables: Background and Sociodemographic Characteristics

Socioeconomic origins is measured by two items: the first is respondent's recollection of whether he or she grew up poor (1 = yes; 0 = no).[4] The second is mother's education, which is coded in years of schooling completed. In addition, two sociodemographic characteristics are assessed: respondent's age is coded in years, and region of current residence is dummy coded as "North," "West," and "South," with "Midwest" serving as the reference category.

Independent Variables: Human Capital Characteristics

Three human capital characteristics are included in the model. The first is educational attainment, which is dummy coded into "high school" and "some college," with "less than high school" serving as the reference category. The second is time spent with present employer, measured by the number of years and months respondent has worked for present employer.[5] The third is experience with other employers (coded in months) since entry into the labor market.

Independent Variables: Workplace and Labor Market Characteristics

The influence of three workplace and labor market characteristics that are documented sources of racial inequality in economic rewards are assessed. First, employment in the public sector is measured by a dummy variable, with the private sector serving as the reference category. Second, the influence of occupational status is assessed by coding respondent's census-based detailed occupation into Duncan SEI [socioeconomic index] scores. Third, the effect of placement in a segmented labor market is assessed by including a dummy variable for employment in the core sector; those employed in the peripheral sector serve as the reference category.

Finally, the primary method of data analysis in this study consists of a hierarchical OLS [ordinary least squares] regression procedure in which each successive block of independent variables is entered at separate stages. This method permits an assessment of zero-order effects as well as the independent effects of each of the subsequent blocks of independent variables on earnings. Regression equations were estimated separately for African American and white males for 1975, 1982, 1985, and 1992.

RESULTS

Table 1 reports the results from the OLS regressions for the determinants of earnings among both cohorts of African Americans and white males (descriptive results for all variables in the analysis are in Table 3).

The first set of findings does not support the prediction from the declining significance of race thesis that racial inequality progressively diminishes over the early work career: there are increases in the income gap favoring whites in the five-year period for both cohorts of African American and white males. In particular, the unstandardized coefficients (b's) indicate that among the earlier cohort the gap favoring whites in 1975 after all controls are introduced is $4,770 ($24,963–$20,193). However, seven years later, at the final stage of the regression analysis, the gap has increased to $6,731 ($29,244–$22,513). For the more recent cohort there are similar results: in 1985 the earnings gap between white and African American males in the final stage of the regression analysis after workplace variables are introduced is $6,338 ($28,676–$22,338). However, seven years later, the gap increased to $9,524 ($33,107–$23,583).

In addition, a second set of findings from the regressions do not support the prediction from the Wilson thesis that racial inequality should be less pronounced among cohorts of workers who entered the labor force later in the post-1965 civil rights era. First, the racial gap in earnings at both stages of the career span is more pronounced among the more recent than the earlier cohort. Specifically, at the final stage of the regression analyses, the racial gap in earnings is approximately $1,700 greater among the more recent than the earlier cohort at the outset of the five-year period (i.e., 1985 vs. 1975). Further, the racial gap in earnings increases to almost $3,000 by the end of the seven-year period (i.e., 1992 vs. 1982). Second, the racial gap increases at a greater rate in the seven-year period among the more recent cohort. Specifically, between 1975 and 1982 the racial gap increased by approximately $2,000, while between 1985 and 1992 the gap increased by approximately $3,200.

A question that sheds additional light on patterns of racial differences in earnings for the two cohorts of African American and white males is whether the "cost" of being African American has declined across the 1975–82 and 1985–92 periods. Specifically, this involves assessing across both periods the dollar

TABLE 1

OLS Regressions of Earnings for Two Cohorts of African American and White Males

	(1) Zero-Order Effects		(2) (1) + Background-Sociodemographic Variables		(3) (2) + Human Capital Variables		(4) (3) + Workplace Variables	
	(b)	(beta)	(b)	(beta)	(b)	(beta)	(b)	(beta)
				Earlier Cohort				
1975								
African American	20,993***	.37	20,665***	.35	20,216**	.25	20,193**	.23
	(.07)		(.08)		(.08)		(.09)	
White	26,193***	.34	25,437***	.31	25,101***	.29	24,963***	.28
	(.06)		(.07)		(.07)		(.08)	
R^2								
African American			.10		.16		.32	
White			.05		.09		.30	
1982								
African American	24,318***	.37	24,222**	.27	24,103**	.25	22,513**	.23
	(.08)		(.11)		(.11)		(.11)	
White	30,555***	.31	30,427***	.31	29,721***	.29	29,244***	.28
	(.09)		(.08)		(.08)		(.07)	
R^2								
African American			.14		.25		.39	
White			.13		.22		.35	
				More Recent Cohort				
1985								
African American	23,936***	.35	23,507**	.30	22,707**	.28	22,338*	.24
	(.08)		(.10)		(.11)		(.11)	
White	30,518***	.33	29,682***	.31	29,246***	.30	28,676***	.29
	(.09)		(.08)		(.10)		(.12)	
R^2								
African American			.09		.15		.37	
White			.05		.10		.33	
1992								
African American	25,323**	.28	25,006**	.26	24,333**	.24	23,583*	.23
	(.11)		(.10)		(.11)		(.11)	
White	34,448***	.34	34,102***	.32	33,665***	.30	33,107***	.27
	(.10)		(.12)		(.11)		(.09)	
R^2								
African American			.10		.25		.39	
White			.11		.19		.36	

Note: *p<.05; **p<.01; ***p<.001 for two-tailed tests. Numbers in parentheses are standard errors.

amount that African Americans would have earned if employers had rewarded their achievements and characteristics at the same rate as they rewarded whites. To accomplish this task, the method of indirect standardization was used in which the mean scores of African Americans on the vector of independent variables were substituted into the regression equations for whites.[6] Table 2 reports the results of this procedure for African Americans across the 1975–82 and 1985–92 periods.

TABLE 2

Standardization Procedure for Earnings for Two Cohorts of African Americans

	Mean Earnings	*Expected Mean Earnings*	*Difference*	*Percentage Gap*
		Earlier Cohort		
1975	$17,585	$20,775	$3,190	15.4
1982	$19,902	$24,613	$4,711	19.1
		More Recent Cohort		
1985	$22,051	$26,704	$4,653	17.4
1992	$25,450	$33,202	$7,752	23.3

The findings provide further confirmation for the results thus far reached about the Wilson thesis. First, the cost of being African American increases across both seven-year periods. Specifically, had African Americans in the earlier cohort enjoyed the regression coefficients and intercepts of whites while retaining their own values on the independent variables, they would have earned an additional $3,190 in 1975 and $4,711 in 1982. Further, African Americans in the more recent cohort would have earned an additional $4,653 in 1985 and $7,752 in 1992. Second, the cost of being African American is greater at both the outset and the conclusion of the later seven-year period. Specifically, the penalty for being African American is approximately $1,500 ($4,653–$3,190) greater in 1985 than in 1975 and approximately $3,000 greater ($7,752–$4,711) in 1992 than in 1982. Finally, the cost of being African American increased by a greater amount over the seven-year period among the more recent cohort. In this vein, the cost increased by approximately $3,000 over the 1985–92 period, while it increased by nearly $1,500 over the 1975–82 period.

In addition, to give further meaning to the findings from the standardization analysis, Table 2 provides the percent gap between the mean and expected earnings across both the 1975–82 and 1985–92 periods. The percentage differences provide support for the interpretation drawn from the absolute dollar amounts: the relative penalty for being African American increases across both seven-year periods (15.4% in 1975 to 19.1% in 1982; 17.4% in 1985 to 23.3% in 1992). Further, the relative cost of being African American is greater at both stages of the later seven-year period (17.4% in 1985 to 15.4% in 1975; 23.3% in 1992 to 19.1% in 1982). Finally, the relative cost of being African American increased by a greater amount (5.7 to 3.9%) among the more recent than the earlier cohort.

CONCLUSION

The racial gap in earnings over the early career years among two cohorts of incumbents in middle-class occupations is structured in a manner that is contrary to predictions from the declining significance of race thesis. First, the earnings gap widens over a seven-year period among both the earlier and the more recent cohorts (H1). Second, the racial gap in earnings is more pronounced among the more recent cohort than among the earlier cohort (H2). Specifically, the gap is larger at the outset of the seven-year period and accumulates more between 1985 and 1992 than between 1975 and 1982.

Significantly, a plausible interpretation of the findings emerges from recent sociological research that has identified a range of dynamics that drive racial inequality in the American workplace. First, operating to widen the racial gap in earnings across the early work career for both cohorts are several institutionalized discriminatory employment practices that operate across components of the segmented labor market. For example, white employers' concern with such phenomena as maintaining a stable workforce (Pettigrew and Martin 1987) and a loyal customer/client base (Pettigrew 1985), as well as their tendency to comply minimally with EEO [equal employment opportunity] mandates (Burstein 1985), results in the restriction of African Americans from early-career stages to "race-conscious" jobs in which work-related tasks are performed in contexts that are less valued in organizations and within work roles that are designated as subordinate to whites (Collins 1989, 1993). Further, not to be overlooked in accounting for the accumulation of economic disadvantage is the systemic practice of African Americans receiving unfairly low pèrformance evaluations because of white employers' penchant for falling prey to social psychological processes including "statistical discrimination" (Wilson 1997) and "attribution bias" (Pettigrew and Martin 1987).

Second, broad-based period effects in the post-1980 period may explain the pronounced accumulation of racial disadvantage over the early career years among the more recent cohort. In particular, cumulative and adverse race-specific effects on the material outcomes of African Americans are a consequence of the well-documented retreat from enforcement of civil rights (Burstein 1985; Myers 1997). Further, the well-documented acceleration of massive industrial restructuring in the post-1980 period has disproportionately placed African Americans in newly created, unfavorable occupational niches in the American economy that are characterized by relatively small numbers of both internal labor markets and positions that offer favorable returns to human capital investments (Sasson 1988; Waldinger 1996).

TABLE 3

Descriptive Statistics for PSID Sample

Earlier Cohort

	1975				*1982*			
	African American (N = 181)		*White (N = 342)*		*African American (N = 181)*		*White (N = 342)*	
	Mean	*SD*	*Mean*	*SD*	*Mean*	*SD*	*Mean*	*SD*
Dependent variable								
Earnings	18,340	7,050	22,719	7,675	18,993	8,182	25,777	9,894
Independent variables								
Background								
Region								
South	N = 40		N = 85					
North	43		104					
West	30		76					
Poor	(Yes = 94)		(Yes = 135)					
Mother's education	9.7	2.3	11.8	2.2				
Age	23.6	4.1	23.4	3.9				
Human capital								
Education	12.16	2.5	12.8	2.7				
With Employer	0.4	0.6	0.5	0.3	5.8	2.2	5.4	2.3
Other Employer					1.6	0.06	1.5	0.5
Workplace								
Occupational status	58.3	5.3	61.7	5.1	60.8	5.2	66.3	5.1
Public sector	N = 111		N = 165		N = 109		N = 157	
Core sector	55		139		57		140	

More Recent Cohort

	1985				*1992*			
	African American (N = 207)		*White (N = 399)*		*African American (N = 207)*		*White (N = 399)*	
	Mean	*SD*	*Mean*	*SD*	*Mean*	*SD*	*Mean*	*SD*
Dependent variable								
Earnings	22,882	8,443	28,108	9,945	27,113	12,009	33,820	13,634
Independent variables								
Background								
Region								
South	N = 40		N = 87					
North	58		92					
West	37		75					
Poor	(Yes = 101)		(Yes = 147)					
Mother's education	10.5	2.2	11.7	2.1				
Age	23.8	3.8	24.1	3.8				
Human capital								
Education	12.5	2.5	12.8	2.4				
With Employer	0.5	0.3	0.4	0.7	5.2	2.3	5.8	2.8
Other Employer					1.7	0.6	1.6	0.7
Workplace								
Occupational status	57.2	4.8	62.9	5.7	62.5	5.6	68.5	4.7
Public sector	N = 123		N = 150		N = 120		N = 154	
Core sector	58		143		56		148	

Finally, we emphasize that further research on inequality over the work career can fill out our understanding of the adequacy of the portion of the declining significance of race thesis that relates to the African American middle class. In particular, future work should specify the influence of the causal agents identified in this study in accounting for gaps in earnings and an additional range of socioeconomic outcomes across both the early- and later-career years. In this regard, we believe that analyzing data from specific firms best provides the opportunity to directly assess the influences of such factors as discriminatory employment practices, levels of commitment to enforcing equal opportunity laws, and sorting practices into a rapidly changing American occupational structure. Further, examinations of inequality over the career span should undertake similar analyses for females, who in the last several decades have experienced growing representation in the middle-class job structure. Overall, we look forward to these efforts: they are crucial if we are to have an adequate basis for assessing one of the most controversial theoretical formulations in sociology.

NOTES

1. Any possibility of including females in the analyses was precluded by sample size. Specifically, there were too few African American and white females whose early career spans the 1975–82 and 1985–92 periods to sustain quantitative analyses.
2. The PSID keys occupational information from every wave to the 1970 census occupational scheme. Major changes in census occupational classifications that began in 1980 precluded translating the 1970 detailed occupational codes assigned by the Institute for Survey Research at the University of Michigan into the more modern classification scheme.
3. To check on model specification and ensure that results were not confounded by heteroscedasticity the Cook-Weisberg test of the assumption of common error variance was performed for all regression analyses. In all instances X^2 statistics of .01 were obtained and had corresponding P values that ranged from .717 to .788, indicating low levels of heteroscedasticity. The results of the Cook-Weisberg tests are available from the authors on request.
4. Missing values for both African Americans and whites on all independent variables were coded to racial group means.
5. A recognized limitation of this study is the failure to factor into regression analyses an indicator of cognitive skills, an important human capital characteristic (Farkas and Vicknair 1996). Unfortunately, such an indicator is not available in the PSID.
6. An alternative method to estimate discrimination-produced inequity is to substitute the White mean into the African American regression equation (Farley 1996). This method tends to yield higher estimates of discrimination, since it determines the cost of being African American with an average white background. However, closer to common conceptions of discrimination is the method adopted in this study, which yields lower estimates by asking what does being African American

cost with having an average African American background (Pettigrew and Martin 1987).

REFERENCES

Burstein, Paul. 1985. *Discrimination, Jobs and Politics.* Chicago: University of Chicago Press.

Cancio, A. Silvio, T. David Evans, and David Maume. 1996. "Reconsidering the Declining Significance of Race: Racial Differences in Early Career Wages." *American Sociological Review* 61: 541–66.

Collins, Sharon. 1989. "The Marginalization of Black Executives." *Social Problems* 36: 317–31.

_____. 1993. "Blacks on the Bubble: The Vulnerability of Black Executives in White Corporations." *Sociological Quarterly* 34: 429–47.

Farkas, George and Kevin Vicknair. 1996. "Appropriate Tests of Racial Wage Discrimination Require Controls for Cognitive Skill: Comment on Cancio, Evans, and Maume." *American Sociological Review* 61: 557–60.

Farley, Reynolds. 1984. *Blacks and Whites: Narrowing the Gap?* Cambridge, MA: Harvard University Press.

_____. 1996. *State of the Union: America in the 1990's.* New York: Russell Sage Foundation.

Hill, Martha. 1992. *Users' Guide to the Panel Study of Income Dynamics.* Ann Arbor: Institute for Survey Research, University of Michigan.

Hout, Michael. 1984. "Occupational Mobility of Black Men: 1962–1973." *American Sociological Review* 49: 308–23.

Marini, Margaret. 1997. "The Gender Gap in Earnings at Career Entry." *American Sociological Review* 62: 588–604.

Moen, Phylis, Donna Dempster-McClain, and Robin Williams. 1992. "Successful Aging: A Life-Course Perspective on Women's Multiple Roles." *American Journal of Sociology* 97: 1612–38.

Myers, Samuel, ed. 1997. *Civil Rights and Race Relations in the Post Reagan-Bush Era.* New York: Praeger.

The Panel Study of Income Dynamics. Wave XX. Ann Arbor: Institute for Social Research, University of Michigan.

Pettigrew, Thomas. 1985. "New Black-White Patterns: How Best to Conceptualize Them." *Annual Review of Sociology* 11: 329–46.

Pettigrew, Thomas and Joanne Martin. 1987. "Shaping the Organizational Context for Black American Inclusion." *Journal of Social Issues* 43: 41–78.

Rosenfeld, Rachel. 1992. "Job Market and Career Processes." *Annual Review of Sociology* 18: 39–61.

Sasson, Saskia. 1988. *The Mobility of Labor and Capital.* Cambridge: Cambridge University Press.

Settersten, Richard and Karl Mayer. 1997. "The Measurement of Age, Age Structuring, and the Life Course." *Annual Review of Sociology* 23: 233–61.

Smith, Ken and Phyllis Moen. 1988. "Passage through Midlife: Women's Changing Family Roles and Economic Well-Being." *Sociological Quarterly* 29: 503–24.

Thomas, Melvin. 1993. "Race, Class, and Personal Income: An Empirical Test of the Declining Significance of Race Thesis, 1968–1988." *Social Problems* 40: 328–42.

Thomas, Melvin, Cedric Herring, and Hayward Derrick Horton. 1994. "Discrimination over the Life-Course: A Synthetic Cohort Analysis of Earnings Differences between Black and White Males, 1940–1990." *Social Problems* 41: 608–28.

Waldinger, Roger. 1996. *Still the Promised City: African Americans and New Immigrants in Postindustrial New York.* Cambridge, MA: Harvard University Press.

Wilson, George. 1997. "Payoffs to Power among Males in the Middle Class: Has Race Declined in Its Significance?" *Sociological Quarterly* 38: 607–22.

Wilson, William. 1978. *The Declining Significance of Race: Blacks and Changing American Institutions.* Chicago: University of Chicago Press.

CHAPTER 9 The Legal Institution

9.1 MICHAEL HUSPEK, ROBERTO MARTINEZ, AND LETICIA JIMENEZ

Violations of Human and Civil Rights on the U.S.-Mexico Border, 1995 to 1997: A Report

One of the most controversial issues confronting policing in the United States is the use of excessive force. A number of high-profile police brutality cases have renewed concerns of misconduct by law enforcement officers. While many social critics contend that police brutality does not occur as often as some people might think, others contend that police brutality is endemic to American policing and not simply comprised of isolated incidents of rogue cops getting out of control. Many qualitative studies show that nonwhite minorities, drug offenders, and homosexuals are disproportionately victimized through police misconduct. Although the true extent of police use of excessive force is unknown, according to Amnesty International in a 1998 report entitled *Shielded From Justice: Police Brutality and Accountability in the United States,* there were over 3,000 federal criminal civil rights cases referred to the U.S. federal judicial district in 1996 involving police misconduct. Yet there is little accountability for police brutality —less than 100 of the cases were sent to grand juries for prosecution. Federal law enforcement officers are repugnant in their proliferation of brutality and lawlessness toward private citizens, often engaging in deadly force and physical and verbal abuse and intimidation.

One aspect of immigration that has yet to surface in the national debate on immigration to the United States is the extent to which immigrants are victims of police violence. One reason for this may be that much of the violence against immigrants is precipitated by law enforcement agents who continue to escape criminal culpability. In the following selection from "Violations of Human and Civil Rights on the U.S.-Mexico Border, 1995 to 1997: A Report," *Social Justice* (Summer 1998), Professor Michael Huspek of California State University at San Marcos and Roberto Martinez and Leticia Jimenez of the U.S.–Mexico Border Program with American Friends Service Committee in San Diego, California, consider complaints from 267 individuals whose civil rights have been violated by various law enforcement agencies patrolling the United States–Mexico border. Their research reveals that the violations range from illegal searches, to physical and psychological victimization, to child abuse and murder. They suggest that law enforcement officers must receive better training and monitoring, that an external review board must be instituted to deal with public complaints of police lawlessness on the border, and that "the relationship between immigration and law enforcement policies be placed at the top of the agenda for national debate."

Key Concept: police lawlessness, the U.S. Border Patrol, and the United States–Mexico border

This report considers a number of complaints by persons who maintain that law enforcement officials have violated their human and civil rights. The violations include illegal search of persons and their private property, verbal, psychological, and physical abuse of persons, child abuse, deprivation of food, water, and medical attention, torture, theft, use of excessive force, assault and battery, and murder. The complaints are directed at a number of law enforcement agencies located principally in Southern California, including the U.S. Border Patrol, U.S. Customs, U.S. Port Security, the Sheriff's Departments of San Diego, Vista, San Marcos, Fallbrook, and Riverside, the San Diego Police Department, the California Highway Patrol, and the California National Guard. The Immigration and Naturalization Service (INS), including the U.S. Border Patrol, is mentioned most frequently in the majority of complaints. The subjects responsible for voicing the complaints include 267 individuals who are highly diverse with respect to age, social class, gender, life ambition, and legal status. Many are undocumented immigrants, but many others are holders of valid border crossing cards as well as citizens and legal residents of the United States. All of the subjects share an Hispanic ethnicity.

The complaints were collected in two ways. First, during 1996, the San Diego office of the American Friends Service Committee (AFSC) charted a decline in the number of human and civil rights abuses reported on the northern side of the California/Baja California border. In the same year, an increase in the number of reports of abuse on the Mexican side of the border suggested that victims of abuse were being apprehended and deported before they could file reports with human rights workers in the United States. In December 1996, therefore, the AFSC-San Diego met with human rights representatives from Baja California to formulate a strategy for interviewing migrants immediately after they were deported to Mexico by U.S. authorities. As a result of this meeting, students from the Universidad Autónoma de Baja California conducted interviews from January to April, 1997, at the Tijuana, Tecate, and Mexicali ports of entry. The binational study documented 204 cases of abuse.

Second, staff of the AFSC-San Diego office carried out 63 interviews of victims of human and civil rights abuses for the years 1995, 1996, and 1997. During the course of these interviews, respondents were encouraged to provide detailed narratives that identified the nature of the abuses and the contexts within which they occurred. Each narrative is highly individualized, offering a uniquely human story that provides a glimpse of the queries, shouts, interrogations, and threats that were used in the course of the law's applications, as well as the felt humiliation, intimidation, frustration, fear, and other life interruptions such applications imposed upon narrators and their family or friends. The narratives also form a collection; considered in conjunction with the binational study, they validate the following statements:

1. That violations of persons and their most basic rights by law enforcement officials are a routine occurrence;
2. That there is a pattern in the delivery of wrongful law enforcement practices;
3. That an identifiable logic motivates and legitimates such delivery; and
4. That the delivery and logic of law enforcement practices together may amount to a routinized infliction of terror upon persons who are targeted by the practices or who feel themselves likely to be so targeted.

The remainder of this report further develops and provides illustrative support for the above statements. The report begins by focusing on the complaints raised by 204 persons released into Mexico after being apprehended by agents of the U.S. Border Patrol, the INS, U.S. Customs, and other law enforcement agencies. The report emphasizes the nature of the complaints and their statistical frequency, but also draws upon the additional 63 narratives to supply meaningful content to the complaints and to address the substantive practices of law enforcement at the specific points of their application. Insofar as the practices are revealed to be patterned, an attempt is made to describe the logic that motivates and legitimates the practices as well as their consequences.

Second, in an attempt to explain the nature of abusive law enforcement practices and the logic that drives them, the report offers an overview of the general climate of law enforcement in the southwest region of the United States.

Recent developments throughout the region include a steady build-up of military and police personnel, an increased integration of military and police units, heightened deployment of surveillance technology, intensified criminalization of activities related to illegal immigration, and an inflamed rhetoric that both vilifies targeted subjects and legitimates the tactics used by law enforcement agencies against them. The report concludes with a set of recommendations as to what is needed in the way of practical, remedial policies.

I. HUMAN AND CIVIL RIGHTS ABUSES AND THEIR CONTENTS

Human and civil rights violations by law enforcement officials have long been a regular feature in the southwest region of the United States. This is especially true of the United States Border Patrol, whose agents have demonstrated a penchant for cruelty and violence toward those they have been commissioned to hunt down and apprehend. The forms of conduct range from the labeling by Border Patrol agents of the undocumented immigrants they apprehend as "tonks," in reference to the sound of a flashlight striking a human's skull, to unwarranted discharging of firearms (ILEMP, 1992). Concerning the latter, a recent study by Americas Watch (1992: 9) reports that "since 1980, Border Patrol agents have shot dozens of people along the U.S.-Mexico border, killing at least eleven and permanently disabling at least ten." The study goes on to state that further killings resulted from a joint Border Patrol-San Diego Police task force, referred to as the Border Crime Prevention Unit. From 1984 to 1989, members of the task force were involved in 26 shooting incidents in which 19 people were killed and 24 wounded.

Many complaints detailed in this report point specifically to what appears to be a continuation in recent years of violent and abusive conduct on the part of law enforcement officials. This statement finds backing in the binational study's statistical breakdown of statements by 204 persons released into Mexico after being apprehended: 43% reported witnessing excessive use of force either to themselves or to others; 12% reported instances of physical/sexual abuse; 23% reported hearing verbal abuse; 11% reported being made to hear racial insults; 46% reported denial of food or water; 14% reported denial of medical attention; 21% reported being recklessly transported; and 15% reported having been threatened.

A. In No Man's Land: Flight and Punishment; Surrender and Punishment

Reported abuses often refer to the treatment undocumented immigrants receive after being intercepted in remote areas. On the one side are enforcement agents who are assigned to hunt down and capture illegal immigrants, which may entail traversing dangerous terrain, made even more dangerous once the hunters and hunted enter into the heat of a chase. On the other side are undocumented immigrants who may have a great deal to lose upon being apprehended. In addition to financial loss (e.g., coyote fees) and possible imprisonment, there may be strong emotional factors at work. At one moment, they are concealed under cloak of darkness in the isolated wild, only to be struck by utter panic in the next upon being sighted in the search beams of a hovering helicopter or pursuing Ford Bronco. Because the undocumented immigrant may have been the victim of violence in the past, or has heard about violence being directed against others, fear may also come into play. In any event, the undocumented immigrant, having been detected, must make a rapid calculation: Do I attempt to flee, or do I submit?

Running places the targeted subject at great risk, for upon being captured one may receive physical punishment from angry law enforcement officers. So attests Francisco Valdez Lopez who, after being apprehended along the U.S.-Mexico border in July 1995, had a foot placed upon his head as he was forced to the ground and handcuffed. First threatened with death by a Border Patrol agent, he was then beaten with closed fists and batons by a number of agents, causing his nose and mouth to bleed. In February 1995, Juan Carlos Guzman Velasquez also ran after Border Patrol agents spotted him smuggling undocumented immigrants through the San Clemente checkpoint. Wrestled to the ground and handcuffed, he was then punched and had his head slammed into the ground repeatedly. One agent pulled his hair back and punched him in the face. The beating Guzman sustained was so severe that he was transferred to a hospital, though the Border Patrol's formal written account of the incident neglected to mention the injuries.

After hopping the border fence at a railroad crossing near the San Ysidro Port of Entry in July 1996, Jorge Soriano Bautista also ran, until he was hit hard in the back by a Ford Bronco that pursued him, knocking him to the ground and causing him to lose consciousness. Upon regaining consciousness, Bautista heard his arm snap while being handcuffed by a Border Patrol agent, and he again lost consciousness. Bautista was given no medical attention for either his broken arm or the blow to his body caused by the Ford Bronco. Instead, he was returned to the border and stuffed by agents back under the fence onto the Mexican side where he later received medical attention at a Tijuana hospital.

Even if the targeted subject does not run, he or she may nevertheless suffer violence at the hands of arresting officers. In June 1996, Sergio Ponce Rodriguez stopped when he was so ordered after having crossed the border near Tecate, but he was then beaten to the ground by a Border Patrol agent and kicked several times in the head. In February 1996, Carlos Sanchez Zamora stopped upon being commanded to do so, yet he too was kicked repeatedly in the ribs and hit on the arm with a baton. In January 1996, Roman Gonzalez Garcia, after stopping and being handcuffed near the San Ysidro Port of Entry, was pulled up by the handcuffs while at the same time an agent stomped on his ankle with his entire weight, breaking the ankle. Near Campo in August 1995, after Rogelio Hernandez was stopped by Border Patrol agents, his head, hip, and testicles were injured as he was pulled out of his car window by the hair and arm. Agents then threw him to the ground, jumped on his back with their knees, beat him with batons, and held his face in the dirt, almost smothering him. All the while, the agents directed obscenities and racial insults at him, including "stupid Mexican."

Verbal abuse seems to frequently accompany the excessive use of force; the binational study indicates that almost half the time such abuse is punctuated with racial insults. Along the border in September 1995, while Jorge Hernandez Samano was being beaten with closed fists and batons by three Border Patrol agents, a fourth agent approached and asked, "Why do you want to run, ... wetback?" Yet another agent hit Hernandez on the head with a flashlight, opening a wound. Near the San Ysidro Port of Entry in February 1996, as Carlos Sanchez Zamora was being kicked by a Border Patrol agent, the agent said: "Shut up, ... Mexican; son of a bitch, I'm tired of Mexicans. Stop or I will be killing one or somebody." In May 1995, in East San Diego County, as Jesus Hector Gaspar Segura attempted to dissuade a Border Patrol agent from hitting a woman companion with a long black club, the agent retorted that "migrants smell" and then stated several times: "... you *hediondos* [stinking persons]."

After violence is inflicted upon persons, efforts may be made to conceal the nature of the resultant injuries as well as how they were sustained. Jorge Soriano Bautista was stuffed by Border Patrol agents back under the border fence where he was left on his own to seek medical treatment for his broken arm. Jesus Hector Gaspar Segura was beaten severely enough to warrant professional treatment of his wounds, yet the Border Patrol agent who beat him warned against Gaspar mentioning the beating to anyone. Ramon Gonzalez Garcia, whose ankle was broken by a Border Patrol agent, was turned over to Grupo Beta in an ironic show of cooperation between U.S. and Mexican law enforcement agencies. Juan Carlos Guzman Velasquez was beaten so badly by Border Patrol agents as to require hospitalization, yet his injuries received no mention on the Border Patrol's report (I-213) form. Alberto Muñoz Juarez, whose chest was pinned against the U.S.-Mexico border fence by a Ford Bronco in October 1995, was told he would not be deported if he decided against filing charges.

If serious injury is inflicted upon an undocumented immigrant, life can become very difficult. Consider Juan Carlos Lizalde Yanez, who in October 1995 was marched up a mountainside, placed into a vehicle, and handcuffed without his body being fastened by a seatbelt. During the bumpy ride, Border Patrol agents went at a very high speed, causing Lizalde to be tossed around in the back of the vehicle and to hit his head repeatedly on the roof of the vehicle. Once the Border Patrol agents saw Lizalde vomiting and showing other signs of discomfort, they took him to a hospital where it was determined he had suffered a stroke that paralyzed him. Three days later, and still paralyzed, he was asked by Border Patrol agents to sign voluntary departure forms, which he refused to do. Both the Border Patrol and hospital administrators were apparently anxious to shuffle Lizalde back to Mexico. While at the hospital, Lizalde suffered frequent physical and mental abuse from an attending physician. He was left to lay in his own waste, staff neglected to change his clothes and bed pan, and refused him bathroom or shower privileges. Eventually, Lizalde was put out on the street and today remains paralyzed on the entire left side of his body.

B. The Gaze, Queries, and Commands

Most of the above applications of law enforcement practice occurred in the field, along the border, in no-man's-land, where agents' suspicions are unlikely to be challenged and where witnesses to their actions are likely to be scarce. There are, however, numerous other points of contact between law enforcement officials and the persons they target: at ports of entry and inland checkpoints, along U.S. roads and highways, in fields and campsites, at weddings and funerals, and in homes and workplaces. Such areas admit of greater ambiguity for authoritative intervention. Has the subject done anything to warrant questioning? Is the subject documented? Are the documents genuine or not? Does the subject have a criminal record? Might the subject be in the process of committing a crime? Is the subject telling the truth, or not?

To reduce such ambiguity, law enforcement officials must first interrupt a subject's movements. This is usually followed by a prolonged and studied gaze used to identify the subject's ethnic markings, as well as any physical signs of nervousness, such as fidgeting or sweating.[1] Questions may then be used not only as an invitation for the subject to disclose various types of information, but also to elicit a language marker—Does the subject speak English?—or to detect lies, contradictions, overt gaps, or silences in the subject's accounts. Commands may also come into play, requiring the subject to reveal papers and possessions or to proceed to a secondary inspection site where a body search may be conducted.

For the person who is targeted, a great deal may be at stake. The gaze, query, or command can ultimately result in separation from loved ones, loss of income or possessions, deportation, or incarceration. When inspection occurs at a port of entry, it may also mean that the subject is denied entry into the United States, as well as having papers and other belongings confiscated. This is what happened to Brenda Catalina Ramos, an 18-year-old U.S. citizen who was detained in November 1996 while attempting to pass through the San Ysidro Port of Entry despite showing INS officers her birth certificate, social security card, and California ID. She was taken to a room and surrounded by seven inspectors who, over 5 hours, grilled her, laughed at her replies, and threatened to imprison her and her mother unless she confessed to being an illegal alien. Frightened and crying, Ramos falsely confessed. After being sent to an INS detention center in Las Vegas, she was returned to San Diego and then deported by an immigration judge. INS officers confiscated all of her valid documentation of U.S. citizenship.

A similar experience befell Abel Arroyo in June 1995 at the same port of entry. A 19-year-old U.S. citizen who attended the San Diego Regional Center for the Developmentally Disabled, Arroyo went on a brief shopping trip to Tijuana. Upon returning to San Diego through the San Ysidro Port of Entry, he declared his U.S. citizenship and showed his birth certificate, state ID, and social security card. INS agents taunted Arroyo, hurled racial insults at him, and then punched him in the stomach. For seven hours he pleaded with officers to be allowed entry, but to no avail. Without identification documents, he then wandered the streets of Tijuana for days until he met a man who agreed to smuggle him across the border for a fee. Eleven days after being denied entry into his own country, Arroyo was smuggled across the border and reunited with his family.

Even for the subject who is innocent of any criminal wrongdoing, contact with authority may prove to be more than a casual encounter. Beyond the inconvenience of being stopped, inspected, or queried, there is the possibility that the encounter may escalate into something painfully more threatening. It may be fear of this type of escalation that prompts those who are relatively free of markings of suspicion to render themselves both visible and vocal to the inspecting official by removing sunglasses, saluting, waving, verbally hailing, or giving a robust "thumbs up." However, for subjects who bear markings that draw suspicion—skin color or other physical appearances—fear of an escalated encounter with authority may produce uncertainty with respect to how to respond. For example, the tendency might be to conceal one's more visible markings by shrinking before authority's intrusive gaze. Alternatively, in response to an official's query, one might minimize one's verbal offerings for fear that traces of an accent or an inability to speak English with facility might provoke heightened suspicion from the inspecting official. Either stratagem might be ill-conceived, however: shrinking from the gaze may heighten the official's suspicion and suppressing information may be viewed as indication of guilt.

On the other hand, to possess the markings of suspicion and to return the gaze or to counter the query with a question of one's own may invite harsh recriminations. This was the experience of Raul Nuñez, who in May 1997 asked a Riverside Sheriff's deputy a question as to the nature of the problem that prompted the deputy's attention. After Nuñez was commanded by the deputy to "shut [his] mouth and step inside," he was then sprayed in the face with mace. When Nuñez's son, Victor, asked for the deputy's badge number, the deputy countered with: "Are you trying to be a smart ass, [you] punk?..." In August 1997, Jose Gonzales was arrested after he asked a sheriff's deputy his name and to whom he could complain about the treatment he was receiving. In July 1997, as Rigoberto Lopez and his friend, Emigdio, were entering the U.S. at the San Ysidro Port of Entry, the men were directed by U.S. Customs officials to secondary inspection. When they asked for the rationale, orders to spread their legs were accompanied with kicks and shoves. Emigdio was struck in the testicles by a U.S. Customs agent while both men were continually being yelled at to keep quiet and not ask any questions. In September 1997, Noel Alarid asked two INS officers at the San Ysidro Port of Entry why he needed to be queried further in an office and whether he had done anything wrong. The officers simply grabbed his arm, and in response to Alarid's protestations, began slamming him against one wall, then another. In April 1995, after David Garcia Cruz was apprehended by Border Patrol agents at the San Clemente checkpoint, he dared to glance at the badge of one of the agents. The agent retaliated by punching Garcia three times in the chest, causing a visible indentation in the rib area, and then laughing at him.

C. Intensified Tactics

Once the dynamic between officials and the subject under their suspicion is intensified, the scrutinizing gaze may be replaced by a thorough search of the subject's body and possessions; queries may be converted into a full-fledged interrogation. Commands come increasingly into play as subjects are ordered to exit vehicles and submit to an assortment of authoritative probes.

Commands interpellate the subject as a possible criminal who may be dangerous and in need of restraint. This process may be humiliating when performed upon the subject while friends or family members are forced to observe; when performed upon the subject in isolation from friends or loved ones, the process may be frightening. No doubt, such was the case for the Sandoval family and friends who in May 1995 were directed by U.S. Customs officials to secondary inspection where the mother, father, their two teen-aged sons and two young women (aged 14 and 15) were all questioned separately after being made to remove their shoes and socks. Or consider 14-year-old Jessica Patricia Soto and her mother, both U.S. citizens, who were separated from one another as they attempted passage through the Otay Mesa Port of Entry in May 1995. After Jessica became nervous in response to INS officials' questions, she was shoved and pulled into an office while being kneed and called a "bitch." Once in the office, Jessica was grabbed by the neck by a male officer and had her face shoved into a corner. All the while, Jessica's mother could hear her daughter's pleas for help, but could not go to her.

As authority steps up its tactical applications, the subject's previously predictable world is quickly transformed into one of insecurity and fear. Eighteen-year-old U.S. citizen Brenda Catalina Ramos was questioned at the San Ysidro Port of Entry in a rapid-fire manner over a five-hour period by no less than seven different INS agents. During this time she was accused of lying, possessing phony documentation, and being from the Philippines (because of her slanted eyes). In August 1996, Pedro Sanchez was queried by Border Patrol agents at his workplace in San Diego. He showed his green card and social security card, but the agents questioned the authenticity of the latter and asked Sanchez repeatedly, "Where did you buy it?" and "How much did you pay for it?" Juan Carlos Aguirre Zazueta attempted to use a valid passport to pass through the San Ysidro Port of Entry in May 1996. When he attempted to assure a U.S. Customs official of the passport's authenticity, however, the official slapped him on the forehead and insisted that Aguirre tell the truth. Later, the official threw the passport into the trash. Juan Ramon Avalos, a U.S. citizen, had the authenticity of his documents questioned by INS agents during his attempt to pass through the San Ysidro Port of Entry in August 1995; yet when Avalos attempted to respond to an agent's queries, he was told to "shut up." At the same port of entry in July 1997, Berta Alicia Chavez, a U.S. citizen, drew attention to herself on account of not speaking English. INS agents then threatened to imprison her unless she signed papers testifying that her documentation was fraudulent. After signing the papers, Chavez was deported and had to wait several days before her family eventually proved her citizenship. Katarina Galvan Ledezma, also a U.S. citizen, ran into similar difficulty at the same port of entry since she lacked full command of the English language. After threatening Ledezma with jail unless she admitted to lying, U.S. Customs officers took her birth certificate and state ID card and sent her and her family back to Tijuana.

Such interrogating procedures may have the effect of making the targeted subject feel inferior. In fact, this might be their logic: to reduce the subject's confidence so that a range of tactics might be more effectively applied. By the same logic, should the subject object to the rough treatment or the shouts or the threats, officials may interpret such assertions of personhood as a resistance that is to be countered by an application of (increased) force. A torrent of violence may then result. In August 1997, for example, 83-year-old Mrs. Ruiz witnessed San Diego Police officers roughing up her son in response to his insistence that he be told why he was being ordered to "hit the ground." When Mrs. Ruiz begged the officers to stop slamming her son's head into the ground, she was kicked in the stomach twice by an officer and then knocked to the ground. In June 1997, Beatrice Avila, a legal resident of the United States, encountered a similar experience involving the Border Patrol. Objecting to the intimidating behavior of Border Patrol agents, her arm was twisted behind her as she was thrown face down to the ground, injuring her chin and face. While handcuffed and lying prone on the ground, Avila was then kicked by an agent in the back and leg.

In May 1995, when 14-year-old Denise Elizabeth Garcia Velez, a U.S. citizen, attempted to enter the United States at the Otay Mesa Port of Entry, she showed her Los Angeles birth certificate. This apparently upset a U.S. Customs Official who yelled, "Stupid bitch! I don't want to see your stupid trash." Denied entry, Garcia was then pushed out of the inspection office. When she protested, the agent sprayed her eyes with pepper spray and asked her if it hurt. Fifteen-year-old Noel Alarid, also a U.S. citizen, protested when INS officers at the San Ysidro Port of Entry directed him to secondary inspection and grabbed his arm. Three officers responded by slamming him against the wall. Witnesses observed that Alarid struggled with the officers, but would periodically stop struggling, which seemed to provoke even greater use of force from his assailants. Alarid's cousin, Ramon, who was witnessing the violence, was commanded to leave the scene when he told officers to stop hurting Noel. When an officer grabbed for Ramon's hand, Ramon kept his arm firm. Despite being placed in handcuffs, Ramon continued to insist that the officers stop hurting Noel. The officers yelled at him to "shut... up," and they then tightened the handcuffs on his wrists. Both Noel and Ramon were placed in holding cells. Noel was placed alone in a small cell that reeked from toilet paper and garbage that lay scattered on the floor. Ramon was placed in a crowded cell with approximately 15 other men. The toilet in this cell had no seat and there was no toilet paper. The smell inside the cell was so bad that the men were using blankets to cover their noses.[2]

Jesus Payan, a U.S. citizen, made the mistake in December 1994 of getting angry when an INS agent at the San Ysidro Port of Entry denied him entry into the United States and told him to "go back to Mexico." After Payan told the agent to ["go away"], the agent ran after him and grabbed him by the neck until several other agents arrived. With Payan's friends watching, the agents slammed his head twice against the edge of a table. At the same port of entry, U.S. citizen Luisa Torres Garcia was treated as if she were resisting when, falling as a result of her neck being grabbed and her arm being pulled behind her, she reached toward an officer for balance. For this action she was accused of striking the officer.

Asserting one's rights and personhood in the way of asking for explanations or rationale for the treatment they are receiving is often mocked or ignored by officials. At the Tecate Port of Entry in March 1995, an INS officer threatened to seize Eva Gonzalez Mendoza's valid U.S. passport. When she asked for a rationale, the officer stated that he did not need a reason. He then seized the passport and refused to listen while Mendoza begged for her document back so she could take her child, a U.S. citizen, to a U.S. doctor. Mendoza never learned why her passport was cancelled, though the officer's report indicates that she shouted and refused to follow orders, both of which she has subsequently denied. In October 1997, when Juan Manuel Moreno was being beaten by Vista Sheriff's deputies who took turns kicking him, his girlfriend asked for an explanation. One of the deputies responded: "Because we don't like Mexicans." When Noel and Ramon Alarid's friends and relatives were overheard discussing human rights, an INS officer shouted: "What... rights? You don't have any... rights!"

D. Patterned Delivery of Law Enforcement Practices

In all likelihood, the experiences of so many over a three-year period are not exceptional cases, but representative of a general pattern of occurrences. The 204 statements collected as part of the binational study over a relatively brief period of time provide support for the above claim. The narratives also offer substantial evidence that it is not the absence of civil and human rights abuses that explains a "mere" 63 complaints being filed through the San Diego AFSC office, but more likely the fear and intimidation tactics that are directed against targeted subjects.[3] In an atmosphere where physical and verbal abuse are being inflicted upon persons, the threat becomes commonplace. Thus, in June 1996 near Tecate, after Sergio Ponce Rodriguez was kicked by a U.S. Border Patrol agent at least seven or eight times, he was told to run while the agent had his hand placed on his service revolver as if it were a dare. In February of the same year, near San Ysidro, Carlos Sanchez Zamora endured kicks and racial taunts while one of the agents had his service revolver pointed at him. In August 1995 along the border, as Francisco Valdez Lopez was bleeding at the nose and mouth from Border patrol agents' closed fists and batons, he was told they were going to kill him. In October 1997, while her car was being directed to secondary inspection at the San Ysidro Port of Entry, a U.S. Customs inspector warned Angelica Navarro that he would "shoot her" if she did not slow down.

Even to witness the lawless behavior of agents is enough to warrant a threat. Such was the case with Rosario Cardenas and Maggie Bauer who in November 1996 were shaken after viewing the rough treatment a young man was receiving at the hands of several INS agents at the San Ysidro Port of Entry. When the witnesses inquired as to the reasons for such behavior, one agent... gave them the middle finger, while another agent yelled, "get ... out of here" and placed his hand on his service revolver. The effects of such threats should not be underestimated: in August 1995 they caused Jorge Hernandez Samano, after receiving a severe beating from four Border Patrol agents, to state that his numerous injuries were caused when he was climbing into a Border Patrol van after being apprehended along the border.

This recognition of human and civil rights abuses as routine occurrences discloses the workings of a logic of law enforcement as it is constituted by practices aimed against a select group of targeted subjects to interrupt their previously free passage, direct a searching gaze upon them, to query and issue authoritative commands to them, and to detain them or to apply other modes of restraint. Each of these practices can be backed by authoritative legitimation. Nevertheless, it is impossible to judge them without recognition that they are directed selectively only against some subjects to the exclusion of others. Further, inasmuch as the practices tend to exceed just limits—the limits of a person's body or one's right to privacy, or one's right to be secure from authoritatively instituted physical or verbal abuse—so they may have cumulative effects upon those who are most frequently targeted.

The effects themselves are fraught with fear and indecision. When the helicopter's search light beams down on its prey, the subject can hardly know whether to run or submit when it appears that excessive punishment may be inflicted regardless of the decision that is made. Once the authoritative gaze is directed upon the subject, does one shrink from it and thereby attempt to conceal visible markings of one's identity? Or does one return the gaze and, by so doing, offer an invitation to harassment or abuse? As the subject is queried from all sides, asked personal or irrelevant questions, or told that one is lying, does one cower and disclose all that is asked, perhaps even signing false confession papers? Or does one counter with questions of one's own that seek a rationale for having such queries directed at oneself, despite the near certainty that such countering will provoke further assaults upon one's sense of personal dignity? When authoritative commands to submit are questionable, does one acquiesce despite the humiliation this entails? Or does one resist with the knowledge that to do so might provoke a brutal response?

The logic that generates practices that produce these kinds of seemingly no-win life dilemmas transgresses the established limit of law. Perhaps the most important question is why it does this. What is it that prompts and normalizes this transgressing logic?

II. EXPLANATIONS

The general atmosphere of law enforcement in Southern California provides some explanation for the frequency of complaints regarding civil and human rights violations. This atmosphere consists of a steady build-up of military and police personnel, increased integration of military and police units, heightened deployment of surveillance technology, intensified criminalization of activities related to illegal immigration, and inflamed rhetoric that vilifies targeted subjects and legitimates the tactics used by law enforcement agencies. Contributing most to these developments has been Operation Gatekeeper, a federal project launched by the Clinton administration in October 1994 in response to the high numbers of undocumented immigrants entering the United States across what is referred to as the San Diego Sector.[4] Behind a steadily increasing amplification of presidential and congressional support, the presence of the operation has expanded dramatically over a short period of time. This includes sizable increases in law enforcement personnel and a formidable build-up of surveillance and control technology. In the San Diego area, for example, over the past year 1,665 Border Patrol agents have been supplemented by an additional 462 additional hires (Doyle, 1997). Congress has also committed at the national level a minimum of 1,000 additional Border Patrol agents per year over the next five years (GAO, 1997). This new force is being equipped with an increasingly sophisticated arsenal of law enforcement equipment consisting of "improved image enhancement vehicles," portable electronic ground sensors, infrared night scopes, sophisticated surveillance helicopters, low-level light television cameras, and high-power stadium-style lighting used to illuminate sections of a triple wall, developed over 1996 and 1997 at a cost of $8.6 million, that separates the U.S. from its Mexican neighbor *(Ibid.)*. A recent Government Accounting Office (GAO) report states that since 1994, "the San Diego sector alone acquired an additional 28 infrared scopes, about 600 underground sensors, about 500 vehicles, about 600 computers, and several advanced computer systems" (1997:23).

At least as notable as the build-up of personnel and technology has been the increased integration of military and police forces. Thus, the Border Patrol, a paramilitary force that has been given expanded law enforcement powers since the late 1980s, routinely receives added support from military, police, and other enforcement agencies (Dunn, 1996; Palafox, 1996). The support is made visible in coordinated maneuvers and joint operations involving the Border Patrol and U.S. Army, Air Force, and Marines. Further, on any given day the National Guard, whose primary task is to build and maintain the wall, may provide the Border Patrol with tactical ground and aviation support. Further plans are also underway for deploying the National Guard in other capacities, which may include manning night-vision scopes, maintaining electronic sensors, assisting with communications and transportation, and conducting aerial surveillance of border activities (U.S. House Hearings, 1995). The Border Patrol also integrates its efforts with some 135 local police and sheriff's deputies who provide escort during nighttime missions. In 1997, U.S. Forest Service personnel were also enlisted to set up and staff inland checkpoint stations for purposes of stopping and interrogating visitors of national parks.

The intensification of law enforcement activity has been fueled by a rhetoric of fear (e.g., Calavita, 1996; Mehan, 1997).[5] This rhetoric, which feeds upon the idea of the dangerousness of the immigrant population, has been made concrete by recent law and a revamped charging policy that effectively increases the criminalization of the immigrant population. Special emphasis has been placed on prosecuting those who have committed "serious felonies," such as for illegally transporting aliens, which can earn sentences of up to five years for a first offence and up to 15 years for a second, as well as for attempting illegal entry with prior felony conviction, which typically earns a two-year sentence, for attempting illegal entry by means of document fraud, which is prosecuted as a felony with a two-year maximum sentence, and for attempting illegal entry after having been previously arrested for a similar act (U.S. Code, Title 8).

Beyond providing a rationale for stepped-up law enforcement, the prevailing rhetoric also has enabled military and police agencies to sidestep otherwise problematic constitutional constraints. Thus, although the National Guard is constitutionally prohibited from enforcing federal immigration laws, it is empowered to provide counterdrug support along the border to federal agencies in the way of "photo reconnaissance," "intelligence analysis," and "aviation support for night thermal imagery" (U.S. House Hearing, 1995:145). Similarly, although U.S. military forces are prohibited by law from pursuing and apprehending suspected criminals within the U.S. interior, they do have jurisdictional authority in marijuana eradication efforts and so are deployed in tandem with the Border Patrol to monitor and surveil suspected criminal activities as well as to assist in the pursuit of criminal suspects (Dunn, 1996; Palafox, 1996). A most telling example of this has been Joint Task Force Six (JTF–6), which was responsible for the fatal shooting of Emanuel Hernandez in Texas as he tended his goats along the U.S.-Mexico border (e.g., Reza, 1997).

The Border Patrol was granted limited authority in 1986 to interdict drugs. The agency may only arrest suspected drug traffickers if they are clearly also suspected of being illegal aliens. To overcome this limitation, local police agencies provide assistance by escorting the Border Patrol on its nightly rounds. The California Highway Patrol is now also regularly called upon for assistance, following a rash of fatal vehicular crashes caused by high-speed chases involving the Border Patrol that led to restrictions on the scope of the agency's authority in this regard.

Spokespersons for various law enforcement agencies claim that the stepped-up campaigns of militarization of the border, criminalization of immigration-related activities, and the integration of military, paramilitary, and police units have been highly successful. The once highly visible flow of undocumented immigrants in and around the San Diego area has been dramatically reduced, with traffic redirected into the mountains, deserts, and vast stretches of no-man's-land to the east. Further, in the past year alone over 110,000 illegal immigrants have been ousted from the United States. California leads the way with the expulsion of over 46,000 people. This represents a 35% jump in deportation of criminals and a 93% jump in deportation of noncriminals (GAO, 1997).

However, critics have pointed to the costs of such proclaimed successes, emphasizing how Operation Gatekeeper has induced changes in behavior among the tens of thousands of undocumented immigrants pulled by the jobs magnet in the U.S. (Huspek, 1998). The rechannelling of immigrant traffic to the perilous eastern terrain has brought with it immense human tragedy. In the nighttime pitch of the mountains, falls resulting in injury are common, as are snakebites. Because the trek across the border now may take up to four days and nights, those setting out without adequate provisions are especially at risk. Climatic conditions in the mountains and desert also tend to be harsh and unpredictable. Thirty-eight immigrants are known to have died in 1996 while attempting to traverse the rugged landscape, with the causes of their deaths being primarily dehydration (in the summer desert heat) and hypothermia (in the cruel mountain snow and cold). In 1997, at least 85 people are known to have died while attempting passage. Countless others have surely disappeared after falling into rocky crevices or wandering disoriented in vast stretches of no-man's-land.

Other shifts in behavior are indicated by a heightened desperation among those who are targeted by U.S. law enforcement agencies. Perhaps most dramatic has been the resort by coyotes to increasingly risky means of avoiding arrest. For example, there has been a marked upswing in vehicular crashes following chases that involve fleeing immigrants and law enforcement agencies. In the San Diego area alone, six violent wrecks that left at least 15 dead and 68 injured have occurred since the inception of Operation Gatekeeper.[6] Despite ongoing construction of the triple wall, coyotes have recently resorted to daring daylight border crossings; after high-speed chases into congested neighborhoods, the fleeing truck or van unloads dozens of clients who then flee on foot.

The state has pointed to the immigrants' increasingly desperate acts to legitimate its own build-up of forces. Specifically, as new behaviors are adopted by those targeted by stepped-up police and military tactics, the state further extends the net of its criminalization categories. This is especially true for coyotes, who have been increasingly spotlighted as a primary source of blame. Thus, the unabated heavy influx of undocumented immigrants is said to be due to the greed and desperate cunning of the coyote. If incidents of drug smuggling have risen along the borderlands and into the interior, this is said to be because coyotes are forcing their clients to carry drugs as partial payment for their passage. If injuries and deaths are on the upswing, this is because smugglers take them into dangerous environs and then leave them to die. Since passage of the 1996 Illegal Immigration Reform and Immigrant Responsibility Act (IIRIRA), the penalty for high-speed vehicular flights or evading immigration checkpoints carries a penalty of up to five years and is grounds for deportation of noncitizens, regardless of status. The U.S. Attorney for the Southwest Region of the United States, Alan Bersin, has repeatedly gone on public record in support of capital punishment for coyotes whose activities result in fatalities.

Stepped-up militarization and policing have contributed to increased law enforcement presence throughout the community: more white Ford Broncos are now positioned along the borderline; more surveillance helicopters are in the sky; more joint operations are being conducted along the border; more inland checkpoints are being installed.[7] With intensified criminalization policies aimed at immigration-related activities, the potential offenses loom larger in the estimates of the targeted subjects as well as those who are commissioned to apprehend and detain them. This may be contributing to even more desperate evasion tactics by the former and more drastic enforcement measures by the latter (Huspek, 1998). In this state of heightened alert, law enforcement officials increasingly encounter their targeted subjects in remote stretches of mountain and desert terrain where, outside any effective monitoring controls, the fear and panic of targeted subjects and the anger and fear of enforcement officials may combine to contribute to an increasingly volatile situation.

It is important to acknowledge how such an atmosphere might be felt by those most frequently targeted by militarization, criminalization, and inflamed rhetoric. Nearly 70% of California's agricultural labor force now consists of undocumented workers. Yet, the state has done virtually nothing to police employers who knowingly hire undocumented workers. In fiscal 1997, there was not a single prosecution of an employer of undocumented workers in San Diego County (Huspek, 1997). Further, as grounds for denying California growers' requests for a guest worker program, top government officials pointed to the adequate labor supply already represented by undocumented workers in the state and projected no discernable decline in the available labor force. As such, undocumented workers seeking to satisfy personal or familial economic need may have some understanding of the ready economic demand for his or her services and the government's own complicity in sustaining existing labor-capital arrangements. Consider, too, that many of these tens of thousands of workers may have labored on U.S. soil for many years.[8] We can only imagine the dissonance that must be felt for undocumented immigrants whose labor is so valued, but who must render themselves invisible, skulking from campsite to workplace and back under cover of darkness.

Finally, consider the legal resident or U.S. citizen who perhaps has struggled over most of a lifetime to attain such a status. One can imagine the sense of righteous indignation in the face of law enforcement officials who show negative dispositions toward persons of Hispanic appearance. This might contribute to the likelihood of escalated tension during points of contact between the subject and law enforcement officials. For their part, officials may be inclined to place the targeted subject of their gaze into one of the many categories that stepped-up criminalization has provided. Short of easy categorization, and faced with a person who may not be showing what in the official's estimate is proper deference to authority, there may be the temptation to provoke some form of conflict that ultimately proves to "confirm" the official's predisposition. In short, if the person does not readily fall into an available criminalization category (beyond ethnic appearance), perhaps some provocation will incite an act of resistance to produce an applicable category where none had existed before.

III. RECOMMENDATIONS

Law delegates to enforcement agencies material and symbolic means of authoritative intervention into people's lives. Frequently, such interventions are violent. This may involve directing an intrusive, inspecting gaze upon subjects, questioning, interrogating, and judging them, searching their personal belongings, including their bodies and private body parts, imposing physical restraints upon them, as well as confiscating personal belongings, money, and documents, inflicting physical harm upon them, incarcerating them, and, in extreme instances, executing them.

With such means of violence and control at their command, law must place proper constraints upon the agents vested with the authority to enforce the law. There are boundaries that simply cannot be transgressed. The law is not to be enforced arbitrarily, or selectively against some while a blind eye is turned toward others. Above all, law enforcement officials cannot abrogate subjects' human and civil rights. To do so constitutes a breaking of the law, a form of lawlessness that instills terror in us all. If the officials entrusted with enforcement routinely violate the law, then we must all live in fear. It is imperative, therefore, that officials are carefully selected, trained, and monitored so as to ensure that they conduct themselves in a highly professional manner. Perhaps most important, they must be made accountable to the public they are commissioned to serve.

The data compiled in this report suggest that law enforcement in the southwest region of the United States may be verging on lawlessness. This statement receives fuller support from announcements emanating from the INS. In December 1997, John Chase, head of the INS Office of Internal Audit (OIA), announced at a press conference that public complaints to the INS had risen 29% from 1996, with the "vast majority" of complaints emanating from the southwest border region. Over 2,300 complaints were filed in 1997 as opposed to the 1,813 complaints filed in 1996. Another 400 reports of "minor misconduct" were placed in a new category. Chase was quick to emphasize, however, that the 243 "serious" allegations of abuse and use of excessive force that could warrant criminal prosecution were down in 1997, as compared with the 328 in 1996. These "serious" cases are considered to be distinct from less serious complaints, such as "verbal abuse, discrimination, extended detention without cause."

On the day Chase spoke to the press, the INS also issued a spate of press releases detailing the Action Plan being implemented in response to recommendations specified in the Final Report of the INS' Citizens' Advisory Panel. According to the INS, much of the Action Plan has already been implemented. The plan consists of increasing the information made available to the public, expanding dialogue between the INS and community groups, enhancing dissemination of INS information, increasing public knowledge about complaint procedures, improving complaint process case management, using a complaint database as the basis for personnel decisions, offering greater consistency in INS disciplinary actions, and incorporating local community-based training of INS staff.

Such changes are to be commended, particularly in an increasingly volatile atmosphere of militarization, criminalization, and anti-immigrant rhetoric. Better training and monitoring are clearly needed since agents are being placed in the field at an unprecedented rate. The steady rise in state funding, coupled with increasing points of contact between agents and the public, makes it essential for the community to have a better understanding of the application, logic, and effects of law enforcement practices. Such measures, moreover, need to be implemented not only for the INS, but also for U.S. Customs and all other law enforcement agencies whose operations are continually being integrated with the INS in response to the war against undocumented immigrants.

This report on human and civil rights violations by law enforcement agencies strongly emphasizes, however, that such proposed changes do not go nearly far enough in the right direction. Most vitally needed is an external review board—with genuine citizen participatory input—that can objectively determine the validity of complaints. This need is patent in light of the track records of the two offices most responsible for dealing with public complaints: the INS' OIA and the Office of the U.S. Attorney of the Southern District.

The experience of the American Friends Service Committee in San Diego is that complaints are routinely buried within the OIA. The U.S. attorney's office fares no better. In response to all 63 AFSC-assisted complaints filed at different times over the 1995 to 1997 period, an identical form letter was received that stated: "After careful review... we have concluded that there is insufficient evidence to establish a prosecutable violation of the federal criminal civil rights statutes." This standardized response raises a question: How can an office commissioned to implement and defend law enforcement policies and practices be independent in its investigations? The abysmal record of case review by the U.S. attorney's office suggests that the office is not adequately suited for the task.

Beyond institution of an external review board, further discussion needs to be devoted to the frequency and nature of abuses being committed by law enforcement personnel. Perhaps the most obvious and disturbing inference to be drawn from both data sets is that law enforcement in the southwest region of the United States is being applied discriminatorily against Hispanics. This appears to be true irrespective of the subject's citizenship or other forms of documented identity. This is not to state that all law enforcement practices are racially motivated or to claim that all law enforcement agents who engage in such practices are driven by racist sentiments or beliefs. Yet the number and frequency of complaints, as well as their contents, are sufficient to suggest that law enforcement practices are being applied discriminatorily against some, but not others, and that the practices are driven by a logic that is racially discriminatory. Further, the effects of the practice are understandably felt to be racist by those toward whom the practices are often directed. Indeed, as to the latter, the application and logic of law enforcement practices may amount to a routinized infliction of terror upon the persons it targets and upon those who feel themselves likely to be so targeted.

The current process of distinguishing "serious" abuses, such as rapes or shootings, from "less serious" abuses is inadequate. Verbal abuse, discrimination, and extended detention without cause must be treated as the crimes that they are. What distinguishes the verbal abuses that frequently accompany excessive use of force by law enforcement officials from hate crimes? In an atmosphere where immigrant strawberry pickers have been sighted between the crosshairs of an intensified criminalization strategy, it seems fitting that law enforcement officials' violations of the law also be treated as crimes and not merely as forms of institutional misconduct. Indeed, law enforcement officials need to be fully aware that such violations take on a greater magnitude when they are committed by the personnel whom we entrust with the authority to intervene in so many ways in our lives.

Finally, this report is limited in scope in that it restricts itself to human and civil rights abuses by law enforcement officials in the southwest region of the United States. Nevertheless, the report notes that the number and type of abuses are best understood only when considered within an atmosphere of heightened militarization and policing of our border and interior regions, intensified criminalization of undocumented immigrants, and an increasingly inflamed anti-immigrant rhetoric. As such, this report is intended to stand as a sobering counter to claims from the INS and U.S. attorney's office that we are deporting more illegal aliens and incarcerating more criminals than ever before. We conclude with the recommendation that critical questions involving the relationship between immigration and law enforcement policies be placed at the top of the agenda for national debate. To what lengths are law enforcement agencies resorting in their zeal to apprehend and convict? And how far will the general public permit them to go?

NOTES

1. Based upon an interview conducted January 7, 1998, with Senior Border Patrol Agents Farrens and Villareal at the Temecula checkpoint.
2. Since September 1997, when Noel and Ramon were incarcerated, conditions of the holding cells have not improved. The AFSC-San Diego office continues to hear of 30 to 50 people being kept in a single cell that measures no more than 10 feet wide by 25 feet long. Each cell has only one toilet and no shower or bathing facilities. No beds are provided; people are given a blanket and are required to sleep on the floor. All inhabitants must relieve themselves, and female inhabitants must attend to their feminine hygiene needs, in full view of others. Because trash receptacles are not provided, the floor is frequently covered with litter.
3. Other problems abound. States Nuñez (1992:1577): "alien victims often will not report incidents of confrontation or abuse. Fears of discovery and deportation lead many illegal aliens to believe that the better course is to not report such incidents." He continues: "because the undocumented immigrant's mere presence in this country is viewed as 'illegal,' courts and scholars are faced with the dilemma of whether the 'illegal alien' should be afforded the same constitutional and civil rights as citizens and legal resident aliens" (p. 1578).
4. Along with similar operations—Operation Safeguard in Tucson, Operation Hold the Line in El Paso, and the recently mobilized Operation Rio Grande in Brownsville—Operation Gatekeeper draws from a federally allocated fund of $3.1 billion, nearly twice the $1.6 billion allocated in 1993, and almost four times the $807.8 million allocated in 1988 (Dunn, 1996:35). The San Diego sector is a 66-mile stretch along the U.S.-Mexico border that runs eastward from the Pacific Ocean into desert and mountain areas.
5. State officials have shown a strong penchant for using war terms when discussing border issues. In the context of eliciting support for death penalty sentences for smugglers of aliens whose actions result in death for their clients or others, U.S. Attorney for the Southwest Region, Alan Bersin, announced: "We are declaring war on them" (Gross, 1996). U.S. Attorney General Janet Reno has also repeatedly stressed that the U.S. "will not surrender" the border to aliens (U.S. Senate Hearings, 1994). Perhaps such terms are unavoidable when so much of Operation Gatekeeper involves the use of U.S. military forces for purposes of offering "ground tactical and aviation support," operations that are assessed according to whether they are, in the words of Deputy Commander of the California National Guard, General Edmund Zysk, "militarily sound" (U.S. House Hearings, 1995). States Mehan (1997:267):

   During the Cold War, the state constructed an external enemy, a military enemy, to discipline the citizenry. Now the state and aligned elites are directing our gaze inward, constructing an economic enemy, one who lives among us, but is not part of us.

6. On June 13, 1996, a fleeing van carrying suspected illegal aliens crashed, killing one and injuring 12; on April 26, 1996, a fleeing van carrying suspected illegal aliens crashed, killing two and injuring 19; on April 6, 1996, a fleeing pick-up truck carrying suspected illegal aliens crashed, killing eight and injuring 17; on September 1, 1995, a fleeing car carrying suspected illegal aliens crashed, leaving one dead and several others injured; on April 19, 1995, a fleeing van carrying suspected illegal aliens smashed into a pick-up truck, leaving three dead and 16 injured (Hunt, 1996).
7. According to a GAO report (1997:15), "the number of Border Patrol agents on board along the southwest border increased 76% between October 1993 and July 1997."
8. John Locke's (1960:329) words may be apposite here:

   The Labour of his Body, and the Work of his Hands, we may say, are properly his. Whatsoever then he removes out of the State that Nature hath provided, and left it in, he hath mixed his Labour with, and joyned to it something that is his own, and thereby makes it his Property. It being by him removed from the common state Nature placed it in, hath by this Labour something annexed to it, that excludes the common right of other Men. For this Labour being the unquestionable Property of the Labourer, no Man but he can have a right to what that is once joyned to, at least where there is enough, and as good left in common for others.

CHAPTER 10 The Family Institution

10.1 TERRY A. CROSS, KATHLEEN A. EARLE, AND DAVID SIMMONS

Child Abuse and Neglect in Indian Country: Policy Issues

Child victimization is pervasive in the United States. Since 1976 reported cases of child victimization have increased over 300 percent, with 3.1 million cases occurring in 1996 alone. Data from the U.S. Department of Health and Human Services reveal that 46 percent of all child victimization cases involve child neglect, 21 percent are cases of physical abuse, 11 percent concern sexual abuse, and 5 percent of the cases have to do with the emotional maltreatment of children. Some 17 percent of all child abuse cases involve other, less common forms of victimization, including medical neglect, abandonment, congenital drug addiction, and threatened physical harm. The National Advisory Commission on Child Abuse and Neglect estimates that some 2,000 children per year die because of parental ill-treatment.

Child victimization occurs across all levels of the American class structure and across all racial groups. Yet child abuse and neglect are far more prevalent in White families than in non-White families. More than 55 percent of all reported cases of child abuse and neglect take place in White families, about 26 percent are in Black families, nearly 10 percent are in

Latino families, about 1.4 percent are in Native American families, and roughly 0.8 percent occur in Asian families. The number of child abuse cases occurring in Black and Native American families, however, are disproportionate to their representations in the general population. Also, while child abuse cases among Latinos are nearly proportionate to their total representation in the general population, child victimization among White and Asian families is underrepresented compared with their overall representation in the U.S. population.

In the following selection from "Child Abuse and Neglect in Indian Country: Policy Issues," *Families in Society* (January 2000), executive director Terry A. Cross and program specialist David Simmons of the National Indian Child Welfare Association in Portland, Oregon, and assistant professor of social work Kathleen A. Earle of the University of Southern Maine in Portland, Maine, address child abuse and neglect policy issues specifically facing Native American families. These researchers argue that increasing rates of child abuse and neglect in Native American tribal communities are the result of an institutional bias by the dominant society in dealing with cultural variation in child-rearing practices and customs among Native Americans as well as the inability of Native American tribes to take advantage of the same child welfare opportunities afforded other children in the United States.

Key Concept: child abuse and neglect, and Native American child-rearing practices and public policy

Abstract: Although Native People have been able to maintain many of their traditional child protective mechanisms, these have been eroded over time by forces largely outside of tribal control. The passage of the Indian Child Welfare Act in 1978 provided an opportunity to return the care of Indian children to their people. Yet, over twenty years later, there remain issues that prevent its full operationalization. This paper identifies some of the major policy issues that need to be addressed in order to provide the same opportunities to American Indian children as are given to other children in the US. in the area of child welfare.

American Indian tribes in the United States have some of the oldest and most positive traditions regarding the protection of children and yet only recently have they had the capacity to exercise those traditions in the form of programs. Tribes are sovereign governments and, like states, have the right to pass and enforce their own child protection laws. This right was not recognized or encouraged before the nineteen seventies. Today, almost all tribes operate some form of child protection services. Many have their own tribal codes, court systems, and child welfare programs and many more tribes would if it were financially feasible.

Even if their programs were fully operational, tribal services would reach less than half of all American Indian children. Public and private mainstream child welfare agencies will always serve Indian children since more than half of the Indian population now lives off reservation. Mainstream agencies need information on effective cross-cultural services, compliance with the Indian Child Welfare Act, and how to collaborate successfully with tribal programs. This paper is intended to provide an overview of historical issues regarding child protection, the problem of abuse among Native Americans, and several strategies for enhancing child protection both at the tribal level and in mainstream public and private agencies.

A HERITAGE OF CULTURAL CHILD PROTECTION

Protecting children from abuse and neglect so that they can thrive and mature is the most fundamental child welfare service that a society can provide. Historically, Indian communities had well-developed customs and traditions regarding child rearing that produced a natural system of child protection. This system was easily enforced within the extended family where parents and children were under the watchful eyes of relatives and elders. Responsibilities for rearing children were often divided among extended family and community members.

In traditional Indian spiritual belief systems, all things had a spiritual nature that demanded respect. Children were not viewed as their parents' property, but were considered gifts from the Creator, endowed with an intrinsic value based on their relationship to the Creator. Thus, respect was extended to children as well as to the earth and creatures from the land, sea, and sky. According to Lewis (1980), mutual respect was highly valued within Indian cultures:

> This respect is the key word in the relationship between Indian children and their parents, it lies at the center of a person's relationship to nature and to the Creator, respect for the elders, respect for the child, respect for all living creatures in life. Respect is really the foundation of discipline and authority, it is basic to every kind of learning as well as to the enjoyment of life (p. 3).

As children were respected, so were they also taught to respect others. It has been said that Indian child-rearing methods were marked by extraordinary patience and tolerance. That is, Indian children were usually brought up without restraint or severe physical punishment. Obedience was achieved through moral or psychological persuasion, building on tribal beliefs in supernatural beings. Many tribes had stories of supernatural beings who watched children and punished them when they were disobedient. Through the telling of myths and legends, children were given clear expectations about desired behavior and the consequences for deviant behavior.

Unlike the dominant society with its strong tradition of "spare the rod and spoil the child," Indian child-rearing practices emphasized self-discipline. The management of behavior came not from fear of reprisal from a parent, but from the fear and respect for something far greater, for example, a supernatural being. Respect for children and self-discipline, coupled with an extended family system where parenting responsibilities were spread among many individuals, meant that child abuse and neglect were seldom problems in traditional tribal settings.

LOSS OF CHILDREN AND CAPACITY TO PROTECT

These aspects of traditional Indian child rearing were vulnerable to the influence of the dominant society. Since the earliest colonization of this continent, most attempts to "civilize" Indian people focused on Indian children. For example, in 1609, the Virginia Company, in a written document, authorized the kidnapping of Indian children for the purpose of civilizing local Indian populations through Christianity.

The "Civilization Fund Act" was an early first federal law that directly affected Indian children. Passed by Congress in 1819, it provided grants to private agencies, primarily churches, to establish programs to "civilize the Indian." The goal of substituting "the social for the savage state" (Elbert Herring, first commissioner of Indian Affairs, 1832) was continually pursued by federal officials and lawmakers. The Indian Peace Commission, in 1868, reviewed the causes of Indian hostilities and recommended bringing Indians into white civilization as a solution to their differences:

> Now, by educating the children of these tribes in the English language, these differences would have disappeared, and civilization would have followed at once. Nothing then would have been left but the antipathy of race, and that too is always softened in the beams of a higher civilization (Prucha, 1990, p.107).

In support of this policy, both the government and private institutions developed large militaristic or mission boarding schools for Indian children. Off reservation boarding schools were established where native children were taken by force. Once there they were forbidden to use their native language or customs, or even their Indian names, which were replaced by Christian names (Nabokov, 1991). Many of these institutions housed more than a thousand students ranging in age from three to thirteen. The out-of-home placement and isolation of children engendered by these schools led to a loss of self and in many cases to dysfunctional behavior (George, 1997). Many left years later with no clear identity, either white or Indian.

The practice of removing Indian children from their families and communities flourished. In 1884, the "placing out" system placed numerous Indian children on farms in the East and Midwest in order to learn the "values of work and the benefits of civilization" (Breamner, 1970). Through beginning of the 20th century, stories have been told of bonuses used to encourage boarding school workers to take leaves of absence and secure as many students as possible from surrounding reservations.

By 1900, the rearing of Indian children was largely under the control of the federal Bureau of Indian Affairs [BIA]. Tribes had been effectively stripped of all but the last vestiges of the natural systems of child protection. Over the next half-century oppression, alcoholism, disease, and poverty were allowed to flourish and child abuse and neglect had fertile ground in which to take root.

IMPACT OF HUMANITARIAN EFFORTS

With the last of the Indian wars more than a half century behind it, white America began to take a romantic view of Indian culture. The social problems of Indian families and children, primarily in the eastern half of the country, began to receive new attention. A new era of liberalism changed the focus of private agencies to humanitarian relief. However, these humanitarian gestures were again aimed at saving children and were largely conducted without consultation with Indian communities or respect for Indian culture. These efforts were motivated by the continuing belief that assimilation was the only realistic alternative for Indian children and that tribes were unable to protect their own.

Public Law 280, passed by Congress in 1953, reflected this new attitude. Under this law, most civil and criminal jurisdiction passed from the federal government and local tribe to the state in which the reservation was located (Canby, 1988). Although not all tribes and states were affected by this law, most were. The motivation behind the law was, in part, to make Indian people eligible for state-administered services such as public assistance and child welfare services. The law further eroded tribal authority and capacity to protect children.

Throughout the 1950s and 60s, transracial adoptions, primarily within the private sector, were widespread. In 1959, the Child Welfare League of America (CWLA), the standard-setting body for child welfare agencies, in cooperation with the Bureau of Indian Affairs, initiated the Indian Adoption Project. As a result of this project, 395 Indian children were placed for adoption with non-Indian families in eastern metropolitan areas (Georges, 1997; Mannes, 1995). Little attention was paid, either by the Bureau of Indian Affairs or CWLA to providing services on reservations that would strengthen and maintain Indian families. The program served as a model to the rest of the nation with near tragic results.

A survey by the Association on American Indian Affairs in the 1970s found that 25% to 35% of all native American children had been separated from their families (Georges, 1997). In 16 states in 1969, 85 percent of the Indian children were placed in non-Indian families (Linger, 1977). From 1971–72 approximately 35,000 Indian children lived in institutional settings, more than 68 percent of these in BIA administered schools (Metheson, 1996). The tragic, long-range effects of the placement of thousands of Native People away from their homes were only beginning to be realized. These include not only effects on individuals (Fanshel, 1972; Robin, Rasmussen, & Gonzalez-Santin, 1999), but also consequences for the cohesion and well being of entire communities of Native People.

TRIBES REASSERT AUTHORITY

In a response to the overwhelming evidence from Indian communities that the loss of their children meant the destruction of Indian culture, Congress concluded that "there is no resource that is more vital to the continued existence and integrity of Indian tribes than their children," (25 U.S.C.A. § 1901–1963). The Indian Child Welfare Act, reaffirming tribal authority to protect their children, was passed in 1978 (P.L. 95–6087). The unique legal relationship that exists between the United States government and Indian tribes and the advocacy of Indian people made it possible for Congress to adopt a new national policy. Because of their sovereign nation status, Indian tribes are nations within a nation. The Constitution of the United States provides that "Congress shall have power to regulate commerce with Indian tribes" (U.S. Const. Art. 1, § 8, cl. 3). Through this and other constitutional authority, Congress has plenary power over Indian affairs, including the protection and preservation of tribes and their resources.

Under the Indian Child Welfare Act, tribal courts have exclusive jurisdiction over adoption and placement of Indian children who live within the reservation of their tribe, unless some federal law such as P.L. 280 provides to the contrary. They also have jurisdiction over proceedings involving any Indian child who is the ward of the tribal court, regardless of where the child lives (Canby, 1988). The Act sets up requirements and standards for child-placing agencies to follow in the placement of Indian children, including, among other things, providing remedial, culturally appropriate service for Indian families before a placement occurs, notifying tribes regarding the placement of Indian children and, when placement must occur, it requires that children be placed in Indian homes. Because most people who work within the system are not aware of the provisions of this act, there is an assumption that the state can proceed as usual with native as well as non-native children.

CHILD ABUSE AND NEGLECT AMONG NATIVE PEOPLE TODAY

Despite a long history in which the natural system protected children, child abuse and neglect are serious problems in many present-day Indian families. Disproportionately large numbers of Indian children experience factors that increase risk for child abuse and neglect.

- 45 percent of Indian mothers having their first child are under the age of 20, compared to 24 percent of U.S. all race mothers (Indian Health Service, 1997).
- 38 percent of Indian children age 6 to 11 live below the poverty level, more than twice the number for the U.S. all races age group, which is 18 percent (Indian Health Service, 1997).
- 27 percent of all Indian households are maintained by a female householder (single parent), compared to 16 percent for U.S. all races (Bureau of the Census, 1993).

- From 1992 to 1995, American Indians and Asians were the only ethnic groups to experience increases in the rate of abuse or neglect of children under age 15, as measured by incidents recorded by state child protective service agencies. The increase in reported incidents involving American Indian children (18 percent) was more than three times as large as that for Asian children (6 percent) (National Child Abuse and Neglect Data System).
- The vast majority of tribal communities would be characterized as rural, with many covering broad areas that create a sense of geographic and sometimes social isolation. This is especially true where services and recreational/community activities are difficult to access.

  Indian children in the United States are placed in substitute care at a much higher rate than is the average for all other children in the nation.
- 12.5 out of every 1,000 Indian children are placed in substitute care, compared to 6.9 out of every 1,000 children from all races (Child Welfare League of America, 1996, 34 states reporting substitute care data).

ATTRIBUTION OF CHILD ABUSE AND NEGLECT IN NATIVE AMERICAN COMMUNITIES

Ishisaka (1978) speculated that Native American parenting practices may be inappropriately interpreted as neglect because of cultural differences. A parent's relative silence, non-interference, and permissiveness with their children may be wrongly interpreted as emotional neglect. The willingness of the Indian mother or father to allow a child to live with a relative is often seen as abandonment.

Among children in the dominant society, research strongly suggests a correlation between incidence of child abuse and neglect, and socioeconomic stressors, such as unemployment, alcoholism, and poverty. Studies have found that modernization, poverty, situational stress, poor parenting skills, alcoholism, unusual perceptions of children, and divorce constitute factors associated with maltreatment (Fischler, 1985). Given the extent of these problems in the Native American community, one might expect the problems of child abuse and neglect to be much more serious than they are reported to be. However, experience tells us that the natural child protections still operate to a large degree despite the weakening of the traditional extended family structure. Aunt and uncles, grandparents, and others are still the primary resource for child abuse prevention in Indian communities.

Relocation Programs

The relocation of tribal members that began with the Indian Removal Act of 1830 continued with the relocation and termination policies of the U.S. government in the 1950s and 1960s. Under these policies of assimilation, the U.S. government severed the federal relationship of sixty-one tribal groups (they were later re-instated) and lured tens of thousands of Indians to urban areas with the promise of apartments, jobs, and schools for their children. The movement of large populations of Native Americans into urban areas has turned out to have been very destructive. Indians living in cities face both the dissolution of family ties and a greater impact of being a minority, which has contributed to the rising incidence of child abuse and neglect. Urban Indians sometimes become abusive of their children as they are confronted by additional traumas of city life and the absence of family support.

Learned Abuse Patterns

Child abuse in the dominant society has been related to its tradition of harsh physical punishment and parental ownership of children. Native Americans have no such tradition. Without a tradition of punitive child-rearing practices among the Native American cultures, we must consider where the concepts of child abuse and neglect have been "learned." There are several possible answers. One possibility is that the tribes learned the abuse by being abused, neglected, and exploited as a people. Another more concrete answer stems from government policies; especially those aimed at assimilation, which separated Indian people from the traditional supports that helped minimize social problems. We know that as many as half of all Indian people in this century have been reared outside of their tribal communities in boarding schools or foster homes. Discipline was often harsh and devoid of nurturing in boarding schools. Physical and sexual abuse were a common boarding school experience. Personal experiences such as these, coupled with the breakdown of the extended family and spiritual belief-systems, the loss of tribal economies, and the introduction of alcohol served to create an environment where child abuse and neglect could develop and continue to exist in Indian communities.

STRENGTHENING TRIBAL SERVICES: POLICY ISSUES

The ICWA was a huge step in the right direction. However, being given the right to provide a service does not mean that the funding, desire, or know-how will come together in a timely way. For Indian tribes, program development has been hampered by lack of funding, jurisdictional barriers, lack of trained personnel, lack of information about the extent of the problem, lack of culturally appropriate service models, and community denial. Despite these obstacles, tribes have been able to develop services to a degree beyond what a reasonable person would believe possible. The struggle is still new and while great strides have been made most of the work is yet to be done.

Resource Barriers

As is clearly evident, lack of stable and adequate funding for tribal child welfare programs has proven to be one of the most serious barriers to tribes' ability to protect their children. With the passage of the Indian Child Welfare Act a new grant program (ICWA Title II) became available to tribes for development and operation of child welfare services. However, the funding was inadequate to fund even 25 percent of the need. Tribal programs that were funded received year to year grants. Just as tribal programs began to develop they would suddenly be faced with the loss of Indian Child Welfare Act funds causing staff to be laid off and the disruption of child welfare services indefinitely. Not until 1993 were adequate funds appropriated to allow each tribe even one caseworker. With the available child welfare funding from the Bureau of Indian Affairs being very limited, tribes have looked to other federal agencies that provide funding for child welfare services.

In 1990, the Indian Child Protection and Family Violence Prevention Act established new federal requirements for reporting and investigating cases of child abuse involving Indian children on tribal lands. It also required background checks for those working with or having direct control over Indian children on reservations. The law also authorized funding for grant programs for tribal child abuse prevention and treatment, although Congress has never appropriated more than a token amount of funding.

The majority of the most stable, ongoing child welfare funding is administered by the Administration for Children and Families under the Department of Health and Human Services [DHHS]. Here the federal government's largest sources of child welfare funding, all of which are Social Security Act programs, are found. They are as follows: Title IV-E Foster Care and Adoption Assistance; Title IV-B (subpart 1) Child Welfare Services; Title IV-B (subpart 2) Promoting Safe and Stable Families; Title XX Social Services Block Grant. These programs provide billions of dollars of funding which can be used to support child welfare services. They are designed to promote the well-being of all children in the United States; however, most of these programs were designed with little or no consideration given to issues of tribal culture, service delivery systems, or the government-to-government relationship that exists between tribes and the state and federal governments. Consequently, tribes have encountered significant barriers to funding access. Following is a discussion of these four major programs in relation to services for American Indian children and families.

PROGRAM: TITLE IV-E FOSTER CARE AND ADOPTION ASSISTANCE. While Congress intended for the Title IV-E program to serve all eligible children in the United States, Indian children under the jurisdiction of a tribal court do not have an entitlement to this important program afforded other children. The statute provides services only for income-eligible children placed by states and public agencies with whom states have agreements.

It may have been a drafting oversight that the Foster Care and Adoption Assistance Act of 1980 made no provision for funding of children placed by tribal courts nor for tribal governments to administer Title IV-E funds and seek reimbursement for foster care and adoption services provided Indian children under their jurisdiction.

There are approximately 405,000 Indian children who live on or near their tribal lands. While not all of these children will need foster care or adoption services, the most recent data suggest that approximately 6,500 of these children will be placed in substitute care during a fiscal year. Based on the characteristics of Indian children in care as identified through case reviews by Bureau of Indian Affairs staff and tribal child welfare administrators, it is estimated that between 3,900 and 4,600 of these children meet the eligibility criteria of Title IV-E.

Not wanting to leave children in harmful situations, tribes have had to resort to alternative vehicles for protecting children who must be removed from their homes. A common method is the placement of Indian children in unsubsidized homes. This often requires the good will of a family in the community who will commit their personal resources, time and home to a foster care, legal guardianship, or pre-adoptive placement for a needy child. Even though the commitment is made with love, the vast majority of these families find this event to be stressful and sometimes unworkable after a period of time, especially when considering the number of Indian families on tribal lands who live in or close to poverty.

PROGRAM: TITLE IV-B, SUBPART 1 CHILD WELFARE SERVICES. While the regulations were revised in 1996 to allow all tribal governments eligibility to submit plans for funding under this program, 477 out of the 558 eligible tribal governments receive less than $10,000 per fiscal year. At least half of this number receives amounts under $5,000 per fiscal year. In order to develop effective programs that can make a difference in preventing child abuse and neglect, all tribal governments must have access to a base level of funding. Funding to provide services is in short supply. Jurisdictional and geographic barriers, among other things, make it difficult to access services outside the community, and the overall need for these types of services continues to increase, despite tribe's best efforts to address child abuse and neglect issues.

Need-based funding for tribal governments must take into account not only the level of need in the target population (beyond just raw population numbers), but also the level of funding necessary to establish an effective program and services. The bare minimum needed to establish a child abuse and neglect prevention program in any tribal community is approximately $80,000. This would provide salary and fringe for one full-time position, office space, utilities, equipment and supplies, training, indirect costs and job-related travel expenses. While Title IV-B would not be the only source of revenue to support this program, it is necessary that IV-B support a significant portion. Other tribal sources of income, such as the Indian Child Welfare Act, Title II funding, are needed to support other child welfare-retated services, in particular, responses to notices of child custody proceedings in state courts involving tribal member children. No other consistent, stable source of funding is available for tribal governments to pursue this important mission.

Another important element of need-based funding is the level of requirements that come with a federal program. Mandated reporting, collection of data and other types of program requirements should be included in establishing an accurate picture of the workload associated with any program. Title IV-B, Subpart 1, is not particularly difficult from a reporting or data collection standpoint, but it does require significant work in meeting federal requirements associated with Section 422 of the Social Security Act. Both tribes and states must ensure that "foster care protections" are provided to every child that is in an out-of-home placement under the jurisdiction and care of the grantee. In most cases these protections are good practice in child welfare; nonetheless, they do require significant amounts of time from case management staff, the child welfare administrator, and court personnel. The majority of tribes are only eligible for extremely small grants, less than $10,000 in most cases. Meeting the federal mandates for foster care protection, while desirable, is not reasonable for a grantee of this size.

Clearly, tribes are interested in this program, as the number of tribal grantees has risen from 59 in fiscal year 1993 to approximately 182 in fiscal year 1997. The challenge for DHHS is to make this valuable program attractive to more tribes by creating a base level of funding for every tribe, regardless of size, that will provide every tribal community with the opportunity to establish a quality child abuse and neglect prevention program.

Jurisdictional and geographic barriers also make it difficult to maintain a critical level of services in Indian country. State governments are often hesitant to provide services on tribal lands because they lack jurisdiction, causing tribal members to drive long distances to receive what state services may be available outside of the reservation. In some parts of the country it is not uncommon for a tribal family to be expected to commute over 200 miles each way to receive services, many times with no assistance available to help with transportation costs.

When states and tribes try to work together, agreements are necessary to sort out jurisdictional and service related issues. Sometimes these agreements themselves are a barrier when the parties cannot find a way to address issues such as resource allocation, jurisdiction and appropriate methods of delivering services to community members. Even after agreements have been established, there can be difficulties in maintaining quality assurance and compliance with the terms of the agreements. In other words, this approach to serving Indian children and families may work in the interim, but as a long-term solution it requires many more resources, both administrative and real dollars, than direct funding of tribal governments to ensure that quality services are available.

PROGRAM: TITLE IV-B, SUBPART 2, PROMOTING SAFE AND STABLE FAMILIES. This program is part of an overall federal system of child welfare funding designed to support a more comprehensive array of program services in child welfare. Title IV-B, Subpart 2, helps promote services to prevent the removal of children from their homes, reunify them with their families after removal when possible and provide services to support adoption when return to the home is not possible. This funding has been a good fit for tribes who have been eligible to receive grants, but with only a small portion (10 percent) of the total number of federally recognized tribes eligible. The program has had little impact on the overall need for these services in tribal communities across the United States. One of the primary purposes of the program was to stimulate systems change, a goal that is definitely needed in child welfare, but again the small amount of funding (averaging under $20,000 per grantee) and restricted eligibility has made it very difficult to create and sustain any meaningful change.

The statistics and issues described above that create higher risk for child abuse and neglect and the need for foster care and adoption assistance services (see Title IV-B, Subpart 1, and Title IV-E justifications) are strong indicators of the need for this type of program in tribal communities. Much like the situation for foster care and child abuse prevention, tribal governments do not have equitable access to sources of stable and reliable funding to promote Title IV-B, Subpart 2, services. Funds are either non-existent or have restrictions on what kinds of activities can be provided that prohibit their use. Flexibility, something that the Title IV-B, Subparts 1 and 2 programs provide, is definitely needed. Tribal governments, like states, need to be able to offer a variety of services to meet the diverse needs of their citizens and avoid the service fragmentation that often occurs in resource-poor communities. With tribal governments taking more and more service responsibility (e.g., TANF [Temporary Assistance for Needy Families]) it is even more important than ever. Otherwise, Indian children and families will continue to be some of the most neglected children, in terms of service access, of any children in the United States.

PROGRAM: TITLE XX SOCIAL SERVICES BLOCK GRANT. The Title XX Social Services Block Grant is a national program that was intended to provide social services for children and families throughout the United States. However, funding from Title XX is allocated only to state and territorial governments. Consequently, Indian children and families on reservations or trust lands receive virtually no benefit from this national program.

Tribal governments—whose communities have some of the greatest needs of any population in the United States—were given virtually no thought during the development in 1981 of a number of federal block grants, and as a result, tribes receive very little benefit from them. Most of these 1981 block grant programs 1) contained no provisions for funding to tribes: 2) were based on formulas which by definition left most tribes out of the funding loop: or 3) provided tribes with a very marginal level of funding. Most notable among the block grants that ignored the needs of tribal governments is the Title XX Social Services Block Grant. In order for tribes to receive funding under these programs, they have had to rely on states to share a portion of their allocation. This option has been available in only a handful of states and in amounts that are extremely small.

IMPROVING TRIBAL ACCESS TO FEDERAL CHILD WELFARE FUNDING

The underlying objectives for any program that is going to serve tribal communities effectively is that the funding source should provide:

- Direct access of funds for tribes. This can be accomplished through legislatively prescribed tribal set-asides or reserved funding as has been done in a number of programs. Most notable is the Child Care and Developmental Block grant. This type of funding stream is the most effective at assuring stable, continuous funding for tribes that promote a true government-to-government relationship.

- Funding formulas for the distribution of tribal funds that emphasize not only need and equity, but also the administrative capacities of tribes. Again, the Child Care and Developmental Block grant, reauthorized and expanded under welfare reform is a good example of this type of approach. This block grant program allows the secretary of the U.S. Department of Health and Human Services to provide up 2 percent but not less than 1 percent of block grant funds for tribal grants. So far the Secretary had allocated the maximum amount. This program utilizes a funding formula that provides a base amount for every tribe so that tribes of all sizes can operate at least a minimal program according to the goals of the program. Application and reporting requirements are matched to tribes' scale of economy for administrative capacity.
- Regulations that provide tribes the ability to design and operate a program that meets the unique circumstances and values of their communities. Too often federal programs have failed to transfer the original intent of their programs to tribal communities that were included in the distribution of funds. This has primarily been because of over regulation of these programs that required activities or services that did not fit with the tribal communities' needs, values, or administrative capacity. Where regulations have strived to give the community control and flexibility over the types of services that can be offered, tribal responses to child abuse and neglect have proven to be effective in their outcomes, while still meeting the federal programs' goals.
- Streamlined application procedures and more realistic reporting requirements have also proven beneficial for tribes by helping tribes dedicate more time to the provision of effective services and less time to "recreating the wheel." Often lengthy and separate applications are required for multiple funding sources that provide similar services in the tribal community, which creates a drain on limited administrative resources.

JURISDICTIONAL ISSUES

Most state governments provide little assistance to tribes in funding their child welfare programs. While a few states have attempted to share small portions of either their federal or state child welfare funds, there continue to be problems connected with the receipt of these funds for tribes. Common problems for tribes include the small amount of funds available compared to the administrative efforts required, and the significant compromises in tribal sovereignty that are a result of agreements that states require for receipt of funds.

Many state agencies take the position that once jurisdiction over a child's case is transferred to a tribe, the state is no longer involved and thus has no fiscal responsibility. This may lead to later jurisdictional issues between the states and the tribes. For example, since tribes are not eligible for direct funding for foster care placement, tribes cannot place that child in foster care and turn to the federal government to fund it; the jurisdiction must be returned to the state (Jones, 1999).

Where tribally based ICW programs have been established, there are still battles with state providers over what those services should look like. Culturally based, tribally operated services, for example, would allow a permanent placement of an Indian child with relatives, while these kinship placements are mistakenly viewed by the non-Native child welfare system as foster care situations. In addition, despite the intent of the ICWA to return jurisdiction to the tribes, there are many Indian children and youth who, for a number of reasons, do not fit into the provisions of this act. There are also small tribes for whom the BIA continues to administer child welfare programs due to their small size and lack of resources. In addition, there are a number of non-tribal, nonprofit agencies, primarily in urban areas, that serve Indian children and families of various tribes (Mannes, 1993).

RECOMMENDATIONS

People in Indian country see child maltreatment as a problem and have a desire to do something about it, so much so that they find ways to protect children even when no specific funds are available. Unfortunately, lack of resources usually means little, if any, evaluation of effectiveness on these efforts. Despite not having reliable data to guide resource allocation, child welfare, behavior and mental health, wellness programs, education programs and other programs are all incorporating various forms of child abuse prevention and intervention services. Multiple approaches are employed in these efforts. Cultural strengths are a cornerstone, with all other prevention approaches being adapted to fit cultural norms and expectations.

To the extent we can do something in Indian communities about substance abuse and poverty, we can go a long way toward prevention of child neglect. While they are not currently counted as child maltreatment prevention programs, substance abuse programs should be considered an important component of child neglect prevention and intervention. Programs such as Healthy Nations and the work of the National Association of Native American Children of Alcoholics (NANACOA) are making important contributions in this area. Gregg Borland, chairman of the Cheyenne River Sioux Tribe, describes the problem of neglect and abuse as intertwined with substance abuse and adds cultural neglect as an additional form of neglect among Indian families (Borland, Indian Country Today, 1995).

With the well-known impact of poverty and multiple problems on child abuse and neglect, we have yet to realize the impact of welfare reform legislation passed in 1996. As Indian families reach the end of their eligibility for TANF, we may see a sharp increase in rates of neglect and resulting placements. We are already seeing an increase in the number of children falling below the poverty level. A careful study of the impact of welfare reform on child maltreatment needs to be conducted in Indian Country.

Given the context of sharply increasing reports of maltreatment, child protection programming must be expanded in American Indian communities. Every American Indian leader needs to know that this is a growing problem that threatens the well being of the whole tribal community. Every policy maker needs to be aware that, given the resources, Indian people can and will engage in prevention and intervention efforts. Every Indian advocate, program director and staff person needs to know that evaluation of these efforts, no matter how modest, is essential to their survival.

While Indian people have a heritage for child protection, we also have a growing problem with child abuse and neglect. If we are to survive as nations, we must turn this around. We need resources, and we need to support the people who put their caring into action. To that end, the National Indian Child Welfare Association recommends:

- That the U.S. Department of Health and Human Services and the Bureau of Indian Affairs provide greater access to child welfare and child abuse prevention funds. This could include expanding tribal access to grant funds under the Child Abuse Prevention and Treatment Act and social services funding from the Bureau of Indian Affairs and by making tribes eligible for the Social Services Block Grant program.
- That Title IV-B, Subpart 1, Child Welfare Services regulations be amended to create a base level of funding of no less than $20,000 per fiscal year for all tribes. While the regulations were revised in 1996 to allow all tribal governments eligibility to submit plans for funding under this program, 477 out of the 558 eligible tribal governments receive less than $10,000 per fiscal year. At least half of this number receives amounts under $5,000 per fiscal year. In order to develop effective programs that can make a difference in preventing child abuse and neglect, all tribal governments must have access to a base level of funding.
- Increased funding for comprehensive evaluation and dissemination of resulting knowledge. This could be accomplished through special initiatives from foundations interested in outcome evaluation with projects that evaluate several tribal efforts at once.
- That Public Law 95–608, the Indian Child Welfare Act, Title II tribal child welfare services and programs, be funded to the level originally authorized.
- That Public Law 101–630, the Indian Child Protection and Family Violence Prevention Act, Title IV grant programs for prevention and treatment of child abuse, be funded at the authorized level.
- That promotion and support of service methods that are culturally based and strengths focused be made a priority.
- That training, technical assistance and resources that are fully funded and Indian specific be made available to Indian tribes and that federal agencies funding child welfare (HHS, BIA and IHS) on American Indian reservations allocate adequate resources for evaluation and technical assistance.

- That tribal access to children's trust fund type funding for child abuse prevention become a reality. It is recommended that a national effort be made to establish a children's trust fund for child abuse prevention, which could be funded by private and tribal contributions, which would be matched by federal dollars. This would require an amendment to the Child Abuse Prevention and Treatment Act, allowing matching funds for such a trust fund.
- That there be greater dissemination of information about models that work in Indian country. Foundations, federal agencies and tribes can all support the dissemination of materials through supporting Indian publications and Web pages, as well as Indian colleges and libraries. Grants, contracts, and subscriptions will help support the national and regional efforts to get culturally specific information into the hands of the people who need it.
- That HHS and the BIA adopt a needs-based budgeting process that deals with the real needs of Indian people. Need-based funding for tribal governments must take into account not only the level of need in the target population (beyond just raw population numbers), but also the level of funding necessary to establish effective programs and services.

CONCLUSION

The purpose of this paper has been to inform and instruct child protection policy makers and professionals outside Native American culture about the child abuse and neglect policy issues faced by Indian people. A strong heritage of child protection has existed among Indian peoples. Various factors from within and from outside the culture have diminished this natural system of child abuse prevention somewhat. Yet it still survives (Cross, 1995). Today, child abuse and neglect are serious problems for Native People, as they are for the rest of the nation. The conditions known to contribute to risk are extreme in most Indian communities. Solutions from outside have a dismal record of not only failure but of furthering the break-down of the culture. Boarding schools, relocation, and inappropriate child placement practices are among the contributing factors.

Child protection policy makers are urged to learn the principles of tribal sovereignty and government to government communication, to value the Indian culture, to be aware of the values of the mainstream and of the dynamics created by the differences between the cultures, to learn about Indian culture and to adapt child welfare policy and funding streams to better fit the cultural context of Indian communities. Strategies for working cross-culturally with Native American communities will require not only sensitivity but heightened awareness, inclusion of Native People in all aspects of planning, child protection, networking or bridge building between the cultures and, most importantly, empowerment of Native People to create and implement their own unique cultural solutions. Culturally relevant approaches should and will be defined from within the culture itself. It is up to the mainstream child protection field to honor, endorse, and legitimize tribal efforts in the eyes of funders and policy makers.

REFERENCES

Breamner, R. H. (Ed.) (1970). *Children and Youth in America, Vol. I.* Cambridge: Harvard University Press.

Bureau of Indian Affairs, U.S. Dept. of the Interior (1999). *Child Protection Handbook: Protecting American Indian/Alaska Native Children.* Washington, D.C.

Canby, W.C. (1988) *American Indian Law in a Nutshell.* St. Paul: West Publishing Company.

Devore, W., & Schlesinger, E.G. (1989). *Ethnic-Sensitive Social Work Practice, 2nd Edition.* Columbus, OH: Charles E. Merrill.

Cross, T.L. (1995) Understanding family resiliency from a relational world view. In H.I. McCubbin, E. A. Thompson, A.I. Thompson, & J.E. Fromer (Eds.), *Resiliency in Ethnic Minority Families, Vol. I.—Native and Immigrant American Families* (pp. 143–157). Madison, WI: University of Wisconsin.

Fanshel, D. (1972) *Far From the Reservation: The Transracial Adoption of American Indian Children,* Metuchen, New Jersey: The Scarecrow Press.

Fischler, R.S. (1985). Child abuse and neglect in American Indian communities. *Child Abuse and Neglect, 9* (1). 95–106.

George, L.J. (1997). Why the need for the Indian Child Welfare Act? *Journal of Multi-Cultural Social Work, 5,* 165–175.

Horejsi, C., Heavy Runner Craig, B., & Pablo, J. (1992). Reactions by Native American parents to child protection agencies: cultural and community factors. *Child Welfare, 62* (4), 329–342.

Ishisaka, H. (1978). American Indians and foster care: Cultural factors in separation. *Child Welfare, 57*

Jones, B.J. (1999). Transfers of jurisdiction under the ICWA: Tribal considerations. Pathways Practice Digest, National Indian Child Welfare Association, May/June. P.8.

Linger, S. (1977) The Destruction of American Indian Families. New York: Association on American Indian Affairs.

Lewis, R. (1980) *Strengths of the American Indian Family,* Resource Paper (Tulsa, Oklahoma: National Indian Child Abuse and Neglect Resource Center).

Mannes, M. (1993). Seeking the balance between child protection and family preservation in Indian Child Welfare. *Child Welfare, 72* (2), 141–152.

Mannes, M. (1995). Factors and events leading to the passage of the Indian Child Welfare Act. *Child Welfare, 74* (1), 264–282.

MacEachron, A.E. (1994). Supervision in tribal and state child welfare agencies: professionalism, responsibilities, training needs, and satisfaction. *Child Welfare, 73* (2), 117–128.

Metheson, L. (1996). The politics of the Indian Child Welfare Act. *Social Work, 41,* (2), 232–235.

Miller, J.L., & Whittaker, J.K. (1988). Social services and social support: Blended programs for families at risk of child maltreatment. *Child Welfare, 67* (2), 161–174.

Nobokov, P. (1991). *Native American Testimony: A Chronicle of Indian-White Relations from Prophecy to the Present,* 1492–1992. New York: Viking Penguin.

Prucha, F.P. (1990) *Documents of United States Indian Policy,* 2nd Edition, Expanded. Lincoln: University of Nebraska Press.

Robin, R.F., Rasmussen, J.K., & Gonzalez-Santin, E. (1999). Impact of childhood out-of-home placement on a Southwestern American Indian tribe. *Journal of Human Behavior in the Social Environment,* 2 (1/2), 69–90.

Schinke, S.P., Schilling, R.F, Gilchrist, L.D., Bobo, J.K., Trimble, J.E., & Cvetkovich, G.T. (1985). Preventing substance abuse with American Indian youth. *Social Casework, 66,* 213–217.

Ware, D.W., Dobrec, A., Rosenthal, J.A., & Wedel, K.R. (1992). Job satisfaction, practice skills, and supervisory skills of Indian Child Welfare programs. *Child Welfare, 71* (5). 405–418.

10.2 YANICK ST. JEAN AND JOE R. FEAGIN

The Family Costs of White Racism

Racism is an ideology. An ideology entails a set of ideas. The main idea that corresponds to the ideology of racism in U.S. society is that members of the White dominant group believe that members of non-White subordinate groups are inherently inferior people. Racial discrimination is one outcome of a racist ideology. Racism and its racist ideologies remain pervasive in contemporary society. Indeed, consistent patterns of institutionalized racial discrimination result in the systematic denial of non-White minority members of U.S. society from fully and equally participating in its major institutions. Discrimination and segregation lead to limited educational, occupational, and economic opportunities for members of minority groups. One concern of many sociologists of race and ethnic relations is identifying the coping mechanisms that non-White Americans develop to deal with institutionalized racism in their daily lives.

In the following selection from "The Family Costs of White Racism: The Case of African American Families," *Journal of Comparative Family Studies* (Summer 1998), associate professor of sociology Yanick St. Jean of the University of Nevada, Las Vegas, and professor of sociology Joe R. Feagin of the University of Florida draw upon in-depth interviews with 209 middle-class Black Americans from several regions of the country to analyze how Black people cope with White racism. The narratives presented in the article reveal that a formidable coping mechanism for the majority of Black people who are victimized by White racism is to discuss racist incidents with family members. That is, discussing experiences with discrimination strengthens family bonds and diminishes the pain that individuals feel from racist encounters. Kinship associations also "revive collective memories of suffering." Although reliance on kinship bonds may diminish the brutalizing effect of White racism for Black people, research has also identified the adverse effects of White racism on Black families.

Key Concept: coping mechanisms against White racism, the cost of White racism to Black families, and kinship bonds

For most people there is a collective memory of the family, one that is revived in the present through contact with others. Insights into this memory, and knowledge of the ways it is transmitted, can unveil the impact of White racism on the family lives of African Americans. If, as Halbwachs (1992:56) writes, "there operates a feeling, both obscure and precise, of kinship, which can arise only within the family and which can be explained only by the family," then memories of an unjust past, together with new experiences of racial discrimination, are likely released in this family haven of "unconditional acceptance" (Bellah et al., 1985:87). The greater the sense of injustice, the more likely that pain suffered will be shared in a setting where family members "can count on other members" (Bellah et al., 1985:87). It is precisely this unselfish nature of family life that can make the impact of racism even more damaging. Whenever the feeling of kinship is present, the brutal effects of racism can be more widespread.

Eased by acceptance, past family sufferings will flow into present situations, validating a family language and heritage. From present situations, a family past can more easily be reconstructed. This remembrance of things past is a key to appreciating the totality of the family experience and to entering the "family spirit." For example, Grier and Cobbs (1968) suggest that "the problem of the Black family is a latter-day version of the problem faced by the slave family." Drawing from Gutman (1976) and McAdoo (1988), Feagin and Sikes (1994) encourage the "remembrance of things past," stressing the continuity of the Black family through time as protector and supporter, but also noting the potentially taxing effects of sharing a memory of oppression with other kin.

Familial memories are dynamic "models, examples, and elements of teaching… express[ing] the general attitude of the group" (Halbwachs, 1992:59). Memories are a family's "traditional armature," its "vision of the world" (Halbwachs, 1992; Namer, 1993). Memories are unique because they precede the present and have the ability to outlive every member of a family. Despite the fact that "we live in a society that encourages us to cut free from the past" (Bellah et al., 1985:154), a family's memory is crucial to its identity and to its members' identities.

There is a well-documented and direct relationship between dissatisfaction at work and family dissatisfaction (Staples and Johnson, 1993; Jackson, 1991). Since for most African Americans, current discrimination in the workplace and in other sectors of the society mirrors a tragic past, understanding the collective memory of the Black family—where racialized pain *is presentized* (Halbwachs, 1992)—helps trace the impact of racism on families.

THE RESEARCH PROBLEM

With two-parent households in decline since the 1960s (Edwards, 1992), the Black family is often said to be very troubled. In 1997 just under half (45.5 percent) of all Black families were married couples, a decrease of 10 percent since 1980 and 23 percent since 1970 (U.S. Department of Commerce, 1998:2,

1995:xiii). In 1997 about 47 percent of Black family households were female-headed, an increase of 7 percent since 1980 and 19 percent since 1970 (U.S. Department of Commerce, 1998:2, 1995:xiii). This trend, which is also evident for White families (Dickson, 1993), is so much more pronounced for Black Americans that many social scientists have long concluded that there is cause for alarm.

Despite these gloomy forecasts, a view from inside suggests that most families at all class levels remain strong and central to Black communities. Men and women rely on kin when affected by the brutality of racism. They receive support from families, described as sounding boards, as frames for interpreting their world and as easing encounters with humiliation. This view is a sharp contrast to the traditional portrayal of the Black family as a "tangle of pathologies" (U.S. Department of Labor, 1965), a biased view criticized by social scientists for ignoring family strengths (Feagin, 1968; Billingsley, 1968; St. Jean and Feagin, 1998).

Yet, despite the rebuttal, all is not well. The Black family pays a serious price for buffering against racism. Below, we assess that price and probe into recollections of middle-class Black Americans. We consider how discussing experiences with discrimination not only reinforces family bonds and reduces individual pain, but also creates and revives collective memories of suffering.

RESEARCH PROCEDURES

This analysis draws on a national study of the experiences of middle-class African Americans with racial discrimination (Feagin and Sikes, 1994). This study involved in-depth interviews with 209 middle-class Black Americans in sixteen cities in several regions of the country. Those interviewed were selected, in a snowball design with dozens of different starting points, from the ranks of the Black middle class.[1]

To assess the role of the Black family in dealing with racism, we draw data primarily from responses to key questions in the interview: "How have your friends and family helped you in dealing with discrimination and its frustrations?" "Could you give me examples?" "Do you discuss these obstacles with family or friends often?" We examined each interviewee's responses for relevance to family questions, leaving out discussions of friends. This yielded detailed statements from 72 females and 73 males. The median age of the females is 39 years and of males, 42 years. The median income of females is $44,000; for the men, it is the "over $55,000" category. Virtually all have occupied, currently occupy, or will soon occupy white-collar positions.[2]

In response to the question about seeking support from relatives in dealing with discrimination, the overwhelming majority of both men and women (86 percent and 90 percent, respectively) said they habitually seek support from their families. Most others sometimes sought and received support from kinfolk or a spouse. The overwhelming majority of men and women who speak in these narratives found that discussing incidents with the family helps in coping with White racism.

THE ROLE OF THE FAMILY AS SOUNDING BOARD

Let us begin with an example of the type of racial encounter likely to generate a need for family support:

> [This woman and I were] talking about vacations and she said that her kids came back with nigger lips... I thought for sure I didn't hear it. And everyone got quiet. I was the only Black in the group. And she was my student teacher [laughs]... The conversation just stopped... Eventually... she apologized. She said, "... I'm not that way. We used to talk like this with family, but I've been around you long enough, and you know I'm not that way... And I just wanted to say I am so sorry.[3]

The respondent recalls her reaction: "I was shocked, because I'd never heard of nigger lips before [laughs] and I'm learning how they [Whites] really describe us behind our backs." Not meant as an insult, this "slip of the tongue" is nevertheless painful. It suggests how racial insensitivity often permeates White life, and that it is so unconsciously rehearsed, it can spring unexpectedly into public discourse.

Seeking relief from distress, this respondent immediately turns to her family, a common Black response for daily insults: "At home I told my husband and I told my kids, and we sat around and we talked about it." The family is an extraordinarily important sounding board, a safe and affectionate setting where encounters with racial discrimination are shared, reassessed and validated. Its significance is manifest in the following statement by a male respondent: "I don't start living until I leave the office, and I get in my family." In the family setting, men and women alike discuss their concerns and leave that home "castle" restored by the exchange. This is an important process of healing, a reminder of the past when "the slave drew on the love and sympathy of... [kin] to raise his spirits" (Blassingame, 1979:191).

For African Americans, family support has a long tradition going back to the first days of the slave trade (Blassingame, 1979; Staples and Johnson, 1993). There are few limits to the caliber of this family support. "Close [family] relationships provide the economic and moral support that assist in day-to-day living as well as in times of crisis" (Little John-Blake and Darling, 1993:462). Generous offers of personal maintenance are common, as in this account: "[Members of my family] are the ones that kind of stuck by me... hey, quit that job and we'll help take care of you." Most respondents seek inspiration from their kinfolk, including encouragement to move forward despite the difficulties of the day. One respondent explains:

> My family's always been... there for me no matter what the circumstances or situations, or how dark the cloud, there was always a way that we, as a family, were going to move through this. So, I never had a crisis, or felt that I was alone, that I had to face it all by myself. We're very close-knit, and we've sort of helped each other all of our lives... If... I have a bad day, if somebody says something to me... I can go home, call somebody on the phone, and we'll talk... and come to some conclusion. In everything in my life, they have always been there and been supportive.

With each respondent's statement, we see how powerful the "feeling of kinship" is and how it binds people together in close-knit networks of support. If in its initial moment discrimination is individual, it is rapidly transformed into a family issue whose resolution derives from collective reflection and comment.

Neither distance nor financial cost is a deterrent to access the sounding board provided by family. Like the previous respondent who "go[es] home, call[s] somebody on the phone, and ... talk[s]," another woman reveals: "Occasionally my phone bill reflects the fact that I'm upset and I've been calling folks, and moaning." Closeness is worth the expense, for as in the slavery and segregation past (Blassingame, 1979; Genovese, 1974), it continues to be a powerful strategy for survival:

> I think our family unit has been ... the reason we have survived.... We pray together, we stay together, we fight together, we argue together, but we do that within the confines of our homes. We talk and process, we help each other. My family is very clannish, and we do everything together.

Despite its soothing effects, family closeness is not free of personal conflicts. Not surprisingly, behind closed doors, Black families fight just like other families. Yet this normal family conflict takes place in troubled racial contexts unknown to White families.

Enormous value is placed on sharing daily woes with kin and on receiving from them constructive feedback and strong expressions of belonging. These conclusions are applicable to men as well. In the next two comments, Black men report they are positively influenced by families:

> [Members of my family] give me ... [the] warm emotional support one needs, [support] that says, "Keep pushing. Don't give up. Hang in there, and don't let things make you do things you'll regret later. Just do the positive thing and recognize that it's going to take a long time."

> When the war is over ... I want to rest. And my family has been supportive in providing ... an atmosphere where I could get away from the battles and sort of stock enough energy to go back out there ... Family ... have created an escape valve ... for some of the tensions that go along with being involved in the struggle.

Comments on not giving up and on stocking enough energy highlight the taxing impact of modern racism. This man's family helps him to heal after emotionally draining encounters. The military terms here and in other respondents' comments, the concepts of "war" and "battles," indicate the painful labor and effort that a racist environment imposes on African Americans seeking to survive in a White-dominated society. Similar thoughts are expressed sharply by another male:

> To surround yourself with family ... is a way you reinforce yourself that you're all right.... I think ... it ... is the key for surviving ... At the end of a long day, or at the end of a bad experience, they say to you that you're all right ... by how you're treated. And ... that second sense tells you that you're in a warm and accepting environment.

When sensibilities are crushed, the family acts as a sounding board. The family struggles alongside each of its members to preserve individual and collective dignity.

DAMAGING EFFECTS ON THE FAMILY

The family suffers from being a sounding board for everyday discrimination. It is in the context of family that encounters with racial discrimination are transformed into serious collective grief. One female respondent put it thus:

> Anything that happens to [my family]... is going to have some effect on me. If the door is slammed to one member of my family, it's eventually... going to slam on me too... That's my father the door's being slammed on, it's my brother, it's my nephew. I can't turn my back on that.

Evident in the statement is a broad sense of kinship recalling the oppressive past of African Americans. Encounters with discrimination are seldom just a personal matter. A victim of racial humiliation frequently shares the account with family to lighten the burden, and this sharing creates a domino effect of anguish rippling across an extended group (Feagin and Sikes 1994:16). Discrimination remembered by a relative has consequences for other relatives who, forced through that same ordeal, may be as affected. Even as affectionate family understanding lessens individual pain, grief spreads rapidly, crushing kin who suffer because of their link to the sufferer. This is where racism turns the positive and soothing feeling of kinship into a severe collective trauma. Aside from this adverse effect, the Black family appears successful as a sounding board, absorbing—if only partially—the brutal effects of racial degradation and humiliation.

INTERPRETATIONS OF PAST AND PRESENT WORLDS

The African American family also struggles to provide its members with a particular reflection on and understanding of past and present Black experiences with racism (Grier and Cobbs, 1968; Staples and Johnson, 1993). One respondent explains the connection across generations: "My children especially have been in a world where they haven't experienced the things that I've experienced. I try to relate to them the struggles that have gone on, so that they will remember... where we've come from, and... appreciate where we are." This "where we've come from" includes interpretations of the lived experiences of one's ancestors with discrimination. Past generations are part of the family heritage and identity; they are points of reference against which to measure recent experiences (Namer, 1987). Exploring the lives of one's family members, including the deceased, links family memories across time and assigns relevance to "where we are" in the present. Blassingame (1979:181) notes that during slavery, "memories of Africa were important in the development of self-awareness in slave children." Younger generations benefit from exposure to the racialized past and secure a pool of examples from which to abstract meaning and coping strategies in their own struggles with racism. These discourses with parents and other relatives historicize the present. Indeed, for African Americans of any age, the similarities between past and present are striking, as one respondent underscores: "[The experiences are] all a little different, but it's the same kind of scenario."

The collective memory of the family is a museum where pieces that are added daily renew an old collection, giving younger generations an immediate grasp of the total kinship experience. A parental summation can answer, as one parent put it, "questions [they] may have as to why these kinds of things continue to happen." Collective memories portray, if not transfigure, brave individuals who have conquered past discrimination, thereby earning a proud place in the pantheon of a family's heritage. Family memories are thus "models, examples, and elements of teaching."

Another man illustrates this point, sharing an important lesson that he learned from his family—a lesson likely to protect his self-esteem:

> [The family has helped] in trying to point out that those comments aren't necessarily directed at me as a person; that those are just preconceived notions that a particular group has been trained to believe about another group.... It's nothing that I'm doing or nothing that I should try to change.

This respondent learned that individual African Americans are exposed to racial humiliation because of the position of *their group* within the U.S. racial structure and because of stereotyping that is part of the White ideology of racism. Note too that the linkage to a dominated past is still alive in the social memory of his family. This potentially enabling vision is acquired through participation in the "feeling of kinship."

LAPSES OF MEMORY

While remembrance has positive consequences for interpreting a racialized world, some in the younger generations may know little, if anything, about their familial or community past. Within families, memories of discrimination may be dimmed or silenced, and a certain amnesia may prevail, as one parent put it: "A lot of parents make mistakes because they don't inform their children of the past." In many cases, parental silence is a way to avoid inflicting the pain of past racism on younger generations. Yet, this "amnesia" has negative consequences. For the children it means an absence of information and experience from which to draw understandings of present experiences with Whites. It leaves young people with no anchor to ground themselves to their family roots, and it can mean a serious lack of knowledge about cultural realities and expectations. It also entails little understanding of the dominating memory and thus little or no knowledge of ways to limit the flow of the painful past into the present.

As one respondent perceptively notes, the value of knowing about one's predecessors cannot be overestimated:

> This past weekend, I went to a family reunion, and we traced our family's roots and we had a chance to all sit around and talk about the kinds of values that are important.... We talked about the people who were slaves.... They lived through Jim Crow, through the Depression, and found their way through the... sustaining philosophies, the sustaining wisdom, love, family, and support.... You are always making a move to make the wound heal. You also understand how to avoid wounds.

To be isolated either from the sustaining family spirit and the collective memories is to be removed from one's heritage, the protective character of its armature, and its vision of the world. Such isolation can throw an individual into a "Tower of Babel" where no one speaks the same language and where present racial "wounds," the humiliations, are not prevented or contextualized by collective experiences.

The uninformed and isolated young person may "operate under an illusion" and live in a dream world. For it is indeed "in the dream that the mind is most removed from society" (Halbwachs, 1992:42), a point this respondent explores:

> That's what worries me about some of these kids today. I'm not sure that they know what [racism] is... I think it manifests itself differently now than it did when I was growing [up]... There was no question that you were different, and now I think these kids are operating under the illusion that they're the same, and they're not. And so the first time it hits 'em in the face they don't know how to deal with it because: a) they haven't been told that it's there, and b) what do you do if it does happen? And sometimes it's a date and sometimes it's the prom and... the [White] mother finds out that he's Black and... bar the door, right? [Laughter]

This theme is found in other interviews. As one male respondent notes, "We can't live in the fantasy world." Yet the scars of oppression can affect memories themselves. Certain spots in family memories can be missing or "fragments of memory too mutilated... to allow us to recognize them" (Halbwachs, 1992:41). The absence of "true sensations such as those which we experience when we are not asleep" (Halbwachs, 1992:41) can result from a numbness to suffering, which can be a panacea, but only for a while. Ultimately, there will be a feverish, frantic awakening of the young Black individual to the reality of oppression and struggle. If the Black family is to play its role effectively as protector of individuals and accurate mirror of the past, the generational memories of racial experiences must be transmitted across generations, however brutal their character.

While displaying sharp insights into the workings and failings of the family, most respondents portray their own families as sources of strength, as buffers against personal rage, pain and humiliation. They focus on the positive outcomes of the family spirit in their lives and deplore conditions, hostilities or attacks that try to thwart endeavors by that family institution to protect its members and mirror their world more effectively.

SOURCES OF TENSION AND EFFECTS OF MEMORY

Today, two significant issues face the Black family: 1) the decline in extended family structures, and 2) the work-role reversal. Our respondents raised these issues in their commentaries. Among African Americans, the extended family is not an American creation. It was brought from Africa (Herskovits, 1990:167; Ani, 1994). The extended structure has often been researched by scholars (Staples, 1994; Staples and Johnson, 1993). As that structure has been transformed, its capacity to play a supportive function against racism has been imperiled. While they are aware of this problem, the respondents nonetheless reaffirm a need for Blacks to work not only to maintain a supportive family system, but also to develop a stronger sense of the African American group. One respondent comments critically:

> There are not enough of us who are stable enough to give the kind of support that an individual who is faced with a discriminating kind of situation would need to have. And that's because... in a lot of situations, there's only single parents, and that person is most often a woman that raises kids, and they don't have that kind of cohesiveness that you need to have, not as a family and not as a group. We're nothing compared to what Jewish people are like, they're very supportive. And we're not like that, and I don't know why we're not like that.

Also stressed by respondents is a need to "return to things past," to recapture a lost vision of the world and thus strengthen the family unit:

> We need to stick to our own value systems like we did back in the other era, because as long as we did that we had strong family ties... A family to me does not have to be the husband and the wife, it could be grandma there, the aunts... We're not all together like we used to be, where if you didn't bring home a paycheck... this week because you got fired, or you were ill and they didn't have sick leave time... you can go over to Momma's or Aunt Josie's or Aunt Clara's... Uncle Bud, and get you a meal. And they will put their pennies together to make sure that you could keep whatever that little bit that you had acquired. But we don't have that too much anymore, because it's I, me and mine. I want to stand alone... It's so individualistic... And that kind of hurts.

These insights underscore the point that family changes are more than a matter of increasing single-parent families. The changes also represent a decline in "communalism" (Blassingame, 1979:148). That is, in many American families —Black and White—we no longer see interdependent collectivities carefully looking out for and protecting the needs of each member (LittleJohn-Blake and Darling, 1993), but rather modern assimilated families that are little more than a collection of individuals looking for self-fulfillment. The solution suggested is returning to the communal family identity, to a sense of mutual cooperation that is more fitting to the needs of African Americans today.

WORK ROLE REVERSAL

Another major source of family trials and tensions is the ability of Black women to get jobs when Black men cannot (Gaiter, 1994; Roberts, 1994; Bernstein, 1995).[4] One respondent explains that "when [Black men] can't get a job to take care of their families... it creates a lot of friction.... And some men walk away because they can't take the pressure anymore." Another male interviewee explains how men may react to the greater workplace success of women:

> We [Black men] have an ego problem, and I don't think it's because we're Black men, it's just because we're men. We're perceived as the breadwinner, so we have to be top dog. We can't be married happily to a woman who has a higher position.

Black men often have difficulty in accepting that their wives earn more (Gaiter, 1994). In such cases Black men, like their White counterparts, have accepted prevailing gender-role expectations and feel emasculated. They feel inferior and "do not perceive themselves... to be marriage material" (Dickson, 1993:477).

While some men partially blame Black women for their situations (Dickson, 1993:482), most blame society:

> [Black men have] been demoralized. Our male image has been crushed and a lot of it has come from within ourselves. I'm not saying that there is a conspiracy of White America... but... many of the things that have developed from the slave mentality until now, have been to crush the spirit and the image of the Black man. And so, it has been a very successful move.

These negative reactions to gender-role reversal do not occur in social isolation. They are rooted in certain aspects of the dominant Anglo culture, which have been absorbed by Black Americans, that assign gendered roles to men and women (Dickson, 1993:483). Such negative reactions are shaped by the reality of Black men living in a sexist framework, as this respondent notes: "Black males live in a sexist society, a sexist culture, that doesn't let Black males express themselves... And I think that causes Black males a lot of problems besides just their oppression as Black males."

Some research findings (Willie, 1993:456) suggest that the typical Black family is an "egalitarian family in which neither spouse has continuing ultimate authority." However, our respondents indicate that many Black families have husband/wife roles that are not clearly defined and are in fact being continuously negotiated. One respondent explains: "I mean, we're experiencing problems, you've got the discrimination out there, the racism out there, [men and women] both have it the same. And now we come home and we're getting to the battle of the roles." The home can mirror the workplace and be a place of struggle over gender roles, as this respondent underscores:

> Black women have always worked, not in the jobs that they would prefer, but Black women have always worked... Black women have had no choice.... And when the Black male was somewhere else for whatever reasons, there was still a family that needed to be fed... [But] when you try to function equally at the same time, there will be a rebellion by one or the other. And I think our homes are in rebellion.

It appears that gender equality is not yet a domestic reality for many African American families.

Moreover, we should note that some Black men do not consider the disparity between their own income and that of their wives as having a negative impact on their marriages:

> Money is money, I don't care who's making it. [Laughs.] That time my wife made more money than me, fine... Keep it working! [Laughs.] I don't care if you are making five *times*. The same roof you're under, I'm going to be under. Same air conditioning you feel, I'm going to feel. You're going fishing, I'm following... no problem.

But this attitude seems to represent a minority view. The interviews suggest that many Black men are humiliated by the work-role reversal and react to it in ways that can negatively affect their families. Indeed, many Black respondents contend that the work-role reversal has long represented a calculated way for White society to destroy the Black family:

> The struggle between Black America and White America is the family. And the thing that White America... saw in Black America was strong family roots. And they knew that the way to do that was to castrate the male from the family. In the slave mentality, the thing was that you castrated the male out of the family and made the woman strong, because she had to become the image in the family. So, it separated the family.

The reversal has a traceable heritage and leads not only to family separations but also to attempts by Black men to look elsewhere for empowerment.

Seeking Areas of Empowerment

One respondent speaks very articulately on the male empowerment issue. She notes that because Black men are subject to "whims and cruelties of White men," they may make up for racial humiliation by seeking power in other spheres, by "taking on a lot of White male attitudes and characteristics" and by behaving as would a White male in their position. She adds,

> I've seen Black males in the workplace where they took a lot of bull... a lot of racism, abusive kinds of things and they will go into their churches and serve on the deacon board and turn around and do the same kinds of things to some of their congregationists or parishioners in the church.

Black community organizations, including churches, represent alternative routes to power for the oppressed, a situation which must be gauged in Black man's total experience: "I feel for Black men... because every day... they've got to tuck their pride in their pockets and they've got to kiss ass. If I'm experiencing the kinds of little, bitty, little jabs that are happening, what are our Black men experiencing?" One answer is *rage,* a deep-seated rage that this man describes:

> I'm a very dangerous person now, [laughs] I am. And I tell people I'm dangerous, because I really won't take anything off a White person. I will knock his ass off, and smile, and be just as happy. If necessary I will kill him, and go to jail. It's all right, I'm going to die anyhow, but I could die happy.

Despite this powerful comment, rage is often not directed at the White aggressor. Instead, many Black men transfer rage to their loved ones, to those closely positioned in the family space such as a spouse.

"Little Murders," Every Day

When present, family abuse by Black men is likely a response to the daily jabs, to the "little murders" every day, as one older respondent describes it. These little murders by Whites accumulate over time.[5] The men are mistreated by Whites and, in turn, they mistreat.

> What do we expect will come home to us in the evening when they've been beaten up all day long, emotionally and mentally?... And I feel for [Black women]. I feel for them.... Unfortunately... too many of our brothers take out the pain on us... I don't want you to mistreat me because you've been mistreated. And that's what's happening, unfortunately, in Black America.

Driven by humiliation, Black men may seek alternative ways of proving their worth to themselves and to the society: "That's where the lying and the spying... and the cheating and the infidelity and all that stuff comes in... Because they are under that kind of emasculation all day, every day, on someone else's job."

Not only do wives suffer indirectly from pain endured by their husbands, but also from the men's displaced expressions of indignation that may have developed into abuse of family members. These angry reactions, which likely presentize the past, are registered in the collective memory of the family.

The incidence of violence is apparently increasing in Black families (Staples, 1994). Hampton et al. (1989:977) observe that in 1985 the "rate of abusive violence toward Black women... was slightly more than twice the rate of severe violence toward White women," and that Black women make up a disproportionately "high percentage of shelter residents." Although these findings do not necessarily point to increasing violence, or represent the situations of middle-class Black families, the workplace experiences of middle-class Black men (Staples and Johnson, 1993; Cose, 1995) suggest there is a problem of displaced rage. As one middle-class Black woman explains eloquently to the interviewer:

> We [Black women] have a double whammy on us. We've got to come here [to work] and be a part of the system all day long, and then we take the brunt of it and go home just exhausted from what we've had to go through all day long, and then you've got to... take it from him, because we've got to hear it a second time. We've got to hear the pain we've felt all day, then we've got to hear the pain from them that they've felt all day. And not only hear it... but be a part of it when they can't handle it and we get in the middle of it, and then they must use us and abuse us.

The statement points to countless emotional pressures facing Black women. It is in the home that workplace sufferings are shared. But often, as one woman notes, it is at home that sufferings are acted out:

> We're the only thing that they [Black men] think they have control over. They can't control the system, they can't control the White man or the White woman, so they come home, we're their wife... and... they think that maybe somebody else has got to feel the brunt of this. Someone gave it to me, the monkey on my back, I'm going to give you the monkey off my back.

As male anger is displaced onto a spouse, family chaos usually prevails, thereby ruining some of the cherished and supportive relationships. One man notes that

> If you can't let it out at work or between work and home, you're only going to have one other place to do it. And that's the family.... Corporate America is getting to be the biggest input to single-parent families now.

Chances for a serious confrontation between men and women are increased by the fact that Black women tend not to accept spousal mistreatment. They tend to fight back (Hampton et al., 1989). They are often involved in marital separations and divorces (Dickson, 1993). Staples and Johnson (1993) conclude that during the 1990s, "Black males and females have had a more difficult time in establishing and maintaining relationships" (Dickson, 1993:474). In a direct address to men, one respondent sums up the attitude of Black women towards abuse: "I demand respect. You will not mistreat me because you have been mistreated. You will not do it to me. I will be alone first before I'll allow you to do that." If extended and nuclear family structures decline further, so may the role of the Black family as protector and sounding board. In this new setting, it becomes more difficult to pass on the collective memory of the family, benefit from its armature, and build family identity.

Even if family structures were not troubled, there would still be the problem created by racism. Because the family setting is a source for validating experiences and putting them into communal memory, it frequently inserts debilitating life moments into that memory. Yet, Black resistance against this oppressive memory of the Black family can take the form of a determined "counter-memory" (Foucault, 1977). Often African Americans say a firm "NO!" to negative images of the Black family in the White mythologies.

SUMMARY AND CONCLUSIONS

Our data clearly indicate that racism has major costs for African American families. Using a collective memory approach, our analysis has explored the consequences of racism for Black family life. We can enumerate briefly our major suggestions and conclusions:

1. There is a "feeling of kinship" characterizing the Black family that invites the disclosure of emotions either too painful or too powerful to be revealed in other settings, and thus buffers some of the pain resulting from workplace and other racial deprivations and humiliations. African American men and women are protected by family support and intervention.
2. This feeling of kinship has an adverse effect as well. It transfers pain from kin to kin, indirectly making every member of the family vulnerable to more harm from White bigotry and discrimination. Each family member pays an emotional price for the experiences of other kinfolk who must deal with racial humiliations. Black men and women appear equally at risk.
3. To retain the feeling of kinship, a strong collective family identity is paramount. A viable collective memory of the family, the summation of total kinship experience, can help preserve that family identity.
4. Yet, when the recollections are painful, some collective family amnesia may arise. In such situations, younger and dissociated members will probably lack a strong feeling of kinship and, consequently, have less access to the Black family's traditional armature and vision. They will also be less fluent in the critical family language.
5. The decline in extended family structures reduces the scope of family support, weakens the feeling of kinship, and thus may keep the family group from effectively transmitting to its members the totality of the Black heritage. This modified structure can intensify the experience of amnesia and weaknesses in individual responses to racial humiliations.
6. The work role reversal can weaken family structures, the feeling of kinship and, through displaced anger, encourage spousal abuse, marital infidelities, and family separations. This situation can also intensify the experience of communal amnesia.

7. Men in the sample tended to focus on the influence of historical factors on Black women; and women in the sample, on the cultural oppression of Black men as antecedents to family tensions. But both men and women agree that displaced indignation and anger by Black men over racist conditions outside the family are a determining factor in family difficulties. More research is needed on the reactions of middle-class Black women to discrimination and to treatment in home settings.

Our analysis provides strong evidence of a feeling of kinship, a family spirit binding Black men and women to their kin. We also find indications of a burden on that family spirit, one expressed long ago by an enslaved Black girl (Brent, 1861:304): "It has been painful to me... to recall the dreary years I passed in bondage. I would gladly forget if I could. The retrospection is not altogether without solace." A memory of oppressions can be oppressive. The more validation from kin, the more vibrant and disquieting the memory. Oppressive memories may so organize one's historical memory as to supersede more pleasant memories of the past.[6]

NOTES

1. A collective memory suggests only a "remembrance" of things past, and need not coincide with social or historical memories. Whereas this study makes occasional reference to the literature on slavery and the Black family, it is concerned primarily with the recollections of its middle-class participants, and thus takes every step to protect these recollections.
2. We also searched through all questions in the interview for discussions of the impact of racism on family life and found additional statements.
3. Some quotes have been lightly edited for grammar.
4. Staples and Johnson (1993:64) suggest otherwise.
5. Women may abuse men too, though Hampton (1989) notes there is little research in this area.
6. The dominance of a memory of oppression, its effect on Black women writers, and their writings about the family are evident in Alice Walker's *The Color Purple* (1982) and L.E. Scott's *Black Family Letters from Boston* (1993).

REFERENCES

Ani, Marimba. 1994. Yurugu: An African-Centered Critique of European Cultural Thought and Behavior. Trenton, NJ: Africa World Press.

Bellah, Robert. N., Richard Madsen, William M. Sullivan, Ann Swidler, and Steven M. Tipton. 1985. Habits of the Heart: Individualism and Commitment in American Life. New York: Harper and Row.

Billingsley, Andrew. 1968. Black Families in White America. Englewood Cliffs, NJ: Prentice.

Bernstein, Jared. 1995. Where's the Payoff? Washington, D.C.: Economic Policy Institute.

Blassingame, John W. 1979. The Slave Community: Plantation Life in the Antebellum South. New York: Oxford University Press.

Brent, Linda. 1861. Incidents in the Life of a Slave Girl: Written by Herself. Edited by Maria L. Child. Boston, MA: Published by the author.

Cose, Ellis. 1995. The Rage of a Privileged Class. New York: Harper Collins.

Dickson, Lynda. 1993. "The future of marriage and family in Black America." Journal of Black Studies 23: 472–491.

Edwards, Gabrielle I. 1992. Coping with Discrimination. New York: Rosen.

Feagin, Joe R. 1968. "The kinship ties of Negro urbanities." Social Science Quarterly 49 (1968): 660–665.

Feagin, Joe R. and Melvin P. Sikes. 1994. Living with Racism: The Black Middle-Class Experience. Boston, MA: Beacon.

Foucault, Michel. 1977. Language, Counter-Memory, Practice, Selected Essays and Interviews. Edited by Donald F. Bouchard. New York: Cornell University Press.

Gaiter, Dorothy J. 1994. "The gender divide: Black women's gains in corporate America outstrip Black men's." Wall Street Journal, March 8, p. Al.

Genovese, Eugene D. 1974. Roll, Jordan, Roll: The World the Slaves Made. New York: Random.

Grier, William H. and Price M. Cobbs. 1968. Black Rage. New York: Basic Books.

Gutman, Herbert. 1976. The Black Family in Slavery and Freedom, 1750–1925. New York: Random.

Halbwachs, Maurice. 1992. On Collective Memory. Chicago, IL: University of Chicago.

Hampton, Robert L., Richard J. Gelles, and John W. Harrop. 1989. "Is violence in Black families increasing? A comparison of 1975 and 1985 National Survey Rates." Journal of Marriage and the Family 51: 969–80.

Herskovits, Melville J. 1990. The Myth of the Negro Past. New York: Harper and Row.

Jackson, James S. 1991. Life in Black America. Newbury Park, CA: Sage.

LittleJohn-Blake, Sheila M. and Carol Anderson Darling. 1993. "Understanding the strengths of African American families." Journal of Black Studies 23: 460–471.

McAdoo, Hariette. 1988. Black Families. Beverly Hills, CA: Sage.

Namer, George. 1987. Mémoire et société. Paris: Méridiens Klincksieck. 1993 "Mémoire sociale, sociologie, culture." Paper presented at the 31st Congress of the International Institute of Sociology, Sorbonne (Paris, France).

Roberts, Sam. 1994. "Black women graduates outpace male counterparts: Income disparity seen as marriage threat." The New York Times, October 31, p. A12.

Scott, L.E. 1994. Black Family Letters from Boston. New Zealand: Bent.

Staples, Robert. 1994. The Black-Family: Essays and Studies. Belmont, CA: Wadsworth.

Staples, Robert and Leanor Boulin Johnson. 1993. Black Families at the Crossroads, Challenges and Prospects. San Francisco, CA: JosseyBass.

St. Jean, Yanick and Joe R. Feagin. 1998. Double Burden: Black Women and Everyday Racism. New York: M. E. Sharpe.

U.S. Department of Commerce. 1995. Household and Family Characteristics: March 1994. Washington, D.C.: Government Printing Office. 1998 Household and Family Characteristics: March 1997, Washington, D.C.: Government Printing Office.

U.S. Department of Labor. 1965. The Negro Family: The Case for National Action. Washington, D.C.: Government Printing Office.

Walker, Alice. 1982. The Color Purple. New York: Harcourt.

Willie, Charles Vert. 1993. "Social theory and social policy derived from the Black family experience." Journal of Black Studies 23: 451–459.

CHAPTER 11 The Institution of Health and Medicine

11.1 PAMELA D. BRIDGEWATER

Reproductive Freedom as Civil Freedom

The institution of health and medicine has helped to perpetuate social inequality in the United States by rationing health care according to a person's ability to pay, by providing inadequate and inferior health care to poor people, and by failing to establish structures that can meet health needs in ways that are acceptable to all patients. For example, women's health issues in the United States have suffered serious neglect. Controversies surround the toxicity of silicone breast implants, the high rate at which hysterectomies are performed on women, and the exceptionally high frequency with which cesarean sections are performed during childbirth. Many people feel that government agencies that are designed to ensure safe medicines and medical procedures cannot be trusted. In April 1992, for example, the Food and Drug Administration (FDA) announced a prohibition on any further silicone breast implant surgeries. Despite its own scientific research of the cancer risk to patients with silicone implants, the FDA's ban failed to mention the risk to 2 million women who had had the implants since the early 1980s. The American Society of Plastic and Reconstructive Surgery, the American College of Radiology, and the American Medical Association adamantly opposed the ban on silicone implants. Dow Corning and Bristol-Myers Squibb corporations have had *secret* evidence of the carcinogenicity of silicone implants since the early 1960s, yet they still marketed the implants with assurances of safety. It was only after the implants had been manufactured and put into patients that the industry admitted that there was a cancer risk to patients.

In the following selection from "Reproductive Freedom as Civil Freedom: The Thirteenth Amendment's Role in the Struggle for Reproductive Rights," *The Journal of Gender, Race, and Justice* (Spring 2000), Pamela D. Bridgewater, an assistant professor in the Northeastern University School of Law, contends that the "Norplant crisis" continues to be at the forefront of women's health issues in that it poses a significant danger to women's reproductive freedom. She suggests that legal scholars should use the antislavery amendment to restructure women's contemporary reproductive freedoms along a historical continuum to include the history of reproductive abuses suffered by female slaves—"to analyze these abuses as badges of slavery—badges the Thirteenth Amendment is designed for and should be used to eradicate."

Key Concept: female reproductive rights, Norplant implantation, and the Thirteenth Amendment

I. INTRODUCTION

I am my father's daughter. From my approach to teaching to my method of choosing my fruit or my friends, I am ever mindful of the ways in which my father is responsible for who I am. Yet despite the constant reminders, I am frequently amazed at the depth of his influence, especially in regards to my life as a lawyer. My father's influence on my legal perspective regarding issues of reproductive freedom has been particularly important in my personal and professional development. Specifically, my adherence to the proposition that reproductive abuse occurs along a historical continuum is largely the result of my father's encouragement of me to consider everything in its appropriate historical context.

These lessons proved especially influential in shaping my thoughts about the frequent judicial and legislative regulations of women's bodies through mandating the use of the contraceptive Norplant in certain situations. Although the "Norplant crisis"[1] does not seem to pose the precise threat to reproductive freedom now that it did in the early nineties, the underlying threat to reproductive freedom still exists. As such, we should still be thinking and talking about Norplant, because many women continue to suffer physically and emotionally both from Norplant implantation and from the inability to remove the device. Additionally, the vast popularity of the device as a tool against women, specifically poor and incarcerated women, poses great danger to women's health and the pursuit of reproductive freedom. The motivations for the popularity of conditioning receipt or maintenance of certain liberties on the use of Norplant, and the absence of an effective legal response to these uses, should still be of great concern to those of us working for the attainment of reproductive freedom.

II. THE CALL

My perception of the Norplant crisis changed dramatically following a telephone conversation with my father. At the time the conversation took place, I was a frantic and overwhelmed first-year law student. However, learning of a California case where a judge offered Norplant implantation as a condition of probation to a person named Darlene Johnson[2] enhanced my usual state of frenzy. The decision, having come within months of FDA approval of the contraceptive in December 1990,[3] stunned everyone concerned about reproductive freedom—from grassroots organizers and abortion clinic defenders to lawyers and scholars.[4] Clearly, reproductive freedom was under attack.

In the midst of this turmoil, my father phoned. At some point during the first few minutes of our conversation, my father picked up on my inability to carry on a meaningful conversation. "Is anything wrong?" he asked. "Everything's wrong," I replied. I went on to explain with feigned familiarity that "some judge said that Darlene had to get Norplant in order to get out of jail." He asked with genuine concern, "Darlene who?" I answered, "Darlene Johnson." I knew the wheels were turning and my dad was poised for action, but true to his nature, he needed more information before he joined me in my hysteria. "Darlene Johnson... Johnson... hummm, who are her people?" he asked. I responded, somewhat irritated, "I don't know her. She lives in California. I heard about the case in school." My dad took an all too familiar deep breath and said, "Speaking of school, how are your classes?" "Classes!?!" I screamed to myself (of course). I said to him, "I need to go. I'll call you back later."

After our conversation, I continued to consider the implications of my father's question, "Who are her people?" Who *are* Darlene Johnson's people? The question mainly troubled me because I was under the impression that this type of question was irrelevant in the objective atmosphere of law school. Yet as I analyzed the question more, it seemed desperately important that I generate a response. I now believe that questions similar to my dad's are essential to understanding the needs of those who are most vulnerable to reproductive abuse. Analyzing reproductive abuse on a historical continuum has the marvelous potential to bring about more inclusive, perhaps stronger, reproductive freedom as it would require an exploration of who the targets of reproductive abuse were (are), as well as who was (is) perpetuating the targeting and how. A historically based inquiry can teach us why targeting the reproductive capacities of particular women continues to be regarded as a viable option in attempts to bring dominant society's political and social objectives to fruition.

In this piece I will take a closer look at the ways in which the Norplant crisis gave rise to an opportunity to consider alternative doctrinal models in the reproductive rights context. Specifically, I suggest that the Thirteenth Amendment potentially provides protection against modern manifestations of reproductive slavery. Further, I advocate that a Thirteenth Amendment challenge is possible only if the current reproductive historiography is expanded to include and analyze the practice of slave breeding during the American slavery era. Ultimately, I suggest that using the Thirteenth Amendment to protect against modern reproductive abuses, such as legislatively and judicially regulated uses of Norplant, via the history of slave breeding, would place reproductive freedom on par with other forms of civil freedom, as well as place the reproductive experiences of women of African descent on par with those of white women.

Expanding reproductive historiography to include slave breeding offers an opportunity to develop an inclusive reproductive rights discourse which speaks to the reproductive realities of everyone. Such inclusion is vital to the pursuit of reproductive freedom because the continued negation and marginalization of many women leaves them vulnerable to abusive reproductive practices, policies and laws.[5] Further, if the historiography is not expanded, the mainstream reproductive rights movement will and should continue to be criticized for failing to address the needs of women who are not middle-class and white.[6] The legal and political responses to the Norplant crisis are illustrative of the consequences of a narrow reproductive rights history and the limited agenda informed by that history.

III. THE CRISIS

In 1990, Norplant was hailed as the pharmaceutical contraceptive advancement of the century.[7] Notwithstanding the early concern over the safety of Norplant,[8] it was not long before Norplant was suggested as a viable method of behavior modification for certain groups of women.[9] Over the objection of the many women, physicians, and women's healthcare activists who voiced concern over its safety and impact on particular segments of women,[10] welfare reform advocates and legislators argued that connecting birth control to public assistance programs would overcome the "cycle of poverty" arguably found in certain subcultures by conditioning receipt or maintenance of benefits on the implantation of Norplant.[11] Further, many legislators argued that resolving the problem of generational poverty via Norplant would lighten the tax burden on their constituents.[12] Additionally, commentators also opined that Norplant would generally decrease welfare dependency.[13] The commonality among these approaches concerning the use of Norplant is that they considered the reproductive capacities of socially, politically and economically disadvantaged women as a mechanism to further the objectives of society as a whole.[14]

Many women's reproductive healthcare activists opposed governmental uses of Norplant immediately after program implementation.[15] Many advocates argued that contraceptive policies which targeted women on public assistance and women convicted of child abuses were modern day versions of eugenics.[16] The initial premise of the eugenics movement was that society could be improved by *encouraging* reproduction among desired classes of people.[17] The flip side of the eugenics movement was that sterilization was used to stop certain classes of people from reproducing if they carried traits that were socially undesirable.[18] By the end of the eugenics experiment more than 60,000 alcoholics, mentally and physically disabled, poor and institutionalized people had been forcibly sterilized.[19]

Opponents argued that Norplant incentives and conditions essentially sought to re-institute eugenics by decreasing reproduction among women on public assistance and women convicted of child abuse because those classes of women were socially undesirable.[20] They argued that such manipulation was indefensible and unconstitutional under present constitutional protections.[21] While this was an important approach to take, it nonetheless missed an opportunity to reverse the exclusion of women of color from the mainstream reproductive rights discourse. Further, few commentators connected Norplant incentives and its commodification of reproduction to the practice of slave breeding during the American slavery era. As such, the mainstream, historically-based opposition to Norplant was largely unresponsive to the critique that reproductive rights discourse protects the interests of privileged white women by employing a narrow scope of reproductive history that excludes the reproductive abuses endured by women of color.

The constitutional challenges to Norplant were also problematic. The most frequently advanced argument in opposition to Norplant conditions and incentives was that such governmental uses of Norplant violated notions of privacy protected by the Fourteenth Amendment.[22] Opponents contended that governmental uses of Norplant were coercive[23] because judges and legislators were essentially dangling "carrots" of money and freedom in the faces of poor women and women convicted of child abuse, and such coerciveness violated the women's right to privacy in reproductive matters.[24]

Critics of the privacy framework in the reproductive rights doctrine have long questioned its appropriateness because it is based on a liberal ideal of reproductive freedom and choice.[25] However, this critique—the notion that privacy itself is antithetical to women's needs and interests in a world where women's sexuality is still dominated by men and poor women cannot access reproductive services necessary to exercise their privacy rights—is ill-suited to bring about reproductive freedom for all women.[26] For example, while many reproductive rights advocates argue for less government involvement in women's ability to receive certain services, they often ask for government funding of other services for women who would otherwise be unable to receive these services.[27] For these women, the right to "choose" reproductive services, such as abortion, is meaningless because they cannot afford the procedure.[28] As a result, choice rhetoric within the privacy doctrine can often operate in diametric opposition to the reproductive needs of poor women.[29] As critics point out, reproductive rights advocacy grounded on the idea of choice fails to deal with the question of access and resources and transforms the valuable concept of choice into a double-edged rhetorical sword.[30] According to choice-rhetoric, a woman ideally makes decisions regarding reproductive matters based on her private circumstances.[31] However, those private circumstances are rarely the central focus of choice analysis.

Other constitutional challenges to Norplant incentives and conditions focused on the identity of those affected. Specifically, opponents argued that such policies were violative of the Fourteenth Amendment's Equal Protection Clause.[32] The argument was based on the fact that government-sponsored uses of Norplant constituted gender discrimination because men were not asked to endure similar restrictions on reproduction.[33] For example, fathers on public assistance were not faced with a comparable requirement although they might have engaged in similar conduct. Although gender classifications are subject to intermediate level scrutiny,[34] it was the approach that offered the best chance of opposing Norplant incentives successfully. The race-based claims, though cogent, were not treated as having much potential in the fight against Norplant.[35] Opponents argued that the conditions and incentives disproportionately impacted women of color because of their heightened vulnerabilities to abuse within the criminal justice system and racial discrepancies in screening mechanisms.[36] As such, any curtailment of the reproductive capacities of these women would amount to an unconstitutional race classification.

The arguments regarding unconstitutional racial classifications underscored significant obstacles within the current fight for identity-based constitutional protection under the Equal Protection Clause. First, so long as defenders of such policies could show that white women were also subject to Norplant use, the practice would likely pass constitutional muster, thus undermining the unconstitutional racial classification claim. Second, given the clear judicial hostility to identity-based claims, the viability of a disparate impact analysis was questionable, at best. As such, most commentators conceded that the search for protection under the current application of the Equal Protection Clause either for race or gender would not fare well.[37]

Despite justifiable pessimism regarding the success of such claims, advocates fought against Norplant with admirable veracity and cogency.[38] However, an unfortunate commonality existed in each argument: frustration with the current framework of reproductive rights doctrine as a vehicle to achieve and protect reproductive freedom for women most vulnerable to Norplant policies.[39] As a result, many reproductive rights advocates joined others who had experienced the declining effectiveness of the Equal Protection doctrine in the search for alternative theories upon which to launch substantive challenges to offensive practices.[40]

I suggest that advocates' efforts to find a more viable legal doctrine on which to base claims for reproductive freedom should include consideration of the Thirteenth Amendment.[41] To utilize the Thirteenth Amendment one must show that the conduct at issue either existed during slavery or is a badge or incident of slavery.[42] This was not a difficult task, as my search for Ms. Johnson's people led me to the history of reproductive abuse during the American slavery era. Specifically, I found Ms. Johnson's people to be among the women slaves forced to reproduce in order to increase the financial standing of their owners, thereby supplementing the slave industry as a whole.[43] Restructuring reproductive freedom's historical continuum to include the history of reproductive abuses suffered by women of color allows an opportunity to analyze these abuses as badges of slavery—badges the Thirteenth Amendment is designed for and should be used to eradicate.

IV. THE SEARCH

My decision to join Thirteenth Amendment proponents proved to be consistent with my quest to find out more about Ms. Johnson's people. The details made available to the public were few; however, I knew that Ms. Johnson was an American woman of African descent who had several children.[44] This was enough information to support an exploration into the reproductive histories of Black women in America. My search yielded proof of my contention that coercing women to alter their reproductive capacities to further the economic objectives of the dominant society was somehow correlated to the current Norplant crisis. Instead of forcing multiple births based on the need for Black bodies to provide free labor, Norplant incentives and conditions are attempting to limit the birth of Black bodies in the name of fiscal conservatism.

Historically, female slaves were expected to do the same work as male slaves while carrying the additional burdens of sexual abuse and exploitation of their reproductive capabilities.[45] These sexual and reproductive exploitations of female slaves occurred in several forms, but none was more vital to the maintenance of the institution of slavery than the practice of slave breeding.[46]

Fundamentally, slave breeding can be thought of as a type of animal husbandry wherein the slave owner, much like the owner of a cow, "encourages" reproduction in order to realize a profit from his economic investment. Slave breeding can also be defined as a systematic sexual and reproductive exploitation of female slaves made possible by force, coercion and oppression, all done for the socio-economic uplift of slave owners.[47] This definition is based on an economic model of slavery premised on the understanding that slave owners, concerned with maximizing profits, were aware that their slaves, as chattel, could be subjected to whatever conditions, practices or processes were necessary to achieve owners' economic objectives and solidify their domination.[48]

Slave breeding was an integral component of the North American slave trade resulting from the increasing demand for slave labor.[49] The eventual close of the international slave trade in 1808 made breeding a viable option for slaveholders wanting to sustain a labor market.[50] Implicitly, after 1808 slave owners saw the intentional breeding of slaves for profit as a more viable and economically efficient alternative to the importation of slaves.[51]

Generally, slave owners' interest in increased slave reproduction was furthered through two methods. The most common method of slave breeding was a strict system of punishments and rewards.[52] Although slave breeding required slave owners to dehumanize slaves and view them as commodities existing solely for the master class' economic benefit,[53] slave owners were nevertheless aware of the slaves' humanity.[54] Given this awareness, slave owners often appealed to the female slaves' interest in avoiding severe punishments and their interest in earning rewards.[55] Alternatively, slave owners recognized both the utility of sexual abuse[56] and community influence[57] in achieving satisfactory reproduction rates from their female slaves. Therefore, the utilizations of sexual abuse and the manipulation of community stigmatization were jointly the second most common method slave owners employed to increase female slave reproduction.

Like her male counterpart, nearly every aspect of the female slave's life was governed by her owner and his agents.[58] As such, the threat and use of punishments, physical and otherwise, were ever present as a method to increase reproduction.[59] In most cases, the female slave understood this vulnerability and often reproduced in order to avoid the wrath of those who exercised control over her life.[60]

There is evidence that the type, severity and frequency of punishments received by female slaves were directly related to the increased interest in slave reproduction.[61] The treatment of infertile slaves highlights the relationship between reproduction and increased punishment.[62] Female slaves who did not yield to the reproductive wishes of their owners were often subjected to a heightened degree of cruelty,[63] regardless of whether it was because female slaves choose not to reproduce or because they did not possess reproductive capabilities.[64]

An infertile female slave became the outcast of the plantation.[65] While contempt for infertile slaves often resulted in abuse as punishment, being placed on the slave market resulting in physical separation from family and friends was also a form of punishment for infertility.[66] Further, slaves purchased for breeding who could not fulfil their intended purpose were considered economic losses.[67] In an effort to regain their initial investment costs, many displeased slave owners sold infertile slaves to unsuspecting buyers.[68] Unless the fraud was discovered, the slave's new owner was likely to punish the slave for insolence.[69] However, more often than resorting to punishment, slave owners opted for a reward system to coerce female slaves into reproducing.[70] Slave owners offered gifts such as dresses, more food and less work.[71] Further, some slave owners made good on their promises to free female slaves after the slaves gave birth to a certain number of children.[72] In light of most slave owners' interest in increasing the slave population, female slaves knew that surrendering control over their reproductive capacity was a way to avoid punishment, as well as to better the material conditions of their lives and those of their families and community.[73]

Even though breeder slaves were often able to improve the conditions of their lives by reproducing frequently, many were aware that receipt of benefits was directly related to their ability and willingness to further the slave owners' interests in reproducing slaves and maintaining slavery.[74] The benefits that breeder slaves received for reproducing were correlated to the benefit to the larger social order aimed at maintaining the institution of slavery.[75] For example, when a pregnant slave woman was spared brutal beatings or excused from fieldwork, the leniency she received was often due to her owner's concern for her well-being as his property, but also of the property interest growing within her.[76] The interest being protected was increased of wealth and the maintenance of the existing social structure which would facilitate further increases of wealth.[77] The tokens of the slave owner's gratitude given to slave mothers served to perpetuate the notion that childbirth was good for him and therefore good for her.[78] However, it is important to note that the calculus for determining "good" included only one factor: the interests of the master class, both individually and collectively.

Slave breeding and slave owners' concerns over maintaining the right to breed slaves reached an identifiable peak during the height of the abolitionist movement[79] which by the mid-1800s had commenced a frontal attack against the sexual abuse of slaves.[80] Like slave owners, abolitionists recognized the important role sexual and reproductive exploitation of female slaves played in the maintenance of the slave industry.[81] In fact, in the twenty years prior to the Civil War, the sexual abuse of female slaves was a prominent theme in abolitionist propaganda.[82]

V. THE CHALLENGE

Against the historical backdrop of the slave market that exploited its primary participants by requiring them to barter their reproductive capacity for increased benefits or decreased punishments, the similarities between slave breeding and Norplant conditions and incentives become easier to ascertain. Like female slaves forced to breed, women faced with Norplant incentives and conditions are asked to exchange their reproductive capacities for financial gain or decreased jail time. Thus, because the nature of the harms and tactics are similar, it is appropriate to invoke the Thirteenth Amendment to eradicate injustice in the current situation, as it was in the exploitation of slaves.

The history of slave breeding not only informs us of an overlooked aspect of reproductive exploitation, but it also offers the opportunity to invoke the Thirteenth Amendment which was specifically designed to eradicate slavery and its badges and incidents.[83] Because slave breeding essentially and necessarily included reproductive manipulation, it is not analytically unsound to argue that such practices are offensive to the notions of freedom and liberty embodied in the Thirteenth Amendment—freedoms and liberties the Amendment was arguably designed to protect.

On its face the Thirteenth Amendment's revolutionary potential is undeniable.[84] However, while the Thirteenth Amendment is endowed with, and perhaps encumbered by, substantial historical relevance and symbolic meaning, few scholars actually know the precise dimensions of the constitutionalized freedom it embodies.

The argument for a broader reading of the Thirteenth Amendment is based on the premise that the maintenance of the institution of slavery necessarily included a wide range of practices and conditions in addition to forced physical servitude.[85] It therefore follows that because slavery was more than merely a legal status of servitude, the Amendment, designed to abolish slavery, must necessarily eradicate more than forced labor.[86] In fact, one member of the Thirty-Eighth and Thirty-Ninth Congresses saw the Amendment as going beyond forced labor to eradicate matters of sexual, familial and reproductive components of slavery.[87] For example, Senator Harlan of Iowa included in his delineation of the incidents of slavery the breach of the conjugal relationship, the abolition of the parental relation, and robbing offspring of the care and attention of their parents, thereby securing to slaves their natural right to the endearments and enjoyment of family ties.[88] Recognizing the wide range of slavery practices and conditions, Harlan's comments exemplify the desire to remove not just the barriers of physical servitude, but also to remove slavery badges in their entirety.

If one accepts the historical interpretation of slavery as an expansive concept, and moreover that the framers of the Thirteenth Amendment understood this and drafted an equally expansive amendment, then one would also justifiably expect to find a doctrinal evolution that closely mirrors the expansive aspirations of the Thirty-Eighth and Thirty-Ninth Congresses.[89] This expectation, however, does not mirror the reality of the Amendment's doctrinal evolution.

After nearly a century of narrow application of the Thirteenth Amendment, it was not until *Jones v. Alfred H. Mayer Co.*[90] that the 1968 Supreme Court recognized the Amendment's potentially broad application. In *Jones*, the Court expanded Congress' authority to identify and eliminate badges and incidents of slavery through legislation.[91] Particularly important to the development of Thirteenth Amendment jurisprudence, the *Jones* Court delineated three lines of reasoning that supported a broad reading of the Amendment. First, the Court affirmed the notion that a condition or practice can be found violative of the Thirteenth Amendment even though the precise condition or practice did not exist during slavery.[92] Second, the Court held that a practice can be deemed violative of the Thirteenth Amendment even if there is no specific reference to the practice in the congressional debates.[93] Finally, the Court relied on the history of slavery and the legislative history of the Amendment to establish that Congress has the power to apply the Thirteenth Amendment broadly.[94] Ultimately, the *Jones* Court established the test for a Thirteenth Amendment violation merely as whether Congress could rationally determine that a proscribed practice is a badge or incident of slavery.[95]

With this holding, the Thirteenth Amendment was resurrected, extended and created a great deal of optimism in advocates fighting for social change. The Court affirmed that section one of the Thirteenth Amendment extended beyond a mere prohibition of the legal ownership of humans and interpreted the two sections of the Amendment as serving different, but related, purposes.[96] Section one was meant clearly and unambiguously to abolish slavery and involuntary servitude and establish universal freedom, granting the Court the power to enforce those prohibitions.[97] Section two, on the other hand, was "a particularized version of the Necessary and Proper Clause, applicable to [section one] of the Thirteenth Amendment."[98] Under section two, Congress could address the continuous social consequences of slavery and indentured servitude, including the badges and incidents of slavery.[99] The Court's approach to the meaning and scope of the text of each section of the Amendment was a drastic departure from its narrow textual analysis in the *Civil Rights Cases*.[100] Subsequently in case dicta, the Court has generally followed the *Jones* approach.[101]

Under *Jones*, application of the Amendment no longer turns on a narrow understanding of slavery, one devoid of any consideration of a broader conception of freedom.[102] *Jones* made possible the idea that Congress and the courts should be expected to identify and counteract modern day manifestations of systemic racial domination. For Thirteenth Amendment purposes, in finding that the private acts of housing discrimination are sufficiently connected to past segregation laws and customs emanating from the racial domination characteristic of slavery, the *Jones* Court marked a startling departure from the limited application of the Thirteenth Amendment only to situations of compulsory labor.[103]

Additionally, the *Jones* Court reshaped existing Thirteenth Amendment doctrine by reanalyzing the legislative debates over the Civil Rights Act of 1866.[104] The Court held that "Congress has the power under the thirteenth Amendment rationally to determine what are the badges and the incidents of slavery, and the authority to translate that determination into effective legislation."[105] This included the "sort of positive legislation that was embodied in the 1866 Civil Rights Act."[106]

The statute at issue in *Jones*, 42 U.S.C. § 1982 (1968),[107] was intended to eliminate race as a factor in real and personal property ownership and transactions.[108] In affirming the constitutionality of the statute on Thirteenth Amendment grounds, the Supreme Court stated that "when racial discrimination herds men into ghettos and makes their ability to buy property turn on the color of their skin, then it too is a relic of slavery."[109] Justice Douglas, in his concurring opinion, listed other badges of slavery to show how "[slavery] has remained in the minds and hearts of many white men," in spite of its legal abolition.[110] The Court also looked to dicta in the *Civil Rights Cases* to support a broader reading of the Thirteenth Amendment.[111] Especially important were Justice Bradley's words acknowledging the Amendment's protection against "badges of slavery," and "relic[s] of slavery," and its power to protect "freedom" and "fundamental rights."[112] The Court focused on what the Amendment guarantees instead of what it prohibits.[113] Viewing slavery as the opposite of freedom, the Court based its holding on the "promise of freedom."[114]

The textual analysis and historical methodology set forth in *Jones* created a foundation upon which many contemporary theorists and advocates argue for expansive interpretations of the Thirteenth Amendment.[115] However, the Court has repeatedly declined to adopt a bounded definition of slavery that supports a broad reading of the Amendment.[116] According to these theorists, other indicators of the expansiveness of the Thirteenth Amendment include that: (1) under *Jones*, the first section of the Amendment is self-executing and therefore does not require additional legislative or judicial action to take effect;[117] (2) the Amendment applies to everyone regardless of race;[118] and (3) it applies to private as well as to state action.[119] The precise force of the first section remains unclear, as in the vast majority of Thirteenth Amendment cases courts have construed legislation enacted under the second section and not under the first section of the Amendment.[120] Many commentators urging greater use of the Thirteenth Amendment argue that the lack of a rigid doctrine surrounding the first section leaves it open to endless possibilities.[121] This openness may be useful to scholars in overcoming a major obstacle in the reproductive context—the issue of "choice." Thus, *Jones* provides an unchartered course from which to explore the breadth of the Thirteenth Amendment in connection to freedom of choice issues.

VI. THE CONNECTION

While the Norplant crisis created by probation conditions and welfare incentives has subsided, it was the litigation regarding its safety, though largely unsuccessful,[122] that ultimately led to Norplant's disuse by governmental agencies and courts.[123] Because of these safety concerns, the ideological justifications for restricting the reproductive capacities of women on welfare and convicted of child abuse remain intact. Therefore, similar proposals are likely to reappear upon the advent of new contraceptives that offer the same degree of control and manageability of women's reproductive freedom as those created by the Norplant crisis.

If this prediction materializes and the next contraceptive merely replaces Norplant as courts and legislatures propose similar uses, we will experience yet another phase along the continuum of reproductive abuse. On the other hand, the opportunity will arise again for advocates and scholars to expand reproductive historiography to include the histories of those traditionally subjected to reproductive abuse. Taking advantage of this opportunity proscriptively rather than as a reaction to the next reproductive threat could lead to a better protection of the most vulnerable in our society. By connecting modern manifestations of reproductive abuse to the practice of slave breeding it will be possible to explore the Thirteenth Amendment's usefulness in protecting reproductive freedom.[124]

A market where a woman, because of her status as a recipient of public assistance or a parolee from child abuse convictions, is offered money in exchange for her reproductive capacity compares substantially to a market in which a woman, because of her status as a slave, is offered gifts in exchange for her reproductive freedom.[125] It matters not that slave breeding promoted reproduction, while Norplant conditions and incentives attempt to restrict reproduction. Both situations involve the government's manipulation of reproduction to advance the interests of the powerful via the procreative control of the less powerful.

Like the female slave, women faced with Norplant conditions and incentives are forced into a market where one's reproduction is the currency. The techniques are the same—the government identifies the needs of the less powerful and conditions the satisfaction of their needs upon their willingness to relinquish their reproductive self determinism. As such, women are at the mercy of the government in much the same way as slaves were at the mercy of owners who exercised sole discretion regarding whether to meet the needs of their slaves. Slave owners interested in reproduction, in ways similar to the courts and legislatures who favored Norplant, would condition their offering of benefits upon whether the slaves satisfactorily altered their reproductive capacities.

Finally, the transaction costs and payments are the same: reproductive freedom for an opportunity to better the material conditions of one's life. Female slaves, given their desperate conditions and substantial needs, often submitted to the will of the slave owner.[126] This transforms reproduction into a negotiable instrument in the market that maintains the institution of slavery. Like female slaves forced to breed for a new dress, more food, or benefits for family members, women offered Norplant incentives or conditions for increased benefits or probation must also submit to the will of legislatures and judges by surrendering their reproductive control as a condition of subsistence level assistance. The government forces the women to use their reproductive capacity as a negotiable instrument to purchase more food, pay a light bill or to purchase freedom from jail in order to care for the children at home—a benefit Darlene Johnson bought with her agreement to have Norplant implanted as a condition of probation.

Market-based reproduction is arguably a relic of slavery; therefore, it is hard to explain why courts refuse to apply the Thirteenth Amendment to conduct which exists either along a historical continuum from slavery to now or against conduct that constitutes modern manifestations of slavery. Many view the Thirteenth Amendment as dead or dormant because the judiciary has underutilized, and inconsistently applied, the Amendment.[127] Whatever the precise reasons, the Thirteenth Amendment has never achieved its full revolutionary potential.

Yet, several scholars continue to urge the Thirteenth Amendment's relevance in today's legal landscape.[128] As Professor Julie Nice points out, since most Thirteenth Amendment decisions interpreted the statutory prohibitions enacted under the second section of the Amendment, the precise scope of the Thirteenth Amendment remains undefined.[129] This creates an opportunity for creative litigators and legal scholars to attempt to persuade courts that a particular practice or condition violates the Thirteenth Amendment.

VII. CONCLUSION

My search for a response to my father's question has brought me full circle. By exploring the history of slave breeding, I have a better sense of Darlene Johnson's people. They are the women who were forced to barter their reproductive capacities in hopes of lessening the daily tortures of slavery. They are the women and men who fought to eliminate slavery and all of its badges and incidents. They are the women and men who were forcibly sterilized in the name of eugenics. Her people endured the oppressive reproductive policies of the 1970s.[130] They are the women of today who are asked to choose between Norplant implantation and assistance in feeding their babies or probation instead of jail time. Finally, Ms. Johnson's people are those of us who are willing to expand reproductive historiography to address the interests of the traditionally marginalized and excluded. Without this expansion, no one will be able to fully understand the needs and interests of those who need protection. Such an understanding is essential in order to achieve real and lasting reproductive freedom.

The search for Ms. Johnson's people, motivated by my father's love of history and context, continues to influence my pursuit of reproductive freedom for all women. After this search, I realized the importance of broadening the reproductive discourse by focusing on slave breeding as practiced in the antebellum South. The growing number of scholars who recognize the current vitality and potential power of the Thirteenth Amendment can join those who challenge Norplant incentives and other reproductive abuses. The result could potentially build bridges, make connections, give a voice to the silenced and serve as a history for future reproductive freedom challenges.

These expansions and theories are not without substantial challenges of their own, nor do they offer a cure all for the problems facing the Darlene Johnsons of the world. However, in this age of ever increasing threats and dangerous set backs to reproductive freedom, we must gain strength from the victory in telling the story of the once silenced voices in order to correct the record and speak the truth. However, I must confess that this suggestion is not completely my own, but it is yet another example of the ways in which I am my father's daughter.

NOTES

1. The "Norplant crisis" is a catchall phrase I will use to refer to the sudden popularity of the contraceptive soon after it was approved by the United States Food and Drug Administration (FDA) in 1990. In this essay, the use of the phrase specifically refers to the judicial and legislative conditioning of receipt or maintenance of welfare benefits and personal liberties on the required use of Norplant.
2. People v. Johnson, No. 29390 (Cal. Super. Ct. June 2, 1991), *cited in* DOROTHY ROBERTS, KILLING THE BLACK BODY 110–52 (1997). Ms. Johnson, a mother of four children, was convicted of child abuse. *Id.* at 151. Before offering Norplant as condition of her probation, Judge Broadman referred to Ms. Johnson's status as a recipient of public assistance in addition to noting that she was the mother of "illegitimate" children. *Id.* On appeal, the case was dismissed as moot because Johnson was returned to prison for violating the terms of her parole for testing positive for drugs. *Id.; see also* Julie Mertus & Simon Heller, *Norplant Meets the New Eugenicists: The Impermissibility of Coerced Contraception,* 11 ST. LOUIS U. PUB. L. REV. 359, 364–67 (1992) (describing the boundaries of judicial power exemplified in People v. Johnson.).
3. ROBERTS, *supra* note 2, at 105.
4. *See, e.g.,* Joyce Price, *Forced Norplant Use Assailed,* WASH. TIMES, Apr. 2, 1992, at A5 (reporting that trustees of the American Medical Association commented that forcing a child abuser to take Norplant probably creates several constitutional violations); Steven S. Spitz, *The Norplant Debate: Birth Control or Woman Control?,* 25 COLUM. HUM. RTS. L. REV. 131 (1993) (stating that *People v. Johnson* was not the first time that a judge tried to inhibit a woman's reproductive rights as a condition of probation).
5. The reproductive history of white women has largely been seen as the only relevant history in reproductive rights discourse. *See, e.g.,* Marlene Gerber Fried, *Introduction* to FROM ABORTION TO REPRODUCTIVE FREEDOM: TRANSFORMING A MOVEMENT ix, x–xi (Marlene Gerber Fried ed., 1990).
6. *See* ROBERTS, *supra* note 2, at 6 (criticizing the dominant view of reproductive liberty, arguing in part that the view "is primarily concerned with the interests of white, middle-class women").
7. *Id.* at 105.

8. Simply put, Norplant failed miserably in its attempt to provide women with safe, trouble free, affordable and effective long-term contraception. In addition to its significant side effects and contraindications, Norplant has proved to be inundated with problems. Severe depression, excessive vaginal bleeding, ovarian cysts, and a plethora of removal problems top the list of adverse consequences over a quarter of a million women endure because of Norplant use. *See Norplant Survives Lawsuits in Texas,* MED. MATERIALS UPDATE, May 1, 1997, *available in* 1997 WL 9760970. In response to these problems, many injured women have brought product liability claims against the drug's manufacturer, Wyeth-Ayerst, a subsidiary of American Home Products. *Id.* In an effort to control the barrage of disgruntled Norplant users, the current claims were consolidated for trial before U.S. District Judge Richard A. Schell. *Id.* The claims include allegations of product defect, negligence, misrepresentation and breach of warranty for failing to warn doctors of the seriousness of the side effects. *Id.*

9. Walter A. Graham, *Norplant Can Aid Mothers,* USA TODAY, Feb. 16, 1993, at 10A. *See also* ROBERTS, *supra* note 2, at 6–7 (quoting Donald Kimelman, *Poverty and Norplant: Can Contraception Reduce the Underclass?,* PHILA. INQUIRER, Dec. 12, 1990, at A18).

10. Price, *supra* note 4, at A5 (describing the American Medical Association's condemnation of the proposed uses of Norplant). For more commentary detailing the early concerns over Norplant's safety, see generally Jeanne L. Vance, *Womb for Rent: Norplant and the Undoing of Poor Women,* 21 HASTINGS CONST. L.Q. 827, 831 (1994); Douglas A. Berman, *The Rights and Wrongs of Norplant Offers,* 3 S. CAL. REV. L. & WOMEN'S STUD. 1, 3–8 (1993); Mertus & Heller, *supra* note 2, at 360–71.

11. *See, e.g.,* Vance, *supra* note 10, at 829 (discussing a Louisiana bill that would pay an initial $100 "grant" and $100 per year thereafter to women on welfare who obtain a Norplant implantation). All states have incorporated Norplant into their Medicaid programs to increase poor women's access to Norplant. *Id.* at 831. Because Medicaid already covers the cost of implanting Norplant, it is unlikely that the Norplant incentives are aimed at defraying the cost of implantation. *Id.* It seems likely that the states are pursuing goals other than just providing accessible birth control to needy persons, such as ending the cycle of poverty. *Id.* at 832; *see also* Karin E. Wilinski, Note, *Involuntary Contraceptive Measures: Controlling Women at the Expense of Human Rights,* 10 B.U. INT'L L.J. 351, 361 (1992) (describing Kansas' proposed welfare reform bill that would provide Norplant at no cost to women on welfare and provide them with a $500 cash bonus upon implantation and $50 per year thereafter).

12. *See* C.J. Fogel, *Duke Bill for Welfare Moms Clears Louisiana House Panel,* GANNETT NEWS SERVICE, May 23, 1991, *available in* LEXIS, News Library, MAJPAP File (noting that Louisiana Representative David Duke advocated that offering incentives to welfare mothers to not have children could save the state hundreds of millions of dollars over the next 16 years); *Primetime Live: End of Innocence* (ABC television broadcast, Sept. 9, 1993) (noting South Carolina legislator Roland Corning's claim that mandating Norplant use from women on public assistance could possibly save taxpayers in his state nearly $36 million in welfare and medical costs in the first year); *see also* Celia W. Dugger, *On the Edge of Survival: Single Mothers on Welfare,* N.Y. TIMES, July 6, 1992, at A1 (reporting that the state of New Jersey has adopted laws that will allow women to keep welfare benefits if they marry, but discourage births by denying increases in Aid to Families with Dependent Children (AFDC) benefits for each new childbirth).

13. Less conservative political figures also touted the fiscal feasibility of Norplant incentives. For example, consider Marion Barry's statement made shortly after regaining office as the mayor of Washington, D.C.:

    [Y]ou can have as many babies as you want... if you don't ask the government to take care of them. But when you start asking the government to take care of them, the government ought to have some control over you... [and] if they want the government to take care of their children, I would be for something like Norplant, mandatory Norplant.

    Katha Pollitt, *Subject to Debate: Political Ramifications of Children Out of Wedlock*, NATION, Jan. 30, 1995, at 120 (quoting Marion Barry in an interview with Sally Quinn of the *Washington Post*). The focus on reproduction and women who receive public assistance was further manifested in the Personal Responsibility Act H.R. 4, 104th Cong. § 105 (1995). The preamble of the Act states that its purpose is "to restore the American family, reduce illegitimacy, control welfare spending and reduce welfare dependence." *Id.*

14. In 1992 during a speech to welfare recipients, George Bush informed women on welfare of the responsibility they bore because they received public money. *Blaming the Resourceless*, WASH. POST, Apr. 19, 1992, at C6. According to Bush, these responsibilities to society included working or looking for work, getting job training and "get[ting] their lives in order." *Id.*
15. Doctors were among the first who opposed government uses of Norplant. *See, e.g.*, Price, *supra* note 4, at A5; Faye Wattleton, *Perspective on Race and Poverty; Using Birth Control as Coercion; To Compel or Deny Contraceptive Use, Such as Norplant, Is Immoral, Inhuman and It Targets the Poor*, L.A. TIMES, Jan. 13, 1991, at M7. For discussions opposing Norplant use in either the public assistance or the criminal justice context, see Catherine Albiston, *The Social Meaning of the Norplant Condition: Constitutional Considerations of Race, Class and Gender*, 9 BERKELEY WOMEN'S L.J. 9, 22–24 (1994); Tracy Ballard, *The Norplant Condition: One Step Forward or Two Steps Back?* 16 HARV. WOMEN'S L.J. 139, 171 (1993); Berman, *supra* note 10, at 3; Janet F. Ginzberg, *Compulsory Contraception as a Condition of Probation: The Use and Abuse of Norplant*, 58 BROOK. L. REV. 979 (1992); Mertus & Heller, *supra* note 2, at 359; Spitz, *supra* note 4, at 131.
16. *See, e.g.*, Albiston, *supra* note 15, at 22–24.
17. For detailed discussions of the role and history of eugenics in the United States, see DANIEL J. KEVLES, IN THE NAME OF EUGENICS: GENETICS AND THE USES OF HUMAN HEREDITY 8 (1985); PHILIP R. REILLY, THE SURGICAL SOLUTION: A HISTORY OF INVOLUNTARY STERILIZATION IN THE UNITED STATES 2 (1991).
18. *See* Buck v. Bell, 274 U.S. 200, 207 (1927) (upholding a state forced sterilization policy as constitutional under the Fourteenth Amendment and commenting that "[t]hree generations of imbeciles are enough").
19. *See* REILLY, *supra* note 17, at 2.
20. *See, e.g.*, Mertus & Heller, *supra* note 2, at 359 (connecting the historical concept of eugenics to modern Norplant proposals).
21. For a more detailed discussion of the Norplant crisis, see Albiston, *supra* note 15; Ballard, *supra* note 15; Douglas Berman, *The Rights and Wrongs of Norplant Offers*, 3 S. CAL. REV. L. & WOMEN'S STUD. 1 (1993); Joan Callahan, *Contraception or Incarceration: What's Wrong with This Picture?*, 7 STAN. L. & POL'Y REV. 67 (1995–1996); Laurence Nolan, *The Unconstitutional Conditions Doctrine and Mandating Norplant for Poor Women on Welfare Discourse*, 3 AM. U. J. GENDER & L. 15 (1994); Vance, *supra* note 10; Wilinski, *supra* note 11; Skinner v. Oklahoma *ex rel.* Williamson, 316 U.S. 535, 538

(1942). The Supreme Court noted that procreation was fundamental to the very existence of a race, and that "[t]he power to sterilize... may have subtle, far-reaching and devastating effects. In evil or reckless hands [sterilization] can cause races or types which are inimical to the dominant group to wither and disappear." *Id.* at 541.

22. *See* Albiston, *supra* note 15, at 43–50 (referring to the Due Process Clause of U.S. CONST. amend. XIV § 1: "No state shall... deprive any person of life, liberty, or property, without due process of law").

23. *See* Mertus & Heller, *supra* note 2, at 370 (stating that "legislative incentives virtually ensure that some women's decisions will be made on the spur of the moment, for the sake of the monetary [']bonus[']").

24. *See* Albiston, *supra* note 5, at 11–12.

25. *See* ROBERTS, *supra* note 2, at 294–312 (providing a cogent discussion of problems associated with the privacy doctrine relating to reproductive rights of poor women and women of color).

26. *See* Rhonda Copelon, *From Privacy to Autonomy: The Conditions for Sexual and Reproductive Freedom, in* FROM ABORTION TO REPRODUCTIVE FREEDOM: TRANSFORMING A MOVEMENT, *supra* note 5, at 27, 33.

27. *See id.* at 38; *see also* Marlene Gerber Fried, *Transforming the Reproductive Rights Movement: The Post-Webster Agenda, in* FROM ABORTION TO REPRODUCTIVE FREEDOM: TRANSFORMING A MOVEMENT, *supra* note 5, at 1, 6.

28. *See* Maher v. Roe, 432 U.S. 464, 469 (1977) ("The Constitution imposes no obligation on the States to pay for pregnancy-related medical expenses to indigent women."); Harris v. McRae, 448 U.S. 297, 326 (1980) (stating that the government may prohibit the use of Medicaid funds for medically necessary abortions for poor women).

29. April L. Cherry has focused extensively on the dilemma of choice rhetoric within the reproductive rights discourse. *See, e.g.*, April L. Cherry, *Choosing Substantive Justice: A Discussion of "Choice," "Rights" and the New Reproductive Technologies,* 11 WIS. WOMEN'S L.J. 431, 432–36 (1997) [hereinafter Cherry, *Choosing Substantive Justice*] (discussing the difficulty of engaging in serious debate about choice rhetoric because women's reproductive rights are so fragile); April L. Cherry, *A Feminist Understanding of Sex-Selective Abortion: Solely a Matter of Choice?*, 10 WIS. WOMEN'S L.J. 161, 219 (1995) (questioning the value of choice in the context of allowing women to abort based on gender in a patriarchal society).

30. Cherry, *Choosing Substantive Justice, supra* note 29, at 435 (positing the notion that focusing on a woman's choice deflects attention from the more important problem of the denigration of women as a social group).

31. *See id.* at 433–35.

32. *See* Albiston, *supra* note 15, at 34; *see also* U.S. CONST. amend. XIV, § 1 ("No State shall make or enforce any law which shall... deny to any person within its jurisdiction the equal protection of the laws.").

33. *See* Albiston, *supra* note 15, at 34; Mertus & Heller, *supra* note 2, at 371.

34. *See* Craig v. Boren, 429 U.S. 190, 198 (1976) (noting that "previous cases establish that classifications by gender must serve important governmental objectives and must be substantially related to achievement of those objectives").

35. *See, e.g.*, Dorothy E. Roberts, *Punishing Drug Addicts Who Have Babies: Women of Color, Equality and the Right of Privacy,* 104 HARV. L. REV. 1419, 1451–52 (1991) (noting that the Supreme Court has interpreted the Equal Protection Clause of the Constitution as affording protection when state action is performed with a discriminatory intent).

36. *See id.* at 1432–33 (citing studies that healthcare professionals are more likely to report drug use among women of color than drug use of wealthy white patients).
37. *See* Albiston, *supra* note 15, at 25.
38. For example, Dr. Sheldon J. Segal, Norplant's inventor, sent a letter to the *New York Times,* "unequivocally opposing the use of Norplant for any coercive purposes," ROBERTS, *supra* note 2, at 106.
39. Presumably, the application of the unconstitutional conditions doctrine to challenge governmental use of Norplant was a response to the limitations of traditional reproductive rights doctrine. *See, e.g.,* Kathleen M. Sullivan, *Unconstitutional Conditions,* 102 HARV. L. REV. 1413, 1415, 1426 (1989). Several commentators argued that Norplant conditions and incentive proposals that condition a benefit on the relinquishment of one's fertility amounts to an unconstitutional condition. *Id.;* Ballard, *supra* note 15, at 171. The doctrine of unconstitutional conditions is based on the principle that the state cannot do indirectly that which it cannot do directly. *Id.*
40. *See, e.g.,* Cherry, *Choosing Substantive Justice, supra* note 29, at 435–36 (discussing reproductive technologies and the frustration resulting from the intersection of individuals' actions and their subsequent broad-reaching and potentially dangerous effects).
41. "Neither slavery nor involuntary servitude, except as a punishment for crime whereof the party shall have been duly convicted, shall exist within the United States, or any place subject to their jurisdiction." U.S. CONST. amend. XIII, § 1.
42. *See* Commonwealth v. Local Union No. 542, Int'l Union of Operating Eng'rs, 347 F. Supp. 268, 301 (E.D. Pa. 1972) ("The purpose of the Thirteenth Amendment was not merely abolishing the physical cruelties of slavery, but its purpose was to also eradicate those 'badges and incidents of slavery.' ") (citation omitted).
43. *See* Dorothy E. Roberts, *Blackcrit Theory and the Problem of Essentialism,* 53 MIAMI L. REV. 855, 858 (1999) ("The institution of slavery gave whites a unique economic and political interest in controlling Black women's reproductive capacity.").
44. *See* William Booth, *Judge Orders Birth Control Implant in Defendant,* WASH. POST, Jan. 5, 1991, at A1.
45. DEBORAH GRAY WHITE, AR'N'T I A WOMAN?: FEMALE SLAVES IN THE PLANTATION SOUTH 14 (1985).
46. Historians Robert Fogel and Stanley L. Engerman, in their 1974 book entitled *Time on the Cross: The Economics of American Negro Slavery,* attempted to debunk the myth that systematic breeding of slaves accounted for a majority of slaveholders' profits. ROBERTS, *supra* note 2, at 27. Ultimately, the historians did not dispute whether slave breeding occurred nor the significance it played in sustaining the institution of slavery. *Id.*
47. This definition is consistent with other scholars' articulation of the components of the practice. *See, e.g.,* Gerald Norde, From Genesis to Phoenix: The Breeding of Slaves During the Domestic Slave Era 1807–1863 and Its Consequences 30 (1985) (unpublished Ph.D. dissertation, University of Delaware) (on file with author) (asserting that the practice of slave breeding was essential to the maintenance of a profitable and thus viable market in slaves); Richard Sutch, *The Breeding of Slaves for Sale and the Westward Expansion of Slavery, 1850–1860, in* RACE AND SLAVERY IN THE WESTERN HEMISPHERE: QUALITATIVE STUDIES 173, 173–75 (Stanley L. Engerman & Eugene D. Genovese eds., 1972) (describing slave breeding as a system of force and coercion designed to increase the birth rate for profit); WHITE, *supra* note 45, at 100–01 (documenting the effects of slave breeding on women in slavery and the relative value assigned to female slaves based upon their breeding capacities).
48. Sutch, *supra* note 47, at 173–75.

49. There were also clear social interests furthered by slave breeding. *See* PATRICIA HILL COLLINS, 2 BLACK FEMINIST THOUGHT: KNOWLEDGE, CONSCIOUSNESS, AND THE POLITICS OF EMPOWERMENT: PERSPECTIVES ON GENDER 50–51 (1990) (stating that the reproductive control of slave women was "important to the maintenance of race, class, and gender inequality").

50. Plantation owners concerned over the extent to which the 1808 prohibition on the importation of slaves would limit their ability to benefit from slave labor systematically engaged in slave breeding. *See e.g.*, JOHN HOPE FRANKLIN & ALFRED A. MOSS, JR., FROM SLAVERY TO FREEDOM: A HISTORY OF AFRICAN AMERICANS 115–17 (7th ed. 1994). Additionally, the combined effects of increased labor needs of the plantation South, abolitionist opposition to the international slave trade and western expansion are believed to be factors which ultimately led to the need for slave breeding. *See, e.g.*, Sutch, *supra* note 47, at 176.

51. *See, e.g.*, Sutch, *supra* note 47, at 196–98 (concluding that many American slave owners systematically bred slaves for domestic sale, with the intention of maximizing the slave owners' incomes and profits).

52. *See* ROBERTS, *supra* note 2, at 25–27.

53. *See* Sutch, *supra* note 47, at 182.

54. *Id.* (describing slaveholders' willingness to interfere in their slaves' lives and dehumanize those slaves to sustain the slaveholders' profits).

55. *See* ROBERTS, *supra* note 2, at 25 (noting that slaveholders rewarded pregnant slaves with extra rations or leisure time, but punished slave women who did not conceive).

56. *Id.* at 30.

57. *See id.* at 26 ("Even without . . . concrete rewards, slave women felt pressure to reproduce.").

58. *See id.* at 35 (discussing slaveholders' control over their slaves' reproduction and child-rearing strategies).

59. *See* WHITE, *supra* note 45, at 102.

60. A number of female slaves did choose to resist the sexual and reproductive exploitation of the master class. *See Resistance, in* WE ARE YOUR SISTERS: BLACK WOMEN IN THE NINETEENTH CENTURY 56, 56–69 (Dorothy Sterling ed., 1984). Whether it was by murdering their owners, running away, infanticide or self-imposed abortions, it is clear that there were some female slaves who thought it better to risk personal safety than to add to the slave population. *Id.*

61. *See, e.g.*, Sutch, *supra* note 47, at 191 (deliberating why slave owners would sell infertile slave women, but retain those capable of breeding).

62. The treatment of infertile female slaves offers the best example of the relationship between reproduction and increased punishment because female slaves who attempted to exercise reproductive autonomy were often raped or otherwise forcibly impregnated. *See generally* Jennifer Wriggins, Note, *Rape, Racism and the Law*, 6 HARV. WOMEN'S L.J. 103 (1983). Also, considering the treatment of infertile slaves versus that of fertile ones is a useful tool in helping scholars determine the different motivations that resulted in different types of punishment for slaves.

63. *See* WHITE, *supra* note 45, at 100–02. Slave owners also had the power to present sticks instead of carrots if slaves did not cooperate with reproduction directives. *Id.* While the sale of infertile women was a major stick, some resorted to outright force to induce reproduction. *Id.*

64. *See* HERBERT G. GUTMAN, THE BLACK FAMILY IN SLAVERY AND FREEDOM, 1750–1925, at 80 (1976). We now know that many slave women were infertile or unable

to carry babies to term. *Id.* There are many theories as to what caused such conditions among slave women. *Id.* However, many slave owners attributed their slaves' infertility and low birth rates as acts of willfulness. *Id.*

65. *See* Catherine Clinton, *Caught in the Web of the Big House: Women and Slavery, in* 1 BLACK WOMEN IN UNITED STATES HISTORY: FROM COLONIAL TIMES THROUGH THE NINETEENTH CENTURY 225, 229–30 (Darlene Clark Hine ed., 1990) (giving examples of the abuse dealt to women who refused to submit to the brutal desires of their owners).

66. *See id.*

67. *See, e.g.*, ROBERTS, *supra* note 2, at 26 (citing BELL HOOKS, AIN'T I A WOMAN?: BLACK WOMEN AND FEMINISM 40–41 (1981)) ("Where fruitfulness is the greatest of virtues, barrenness will be regarded as worse than a misfortune, as a crime and the subjects of it will be exposed to every form of privation and affliction. Thus deficiency wholly beyond the slave's power becomes the occasion of inconceivable suffering.").

68. "Infertile women . . . [were] treated like barren sows and . . . passed from one unsuspecting buyer to the next." WHITE, *supra* note 45, at 101. "If a woman weren't a good breeder, she had to do work with de men. But Moster tried to get rid of a woman who didn't have chillun. He would sell her and tell de man who bought her dat she was all right to own." *Voices: Slave Auctions, Forced Breeding, Rape and Runaways, in* BULLWHIP DAYS: THE SLAVES REMEMBER 286, 296 (James Mellon ed., 1988) (quoting James Green).

69. *See, e.g.*, WHITE, *supra* note 45, at 101–02 (quoting JUDICIAL CASES CONCERNING AMERICAN SLAVERY AND THE NEGRO 65, 69, 79, 164, 195, 204, 213–14, 292, 523, 541 (Helen T. Catterall ed., 1968)). Fraud was common in the sale of infertile women, so much so that legal policies were established for dealing with such cases. *Id.* One policy stated that "[i]f a buyer took possession of a woman who had been certified as fit to bear children by the seller, and it could be demonstrated that the seller knew the woman was incapable of having children, the sale was voided and the proceeds were refunded." *Id.*

70. *See supra* notes 52–55 and accompanying text.

71. *See supra* note 55 and accompanying text.

72. *See generally* 6 THE AMERICAN SLAVE: A COMPOSITE AUTOBIOGRAPHY, SUPPLEMENT SERIES 1 (George P. Rawick ed., 1977) (describing accounts of female slaves who were promised freedom after giving birth to a number of children).

73. *See* ROBERTS, *supra* note 2, at 26 (describing slave women's pressure to conceive in order to avoid being sold or to gain relief from their work loads).

74. *See* WHITE, *supra* note 45, at 99: *Courtship and Family Life, in* WE ARE YOUR SISTERS: BLACK WOMEN IN THE NINETEENTH CENTURY, *supra* note 60, at 31.

75. *See, e.g.*, COLLINS, *supra* note 49 and accompanying footnote text.

76. One example of the treatment women received while pregnant is the method used for whipping pregnant slaves. The overseer would dig a hole in the ground and then order the woman to lie down with her stomach in the hole so as not to injure the unborn child. *See* ROBERTS, *supra* note 2, at 39–40 (quoting Michael P. Johnson, *Smothered Slave Infants: Were Slave Mothers at Fault?*, 47 J. S. HIST. 493, 513 (1981)).

77. *See* Johnson, *supra* note 76, at 513.

78. *Id.*

79. During the abolitionist movement, slave owners were motivated to enter the public debate in support of slavery because of their fear of losing access to the sexual

and reproductive capacities of female slaves. *See* JOHN DIXON LONG, PICTURES OF SLAVERY IN CHURCH AND STATE 263 (Negro University Press 1969) (1857).

80. Former slave and famous abolitionist Frederick Douglass spoke specifically and intimately about the sexual and reproductive components of slavery. FREDERICK DOUGLASS, NARRATIVE OF THE LIFE OF FREDERICK DOUGLASS, AN AMERICAN SLAVE 49 (Houston A. Baker, Jr. ed., Penguin Books 1982) (discussing the rumor that his master was his father, Douglass stated that regardless of the truthfulness of the rumor, "the fact remains, in all its glaring odiousness, that slaveholders have ordained, and by law established, that the children of slave women shall in all cases follow the condition of their mothers"). *See generally* EUGENE D. GENOVESE, ROLL, JORDAN ROLL (First Vintage Books Edition 1976) (1972) (discussing abolitionists' discourse regarding the sexual exploitation of female slaves).

81. *See generally* Jacobus tenBroek, *Thirteenth Amendment to the Constitution of the United States: Consummation to Abolition and Key to the Fourteenth Amendment,* 39 CAL. L. REV. 171, 202 (1951) (stating that "[the meaning of the Thirteenth Amendment] is to be gathered from the comprehensive goals of the abolitionist crusade"). *Id.* at 176–79 (remarking that the anti-slavery movement contributed greatly to the success of the Thirteenth Amendment and that insight on the intention of the framers in drafting the Thirteenth Amendment can be gained from surveying the issues addressed by abolitionists of the day).

82. *See* JOHN D'EMILIO & ESTELLE B. FREEDMAN, INTIMATE MATTERS: A HISTORY OF SEXUALITY IN AMERICA 101 (1988) ("Incidents of brutal rape and sadistic beatings of slave women, [were] popularized in nineteenth century abolitionist literature. . . . "); *see also* CHARLES OLCOTT, SLAVERY AND ABOLITION: TWO LECTURES ON THE SUBJECTS OF SLAVERY AND ABOLITION 112 (Black Heritage Library Collection 1971) (1838) (discussing how white males sexually abused female slaves to produce mulatto children who became the most marketable slaves); SLAVE TESTIMONY: TWO CENTURIES OF LETTERS, SPEECHES, INTERVIEWS, AND AUTOBIOGRAPHIES 225 (John W. Blassingame ed., 1977) (discussing accounts of female slave abuse); WENDELL PHILLIPS, *Philosophy of the Abolition Movement, in* SPEECHES, LECTURES AND LETTERS 98 (Negro University Press 1968) (1863) (evidencing that the sexual and reproductive abuse of female slaves gave rise to substantial abolitionist commentary).

83. Douglas Colbert contends that a modern application of the Thirteenth Amendment is dependent upon one's knowledge of the history of slavery. *See, e.g.,* Douglas Colbert, *Liberating the Thirteenth Amendment,* 30 HARV. C.R.-C.L. L. REV. 1, 1 (1995) ("By linking present racial discrimination to this nation's history of slavery and apartheid, a Thirteenth Amendment analysis uniquely addresses existing racial and economic injustice as modern relics and badges of slavery.").

84. *See* Bobilin v. Board of Educ., 403 F.Supp. 1095, 1101 (D. Haw. 1975) ("[T]he elimination of African slavery, while the prime motivating cause of the Thirteenth Amendment, nevertheless does not demark the outer limits of [this] Amendment's application."); Sethy v. Alameda County Water Dist., 545 F.2d 1157, 1160 (9th Cir. 1976) ("The Thirteenth Amendment is not a mere prohibition of discriminatory state laws, but an affirmative declaration that all vestiges of slavery [are] illegal.").

85. *See, e.g.,* Turner v. Unification Church, 473 F.Supp 367, 375 (D.R.I. 1978), *aff'd,* 602 F.2d 458 (1st Cir. 1979) ("Involuntary servitude usually includes both elements of physical restraint and complete psychological domination.").

86. *See* Akhil Reed Amar & David Widawsky, *Child Abuse and the Thirteenth Amendment,* 105 HARV. L. REV. 1359, 1370 (1992). Amar and Widawsky state that since forced labor does not exhaust the meaning of slavery, the sweeping words and vision of the Amendment prohibited not only forced labor for the master's economic enrichment,

but all forms of chattel slavery. *Id.* at 1359. As such, they contend that an accurate definition of slavery under the Thirteenth Amendment should reflect how slaves interpreted their condition. *Id.* at 1370.

87. *See* tenBroek, *supra* note 81, at 177–78 (citing CONG. GLOBE, 38th Cong., 1st Sess. 1439, 1440, 2989, 2990 (1864)).

88. *Id.*

89. For recent articles supporting the use of the Thirteenth Amendment as a challenge to a variety of modern conditions, see Amar & Widawsky, *supra* note 86; Jennifer Conn, *Sexual Harassment: A Thirteenth Amendment Response,* 28 COLUM. J.L. & SOC. PROBS. 519 (1995); Samantha Halem, *Slaves to Fashion: A Thirteenth Amendment Litigation Strategy to Abolish Sweatshops in the Garment Industry,* 36 SAN DIEGO L. REV. 397 (1999); Marcellene E. Hearn, *A Thirteenth Amendment Defense of the Violence Against Women Act,* 146 U. PA. L. REV. 1097 (1988); Andrew Koppelman, *Forced Labor: A Thirteenth Amendment Defense of Abortion,* 84 NW. U.L. REV. 480 (1990); Marco Masoni, *Green Badge of Slavery,* 2 GEO J. ON FIGHTING POVERTY 97 (1997); Julie A. Nice, *Welfare Servitude,* 1 GEO J. ON FIGHTING POVERTY 340 (1994); Joyce McConnell, *Beyond Metaphor: Battered Women, Involuntary Servitude and the Thirteenth Amendment,* 4 YALE J.L. & FEMINISM 207 (1992); David Tedhams, *The Reincarnation of "Jim Crow": A Thirteenth Amendment Analysis of Colorado's Amendment 2,* 4 TEMP. POL. & CIV. RTS. L. REV. 133 (1994).

90. 392 U.S. 409 (1968).

91. *Id.* at 439.

92. *Id.* at 444–49 (Douglas, J., concurring).

93. *Id.* at 441–43.

94. *Id.* at 440–43.

95. *Id.* at 439.

96. *Jones,* 392 U.S. at 439.

97. *Id.* at 438–39.

98. *See id.* at 439 (noting that the Thirteenth Amendment abolished slavery and regardless "[w]hether or not the Amendment itself did any more than that . . . it is clear that the Enabling Clause of that Amendment empowered Congress to do much more . . . ").

99. *See generally id.*

100. 104 U.S. 3, 25 (1883) (invalidating the Civil Rights Act of 1875 because Congress did not have authority to legislate against social segregation in public accommodation).

101. *See* City of Memphis v. Greene, 451 U.S. 100, 124–26 (1981) (affirming Congress' power to define badges and incidents and enact legislation accordingly); *see also* Runyon v. McCrary, 427 U.S. 160, 179 (1976) (quoting *Jones,* 392 U.S. at 443) (finding that Congress has the power to prohibit discriminatory admissions policies at private schools, so that "a dollar in the hands of a Negro will purchase the same thing as a dollar in the hands of a white man").

102. The Thirteenth Amendment was as revolutionary as the Civil War in that it turned issues that were considered purely a function of state governments into interests that were within the province of the federal government. DONALD E. LIVELY, THE CONSTITUTION AND RACE 41 (1992).

103. *Jones,* 392 U.S. at 439.

104. The Act states:

> [A]ll persons born in the United States... are hereby declared to be citizens of the United States; and such citizens, of every race and color, without regard to any previous condition of slavery or involuntary servitude... have the same right[s]... and... full and equal benefit of all laws... as is enjoyed by white citizens[.]

Enforcement Act of 1870, ch. 114, § 18, 16 Stat. 140, 144 (1870) (current version at 42 U.S.C. §§ 1981–1982 (1987)).

105. *Jones,* 392 U.S. at 440.

106. *Id.* at 439–40.

107. "All citizens of the United States shall have the same right, in every State and Territory, as is enjoyed by white citizens thereof to inherit, purchase, lease, sell, hold, and convey real and personal property...." 42 U.S.C. §§ 1981–1982 (1987).

108. *Jones,* 392 U.S. at 413.

109. *Id.* at 442–43.

110. *Id.* at 445 (Douglas, J., concurring).

111. The Court quoted:

> The constitutional question in this case, therefore, comes to this: Does the authority of Congress to enforce the Thirteenth Amendment "by appropriate legislation" include the power to eliminate all racial barriers to the acquisition of real and personal property? We think the answer to that question is plainly yes.... For this Court recognized long ago that, whatever else they may have encompassed, the badges and incidents of slavery—its "burden and disabilities"—included restraints upon "those fundamental rights which are the essence of civil freedom...."

Id. at 439, 441 (quoting The Civil Rights Cases, 109 U.S. 3, 20, 22 (1883)).

112. *Id.* at 441–43.

113. *Id.*

114. *Jones,* 392 U.S. at 443. *Jones* left the question of the reach of the first clause unanswered, *Id.* at 439. Therefore, the scope of what liberties are regarded as a form of freedom in the first clause, which is self-executing, is not clearly bounded. *Jones* also explicitly overruled *Hodges v. United States,* 203 U.S. 1, 18 (1906), which determined that neither a mere personal assault or trespass, nor appropriation operates to reduce a person to a condition of slavery. *Jones,* 392 U.S. at 441 n.78.

115. For more thorough discussions of the promise of *Jones,* see Colbert, *supra* note 83, at 2–3; Conn, *supra* note 89, at 545; Halem, *supra* note 89, at 453 n. 106; Koppelman, *supra* note 89, at 498–99; Masoni, *supra* note 89, at 104.

116. *See* United States v. Kozminski, 487 U.S. 931, 942–44 (1988) (recognizing that while slavery as a broad concept under the first section of the Thirteenth Amendment, previous courts had declined the opportunity to define the term and deciding to follow those courts' disinclination).

117. *Jones,* 392 U.S. at 439 ("'By its own unaided force and effect,' the Thirteenth Amendment 'abolished slavery, and established universal freedom.'") (quoting The Civil Rights Cases, 109 U.S. 3, 20 (1883)).

118. This was also reflected in the congressional debates when Rep. E.C. Ingersoll of Illinois declared that the Amendment meant "that rights of man-kind, without regard to color or race, are respected and protected." G. SIDNEY BUCHANAN ET AL., THE

QUEST FOR FREEDOM: A LEGAL HISTORY OF THE THIRTEENTH AMENDMENT 9 (1976) (quoting CONG. GLOBE, 38th Cong., 1st Sess. 2989–90 (1864)).

119. *Jones,* 392 U.S. at 441–43.

120. *See, e.g.,* Nice, *supra* note 89, at 344 (stating that "[m]ost Thirteenth Amendment decisions... have interpreted... statutory protections enacted by Congress pursuant to the second section of the Amendment").

121. *See generally* Lauren Kares, *The Unlucky Thirteenth: A Constitutional Amendment in Search of a Doctrine,* 80 CORNELL L. REV. 372 (1995) (describing the difficulty litigators, courts and scholars have had in interpreting and applying the Thirteenth Amendment given its textual ambiguities and its uneven doctrinal development).

122. *See, e.g., Norplant Survives Lawsuits in Texas, supra* note 8.

123. For example, in their most recent edition of the popular guide to women's health, *Our Bodies, Ourselves,* the editors at the Boston Health Book Collective specifically warn women against using Norplant given its safety record and problems associated with removal. THE BOSTON WOMEN'S HEALTH BOOK COLLECTIVE, OUR BODIES, OURSELVES FOR THE NEW CENTURY: A BOOK BY AND FOR WOMEN 318–22 (1998).

124.

> Careful investigation and research can expose previously overlooked, neglected, or even unknown facts that would aid in establishing a Thirteenth Amendment claim. Then... plaintiffs can try to "connect the dots" and compel a court to grasp the true cultural meaning of the act. By equating [the practice or condition] with elements fundamental to slavery or by tracing the origins of such discrimination to slavery and its aftermath, plaintiffs will, at the very least, expand the record and refocus the court's inquiry.

Masoni, *supra* note 89, 117.

125. Patricia Hill Collins makes precisely this point when she states that the "welfare mother" image is "[e]ssentially an updated version of the breeder woman... [which] provides an ideological justification for efforts to harness Black women's fertility to the needs of a changing political economy." COLLINS, *supra* note 49, at 76.

126. *See generally supra* note 73 and accompanying text.

127. *See, e.g.,* Kares, *supra* note 121 (arguing that "[t]he absence of a uniform standard for finding involuntary servitude renders the rights of recourse available under the Thirteen Amendment unpredictable and largely useless").

128. *See, e.g.,* Nice, *supra* note 89, at 344 (discussing the viability of the Thirteenth Amendment in current legal matters).

129. *Id.*

130. *See* ROBERTS, *supra* note 2, at 90 ("During the 1970s sterilization became the most rapidly growing form of birth control in the United States.... It was a common belief among Blacks in the South that Black women were routinely sterilized without their informed consent and for no valid medical reason.").

PART FOUR

Race and Ethnicity in Popular Culture and Community

On the Internet . . .

Sites appropriate to Part Four

The Center for Equal Opportunity, a nonprofit research institution, is a project of the Equal Opportunity Foundation. It sponsors conferences, supports research, and publishes policy briefs and monographs on issues related to race, ethnicity, assimilation, and public policy. The site includes information on racial preferences, immigration and assimilation, and multicultural education.

`http://www.ceousa.org`

The DePaul University's Diversity Forum pursues the preservation, enrichment, and transmission of knowledge and cultures across a broad scope of academic disciplines and human endeavors. This site includes resources on race, gender, religion, ethnicity, sexual orientation, size/weight, age, and disability. You can also submit questions to the Diversity Advice column.

`http://diversity.depaul.edu/index2.html`

The Michigan Electronic Library Multicultural Links site is an excellent resource. Over 80 sites are referenced, including minority and diversity links, African American resources, Asian American resources, Latin American resources, and Native American resources.

`http://mel.lib.mi.us/social/SOC-cultures.html`

CHAPTER 12 The Media

12.1 DONALD TRICARICO

Read All About It!

Italian Americans are the fourth largest White ethnic group in the United States, making up roughly 6 percent of the U.S. population. Although Italians began migrating to the United States during the colonial period, the largest immigration of Italians took place between 1880 and 1920, when some 4 million southern Italians came to the United States to escape economic stagnation and political and social mistreatment by an oppressive government. They soon formed ethnic enclaves primarily in the Northeast known as "Little Italys," and they sought low-skilled jobs in public works projects. Several scholars point out that early in the historical migration of Italians, U.S. society perceived them as an intellectually inferior ethnic group. Italian Americans were quickly portrayed as associated with organized crime syndicates. The media have furthered this "gangster" image of Italian Americans with such movies as *The Godfather, The Untouchables, Goodfellas,* and *Prizzi's Honor.*

The following selection from "Read All About It! Representations of Italian Americans in the Print Media in Response to the Bensonhurst Racial Killing," an original essay written for this book, exemplifies how old stereotypes about Italian Americans may resurface in some muted form during periods of ethnic conflict. In it, Donald Tricarico states that media accounts of the Bensonhurst racial killing in 1989 "invoked a stigmatized version of Italian American ethnicity, emphasizing themes of bigotry, criminality and social disorganization." Furthermore, Tricarico considers the media's treatment of Italian American stereotypes in the context of "deviance construction" and "identity politics."

Key Concept: Italian Americans, mass media culture, deviance construction, racial status, and symbolic ethnicity

Abstract: Mass media culture is a key site for the construction of ethnic identity. This article examines representations of Italian Americans in the print media in relation to the Bensonhurst (Brooklyn) racial killing in 1989. It maintains that media accounts invoked a stigmatized version of Italian American ethnicity, emphasizing themes of bigotry, criminality and social disorganization. Media representations are understood in the context of deviance construction and identity politics; in particular, foregrounding Italian American ethnicity compartmentalized racial guilt. Finally, implications of this media episode for Italian American identity are considered, with special reference to issues of racial status and "symbolic ethnicity".

Ethnic identity is variable and fluid; boundaries, cultural referents, and modes of expression are negotiated in response to shifting circumstances. Identity negotiation is inherently political, with individuals and groups positioning themselves for scarce resources. Outcomes are a product of "the opportunities and constraints" that contestants encounter at a particular time and place, and the cultural capital that they "bring to that encounter" (Cornell and Hartmann, 1998: 195).

Media culture is a prominent "construction site" for ethnic identity (Cornell and Hartmann: 195). Representations in the mass media constitute a significant "external boundary" for ethnic group identity, indicating a disposition to make ethnicity relevant and to invest it with certain cultural meanings (Royce, 1982: 2–5). Media representations reflect particular social interests and ideologies (Ferguson, 1998: 130; Grossberg et al., 1998: 178–183). Establishment media, in particular, have traditionally acted as "guardians of controlling value systems" (Schemerhorn, 1970: 12). The "cultural stories" about ethnic groups comprise a major store of knowledge held by outsiders (Lipsitz, 1998); distilled into stereotypes, they "underlie and condition interaction" in multiethnic societies (Lyman and Douglas, 1973: 347).

This article examines the media representations of Italian Americans in response to the killing of a Black teenager in the Bensonhurst section of Brooklyn on August 23, 1989, an event that has been characterized as "one of the most infamous bias incidents in recent history" (Pinderhughes, 1997: 2). A consideration of Italian American ethnicity accompanied the news reports and commentary on the killing, the protest marches and the subsequent court cases. This *public discourse,* which spanned the better part of one year, comprised an "external boundary" that has special relevance for ethnic identity development.

Contemporary discourse about ethnicity in the mainstream media, informed by the implicit acceptance of multicultural diversity, tends to be celebratory and to specifically avoid negative generalizations. Thus, a local PBS station has produced a documentary film series on American ethnic groups that

> tries to create a kind of warm and fuzzy photo-album profile of each ethnic group and has a tendency to praise that group to the heavens, often citing the same virtues across the board: strong work ethic, solid family values, religious piety and the ability to make great food. (Berger, 1998).

In a society where racial and ethnic tolerance is legally and morally constrained, untoward characterizations of racial and ethnic groups are typically kept off the public stage. Once a despised immigrant minority, Italian Americans have lately received their share of ethnic celebration in the media. The above-mentioned PBS series celebrated them with two installments. A *New York Times Magazine* cover story in 1983 (Hall) trumpeted "the new respectability" of Italian Americans in mainstream life *without* compromising ethnic values like personal warmth and family cohesion. Even the tenement slums that were the bane of reformers like Jacob Riis and fodder for urban developers like Robert Moses are now cherished in the press. Recently, the *Times* carried two stories about neighborhoods in lower Manhattan that were settlements during the period of mass immigration from Italy before World War One, portraying them as colorful places for its readers to live:

> Historically, this northern edge of Little Italy was a sleepy family neighborhood, home to several waves of immigrants who settled in its five- and six-story tenement buildings. Some of them moved up and out, but others turned into the gray-haired grandmothers who still sit out on the sidewalk in pleasant weather. (Cohen, 1998)

> Like Mrs. Maggio, Tony Dapolito recalls a simpler time. His Vesuvio Bakery is an institution in the neighborhood.... During business hours the man some call the Mayor of Greenwich Village holds court, giving treats to babies, catching up and talking politics with a seemingly endless stream of people. (Lappe, 1998)

Bensonhurst has been acclaimed for its ethnic culture, although it has generated considerably less interest than the historic Manhattan neighborhoods settled during the mass migration from Italy. Two years after the Yusuf Hawkins killing, a *Times* food critic writing about the late summer zucchini harvest in backyard gardens portrayed Bensonhurst as "a living Italian neighborhood" where families make red wine and "there are first communion celebrations that cost a year's rent"; the article featured a local restauranteur who not only puts zucchini on the menu but sings opera for his customers (O'Neill, 1991). Images such as these were conspicuously missing in the media response to the Hawkins killing, which is not remarkable given the circumstances of a "racial killing". What is remarkable in light of the current etiquette of public discourse about ethnicity was the negative representations of Italian American group life and identity.

This media discourse about Italian American ethnicity is significant given the increasingly accepted view in American sociology, evidenced in texts on racial and ethnic relations, that Italian Americans and European ancestry groups in general have only trivial interest as ethnic subjects. A neo-assimilationist paradigm has subsumed Italian American ethnicity within a "dominant group" ethnicity; to this extent, Italian Americans as a group are believed to have largely metamorphosed into *white,* or *Euro,* Americans (Doane, 1999; Hollinger, 1999).

The "media spectacle" (Kellner, 1995) that followed the Bensonhurst incident did not subscribe to this scenario. Given the central assumption of a "racial killing", there was ample room to construe events in terms of race relations. While race figured prominently, it was not a sufficient explanation. At times, nationality was juxtaposed to race, with Bensonhurst residents depicted as both Italian American and white. There were also times when nationality mattered more than race, and even confounded or contradicted it with scenarios in which Italian Americans were "less than white" (Roediger, 1994). Characterizations of ethnic group life in Bensonhurst as primordial and communal did not fit a "dominant group" model in which ethnicity is "optional" and "symbolic" (Waters, 1990; Gans, 1999).

This article is concerned with the cultural process of labeling "that is crucial to the construction of ethnicity" (diLeonardo, 1984:23). It pursues three interrelated issues. First, it distills the media "stories" that "constructed" an Italian American ethnicity in relation to the Bensonhurst "racial killing"; these accounts featured themes of social marginality and deviance, "re-presenting" Italian Americans in terms of the stigma historically reserved for a disparaged immigrant group. Second, the article asks why deviant meanings were appropriated as the epitome of Italian American ethnicity and, even more fundamentally, why Italian American identity mattered, or was foregrounded, in media accounts of a "racial killing"; these questions warrant a consideration of the interests and agendas that social actors bring to such "encounters" (Cornell and Hartmann, 1998) and, more generally, "the processes that motivate ethnic boundary construction" (Nagel, 1999). Finally, since ethnicity is negotiated across a "double boundary" (Royce, 1982), the article ponders the implications of this episode of media representations for the identity strategies of Italian Americans.

STAGING ETHNICITY: PLACING ITALIAN AMERICANS AT THE SCENE OF THE CRIME

The event that occasioned this media encounter was the shooting death of a Black teenager on August 23, 1989. Sixteen year old Yusuf Hawkins and three teen age friends travelled to Bensonhurst by subway from the East New York section of Brooklyn to look at a used automobile that was for sale. Approaching the corner of Bay Ridge Avenue and 20th Avenue shortly before 9:30 PM, they were confronted by as many as twenty five youths from the neighborhood. The latter intended to engage Black and Hispanic males who were invited to a sixteenth birthday party for Gina Feliciano; Feliciano reportedly had "jilted" someone in the Bensonhurst contingent, Keith Mondello, for "a Black lover". It was Mondello who assembled the neighborhood group to seek revenge. The unsuspecting Hawkins and his friends were mistaken for Feliciano's guests. As matters spun out of control, four shots were fired from a handgun and Hawkins was struck twice in the chest (see Stone, 1989 for an overview of the incident).

The killing spawned a protest march on August 26 through the streets of Bensonhurst organized by Black activist organizations under the leadership of Reverend Al Sharpton and the Reverend Herbert Daughtry. More than three hundred demonstrators clashed with local residents, with police in riot gear caught in between. Newspapers and television produced incendiary visual images of the hecklers, most of whom were young males, insulting Black marchers with conspicuous displays of watermelons and the chant of "Go home, niggers, go home" (Harney and Lubrano, 1989). This event had a special significance for the media narrative, not only because it compounded the tragedy of a "racial killing", but because it put the media spotlight on the Bensonhurst community.

The Bensonhurst case resulted in extensive coverage in the print media, the bulk of it reporting on the circumstances of the killing and the subsequent criminal trials (the incident was also the subject of a documentary film narrated by Shelby Steele, "Seven Days in Bensonhurst" that first aired on PBS on May 15, 1990). New York City newspapers were obviously a major forum and this article will focus on those publications; an INFOTRAC search yielded 147 entries associated with the name "Yusuf Hawkins" from *The New York Times* alone. The incident received feature coverage in national news magazines like *Time* and *Newsweek* and was the subject of a cover story in *New York Magazine.* Essays appeared in both *Harper's Magazine* and *Partisan Review,* publications appealing to a cultural elite. The incident was the subject of a book by a free-lance journalist (DeSantis, 1991). Published well after the "media spectacle", it focused on the lives of *dramatis personae* into the inital round of court trials and is significant for muting the ethnic angle.

This discussion is not interested in the Bensonhurst incident itself, nor in media accounts of that incident, but in the way Italian American ethnicity was portrayed in the mainstream print media in response to that incident. Ethnic framing was not evident in every story about Bensonhurst, even those in which ostensibly Italian American actors (i.e., individuals identified by Italian surnames) were present. Most, although not all (e.g., Hamill, 1989), accounts conceptualized the incident as a racial drama in which Bensonhurst residents were cast as "whites":

> 'The black people don't belong here', a white teen-age girl said as she stood on the corner of 20th Avenue and 68th Street, not far from where Yusuf Hawkins was killed. (Terry, 1989)
>
> Bishop Francis J. Mugavero of the Roman Catholic archdiocese of Brooklyn yesterday questioned the decision of some clergymen to conduct protest marches last weekend in Bensonhurst, where a black youth had earlier been shot to death after being chased by a white gang. (Glaberson, 1989)

Bensonhurst residents were also framed by social *class,* although largely to modify racial and ethnic identity:

> Both Bensonhurst and the area of East New York where Mr. Hawkins lived are communities of blue-collar workers, many in construction or holding municipal jobs. (Kaufman, 1989)

> Such comments do not surprise Joanne Carretta, a 26-year-old white woman who has lived in the largely white, working-class neighborhood all of her life. (Terry, 1989)

A class analysis was salient in a November 1989 *New York Magazine* article (Stone, 1989) that emphasized the effects of dislocations in the city's economy on working class communities. Michael Eric Dyson in *The Nation* (1989: 302) utilized a class perspective in juxtaposing "the two racisms"—the racial violence of "tightly-turfed, blue-collar communities" like Bensonhurst and "its less visible but just as vicious middle- and upper-class counterparts".

While acknowledging that Italian Americans were positioned in terms of *race* and *class,* this discussion is specifically interested in the way that *ethnicity* was constructed. This recognizes that there was a "story" about Italian Americans within the Bensonhurst narrative. Certain accounts were notable for the composition of this other story. *The New York Times* published two investigative features within a week of the murder in which the ethnicity of Italian Americans was designated, on page one, as a major plot element (Bohlen, 1989; Kifner, 1989). The newspaper columnists Pete Hamill (1989) and Amy Pagnozzi (1989) offered ascerbic commentaries in the vernacular of ethnic stereotypes. *The Village Voice,* an "alternative" weekly rooted in the bohemian culture of Greenwich Village, published related investigative features on the violent character of Italian American life in Bensonhurst in the September 5, 1989 edition. The memoirs of two former residents of Bensonhurst that were published, respectively, in *Harper's Magazine* in March 1990 and in *Partisan Review* in the summer of 1990 used the killing as a pretext to deconstruct Italian ethnic culture.

From the outset, news reports situated Italian Americans in the unfolding narrative of a "racial killing". Individuals and groups were explicitly framed by their Italian ancestry and heritage. For example, it was noted that the parents of the alleged killer (Joey Fama) "had emigrated from Italy and spoke only Italian at home" (Bohlen, 1989). Ethnicity could also be inferred from the perception of ostensibly Italian surnames, a strategy with limitations as evidenced by a defendant named Mondello whose mother was "originally Jewish" (Stone, 1989). Notwithstanding these glitches, ethnic credentials were liberally reserved for local actors. Thus, the defendants and other Bensonhurst locals were identified as "the children and grandchildren of immigrants from Italy" (Hamill, 1989). The "community" of Bensonhurst was perceived as "predominantly Italian American", with a population that "still lives in a web of traditions and rituals, many of them transplanted from Italy" (Bohlen, 1989). Frequent allusions to the old country underscored the *essentially* Italian American character of Bensonhurst. A front page *New York Times* (Kifner, 1989) feature one week after the killing threw this ethnic dimension into sharp relief in the lead paragraph:

> Banners and lights of red, white and green—the colors of the Italian flag—hang along 18th Avenue in Bensonhurst for the feast of Santa Rosalia. Normally the neighborhood's biggest event of the year, the feast is overshadowed now by the murder of Yusuf K. Hawkins, a black youth who had ventured into the neighborhood to look at a used car and was surrounded by a crowd of white youths and gunned down.

Italian ethnicity was tacitly invoked with references to popular cultural imaging such as street festivals and lawn shrines (Kifner, 1989; Quindlen, 1989; Bohlen, 1989). Local Italian Americans were identified by "elaborate hairdos" (Kifner, 1989) and "ankle bracelets" (Pagnozzi, 1989). Vernacular labels referenced to problematic stereotypes were used for Italian Americans:

> You can still hear Jimmy Roselli singing on the jukebox of the Vegas diner, home away from home to Bensonhurst's *cugines* and *cugettes*. (Pagnozzi, 1989)

A leading role in the narrative was assigned to the "Mafia", a central category for apprehending the meaning of Italian Americans in the popular culture (Kifner, 1989; McAlary, 1989; George, 1989). Allusions to popular films like *Goodfellas, Do The Right Thing,* and *Saturday Night Fever* lent additional credibility to ethnic framing (Dyson, 1989; Lee, 1989). Blurring the distinction between fiction and reality was a signature element of the "media spectacle". In a guest column written for *The New York Daily News* (1989), Spike Lee uses the comments of a character in a film to explain the animus of Yusuf Hawkins' killers: "Pino, the racist son in 'Do The Right Thing', tells Sal, his father, 'We should stay in Bensonhurst and the niggers should stay in their neighborhood' ". In the column, Lee, who was a visible participant in the first protest march staged in Bensonhurst, noted that the film's script was drawn from [the] Howard Beach incident in 1986—a case of life (Bensonhurst) imitating art ("Do The Right Thing") imitating life (Howard Beach).

ETHNIC FRAMING

The mass media "make meanings" in the sense that "codes" are employed to "interpret reality" (Grossberg et al., 1998: 178). These interpretations of reality are *representations*. As Grossberg et al. (179) point out,

> The word *representation* literally means 're-presentation'. To represent Something means to take an original, mediate it, and play it back.

In the Bensonhurst narrative, several representations emerged to frame Italian American actors:

1. *provinciality* and *bigotry;*
2. *criminality,* and;
3. *social disorganization.*

These themes comprised an "interpretive framework" (Ferguson, 1998: 132) that supplied the main scaffolding for the "story" about Italian Americans embedded in the Bensonhurst murder drama. They purported to inform the public who Italian Americans were as an ethnic group, and who they were not. The interpretations that were offered precluded or overshadowed alternative ways of characterizing Italian American identity.

PROVINCIALITY AND BIGOTRY

Twentieth Avenue in Bensonhurst starts in the Hudson River, where it is called Gravesend Bay, only a couple of miles from the Atlantic Ocean. You can see the ocean across the Belt Parkway, but Bensonhurst rarely looks. (Sullivan, 1990: 13).

A major thread in the Italian American story stresses the group's social and cultural isolation. The first two feature stories in *The New York Times* referred to Bensonhurst as "a closed community", a theme that echoed in synonyms such as "insular", "provincial", and "tightknit" (Kifner, 1989; Bohlen, 1989). DeMarco-Torgovnick, a professor of English at Duke, elaborated the isolation theme in a memoir written for *Partisan Review.* A cultural insider who escaped via an academic career and an exogamous marriage, she contended that "Italian Americans in Bensonhurst are notable for their cohesiveness and provinciality" (1990: 458). She described a way of life that "tends toward certain forms of inertia" and envelops residents, including her own parents, in an almost pathological fear of "change" (459). *New York Post* columnist Amy Pagnozzi similarly portrayed the life choices of young Italian Americans as circumscribed and "predictable":

> The typical *cugette* might work in Manhattan as a secretary or receptionist while she waits to be married to the typical *cugine,* who might get a job at the airlines or in construction or on the police force.
>
> And they marry: definitely within their race, almost definitely to an Italian, probably to someone from the neighborhood.

The "provinciality" of Bensonhurst was underscored by distinctions of cultural taste.[1] A *Times* reporter remarked on the "plastic pink flamingos and ceramic madonnas" found in some front yards (Terry, 1989). Even Andrew Sullivan's alternative interpretation Bensonhurst Italian Americans slipped a comment on the local taste culture with a description of "a statue of Our Lady of Guadelupe on the lawn, covered in cellophane to protect her from the rain". Another *Times* reporter called attention to young girls with "elaborate hairdos and names spelled out in gold necklaces" (Kifner, 1989). Cultural distinctions assumed an invidious dimension in the columns. *New York Post* columnist Pagnozzi (1989) sarcastically described a neighborhood landscape in which "big catering houses are as plentiful as the auto supply shops" (Pagnozzi, 1989).

In a column inspired by ugly altercations between Bensonhurst residents and predominantly Black protest marchers, *The Post*'s Pete Hamill (1989) derisively catalogued local styles like "tatoos" and the "Guido cut, the hair cut straight across the back of the neck". Demonstrating the ear of Bernard Shaw's Professor Higgins, Hamill reserved extended comment for the local jargon,

> the few words and phrases that make up the language of Guidoville: "Ey, wah, ming, mah... 'Ey, I like ta get some a dat... Whassamatta wit you, Joonyuh... I truckin' tole huh, I says to huh, I says, I dough wan no truckin' backtawk, and den I slap huh in da truckin' mout', I mean, in the mout', cause dat's all a trucking broad respects, a rap in da mout... Huh mudthuh tells huh to be home oirly, says ta huh, Who you truckin' gonna listen ta, ya truckin' mudthuh aw me? Mah..."

The portrayal of Italian American "insularity" entailed the repudiation of core middle class, American values. Underscoring the false arrogance of "Guidoville", Hamill wrote that

> The Guido decides early that homework is for jerks. So is work... Go to a library? Read a book? Finish high school? Go to a university? *Figget abo't it!* Om gonna go work construkshun, eight bills an hour!

Although Hamill attempts to distinguish "Guido" from the majority of "respectable" people in Bensonhurst, this was undermined by the use of group stereotypes for Italian Americans.

In a less strident voice, Grizzuti-Harrison (1990: 75) recalled that, in her day, "Italians didn't believe in college because it threatened family authority", adding that "this has not changed". Interestingly, Grizzuti-Harrison and DeMarco-Torgovnick both drew invidious contrasts in regard to Jewish culture and credit their relationships with Jews and liberal Jewish values for liberating them from the oppressiveness of Italian American life in Bensonhurst. Likewise, a CBS television producer named Alan Wiseman (1989) maintained in a *Times* Op-Ed piece that he took refuge in his father's Jewish heritage to escape the obtuse pettiness of his mother's Italian American ancestral culture. DeMarco-Torgovnick, who went on to become a professor at Duke University, found it difficult merely to visit Bensonhurst, the community where she grew up; a stay at her parental home for "several days" when her father is hospitalized by a stroke is enough to make her feel like she is "going to go crazy" (1990:465).

"Insularity" and "provincialism" were not portrayed merely as cultural eccentricity, but were linked to compelling moral issues. In particular, the media narrative underlined a tribal morality that featured exclusion of strangers. This tribalism was evident in the assertion of a "neighborhood loyalist" interviewed by Bauman and Chittum in *The Village Voice* (1989): "This neighborhood has been Italian for 100 years and it's not going to change". *Times* Op-Ed columnist Anna Quindlen (1990) purported to capture the essence of communal *amorality* in the blasé remark of an elderly woman that the media attention and the protest marches "had ruined the feast of Santa Rosalia".

DeMarco-Torgovnick identified this dark side of Italian American insularity and provincialism, adding that "only the slightest pressure turns those qualities into prejudice and racism" (1990: 458). Grizzuti-Harrison (1990: 71) portrays Bensonhurst Italian Americans as "so embattled": "the 'Americans', the Jews, the others—were out to get them", although the frequency of "internecine fights" leads her to conclude that mistrust and fear dominated relationships *within* the ethnic group as well (71). Memories were retrieved depicting a strong animus toward Jews. Grizzuti-Harrison maintained that "almost all" of her "Italian neighbors were casually anti-semitic" (1990: 77). This corroborated Alan Wiseman's *Times* Op-Ed piece (1989) which depicted the pervasiveness of anti-semitism in the Flatbush (Brooklyn) Italian American community of his youth. Wiseman proceeds to establish its more violent proclivities, including a vivid recollection of orthodox Jewish children receiving "a regularly scheduled pummeling every Friday outside the rectory" at the hands of older Italian American youth.

These personal experiences with anti-semitism established a precedence for Italian American "racism and prejudice". The most egregious manifestation of Italian American tribalism in the media narrative was the deep hostility toward Blacks. A front page *New York Times* story immediately following the killing reported "blunt expressions of racism" in "interviews with dozens of Bensonhurst residents" (Kifner, 1989). Another *Times* reporter described local residents "flaunting a racism so blunt that it shocked even veterans of the civil rights movement in Mississippi" (Bohlen, 1989). These and other articles established the overt ("blunt") and ordinary character of Italian American racial bigotry. Thus, "Richie, a clerk from an auto-supply store" concludes that the girl (Gina Feliciano) whose birthday party set the stage for the murder should be faulted for the killing because "Any girl who brings blacks into this neighborhood is asking for trouble" (Pagnozzi, 1989). Even a venerable senior citizen like DeMarco-Torgovnick's father, when challenged to morally respond to the killing, can casually and unequivocally remark that Blacks "don't belong" in the neighborhood (1990:459). Once sentiments such as these were recorded, characterizations of Bensonhurst Italian Americans as "tightknit" and "insular" have to be read as coded representations of racist sentiments aimed at Blacks and other racial minorities.

Although racism was perceived as endemic to the community and ethnic culture, young males were portrayed as the agents of racial aggression. Street violence in Bensonhurst and in other Italian American areas like Howard Beach, in fact, was perpetrated by males in their late teens and media accounts described them as inveterately hostile to Blacks and other minorities. Indeed, racial violence was depicted as the consummate expression of their peer group life and their role in the community (Baumann and Chittum, 1989; see also Pinderhughes, 1997). In a *Village Voice* article, these young males, "armed with baseball bats", were portrayed as having "taken their battle [with racial minorities] to the streets" (Bauman and Chittum, 1989).[2]

The portrait of embedded bigotry was tempered in a *New York Magazine* story which maintained that tolerance for nonwhites had significantly improved in the years immediately preceding the killing (Stone, 1989). The article noted that, despite some organized opposition, the nonwhite residential population of Bensonhurst had been increasing. It also pointed out the apparently contradictory fact that a nineteen year old Black man (Russell Gibbons) was part of the mob that confronted Yusuf Hawkins and his friends. After recounting "anecdotes of racism", Andrew Sullivan's article in the *New Republic* (1990) reported that racial mixing in Bensonhurst was more common than what was portrayed in media accounts immediately following the killing.

On the whole, however, the perception of racial tolerance was overwhelmed by the weight of images that framed Italian Americans as racists; one journalist overgeneralized "racist incidents" in communities like Bensonhurst and Howard Beach into a trend whereby "blacks have been murdered in predominantly Italian neighborhoods" (Haalasa, 1989). Discrepancies with the dominant interpretation that cast the killers as Italian Americans and Italian Americans as racists were muted or swept aside (see below).

CRIMINALITY

The Bensonhurst "media spectacle" made criminality an integral element of both the killing and local Italian American life. An especially significant role was attributed to the "Mafia". Mafia employment was portrayed as highly desirable to young males.

> Would-be wiseguys talk in hushed tones about an uncle who's "connected", a cousin who's "involved", hoping to be set up for life... (Pagnozzi, 1989).

A *Village Voice* article uncovered a "hard-core" element striving for "a position in 'La Cosa Nostra'"; one "wannabe gangster", a twenty year old named "Frank", was portrayed as auditioning for local "wiseguys" by committing small-time crime (Bauman and Chittum, 1989). According to *Daily News* columnist Mike McAlary (1989), "In Bensonhurst, as in Howard Beach, we now have wiseguys and wannabe gangsters all over the place". In a national weekly magazine, a song by Melvin Gibbs called "Howard Beach Memoirs" was recalled for the lyrics: "Ethnically, the only thing these white Italian youth have to look up to is gangsters" (Haalasa, 1989). *Village Voice* reporters remarked that street violence aimed at nonwhites by Italian American youth was "[f]ortified by their faith in the Godfather myth" (Bauman and Chittum, 1989).

Mafia influence was portrayed as having more far reaching significance. A *Village Voice* article reported that "the Mafia presence still pervades Bensonhurst, cloaking the neighborhood in ostentatious secrecy, like the tinted windows of the stretch limousines that line 18th Avenue" (Bauman and Chittum, 1989). A *New York Times* story noted that "Federal prosecutors say the Mafia... has a strong presence in the community" and that the Mafia was part of the cultural baggage "transplanted from Italy" (Bohlen, 1989). Bauman and Chittum (1989) eased the Mafia into the local landscape:

> A few blocks from their corner is the old bakery where the "Pizza Connection" heroin busts were made. At 74th Street and 18th Avenue is the Caffe Giardino, allegedly owned by Giuseppe Gambino, nephew of Carlo, who served as "boss of bosses" in New York until his death in 1976.

There is also the impression that Mafia codes are embedded in a shared culture or, perhaps, vice versa. The opening paragraph in DeMarco-Torgovnick's essay (1990) makes the case that the Mafia has historically received legitimation from Bensonhurst Italian Americans for excluding Blacks:

> The Mafia protects the neighborhood, our fathers say, with that peculiar satisfied pride with which law-abiding Italian Americans refer to the Mafia: the Mafia protects the neighborhood from "the coloreds". In the fifties and sixties, I heard that information repeated in whispers, in neighborhood parks and in the yard at school in Bensonhurst. The same information probably passes today in the parks (the word now "blacks", not "coloreds")...

While the reluctance of the local population to give testimony in the case can be attributed to Mafia intimidation, the term "Bensonhurst amnesia" used by prosecutors and the press implied complicity on the part of Bensonhurst residents in Mafia moral codes (Roberts, 1989; see also Pinderhughes, 1997).

For the most part, however, it is a "wiseguy" street culture with indirect and latent ties to the Mafia that is the centerpiece of the criminality motif. Bauman and Chittum (1989) elaborated on the menacing character of these youth, especially their commitment to violence:

> "For some reason, I'm up all the time", says Frank. "I just like to abuse people".
>
> Even when the guys on the corner are not doing anything to attract police attention, they play at being wiseguys. Most of them own BB guns. And on a really slow night, they meander down to Gravesend Bay and shoot at rats—"target practice" for more serious games.

The article emphasized the inveterate ruthlessness of their ways. Sal, "a young enforcer for the mob", sent a message to local "crackheads":

> Sal soon caught up with the next kid. He stabbed him in the throat—slit him—17 stitches.

The authors concluded that the predatory disposition of these youth meant that "pedestrians", not just Blacks, were vulnerable to "group harassment" in Bensonhurst. In fact, they cautioned that the "wiseguy" menace was being exported to upscale neighborhoods when the member of one crew bragged about "going over to the Village to beat up some Yuppies" (Bauman and Chittum, 1989). As discussed below, the violent nature of menacing Italian American youth was later elaborated by a "feral" metaphor that sounded notes of dehumanization and primitive danger (Roberts, 1990; Letwin, 1989).

"Wiseguy" street culture was the link between the Mafia (*the* mob) and "the mob" of neighborhood youth that confronted Yusuf Hawkins and his friends. It was noted in the first news reports that the youth who allegedly shot Yusuf Hawkins had relatives with affiliations to a Brooklyn crime family; a certain uncle allegedly helped him flee the city and acted to suppress harmful testimony against him (Kifner, 1989). In addition, the youth who assembled the neighborhood mob was rumored to have been sponsored by the Mafia as a low-level drug dealer (Stone, 1989).

SOCIAL DISORGANIZATION

A third frame in the media narrative depicts an Italian American community in disarray and in eclipse. In this scenario, Bensonhurst is "the last Italian neighborhood in the city" (George, 1989). It is portrayed as imminently threatened by unwelcome outsiders, especially immigrants from Asia, the Caribbean, and Central America. This had, in fact, been occuring, as Italian Americans continued to leave for more suburban settings. Interestingly, the media narrative largely ignored processes of acculturation and upward mobility, which is difficult to reconcile with the assumption of cultural backwardness.

Notwithstanding this discrepancy, Bensonhurst was portrayed as being on the brink of ethnic succession by racial minorities. This succession was seen as corroding Italian American institutions. *A Village Voice* story delineated an apocalyptic scenario where "remaining white homelands" like Bensonhurst "turn into Third World Villages", "the local pizzerias will sell beef patties", and new ethnic "mafias" operate the rackets; this prospect was expected to exacerbate "the anxiety of the working class Italian teen in Bensonhurst, getting bum-rushed culturally if not physically every day of his life" (George, 1989).[3]

Disorganization assumed an economic dimension that was most consistently developed by Michael Stone in *New York* magazine (1989; see also Dyson, 1989). Stone linked the eclipse of Italian American Bensonhurst to the erosion of the city's blue-collar economy, in particular, the shrinking of the manufacturing sector and the loss of union jobs. With "an economy in the toilet" (Quindlen, 1990), youth were portrayed as particularly anomic and desperate. It was reported that the school drop-out rate was burgeoning and that Italian Americans, in fact, had the highest rate among the city's white populations; none of the youthful defendants in the Hawkins killing were enrolled in school (Stone, 1989). A link was established between a high school dropout rate and high rates of unemployment on the one hand, and an increase in violent crime (30% in the five years prior to the Hawkins killing) and the use of illegal drugs on the other (Stone, 1989; see also Bauman and Chittum, 1989). A number of journalists, including Maria Laurino (1989) who subsequently became a speech writer for David Dinkins during his mayoralty, concluded that these developments had created "an underclass" among Italian American youth. The stigma attached to this label made Italian American youth even more dangerous (see below).

Bensonhurst was portrayed as under siege from the *inside* as well as the outside. A *Village Voice* feature created the impression of an ominous state of affairs in which gangster culture ruled; according to the article, the "calm surface" of the neighborhood belied a situation where "sudden death from less than natural causes is not unusual" (Bauman and Chittum, 1989). By all appearances, "wiseguys" had a free rein, intimidating solid citizens and inhibiting civic responsibility (Roberts, 1990; Hamill, 1989). As long as residents obeyed local codes, the violence under the "surface" was mainly spent in tribal conflicts among "wiseguys".

Other accounts portrayed divisiveness as a communal trait. Thus, DeMarco-Torgovnick (1990: 458) called attention to "Italian Americans' devotion to jealous distinctions and discriminations". Grizzuti-Harrison (1990: 71) illustrated one of the more significant intraethnic divisions, reflected in the animosity and resentment on the part of Italian Americans for Italian immigrants:

> "We got this big influx of Italians from the Old Country—geeps. They're not like us. They got a chip on their shoulder.... The geeps are here three years, and they got money to buy a four-family house. That's all they think about is money. They never heard of going to the movies. They never heard of anisette. They never even heard of coffee. What kind of Italian is that?"

Bauman and Chittum (1989) gave internecine divisions a bellicose cast.

> According to Frank, Brooklyn Italians hate Long Island Italians, Long Island Italians hate Jersey Italians, and they all hate Staten Island Italians. Furthermore, Brooklyn Italians from different turfs are obliged to knock heads. "If different Avenues are at a club, they always have to fight each other".

In these portrayals, the image of a cohesive ethnic community—"a world of tightknit families" (Kifner, 1989)—is regarded with a cynical eye. There is an inference that, in contrast to mainstream American community, social commitment is seriously deficient in Bensonhurst, even within the ethnic group. Communal solidarity (i.e., what makes families "tightknit") in Bensonhurst was depicted as essentially a war of all against all (and "all" against Blacks, Jews, etc.), a scenario that resonates with the "long discredited", though apparently still resilient, Banfield thesis of *amoral familism* (see Filippucci, 1996: 54; Tricarico, 1984b). Outsiders reading these accounts could infer that the "last Italian neighborhood" in New York City had descended into anarchy.

LABELING ITALIAN AMERICANS DEVIANT

Motifs of racial bigotry, criminal violence and social disorganization framed Italian American ethnicity as a "social problem". To that extent, the "construction" of an ethnic boundary was simultaneously a process of "deviance construction" (Schur, 1984: 28; Becker, 1963; Gusfield, 1981). In the Bensonhurst case, media accounts positioned Italian Americans outside of mainstream cultural life; their cultural *otherness* was evidenced in matters ranging from consumption styles (e.g., pink flamingos and jogging suits) to speech patterns (e.g., "broken" English). Cultural *difference* was then linked to moral *deviance,* in particular criminal violence and racial bigotry. Indeed, Italian American identity was *stigmatized* by the very fact of being referenced to a "racial killing" and an ensuing "moral panic". "Cultural stories" that associated Italian American peoplehood with "stigma-laden definitions" were legitimated by the establishment media and disseminated into the public discourse (Schur: 5–12).

Alternative, empowering motifs for constituting Italian American ethnicity were contained or omitted.[4] Nowhere in the "media spectacle" was credibility accorded to a viable ethnic culture based on the shared family traditions that have historically anchored the moral order of urban Italian American communities (Tricarico, 1984b: 20–32). For the most part, the mainstream narrative left little room for the views of Italian Americans, with the exception of those prepared to corroborate the deviance paradigm (see below). The tone of these accounts implied that Italian Americans were not privy to the discussion taking place about them, perhaps even that they lacked the cognitive requirements for access to literate publications like *The New York Times* and *Partisan Review.*

The *problem* of Italian American ethnicity was elevated to the status of a "moral panic" when the Bensonhurst incident was linked to highly publicized issues of street violence associated with Black and Latino teenagers (Letwin, 1989; Stein, 1990). More specifically, Italian American teenagers like those involved in the killing were likened to the "wilding crews" held responsible for the "epidemic" of street crimes in the city, especially "the Central Park jogger case".[5] "Feral" metaphors portrayed the "Bensonhurst boys" as displaying "an animal energy" and "forming pack groups" that threatened whites in upscale neighborhoods (Bauman and Chittum, 1989). A *New York Times* columnist detected "similarities between the feral youth of Bensonhurst and their Black and Hispanic counterparts" (Roberts, 1990). Perceived "similarities" to African American and Latino youth led a *Village Voice* writer to label "Italian American kids, the third underclass in the city right now" (Laurino, 1990). This comparison effectively slotted Italian American youth into the "media images and political discourse" that routinely links nonwhites to social pathology and represents whites as "besieged" (Lipsitz, 1997: 112). Linked to a culture of underclass pathology, young Italian American males were represented as having crossed the color line.[6]

The moral panic specifically targeted Italian American youth identified as "Guidos". An Italian proper name, "Guido" designated an Italian American style within local youth culture (Tricarico, 1991). In the press, however, "Guido" became a category of deviance. The youth who allegedly fired a handgun at Yusuf Hawkins was identified as "a typical Guido" in a *Village Voice* article (Dobie, 1989). "Guido" was elaborated as an ethnic epithet in Pete Hamill's column in *The New York Post* (1989); Hamill's portrayal of "the boys from Guidoville" as "snarling imbeciles" put *into print* what is typically said in private discourse ("behind their backs").

With this depiction in the press, youth cultural style became a conspicuous marker for social deviance and moral degeneration (see also Pagnozzi, 1989; Quindlen, 1990). Feral references might have become more prominent were it not for availability of Mafia imagery and the casting of Italian American teenagers as "wannabe wiseguys". When John Gotti's brother Gene was depicted in a "Fila jogging suit", "Guido" style acquired Mafia connections (Pagnozzi, 1989; see also Tricarico, 1991). Still, it was the comparisons to "wilding" Blacks, even more than the Mafia, that made "Guido" a *public* peril because "Guidos" were not Black, crass stereotypes could not be construed as racist. The press had created a new "folk devil" (Cohen, 1980), with the "Guido" as contemporary version of the notorious "Dago".

The overall narrative did not exclude alternative images. Andrew Sullivan's article in *The New Republic* (1990) went the furthest in this regard. Sullivan managed to find people like "Father Barozzi... a genial Italian... making a genuine effort to counter bigotry";

> Or take Gerard. Born and brought up in Bensonhurst, he's a wiry, almost nerdy Italian in early middle age who made it to Columbia College and Law School. He went to Wall Street as a corporate tax lawyer, but in his twenties decided to do something for his old neighborhood and started a basketball team for local youth.(16)

Sullivan called attention to "the easy racial mixing on the street", although noting that since Bensonhurst had "virtually no Black residents at all", this mainly pertained to those for whom Bensonhurst was a workplace in the daytime. In contrast to Hamill's gratuitous reference to a moral "bourgeois" majority in Bensonhurst, Sullivan inspired a credible belief that "another Bensonhurst clearly exists" (17).

However, representations that countered the dominant "interpretive framework" were scarce, especially in the establishment press at the height of the "media spectacle". Sullivan's essay was published almost a year after the killing and, in fact, was offered as a reflection on the "hysterical media" (13). Even then, he cautions that it is "not clear" which Bensonhurst "will emerge from the agony of the last few months" (17). It should also be noted that images of "another Bensonhurst" were not specifically linked to Italian American culture. Thus, while Sullivan locates moral Italian Americans, he does little to redeem Italian American ethnicity .

ETHNICITY AND IDENTITY POLITICS

The Bensonhurst incident occasioned the construction of Italian American ethnicity in the print media as a *social problem*. It remains to inquire about "the processes that motivate ethnic boundary construction" (Nagel, 1999:58). The intention to invoke ethnicity and the manipulation of ethnic meaning reflects interests and strategies that fluctuate with changing circumstances (Cornell and Hartmann, 1998: 77). Media representations in the Bensonhurst case can be referenced to "ideological choices" (Grossberg at al., 1998: 178–179) that reflected organizational and personal agendas at a particular historical juncture.

The murder of Yusuf Hawkins was imbued with strategic significance for a Black identity politics. It became a platform for the populist ethnic entrepreneur and political activist Reverend Al Sharpton who led civil rights marches through Bensonhurst; Sharpton was stabbed at one of the marches by a young Italian American man who was part of the crowd. Sharpton was determined to create and manipulate a "media spectacle" (Steele, 1990). Without a prominent leader with a savvy media strategy, the Bensonhurst incident, like the racial killing in Howard Beach in 1986, may not have acquired a compelling public profile. These two episodes can be contrasted with the death of a Black vocational high school student in a playground fight with local Italian American youth in the South (Greenwich) Village in the 1970s (as in Bensonhurst, there were rumors in the neighborhood that the Mafia spirited the Italian American boys into hiding). That incident generated only token media attention and had no political fallout (see Tricarico, 1984b: 97–101).

Circumstances were quite different in 1989 for other reasons. The Bensonhurst "racial killing" took place just days before the Democratic mayoral primary and two months before the general election. It made a powerful case for the election of the city's first African American mayor who could, perhaps, soothe Black anger and alienation while salving white liberal guilt and keeping the populist Al Sharpton at bay. Dinkins' Republican opponent was Rudy Giuliani whose ethnic connection to Italian American Bensonhurst may have accentuated the perception that he was not sensitive to racial minorities; Giuliani's racial politics, at the same time, may have reinforced the stereotype of Italian American racial bigotry.

Other issues in the mayoral election imparted a racial cast to the Bensonhurst incident. Notwithstanding an Italian surname, Giuliani is not typified as an Italian American on the public stage (he provoked the ire of many Italian Americans when he threatened to shut down the city's most popular street *festa* for alleged Mafia ties). Politically, he has been prominently framed by racial divisions between whites and Blacks (e.g., the 1999 killing of African immigrant Amadou Diallo by four undercover police officers with the controversial Street Crimes Unit); to this extent, Giuliani's racial politics resonated with Italian Americans as *whites*. In the context of the 1989 mayoral election, Black leaders like Al Sharpton and Herbert Daughtry *whitened* both the issues and the cast of characters in Bensonhurst to fit a racial scenario. Prominent liberal political columnists projected a Dinkins victory as vindication for racial violence and the evils of *white racism* more generally (Klein, 1989; Roberts, 1989).

Media outlets may be assumed to pursue their own "agendas". According to Ferguson (1998: 56), media representations are "usually undertaken without reflection or consideration". Lule (2000: 356) suggests the influence of taken-for-granted cultural understandings, noting that representations "may result in part from the press' limited and limiting cast of symbolic types". Regardless of whether media outlets pursued an "intentional agenda" (Ferguson, 1998: 56), coverage of the Bensonhurst incident *exposed* an external ethnic boundary.

Notwithstanding the establishment media's ethnocentrism, deliberate decisions were made inside media organizations to invoke Italian American ethnicity as relevant to a "racial killing" and to allow certain images to proliferate in the public discourse. It is instructive to note that ethnicity was *not* invoked in a front page *Times* article about the history of "racial violence" in the intergroup relations of Hasidic Jews and Blacks in Crown Heights. Indeed, although the Hasidim were essentially described as insular and exclusive, ethnic cultural traits did not inform an "interpretive framework" in the narrative of the community's conflict with Blacks (Yardley, 1998). Similarly, the *Times* did not invoke ethnicity to frame the "roving bands" of young men that sexually assaulted as many as fifty women near Central Park immediately following the National Puerto Rican Day Parade, in an incident that recalled the "wilding" panic of 1989 (Rashbaum and Chivers, 2000). Accompanying pictures of the participants culled from videotapes suggested that ethnic framing was plausible. However, the *Times* portrayed the suspects as without any defining ethnicity: "the police yesterday arrested six young men, from all around the region and all walks of life, and charged them in the rampage of sexual assaults Sunday in Central Park" (Rashbaum, 2000). A week after the riot, a front page story reinforced a perspective that deemphasized ethnicity:

> Just as a thundercloud is fueled by moisture and heat, Sunday's attacks on women in Central Park were fueled by an alchemy of alcohol, marijuana, oppressive weather, testosterone and lapses police strategy, tactics and communication. (Barstow and Chivers, 2000)

In the Bensonhurst case, the significance of being Italian American was often exaggerated in media accounts. For example, the "mob" that confronted Yusuf Hawkins was not ethnically homogeneous. Of the six defendants in the murder case, one had a German surname (Charles Stroessler) while another, the alleged "ringleader" (Keith Mondello), was half Jewish (Stone, 1989). A young Black man (Russel Gibbons) admitted to have carried baseball bats to the attack. However, this diversity was muted during the "media spectacle". It took more than three years for a reporter to ask

> "the most obvious question: What was a black man doing with a group of white guys who intended to beat up a group of black guys for coming into their neighborhood?" (Gelman, 1992)."They're my friends", he answered. "We do everything together. If I was in trouble, Keith Mondello would come to my side. I was there for him." (Gelman, 1992)

An "interpretive framework" that privileged Italian American ethnicity could not effectively assimilate this information (the discrepancy created by Gibbons' racial identity was significantly allieviated when criminal charges against him were dropped in a plea bargain). The stereotypes that dominated the narrative, legitimated by the popular culture, created the appearance that the individuals who comprised the mob, regardless of their actual ethnic and racial identities, were *acting* Italian American.

Deviance labeling is typically grounded in "the definers' perception that the deviants pose some kind of threat to their specific interests or overall social position"; devaluation and stigmatization processes operate to keep deviants "under control, or in their place" (Schur, 1984: 8–9). In the Bensonhurst case, media representations of Italian Americans similarly established invidious contrasts that are at the core of ethnic constructs (Cornell and Hartmann, 1998:20). By invoking and, then, devaluing Italian American ethnicity, blame was compartmentalized—a "cognitive device" that deflected blame from *white* Americans (Pinderhughes, 1997: 23; Zack, 1998: 63). Insofar as establishment media serve as the "guardians" of mainstream morality (Schemerhorn, 1970: 12), the privileging of Italian American ethnicity reverberated for a "moral economy of racism" (Lipsitz, 1997). This moral calculus was identified by Shelby Steele in a PBS documentary, "Seven Days in Bensonhurst" (1990), which aired almost eight months after the killing:

> It is now as disturbing for a white to be called a racist, as it is for a black to be called a nigger. By making a special show of concern for Hawkins, whites could demonstrate their racial innocence, if for no other reason than to fight off the charge of racism. Where race is concerned, innocence is power.

The positioning for "racial innocence" may be viewed as a strategy for resource competition" (Nagel, 1999: 58). Moreover, the "scapegoating" of Italian Americans for morally reprehensible acts (Schaefer, 1996: 47) had consequences beyond the assignment of racist guilt. Political and economic claims could also be contained to the extent that racist violence could be construed as an isolated, Italian American problem rather than a societal problem. This "problem" with Italian Americans disguised a "problem" that is quintessentially American (Lipsitz, 1997; Dyson, 1989). Racial violence in Bensonhurst made *white* racism translucent, which was a *problem* in its own right that invited censure. To the extent that Italian Americans strive to be white, the dominant position in the American racial hierarchy, attributing racial ambiguity to Italian Americans can be construed as a punitive response.

An "interpretive framework" based on *ethnic* deviance preempted explanations based on race. Except for an essay by African American Studies professor Michael Eric Dyson in *The Nation* (1989), establishment media did not frame the "racist" attitudes and behavior of Bensonhurst residents as *racial deviance,* even when they were identified as "white"; although Bensonhurst Italian Americans could be categorized as white, their racism was attributed to their ethnicity. They were also portrayed as acting "blue-collar" or "working class", although, class deviance was largely confounded with ethnicity. Deviant cultural distinctions, such as "broken" speech and "high" hair, are also class signifiers, as is the "blue-collar" occupational profile attributed to "Guidos" and "cugines" (Hamill, 1989; Pagnozzi, 1989). Similarly, the socioeconomic status of Bensonhurst Italian Americans, which made them vulnerable to structural changes like the decline of a manufacturing economy, exacerbated their purported ethnic predisposition to "problem" behaviors like racism (Stone, 1989).

Deviance labelling was promoted by the "moral panic" associated with "wilding" crimes. The use of feral metaphors in the public discourse illustrates the extent of the "moral panic" in the city at the time (Letwin, 1989). A connection between random sexual assault, such as in the Central Park jogger case, and the "turf" fights that characterized both the Bensonhurst and Howard Beach incidents, was a stretch. Nevertheless, Italian American youth appear to have been swept up in the fervor. Embedded ethnic stereotypes made them vulnerable to inclusion in "wilding" imagery. The emergence of ethnic epithets like "Guido" in the establishment press also revealed the moral panic that surrounded Italian Americans.

Representations of Italian Americans can also be linked to media agendas in the 1989 mayoral election. A guest column written by film maker Spike Lee in *The Daily News* (1989) explicitly placed the event in an electoral context. The depiction of Italian Americans as anti-semitic in Wiseman's *Times* Op-Ed essay may have been intended as a message to elements in the city's large and influential Jewish population, struggling to salvage a tradition of liberalism in a trying period for Black-Jewish relations. A vote for Dinkins, who was endorsed by *The Times*, relected a commitment to this tradition. It should be noted that support for Dinkins did not include orthodox Jews in Crown Heights and Williamsburgh who were embroiled in racial conflicts in their own neighborhoods and have been among the most consistent supporters of Guiliani's mayoralty (Yardley, 1998). Since the mayoral contest symbolically "re-presented" the ethnic issues played out in the streets of Bensonhurst between African Americans and Italian Americans, blame for the racial hostility of Italian Americans in Bensonhurst could be transferred to Rudy Giuliani who shared in an ethnic heritage that was framed as morally dubious.

Even without the play of "intentional agendas", issues of power and ideology are implicit in the "interpretive repertoires" of the media (Ferguson, 1998: 30–32). In the Bensonhurst case, media power was evidenced in the way that representations of Italian Americans were "imposed" rather than negotiated through "dialogue" (Ferguson, 1998: 168). The *Times* did not publish an Op-Ed piece that balanced the blatantly incriminating essay by Alan Wiseman and printed only four response letters, none of which critically challenged to Wiseman's logic and motivation (see below). The *Times* did not give Italian Americans an opportunity to write their own story. It is noteworthy that when Italian Americans were given significant space in the establishment media, in particular Grizzutti-Harrison in *Harper's* and DeMarco-Torgovnick in *Partisan Review*, their essays collaborated in disparaging Italian Americans from inside the ethnic boundary.

Deviance labeling is facilitated by a power imbalance, in particular, a perception that there would not be commensurate responses to "counter stigmatization" (Schur, 1984: 8). In the Bensonhurst case, a power imbalance was rooted in the historical subordination of Italian Americans in the American system of ethnic stratification, featuring a "discursive reserve" (Ferguson, 1998: 130) of hurtful cultural stereotypes. Moreover, Italian American advocates may not have possessed the necessary leverage to "represent" the group in the mainstream media, for example, to obtain Op-Ed space in the *Times*. An Italian American anti-defamation group did secure a private meeting with Pete Hamill and *The New York Post*, presumably reacting to the most egregious expression of ethnic antipathy in the media spectacle, and on the part of a writer prominently identified with a historic ethnic rival. Nevertheless, an Italian American response to "Guidoville" was not incorporated in the public record.

There is also the possibility that capable ethnic entrepreneurs, and mainstream Italian Americans more generally, were intimidated by the media "panic" and reluctant to publicly align with the spoiled ethnicity of Bensonhurst Italian Americans, especially "Guido" youth (Vecoli, 1996: 14). To this extent, the Bensonhurst incident may have exposed invidious status and cultural distinctions among Italian Americans; upward mobility and assimilation have historically been predicated on "escaping" blue-collar, ethnic neighborhoods like Bensonhurst.

Aside from institutional agendas, the Bensonhurst "media spectacle" was fueled by an opportunistic *personal* politics. This was reflected in recollections submitted to the public record by wounded insiders who defected from the ethnic community. They had personal scores to settle and the moment was propitious; they were given access to prominent publications to vent personal troubles that overlapped with public issues. Both Grizzuti-Harrison and DeMarco-Torgovnick, for example, harbored deep grudges against Bensonhurst's ethnic culture for perceived personal oppression; the latter still claims to be traumatized by "the conditions of [her] youth" (1990: 466). In Alan Wiseman's *Times* OpEd piece (1989), the denigration of Italian Americans (his comments are not confined to Bensonhurst) originate in a family conflict, in particular, his maternal grandfather's disappointment with his mother for "marrying a Jew", and the bullying of Jewish schoolboys by tough "Italian kids" in the old neighborhood. His conviction that Italian Americans were capable of racial violence in Bensonhurst, even though he admitted that he did "not know what really happened", is based on the actions of other Italian Americans in some other place and at some other time.

ETHNIC IDENTITY CRISIS

Media representations of Italian Americans in Bensonhurst racial killing reflected "a particular kind of identity" (Cornell and Hartmann, 1998: 184). What it meant to be Italian American was conveyed by a cognitive distortion (i.e., ethnic stereotypes); certain traits found in every population, like insularity and racial intolerance, were made salient while others were minimized or consigned to insignificance. By linking racial violence to a shared culture, responsibility was generalized from the individuals who authored a racial attack to an Italian American community, and then to Italian Americans *as an ethnic group.* Overgeneralizations simplified a complex ethnic reality, an outcome facilitated by the uneven distribution of knowledge about constituent groups in multiethnic societies (Lyman and Douglas, 1973: 347). Media "re-presentations" constituted an "ideological choice" in which "a particular way of seeing" was privileged; representations of Italian Americans were *ideological* also to the extent that "the mediated character of this construction" was concealed (Grossberg et al., 1998: 182–183).

The "fundamental" advantage of group identity is arguably its ability to lend the individual "some measure of esteem" (Isaacs, 1975: 95). To this extent, the Bensonhurst "media spectacle" became problematic for an identity development that struggles to reconcile with higher status levels and mainstream life-styles (Tricarico, 1984a). At other times and under different circumstances, the mainstream media has conspicuously elevated the prestige of Italian Americans and their ethnic heritage (Hall, 1983). In the Bensonhurst "media spectacle", however, there was a cast of disreputable Italian American characters such as *Guidos* and *cugines, wiseguys* and *mafiosi, feral youth* and, perhaps most prominently, *racists.* As an ethnic group, Italian Americans were accorded a "cultural deficiency" in contradistinction to the mainstream and, in essays by Grizzutti-Harrison, DeMarco-Torgovnick, and Wiseman, to a "model minority" (Brodkin, 1998: 150). The construction of a spoiled ethnic identity featured an incompatibility with the basic moral assumptions of a liberal society.

The Bensonhurst media spectacle also revisited the historical problem of Italian American racial positioning. Identifying Italian Americans by their nationality has historically signified that [they] were "less than white" (Barrett and Roediger, 1999: 146). As Brodkin (1998: 55) suggests in a study of American Jewish ethnic and racial identity, "nonwhite racial assignment" seems to be a function of what the group happens to be "doing" at the time. The Bensonhurst case suggests that Italian Americans run the risk of *acting* nonwhite when they remain in the inner city, oppose school, and cultivate a tough street code, a risk that may be enhanced for Italian Americans who are dark-skinned. Historically, Brodkin (58) observes that "Italian culture is not prefiguratively white, in the way Jewish culture—which [Nathan] Glazer has described as like Anglo-Saxon Protestant culture in valuing individualism and ambition—is".

Bensonhurst Italian Americans aggressively identified themselves in public displays as "white", often submerging their nationality background. They believed that they were *acting white* by expressing hostility toward blacks along racial lines. Thus, the watermelons brandished at Black protest marchers by Bensonhurst residents represented a preference for American *racial* symbolism; the corruption of the Italian word for eggplant, "mulignan", is commonly used by Italian Americans within the group as a racial epithet for Blacks.

However, the media narrative not only foregrounded nationality but also blurred racial boundaries. Racial ambiguity is suggested in allusions to Bensonhurst Italian Americans as the "white tribe" (George, 1989) and "the other white New York" (Stone, 1989). Italian American teenagers were actually portrayed as having crossed over the racial boundary. As "white homeboys" (George, 1989) and "feral youth" (Roberts, 1990), they were slotted into categories that designated Black and Latino youth. The conferring of an "underclass" status (Laurino, 1989) further solidified a nonwhite profile, referencing Italian American teenagers to the stereotypes of urban fear and danger typically reserved for African Americans and Latinos (Miller and Levin, 1998: 230).[7] Ironically, this *darkening* of Italian Americans undermined the scenario of a "racial killing".

One of the ways "borderline whites" have qualified for whiteness has been to demonstrate hostility toward nonwhites (Frye, 1998: 231; Barrett and Roediger, 1999: 152). To this extent, Bensonhurst Italian Americans were following a historical script for racial inclusion. However, it appears that this time, the storyline included a cruel twist. It was disconcerting enough to be censured as "racists" for doing the dirty work of *whiteness* in "the larger American racial discourse" (Brodkin: 151). Racial belligerence resulted in having their racial credentials questioned.

It is likely that the identity crisis occasioned by the Bensonhurst incident is conditional for a particular expression of Italian American ethnicity, a development associated with the urban enclave. An artifact of immigrant adaptation to the city, enclave ethnicity has social and moral features that are "ideologically" incompatible with mainstream "liberal" culture (Rieder, 1985). In this form, ethnicity is less "symbolic" and "optional" (Waters, 1990) than "primordial" and "thick" (Cornell and Hartmann, 1998: 77). From a mainstream perspective, Italian American group life has historically been regarded as "culturally deficient" and even pathological (Brodkin, 1998: 150). It has never been platable within the cultural mainstream, including the establishment media, until it has been sufficiently commodified, that is, until the middle class was able to buy into a *symbolic* ethnic experience. Commodification has been predicated on the exodus of Italian Americans themselves for mainstream settings and the eclipse of enclave institutions (Tricarico, 1984b: 156–167).

In New York City, historic Italian American enclaves have increasingly been packaged for the cultural consumption of the affluent and cosmpolitan. In 1974, the Lower East Side/Mulberry Street Italian American neighborhood was designated by the New York City Planning Commission as the city's official "Little Italy"; this landmark status enshrined a restaurant economy as the symbol of Italian American life at the very moment that the neighborhood was being absorbed by Chinatown. The ongoing gentrification of downtown Manhattan has more recently spawned a real estate concoction called NOLITA, an acronym that stands for "North of Little Italy" (it is actually within the limits of the historic ethnic community). The name attempts to capitalize on the cachet of the SoHo development in the 1970s (acronyms are the nomenclature of gentrification in lower Manhattan) in order "to attract a young and trend-setting clientele of artists and professionals"; with upscale newcomers poised to inherit the neighborhood, an article in *The New York Times* real estate section described the residual Italian American population as a residential amenity (Cohen, 1998). Although historic downtown neighborhoods may soon have more Italian restaurants than Italian Americans, media culture can perhaps stand in for a neighborhood culture:

> Grand Ticino, the homey Italian restaurant featured in "Moonstruck" (1987), is on Thompson Street, a couple of blocks below the park. This is where Danny Aiello proposed to Cher, and where Olympia Dukakis arrived for dinner alone... (Gates, 2000)

Unlike ethnically depopulated and gentrified Manhattan neighborhoods like the South (Greenwich) Village and "Little Italy", "a living Italian neighborhood" (O'Neill, 1991) in Bensonhurst was not available as a commodified and symbolic enclave experience. Through the 1980s, the communal character of Bensonhurst reflected the working class and ethnic strategies of a large and dense Italian American population. The *otherness* and deviance attributed to Bensonhurst by the establishment media was fundamentally a response to these urban strategies which Suttles (1968) locates as the core of a "defended neighborhood". In this scenario, a "moral order" in Bensonhurst was structured by the interplay of ethnicity, race and class within segmented urban spaces; "Greater Bensonhurst" was itself segmented into myriad "defended neighborhoods" with units as small as the block. Within these spatial units, insiders are defined as relatively trustworthy and outsiders are either superfluous or threatening. Blacks were threatening in Bensonhurst primarily because of the acceptance of *American* racial discourses. Racial threat had an immediacy because demographic shifts portended integration and even succession by nonwhites (Green et al., 1998). Racial belligerence was confined to an element of the community that was both structurally vulnerable (e.g., unemployment or underemployment). This vulnerability promoted a "turf" consciousness, as competition for scarce resources (e.g., "respect") was centered on the locality; thus, young males with little mainstream social capital served as the principal agents of a "defended neighborhood" culture.

Italian American neighborhoods have historically played a "middleman" role in the "racial discourse" of New York City. They have created a strategic buffer between more affluent and educated whites intent on reclaiming the inner city and low status Blacks and Latinos. They have done this by stabilizing real estate values and by discouraging predatory street behavior. "Street work" has been the specialized role of tough Italian American youth, backed up the Mafia (Tricarico, 1984b: 67–69). Jonathan Rieder's study of Canarsie (1985) in the 1980s noted that Italian Americans served as "Jewish muscle" in a neighborhood that was experiencing racial succession; this allowed Jewish Americans to resolve the contradictions between opposition to racial integration and a signature liberalism, although a tough street response eventually emerged with the formation of the Jewish Defense League. Artists and incubating professionals (*yuppies*) moving into the South Village in the 1970s appreciated the vigilance of cornerboys, without actually condoning physical violence (Tricarico, 1984: 102–111). Although it occasionally posed problems for newcomers, the "street work" of Italian American cornerboys has made gritty inner city neighborhoods safe for gentrification. In contrast to areas like the South Village which have locational or architectural significance, Bensonhurst held virtually no appeal for bohemians or gentry. Its peripheral status to the material and social concerns of strategic urban actors may have facilitated a moral repositioning of Italian Americans, in particular the criminalization of "Guido".[8]

Nevertheless, the Bensonhurst "media spectacle" holds out the possibility that the *otherness* and deviance associated with the urban Italian American neighborhood can be generalized to Italian American ethnicity. As this media episode suggests, the "discursive reserve" of stereotypes that stigmatize Italian Americans lies just below the surface of American popular culture. Because it activated stereotypes of a "thick" and deviant ethnicity, the Bensonhurst incident may have occasioned a major setback for a mainstream identity development. Indeed, assimilated Italian Americans may have been astounded by the recrudescence of public discourse that, after all these years, portrays Italian Americans as a stigmatized other (i.e., an "underclass" that is "not yet white").

These characterizations would seem to preempt inclusion in a "dominant group ethnicity". They also pose status dilemmas for a mainstream "symbolic" ethnicity (Gans, 1999). Ethnicity is not always available "how and when it suits" the individual (Royce, 1982: 3). Under certain circumstances, ethnic identity can be invoked by powerful others; ethnic meanings can be elaborated to "suit" *their* purposes, which may include stigmatization. Although instrumental exploitation of Italian Americans (e.g., as "dago" labor) may no longer be prevalent, this does not preclude "expressive depreciation" (Suarez-Orozco, 1987). Thus, the Bensonhurst "media spectacle" created an external boundary of invidious cultural and moral distinctions.

Representations of Italian Americans in the print media in response to the Bensonhurst incident reveal that the "ways in which a person is, or wishes to be, known by certain others" can become highly politicized under certain kinds of "circumstances" (Cohen, 1993: 195–197). "Post-modern" ethnicity appears to be "contested terrain"; the construction of ethnic identity has to contend with media images and discourses that have a tacit ideological character (Kellner, 1995: 2–3). Audiences "may resist the dominant meanings and messages... and use their culture to empower themselves and to invent their own meanings, identities, and forms of life" (Kellner: 3). For mainstream Italian Americans, then, ethnic identity construction has involved the manipulation of themes that can be reconciled with an upgraded socioeconomic status (Tricarico, 1984a). Media representations remain "part of the world they encounter, part of what others say they are, and therefore part of the weight they carry" (Cornell and Hartmann, 1998: 184). In particular, the media have the power to effect the "reproduction" of existing prejudices and stereotypes in the popular culture (Ferguson, 1998: 61). With so much at stake, media culture will remain a prime venue for identity politics, ethnic and otherwise, in a "post-modern" society.[9]

NOTES

1. Juliet Schor (1998) argues quite convincingly that the popular cultural mainstream in America is now represented by the taste preferences of the *upper* middle class. The *New York Times* articles on the subject of Bensonhurst have to be understood in relation to advertisements elsewhere in the paper for Armani suits and Rolex watches.
2. A study by Pinderhughes (1997) of Italian American teenagers in a turf-related gang in the Kings Highway section of southern Brooklyn offers a graphic depiction of racial dynamics at street-level. While he is correct to emphasize that the gang was supported by community norms and ideology, it can not be inferred that racism and racial violence define a dominant moral posture in the community.
3. George, an African-American who is an expert on Black popular culture, was playing with the symbolism of the pizzeria as it figured in both the Howard Beach racial killing in 1986 and Spike Lee's response to that incident in the film *Do The Right Thing.* The Lee film subsequently became a frame of reference for events in Bensonhurst, and Lee himself made inferences as a guest columnist for the *The Daily News.*
4. Favorable characterizations of Italian Americans (e.g., as "hardworking") were overwhelmed by negative associations (see Freitag, 1989). Recent identity development on the part of Italian Americans involves a displacement of negative images associated with a pariah immigrant group by images compatible with mainstream, upscale status (see Tricarico, 1986).

5. One of the more infamous incidents was the sexual assault of a female jogger (routinely identified as an "investment banker") in Central Park by a "wilding" mob of Black and Hispanic teenagers (see Stein, 1990; Pinderhughes, 1997). Fuel was added to the fire with random needle attacks on pedestrians in Manhattan neighborhoods.
6. Press accounts did not acknowledge the appropriation of gangster imagery in both Black and Hispanic youth culture, in the form of the "gangsta" and "hood" personas respectively (Stein, 1989; Roberts, 1990).
7. Italian American youth in the city's neighborhoods have historically developed a street culture organized around a sense of place, or turf, and featuring both the pose and substance of aggression. It appears, especially more recently, to have been influenced by Black and Hispanic youth culture on the level of style (see Tricarico, 1991).
8. Artists and "bohemians" have historically found Italian American neighborhoods in the city appealing. The area below Washington Square Park, for example, afforded inexpensive housing and restaurants in the 1950s, and again in the 1960s and 1970s with the development of the SoHo artists' community. In the 1970s, the first wave of newcomers who were typically in their twenties and early thirties and incubating professional careers were also drawn by the belief that Italian neighborhoods were relatively free of street crime. Moreover, they evidenced little moral conflict over how neighborhood peace was secured. Gentrification did not displace restaurants and shops that were able to stage a commodified ethnic experience suitable for cosmopolitan residents and visitors *without* a working class ethnic community (see Tricarico, 1984b).
9. George Will used his column in the *Washington Post* (1993) to belittle the idea that affirmative action was needed at the City University of New York to educate "Dumb Guys Named Guido". Italian American politicians conspicuously resorted to ethnic identity politics to aid the electoral causes of Italian American candidates in 1998. In particular, Mayor Giuliani issued a complaint at a news conference about "a pattern" of anti-Italian American slurs which was followed by a challenge: "Italian Americans have to stand up, they have to say they're not going to put up with this" (Lambert, 1998).

REFERENCES

Allport, G. 1958. *The Nature of Prejudice.* Garden City: Doubleday.

Barrett, J. R. and D. Roediger 1999. "Inbetween Peoples: Race, Nationality, and the 'New Immigrant' Working Class". *Majority and Minority*. Edited by N. Yetman. Boston: Allyn and Bacon (144–159).

Barstow, D. and C. J. Chivers. 2000. "A Volatile Mixture Exploded Into Rampage in Central Park". *The New York Times* (June 17).

Bauman, M. and S. Chittum. 1989. "Married to the Mob", *The Village Voice* (September 5): 40–41.

Becker, H. 1963. *The Outsiders*. New York: Free Press.

Berger, W. 1998. "It's Not Just a Myth: They Do Speak With Their Hands", *The New York Times* (August 2).

Bohlen, C. 1989. "In Bensonhurst, Grief Mixed With Shame and Blunt Bias", *The New York Times* (August 28).

Brodkin, K. 1998. *How Jews Became White Folks.* New Brunswick, N.J.: Rutgers University Press.

Cohen, A. P. 1993. "Culture and Identity: An Anthropologist's View", *New Literary History,* vol. 24, no. 1 (Winter).

Cohen, J. 1998. "A Slice of Little Italy Moving Upscale", *The New York Times* (May 17).

Cohen, S. 1980. *Folk Devils and Moral Panics.* London: MacGibbon and Kee.

Cornell, S. and D. Hartman. 1998. *Ethnicity and Race.* Thousand Oaks, CA: Pine Forge.

DeMarco-Torgovnick, M. 1990. "On Being White, Female, and Born in Bensonhurst", *Partisan Review,* vol. LVII, no. 3 (Summer): 456–466.

DeSantis, J. 1991. *For The Color of His Skin.* New York: Pharos Books.

di Leonardo, M. 1984. *The Varieties of Ethnic Experience.* Ithaca: New York.

Dobie, K. 1989. "The Boys of Bensonhurst", *The Village Voice* (September 5): 34–39.

Doane, A. W. 1999. "Dominant Group Ethnic Identity in the United States: The Role of 'Hidden Ethnicity' in Intergroup Relations", *Majority and Minority.* Edited by N. Yetman. Boston: Allyn and Bacon (72–86).

Dyson, M. E., "The Two Racisms". *The Nation,* vol. 249, no. 9 (300–302).

Ferguson, R. 1998. *Representing 'Race'.* London: Arnold.

Fillipucci, P. 1996. "Anthropological Perspectives on Culture in Italy", in *Italian Cultural Studies.* Edited by D. Forgacs and R. Lumley. Oxford (52–71).

Freitag, M. 1989. "Bensonhurst on Stage: Plot Is Sadly Familiar, Playwright Says", *The New York Times* (October 2).

Gans, H. 1999. "Symbolic Ethnicity: The Future of Ethnic Groups and Culture in America", *Majority and Minority.* Edited by N. Yetman. Boston: Allyn and Bacon (417–430).

Gates, A. 2000. "Bright Lights, Bright City… Action!", *The New York Times* (May 15).

Gelman, M. 1992. "Bensonhurst 'Crime Scene': A Black Man Is Part of the White Mob", *Newsday* (September 17).

George, N. 1990. "Brooklyn Bound", *The Village Voice* (May 29): 27–28.

Glaberson, W. 1990. "A Black From Bensonhurst Tells of Carrying Bats to White Friends", *The New York Times* (April 25).

Green, D.P. et al. 1998. "Defended Neighborhoods, Integration, and Racially Motivated Crime". *American Journal of Sociology* vol: 104, no. 2 (September): 372–403.

Grizzuti-Harison, B. 1990. "Women and Blacks in Bensonhurst", *Harper's Magazine* (March): 69–82.

Grossberg, L., E. Wartella, and D.C. Whitney. 1998. *MediaMaking.* Thousand Oaks, CA: Sage.

Gusfield, J. 1981. *The Culture of Public Problems.* Chicago: University of Chicago Press.

Haalasa, M. 1989. "Be Black and Rock", *New Statesman and Society* (November 24).

Hall, S. S. 1983. "The Italian Americans: Coming Into Their Own", *The New York Times Magazine* (May 15).

Hamill, P. 1989. "The Lesson of Howard Beach Was Lost on the Punks of Guidoville", *New York Post* (August 29).

Harney, J. and A. Lubrano. 1989. "Tension up as Marchers, Residents Trade Taunts". *The Daily News* (August 27).

Hollinger, D. 1999. "Postethnic America", *Majority and Minority.* Edited by N. Yetman. Boston: Allyn and Bacon (122–130).

Isaacs, H. 1975. *Idols of the Tribe*. New York: Harper and Row.

Jacobson, M. F. 1998. *Whiteness of a Different Color*. Cambridge: Harvard University Press.

Jordan, G. E. 1989. "100 Marchers Decry Slaying: 250 Police Keep the Peace in Bensonhurst Protest", *Newsday* (August 28).

Kaufman, M. T. 1989. "Despair Comes Twice to a Brooklyn Family", *The New York Times* (August 26).

Kellner, D. 1995. *Media Culture*. London and New York: Routledge.

Kifner, J. 1989. "Bensonhurst: A Tough Code in Defense of a Closed World", *The New York Times* (September 1).

Klein, J. 1989. "The Real Thing", *New York Magazine* (November 13): 16–20.

Lambert, B. 1998. "Mayor Says Democrats Have Made Slurs", *The New York Times* (October 25).

Lappe, A. 1998. "Two Way Street", *The New York Times* (October 18).

Laurino, M. 1990. "Dinkins on the Defensive", *The Village Voice* (May 29): 15–16.

Lee, S. 1989. "The Right Thing: Self-Defense, Vote", *The Daily News* (September 21).

Letwin, M. 1989. "N.Y. Justice: Not Color-Blind", *The New York Times* (September 29).

Lewis, N. "Bishop Questions Protest Marches in Racial Slaying", *The New York Times* (August 30).

Lipsitz, G. 1998. *The Possessive Investment in Whiteness.* Philadelphia: Temple University Press.

Lule, J. 2000. "The Rape of Mike Tyson", *Structured Inequality in the United States.* Edited by A. Aguirre, Jr. and D.V. Baker. Upper Saddle River: Prentice-Hall (355–369).

Lyman, S. and W. Douglas. 1973. "Ethnicity: Structure of Impression Management", *Social Research*, vol. 40, no. 2 (Summer): 344–365.

McAlary, M. 1989. "Gangs had Capo-tal Role Models", *New York Post* (August 27).

Miller, J. and P. Levin. 1998. "The Caucasian Evasion: Victims, Exceptions, and Defenders of the Faith", in *Images of Color, Images of Crime*. Edited by C. R. Mann and M. S. Zatz. Los Angeles, CA.: Roxbury Publishing Company (217–233).

Nagel, J. 1999. "Constructing Ethnicity: Creating and Recreating Ethnic Identity and Culture", in *Majority and Minority*. Edited by N. Yetman. Boston: Allyn and Bacon (57–71).

O'Neill, M. 1991. "Taming Bensonhurst's Annual Zucchini Glut", *The New York Times* (September 4).

Orsi, R. 1993. "The Religious Foundations of an Inbetween People", *American Quarterly*, vol. 44, no. 3 (September): 313–347.

Pagnozzi, A. 1989. "Blaming the 'Evil Woman' in Race Death", *New York Post* (August 30).

Pinderhughes, H. 1997. *Race in the Hood*. Minneapolis: University of Minnesota Press.

Quindlen, A. 1990. "A Changing World", *The New York Times* (May 5).

Rashbaum, W. K. 2000. "Six Identified in Videos Are Arrested in Central Park Sex Attacks". *The New York Times* (June 16).

Rashbaum, W. K . and C. J. Chivers. 2000 "Photos of 7 Men Sought in Melee". *The New York Times* (June 15).

Rieder, J. 1985. *Canarsie: The Jews and Italians of Brooklyn Against Liberalism.* Cambridge: Harvard University Press.

Roediger, D. R. 1994. *Toward the Abolition of Whiteness.* New York: Verso Books.

Roberts, S. 1990. "The Feral Youth and Amnesiacs Of Bensonhurst", *The New York Times* (May 3).

Royce, A. P. 1982. *Ethnic Identity: Strategies for Diversity.* Bloomington: Indiana University Press.

Schaefer, R. 1996. *Racial and Ethnic Groups.* New York: Harper Collins.

Schermerhorn, R. A. 1970. *Comparative Ethnic Relations.* New York: Random House.

Schor, J. 1998. *The Overspent American.* New York: Basic Books.

Schur, E. 1984. *Labelling Women Deviant.* New York: Random House.

Singleton, D. 1989. "Tension up as Marchers, Residents Trade Taunts", *New York Daily News* (August 27).

Steele, S. 1990. "Seven Days in Bensonhurst" (a documentary film). *PBS* (May 15).

Stein, A. 1990. "Wilding Is a Crime, Except in Law", *The New York Times* (January 13).

Stone, M. 1989. "What Really Happened In Bensonhurst", *New York Magazine* (November 6): 44–56.

Suarez-Orozco, M. M. 1987. "Transformations in Perception of Self and Social Environment in Mexican Immigrants". In *People in Upheaval.* Edited by S. Morgan and E. F. Colson. Staten Island, N.Y.: Center for Migration Studies (129–143).

Sullivan, A. 1990. "The Two Faces of Bensonhurst: A Report from the Neighborhood". *The New Republic,* vol. 203, no. 1 (July 2): 13–17.

Suttles, G. 1968. *The Social Order of the Slum.* Chicago: University of Chicago Press.

———— 1972. *The Social Construction of Communities.* Chicago: University of Chicago Press.

Terry, D. 1989. "Sorrow and Bitterness", *The New York Times* (August 31).

Tricarico, D. 1984a. "The 'New' Italian American Ethnicity", *Journal of Ethnic Studies,* vol. 12, no. 3 (Fall): 75–94.

————. 1984b. *The Italians of Greenwich Village: The Social Structure and Transformation of an Ethnic Community.* Staten Island, N.Y.: Center for Migration Studies.

————. 1990. "What's in a Name (Guido)? The Emergence of an (Ethnic) Italian American Stereotype". Paper presented at American Italian Historical Association Conference in New Orleans, November 1, 1990.

————. 1991. "Guido: Fashioning an Italian American Youth Style", *Journal of Ethnic Studies,* vol. 19, no. 1 (Spring): 41–66.

Vecoli, R. J. 1995. "Are Italian Americans Just White Folks?" *In Through The Looking Glass.* Edited by M. J. Bona and A. J. Tamburri. Staten Island, N.Y.: American Italian Historical Association (3–17).

Waters, M. 1990. *Ethnic Options.* Berkeley: University of California Press.

Weisman, A. 1989. "Flatbush, 60s; Bensonhurst, '89", *The New York Times* (November 5).

Will, G. F. 1993. " 'Dumb Guys Named Guido' ", *The Washington Post* (November 28).

Yardley, J. 1998. "Jews and Blacks Try to Avoid Reprise of '91 in Crown Heights". *The New York Times* (April 4).

Zack, N. 1998. *Thinking About Race.* Belmont, CA: Wadsworth.

CHAPTER 13 The Race and Ethnic Community

13.1 VICTOR M. HWANG

The Interrelationship Between Anti-Asian Violence and Asian America

Anti-Asian violence has remained pervasive throughout U.S. history. Beginning with the early arrival of Chinese and Japanese immigrants and continuing with the migration of the so-called new wave immigrants—namely, Asian Indian and Southeast Asian groups—bigoted Whites have targeted Asian Americans as scapegoats for the nation's socioeconomic ills resulting from wars and economic competition with Asian countries. Still etched in the the American national consciousness are the brutal racial killings of Vincent Chin, Ming Hai Loo, Navroze Mody, and Hung Truong, as well as the massacre of Southeast Asian schoolchildren in California. Hate mongers have cruelly defaced the homes of Asian Americans and their places of worship. Asian American students continue to suffer racial harassment on U.S. college campuses. The most recent government figures on bias-motivated violence show that some 372 Asian and Pacific Islanders are violently accosted each year, mostly by White people engaged in vicious acts of intimidation, vandalism, assault, robbery, murder, and rape. In California alone, anti-Asian hate crimes constitute 11 percent of the state's 2,000 bias-motivated crimes each year.

A recent report by the U.S. Commission on Civil Rights recounts incidents of bigotry and violence against Asian Americans presently occurring in U.S. society. The report states that the bigotry and violence often waged against Asian Americans results mostly from resentment of their perceived socioeconomic success and a lack of social understanding of the Asian American histories, customs, and religions. Also, the media has contributed to anti-Asian sentiment in the United States by promoting a model minority image of Asian Americans and by failing to provide for positive public understanding of the diversity in the Asian American population. The report notes that the media has given little attention to hate crimes against Asian Americans, thereby hindering the development of a national sense of outrage about bigotry and violence against Asian Americans. Perhaps most important, the report contends that America's political leadership has failed to openly denounce racial bigotry and violence against Asian Americans with strong criminal justice sanctions.

In the following selection from "The Interrelationship Between Anti-Asian Violence and Asian America," *Chicano-Latino Law Review* (Spring 2000), Victor M. Hwang, a staff attorney with the Asian Law Caucus and director of the Hate Violence Project, contends that anti-Asian violence plays a significant role in shaping the character of the Asian Pacific American community and its relationship to the mainstream society. Using the racial violence suffered by Sylvia, a 63-year-old Korean American woman ferociously attacked by a Caucasian man, and swastikas carved into the glass storefronts of Asian American–owned business as cases in point, Hwang reveals how painful and disparaging racial violence is to Asian Americans and their struggle to be acknowledged as equals in U.S. society.

Key Concept: anti–Asian American violence and hate crime

INTRODUCTION

The concept of the Asian Pacific American community is unique in the field of American race relations. Our community is neither united by a common experience such as slavery or by a common language such as Spanish. We are individually Vietnamese Amerasians, second generation South Asian Americans, kibei, third generation Sansei activists born of World War II internees, 1.5 generation Korean Americans, FOBs, JOJs (just off the jet), Pilipino seniors, hapas, Taiwanese nationalists, and more. In many ways, the Hmong veteran escaping persecution from Laos may have much more in common with the political refugee from Guatemala in terms of language and cultural barriers, moral and family values, psychological trauma, job skills and education than with a third generation Japanese American who grew up in Gardena. The Taiwan computer software salesman may identify closer along class and political interests with the German transnational machine parts manufacturer than with a second generation Cantonese seamstress in Chinatown. Our community encompasses differences in ethnicity, religion, language, culture, class, color, immigration history, politics and even race.

What we obviously do have most in common is the way that we look to those outside our community and the way we are treated in America based upon the way we look. Our commonality begins with a recognition that whether you are a first-generation Vietnamese American rollerblading at a park or a second-generation Chinese American celebrating at your bachelor party, you are constantly at risk of being killed without warning or provocation based upon the belief that you are a foreign "Jap." Whether you are second generation South Asian American or a fifth generation Chinatown native, we are faced constantly with the implicit and explicit question, "No, really, where are you from?"

Yet, while anti-Asian violence forces individuals to band together at times for physical or political protection, it plays a much greater role in shaping the Asian Pacific American community than simply acting as the outside threat which drives the flock together. It is not the action of anti-Asian violence which is so important to the development of our community as much as it is the reaction to the incident. For "Asian America" lives not in the Chinatowns or the Little Tokyos, but in the hearts of those who recognize that incidents of anti-Asian violence are not isolated attacks, but are part of the historical treatment of Asians in America for the past two hundred years.

As much as immigration and anti-miscegenation laws work hand-in-hand to control and manipulate the number of Asian immigrants in America to serve the labor needs of the country, the pattern of anti-Asian violence dictates the role and character of our community and its relationship to mainstream society. From the unofficially sanctioned massacres of Chinese mining camps to laws prohibiting the testimony of Chinese witnesses in courts against the murderers, the unspoken policy and history of America has been to erase the experience of Asians in America and to silence the voice of the community. Thus, we have been displaced from our role in American history, from our place in America, and more than two hundred years after the first Asians came to America, we are still being collectively told to go back to where we came from.

It is in our struggle against this pattern of violence and its underlying message of physical, political, and historical exclusion that we find ourselves as Asian Pacific Americans. Not every Asian in America is a member of the Asian Pacific American community. We are born or naturalized as Americans by geographic and legal definitions and we can be distinguished as Asians based upon certain physiological and racial characteristics. But we become Asian Americans as we begin to recognize that we share a common bond and experience with all other Asians in America based upon our history, our treatment and our status as a racial minority in the United States. The formation of the community begins not when ten Asian families happen to live in the same neighborhood, but when one family has been attacked and the other nine rally to their assistance.

The Asian American community is based on an understanding and appreciation of the fact that we have struggled for nearly two centuries against this violence and exclusion in the plantations, in the courts, and on the battlefields. From the early organizing efforts of the Chinese Six Companies in San Francisco to protect the Chinese workers from nativist attacks to the more recent campaigns to bring justice to the killers of Vincent Chin and Kao Kuan Chung, Asian Americans have not always been the silent victims of hate crimes, but have strived to defend and empower our communities in the American tradition.

This paper will discuss the role of anti-Asian violence as a foil and as a catalyst in the development of an Asian American identity and a community. Our community lives in the contradiction, in the friction between competing notions of ethnicity and nationality, in the margins and as a wedge between black and white in American society. It is not a physical community, but one that exists in flashes, in movements, in speeches, in hearts and minds, and in struggle. It is within the heat of the response to these incidents of extreme racial violence that we continue to forge our identity and our sense of community. We build our community in times of crisis by speaking out against the incidents of anti-Asian violence and claiming our piece of history.

However, in times of racial tension, it is sometimes difficult to process the elements of the hate crime to craft an effective and targeted response which serves both the needs of the individual victim as well as empowering the community. In this paper, I will explore two recent incidents of anti-Asian violence as a framework to discussing the crafting and mis-crafting of a progressive community response. I believe we should approach hate crimes in the same way a doctor would approach a medical problem. Prior to making a diagnosis, we need to understand the nature of the injury as well as who has been hurt. Further, without an understanding of the history of anti-Asian violence, hate crimes, and the community, we can do little for either the protection of the individual or the development of Asian America.

ANTI-ASIAN VIOLENCE AND THE INDIVIDUAL: WHAT IS THE INJURY?

Individual victims of hate crimes and their families often suffer injuries far beyond the physical wounds inflicted upon them. It is both the sticks and stones which break our bones and the accompanying words and hateful intent which hurt us. Like a snake's bite, the venomous injuries of anti-Asian violence go far deeper than the physical injury because they are intended to inject a poison to strike at the core of our being. As advocates, we must recognize the injury to the internal psyche as well as the physical injury in crafting a remedy for the individual and the community. Just as you cannot treat a snakebite with a Band-Aid, you cannot treat the hate crime as either a simple crime or an accident.

THE INCIDENT

Sylvia is a 63 year old Korean American who came to the United States as a teenager. She grew up in Washington, D.C., the daughter of a Korean minister and attended an all-white segregated high school. She spent most of her adult years in Arizona as the wife of a university professor where, as she describes it, never thought she experienced much racism in the ivory tower setting. "Oh, every once in a while, my kids would tell me that someone had called them a Chinaman in school or had tried to put them down on account of their race," she said. "But I always told them just to work harder and prove to every one else that they were superior. I knew that we were descendants of a proud people with many centuries of culture and civilization. I never worried much about what the other people thought. I knew we were better."

She never had much contact with African Americans, but says that she always sort of looked down her nose at them since she felt that they tended to complain too much about racism and did not adopt the Asian work ethic to work twice as hard when confronted with racist behavior.

Sylvia moved to California a number of years ago and ironically it was in San Francisco that she experienced her first taste of anti-Asian violence. She was coming out of the Borders Bookstore in Union Square when a 6-foot tall "Timothy McVeigh"-looking Caucasian man ran up to her and said "My mother is not Chinese but yours is." Sylvia was somewhat taken aback, but tried to ignore him while she passed him.

He repeated the remark from behind her and when she did not react, he picked her up from behind and threw her against a nearby concrete wall, shattering her hip. Her assailant then ran away. As she lay there in shock, she was assaulted again in a much more painful and personal way as two Caucasian tourists walked by and in an attempt to be helpful, asked her if she spoke English.

Sylvia noted afterwards that even in an emergency situation, the first thought that crossed the minds of these Caucasians upon seeing an injured Asian woman was not the injury, but the race. "I was so outraged then, I couldn't even respond. Here I lay, on the ground, I was beaten, my hip was shattered, and the first thing they asked me was if I spoke English, not if I was ok, if I needed help, or if they should call an ambulance. The first thing they asked me was if I spoke English—and they were clearly tourists. I was so shocked, I couldn't even say anything."

Sylvia was eventually taken to the hospital and underwent extensive surgery to have her entire hip replaced. But as her physical injuries were treated by the doctors, her psychological injuries remained unattended, festering as she fell into a deep depression. "My co-workers, who were mostly Caucasian, came by to see me and I guess that they were trying to be funny. One of them said something like 'Well, at least you got a new hip.' At that moment, I just felt so angry because they couldn't understand that I was almost killed because of my race. I just didn't think I could ever see them in the same light again."

"[My coworkers] had a hard time saying 'assault'; they felt embarrassed and responsible," according to Sylvia. "The first thing they ask is, 'Did he take your money?" Her friends felt that she was obsessed with the racial nature of the attack and that she should not dwell on the incident. Sylvia, on the other hand, felt like she was unable to talk with them anymore.

The police had talked to a few witnesses, but were unable to develop any substantive leads and, in the opinion of the family, discouraged them from pursuing an active criminal investigation. Time and time again, Sylvia was told by the officer in charge of the investigation it was not worth her while to pursue the assailant, suggesting it was better to forget the incident and simply let old wounds heal. Though witnesses indicated that the assailant had been hanging around the area previously and had harassed other people of color, the police closed their investigation shortly after the incident.

But as time progressed, Sylvia did not just "get over" the racial attack. Her mental health continued to deteriorate to the point where the family contacted the Asian Law Caucus expressing grave concerns over her well being. They were frustrated over the lack of police response, angry over the racist nature of the attack, and distressed over Sylvia's deepening depression.

Initially, I spoke with Sylvia a few weeks after the incident and made some inquiries with the police regarding the status of her case. Although this was clearly a hate crime and had been treated as such by the police department, as is the case with the overwhelming majority of hate crimes, there was little the criminal justice system could do for her since the assailant had not been caught. The police expressed a general resistance to conducting any additional investigation into her case, stating that it was hopeless to pursue a random assault like this. I then worked with Sylvia to put her story into the media since she felt this would encourage greater interest in her case and help her talk through what had happened to her.

THE RESPONSE: WHAT IS THE INJURY?

In treating only her physical injuries, the doctors treated Sylvia the same way they would handle a patient who fell down the stairs or who was in an automobile accident. While the doctors were able to replace her shattered hip, they were unable to give her a replacement for her shattered frame of reference which had helped her in life to interpret, deflect, and respond to racism. In a moment's notice, she was inexplicably attacked and her life drastically changed, all by an idea which she had tried to suppress or ignore for most of her life. In failing to address the underlying cause of the injury, the doctors failed to treat the most serious injury of all—the one to her psyche. As such, Sylvia was left feeling confused and powerless, without the ability to either explain or prevent another unprovoked attack.

The isolated hate crime is particularly venomous because of its seemingly random nature and the inability of the victim to rationalize its occurrence. Even as children, we learn to create mental defenses and white lies to guard against the mental attacks from others. Rationalization is an important defense in our logical world and, as thinking beings, it is important for us to believe that the world is controlled by rationality. By using rational reasons to explain the occurrence of bad things, we can learn from our experiences and change to avoid a reoccurrence. The inability to explain the incident subjects the victim to further trauma because if you can't explain it, there's nothing you can do to prevent it from happening again. The well-documented tendency of victims to blame themselves can often be mitigated by a belief that a change in behavior will prevent it from happening again. We like to think of life events as cause and effect, order and chaos.

Victims of burglary may rationalize that they did not take enough safety precautions and install a better alarm system. Someone who is involved in an automobile accident will try to remember to look both ways next time before crossing the street. But there is nothing you can do to hide your race, skin color, gender, or sexual orientation. There is simply no escape or change in behavior possible for victims of hate crimes and they understand that they have to live with the possibility of reoccurrence without warning. In Sylvia's case and in other similar cases, this helplessness may be exacerbated by the fact that the actual perpetrators are rarely caught.

Moreover, this may be compounded by the fact that victims of hate crimes may have never even viewed themselves as representatives of the community, but in the hate crime they are subject to attack, not as individuals, but as symbols. They are stripped of their individuality and reduced to their race. In Sylvia's case, as she was being attacked, her assailant kept repeating, "My mother is not Chinese, but yours is." Sylvia was not attacked for anything about her, anything she stood for, but on the basis of her birth. Her "crime" in the eyes of the attacker was not acting Chinese, or even being Chinese, but the crime of her ancestors in being born Chinese. The message was direct and terrifying—you are different from me and so you must be hurt.

This is the poison of hate crimes which distinguishes it from other types of victimization. The consistent message of violence directed against Asian Pacific Americans is that you are the foreigner, you do not belong here, you are not an American. This message was one that Sylvia was not prepared to receive as it violently contradicted all of the promises of America she was raised to believe and which she adopted as her own values. Like many immigrants, Sylvia always believed in the ideal of America as the land of equality and opportunity. If you worked hard, you could get ahead, blend in, and be considered an equal. In the instances where she or her family were confronted with racist attitudes, her external response was to work twice as hard to go around the wall of racism, to work harder to prove her worth as an American.

In coming to America, Asians accept the unspoken racial hierarchy which will allow them to succeed up to the point where they hit the glass ceiling. They do not even carry the expectations of parity with whites. As such, they are identified as the "model minority," willing to accept a second-class standard of living as opposed to the African Americans whose civil rights paradigm has demanded an equal playing field. As in Sylvia's case, it is precisely due to this reason that many immigrants look down upon African Americans, because they themselves have made the difficult choice to swallow their pride and accept their status to provide their children with a better future. Sylvia believed that African Americans chose to complain too much and did not work hard enough to fight their way through the wall of racism.

The attack shook Sylvia to the core not only due to the extreme violence, but because it forced her to confront the fact that regardless of the years of work that she put into proving herself, the goodwill offered little protection to her from either the attacker or the tourists who did not view her as an equal American. In an incident lasting less than a minute, one man stripped her of her veneer, her status as an honorary white, and reduced her to her race. Despite years of sacrifice and hard work to form a protective layer of class, assimilation, and privilege, she understood now that she was still as vulnerable as the newly-arrived Asian immigrant or the African American. And, as Sylvia discovered, you could not just turn your back and try to ignore the racism because it would just follow you and haunt you. The advice that she had given herself and her children for years simply did not work and failed to protect her from the brutal assault.

The attack also undermined Sylvia's second learned form of psychological defense of internally strengthening herself against racist attacks by relying upon her heritage as a Korean immigrant. In less severe incidents, Sylvia was able to disregard the incidents and dismiss the rejection by falling back upon the strength of Korean culture. As a first-generation immigrant with some degree of grounding in the Korean culture, she was able to draw strength in the idea that in her true home, she would be regarded as an equal. Therefore, in America, as a guest or sojourner, she could accept second class citizenship. Essentially, Sylvia was saying, "I don't deserve to be treated like a regular American and I don't need to respond to these demeaning attitudes because I have another home in Korea where they treat me like an equal." This is a standard form of mental gamesmanship that we all engage in to protect our sense of pride when denied a certain goal; we always create a lie that we didn't really want it anyway.

However, perhaps due to the passage of time and her tenure in the United States, or perhaps due to the seriousness of her injuries, she was no longer able to ignore the fact that her rights had been violated and that she was not respected as an equal in the country where she had spent the majority of her life. Although Sylvia was originally an immigrant, her fifty years of struggle and survival here in the United States had earned her the right to be recognized as an American, equal and unquestioned. But now, only moments after her physical assault, she was assaulted again verbally by well-meaning by-passers, questioning her identity even before asking about her injuries. From skinhead to good Samaritan, she was viewed as a foreigner, as an outsider, told physically and orally that she did not belong.

The inability to use her birthplace heritage as a source of comfort was a first step towards establishing an identity as an Asian American. The birth of the Asian Pacific American identity begins when the standard tag of "Oh, you speak English so well (for a foreigner)?" is no longer considered a compliment but taken as an insult. However, without a further bridge to developing an Asian American consciousness, she knew only that a door had closed behind her without yet seeing a path before her. Lost and feeling abandoned, Sylvia fell into a depression over the realization that she was homeless, neither Korean nor American. In this nether world, she could no longer claim the protection of her cultural heritage or the promises of American equality.

SYLVIA'S RESPONSE: KNOCKING DOWN WALLS

Metaphorically speaking, Sylvia was thrown against the concrete wall of racial reality, which forced her to re-examine her internal and external defenses which were previously erected to deny or mitigate the existence of racism in her life. In a context far beyond the racial taunts suffered by her children, the seriousness of the injury forced her into a position where she could no longer dismiss the prejudice as irrelevant. The life-threatening nature of her injuries forced her to take a second look not only at racism, but her own responses and attitudes in the past.

Sylvia's response as she gradually healed was to build an entirely new frame of reference in relating to American society incorporating elements of Asian American and cross-cultural studies. Ironically, at the time that she was subject to this hate violence, Sylvia had been taking a class in cross-cultural studies to become a certified ESL [English as a Second Language] instructor. She had actually gone to the Borders Bookstore that day to buy some of the assigned books for the class. She tells me that initially she hadn't put much stock in the class and found many of the African American attitudes to be tiresome. "Why couldn't they just work harder?" I thought, "Why do they always complain so much?"

But as she lay in her hospital bed, one of the African American students from her class made it a special point to visit with her. She watched as he was stopped by the hospital staff and questioned as to his reasons for being at the hospital. And as he made his way to her bed and held her hand, Sylvia began to cry. "And all I could say to him was, 'I'm sorry, I'm sorry, only now can I begin to understand."

Although her attacker was Caucasian, the attack prompted Sylvia to re-examine her beliefs and attitudes towards all of race relations with a particular emphasis on African Americans. By turning to the theories she acquired through cross-racial studies courses, she found a framework for recovery, a new structure for re-evaluating her own life and experiences through the lens of race. After her attack, that which had been theoretical and incomprehensible found form and substance. What had previously existed outside her reality now became her point of view. She read books on Martin Luther King Jr. and other African American leaders, looking to them for answers.

As she began to understand the broader context of racism and race relations in the United States, her incident of hate violence began to seem less a random occurrence. At the same time, it became less painful as she read about the history of African Americans in the U.S. "I just stopped feeling sorry for myself. After all, it had just happened to me for a few times. But this sort of thing was happening to African Americans all the time."

Talking with her children and others about her experiences and newfound framework, she eagerly embraced learning about new cultures and ideas. It was as if she were born again at the age of 63. She told me how recently, in watching a documentary "Once We Were Kings," regarding the life of Muhammad Ali, she broke down weeping in the theatre. "I grew up hearing about this Muhammad Ali and to tell you the truth, we always sort of looked down on him. In the Korean culture, we don't respect physical accomplishments that much—

perhaps it is the Confucian teachings which tell us to respect that which you can accomplish with your brain."

"But now, for the first time, I understand the courage and honor of Muhammad Ali in changing his name and taking a stand for his people. I used to think of him as a braggart. Now, I see him as a hero. I never knew he risked so much. In a way, my biggest regret is that this beating I suffered didn't happen to me 60 years earlier," she laughs. "I now look back on my life and think how blind I was. I now spend time reflecting on my whole life and I think what I might have done different if only my eyes had been opened sooner to the racism in our society. I wish I had been able to do more; to do something about it."

Sylvia credits her exploration and increased understanding of the African American struggle with providing her with the strength and context to fight her way out of her pit of depression. "I don't hate white people. I still don't know that much about black people, but I know more now about where I fit in than I did before."

Sylvia has recovered both physically and psychologically and now continues to attend classes in exploring race relations and cultural studies. After the release of the 1996 National Asian Pacific American Legal Consortium report on violence against Asian Pacific Americans, Sylvia was profiled widely by the media including an appearance on the Lehrer News Hour. She hopes to be certified as an ESL instructor soon and intends to teach new immigrants not only about English, but about America.

SWASTIKAS IN THE SUNSET: WHO IS THE VICTIM?

The Incident:

The Sunset District of San Francisco is an affordable, residential and small business community located in the western section of the city, running above Golden Gate Park along Irving and Judah streets. It is a culturally diverse and middle-class neighborhood with a long-established Irish, Jewish and Russian community and a rapidly growing Asian American immigrant population. The Asian American population of the Sunset District has doubled in recent years and many now refer to the area as the "New Chinatown." The area has historically prided itself on its neighborhood "mom and pop" stores and has been highly resistant to the influx of chain stores and fast food franchises.

In 1996, a Chinese American business owner opened a Burger King franchise in the area, which was immediately met with community resistance, both reasoned and racist. While some residents protested the change in the neighborhood character, others posted flyers calling for "Chinks and Burger King Out of the Sunset." The Burger King was subject to a barrage of vandalism, graffiti, and protests through the following months, continuing to this day.

In February of 1997, an individual or a group of individuals known as the "SWB" or "Sunset White Boys," carved swastikas into the glass storefronts of nearly two dozen Asian American businesses, mostly along Irving Street. The placement and selectivity of the swastikas was particularly ominous in that primarily Asian-owned businesses were targeted and non-Asian businesses were passed over with the exception of a Caucasian-run karate studio with Asian lettering on the storefront. The clinical precision exercised in the choice of the targets indicated a familiarity with the community, leading people to suspect that this was an "inside" job. There were also the biblical overtones of genocide and divine retribution.

The vandalism ranged from small, red spray-painted swastikas accompanied by the initials "SWB" to three-foot high swastikas carved with some sharp instrument into the glass storefronts of several Asian-owned businesses. A great deal of attention and energy was focused in particular upon the Bank of the Orient, with the swastika carved prominently next to the word Orient.

Surprisingly, many of the store owners were immigrants from China and Vietnam who confessed ignorance at the significance of the swastikas. All they knew was that they were vandalized once again, and due to the indifferent or hostile treatment that they had received at the hands of the police in previous cases of vandalism, most failed to even report the occurrence. Many did not even realize that other Asian businesses along the street had suffered similar etchings and more than a week went by without any action being taken. During this time, the swastikas remained prominently displayed to the public.

The swastikas were finally brought to the attention of a Chinese American officer in another jurisdiction who decided to look into it on his own. The Asian Law Caucus was notified through a distant source during the course of the investigation and immediately responded to the location to document the hate vandalism, interview the targeted merchants and offer assistance. On two different occasions, staff and volunteers walked up and down Irving Street, meeting with each of the merchants as well as customers and people in the streets.

Even after I spoke with them, some of the store owners indicated that they did not intend to replace the glass panes defaced with swastikas since vandalism was rampant and they would just be hit again after spending the money. In visiting these merchants, it was chilling to see customers and families coming to the area to shop or do business as usual in broad daylight with each of the storefronts marked by swastikas.

Many of the merchants were reluctant to have their businesses photographed or identified for fear of retaliation. In fact, many were surprised that what they viewed as another routine round of vandalism had attracted outside attention. After speaking with the merchants and documenting the incidents, we alerted the mainstream press. Both print and broadcast media ran widespread coverage on the swastikas even though the vandalism had taken place a week earlier. In response to the media coverage and subsequent public outcry, police and elected officials flocked to the community.

The Response: Who Is the Victim?

The response to a hate crime must be carefully tailored to address both the needs and concerns of the primary victim and also that of the community. A directed and strategic response works to counter the hateful message of exclusion and intimidation. However, in many cases it is unclear at the outset who the primary victim is and towards whom the communal remedy should be directed. Was the true victim of the hate crime the more established Jewish community at large which was forced to confront the painful reminder of the Holocaust? Or was the victim the potential APA (Asian Pacific American) store owner, resident, or customer considering coming into the Sunset District but who was then scared away by the prospect of being racially targeted because of his/her ethnicity? Or was it the San Francisco community at large? The responses of various authorities in this case differed depending upon their determinations on the identity of the victim. While all were successful in achieving some measure of combating hate crimes, no one fully addressed the underlying tensions which created the hate-filled environment.

The Police Response

Typically, the police are focused solely on the apprehension of the criminal and exhibit little sympathy or understanding of the needs of the victim or community. Generally, they are reluctant to categorize any case as a hate crime, perhaps out of an unwillingness to invest the extra time into conducting additional investigation, or perhaps due to a resistance to taint their jurisdiction with an insinuation of racism.

In this case, the police responded exceptionally poorly, which was surprising given the fact that San Francisco Police Department Chief Fred Lau is Chinese American and for years the department maintained a separate investigative unit specifically trained and devoted to working on hate crimes. In response to press inquiries, the police captain incredulously countered that these carvings were not hate crimes since swastikas are anti-Semitic in nature and not anti-Asian. While this initial statement was quickly retracted, the captain then adopted the position that these acts of vandalism were the acts of juveniles and therefore, should not be taken seriously. The acts were dismissed and somehow excused as childish pranks and therefore, not worthy of community discussion and intervention.

Under increasing scrutiny and public pressure, Chief Fred Lau intervened. Several bilingual officers were re-assigned to patrol the Sunset District, the case was turned over to the special hate crimes unit, and general police presence in the area was increased over the short term in an attempt to apprehend the perpetrator(s).

Several juveniles were soon arrested and the newspaper headlines reported that the responsible parties had been found. Conveniently, one of the youths was Pilipino and so the police took the opportunity to declare that this was clearly not a hate crime since one of the suspects was Asian. Weeks later, with smaller fanfare, it was reported that the youths who were arrested—while admitting to general tagging in the neighborhood—did not actually have anything to do with the swastikas. After a few weeks when community and media pressure died down, nothing further was heard from the police regarding their efforts to find the perpetrators.

ASIAN AMERICAN MERCHANTS AS VICTIMS?

One Asian American San Francisco county supervisor organized a highly successful volunteer clean-up day and recruited elected officials, union labor, community members and donations of materials to clean up all of the graffiti, sweep the streets, and replace the glass at no charge to the merchants. Volunteers turned out from all parts of the city and the media flocked. The event removed the obvious signs of hate and arguably sent a message to the perpetrators and the community that such hate violence would not be tolerated and that San Francisco was united in stamping out the signs of racism. The clean-up day was successful in removing the swastikas from public view, in giving the community a chance to directly demonstrate its commitment to fighting hate crimes, and bringing together diverse communities for a day to take a joint stand against hate crimes.

However, while this clean-up day was an unqualified success in removing the physical vestiges of racism, it is questionable as to how successful it was in addressing the underlying attitudes that lead to acts of hate. In addressing the problem as one of vandalism, the effort failed to acknowledge that the swastikas were reflective of ideas and beliefs held much closer to heart of the community. The focus upon the physical element of the hate crime overlooked the intangible factors of prejudice and racial tensions which had created an environment conducive to the racist expression of the swastikas.

On the other hand, one may argue the lesson learned in bringing together diverse communities to tackle a common goal was that the volunteer physical labor itself served as a symbol of the community coming together to fight anti-Asian violence. Undoubtedly, a major part of this effort was intended to impart upon the individual merchants that they were a part of the community and to demonstrate that in times of crisis they could rely upon the community to come to their assistance.

The focus upon these individual merchants was perhaps misplaced in that many of them were unaware of the historical and genocidal significance of the swastikas. Given their political naiveté, it is debatable as to whether or not they were truly the victims of a hate crime and whether or not they could appreciate the reasons for the volunteer response. One merchant told me that the clean-up was a great gesture, but asked why they had not come out before to clean up and whether or not they would come out again when the storefronts were defaced the following week.

Certainly, the store owners were economically and physically the victims of vandalism, but can they also be considered the victims of a hate crime if some failed to understand the intended message of the perpetrator(s)? Given that several did not understand the importance of the symbols, was it critical for the people and politicians to rally behind them in a show of community support?

According to the traditional principles of criminal law and specifically the law around hate crimes, these store owners are the victims of a hate crime. Generally, the definition of a hate crime turns on the intent of the perpetrator and not the understanding of the victim. For example, many jurisdictions hold that a man who is attacked because he is perceived to be gay—even if he is not—would be the victim of a hate crime and the perpetrator could be subject to enhanced penalties. On the other hand, a person who fights with a gay person motivated solely by a dispute over a parking space, would not be subject to a hate crime even if the gay person was subjectively afraid that the dispute was over his sexual orientation. This follows the general principles of criminal law that focuses on the intent of the perpetrator.

However, what makes hate crimes punishable above and beyond the physical act of criminality is the recognition that hate violence carries levels of psychological and emotional impact well beyond the simple commission of the crime. The penalties for hate crimes are more severe because we recognize that based upon a history of racial intolerance, the victims are particularly vulnerable and suffer levels of injuries far beyond the physical and objective damages. A cross-burning on an African American lawn is much more than an act of arson or vandalism. It carries with it the clear threat of further escalation of violence when considered in the context of historical precedent. Thus, when the victim does not understand or is unaware of the message of hate, much of the psychological trauma and venom of the crime is not present and from the individual victim's viewpoint, it becomes indistinguishable from a simple act of vandalism. Here, several of the merchants indicated that they were unaware of the swastikas or their meaning until after the police and media explained to them the significance behind the symbol.

Therefore, should some of the merchants who did understand the message of intimidation and racial hatred and suffered the psychological consequences be considered hate violence victims while the other merchants are not? Should the white karate store owner who also had his store defaced be considered a victim of anti-Asian violence? Clearly, the focus on the individual level makes little sense because the bottom line is that property-based hate crimes such as these are clearly an attack upon the community. Common sense dictates that the use of a swastika defines the incident as one of hate violence given its symbolism for racial hatred and violence regardless of the understanding of the owner of the property. But if the merchants were not particularly intimidated by this act, then was the clean-up perhaps for the benefit of the community as opposed to assisting these particular individuals? After all, the older neighborhood is predominantly Jewish and was certainly put on notice similar to the cross-burning once the swastikas were carved into their community stores. A more cynical and jaded viewpoint would be that the clean-up was not directed at helping the Asian American merchants at all but rather at the larger Jewish community which had to be confronted with these symbols every day.

THE NEIGHBORHOOD/GEOGRAPHIC COMMUNITY AS VICTIM?

A second Asian American county supervisor organized two town hall meetings to facilitate discussions on the placement of swastikas in the community. The events were advertised in several languages to both the Asian merchants and the Sunset community at large. Myself and several other volunteers conducted outreach to the merchants along the Irving corridor in an attempt to encourage their participation in the hearings. A non-Asian leader in hate crimes coalition work was selected to lead the discussions and hate crimes "experts," police, elected officials, media, and community groups were invited to attend.

Nearly two hundred people attended the first town hall meeting, but virtually none of the Asian merchants attended either of the sessions. The discussions were mostly dominated by a number of neighborhood conservation and watch groups from the Sunset community—many of whom were involved and continued to be involved in the efforts to drive the Burger King out of the Sunset District.

The first forum was opened with statements of support from local elected officials and presentations by the hate crimes experts. However, as the discussions progressed and the floor was opened up to those in attendance, the talk quickly turned to combating vandalism generally in the community and the changing character of the neighborhood. The changing character of the neighborhood, of course, was a euphemism for the rapid growth of the Asian American community in the Sunset district, which some say at the expense of the older Jewish Russian community. More neighborhood watch groups and closer cooperation with the police were proposed, a vandalism task force and hotline were discussed, and after the opening few minutes, the discussion of "hate" had been dropped and the audience spoke only of the "crimes."

In a more disturbing segment of the town hall meeting, audience members testified that the real problem contributing to the rise in crime was the fact that the community had changed so much that they did not feel that this was their community anymore. Some attendees remarked that Asian-language signs dominated the streets and you no longer heard English being spoken. Others commented that these "new" residents packed too many family members in a house, did not try to assimilate, hung out only with their own, did not participate in the civic affairs of the community, and generally did not fit into the Sunset character.

It is important to note that this was as much a case of ethnic conflict as it was a dispute between long time residents and newcomers. Some of those who spoke out against the transformation of the neighborhood included established Japanese Americans who could not read the Chinese language signs or understand the foreign languages being spoken on the street.

In an ironic twist, several residents complained that the merchants were at fault for not acting quickly to eradicate the swastikas once they appeared. These residents stated that they were offended that the stores did not act responsibly and rapidly to remove these signs of hate once they were carved on their front windowpanes. The residents who appeared at this public forum indicated that the problem was that the Asians did not participate in the neighborhood watches and other civic duties of the "community" and thus, hate crimes and vandalism were allowed to flourish. In a loosely-controlled forum, the audience had come full circle in scape-goating the victims as the perpetrators, and these were the voices and faces heard that night on the eleven o'clock news.

One resident in particular, who was widely featured during the media coverage of the community forums as a neighborhood leader, was regarded by the Asian American merchants as the leader of the racist and exclusionary forces against them. He had months earlier led the campaign against the Burger King and said to the owner of the Burger King "we don't want your cheap, sleazy, *yellow*, sign here in the Sunset."

In earlier discussions, the Asian American merchants expressed a general disinterest in attending such a forum and noted that the scheduled times conflicted with their business hours. I tried everything to encourage their attendance from pleading to their sense of community, to challenging their ethnic pride, to pitching attendance at the forum as a smart business decision. But I think the true reason why many failed to attend was a premonition that their issues, concerns and needs were not going to be addressed in this public setting. Perhaps the merchants thought they would not be able to communicate the depth of their hopes and fears through an interpreter. Many expressed a fear in becoming involved and subjecting themselves to potential future retaliation. And maybe they already knew who their neighbors were and did not want to walk into a hostile trap.

In trying to open up discussions with the community, the officials had allowed the content of the discourse to shift without moderation and granted legitimacy and press to a particular viewpoint of the community. In empowering a certain segment of the community which was hostile to the "Asian invasion," the town hall meetings served to further divide and separate the community. Sometime between the first and second town hall meetings, several businesses owned by non-Asians displayed signs calling for "No hate crimes in the Sunset, except against Burger King."

All of a sudden, it became clear "who killed Vincent Chin,"[1] these community leaders who had turned out to ostensibly combat hate crimes were in fact perpetuating much of the hate crimes messages in their own homes. No doubt, it was some juvenile that had committed the physical act of vandalism, but the hate was something being taught at home. The town hall meetings ended with the second forum. Nothing ever came of those meetings.

THE CALIFORNIA PUBLIC AS VICTIM?

The final response from the government involved a state assembly member who proposed legislation nearly a year later which would elevate hate crimes to a "wobbler" offense, allowing prosecutors the discretion to charge perpetrators with either a misdemeanor or felony, depending on the seriousness of the offense. In doing so, he cited the growing increase in hate crimes in general and the swastikas in the Sunset, in particular.

In doing so, the legislator also planned a press conference involving leaders of the Asian Pacific American community and other hate crimes professionals designed to send out a message to the community that hate crimes would be prosecuted seriously and the offender would be subject to felony imprisonment.

There is arguably some deterrent value to this legislation to the extent that it would generate some degree of publicity in having a public official condemn the commission of hate crimes. However, following passage of the law onto the books, it is unlikely to have much impact given that only a small fraction of hate crimes are ever solved by the police and an even smaller fraction are ever prosecuted as hate crimes. In San Francisco, there is a hate crimes investigation unit within the police department and a hate crimes prosecution unit within the District Attorney's Office. Yet, out of more than 300 hate crimes reported yearly to the police unit, there were only 13 arrests referred to the District Attorney's office. This resulted in an annual total of only seven convictions for hate crimes, six of which were the results of plea bargains. While the legislation deters the commission of a hate crime in the future by increasing the penalty, even if the perpetrators had been arrested in this case, the imprisonment of these individuals would do nothing to address the underlying tensions within the community.

THE ASIAN PACIFIC AMERICAN COMMUNITY AS VICTIM?

The swastikas were only a symptom of a more deeply rooted problem. The vandalism was neither a juvenile prank, nor a simple act of vandalism, but rather a powerful symbol of communities in conflict and a visible mark of the underlying tensions around a changing demographic in the Sunset District.

Undoubtedly, the commission of the hate vandalism in this case was a juvenile act, but the intent behind the swastikas was not a childish thought, but one shared by a large segment of the community. Asian Americans in the Sunset district were being told both by symbol and by comments made in community forums that they were threatening the integrity and character of the neighborhood, and therefore, should be marked. And in the town hall discussions, while many residents repudiated the specific action taken in this case, no one spoke against the underlying message of racial intolerance and disharmony.

Anti-Asian violence is the friction generated from two communities beginning to rub up against each other where there is no discussion or relationship between the communities. Viewing this situation in a historical context, what happened in the Sunset District was identical to what happened in countless other cities such as Monterey Park in Southern California or Queens in New

York where a fast-growing Asian American immigrant population began to threaten the character of an "older" neighborhood. Like an earthquake, the shifting and overlapping plates build up increasing resentment until there is a sudden release in the form of a hate crime.

On a macro level, anti-Asian violence represents the growing pains of our community as we expand and bump shoulders with neighboring communities. Because we are perceived as new, because we are seen as foreign, we are interpreted as a threat. The 1996 national audit on anti-Asian violence prepared by the National Asian Pacific American Legal Consortium and the Asian Law Caucus documents an increase in hate crimes in the housing projects, in the political arena, in the schools, and in these emerging communities. As our community continues to grow, we can only expect to see a greater incidence of hate violence directed against us.

CONCLUSION

Contrary to what many may think, Asian Americans are not born or naturalized. Anti-Asian violence is the pain prefacing the light which delivers the Asian American identity into our community. It is a recognition not only that you share a common bond and experience with all other Asians based upon your experiences here in the U.S., but that based upon that bond, you have an obligation to act on behalf of the community. The Asian American identity is based upon an understanding that anti-Asian violence has played an integral part in the history of both America and Asian America and that it has always served to exclude and deny us our rightful place. Asian America lives in the struggle for recognition and existence and in combating anti-Asian violence, we fight the message that we do not belong. It is a recognition that the attack upon the individual is an attempt to silence us all and therefore, to break our silence, we must speak up for the individual. Thus, while the community may be defined by the isolation and exclusion by the mainstream, it is also created from the response to anti-Asian violence.

But more than exclusion, it is a recognition that Asian America lives in the hearts of those in our community. The history of Asian Americans reflects the struggle for recognition and equality. Our forefathers planted seeds in the cracks of mountains and they planted dynamite high above the railroads, in concentration camps located in the deserts of Wyoming and Arizona, across the oceans on flotsam and refugee boats, parachuted in from modern jets and seared in the fires of Koreatown. The acres of history that we have tilled have not been welcoming nor fertile, but we have persevered and out of the desert we have taken seed and we have grown. The promise of America is not happiness or equality, but the pursuit of happiness and the opportunity to advocate for equality. In order for us to be recognized as equals, we must struggle to assert our right to sit at the table.

NOTES

1. "Who Killed Vincent Chin?," is a question raised in the documentary by the same name directed by Renee Tajima-Pena and Christine Choy. Vincent Chin was killed by two unemployed autoworkers on June 19, 1982, a week before he was to be wed. The two murderers yelled at Chin "It's because of motherf***ers like you that we're out of work," chased him down a street and one held him while the other beat his head in with a baseball bat. His murderers never served a day in jail and were sentenced to three years probation and a $3000 fine. The case became a symbol for anti-Asian violence in America and the filmmakers raised in their documentary the question of societal responsibility for Chin's death. The high level of Japan-bashing and Asian-bashing promulgated by the auto manufacturers, especially in this period, created an environment conducive to violence and anti-Asian American violence.

13.2 DERRICK BELL

Racism Will Always Be With Us

Racism is an integral part of America's cultural fabric. It is a major social malady that deeply affects the stability of the nation. Some social critics argue that racism is indispensable to the American political and economic structure. In the following selection from "Racism Will Always Be With Us," *New Perspectives Quarterly* (vol. 8, 1991), for example, Derrick Bell asserts that racism is inevitable in American society, where majority rule can effectively maintain control of an ideological framework that defines minorities as expendable. He shows that by compromising minority interests in favor of protecting White interests, the ruling class is able to retain political and economic control in society.

Bell is a professor of law at Harvard University and a former deputy director for civil rights in the Department of Health, Education, and Welfare. His many publications include *And We Are Not Saved: The Elusive Quest for Racial Justice* (Basic Books, 1989).

Key Concept: the inevitability of racism

Racism, like death, will always be with us. It is a permanent fixture of American society, and its effect—if not its form—has been fairly consistent in the US for 350 years.

There is an allegorical story in my . . . book [*Faces at the Bottom of the Well* (1996)] called "The Space Traders," which takes place in the year 2000 and involves an alien people who come to Earth and offer the US gold to pay off all its debts, chemicals to clean up its environment, and inexpensive, safe nuclear fuel to satisfy its energy needs. All the aliens want in return is an agreement that they can go back to their home star with America's black population in tow. Whites can't see these aliens; they can only hear them. But blacks, who can see them perfectly well and who establish that they hold an uncanny resemblance to Ku Klux Klansmen, respond incredulously to the Administration: "What are you doing? Just tell them 'No!' " There are many twists and turns in the story but finally there is a national referendum and by about 70 to 30 percent, the majority votes for the trade.

"The Space Traders" story is futuristic but it is based on fact. In the history of the US, whenever there is a serious difference between contending groups of whites and compromise can be reached by sacrificing the rights of blacks, that is what happens. There were no aliens offering gold when the Constitution was written but there were a good many powerful men who threatened to walk out of the Constitutional Convention and so sacrifice the unity of the nation if blacks were endowed with human qualities, much less rights. There were Northerners who hated slavery but Southerners who said, "either protect slavery or there will be no new federal government." Slavery was protected.

THE THEORY OF MORAL RELATIVITY In 1830, Alexis de Tocqueville wrote: "I do not believe that the white and black races will ever live in any country upon an equal footing. But I believe the difficulty to be still greater in the US than elsewhere. An isolated individual may surmount the prejudices of the religion of his country or his race but a whole people cannot rise, as it were, above itself. A despot who should subject the American and his former slaves to the same yoke might perhaps succeed in co-mingling the races but as long as the American democracy remains at the head of affairs, no one will undertake so difficult a task and it may be foreseen that the freer, that is the more democratic the white population of the US becomes, the more isolated it will remain."

Indeed, the Framers of the Constitution were afraid of majoritarian government; and in *The Federalist,* James Madison urged a large, diverse electorate composed of many factions as the best defense against majority tyranny. Madison's approach is viable as long as coalition building occurs freely across racial lines, but when issues come to be seen across the fault line of race, minorities always pay the highest price.

The fact of contemporary American politics is that ours is a majoritarian system, divided along racial lines and whites tend to oppose those policies blacks support: Affirmative action and civil rights legislation are only the most obvious examples.

One effect of race-based politics is that ideas of justice, equality and morality become infinitely manipulatable based on one's racial perspective—who is doing what to whom, when, where and under what circumstances.

An example: The attack by Los Angeles police on Rodney King last spring shocked the US not because *any* act of police brutality is, in and of itself, immoral and illegal but because we saw it on television and we could no longer avoid the issue. However, the fact of the matter is that the Los Angeles police force has a decades-old reputation—and out-of-court settlements to victims to substantiate the reputation—of brutality toward minorities.

Blacks saw the King beating as a pattern in practice—a graphic comment on the quality of their citizenship. Yet, until a video was made of this brutality in action, most people were willing to look the other way as long as these policemen protected their car stereos and their homes.

Most whites would not vote for police to beat black heads. But if there are police who say that the only way they can do their job and protect property is if they can beat black heads, compromises—meaning the sacrifice of civil rights—will be made.

THE PRINCIPLE OF INTEREST CONVERGENCE If the first principle of political physics is compromise—with blacks always being compromised first—the second principle is that no law is passed that benefits blacks unless that law benefits or at least does no harm to the interests of whites—a principle I call "interest convergence."

The 1954 *Brown v. Board of Education* is a perfect example of interest convergence. I often cite the NAACP and government briefs in the *Brown* case, both of which maintain that abandonment of state-supported segregation would be a crucial asset as we compete with communist countries for the hearts and minds of Third World people just emerging from long years of colonialism. Certainly, it would have been harder to convince the Third World of our superiority if we had continued to have official apartheid built right into the Constitution or its interpretation.

Though Dr. W. E. B. DuBois did not endear himself to civil rights advocates with the following statement, years after the *Brown* decision he observed that "no such decision would have been possible without the world pressure of communism," which he felt rendered it "simply impossible for the US to continue to lead a "Free World" with race segregation kept legal over a third of its territory." In *Parting the Waters,* Taylor Branch notes that the Voice of America immediately translated Justice Warren's opinion into 34 languages for overseas broadcast, while some domestic media outlets fell silent and Universal Newsreels never even mentioned the most important Supreme Court decision of the century.

But the Court, after handing down *Brown* in 1954 then said, "Come back next year and we will tell you how to go about implementing the desegregation ruling." And what they said the next year was that they were going to implement *Brown* very, very slowly. But for the protests, the bus boycott in Montgomery in 1959, the sit-ins that started in 1960, who knows what would have happened to *Brown.*

As it was, *Brown* dealt with the effects of segregation but didn't address its causes. Indeed, *Brown* is an amazing piece of legal writing in that there is an acknowledgement of serious harm but no admission of wrong doing. Segregation just floated down out of the sky; it is bad; we don't know how it got started; we have got to end it. As if racism was an anachronism that could be picked out of society like so many weeds.

Had the Court been serious about the equal educational opportunity *Brown* promised, as well as concerned about white opposition to actual desegregation, it might have approached the issue from the victim's perspective and issued the following orders in *Brown*—orders which would have given priority to desegregating not the students but the money and the control:

1. Even though we encourage voluntary desegregation, we will not order racially integrated assignments of students or staff for ten years.
2. Even though "separate but equal" no longer meets the constitutional equal-protection standard, we will require immediate equalization of all facilities and resources.

3. Blacks must be represented on school boards and other policy-making bodies in proportions equal to those of black students in each school district.

The third point would have been intended to give blacks meaningful access to decision making—a prerequisite to full equality still unattained in many predominantly black school systems. For example, an "equal representation" rule might have helped protect the thousands of black teachers and principals who were dismissed by school systems during the desegregation process.

Had this been the approach, however, the Court never would have reached a unanimous decision. In fact, it probably would not even have gotten a majority to go along with the school desegregation plan.

So, instead, *Brown* essentially equated integration with the effective education black children need. And because *Brown* did not have the power to regulate the behavior of white parents who could afford to move to the suburbs or send their children to private schools, or to redistribute taxes so that a district's tax base would not destine poor areas to inferior educational facilities, 36 years after *Brown* the schools are resegregated and black children continue to receive an inferior education in substandard facilities.

RACE AS METAPHOR Racism, however, is merely a metaphor for what happens to the vast majority of Americans—white, black or brown—on a much larger scale. I am always amazed that problems of race I see dramatically in regard to blacks are present, although less dramatically, for whites also. Rhetoric about equality and justice aside, the failure of these ideals to translate into reality in any meaningful way go well beyond race.

But the "race question" is an extremely powerful diversion. Twenty years ago, economist Robert Heilbroner argued that the reason the US lagged so far behind countries in Northern Europe on issues of housing, prison reform, social security and health care—even though Northern Europe was much less rich than the US—was because those countries were homogeneous and people were able to perceive that, "there but for the grace of God go I."

In our heterogeneous country, it is very easy for those opposed to these programs to argue against them on the basis that prison reform will only coddle the black prisoner; that affirmative action gives jobs to reward lazy minorities who would rather stand on the corner than study; that welfare is being abused by lazy, pathological, drug-abusing black women. The US is able to distance the suffering and relative disadvantage of many whites by arguing that people of color disproportionately and unfairly benefit from social welfare programs. . . .

George Bush used Willie Horton, a black felon, in a national television campaign to scare voters away from his opponent. [North Carolina Senator] Jesse Helms appealed to white voters by showing white hands tearing up a rejection slip, the message being: Blacks, through affirmative action, are stealing your jobs. These two men, who should have been excoriated, were hailed—and elected—though they merely utilized a modern version of a tried-and-true coalition-building tactic: playing to white fears of loss—job, position, prestige, safety—to blacks.

These are only two examples of the fact that those who wish to protect their place within the economic and political status quo need only remind voters that they must stand together against blacks who, through affirmative action or crime, pose a major threat to them all. Racism is a very effective organizing tool.

THE PERKS OF RACISM Tocqueville understood in 1830, and Yale professor Edmond Morgan confirmed in his book *American Slavery, American Freedom,* what most of us today refuse to acknowledge: that there is a significant connection between democracy and discrimination. Both men understood quite clearly that the presence of a class at the bottom in slavery meant that those on top were able to preach the apostrophes of freedom to poor and working-class whites, urge them to vote and be a part of the system, while denying them any real opportunities. We have had variations of this theme ever since.

Except for a few brilliant exceptions such as Tocqueville or Thomas Jefferson, who, considering the evil of slavery, wrote: "I tremble for my country when I reflect that God is just," racism is rarely acknowledged in its then-currently-functioning form. During slavery, there were arguments about how enslavement actually helped slaves. Variations on this argument were used during the days of "separate but equal." We hear more of the same today, except the arguments are negative: Affirmative action actually hurts the self-esteem of blacks; civil rights legislation hurts small businesses.

I have come to the conclusion, after many years, that my obligation is not to overcome racism but to recognize and oppose it. Just as death is inevitable, racism is intractable. It is the failure to develop a realistic perspective on the problem that stymies progress and makes setbacks very discouraging.

We must advocate an infusion of tragedy into our American culture, an understanding of our past and the limits of our shared future.

Certainly, there is tragedy in America vis-à-vis blacks. In failing to acknowledge this we invite side shows: We argue about who is to blame rather than what is to be done; we fight to desegregate the schools, rather than to educate our children; we argue about why Vietnamese immigrant children succeed while blacks remain behind, rather than demanding that all children be well-educated.

This said, the likelihood of getting any unanimous agreement on policies is very poor. However, strategy and tactics are less important than having a sense of what we are fighting. We must first understand the peculiar hold racism has on American society. Then, after we have some understanding, we must use whatever tools we have available to loosen its hold on our lives.

PART FIVE

Responding to Race and Ethnic Oppression

On the Internet . . .

Sites appropriate to Part Five

This *Washington Post* online site contains an article entitled, "A Conversation in Black and White." This article consists of excerpts from an e-mail discussion between the author of a newspaper story entitled, "White Girl?" and a reader. A five-month-long exchange of e-mails excerpted on this site shows how an unusual public exchange turned into an extraordinary personal one.

`http://washingtonpost.com/wp-dyn/articles/A15476-2000Jul20.html`

The Crosspoint site contains links on racism, human rights, Jewish resources, disability resources, gay and lesbian resources, and more. Search by country or subject to learn about international efforts to stop racism.

`http://www.magenta.nl/crosspoint/`

The National Conference for Community and Justice (NCCJ) is a human relations organization dedicated to fighting bias, bigotry, and racism in America. This site provides information on how the organization seeks to transform the nation's communities and workplaces. Also included are links to other human relations, civil rights, human rights, and education organizations.

`http://www.nccj.org`

CHAPTER 14 Responses to Racism

14.1 PAUL BUTLER

Racially Based Jury Nullification

The adjudication of criminal culpability by a jury of one's peers reinforces the notion of fundamental fairness in Anglo-American jurisprudence. The United States adopted the jury system in the Sixth Amendment to the Constitution, by which "in all criminal prosecutions, the accused shall enjoy the right to a speedy and public trial, by an impartial jury." Yet, as one scholar has put it, "If rights are to have real meaning for the great masses of people, we must not only inscribe them in constitutions and statutes—we must support these freedoms by powerful institutions as well." Considerable evidence suggests that throughout the history of American criminal justice, non-White minorities have been methodically disenfranchised from full and equal participation in the jury system. For example, all-White juries have been used selectively to ensure that non-White defendants accused of crimes against Whites received a guilty verdict. Similarly, racist White jurors often refused to convict Whites who were accused of lynching and murdering Blacks during the Jim Crow period of the Deep South. To some scholars, institutionalized racism continues in the American jury system today, and, as a result, the jury system and jury selection are grounded in structural ideas of supremacy and Anglo-controlled institutions.

In the following selection from "Racially Based Jury Nullification: Black Power in the Criminal Justice System," *Yale Law Journal* (December

1995), former U.S. attorney Paul Butler reviews the doctrine of jury nullification and asserts that it is an effective means by which African Americans can rectify the injustices they receive at the hands of the American criminal justice system. Butler suggests that Black jurors can combat the inherent racism in the U.S. criminal justice system by acquitting Black defendants who are accused of committing nonviolent, victimless crimes, despite evidence of guilt.

Key Concept: jury nullification and strategies for combating racism

INTRODUCTION

I was a Special Assistant United States Attorney in the District of Columbia in 1990. I prosecuted people accused of misdemeanor crimes, mainly the drug and gun cases that overwhelm the local courts of most American cities. As a federal prosecutor, I represented the United States of America and used that power to put people, mainly African-American men, in prison. I am also an African-American man. While at the U.S. Attorney's office, I made two discoveries that profoundly changed the way I viewed my work as a prosecutor and my responsibilities as a black person.

The first discovery occurred during a training session for new Assistants conducted by experienced prosecutors. We rookies were informed that we would lose many of our cases, despite having persuaded a jury beyond a reasonable doubt that the defendant was guilty. We would lose because some black jurors would refuse to convict black defendants who they knew were guilty.

The second discovery was related to the first, but was even more unsettling. It occurred during the trial of Marion Barry, then the second-term mayor of the District of Columbia. Barry was being prosecuted by my office for drug possession and perjury. I learned, to my surprise, that some of my fellow African-American prosecutors hoped that the mayor would be acquitted, despite the fact that he was obviously guilty of at least one of the charges—he had smoked cocaine on FBI videotape. These black prosecutors wanted their office to lose its case because they believed that the prosecution of Barry was racist.

Federal prosecutors in the nation's capital hear many rumors about prominent officials engaging in illegal conduct, including drug use. Some African-American prosecutors wondered why, of all those people, the government chose to "set up" the most famous black politician in Washington, D.C. They also asked themselves why, if crack is so dangerous, the FBI had allowed the mayor to smoke it. Some members of the predominantly black jury must have had similar concerns: They convicted the mayor of only one count of a fourteen-count indictment, despite the trial judge's assessment that he had

" 'never seen a stronger government case.' " Some African-American prosecutors thought that the jury, in rendering its verdict, jabbed its black thumb in the face of a racist prosecution, and that idea made those prosecutors glad.

As such reactions suggest, lawyers and judges increasingly perceive that some African-American jurors vote to acquit black defendants for racial reasons, a decision sometimes expressed as the juror's desire not to send yet another black man to jail. This Essay examines the question of what role race should play in black jurors' decisions to acquit defendants in criminal cases. Specifically, I consider trials that include both African-American defendants and African-American jurors. I argue that the race of a black defendant is sometimes a legally and morally appropriate factor for jurors to consider in reaching a verdict of not guilty or for an individual juror to consider in refusing to vote for conviction.

My thesis is that, for pragmatic and political reasons, the black community is better off when some nonviolent lawbreakers remain in the community rather than go to prison. The decision as to what kind of conduct by African-Americans ought to be punished is better made by African-Americans themselves, based on the costs and benefits to their community, than by the traditional criminal justice process, which is controlled by white lawmakers and white law enforcers. Legally, the doctrine of jury nullification gives the power to make this decision to African-American jurors who sit in judgment of African-American defendants. Considering the costs of law enforcement to the black community and the failure of white lawmakers to devise significant nonincarcerative responses to black antisocial conduct, it is the moral responsibility of black jurors to emancipate some guilty black outlaws.

Part I of this Essay describes two criminal cases in the District of Columbia in which judges feared that defendants or their lawyers were sending race-conscious, "forbidden" messages to black jurors and attempted to regulate those messages. I suggest that the judicial and public responses to those cases signal a dangerous reluctance among many Americans to engage in meaningful discourse about the relationship between race and crime. In Part II, I describe racial critiques of the criminal justice system. I then examine the evolution of the doctrine of jury nullification and suggest, in light of this doctrine, that racial considerations by African-American jurors are legally and morally right. Part II proposes a framework for analysis of the kind of criminal cases involving black defendants in which jury nullification is appropriate, and considers some of the concerns that implementation of the proposal raises.

My goal is the subversion of American criminal justice, at least as it now exists. Through jury nullification, I want to dismantle the master's house with the master's tools. My intent, however, is not purely destructive; this project is also constructive, because I hope that the destruction of the status quo will not lead to anarchy, but rather to the implementation of certain noncriminal ways of addressing antisocial conduct. Criminal conduct among African-Americans is often a predictable reaction to oppression. Sometimes black crime is a symptom of internalized white supremacy; other times it is a reasonable response to the racial and economic subordination every African-American faces every day. Punishing black people for the fruits of racism is wrong if that punishment is premised on the idea that it is the black criminal's "just deserts." Hence, the new paradigm of justice that I suggest in Part III rejects punishment for the sake of retribution and endorses it, with qualifications, for the ends of deterrence and incapacitation.

In a sense, this Essay simply may argue for the return of rehabilitation as the purpose of American criminal justice, but a rehabilitation that begins with the white-supremacist beliefs that poison the minds of us all—you, me, and the black criminal. I wish that black people had the power to end racial oppression right now. African-Americans can prevent the application of one particularly destructive instrument of white supremacy—American criminal justice—to some African-American people, and this they can do immediately. I hope that this Essay makes the case for why and how they should.

I. SECRET MESSAGES EVERYONE HEARS

Americans seem reluctant to have an open conversation about the relationship between race and crime. Lawmakers ignore the issue, judges run from it, and crafty defense lawyers exploit it. It is not surprising, then, that some African-American jurors are forced to sneak through the back door what is not allowed to come in through the front: the idea that "race matters" in criminal justice. In this part, I tell two stories about attempts by defense attorneys to encourage black jurors' sympathy for their clients, and then I examine how these attempts provoked many people to act as though the idea of racial identification with black defendants was ridiculous or insulting to black people. In fact, the defense attorneys may well have been attempting to encourage black jurors' sympathy as part of their trial strategies. The lesson of the stories is that the failure of the law to address openly the relationship between race and crime fosters a willful and unhelpful blindness in many who really ought to see and allows jury nullification to go on without a principled framework. This Essay offers such a framework and encourages nullification for the purpose of black self-help.

A. United States v. Marion Barry

The time is January 1990. The mayor of the District of Columbia is an African-American man named Marion Barry. African-Americans make up approximately sixty-six percent of the population of the City. The mayor is so popular in the black community that one local newspaper columnist has dubbed him "Mayor for Life." Barry is hounded, however, by rumors of his using drugs and " 'chasing women.' " Barry denies the rumors and claims that they are racist.

On January 18, 1990, the mayor is contacted by an old friend, Rasheeda Moore, who tells him that she is visiting for a short time, and staying at a local hotel. The mayor stops by later that afternoon and telephones Ms. Moore's room from the lobby of the hotel. He wants her to come downstairs to the lobby for a drink, but she requests that he come up to her room. The mayor assents, joins Ms. Moore in the room, and the two converse. At some point, Ms. Moore produces crack cocaine and a pipe, and invites the mayor to smoke it. He first demurs, then consents, and after he inhales smoke from the pipe, agents of the FBI and the Metropolitan Police Department storm the room. It turns out that Ms. Moore is a government informant, and the police have observed and videotaped the entire proceeding in the hotel room. The mayor is arrested and subsequently charged with one count of conspiracy to possess cocaine, ten counts of possession of cocaine, and three counts of perjury for allegedly lying to the grand jury that had investigated him. The mayor publicly asserts that he is the victim of a racist prosecution.

It is the last week in June 1990. The mayor is on trial in federal court. The judge is white. Of the twelve jurors, ten are African-American. Rasheeda Moore, the government's star witness, is expected to testify. The mayor has four passes to give to guests he would like to attend his trial. On this day, he has given one pass to Minister Louis Farrakhan, the controversial leader of the Nation of Islam. Farrakhan has publicly supported Barry since his arrest, in part by suggesting that the sting operation and the prosecution were racist. When Farrakhan attempts to walk into the courtroom, a U.S. deputy marshal bars his entry. When Barry's attorney protests, the judge states, outside of the jury's hearing, that Farrakhan's " 'presence would be potentially disruptive, very likely intimidating, and he is a persona non grata for the [rest] of this case.' " Rasheeda Moore then takes the stand.

The next day, the Reverend George Stallings appears at the trial with one of Barry's guest passes in hand. Stallings is a black Roman Catholic priest who, the previous year, received extensive publicity when he accused the Catholic Church of being hopelessly racist, left it, and founded his own church. When Stallings reaches the courtroom, the deputy marshal, following the instructions of the judge, does not let him enter. The judge explains, again outside of the jury's hearing, that Stallings is " 'in my judgment, not an ordinary member of the public and his presence would very likely have the same effect as Mr. Farrakhan's.' " The judge also indicates that there are " 'others who fit the same category.' " Barry's attorney asks for a list of those persons. The judge replies, " 'I think you will know them when you see them.' "

In the wake of these two episodes, the American Civil Liberties Union, representing Barry, Farrakhan, and Stallings, files an emergency appeal of the trial judge's decision. It argues that the judge's refusal to allow Barry's guests to attend the trial violated Barry's Sixth Amendment right to a fair trial and the First Amendment rights of the guests. In response, the judge's attorneys state that the judge excluded Farrakhan and Stallings because their presence in the courtroom would send an " 'impermissible message' " of " 'intimidation' " and " 'racial animosity' " to jurors and witnesses. The judge's attorneys argue that the excluded persons' views of the prosecution had been highly publicized and that their appearance at the trial was consistent with Barry's " 'publicly avowed strategies of seeking a hung jury and jury nullification.' " The judge's attorneys argue that Farrakhan and Stallings attended the trial " 'not to view the proceedings or to show generalized concern, but instead to send a forbidden message to the jury and witness.' "

The U.S. Court of Appeals for the District of Columbia Circuit rules that Farrakhan and Stallings should have presented their constitutional claims to the trial judge prior to seeking relief in the appellate court. Accordingly, it remands the case back to the trial judge. Because the trial has been halted pending appeal, however, the D.C. Circuit, in light of the "exigent circumstances," lists several "pertinent considerations" for the trial judge on remand. The considerations mainly concern the judge's power to regulate the attendance of those who threaten physically to disrupt a courtroom. The court does note, though, that:

> No individual can be wholly excluded from the courtroom merely because he advocates a particular political, legal or religious point of view—even a point of view that the district court or we may regard as antithetical to the fair administration of justice. Nor can an individual be wholly excluded from the courtroom because his presence is thought to send an undesirable message to the jurors except that of physical intimidation.

The trial judge hears the message of the court of appeals. In lieu of resolving Farrakhan and Stalling's constitutional claims, he instead seeks assurances from their attorneys that their clients know how to conduct themselves in a courtroom. Indeed, the judge provides the attorneys with his own "special rules" of decorum regarding the trial, stating that "any attempt to communicate with a juror may be punished as criminal contempt of Court." Farrakhan and Stallings's attorneys assure the court that their clients will act with decorum in the courtroom. The trial continues. The mayor is eventually convicted of one of the indictment's fourteen counts (for perjury), but not of the count in which he smoked the cocaine on videotape.

B. The Attorney Who Wore Kente Cloth

It is now June 11, 1992. John T. Harvey, III is an African-American criminal defense attorney who practices in the District of Columbia. Harvey represents a black man who is charged with assault with intent to murder. The case is scheduled for arraignment before a white judge. At the arraignment, Harvey wears a business suit and tie, and his jacket is accessorized by a colorful stole made of kente cloth. Kente cloth is a multihued woven fabric originally worn by ancient African royalty, and many African-Americans have adopted it as a fashion statement and a symbol of racial pride.

In pretrial proceedings, the judge had warned Harvey that he would not be permitted to wear kente cloth before a jury. According to Harvey, the judge told him that wearing the fabric during a jury trial " 'was sending a hidden message to jurors.' " The judge had informed Harvey that he had three options: He could refrain from wearing the kente cloth; he could withdraw from the case; or he could agree to try the case before the judge, without a jury. Harvey's client decided to plead guilty. At the June 11 hearing, however, Harvey refuses to enter his client's plea before the judge because he doubts that the judge will be impartial. The judge then removes Harvey from the case, " 'not on the basis of [the] kente cloth, but on the basis that [Harvey] will not enter a plea which [his] client wishes to enter.' "

The same day, another client of Harvey's is scheduled to go to trial, also for assault with intent to kill, before another white judge. During the voir dire, the judge asks if any of the jurors are familiar with Harvey, whose battle with the other judge was well publicized. Four of the potential jurors know of the controversy. " '[T]he concern we think we have here,' " the judge says, is " 'that we won't influence a juror improperly.' " He also informs them of case law in another jurisdiction suggesting that a court may prevent a Catholic priest from wearing a clerical collar in court. When Harvey asks the judge to inform the potential jurors of contrary cases, the judge refuses. The judge subsequently states:

> "For the record, Mr. Harvey is black. Aside from the courtroom clerk, he is the only black person who is participating in this trial.... He is wearing a so-called kente cloth around his neck, and he has recently received wide publicity, which I am sure he loves. I have wondered with my own conscience whether for me to simply wait for the government or someone else to object is the proper approach to avoid a war with Mr. Harvey, which I am not anxious for—either personally or on behalf of the Superior Court....
>
> I also note that this is costing us all a lot of time... and I don't appreciate it."

Ultimately, the judge allows Harvey to wear the cloth, but he suggests that when Harvey submits an attorney fee voucher to him for approval, he might not allow Harvey to be paid for the time the kente cloth issue has consumed. Harvey's client is tried before an all-black jury and is acquitted.

C. The Judicial and Popular Response: Willful Blindness

As described above, the trial judge's attempt to exclude Farrakhan and Stallings from Barry's trial met with disapproval from the D.C. Circuit. In the case of John Harvey, no higher court had occasion to review the judge's prohibition against the kente cloth, but, as discussed below, much of the public reaction to the judge's prohibition was critical. These responses scorned the trial judge's fears that black jurors might acquit on the basis of racial identification rather than the "evidence." The D.C. Circuit and many observers, however, failed to acknowledge the significance of the "forbidden" message. I believe that this failure was deliberate. It reflected an intention to avoid serious consideration of the issue of black jurors acquitting black defendants on the basis of racial identification. Simply put, the D.C. Circuit and some of the public did not want to face the reality that race matters, in general and in jury adjudications of guilt and innocence.

1. THE D.C. CIRCUIT: WE HATE FIGHTS The D.C. Circuit's per curiam opinion discussed the issue before it as though the judge's concern was that Barry's invitees would cause some type of physical disruption. The court listed a series of five "pertinent considerations," four of which actually were not pertinent because they involved the physical disruption of courtrooms or physical threats to witnesses.

The only relevant consideration was so vague that it was nearly useless: The trial judge must exercise his discretion to exclude people from attending criminal matters "consistently with the First and Fifth Amendment rights of individuals to attend criminal trials." The court's discussion of this consideration is even more ambivalent: No one can be "wholly" excluded from a trial, even if he advocates a point of view that "we may regard as antithetical to the fair administration of justice" or if his presence sends an "undesirable message" to jurors. Because the appellate court did not suggest a procedure for partial exclusion of courtroom spectators, the trial judge's response was to pretend as though he had been concerned all along about physical disruption and subsequently to insist that Farrakhan and Stallings act in accordance with his rules of decorum. In the view of the D.C. Circuit, trial guests should keep their hands and their feet to themselves, but their messages may run amuck. In reality, Farrakhan's and Stallings's manners in the courtroom were an issue created by the appellate court. Ironically, the trial judge's response—the patronizing insistence that Farrakhan and Stallings agree to behave themselves—smacks of racism more than does his initial decision to exclude them from the courtroom.

United States v. Barry suggests that no trial spectator can be barred from a courtroom unless she threatens physically to disrupt the trial. In this respect, the court established a severe restriction on the discretion of judges to control public access to trials. Not all courts have taken this position, however. Two of the few other federal appellate courts that have considered symbolic communication by trial spectators have found it appropriate to regulate this type of communication. In one case, the Ninth Circuit stated that "[w]hen fair trial rights are at significant risk . . . the first amendment rights of trial attendees can and must be curtailed at the courthouse door." In another case, the Eleventh Circuit ordered the retrial of a man convicted of the murder of a prison guard, partly because of the presence, at the first trial, of numerous uniformed prison guards. The court was concerned that the guards' presence posed an unacceptable risk of prejudicing the jurors.

Significantly, the decisions from the Ninth and Eleventh Circuits involved cases in which the presence of the spectators was not thought to implicate race. The D.C. Circuit is the first appellate court to consider a "forbidden" racial message. My intention in noting this distinction is not to criticize the restrictive standard the D.C. Circuit established; indeed, there are potentially troubling implications of standards that allow trial judges more discretion in terms of which "secret" messages to regulate. I suggest, however, that the D.C. Circuit's holding was not mandated by clear constitutional dictates and was not supported by precedent from other federal jurisdictions. Indeed, other appellate courts have considered and regulated the contents of the messages that trial spectators were thought to be sending. Those cases suggest that the D.C. Circuit could have talked about race, and yet it did not.

2. THE SKEPTICS: WHAT'S RACE GOT TO DO WITH IT? The response of a number of commentators to the controversy over John Harvey's kente cloth was disdainful of the trial judge's apprehension about race-based appeals to

black jurors. For example, the *Washington Times* characterized one of the judge's concerns as "[s]heer, unadulterated goofiness." The editorial continued:

> [The judge] apparently believes that the [kente] cloth is no innocent fabric but rather possesses hypnotic powers of seduction, powers that will turn the judicial system on its head and hold jurors in its sway. . . .
>
> . . . . [W]hile most of us common folk are puzzled by this kind of judicial behavior, lawyers are widely inured to the fact that judges are free to act like fools with impunity—even when it is an abuse of discretion, an abuse of power, a waste of time and an injustice to someone who has come before the court seeking justice.

The *Washington Post* opined:

> There is absolutely no reason in logic or law for Judge Scott to tell Mr. Harvey that he cannot wear a kente cloth before a jury—regardless of the jurors' race. The very suggestion is offensive to black jurors, that they somehow lose their judgment and objectivity at the sight of a kente cloth.

The National Bar Association, an African-American lawyers' group, expressed a similar concern, and one black attorney called the judge's actions " 'almost unbelievable' " . . . and wondered why the judge " 'injected race . . . into the trial proceedings by making an issue of the kente cloth. Even the prosecutors in the kente cloth case "remained conspicuously silent" and refrained from endorsing the judge's concerns about the cloth.' "

D. The Forbidden Message Revealed

I am fascinated by the refusal of these actors to take seriously the possibility and legal implications of black jurors' sympathy with black defendants. The criminal justice system would be better served if there were less reluctance to consider the significance of race in black jurors' adjudications of guilt or innocence. The remainder of this Essay argues that race matters when a black person violates American criminal law and when a black juror decides how she should exercise her power to put another black man in prison.

The idea that race matters in criminal justice is hardly shocking; it surely does not surprise most African-Americans. In the Barry and Harvey stories, I believe that it was known by all of the key players: judges, jurors, attorneys, defendants, and spectators. The trial judges in those cases were correct: Somebody —the controversial black demagogue, the radical black priest, the kente-cloth-wearing lawyer—was trying to send the black jurors a message. The message, in my view, was that the black jurors should consider the evidence presented at trial in light of the idea that the American criminal justice system discriminates against blacks. The message was that the jurors should not send another black man to prison.

There is no way to "prove" what Farrakhan's and Stallings's purposes were in attending Barry's trial—nor can I "prove" the intent of the kente-cloth-wearing lawyer. I believe that my theory that they were encouraging black jurors' sympathy is reasonable, based on the relevant players' statements, the trial judge's observations, and common sense and experience. Even if one is unwilling to ascribe to those players the same racially based motivations that I do, acknowledgement and concern that some black jurors acquit black defendants on the basis of race are increasing, as my experience at the U.S. Attorney's Office showed. For the remainder of this Essay, I focus on the legal and social implications of this conduct by black jurors.

II. "JUSTICE OUTSIDE THE FORMAL RULES OF LAW"

Why would a black juror vote to let a guilty person go free? Assuming that the juror is a rational actor, she must believe that she and her community are, in some way, better off with the defendant out of prison than in prison. But how could any rational person believe that about a criminal? The following section describes racial critiques of the American criminal justice system. I then examine the evolution of the doctrine of jury nullification and argue that its practice by African-Americans is, in many cases, consistent with the Anglo-American tradition and, moreover, is legally and morally right.

A. The Criminal Law and African-Americans: Justice or "Just Us"?

Imagine a country in which more than half of the young male citizens are under the supervision of the criminal justice system, either awaiting trial, in prison, or on probation or parole. Imagine a country in which two-thirds of the men can anticipate being arrested before they reach age thirty. Imagine a country in which there are more young men in prison than in college. Now give the citizens of the country the key to the prison. Should they use it?

Such a country bears some resemblance to a police state. When we criticize a police state, we think that the problem lies not with the citizens of the state, but rather with the form of government or law, or with the powerful elites and petty bureaucrats whose interests the state serves. Similarly, racial critics of American criminal justice locate the problem not so much with the black prisoners as with the state and its actors and beneficiaries. As evidence, they cite their own experiences and other people's stories, African-American history, understanding gained from social science research on the power and pervasiveness of white supremacy, and ugly statistics like those in the preceding paragraph.

For analytical purposes, I will create a false dichotomy among racial critics by dividing them into two camps: liberal critics and radical critics. Those are not names that the critics have given themselves or that they would necessarily accept, and there would undoubtedly be disagreement within each camp and theoretical overlap between the camps. Nonetheless, for the purposes of a brief explication of racial critiques, my oversimplification may be useful.

1. THE LIBERAL CRITIQUE According to this critique, American criminal justice is racist because it is controlled primarily by white people, who are unable to escape the culture's dominant message of white supremacy, and who

are therefore inevitably, even if unintentionally, prejudiced. These white actors include legislators, police, prosecutors, judges, and jurors. They exercise their discretion to make and enforce the criminal law in a discriminatory fashion. Sometimes the discrimination is overt, as in the case of Mark Fuhrman, the police officer in the O.J. Simpson case who, in interviews, used racist language and boasted of his own brutality, and sometimes it is unintentional, as with a hypothetical white juror who invariably credits the testimony of a white witness over that of a black witness.

The problem with the liberal critique is that it does not adequately explain the extent of the difference between the incidence of black and white crime, especially violent crime. For example, in 1991, blacks constituted about fifty-five percent of the 18,096 people arrested for murder and non-negligent manslaughter in the United States (9924 people). One explanation the liberal critique offers for this unfortunate statistic is that the police pursue black murder suspects more aggressively than they do white murder suspects. In other words, but for discrimination, the percentage of blacks arrested for murder would be closer to their percentage of the population, roughly twelve percent. The liberal critique would attribute some portion of the additional forty-three percent of non-negligent homicide arrestees (in 1991, approximately 7781 people) to race prejudice. Ultimately, however, those assumptions strain credulity, not because many police officers are not racist, but because there is no evidence that there is a crisis of that magnitude in criminal justice. In fact, for all the faults of American law enforcement, catching the bad guys seems to be something it does rather well. The liberal critique fails to account convincingly for the incidence of black crime.

2. THE RADICAL CRITIQUE The radical critique does not discount the role of discrimination in accounting for some of the racial disparity in crime rates, but it also does not, in contrast to the liberal critique, attribute all or even most of the differential to police and prosecutor prejudice. The radical critique offers a more fundamental, structural explanation.

It suggests that criminal law is racist because, like other American law, it is an instrument of white supremacy. Law is made by white elites to protect their interests and, especially, to preserve the economic status quo, which benefits those elites at the expense of blacks, among others. Due to discrimination and segregation, the majority of African-Americans receive few meaningful educational and employment opportunities and, accordingly, are unable to succeed, at least in the terms of the capitalist ideal. Some property crimes committed by blacks may be understood as an inevitable result of the tension between the dominant societal message equating possession of material resources with success and happiness and the power of white supremacy to prevent most African-Americans from acquiring "enough" of those resources in a legal manner. "Black-on-black" violent crime, and even "victimless" crime like drug offenses, can be attributed to internalized racism, which causes some African-Americans to devalue black lives—either those of others or their own. The political process does not allow for the creation or implementation of effective "legal" solutions to this plight, and the criminal law punishes predictable reactions to it.

I am persuaded by the radical critique when I wonder about the roots of the ugly truth that blacks commit many crimes at substantially higher rates than whites. Most white Americans, especially liberals, would publicly offer an environmental, as opposed to genetic, explanation for this fact. They would probably concede that racism, historical and current, plays a major role in creating an environment that breeds criminal conduct. From this premise, the radical critic deduces that but for the (racist) environment, the African-American criminal would not be a criminal. In other words, racism creates and sustains the criminal breeding ground, which produces the black criminal. Thus, when many African-Americans are locked up, it is because of a situation that white supremacy created.

Obviously, most blacks are not criminals, even if every black is exposed to racism. To the radical critics, however, the law-abiding conduct of the majority of African-Americans does not mean that racism does not create black criminals. Not everyone exposed to a virus will become sick, but that does not mean that the virus does not cause the illness of the people who do.

The radical racial critique of criminal justice is premised as much on the criminal law's effect as on its intent. The system is discriminatory, in part, because of the disparate impact law enforcement has on the black community. This unjust effect is measured in terms of the costs to the black community of having so many African-Americans, particularly males, incarcerated or otherwise involved in the criminal justice system. These costs are social and economic, and include the perceived dearth of men "eligible" for marriage, the large percentage of black children who live in female headed households, the lack of male "role models" for black children, especially boys, the absence of wealth in the black community, and the large unemployment rate among black men.

3. EXAMPLES OF RACISM IN CRIMINAL JUSTICE Examples commonly cited by both liberal and radical critics as evidence of racism in criminal justice include: the Scottsboro case; the history of the criminalization of drug use; past and contemporary administration of the death penalty; the use of imagery linking crime to race in the 1988 presidential campaign and other political campaigns; the beating of Rodney King and the acquittal of his police assailants; disparities between punishments for white-collar crimes and punishments for other crimes; more severe penalties for crack cocaine users than for powder cocaine users; the Charles Murray and Susan Smith cases; police corruption scandals in minority neighborhoods in New York and Philadelphia; the O.J. Simpson case, including the extraordinary public and media fascination with it, the racist police officer who was the prosecution's star witness, and the response of many white people to the jury's verdict of acquittal; and, cited most frequently, the extraordinary rate of incarceration of African-American men.

4. LAW ENFORCEMENT ENTHUSIASTS Of course, the idea that the criminal justice system is racist and oppressive is not without dissent, and among

the dissenters are some African-Americans. Randall Kennedy succinctly poses the counterargument:

> Although the administration of criminal justice has, at times, been used as an instrument of racial oppression, the principal problem facing African-Americans in the context of criminal justice today is not over-enforcement but under-enforcement of the laws. The most lethal danger facing African-Americans in their day-to-day lives is not white, racist officials of the state, but private, violent criminals (typically black) who attack those most vulnerable to them without regard to racial identity.

According to these theorists, whom I will call law enforcement enthusiasts, the criminal law may have a disproportionate impact on the black community, but this is not a moral or racial issue because the disproportionate impact is the law's effect, not its intent. For law enforcement enthusiasts, intent is the most appropriate barometer of governmental racism. Because law enforcement is a public good, it is in the best interest of the black community to have more, rather than less, of it. Allowing criminals to live unfettered in the community would harm, in particular, the black poor, who are disproportionately the victims of violent crime. Indeed, the logical conclusion of the enthusiasts' argument is that African-Americans would be better off with more, not fewer, black criminals behind bars.

To my mind, the enthusiasts embrace law enforcement too uncritically: They are blind to its opportunity costs. I agree that criminal law enforcement constitutes a public good for African-Americans when it serves the social protection goals that Professor Kennedy highlights. In other words, when locking up black men means that "violent criminals . . . who attack those most vulnerable" are off the streets, most people—including most law enforcement critics—would endorse the incarceration. But what about when locking up a black man has no or little net effect on public safety, when, for example, the crime with which he was charged is victimless? Putting aside for the moment the legal implications, couldn't an analysis of the costs and benefits to the African-American community present an argument against incarceration? I argue "yes," in light of the substantial costs to the community of law enforcement. I accept that other reasonable people may disagree. But the law enforcement enthusiasts seldom acknowledge that racial critics even weigh the costs and benefits; their assumption seems to be that the racial critics are foolish or blinded by history or motivated by their own ethnocentrism.

5. THE BODY POLITIC AND THE RACIAL CRITIQUES I suspect that many white people would agree with the racial critics' analysis, even if most whites would not support a solution involving the emancipation of black criminals. I write this Essay, however, out of concern for African-Americans and how they can use the power they have now to create change. The important practicability question is how many African-Americans embrace racial critiques of the criminal justice system and how many are law enforcement enthusiasts?

According to a recent *USA Today*/*CNN*/Gallup poll, sixty-six percent of blacks believe that the criminal justice system is racist and only thirty-two percent believe it is not racist. Interestingly, other polls suggest that blacks also tend to be more worried about crime than whites; this seems logical when one considers that blacks are more likely to be the victims of crime. This enhanced concern, however, does not appear to translate into endorsement of tougher enforcement of traditional criminal law. For example, substantially fewer blacks than whites support the death penalty, and many more blacks than whites were concerned with the potential racial consequences of the strict provisions of the Crime Bill of 1994. While polls are not, perhaps, the most reliable means of measuring sentiment in the African-American community, the polls, along with significant evidence from popular culture, suggest that a substantial portion of the African-American community sympathizes with racial critiques of the criminal justice system.

African-American jurors who endorse these critiques are in a unique position to act on their beliefs when they sit in judgment of a black defendant. As jurors, they have the power to convict the defendant or to set him free. May the responsible exercise of that power include voting to free a black defendant who the juror believes is guilty? The next section suggests that, based on legal doctrine concerning the role of juries in general, and the role of black jurors in particular, the answer to this question is "yes."

B. Jury Nullification

When a jury disregards evidence presented at trial and acquits an otherwise guilty defendant, because the jury objects to the law that the defendant violated or to the application of the law to that defendant, it has practiced jury nullification. In this section, I describe the evolution of this doctrine and consider its applicability to African-Americans. I then examine Supreme Court cases that discuss the role of black people on juries. In light of judicial rulings in these areas, I argue that it is both lawful and morally right that black jurors consider race in reaching verdicts in criminal cases.

1. WHAT IS JURY NULLIFICATION? Jury nullification occurs when a jury acquits a defendant who it believes is guilty of the crime with which he is charged. In finding the defendant not guilty, the jury refuses to be bound by the facts of the case or the judge's instructions regarding the law. Instead, the jury votes its conscience.

In the United States, the doctrine of jury nullification originally was based on the common law idea that the function of a jury was, broadly, to decide justice, which included judging the law as well as the facts. If jurors believed that applying a law would lead to an unjust conviction, they were not compelled to convict someone who had broken that law. Although most American courts now disapprove of a jury's deciding anything other than the "facts," the Double Jeopardy Clause of the Fifth Amendment prohibits appellate reversal of a jury's decision to acquit, regardless of the reason for the acquittal. Thus, even when a trial judge thinks that a jury's acquittal directly contradicts the evidence, the jury's verdict must be accepted as final. The jurors, in judging the law, function as an important and necessary check on government power.

2. A BRIEF HISTORY The prerogative of juries to nullify has been part of English and American law for centuries. In 1670, the landmark decision in Bushell's Case established the right of juries under English common law to nullify on the basis of an objection to the law the defendant had violated. Two members of an unpopular minority group—the Quakers—were prosecuted for unlawful assembly and disturbance of the peace. At trial, the defendants, William Penn and William Mead, admitted that they had assembled a large crowd on the streets of London. Upon that admission, the judge asked the men if they wished to plead guilty. Penn replied that the issue was not " 'whether I am guilty of this Indictment but whether this Indictment be legal,' " and argued that the jurors should go "behind" the law and use their consciences to decide whether he was guilty. The judge disagreed, and he instructed the jurors that the defendants' admissions compelled a guilty verdict. After extended deliberation, however, the jurors found both defendants not guilty. The judge then fined the jurors for rendering a decision contrary to the evidence and to his instructions. When one juror, Bushell, refused to pay his fine, the issue reached the Court of Common Pleas, which held that jurors in criminal cases could not be punished for voting to acquit, even when the trial judge believed that the verdict contradicted the evidence. The reason was stated by the Chief Justice of the Court of Common Pleas:

> A man cannot see by anothers eye, nor hear by anothers ear, no more can a man conclude or inferr the thing to be resolv'd by anothers understanding or reasoning; and though the verdict be right the jury give, yet they being not assur'd it is so from their own understanding, are forsworn, at least in foro conscientiae.

This decision "changed the course of jury history." It is unclear why the jurors acquitted Penn and Mead, but their act has been viewed in near mythological terms. Bushell and his fellow jurors have come to be seen as representing the best ideals of democracy because they "rebuffed the tyranny of the judiciary and vindicated their own true historical and moral purpose."

American colonial law incorporated the common law prerogative of jurors to vote according to their consciences after the British government began prosecuting American revolutionaries for political crimes. The best known of these cases involved John Peter Zenger, who was accused of seditious libel for publishing statements critical of British colonial rule in North America. In seditious libel cases, English law required that the judge determine whether the statements made by the defendant were libelous; the jury was not supposed to question the judge's finding on this issue. At trial, Zenger's attorney told the jury that it should ignore the judge's instructions that Zenger's remarks were libelous because the jury " 'ha[d] the right beyond all dispute to determine both the law and the facts.' " The lawyer then echoed the language of Bushell's Case, arguing that the jurors had " 'to see with their eyes, to hear with their own ears, and to make use of their own consciences and understandings, in judging of the lives, liberties or estates of their fellow subjects.' " Famously, the jury acquitted Zenger, and another case entered the canon as a shining example of the benefits of the jury system.

After Zenger's trial, the notion that juries should decide "justice," as opposed to simply applying the law to the facts, became relatively settled in American jurisprudence. In addition to pointing to political prosecutions of white American revolutionaries like Zenger, modern courts and legal historians often cite with approval nullification in trials of defendants "guilty" of helping to free black slaves. In these cases, Northern jurors with abolitionist sentiments used their power as jurors to subvert federal law that supported slavery. In *United States v. Morris*, for example, three defendants were accused of aiding and abetting a runaway slave's escape to Canada. The defense attorney told the jury that, because it was hearing a criminal case, it had the right to judge the law, and if it believed that the Fugitive Slave Act was unconstitutional, it was bound to disregard any contrary instructions given by the judge. The defendants were acquitted, and the government dropped the charges against five other people accused of the same crime. Another success story entered the canon.

3. SPARF AND OTHER CRITIQUES In the mid-nineteenth century, as memories of the tyranny of British rule faded, some American courts began to criticize the idea of jurors deciding justice. A number of the state decisions that allowed this practice were overruled, and in the 1895 case of *Sparf v. United States*, the Supreme Court spoke regarding jury nullification in federal courts.

In *Sparf*, two men on trial for murder requested that the judge instruct the jury that it had the option of convicting them of manslaughter, a lesser-included offense. The trial court refused this request and instead instructed the jurors that if they convicted the defendants of any crime less than murder, or if they acquitted them, the jurors would be in violation of their legal oath and duties. The Supreme Court held that this instruction was not contrary to law and affirmed the defendants' murder convictions. The Court acknowledged that juries have the... "'physical power'" to disregard the law, but stated that they have no "'moral right'" to do so. Indeed, the Court observed, "If the jury were at liberty to settle the law for themselves, the effect would be... that the law itself would be most uncertain, from the different views, which different juries might take of it." Despite this criticism, *Sparf* conceded that, as a matter of law, a judge could not prevent jury nullification, because in criminal cases "'[a] verdict of acquittal cannot be set aside.'" An anomaly was thus created, and has been a feature of American criminal law ever since: Jurors have the power to nullify, but, in most jurisdictions, they have no right to be informed of this power.

Since *Sparf*, most of the appellate courts that have considered jury nullification have addressed that anomaly and have endorsed it. Some of these courts, however, have not been as critical of the concept of jury nullification as the *Sparf* Court. The D.C. Circuit's opinion in *United States v. Dougherty* is illustrative. In *Dougherty*, the court noted that the ability of juries to nullify was widely recognized and even approved "as a necessary counter to case-hardened judges and arbitrary prosecutors.'" This necessity, however, did not establish "as an imperative" that a jury be informed by the judge of its power to nullify. The D.C.

Circuit was concerned that "[w]hat makes for health as an occasional medicine would be disastrous as a daily diet." Specifically:

> Rules of law or justice involve choice of values and ordering of objectives for which unanimity is unlikely in any society, or group representing the society, especially a society as diverse in cultures and interests as ours. To seek unity out of diversity, under the national motto, there must be a procedure for decision by vote of a majority or prescribed plurality—in accordance with democratic philosophy. To assign the role of mini-legislature to the various petit juries, who must hang if not unanimous, exposes criminal law and administration to paralysis, and to a deadlock that betrays rather than furthers the assumptions of viable democracy.

The idea that jury nullification undermines the rule of law is the most common criticism of the doctrine. The concern is that the meaning of self-government is threatened when twelve individuals on a jury in essence remake the criminal law after it has already been made in accordance with traditional democratic principles. Another critique of African-American jurors engaging in racially based jury nullification is that the practice by black jurors is distinct from the historically approved cases because the black jurors are not so much "judging" the law as preventing its application to members of their own race. The reader should recognize that these are moral, not legal, critiques because, as discussed above, the legal prerogative of any juror to acquit is well established. In the next section, I respond to these moral critiques.

C. The Moral Case for Jury Nullification by African-Americans

Any juror legally may vote for nullification in any case, but, certainly, jurors should not do so without some principled basis. The reason that some historical examples of nullification are viewed approvingly is that most of us now believe that the jurors in those cases did the morally right thing; it would have been unconscionable, for example, to punish those slaves who committed the crime of escaping to the North for their freedom. It is true that nullification later would be used as a means of racial subordination by some Southern jurors, but that does not mean that nullification in the approved cases was wrong. It only means that those Southern jurors erred in their calculus of justice. I distinguish racially based nullification by African-Americans from recent right-wing proposals for jury nullification on the ground that the former is sometimes morally right and the latter is not.

The question of how to assign the power of moral choice is a difficult one. Yet we should not allow that difficulty to obscure the fact that legal resolutions involve moral decisions, judgments of right and wrong. The fullness of time permits us to judge the fugitive slave case differently than the Southern pro-white-violence case. One day we will be able to distinguish between racially based nullification and that proposed by certain right-wing activist groups. We should remember that the morality of the historically approved cases was not so clear when those brave jurors acted. After all, the fugitive slave law was enacted through the democratic process, and those jurors who disregarded it subverted the rule of law. Presumably, they were harshly criticized by those whose interests the slave law protected. Then, as now, it is difficult to see the picture when you are inside the frame.

In this section, I explain why African-Americans have the moral right to practice nullification in particular cases. [I] do so by responding to the traditional moral critiques of jury nullification.

1. AFRICAN-AMERICANS AND THE "BETRAYAL" OF DEMOCRACY There is no question that jury nullification is subversive of the rule of law. It appears to be the antithesis of the view that courts apply settled, standing laws and do not "dispense justice in some ad hoc, case-by-case basis." To borrow a phrase from the D.C. Circuit, jury nullification "betrays rather than furthers the assumptions of viable democracy." Because the Double Jeopardy Clause makes this power part-and-parcel of the jury system, the issue becomes whether black jurors have any moral right to "betray democracy" in this sense, I believe that they do for two reasons that I borrow from the jurisprudence of legal realism and critical race theory: First, the idea of "the rule of law" is more mythological than real, and second, "democracy," as practiced in the United States, has betrayed African-Americans far more than they could ever betray it. Explication of these theories has consumed legal scholars for years, and is well beyond the scope of this Essay. I describe the theories below not to persuade the reader of their rightness, but rather to make the case that a reasonable juror might hold such beliefs, and thus be morally justified in subverting democracy through nullification.

2. THE RULE OF LAW AS MYTH The idea that "any result can be derived from the preexisting legal doctrine" either in every case or many cases, is a fundamental principle of legal realism (and, now, critical legal theory). The argument, in brief, is that it is indeterminate and incapable of neutral interpretation. When judges "decide" cases, they "choose" legal principles to determine particular outcomes. Even if a judge wants to be neutral, she cannot, because, ultimately, she is vulnerable to an array of personal and cultural biases and influences; she is only human. In an implicit endorsement of the doctrine of jury nullification, legal realists also suggest that, even if neutrality were possible, it would not be desirable, because no general principle of law can lead to justice in every case.

It is difficult for an African-American knowledgeable of the history of her people in the United States not to profess, at minimum, sympathy for legal realism. Most blacks are aware of countless historical examples in which African-Americans were not afforded the benefit of the rule of law: Think, for example, of the existence of slavery in a republic purportedly dedicated to the proposition that all men are created equal, or the law's support of state-sponsored segregation even after the Fourteenth Amendment guaranteed blacks equal protection. That the rule of law ultimately corrected some of the large holes in the American fabric is evidence more of its malleability than of its virtue; the rule of law had, in the first instance, justified the holes.

The Supreme Court's decisions in the major "race" cases of the last term underscore the continuing failure of the rule of law to protect African-Americans through consistent application. Dissenting in a school desegregation case, four Justices stated that "[t]he Court's process of orderly adjudication has broken down in this case." The dissent noted that the majority opinion effectively... overrule[d] a unanimous constitutional precedent of 20 years standing, which was not even addressed in argument, was mentioned merely in passing by one of the parties, and discussed by another of them only in a misleading way." Similarly, in a voting rights case, Justice Stevens, in dissent, described the majority opinion as a "law-changing decision." And in an affirmative action case, Justice Stevens began his dissent by declaring that, "[i]nstead of deciding this case in accordance with controlling precedent, the Court today delivers a disconcerting lecture about the evils of governmental racial classifications." At the end of his dissent, Stevens argued that "the majority's concept of stare decisis ignores the force of binding precedent."

If the rule of law is a myth, or at least is not applicable to African-Americans, the criticism that jury nullification undermines it loses force. The black juror is simply another actor in the system, using her power to fashion a particular outcome; the juror's act of nullification—like the act of the citizen who dials 911 to report Ricky but not Bob, or the police officer who arrests Lisa but not Mary, or the prosecutor who charges Kwame but not Brad, or the judge who finds that Nancy was illegally entrapped but Verna was not—exposes the indeterminancy of law, but does not create it.

3. THE MORAL OBLIGATION TO DISOBEY UNJUST LAWS For the reader who is unwilling to concede the mythology of the rule of law, I offer another response to the concern about violating it. Assuming, for the purposes of argument, that the rule of law exists, there still is no moral obligation to follow an unjust law. This principle is familiar to many African-Americans who practiced civil disobedience during the civil rights protests of the 1950s and 1960s. Indeed, Martin Luther King suggested that morality requires that unjust laws not be obeyed. As I state above, the difficulty of determining which laws are unjust should not obscure the need to make that determination.

Radical critics believe that the criminal law is unjust when applied to some antisocial conduct by African-Americans: The law uses punishment to treat social problems that are the result of racism and that should be addressed by other means such as medical care or the redistribution of wealth. Later, I suggest a utilitarian justification for why African-Americans should obey most criminal law: It protects them. I concede, however, that this limitation is not morally required if one accepts the radical critique, which applies to all criminal law.

4. DEMOCRATIC DOMINATION Related to the "undermining the law" critique is the charge that jury nullification is antidemocratic. The trial judge in the Barry case, for example, in remarks made after the conclusion of the trial, expressed this criticism of the jury's verdict: " 'The jury is not a mini-democracy, or a mini-legislature.... They are not to go back and do right as they see fit. That's anarchy. They are supposed to follow the law.' " A jury that nullifies "betrays rather than furthers the assumptions of viable democracy." In a sense, the argument suggests that the jurors are not playing fair: The citizenry made the rules, so the jurors, as citizens, ought to follow them.

What does "viable democracy" assume about the power of an unpopular minority group to make the laws that affect them? It assumes that the group has the power to influence legislation. The American majority-rule electoral system is premised on the hope that the majority will not tyrannize the minority, but rather represent the minority's interests. Indeed, in creating the Constitution, the Framers attempted to guard against the oppression of the minority by the majority. Unfortunately, these attempts were expressed more in theory than in actual constitutional guarantees, a point made by some legal scholars, particularly critical race theorists. The implication of the failure to protect blacks from the tyrannical majority is that the majority rule of whites over African-Americans is, morally speaking, illegitimate. Lani Guinier suggests that the moral legitimacy of majority rule hinges on two assumptions: 1) that majorities are not fixed; and 2) that minorities will be able to become members of some majorities." Racial prejudice "to such a degree that the majority consistently excludes the minority, or refuses to inform itself about the relative merit of the minority's preferences," defeats both assumptions." Similarly, Owen Fiss has given three reasons for the failure of blacks to prosper through American democracy: They are a numerical minority, they have low economic status, and, "'as a discrete and insular' minority, they are the object of 'prejudice'—that is, the subject of fear, hatred, and distaste that make it particularly difficult for them to form coalitions with others (such as the white poor)."

According to both theories, blacks are unable to achieve substantial progress through regular electoral politics. Their only "democratic" route to success—coalition building with similarly situated groups—is blocked because other groups resist the stigma of the association. The stigma is powerful enough to prevent alignment with African-Americans even when a group—like low income whites—has similar interests.

In addition to individual white citizens, legislative bodies experience the Negrophobia described above. Professor Guinier defines such legislative racism as

> a pattern of actions [that] persistently disadvantag[es] a ... legislative minority and encompasses conscious exclusion as well as marginalization that results from "a lack of interracial empathy." It means that where a prejudiced majority rules, its representatives are not compelled to identify its interests with those of the African-American minority.

Such racism excludes blacks from the governing legislative coalitions. A permanent, homogeneous majority emerges, which effectively marginalizes minority interests and "transform[s] majority rule into majority tyranny." Derrick Bell calls this condition "democratic domination."

Democratic domination undermines the basis of political stability, which depends on the inducement of "losers to continue to play the political game, to continue to work within the system rather than to try to overthrow it." Resistance by minorities to the operation of majority rule may take several forms, including "overt compliance and secret rejection of the legitimacy of the political order." I suggest that another form of this resistance is racially based jury nullification.

If African-Americans believe that democratic domination exists (and the 1994 congressional elections seem to provide compelling recent support for such a belief, they should not back away from lawful self-help measures, like jury nullification, on the ground that the self-help is antidemocratic. African-Americans are not a numerical majority in any of the fifty states, which are the primary sources of criminal law. In addition, they are not even proportionally represented in the U.S. House of Representatives or in the Senate. As a result, African-Americans wield little influence over criminal law, state or federal. African-Americans should embrace the antidemocratic nature of jury nullification because it provides them with the power to determine justice in a way that majority rule does not.

D. "[J]ustice Must Satisfy, the Appearance of Justice": The Symbolic Function of Black Jurors

A second distinction one might draw between the traditionally approved examples of jury nullification and its practice by contemporary African-Americans is that, in the case of the former, jurors refused to apply a particular law, e.g., a fugitive slave law, on the grounds that it was unfair, while in the case of the latter, jurors are not so much judging discrete statutes as they are refusing to apply those statutes to members of their own race. This application of race consciousness by jurors may appear to be antithetical to the American ideal of equality under the law.

This critique, however, like the "betraying democracy" critique, begs the question of whether the ideal actually applies to African-Americans. As stated above, racial critics answer this question in the negative. They, especially the liberal critics, argue that the criminal law is applied in a discriminatory fashion. Furthermore, on several occasions, the Supreme Court has referred to the usefulness of black jurors to the rule of law in the United States. In essence, black jurors symbolize the fairness and impartiality of the law. Here I examine this rhetoric and suggest that, if the presence of black jurors sends a political message, it is right that these jurors use their power to control or negate the meaning of that message.

As a result of the ugly history of discrimination against African-Americans in the criminal justice system, the Supreme Court has had numerous opportunities to consider the significance of black jurors. In so doing, the Court has suggested that these jurors perform a symbolic function, especially when they sit on cases involving African-American defendants, and the Court has typically made these suggestions in the form of rhetoric about the social harm caused by the exclusion of blacks from jury service. I will refer to this role of black jurors as the "legitimization function."

The legitimization function stems from every jury's political function of providing American citizens with "the security... that they, as jurors actual or possible, being part of the judicial system of the country can prevent its arbitrary use or abuse." In addition to, and perhaps more important than, seeking the truth, the purpose of the jury system is "to impress upon the criminal defendant and the community as a whole that a verdict of conviction or acquittal is given in accordance with the law by persons who are fair." This purpose is consistent with the original purpose of the constitutional right to a jury trial, which was "to prevent oppression by the Government." When blacks are excluded from juries, beyond any harm done to the juror who suffers the discrimination or to the defendant, the social injury of the exclusion is that it "undermine[s]... public confidence—as well [it] should." Because the United States is both a democracy and a pluralist society, it is important that diverse groups appear to have a voice in the laws that govern them. Allowing black people to serve on juries strengthens "public respect for our criminal justice system and the rule of law."

The Supreme Court has found that the legitimization function is particularly valuable in cases involving "race-related" crimes. According to the Court, in these cases, "emotions in the affected community [are] inevitably... heated and volatile." The potential presence of black people on the jury in a "race-related" case calms the natives, which is especially important in this type of case because "[p]ublic confidence in the integrity of the criminal justice system is essential for preserving community peace." The very fact that a black person can be on a jury is evidence that the criminal justice system is one in which black people should have confidence, and one that they should respect. But what of the black juror who endorses racial critiques of American criminal justice? Such a person holds no "confidence in the integrity of the criminal justice system." If she is cognizant of the implicit message that the Supreme Court believes her presence sends, she might not want her presence to be the vehicle for that message. Let us assume that there is a black defendant who, the evidence suggests, is guilty of the crime with which he has been charged, and a black juror who thinks that there are too many black men in prison. The black juror has two choices: She can vote for conviction, thus sending another black man to prison and implicitly allowing her presence to support public confidence in the system that puts him there, or she can vote "not guilty," thereby acquitting the defendant, or at least causing a mistrial. In choosing the latter, the juror makes a decision not to be a passive symbol of support for a system for which she has no respect. Rather than signaling her displeasure with the system by breaching "community peace," the black juror invokes the political nature of her role in the criminal justice system and votes "no." In a sense, the black juror engages in an act of civil disobedience, except that her choice is better than civil disobedience because it is lawful. Is the black juror's race-conscious act moral? Absolutely. It would be farcical for her to be the sole color-blind actor in the criminal process, especially when it is her blackness that advertises the system's fairness.

At this point, every African-American should ask herself whether the operation of the criminal law in the United States advances the interests of black people. If it does not, the doctrine of jury nullification affords African-American jurors the opportunity to control the authority of the law over some African-American criminal defendants. In essence, black people can "opt out" of American criminal law.

How far should they go? Completely to anarchy? Or is there some place between here and there, safer than both? The next part describes such a place, and how to get there.

III. A PROPOSAL FOR RACIALLY BASED JURY NULLIFICATION

To allow African-American jurors to exercise their responsibility in a principled way, I make the following proposal: African-American jurors should approach their work cognizant of its political nature and their prerogative to exercise their power in the best interests of the black community. In every case, the juror should be guided by her view of what is "just." For the reasons stated in the preceding parts of this Essay, I have more faith in the average black juror's idea of justice than I do in the idea that is embodied in the "rule of law."

A. A Framework for Criminal Justice in the Black Community

In cases involving violent malum in se crimes like murder, rape, and assault, jurors should consider the case strictly on the evidence presented, and, if they have no reasonable doubt that the defendant is guilty, they should convict. For nonviolent malum in se crimes such as theft or perjury, nullification is an option that the juror should consider, although there should be no presumption in favor of it. A juror might vote for acquittal, for example, when a poor woman steals from Tiffany's, but not when the same woman steals from her next-door neighbor. Finally, in cases involving nonviolent, malum prohibitum offenses, including "victimless" crimes like narcotics offenses, there should be a presumption in favor of nullification.

This approach seeks to incorporate the most persuasive arguments of both the racial critics and the law enforcement enthusiasts. If my model is faithfully executed, the result would be that fewer black people would go to prison; to that extent, the proposal ameliorates one of the most severe consequences of law enforcement in the African-American community. At the same time, the proposal, by punishing violent offenses and certain others, preserves any protection against harmful conduct that the law may offer potential victims. If the experienced prosecutors at the U.S. Attorney's Office are correct, some violent offenders currently receive the benefit of jury nullification, doubtless from a misguided, if well-intentioned, attempt by racial critics to make a political point. Under my proposal, violent lawbreakers would go to prison.

In the language of criminal law, the proposal adopts utilitarian justifications for punishment: deterrence and isolation. To that extent, it accepts the law enforcement enthusiasts' faith in the possibility that law can prevent crime. The proposal does not, however, judge the lawbreakers as harshly as the enthusiasts would judge them. Rather, the proposal assumes that, regardless of the reasons for their antisocial conduct, people who are violent should be separated from the community, for the sake of the nonviolent. The proposal's justifications for the separation are that the community is protected from the offender for the duration of the sentence and that the threat of punishment may discourage future offenses and offenders. I am confident that balancing the social costs and benefits of incarceration would not lead black jurors to release violent criminals simply because of race. While I confess agnosticism about whether the law can deter antisocial conduct, I am unwilling to experiment by abandoning any punishment premised on deterrence.

Of the remaining traditional justifications for punishment, the proposal eschews the retributive or "just deserts" theory for two reasons. First, I am persuaded by racial and other critiques of the unfairness of punishing people for "negative" reactions to racist, oppressive conditions. In fact, I sympathize with people who react "negatively" to the countless manifestations of white supremacy that black people experience daily. While my proposal does not "excuse" all antisocial conduct, it will not punish such conduct on the premise that the intent to engage in it is "evil." The antisocial conduct is no more evil than the conditions that cause it, and, accordingly, the "just deserts" of a black offender are impossible to know. And even if just deserts were susceptible to accurate measure, I would reject the idea of punishment for retribution's sake.

My argument here is that the consequences are too severe: African-Americans cannot afford to lock up other African-Americans simply on account of anger. There is too little bang for the buck. Black people have a community that needs building, and children who need rescuing, and as long as a person will not hurt anyone, the community needs him there to help.

Assuming that he actually will help is a gamble but not a reckless one, for the "just" African-American community will not leave the lawbreaker be: It will, for example, encourage his education and provide his health care (including narcotics dependency treatment) and, if necessary, sue him for child support. In other words, the proposal demands of African-Americans responsible self-help outside of the criminal courtroom as well as inside it. When the community is richer, perhaps then it can afford anger.

The final traditional justification for punishment, rehabilitation, can be dealt with summarily. If rehabilitation were a meaningful option in American criminal justice, I would not endorse nullification in any case. It would be counterproductive, for utilitarian reasons: The community is better off with the antisocial person cured than sick. Unfortunately, however, rehabilitation is no longer an objective of criminal law in the United States, and prison appears to have an antirehabilitative effect. For this reason, unless a juror is provided with a specific, compelling reason to believe that a conviction would result in some useful treatment for an offender, she should not use her vote to achieve this end, because almost certainly it will not occur.

B. Hypothetical Cases

How would a juror decide individual cases under my proposal? For the purposes of the following hypothesis, let us assume criminal prosecutions in state or federal court and technically guilty African-American defendants. Easy cases under my proposal include a defendant who possessed crack cocaine, and a defendant who killed another person. The former should be acquitted, and the latter should go to prison.

The crack cocaine case is simple: Because the crime is victimless, the proposal presumes nullification. According to racial critiques, acquittal is just, due in part to the longer sentences given for crack offenses than for powder cocaine offenses. This case should be particularly compelling to the liberal racial critic, given the extreme disparity between crack and powder in both enforcement of the law and in actual sentencing. According to a recent study, African-Americans make up 13% of the nation's regular drug users, but they account for 35% of narcotics arrests, 55% of drug convictions, and 74% of those receiving prison sentences. Most of the people who are arrested for crack cocaine offences are black; most arrested for powder cocaine are white. Under federal law, if someone possesses fifty grams of crack cocaine, the mandatory-minimum sentence is ten years; in order to receive the same sentence for powder cocaine, the defendant must possess 5000 grams. Given the racial consequences of this disparity, I hope that many racial critics will nullify without hesitation in these cases.

The case of the murderer is "easy" solely for the utilitarian reasons I discussed above. Although I do not believe that prison will serve any rehabilitative function for the murderer, there is a possibility that a guilty verdict will prevent another person from becoming a victim, and the juror should err on the side of that possibility. In effect, I "write off" the black person who takes a life, not for retributive reasons, but because the black community cannot afford the risks of leaving this person in its midst. Accordingly, for the sake of potential victims (given the possibility that the criminal law deters homicide), nullification is not morally justifiable here.

Difficult hypothetical cases include the ghetto drug dealer and the thief who burglarizes the home of a rich family. Under the proposal, nullification is presumed in the first case because drug distribution is a nonviolent, malum prohibitum offense. Is nullification morally justifiable here? It depends. There is no question that encouraging people to engage in self-destructive behavior is evil; the question the juror should ask herself is whether the remedy is less evil. I suspect that the usual answer would be "yes," premised on deterrence and isolation theories of punishment. Accordingly, the drug dealer would be convicted. The answer might change, however, depending on the particular facts of the case: the type of narcotic sold, the ages of the buyers, whether the dealer "marketed" the drugs to customers or whether they sought him out, whether it is a first offense, whether there is reason to believe that the drug dealer would cease this conduct if given another chance, and whether, as in the crack case, there are racial disparities in sentencing for this kind of crime. I recognize that, in this hypothetical, nullification carries some societal risk. The risk, however, is less consequential than with violent crimes. Furthermore, the cost to the community of imprisoning all drug dealers is great. I would allow the juror in this case more discretion.

The juror should also remember that many ghetto "drug" dealers are not African-American and that the state does not punish these dealers—instead, it licenses them. Liquor stores are ubiquitous on the ghetto streets of America. By almost every measure, alcoholism causes great injury to society, and yet the state does not use the criminal law to address this severe social problem. When the government tried to treat the problem of alcohol use with criminal law, during Prohibition, a violent "black" market formed. Even if the juror does not believe that drug dealing is a "victimless" crime, she might question why it is that of all drug dealers, many of the black capitalists are imprisoned, and many of the non-black capitalists are legally enriched. When the juror remembers that the cost to the community of having so many young men in jail means that law enforcement also is not "victimless," the juror's calculus of justice might lead her to vote for acquittal.

As for the burglar who steals from the rich family, the case is troubling, first of all, because the conduct is so clearly "wrong." As a nonviolent malum in se crime, there is no presumption in favor of nullification, through it remains an option. Here, again, the facts of the case are relevant to the juror's decision of what outcome is fair. For example, if the offense was committed to support a drug habit, I think there is a moral case to be made for nullification, at least until drug rehabilitation services are available to all.

If the burglary victim is a rich white person, the hypothetical is troubling for the additional reason that it demonstrates how a black juror's sense of justice might, in some cases, lead her to treat defendants differently based on the class and race of their victims. I expect that this distinction would occur most often in property offenses because, under the proposal, no violent offenders would be excused. In an ideal world, whether the victim is rich or poor or black or white would be irrelevant to adjudication of the defendant's culpability. In the United States, my sense is that some black jurors will believe that these factors are relevant to the calculus of justice. The rationale is implicitly premised on a critique of the legitimacy of property rights in a society marked by gross economic inequities. While I endorse this critique, I would encourage nullification here only in extreme cases (i.e., nonviolent theft from the very wealthy) and mainly for political reasons: If the rich cannot rely on criminal law for the protection of their property and the law prevents more direct self-help measures, perhaps they will focus on correcting the conditions that make others want to steal from them. This view may be naive, but arguably no more so than that of the black people who thought that if they refused to ride the bus, they could end legally enforced segregation in the South.

C. Some Political and Procedural Concerns

1. WHAT IF WHITE PEOPLE START NULLIFYING TOO? One concern is that whites will nullify in cases of white-on-black crime. The best response to this concern is that often white people do nullify in those cases. The white jurors who acquitted the police officers who beat up Rodney King are a good example. There is no reason why my proposal should cause white jurors to acquit white defendants who are guilty of violence against blacks any more frequently. My model assumes that black violence against whites would be punished by black jurors; I hope that white jurors would do the same in cases involving white defendants.

If white jurors were to begin applying my proposal to cases with white defendants, then they, like the black jurors, would be choosing to opt out of the criminal justice system. For pragmatic political purposes, that would be excellent. Attention would then be focused on alternative methods of correcting antisocial conduct much sooner than it would if only African-Americans raised the issue.

2. HOW DO YOU CONTROL ANARCHY? Why would a juror who is willing to ignore a law created through the democratic process be inclined to follow my proposal? There is no guarantee that she would. But when we consider that black jurors are already nullifying on the basis of race because they do not want to send another black man to prison, we recognize that these jurors are willing to use their power in a politically conscious manner. Many black people have concerns about their participation in the criminal justice system as jurors and might be willing to engage in some organized political conduct, not unlike the civil disobedience that African-Americans practiced in the South in the 1950s and 1960s. It appears that some black jurors now excuse some conduct—like murder—that they should not excuse. My proposal, however, provides a principled structure for the exercise of the black juror's vote. I am not encouraging anarchy. Instead, I am reminding black jurors of their privilege to serve a higher calling than law: justice. I am suggesting a framework for what justice means in the African-American community.

3. HOW DO YOU IMPLEMENT THE PROPOSAL? Because *Sparf*, as well as the law of many states, prohibits jurors from being instructed about jury nullification in criminal cases, information about this privilege would have to be communicated to black jurors before they heard such cases. In addition, jurors would need to be familiar with my proposal's framework for analyzing whether nullification is appropriate in a particular case. Disseminating this information should not be difficult. African-American culture—through mediums such as church, music (particularly rap songs), black newspapers and magazines, literature, storytelling, film (including music videos), soapbox speeches, and convention gatherings—facilitates intraracial communication. At African-American cultural events, such as concerts or theatrical productions, the audience could be instructed on the proposal, either verbally or through the dissemination of written material; this type of political expression at a cultural event would hardly be unique—voter registration campaigns are often conducted at such events. The proposal could be the subject of rap songs, which are already popular vehicles for racial critiques, or of ministers' sermons.

One can also imagine more direct approaches. For example, advocates of this proposal might stand outside a courthouse and distribute flyers explaining the proposal to prospective jurors. During deliberations, those jurors could then explain to other jurors their prerogative—their power—to decide justice rather than simply the facts. *Sparf* is one Supreme Court decision whose holding is rather easy to circumvent: If the defense attorneys cannot inform the people of their power, the people can inform themselves. And once informed, the people would have a formula for what justice means in the African-American community, rather than having to decide it on an ad hoc basis.

I hope that all African-American jurors will follow my proposal, and I am encouraged by the success of other grass-roots campaigns, like the famous Montgomery bus boycott, aimed at eliminating racial oppression. I note, however, that even with limited participation by African-Americans, my proposal could have a significant impact. In most American jurisdictions, jury verdicts in criminal cases must be unanimous. One juror could prevent the conviction of a defendant. The prosecution would then have to retry the case, and risk facing another African-American juror with emancipation tendencies. I hope that there are enough of us out there, fed up with prison as the answer to black desperation and white supremacy, to cause retrial after retrial, until, finally, the United States "retries" its idea of justice.

CONCLUSION

This Essay's proposal raises other concerns, such as the problem of providing jurors with information relevant to their decision within the restrictive evidentiary confines of a trial. Some of theses issues can be resolved through creative lawyering. Other policy questions are not as easily answered, including the issue of how long (years, decades, centuries?) black jurors would need to pursue racially based jury nullification. I think this concern is related to the issue of the appropriate time span of other race-conscious remedies, including affirmative action. Perhaps, when policymakers acknowledge that race matters in criminal justice, the criminal law can benefit from the successes and failures of race consciousness in other areas of the law. I fear, however, that this day of acknowledgment will be long in coming. Until then, I expect that many black jurors will perceive the necessity of employing the self-held measures prescribed here.

I concede that the justice my proposal achieves is rough because it is as susceptible to human foibles as the jury system. I am sufficiently optimistic to hope that my proposal will be only an intermediate plan, a stopping point between the status quo and real justice. I hope that this Essay will encourage African-Americans to use responsibly the power they already have. To get criminal justice past the middle point, I hope that the Essay will facilitate a dialogue among all Americans in which the significance of race will not be dismissed or feared, but addressed. The most dangerous "forbidden" message is that it is better to ignore the truth than to face it.

14.2 RICHARD DELGADO

Words That Wound

The occurrence of bias-motivated violence has become so pervasive in recent years that the U.S. criminal justice system now recognizes it as a new category of violent personal crime—*hate crime.* Most hate crimes involve intimidation, vandalism, and assaults, but many hate crimes involve murder, attempted murder, and attempted rape. National figures on hate crimes show that in 1995 some 8,610 persons victimized 9,372 persons because of their race, ethnicity, religion, or sexual orientation. However, criminal justice statistics are extremely limited with regard to how much hate crime exists in U.S. society because they do not include figures on hate literature and rallies, graffiti in public places, name-calling, and epithets not associated with assaults and other threats. A major problem with fighting hate crime in the United States is getting law enforcement officers to recognize and understand what a hate crime is. Many victims fail to report hate crimes because they fear reprisal from police officers and other government agencies.

The following selection is from "Words That Wound: A Tort Action for Racial Insults, Epithets, and Name-Calling," *Harvard Civil Rights–Civil Liberties Law Review* (vol. 17, 1982), by Richard Delgado, a professor of law at the University of Colorado at Boulder whose work on critical race theory and the effects of racist speech has led to a new way of thinking about civil rights. In it, Delgado suggests that one way to satisfy the social need for legal redress for victims of racial insults, epithets, and name-calling is to seek a tort remedy in civil court.

Key Concept: tort action for racial insults, epithets, and name-calling

PSYCHOLOGICAL, SOCIOLOGICAL, AND POLITICAL EFFECTS OF RACIAL INSULTS

American society remains deeply afflicted by racism. Long before slavery became the mainstay of the plantation society of the antebellum South, Anglo-Saxon attitudes of racial superiority left their stamp on the developing culture of colonial America. Today, over a century after the abolition of slavery, many citizens suffer from discriminatory attitudes and practices, infecting our economic system, our cultural and political institutions, and the daily interactions of individuals. The idea that color is a badge of inferiority and a justification for the denial of opportunity and equal treatment is deeply ingrained.

The racial insult remains one of the most pervasive channels through which discriminatory attitudes are imparted. Such language injures the dignity and self-regard of the person to whom it is addressed, communicating the message that distinctions of race are distinctions of merit, dignity, status, and personhood. Not only does the listener learn and internalize the messages contained in racial insults, these messages color our society's institutions and are transmitted to succeeding generations.

THE HARMS OF RACISM

The psychological harms caused by racial stigmatization are often much more severe than those created by other stereotyping actions. Unlike many characteristics upon which stigmatization may be based, membership in a racial minority can be considered neither self-induced, like alcoholism or prostitution, nor alterable. Race-based stigmatization is, therefore, "one of the most fruitful causes of human misery. Poverty can be eliminated—but skin color cannot." The plight of members of racial minorities may be compared with that of persons with physical disfigurements; the point has been made that

> [a] rebuff due to one's color puts [the victim] in very much the situation of the very ugly person or one suffering from a loathsome disease. The suffering... may be aggravated by a consciousness of incurability and even blameworthiness, a self-reproaching which tends to leave the individual still more aware of his loneliness and unwantedness.

The psychological impact of this type of verbal abuse has been described in various ways. Kenneth Clark has observed, "Human beings... whose daily experience tells them that almost nowhere in society are they respected and granted the ordinary dignity and courtesy accorded to others will, as a matter of course, begin to doubt their own worth." Minorities may come to believe the frequent accusations that they are lazy, ignorant, dirty, and superstitious. "The accumulation of negative images... present[s] them with one massive and destructive choice: either to hate one's self, as culture so systematically demand[s], or to have no self at all, to be nothing."

The psychological responses to such stigmatization consist of feelings of humiliation, isolation, and self-hatred. Consequently, it is neither unusual nor abnormal for stigmatized individuals to feel ambivalent about their self-worth and identity. This ambivalence arises from the stigmatized individual's awareness that others perceive him or her as falling short of societal standards, standards which the individual has adopted. Stigmatized individuals thus often are hypersensitive and anticipate pain at the prospect of contact with "normals."

It is no surprise, then, that racial stigmatization injures its victims' relationships with others. Racial tags deny minority individuals the possibility of neutral behavior in cross-racial contacts, thereby impairing the victims' capacity to form close interracial relationships. Moreover, the psychological responses of self-hatred and self-doubt unquestionably affect even the victims' relationships with members of their own group.

The psychological effects of racism may also result in mental illness and psychosomatic disease. The affected person may react by seeking escape through alcohol, drugs, or other kinds of anti-social behavior. The rates of narcotic use and admission to public psychiatric hospitals are much higher in minority communities than in society as a whole.

The achievement of high socioeconomic status does not diminish the psychological harms caused by prejudice. The effort to achieve success in business and managerial careers exacts a psychological toll even among exceptionally ambitious and upwardly mobile members of minority groups. Furthermore, those who succeed "do not enjoy the full benefits of their professional status within their organizations, because of inconsistent treatment by others resulting in continual psychological stress, strain, and frustration." As a result, the incidence of severe psychological impairment caused by the environmental stress of prejudice and discrimination is not lower among minority group members of high socioeconomic status.

One of the most troubling effects of racial stigmatization is that it may affect parenting practices among minority group members, thereby perpetuating a tradition of failure. A recent study of minority mothers found that many denied the real significance of color in their lives, yet were morbidly sensitive to matters of race. Some, as a defense against aggression, identified excessively with whites, accepting whiteness as superior. Most had negative expectations concerning life's chances. Such self-conscious, hypersensitive parents, preoccupied with the ambiguity of their own social position, are unlikely to raise confident, achievement-oriented, and emotionally stable children.

In addition to these long-term psychological harms of racial labeling, the stresses of racial abuse may have physical consequences. There is evidence that high blood pressure is associated with inhibited, constrained, or restricted anger, and not with genetic factors, and that insults produce elevation in blood pressure. American blacks have higher blood pressure levels and higher morbidity and mortality rates from hypertension, hypertensive disease, and stroke than do white counterparts. Further, there exists a strong correlation between degree of darkness of skin for blacks and level of stress felt, a correlation that may be caused by the greater discrimination experienced by dark-skinned blacks.

In addition to such emotional and physical consequences, racial stigmatization may damage a victim's pecuniary interests. The psychological injuries severely handicap the victim's pursuit of a career. The person who is timid, withdrawn, bitter, hypertense, or psychotic will almost certainly fare poorly in employment settings. An experiment in which blacks and whites of similar aptitudes and capacities were put into a competitive situation found that the blacks exhibited defeatism, half-hearted competitiveness, and "high expectancies of failure." For many minority group members, the equalization of such quantifiable variables as salary and entry level would be an insufficient antidote to defeatist attitudes because the psychological price of attempting to compete is unaffordable; they are "programmed for failure." Additionally, career options for the victims of racism are closed off by institutional racism—the subtle and unconscious racism in schools, hiring decisions, and the other practices which determine the distribution of social benefits and responsibilities.

Unlike most of the actions for which tort law provides redress to the victim, racial labeling and racial insults directly harm the perpetrator. Bigotry harms the individuals who harbor it by reinforcing rigid thinking, thereby dulling their moral and social senses and possibly leading to a "mildly... paranoid" mentality. There is little evidence that racial slurs serve as a "safety valve" for anxiety which would otherwise be expressed in violence.

Racism and racial stigmatization harm not only the victim and the perpetrator of individual racist acts but also society as a whole. Racism is a breach of the ideal of egalitarianism, that "all men are created equal" and each person is an equal moral agent, an ideal that is a cornerstone of the American moral and legal system. A society in which some members regularly are subjected to degradation because of their race hardly exemplifies this ideal. The failure of the legal system to redress the harms of racism, and of racial insults, conveys to all the lesson that egalitarianism is not a fundamental principle; the law, through inaction, implicitly teaches that respect for individuals is of little importance. Moreover, unredressed breaches of the egalitarian ideal may demoralize all those who prefer to live in a truly equal society, making them unwilling participants in the perpetuation of racism and racial inequality.

To the extent that racism contributes to a class system, society has a paramount interest in controlling or suppressing it. Racism injures the career prospects, social mobility, and interracial contacts of minority group members. This, in turn, impedes assimilation into the economic, social, and political mainstream of society and ensures that the victims of racism are seen and see themselves as outsiders. Indeed, racism can be seen as a force used by the majority to preserve an economically advantageous position for themselves. But when individuals cannot or choose not to contribute their talents to a social system because they are demoralized or angry, or when they are actively prevented by racist institutions from fully contributing their talents, society as a whole loses.

Finally, and perhaps most disturbingly, racism and racial labeling have an even greater impact on children than on adults. The effects of racial labeling are discernible early in life; at a young age, minority children exhibit self-hatred because of their color, and majority children learn to associate dark skin with undesirability and ugliness. A few examples readily reveal the psychological damage of racial stigmatization on children. When presented with otherwise identical dolls, a black child preferred the light-skinned one as a friend; she said that the dark-skinned one looked dirty or "not nice." Another child hated her skin color so intensely that she "vigorously lathered her arms and face with soap in an effort to wash away the dirt." She told the experimenter, "This morning I scrubbed and scrubbed and it came almost white." When asked about making a little girl out of clay, a black child said that the group should use the white clay rather than the brown "because it will make a better girl." When asked to describe dolls which had the physical characteristics of black people, young children chose adjectives such as "rough, funny, stupid, silly, smelly, stinky, dirty." Three-fourths of a group of four-year-old black children favored white play companions; over half felt themselves inferior to whites. Some engaged in denial or falsification.

THE HARMS OF RACIAL INSULTS

Immediate mental or emotional distress is the most obvious direct harm caused by a racial insult. Without question, mere words, whether racial or otherwise, can cause mental, emotional, or even physical harm to their target, especially if delivered in front of others or by a person in a position of authority. Racial insults, relying as they do on the unalterable fact of the victim's race and on the history of slavery and race discrimination in this country, have an even greater potential for harm than other insults.

Although the emotional damage caused is variable and depends on many factors, only one of which is the outrageousness of the insult, a racial insult is always a dignitary affront, a direct violation of the victim's right to be treated respectfully. Our moral and legal systems recognize the principle that individuals are entitled to treatment that does not denigrate their humanity through disrespect for their privacy or moral worth. This ideal has a high place in our traditions, finding expression in such principles as universal suffrage, the prohibition against cruel and unusual punishment, the protection of the fourth amendment against unreasonable searches, and the abolition of slavery. A racial insult is a serious transgression of this principle because it derogates by race, a characteristic central to one's self-image.

The wrong of this dignitary affront consists of the expression of a judgment that the victim of the racial slur is entitled to less than that to which all other citizens are entitled. Verbal tags provide a convenient means of categorization so that individuals may be treated as members of a class and assumed to share all the negative attitudes imputed to the class. Racial insults also serve to keep the victim compliant. Such dignitary affronts are certainly no less harmful than others recognized by the law. Clearly, a society whose public law recognizes harm in the stigma of separate but equal schooling and the potential offensiveness of the required display of a state motto on automobile license plates, and whose private law sees actionable conduct in an unwanted kiss or the forcible removal of a person's hat, should also recognize the dignitary harm inflicted by a racial insult.

The need for legal redress for victims also is underscored by the fact that racial insults are intentional acts. The intentionality of racial insults is obvious: what other purpose could the insult serve? There can be little doubt that the dignitary affront of racial insults, except perhaps those that are overheard, is intentional and therefore most reprehensible. Most people today know that certain words are offensive and only calculated to wound. No other use remains for such words as "nigger," "wop," "spick," or "kike."

In addition to the harms of immediate emotional distress and infringement of dignity, racial insults inflict psychological harm upon the victim. Racial slurs may cause long-term emotional pain because they draw upon and intensify the effects of the stigmatization, labeling, and disrespectful treatment that the victim has previously undergone. Social scientists who have studied the effects of racism have found that speech that communicates low regard for an individual because of race "tends to create in the victim those very traits of 'inferiority' that it ascribes to him." Moreover, "even in the absence of more objective forms of discrimination—poor schools, menial jobs, and substandard housing —traditional stereotypes about the low ability and apathy of Negroes and other minorities can operate as 'self-fulfilling prophecies.'" These stereotypes, portraying members of a minority group as stupid, lazy, dirty, or untrustworthy, are often communicated either explicitly or implicitly through racial insults.

Because they constantly hear racist messages, minority children, not surprisingly, come to question their competence, intelligence, and worth. Much of the blame for the formation of these attitudes lies squarely on value-laden words, epithets, and racial names. These are the materials out of which each child "grows his own set of thoughts and feelings about race." If the majority "defines them and their parents as no good, inadequate, dirty, incompetent, and stupid," the child will find it difficult not to accept those judgments.

Victims of racial invective have few means of coping with the harms caused by the insults. Physical attacks are of course forbidden. "More speech" frequently is useless because it may provoke only further abuse or because the insulter is in a position of authority over the victim. Complaints to civil rights organizations also are meaningless unless they are followed by action to punish the offender. Adoption of a "they're well meaning but ignorant" attitude is another impotent response in light of the insidious psychological harms of racial slurs. When victimized by racist language, victims must be able to threaten and institute legal action, thereby relieving the sense of helplessness that leads to psychological harm and communicating to the perpetrator and to society that such abuse will not be tolerated, either by its victims or by the courts.

Minority children possess even fewer means for coping with racial insults than do adults. "A child who finds himself rejected and attacked . . . is not likely to develop dignity and poise. . . . On the contrary he develops defenses. Like a dwarf in a world of menacing giants, he cannot fight on equal terms." The child who is the victim of belittlement can react with only two unsuccessful strategies, hostility or passivity. Aggressive reactions can lead to consequences that reinforce the harm caused by the insults; children who behave aggressively in school are marked by their teachers as troublemakers, adding to the children's alienation and sense of rejection. Seemingly passive reactions have no better results; children who are passive toward their insulters turn the aggressive response on themselves; robbed of confidence and motivation, these children withdraw into moroseness, fantasy, and fear.

It is, of course, impossible to predict the degree of deterrence a cause of action in tort would create. However, as Professor van den Berghe has written, "for most people living in racist societies racial prejudice is merely a special kind of convenient rationalization for rewarding behavior." In other words, in racist societies "most members of the dominant group will exhibit both prejudice and discrimination," but only in conforming to social norms. Thus, "[W]hen social pressures and rewards for racism are absent, racial bigotry is more likely to be restricted to people for whom prejudice fulfills a psychological 'need.' In such a tolerant milieu prejudiced persons may even refrain from discriminating behavior to escape social disapproval." Increasing the cost of racial insults thus would certainly decrease their frequency. Laws will never prevent violations altogether, but they will deter "whoever is deterrable."

Because most citizens comply with legal rules, and this compliance in turn "reinforce[s] their own sentiments toward conformity," a tort action for racial insults would discourage such harmful activity through the teaching function of the law. The establishment of a legal norm "creates a public conscience and a standard for expected behavior that check overt signs of prejudice." Legislation aims first at controlling only the acts that express undesired attitudes. But "when expression changes, thoughts too in the long run are likely to fall into line." "Laws . . . restrain the middle range of mortals who need them as a mentor in molding their habits." Thus, "If we create institutional arrangements in which exploitative behaviors are no longer reinforced, we will then succeed in changing attitudes [that underlie these behaviors]." Because racial attitudes of white Americans "typically follow rather than precede actual institutional [or legal] alteration," a tort for racial slurs is a promising vehicle for the eradication of racism.

ACKNOWLEDGMENTS

1.1 From Michael Omi and Howard Winant, *Racial Formations in the United States From the 1960s to the 1980s* (Routledge, Kegan & Paul, 1986). Copyright © 1986 by Michael Omi and Howard Winant. Reprinted by permission of Routledge, Inc., part of The Taylor & Francis Group.

1.2 From Beth B. Hess, Elizabeth W. Markson, and Peter J. Stein, "Racial and Ethnic Minorities: An Overview," in Beth B. Hess, Elizabeth W. Markson, and Peter J. Stein, *Sociology* (Macmillan, 1985). Copyright © 1985 by Macmillan Publishing Company, a division of Simon & Schuster, Inc. Reprinted by permission of Beth B. Hess. References omitted.

2.1 From William Julius Wilson, "The Declining Significance of Race," *Society* (January/February 1978). Copyright © 1978 by William Julius Wilson. Reprinted by permission of University of Chicago Press.

2.2 From Joe R. Feagin, "The Continuing Significance of Race: Antiblack Discrimination in Public Places," *American Sociological Review*, vol. 56 (February 1991). Copyright © 1991 by The American Sociological Association. Reprinted by permission.

3.1 From Louis L. Knowles and Kenneth Prewitt, "Institutional and Ideological Roots of Racism," in Louis L. Knowles and Kenneth Prewitt, eds., *Institutional Racism in America* (Prentice Hall, 1969). Copyright © 1969 by Prentice Hall, Inc. Reprinted by permission of Simon & Schuster, Inc.

3.2 From Edna Bonacich, "Inequality in America: The Failure of the American System for People of Color," *Sociological Spectrum*, vol. 9, no. 1 (1989), pp. 77–101. Copyright © 1989 by Taylor & Francis, Inc. Reprinted by permission of Taylor & Francis, Inc. `http://www.routledge-ny.com`.

4.1 From Milton M. Gordon, "Assimilation in America: Theory and Reality," *Daedalus*, vol. 90, no. 2 (Spring 1961). Copyright © 1961 by *Daedalus*, a journal of The American Academy of Arts and Sciences. Reprinted by permission.

4.2 From Ruth W. Grant and Marion Orr, "Language, Race and Politics: From 'Black' to 'African-American,'" *Politics and Society* (June 1996), pp. 137–149. Copyright © 1996 by Sage Publications, Inc. Reprinted by permission.

5.1 From Leobardo F. Estrada, F. Chris García, Reynaldo Flores Macías, and Lionel Maldonado, "Chicanos in the United States: A History of Exploitation and Resistance," *Daedalus*, vol. 110, no. 2 (Spring 1981). Copyright © 1981 by *Daedalus*, a journal of The American Academy of Arts and Sciences. Reprinted by permission. Some notes omitted. This essay is a joint effort by the authors. The listing of names in no way indicates the extent of contribution. Rather, all four authors contributed equally.

5.2 From Leslie Inniss and Joe R. Feagin, "The Black 'Underclass' Ideology in Race Relations Analysis," *Social Justice*, vol. 16, no. 4 (Winter 1989), pp. 13–32. Copyright © 1989 by *Social Justice*. Reprinted by permission. References omitted.

6.1 From Noel Jacob Kent, "The New Campus Racism: What's Going On?" *Thought and Action* (Fall 2000). Copyright © 2000 by *Thought and Action*, the National Education Association Higher Education Journal. Reprinted by permission.

6.2 From Adalberto Aguirre, Jr., "Academic Storytelling: A Critical Race Theory Story of Affirmative Action," *Sociological Perspectives*, vol. 43, no. 2 (Summer

2000). Copyright © 2000 by The Pacific Sociological Association. Reprinted by permission of University of California Press.

7.1 From Margalynne Armstrong, "Protecting Privilege: Race, Residence and Rodney King," *Law and Inequality*, vol. 12 (1994). Copyright © 1994 by *Law and Inequality*. Reprinted by permission.

8.1 From George Wilson and Ian Sakura-Lemessy, "Earnings Over the Early Work Career Among Males in the Middle Class: Has Race Declined in Its Significance?" *Sociological Perspectives*, vol. 43, no. 1 (Spring 2000). Copyright © 2000 by The Pacific Sociological Association. Reprinted by permission of University of California Press.

9.1 From Michael Huspek, Roberto Martinez, and Leticia Jimenez, "Violations of Human and Civil Rights on the U.S.-Mexico Border, 1995 to 1997: A Report," *Social Justice*, vol. 25, no. 2 (Summer 1998). Copyright © 1998 by *Social Justice*. Reprinted by permission. References omitted.

10.1 From Terry A. Cross, Kathleen A. Earle, and David Simmons, "Child Abuse and Neglect in Indian Country: Policy Issues," *Families in Society*, vol. 81, no. 1 (2000). Copyright © 2000 by Families International, Inc. Reprinted by permission of *Families in Society*.

10.2 From Yanick St. Jean and Joe R. Feagin, "The Family Costs of White Racism: The Case of African American Families," *Journal of Comparative Family Studies*, vol. 29 (1998). Copyright © 1998 by *Journal of Comparative Family Studies*. Reprinted by permission.

11.1 From Pamela D. Bridgewater, "Reproductive Freedom as Civil Freedom: The Thirteenth Amendment's Role in the Struggle for Reproductive Rights," *The Journal of Gender, Race and Justice*, vol. 3, no. 2 (2000). Copyright © 2000 by *The Journal of Gender, Race and Justice*. Reprinted by permission.

12.1 Copyright © 2001 by Donald Tricarico.

13.1 From Victor M. Hwang, "The Interrelationship Between Anti-Asian Violence and Asian America," *Chicano-Latino Law Review*, vol. 21 (2000). A version of this article appears in *Anti-Asian Violence in North America* (Rowman & Littlefield, 2001). Copyright © 2001 by Rowman & Littlefield Publishers, Inc. Reprinted by permission of Rowman & Littlefield Publishers, Inc.

13.2 From Derrick Bell, "Racism Will Always Be With Us," *New Perspectives Quarterly* (vol. 8, 1991). Copyright © 1991 by *New Perspectives Quarterly*. Reprinted by permission.

14.1 From Paul Butler, "Racially Based Jury Nullification: Black Power in the Criminal Justice System," *Yale Law Journal*, vol. 105, no. 3 (December 1995). Copyright © 1995 by The Yale Law Journal Company and Fred B. Rothman & Company. Reprinted by permission. Notes omitted.

14.2 From Richard Delgado, "Words That Wound: A Tort Action for Racial Insults, Epithets, and Name-Calling," *Harvard Civil Rights–Civil Liberties Law Review*, vol. 133 (1982), pp. 159–165. Copyright © 1982 by the President and Fellows of Harvard College. Reprinted by permission. Notes omitted.

Index